CARY GRANT

A BRILLIANT DISGUISE

SCOTT EYMAN

SIMON & SCHUSTER
New York London Toronto Sydney New Delhi

Simon & Schuster
1230 Avenue of the Americas
New York, NY 10020

Copyright © 2020 by Paladin Literature, Inc.

All rights reserved, including the right to reproduce this
book or portions thereof in any form whatsoever. For information,
address Simon & Schuster Subsidiary Rights Department,
1230 Avenue of the Americas, New York, NY 10020.

First Simon & Schuster hardcover edition October 2020

For information about special discounts for bulk purchases,
please contact Simon & Schuster Special Sales at 1-866-506-1949
or business@simonandschuster.com.

The Simon & Schuster Speakers Bureau can bring authors to
your live event. For more information or to book an event,
contact the Simon & Schuster Speakers Bureau at 1-866-248-3049
or visit our website at www.simonspeakers.com.

Interior design by Kyle Kabel

Manufactured in the United States of America

1   3   5   7   9   10   8   6   4   2

Library of Congress Cataloging-in-Publication Data

Names: Eyman, Scott, 1951– author.
Title: Cary Grant : a brilliant disguise / Scott Eyman.
Description: First Simon & Schuster hardcover edition. | New York :
Simon & Schuster, 2021. | Includes bibliographical references and index.
Identifiers: LCCN 2020001234 | ISBN 9781501192111 (hardcover) |
ISBN 9781501191398 (trade paperback) | ISBN 9781501192128 (ebook)
Subjects: LCSH: Grant, Cary, 1904–1986. | Motion picture
actors and actresses—United States—Biography.
Classification: LCC PN2287.G675 E94 2021 | DDC 791.4302/8092 [B]—dc23
LC record available at https://lccn.loc.gov/2020001234

ISBN 978-1-5011-9211-1
ISBN 978-1-5011-9212-8 (ebook)

This book is for Edward Sykes Comstock, better known as Ned, the patron saint of film research at the University of Southern California, who has bailed innumerable authors out of impossible difficulties of their own making, including this one. Thanks, pal.

"Everyone tells me I've had such an interesting life, but sometimes I think it's been nothing but stomach disturbances and self-concern."

—Cary Grant

"Style. If you've got it, you don't need much else. If you haven't got it, well . . . it doesn't matter what you've got."

—William Saroyan

CONTENTS

════════════

xi

CARY GRANT

PROLOGUE

F ate rarely writes the perfect ending.

    Eleanora Duse died in Pittsburgh, Pennsylvania.

John Huston died in Middletown, Rhode Island.

And Cary Grant died in Davenport, Iowa.

He had been doing "A Conversation with Cary Grant" for several years, playing second- and third-tier towns, avoiding New York, Chicago, or Los Angeles in favor of Fort Lauderdale, Joliet, and Schenectady. As Grant explained to Douglas Fairbanks Jr., a good friend since they costarred in *Gunga Din*, he did the show for "jam money." Fairbanks found this amusing since, as he would confide, "Cary's still got the first dollar he ever earned."

"A Conversation with Cary Grant" began with eight minutes of film clips, ending with a shot of Grant walking out to accept his honorary Academy Award in 1970. As the screen showed Grant in 1970, a spotlight would hit him striding onto the stage, invariably meeting with thunderous applause. He had maintained the trim figure of his movie star prime; his only apparent concessions to age were a full head of white hair and glasses with heavy black rims. They were identical to the glasses worn by Lew Wasserman, the head of MCA-Universal, who had made Grant extremely wealthy. Grant told Doug Fairbanks that he chose the large rims because he didn't want to go to the trouble of plastic surgery, and the rims covered the bags under his eyes.

1

Grant would take his place on a stool, and after a brief introduction, take questions, generally from women in various stages of emotional distress at being in the same geographic space as Cary Grant.

"You look gorgeous—what's your secret?"

"Who was your favorite leading lady?"

"What was it like to kiss Grace Kelly?"

The answers were, in order, think thin, Grace Kelly, and divine. His least favorite leading lady was Mae West, whose choice of a youthful Grant as her leading man in *She Done Him Wrong* and *I'm No Angel* gave him a large career boost. Nevertheless, he was not grateful. "She was all contrivance, all artifice," he said. "I don't like artifice in a woman."

Occasionally, there were uncomfortable moments. In Stamford, he was asked about both Sophia Loren and Randolph Scott. And in February 1984, while speaking at Johns Hopkins University in Baltimore, things teetered uncomfortably. Before Grant was introduced, the audience was told there would be no photographs and no autographs, the latter a pet peeve since he became a star a half-century before.

That night in Baltimore, the first question came from a man in the rear of the audience. In a put-upon voice, the man begged for an autograph. "I don't give autographs," said Grant, who attempted to be light and casual about it. But the man would not let go, claiming the autograph was for a crippled child who was counting the hours until he had Cary Grant's autograph.

"Yes, yes," said Grant, whose patience was obviously wearing thin. "You're obviously the same man who previously requested an autograph at the stage door. I'd sent word to you then that I'd sign one for you before leaving. But it's the only one I'll sign tonight, I'll tell you that!"

A young man named Greg Mank was in the audience and thought it was possible that Grant might storm off and end the evening prematurely. Grant went on at some length, fretfully talking about how autograph hounds harass celebrities and make it impossible for them to go out in public. But he gradually sensed that the audience was on his side and began to relax. The show continued. He told the audience that, while he wouldn't sign autographs after the show, they were welcome to come to the front of the stage and shake his hand.

That night in Baltimore, and in all the other cities, he was cumulatively charming, funny, and demonstrated excellent recall. He talked about a simple thing like mixing a drink in a scene. You had to mix the drink correctly or someone in the audience would be sure to notice and complain, but at the same time you also had to make sure to hit your marks and remember the dialogue. If you dropped ice cubes in the glass you had to do it gently, so the sound of the ice hitting the glass wouldn't make a distracting sound. He made it sound like a six-ball juggle, a technical and creative burden that was accompanied by a load of tension no matter the level of feigned nonchalance camouflaging a very real professional expertise.

Grant was a marvelously skilled ringmaster at controlling his audience. As far as he was concerned, the shows were a chance to be seen and to be reassured that he was remembered. As if anybody could forget Cary Grant.

Grant's ease in front of audiences confounded his friends, because for most of his life he had been a nervous wreck whenever he had to make any kind of speech in public, no matter how innocuous. Even a prepared speech would give him weeks of anxiety, but over the years he managed quite well with press conferences to promote his films. He would sit amongst the reporters and answer questions in a tone that never strayed far from the light touch people expected from Cary Grant. It was those apparently relaxed sessions with reporters that Grant sought to replicate with "A Conversation with Cary Grant."

He expected the mixture as before when he arrived in Davenport by private plane on Friday evening, November 28, 1986. The Saturday performance would be the thirty-seventh time he did the show. It was the crowning event of a four-day event Davenport called the Festival of Trees, which included carolers, a Filipino dance troupe, a boys choir, fiddlers, and clog dancing, as well as $100-a-person dinner dance and tree auction called "An Affair to Remember." Grant and his wife, Barbara, registered at the Blackhawk Hotel in room 903, then spent a quiet evening in their room.

It was not his first trip to Davenport. More than sixty years before, in September 1925, when he was still Archie Leach, he had been part of a vaudeville act called Robinson, Janis & Leach and had played at Davenport's Columbia Theater for four days.

Saturday morning dawned crisp—it was going to be 50 during the day, a chilly 30 that night. At 2 p.m. Grant and his wife took a walk along the Mississippi River and chatted with people who recognized

him. They came across a restaurant called Archie's, which Grant took
as a good omen. He told his hosts in Davenport that if ticket sales
were insufficient, he would be happy to adjust his fee. Assured that
ticket sales were more than satisfactory, he relaxed.

He was an eighty-two-year-old man in fine fettle. Although he had
a long-standing fear of surgery, he had had few serious illnesses—a
bout with hepatitis in 1949 while shooting *I Was a Male War Bride*,
hernia surgery in 1977, a small stroke a few years before the trip to
Davenport. Other than his hair, the only obvious signs of age were
his voice, which was now sandy compared to the ringing tones of
his acting years, and a very slight stoop that had appeared in the
last year or two. He appeared to be one of nature's miracles, and in
truth he had very few petty vanities for a man of his renown—he
had age spots removed as soon as they appeared, and he darkened
his eyebrows slightly because he felt that white eyebrows limited his
expressiveness.

At 4 p.m., Grant and his wife arrived at the Adler Theatre for a
rehearsal for the 8:30 performance. He set the stool on which he would
sit downstage, close to the audience, and instructed the stagehand, a
man named Jack Dexter, about the necessity of timing his entrance on
the stage to synchronize precisely with his entrance on the film. He
was concerned about the ushers who would handle the microphones
for audience members asking questions. "He was very particular about
what he wanted," remembered Dexter. At about 5 p.m. he apologized
for taking so much rehearsal time and said he would go back to his
dressing room for a moment. "We'll go through it again," he said. But
Grant didn't come back after a few minutes, so the stagehand assumed
that he had decided everything was all right after all.

The trouble had begun while Grant was still rehearsing. At first, he
felt slightly nauseous and unsettled. A photograph of Grant, his wife,
and Dexter before he returned to his dressing room shows Grant looking uncharacteristically disheveled—his tie askew, his hair rumpled.
He's gazing downward and his wife is looking at him with concern.
Shortly afterward Grant began to develop a slight balance issue, at
which point he and Barbara returned to his dressing room, where he
became dizzy and vomited.

Something was clearly wrong. The theater manager was told Grant
would have to cancel the show. "I'm sorry I can't go on," he said several

times according to J. Douglas Miller, the Davenport broadcasting executive who had brought Grant to Davenport. He said it while in the throes of nausea, said it as a stagehand and two policemen carried him to a car to go back to the hotel. He didn't speak as he was driven back to the hotel, but refused to go to the hospital. At this point, Grant thought he had a stomach flu.

Actually, it was a stroke. As the blood slowly leaked into his skull, probably from the midsection or rear of the brain, it began to apply pressure to his brain stem, gradually affecting vital functions—balance, alertness, breathing. What started with headache and nausea was inevitably extending to weakness and clumsiness of the hands—all completely unfamiliar sensations for a man whose absolute command of his body had been a hallmark of his professional life.

Two doctors, Dr. James Gilson, a cardiologist, and Dr. Duane Manlove were called. When they arrived at the hotel suite, they contacted Grant's physician in Los Angeles. It was now clear that this was no stomach flu—Grant's blood pressure was 210 over 130. "By about 8:15 he was beginning to have a lot of pain, but he was still coherent," Manlove remembered. "He was talking about going back to Los Angeles and maybe seeing a doctor there. But I knew that was impossible. . . . He didn't have that much time left to live. The stroke was getting worse. In only fifteen minutes he had deteriorated rapidly. It was terrible watching him die and not being able to help. But he wouldn't let us."

At about 9:15 p.m., an ambulance arrived to take Grant to St. Luke's Hospital. He was still conscious, but deteriorating quickly—a photograph taken as he was being moved shows that Barbara Grant had covered his face, so that his distress couldn't be observed. Barbara kept whispering to him, reassuring him, and Grant whispered back. "I'm sorry," he told her. Barbara Grant placed a call to their friend Kirk Kerkorian, asking for a plane to get Grant back to California and his doctors. Kerkorian started to round up a flight crew. Just about the time he was being admitted to the hospital, Grant fell into a coma. He was immediately placed in intensive care, where his condition continued to deteriorate.

By this time, Gregory Peck, one of Grant's closest friends, had alerted Stanley Fox, Grant's business partner. It was obvious that Kerkorian's plane would take too long to get to Davenport from Los

Angeles. Finally, a Learjet air ambulance was located in Bloomington, Illinois. But it was all too late.

The word had gone out that Grant was ill. By 12:30 a.m., a reporter from the *Chicago Tribune* had arrived at St. Luke's. The reporters were waiting, only to be flummoxed when United Press ran with a bulletin from CNN in London that Cary Grant had died in Davenport, Iowa. There was no confirmation from St. Luke's. One reporter shouted, "It's a hell of a note to learn from London that Cary Grant has died in Davenport." The report originated with Stanley Fox, who had been told by Barbara Harris Grant that her husband had died.

Ten minutes after the United Press story moved, St. Luke's confirmed the story, and the reporters rushed for the phones. Cary Grant had died in the Davenport hospital at 11:22 p.m. He was eighty-two years old. The death certificate, signed by Dr. Gilson, stated that his death was due to "massive intracerebral hemorrhage."

There was no neurological ICU in Davenport, and, allowing for the state of medicine in 1986, even if the stroke had occurred in a major city such as Chicago the outcome would probably not have been any different. If the doctors had somehow managed to save Grant, he would have spent the remainder of his life severely damaged, in a wheelchair.

Decades later, the retired Dr. Gilson said that he doubted Grant could have survived even if he had gone to the hospital immediately, even if he had been able to be magically transported to Los Angeles and Cedars-Sinai. It was, simply, a catastrophic event. "He was still alive [when he got to the hospital] but his brain was so badly damaged that he couldn't talk. One side was totally paralyzed, and his [pupils] were dilated. Cary felt no pain."

As one twenty-first-century doctor said after examining the record, "It was a relatively quick and merciful death."

It was his time.

An hour after Grant's death, the Weerts Funeral Home was called to prepare Grant's body for transportation to California. At 2:45 a.m., the chartered Learjet carrying the body and Barbara Grant left for Los Angeles. When the plane arrived at a remote gate at LAX at dawn, Stanley Fox was there waiting. The body was cremated by the Neptune Society. A few days later, his widow, daughter, and Kirk

Kerkorian took a boat out into Santa Monica Bay and scattered Cary Grant's ashes into the Pacific Ocean.

One of the great legends of the movies was gone. And that was that. Or was it?

PEOPLE SAW THE ASSURED, polished, radiantly alert character that Cary Grant portrayed in movies for close to forty years and naturally assumed that he was that man. It was a reasonable enough supposition; most movie stars play emphasized aspects of themselves filtered through fictional contexts.

In fact, Scott Fitzgerald's dictum that the mark of a first-rate intelligence is the ability to hold two mutually opposing thoughts in your head at the same time was personified by Grant—the most self-invented man in the movies. "He's a completely made-up character and I'm playing a part," Grant would explain. "It's a part I've been playing a long time, but no way am I really Cary Grant. A friend told me once, 'I always wanted to be Cary Grant.' And I said, 'So did I.' In my mind's eye, I'm just a vaudevillian named Archie Leach. When somebody yells 'Archie' on the street I'll look up. I don't look up if somebody calls 'Cary.' So I think Cary Grant has done wonders for my life and I always want to give him his due."

This philosophical awareness of an essential duality took Grant decades to assimilate, and it was accomplished only after sacrificing four marriages, enduring years of therapy, and over one hundred LSD sessions—an experience he came to regard as life-altering.

His specific genius was to project a consistent image of style and grace . . . with a little something extra. As Peter Bogdanovich wrote, Grant "became synonomous with . . . a kind of . . . directness combined with impeccable taste and a detached and subtle wit."

But it was more than that. He was arguably more poised, more *focused* than any movie actor of his generation; he played every emotion except self-pity with a touch of acerbity.

The psychological cross-reference for Archie Leach was Charlie Chaplin, with whom he shared a number of elements—a disturbed mother, an indifferent, alcoholic father, a catch-as-catch-can childhood that led to a youthful infatuation with the music hall and to the movies.

There was also a willingness to repeat themselves within the niche they created, which they both got away with because of a remarkable ability to simulate spontaneity. Like Chaplin, Grant could also project a wary coldness that shadowed the humor and charm, giving his character a sense of dimension it would not otherwise have had.

And there were differences as well. Underneath Grant's fascinating, nonpareil facade was a personality of nearly perpetual anxiety—a perfectly natural response to his experience of life.

On occasion, he would step out of his comfort zone and allow his natural disillusion to show through, seasoned with a touch of bitterness—*Sylvia Scarlett, None But the Lonely Heart, Notorious*, a few others. As the critic David Thomson noted, he would have made a spectacular Archie Rice in *The Entertainer*, and could have brilliantly played the narrow, cheap James Tyrone in *Long Day's Journey into Night* if only because he was a consummate professional with a comprehensive experience of the demeaning byways of low-end show business. He didn't broadcast it, but Archie Leach once worked in Nashville on a bill with four performing seals.

Mainly, he tended to shy away from parts that demanded self-exposure. Similarly, in movies as varied as *Bringing Up Baby, To Catch a Thief*, and *Charade*, he gazed impassively at stunning women, then backed away, leaving the chase to them. Retreat can be funny because of its essential lack of composure; ardor can be tedious because of its sincerity. Aside from this preference for being left alone, he brought the unusual addition of pratfalls and somersaults to romantic comedy, a genre that favors the genteel.

He was always the conspicuous object of desire; his character preferred to be left alone—passion was to be ignored, love was to be endured. When he did want a woman, as in *His Girl Friday*, his character arranged things so that he would be the last man standing—a fait accompli.

Similarly, he tended to emphasize the comedy in "romantic comedy."

What really turned Grant on as an actor was the possibility of fun, so that he could unleash his inner clown, which is why he seemed to stimulate other actors to his own level of attentive intelligence and joie de vivre. And there was something else. He wasn't about his close-ups. He's actually at his best in medium shots, when he's reacting to another performer. "He is always fretting at, muttering against, or edging away from the solitude that stars generally inhaled with the light," wrote David Thomson. "He does not quite talk to the audience or look at the camera, but he communes with the film."

In recent years, most discussion about Grant has moved beyond—or beneath—analyses of his acting skills to the matter of his sexual identity—his years of living with Randolph Scott, insinuating comments by people like Arthur Laurents, who called him "bisexual at best." Gays have been eager to claim Grant as one of their own, while straights have been every bit as insistent about his presumed heterosexuality.

Caught in the middle are skeptics, who ask why a supposedly gay man would marry five times. For that matter, why would a theoretically gay actor in a tightly closeted time go out of his way to appear in hilarious drag—a fetching peignoir in *Bringing Up Baby*, while hopping up and down proclaiming, "I just went *gay* all of a sudden!" Not to mention the title character in *I Was a Male War Bride*?

So much talent, so many mysteries.

This is the story of the man born Archibald Alexander Leach, whose greatest performance was unquestionably as the matchless specimen of masculine charm known as Cary Grant.

PART ONE

1904-1938

"It's important to know where you've come from so that you can know where you're going. I probably chose my profession because I was seeking approval, adulation, admiration and affection."

—Cary Grant, aka Archie Leach

CHAPTER ONE

====================

Like Liverpool, another major English port, Bristol rose to wealth via the slave trade in the eighteenth century. It was a trading port as early as 1051, as attested by a listing in the Anglo-Saxon Chronicle, and by the fourteenth century Bristol was engaged in trading with Spain, Portugal, and Iceland. The oldest building in town is the St. James Priory, dating from 1129, a place of worship for more than nine hundred years.

In 1809, Bristol was transformed by the opening of what became known as the Floating Harbor, which was meant to compensate for the fact that the town had the second highest tidal range in the world. For more than a hundred years, cargo ships would wait for high tide, then sail single file for several miles from the mouth of the Avon River—a different Avon than the one that bisects Stratford—to the port in the heart of the city.

As the ships arrived, Bristol's Old City prospered. It was and is full of cobbled streets, alleys, and Regency townhouses clustered around Queen Square. Bristol is only 125 miles or so from London, but it might as well be five thousand miles. Bristol grew until it had all the benefits of a city, but not so large that it became an intimidating, congested metropolis.

It was in Bristol, on January 18, 1904, that a son was born to Elias James Leach and Elsie Maria Kingdon Leach. "My family name is Leach," he would write, echoing *David Copperfield*. "To which, at my christening, was added Archibald Alexander, with no opportunity for me to protest." He was born at home, at 15 Hughenden Road, a commonplace brick terrace house in the Horfield district. His mother's attendant was a midwife, a more economical alternative than a doctor and a hospital.

Archie was baptized on February 8 at the Horfield Parish Church by the Episcopal vicar E. W. Oakden. The lifelong confusion wrought by warring identities began early—Archie's baptismal certificate records his middle name as Alec, while his birth certificate says Alexander. The baptismal certificate was probably a mistaken contraction— he would always use Alexander on his legal documents.

Elias Leach and his wife had been married on May 30, 1898. At the time, Elias was twenty-five years old, the son of a potter. Elsie was the daughter of a shipwright, and was four years younger than her husband. Elsie's mother, Elizabeth Morgan, was from Newport, Wales, born around 1840.

What all this means is that a definitely working-class ancestry somehow managed to produce one of the world's most convincing representations of an aristocrat, albeit an aristocrat who could summon at will a welcome touch of the gutter.

While Bristol was a prosperous town, Elias Leach did not share overmuch in that prosperity. At the time, and later, Elias Leach pressed men's suits for a living, mostly at Todd's Clothing Factory off Portland Square.

In youth, Elias was handsome, even rakish, while Elsie was also attractive, with the same dark coloring that would be a prominent feature of her son. "My father was a . . . tallish man with a fancy moustache," Archie would remember. "He possessed an outwardly cheerful sense of humor and, to balance it, an inwardly sad acceptance of the dull life he had chosen. My mother was a delicate black-haired beauty, with olive skin, frail and feminine to look upon. What isn't apparent in the photograph is the extent of her strength and her will to control—a deep need to receive unreservedly the very affection she sought to control."

Archie remembered the house where he was born as "a suburban stone house, which, lacking modern heating convenience, kept only one step ahead of freezing by means of small coal fires in small bedroom fireplaces." The house on Hughenden was typical of English homes of the turn of the last century, both provincial and urban. Generations of English children were used to bedrooms where windows would be cracked even in frigid winters, resulting in frost on the windows and a thin sheet of ice in the water glass in the bathroom. The theory was that a bit of the outdoors wouldn't hurt you, but Archie hated the omnipresent cold, which led to a lifetime of lusting after warmth both physical and emotional.

In other respects, the house on Hughenden had its advantages. The street dead-ends into Horfield Commons, a pleasant city park, so little Archie had plenty of room to run, and there wouldn't have been much traffic on the street itself.

Elias did what he could to brighten things up. Archie would remember wild strawberry patches in the land behind his house, and it seems that his father had an instinct for gardening. Elias planted one of those glorious English gardens behind the house—fuchsias and hollyhocks, geraniums and daffodils, crocuses and lilies of the valley. There was an apple tree from which Elias hung a swing, which provoked a fear of heights in Archie.

The Leach family does not appear to have been particularly close; Archie would tell friends that his parents didn't pay much attention to him and would often head to the pub to drink. It was said more as a glum statement of fact than an expression of anger. As with most working-class families, they moved frequently. Before Archie was born, they were at 30 Brighton Street; in 1904 it was 15 Hughendon Road; by 1911, they had moved to six rooms at 5 Seymour Avenue.

That year the census for England and Wales documented Elias and Elsie as thirty-eight and thirty-three years old respectively, married for thirteen years. Elias's occupation was listed as "Tailor's Presser's." The total number of children born to Elias and Elsie was two, the number still living was one, and that survivor was listed as "Archibald Alex. Leach," seven years of age. Also living with the Leaches were three nieces named Lilian, Dora, and Josephine Monk, who were twenty-two, eighteen, and fifteen respectively. All this was agreed and attested to by Elias in his neat, childishly correct hand.

As the census indicated, Archie was the second child born to Elias and Elsie. John William Elias Leach had been born on February 9, 1899, and died two days before his first birthday. The family legend had it that Elsie was holding John when a door slammed on the child's thumb. The nail was torn off and an infection developed. Elsie stayed up night after night to tend the child. When she finally fell into a stuperous sleep, John began convulsing and died. The child's death certificate tells a less complicated story; it lists the cause of death as "tubercular meningitis."

Whether the child's death caused the drinking or was a result of the drinking is impossible to gauge. What is certain is that there was more than the nominal amount of household strife—Archie would speak of arguments and raised voices. "My mother was not a happy woman," he would remember, "and I was not a happy child because my mother tried to smother me with care. She was so scared something would happen to me. . . . She and my father fought about me constantly. He wanted her to let go. She couldn't. I never spent a happy moment with them under the same roof. And that's a *fact*. That's the *truth*."

Archie would spend most of his life coping with this early immersion in stress-filled domesticity. It would leave him both needing and rejecting love and its commitments nearly simultaneously. "I know a thing or two about men and women," he would tell a girlfriend. "And especially how women like to control you."

Archie resembled his father physically—Elias had the same jutting chin as his son—but in most other respects he took after his mother. He had her dark complexion, her deep brown, almost chocolate eyes, and her temperament—brooding, tending toward depressive. It was a temperament that would propel him to the world's heights, but for much of his life it also condemned him to a gnawing sense of dissatisfaction. *Is that all there is?*

In 1908, at the age of four and a half, Archie began attending the Bishop Road School, about a quarter-mile from the house on Hughenden. The school had opened in 1896, and was more or less state of the educational art at the time. It is still in use today, holds about eight hundred children, and remains pretty much state-of-the-art. Archie attended the Bishop Road School until July 23, 1915. Oddly, the Bristol jail was right around the corner, with the prison wall visible as Archie crossed the street to enter the school. The occasional jail escape provided much-needed neighborhood excitement.

Classmates remembered Archie as "scruffy-looking" or as a "pathetic little figure." Basil Varney, who was in the same class as Archie at Bishop Road as well as the succeeding Fairfield School, drew a portrait of a cozy time when the children felt cosseted, World War I or no World War I. A student named Harold Jones remembered that the atmosphere was strict but fair. Students had to raise their caps to the teachers. Peashooters and skates were forbidden, and students couldn't put their hands in their pockets. German prisoners of war would occasionally be driven in lorries past the school to dig trenches in what later became Kings Drive.

Basil Varney said that "To commemorate King George's Coronation [in 1911] we received a tin of chocolates with a picture of the King and Queen Mary on the lid. Also, I received a medal for never being late." The main danger children faced was whooping cough, and there was a "fever van" that would take sick children to the hospital.

Archie seemed to find a niche when he was made the goalkeeper for the recess soccer matches. "If the ball slammed past me, I alone— no other member of the team, but I alone—was held responsible for the catastrophe." At the same time, if he stopped the ball, there was exultation. "I learned the deep satisfaction derived from receiving the adulation of my fellow little men. Perhaps it began the process that resulted in my search for it ever since. No money, no material reward is comparable to the praise, the shouts of well done, and accompanying pat on the back of one's fellow man."

Soccer games aside, Archie's memory of his schooling was a roster of humiliations and disappointments. He remembered that he struck out at arithmetic and at talking to girls. He recorded that he was fascinated by his mother's pinking shears, and that his Christmas stocking would be filled with tangerines and nuts. His favorite toy was a candle-powered magic lantern complete with colored slides that provided the entertainment at the only children's party his parents ever hosted for the boy.

Elias allotted six pence a week for his son's allowance, but his mother would dock him two pence if he spilled any food on the prize tablecloth she would bring out for Sunday meals. Elsie would take her son to the Claire Street Cinema, a posh place catty-cornered from the lavish Hippodrome Theatre in the heart of Bristol.

At the cinema on Claire Street you could take tea while watching the movie. (His father would take him to the movies at the less expensive Metropole.) Archie loved Keystone comedies and the serials. He watched Charlie Chaplin, Fatty Arbuckle, John Bunny, and his particular favorite, Broncho Billy Anderson, the first cowboy star and cofounder of the Essanay Studios. He spoke of raptly attending a Pearl White serial called *The Clutching Hand*, but he was probably thinking of *The Iron Claw*, released in 1916.

He would sum up his early childhood as dour. "I doubt if I was a happy child because, like most people, I conveniently find it difficult to remember those early formative years. . . . Since my parents did not seem particularly happy together . . . the lack of sufficient money became an excuse for regular sessions of reproach, against which my father resignedly learned the futility of trying to defend himself."

And so the casting in the drama of Archie's life began to take place. Men were victims and women—especially needy women—were the oppressors. This provoked a tendency in Archie to hold himself slightly aloof from intimate relationships, the better to extricate himself when things got unpleasant. Archie would always characterize his father as a more or less hapless onlooker in his own life, and marveled at his mother's strength and will to power.

In 1912, Elias told his wife that he had been offered a good job in Southampton, eighty miles from Bristol. The new job had him making uniforms for the British Army. It seems that Elias had also found another woman who just happened to live in Southampton. Within a year he was back in Bristol; however much he was being paid it wasn't enough to sustain two households.

The family strife might have derailed Archie's academics, but despite his memories centering on dolorous failure, the record indicates he was actually smart and attentive, with a native intelligence. His report card dated May 2, 1913, says that he earned 20 out of 20 in Reading, 30 out of 30 in Arithmetic, 10 out of 10 in Writing, 19 out of 20 for Dictation, 20 out of 20 for Drawing, and 18 out of 20 for Conduct. "I am very pleased with this report," his teacher wrote. He was rated first in his class of 41; on his previous report card he had ranked 11th.

But the situation at home was growing worse. Elsie's mental health began to deteriorate. Her fear spiked; she kept all the doors in the house locked, washed her hands incessantly with a stiff-bristled brush. "Where are my dancing shoes?" she would ask, more to herself than anybody else.

One Saturday Elsie took her son to Marks & Spencer. It was the first time Archie remembered being there, and he loved the bounty of it. Archie ran over to the penny bazaar to see what he could get for his pocket change, when he realized his mother wasn't with him. He was suddenly alone and frightened and wanted to cry, but he didn't want to do anything that would embarrass his parents, so he maintained his composure.

After a while, there was still no sign of his mother, so Archie began to cry, but nobody paid any attention; the throngs of people just kept moving past the little boy. Then he felt a hand grab his. He looked up and it was Elsie, who knelt down and looked him right in the face. "You see, Archie, nobody wants you. Nobody came for you, did they? I'm the only one—*the only one*—who cares about you. Nobody else. And don't you ever forget it, because the next time you let go of my hand and wander off, I won't come back."

He would spend the rest of his life coping with the damage inflicted on him in these years. "I think she thought of me as her doll," he would tell a friend late in his life. "Someone totally dependent upon her and only her. She wanted control of me because she couldn't control what had happened to her first son."

Almost all of his relationships with women would be derailed by alternating waves of need and fear, seduction then flight. He would come to regard his mother as a well-meaning psychological assassin. He would spend decades avoiding sitting at his own dining room table, because that was a place of rising tension and impending financial loss. He preferred trays in front of the TV.

All of this could go in only one direction. Elias's drinking increased to the point where he was an alcoholic. Archie would come to believe that it was "his only escape—the only way he could get away from my mother and her constant complaints about money and everything else. . . .

> They constantly fought. Elsie had lived in Clifton, kind of the Beverly Hills of Bristol, and she looked down on the part of town where we lived. It was by no means a slum—it was a good, working-class neighborhood—but it wasn't Clifton and she never let my father forget it. Ever. They were always arguing about money. There just never seemed to be enough of it. That's all they talked about. And she made it seem like it was his fault.

His mother wanted Archie to play the piano and insisted he take lessons—undoubtedly a stretch given the family's thin resources.

Despite all this, his report card indicates that even if he was uninter-ested, he was invariably diligent—a trait that never changed.

When World War I arrived in 1914, Archie did his part by joining the YMCA and being assigned air raid duty—if a siren went off, he had to climb up the gas streetlamps and extinguish them. Although only ten years old, he already was showing signs of wanderlust, accepting any assignment that might involve travel outside his neighborhood.

None of this seemed to soften the home environment. Elias would argue that their son should be out in the streets playing, while Elsie wanted him kept close. The arguments grew worse, until Elias finally did something drastic.

On February 3, 1915, Elsie Maria Leach, thirty-eight years of age, was committed to the asylum at the Bristol district known as Fish-ponds. There were actually two hospitals for the mentally ill in Bristol. One was Stoke Park, a Gothic pile out of a Brontë novel painted an incongruous yellow that sits on a hill looming over the M32 highway in and out of Bristol. It's usually assumed to be the building where Elsie was housed, but Stoke Park was strictly for violent or highly damaged patients. Elsie was interned at Glenside Hospital, reserved for comparatively mild cases, just down the road from Stoke Park.*

The intake document states that Elsie was "very talkative," and goes on to specify the reasons for her commitment. "Husband says his wife Elsie Maria Leach has been queer in her head for some months, thinks that several women are concealed in the house and that they put poison in her food. She hears voices through the wall and thinks [she's] being watched." Under the heading "Dangerous to Herself" is written *No*; under the heading "Dangerous to Others" is written *No*. The variety of insanity is specified as "Mania."

It was all so simple. There appears to have been nobody attesting to Elsie's supposed insanity other than her husband. From Elsie's correspondence in later years, there seems no doubt that she was emotionally and intellectually erratic, although those characteristics could easily have been exacerbated by being incarcerated in a mental institution for more than twenty years. She would not be discharged from Glenside Hospital until July 26, 1936. After that, she would live

---

* Today, part of Glenside Hospital is still used as a mental institution, while the rest of the complex is used for housing student nurses.

on her own for more than twenty years, which indicates she should never have been interned in the first place.

One of the primary issues Elsie seems to have presented was inconvenience. With his wife out of the way, Elias would contract a common-law marriage with a woman named Mabel Johnson, with whom he had a child out of wedlock named Eric Leach in September 1921. It is possible he was already involved with her in 1915.

If Elias had worked to overcome his wife's disappearance and established an intimate relationship with his son, a certain amount of good intentions might be ascribed, but as far as Archie was concerned, his father was always pretty much the same—absent.

And so it was that Archie Leach came home a few weeks after turning eleven to find his mother gone. He asked where she was and the response was a series of vague inferences implying that she had gone to a seaside resort. "I accepted it as one of those peculiarly unaccountable things that grown-ups are apt to do." After several weeks, he realized that she wasn't coming back and the inference shifted from a trip to sudden death. Apparently he never demanded any specifics from his father, who in turn never offered any. Silence descended. So did guilt. Years later, he would describe the awful responsibility he felt over his mother's disappearance—on some level, he believed *he* was the subject of his parents' quarrels, and perhaps even her death. Then and later, there was little happiness to be recalled in his childhood, so he tended to avoid the subject.

Late in his life, during one of his trips to Bristol, he would stand in front of the house at 15 Hughenden Road. "It is true what they say," he began reminiscing. "Sometimes I can't remember what happened yesterday, but I can remember things from my life here that are so clear and vivid.

"The thing I remember most is how cold that upstairs bedroom would get. There was an eiderdown that always slipped off the bed. There's nothing worse than waking up in a cold home, is there?" On rare occasions, he would discuss how lonely he was after his mother disappeared. He would go down to the Bristol docks, wishing one of the freighters would take him far away to someplace warmer, more comforting.

Archie and his father moved to his grandmother's house on Campbell Street, where, he remembered, he didn't see a great deal of her. He remembered his grandmother as "a cold, cold woman."

When Archie had been small, four or five, he remembered his grandmother treating him with affection, but by the time he and his father moved in with her, she had switched to dislike. "At most I was a steady annoyance. At worst, I was a hindrance to her drinking. . . . I was on my own a lot. When I did come home, I'd find her in the upstairs bedroom, usually drunk. The worst words would come out of her mouth. She truly and completely disliked me. I swear I could smell hell on her breath.

"More than that, what I remember about that house was how cold it was. Always. And there was never enough food. Never. She could have cared less if I was fed or clothed properly. So most of the time when I wasn't in school, I was on the streets." He summed up his domestic situation by saying, "I . . . took care of my own needs as best I could."

ARCHIE LATER REALIZED that "no one had an easy time of it, especially my father." One time the landlord came to the door to collect the rent, and Archie never forgot the look of shame on his father's face. He didn't have the money.

Nineteen fifteen was also the year Archie left the Bishop Road School to transfer to Fairfield School, roughly analogous to an American middle school. He would have had to take a test to enter Fairfield, and if he had flunked he would have stayed at Bishop Road. Fairfield was built in 1898 as a series of overlapping gabled structures. The school was coeducational, with a general fee of one pound per term, but 25 percent of the slots were available to non-fee-paying students, which would have included Archie. Acceptance at Fairfield was good but it didn't promise a college education. The Fairfield School was one-fifth private and four-fifths a state school, that is to say government funded.

Archie acknowledged being a nervous child, with two primary fears—knives and heights. The latter is fairly common, but the former derived from watching his father shave and having Elias gesture toward him with the straight razor. He never forgot the startling move, the flash of the light on the razor.

In later life, he would only have a few anecdotes about Elias's accumulated wisdom. Anecdote # 1: "I always fancied shoes, and my father told me, 'If you can't afford good shoes, don't buy any. If you can afford one pair, buy black. If two pair, one black, one brown. But they must be good. That way even if they are old, they will always be seen to be good shoes.'"

Anecdote # 2: Archie had a penchant for "elegant sorts of tweeds and glenurquhart plaids. My father said, 'Don't buy them unless you can afford a lot of suits. Otherwise, people will say, 'Here comes that suit down the road,' rather than Archie.'"

Good advice as far as it goes, which isn't very far. Guidance about clothes isn't guidance about life. On that score, Elias seems to have kept his mouth shut, perhaps because he realized he didn't have any advice worth passing on.

Despite his intelligence, Archie seems to have disliked the regimentation of organized learning, which explains his comprehensively random intake of information as an older man. Archie's memory of Fairfield was of a roughhouse atmosphere: "Either you were a hitter or you got hit." Archie seems to have been a hitter; he had his slingshot commandeered by one of his teachers, who might have been Miss Craigie, a Scottish teacher on whom he developed a crush. Archie's allowance was only a shilling a week, so he took on whatever work he could find—a chemist's shop, taking tickets at a roundabout.

He couldn't afford to buy new textbooks, so bought them second-hand from students who had already taken the courses. This made him realize that college was going to be out of the question. Concurrently, he developed an obsession to be clean. "I washed myself constantly; a habit I carried far into adulthood in a subconscious belief that if I scrubbed hard enough outside I might cleanse myself inside: perhaps of an imagined guilt that I was in some way responsible for the circumstances of my parents' separation."

By this time, Archie knew what he wanted. He wanted out.

"I hung around the wharves hoping to get a job as a cabin boy," he said seventy-odd years later. "I couldn't be a traveling salesman, I was too young to be a commercial traveler. I was too young to join the army. But all I dreamed of was to travel." The only question was where he would go . . . and what he would do.

Bristol was now a city in transition. The streets around the waterfront were dingy from two hundred years of constant use, and the bowers and fruit groves that had grown wild were long gone. By 1915 much of the inner city, especially what Bristol historians would refer to as "the notorious Hanover Street," constituted an embarrassment to the government and many of the commercial businesses.

Archie remembered that his introduction to the intimacy of the stage came courtesy of an electrician who served as a part-time science instructor at Fairfield. The teacher was hired to work on the lighting system at the Bristol Hippodrome and invited Archie to check out his handiwork. The Hippodrome had opened in 1912 at a cost of £32,000, a splendid theater of deep crimson with gold accents, three thousand seats spread over a main floor, and two balconies—the height of Imperial Victorian splendor, part of a long roster of Empires, Coliseums, and Hippodromes built across cities and towns in England in the early years of the twentieth century, most of them designed by Frank Matcham.

The Hippodrome was mostly a vaudeville house—two performances every evening and matinees twice a week. Sometimes the rhythm would be broken by bringing in opera, concerts, a circus, or even a movie. The theater was built with a water tank beneath the stage that held a hundred thousand gallons and could simulate choppy waves, whirlpools, or foaming waterfalls. The theater advertised that the water could be heated to 80 degrees Fahrenheit, although performers who had occasion to work in the tank begged to differ with the advertising.

Perhaps the most awe-inspiring feature of the Hippodrome was a dome above the auditorium that could be opened to let out tobacco fumes and let in cool night air in those years before air-conditioning. In the first year of the Hippodrome's existence, Sarah Bernhardt appeared there in *La Dame aux Camélias*. It was a triumph, except for one performance when Bernhardt's death scene was interrupted by a group of women in one of the boxes who began chanting about voting rights, only to be met by equal amounts of catcalling from men in the audience. The police were called and the protesters were evicted.

But Archie Leach wasn't fascinated by the dome, the tank, or any of the physical accoutrements of the Hippodrome. Rather he was entranced by camaraderie—a feeling of family that had been completely absent from his life until that moment.

"The Saturday matinee was in full swing when I arrived backstage," he remembered, "and there I suddenly found my inarticulate self in a dazzling land of smiling, jostling people wearing and not wearing all sorts of costumes and doing all sorts of clever things. And that's when I *knew*. What other life could there be but that of an actor? They happily traveled and toured. They were classless, cheerful and carefree. They gaily laughed, lived and loved."

Most importantly, there were performers at the Hippodrome who were just about the same age as Archie. A half-century later, he remembered that it would be "An actor's life for me." He hung around until he got a job as a call-boy, telling the performers they had a half-hour until showtime, then fifteen minutes and so forth.

From the Hippodrome, he went to the Empire, where he was hired to assist with the spotlights. The main reason he went after the job was to see the shows for free. He particularly loved the Great David Devant, a magician. The Great Devant was less appreciative of Archie, because the boy was so enthralled by Devant's act that during one performance he allowed the spotlight to drift downward, where it revealed two mirrors under Devant's platform that were the basis of many of the illusions. Archie would always be a great fan of the illusionary arts— decades later he joined the board of the Magic Castle in Hollywood.

At the age of fourteen, he began keeping a rough journal in a small book with the cover legend "The Boy Scout's Note Book and Diary." On the first page, he lists his name as "A. Leach," his address as 12 Campbell St., St. Paul's, Bristol, his height as 5 ft 1/2. On page 73, he records his troop as 1st Bristol, his patrol as Beavers, his boot size as 6. Hat size and glove size are left blank.

The diary mainly attests to his passion for the stage. From January 1 to the 4th he was on holiday from school and spent each night at the Empire. On the 5th he went to King's Hall Old Market, where he saw *Gloria's Romance*, a film with Billie Burke. School started up on the 8th, and he would attend the Empire several nights a week.

A few of his entries from January 1918:

14 MONDAY: "After School I went and bought a new belt. And a new tie. Empire in evening. Daro-Lyric Kingston's Rosebuds."

17 THURSDAY: "Stayed home from school all day. Went to Empire in evening. Snowing."

18 FRIDAY: "My birthday. Stayed home from school. In afternoon went in town. In evening, Empire. Second house . . . out to King's Hall. Snowing . . . Letter from Mary M."

Monday, January 21, was a more typical day: "School wrote letter to Mary M. Empire in evening, not a bad show. Caper at the top of bill. Bail flys around hall 20' long . . . Mr. Macaine gave me pass for 2 in stalls Thursday second House."

By February, he is simply noting "Stayed away," probably from school, possibly from home, perhaps both. "Roamed . . . & went to the pictures. Empire in evening." On Friday, February 15: "Mucked about all day. Went to Panto in evening Allright. Had 2 fish & chips." There are occasional notations about a friend named Stan, but nothing about his father, or any consequences from his repeated absences from school. The high point seems to have been seeing the famous music hall entertainer Vesta Tilley on March 5, and getting her autograph three days later. He kept the autographed photo for the rest of his life.

The diary begins to peter out in April and there are only fragmentary entries after that. A section marked Cash Accounts reveals that he was getting paid occasionally by the Empire in 1917 and 1918, anywhere from 1/9 to 2/6, although whether that's pounds and shillings or shillings and pence is open to question. In a section titled "My Friends," he lists five music hall acts that include "Bart & Bart Comedy Acrobats" and "Charlie Harvey Friend Heave O' Revue." The only friends he bothers to list are Fred Pitts and Cass, or Ciss—his penmanship is sloppy—Hillier.

The diary is interesting for what it doesn't mention as well as for what it does. Like most teenagers, Archie is only interested in what Archie is interested in. There is no notice taken of anything in the world outside of theatricals and school, such as, for instance, World War I. Increasing amounts of time are spent at the Empire, decreasing amounts of time spent at school. The lack of involvement with school, not to mention his father, is obvious. Alternatives to home were sought, and inevitably found.

Nor does he write anything about his missing mother, or any family member outside of two mentions of "Gram," where he goes once for tea and a notation on February 14, where he mentions that the doctor had come to see Gram, "who is bad." Nor does he mention the fact that in 1918 he ran away from home and got kicked out of Fairfield. The overall impression is of an isolated boy left to his own devices and more or less content with that.

The last entry in the diary comes on Saturday, December 21. It is gnomic but enticing, and possibly a preview of coming attractions:

good
dog
do
a
good
TRICK

ARCHIE WAS UNAWARE that his father was keeping his mother informed about their son. On May 5, 1918, Elias wrote Elsie that, "I am very sort [sic] that I have not written to you before you must excuse me once again I am very pleased to say that Archie is going along alright and also that he is in the very best of health and that he is enjoying himself allright. I am very glad that you are getting better which I hope will continue for you. . . . I remain your loving . . ." Elias's mechanical, uninterested recitation of trivialities would be replicated in his occasional letters to his son.

That same year, Archie wrote to Bob Pender under his father's name, inquiring if Pender was interested in taking on an apprentice. Bob Pender—real name Robert Lomas—was born in 1871, part of a second-generation troupe of tumblers. A London *Times* article in the 1850s refers to a "Lomas Troupe," probably headed by Richard John Lomas, Bob's father. By the turn of the century, Bob Lomas had given up the family name and was touring under the name of the Bob Pender Troupe, recognized as one of the finest acts of its kind in the world.

When he got Archie's letter, Pender wrote back, enclosing railroad fare and suggesting that Archie meet the troupe in Norwich. When Archie arrived, some of the boys in the troupe began instructing him in tumbling and basic acrobatics. But Archie hadn't bothered to tell his father he was leaving home. After Archie had spent ten days with the troupe, Elias somehow found out where his errant son was and snatched the boy back to Bristol.

Archie was adamant, so much so that he engineered an event that got him expelled from Fairfield. The date was March 13, 1918. Archie's version of events was that he snuck into the girls' side of the school so he could check out the bathrooms and got caught. After he died, one old classmate reported that he had indeed done that, but that he had added masturbation to his roster of delinquencies. Whatever the degree of transgression, Archie's mission was accomplished: he was now available for a full-time apprenticeship with Pender's troupe. Elias must have been upset, but Archie remembered that both his father and Pender were Masons and that shared bond eventually enabled them to come to an agreement. On August 9, 1918, a contract was drawn up between Pender and Elias Leach concerning his minor son.

The said Robert Pender agrees to employ the son of the said Elias Leach Archie Leach in his troupe at a weekly salary of 10/ a week with board and lodgings and everything found for the stage, and when not working full board and lodgings.

This salary to be increased as the said Archie Leach improves in his profession and he agrees to remain in the employment of Robert Pender till he is 18 years of age or a six months notice on either sides.

Robert Pender undertaking to teach him dancing & other accomplishments needful for his work.

Archie Leach agrees to work to the best of his abilities.

Archie's schooling was over, but his education was just beginning.

CHAPTER TWO

U nlike American vaudeville, which was primarily attended by the
lower and middle classes, English music halls drew customers from
every economic strata. As one historian noted, "Ford Madox Ford
edited his *English Review* in a box at the Shepherd's Bush Empire,
and the King himself preferred an evening of variety at the Empire or
the Gaiety to G. B. Shaw at the Royal Court."

When it came to the working class, the music halls were not ancillary, but primary and had been since the days when the form began
in taverns, which is why the music halls were full of satirical takes on
aristocrats who were generally portrayed as feckless fools.

Archie remembered that Bob Pender was "a stocky, strongly built,
likable man of about 42" who had been renowned as a great Drury
Lane clown. He also liked Pender's wife, Margaret, whom he termed
"kindly." Within three months Archie was not in the audience at the
Empire in Bristol, he was on the stage.

The English music hall was similar to American vaudeville—eight
to ten acts amounting to a variety show lasting for a maximum of
two hours. But there were some differences—American vaudeville
was rigorously policed by the producers and theater owners, who
wanted a family audience and took a very dim view of anything
suggestive or racy. By contrast, the music hall featured performers
who specialized in the risqué such as Marie Lloyd and "Max Miller,
the Cheeky Chappy."

The Pender troupe's schedule for the period when Archie joined in August is exhausting to contemplate. Beginning with Kingston-on-Thames, the troupe played week-long engagements at, in order, Aldershot, London, Aberdeen, Hamilton, Bolton, Walham Green, Canning Town, Chatham, Liverpool, Leeds, Manchester, Aston-u-Lyne, Preston, Dumbarton, and Alexandria. Archie remembered that during the week of November 11, 1918, when the Armistice was declared, he was playing in Preston, a large town east of Blackpool in Lancashire. He was correct—the theater was yet another Hippodrome, and the troupe left for Dumbarton, Scotland, on November 18.

Then it was off to Glasgow for a rehearsal for the Holiday pantomime, which they played through February. Archie would describe the Christmas pantomime as "adapted from the old Italian Commedia dell'arte. Stock clowns, each of whom has a traditional personality. They have marvelous adventures told in action—in pantomime and tumbling. Beginning on Boxing day, which is the first weekday after Christmas, they continue for sometimes 10 to 12 weeks to the great delight of the kiddies." After the pantomime, the company was off for two weeks, followed by bookings in Sunderland, Birmingham, Coventry, Weymouth, and Salisbury.

Shortly after the end of the war, Pender split the company in two, and Archie was promoted from acrobatics to stilt-walking and pantomime. He learned fast. Pender's troupe was what the trade called a "dumb act," meaning they didn't talk. The vaudeville historian Joe Laurie Jr. would write that "In Europe, the dumb act was respected and was usually a featured act and many times a headliner," if only because of the enormous skill on view. Acrobats usually either opened or closed the bill.

As with Fred Karno's troupe, which produced Charlie Chaplin and Stan Laurel, Pender demanded not merely physical grace, but total control even if the performers had to simulate a total loss of control. English acrobats were generally regarded as beginners until they had been working together for at least six months. "Most of the great dumb acts were Europeans," wrote Joe Laurie, "because they had the patience to work for hours, weeks and years to perfect their specialties. . . . The foreign troupes had apprentices who worked for years for just room and board, a few clothes, and maybe a buck or two for spending money. The owner of the act would send the kid's parents a few bucks a week, which they were glad to get while their kid was learning a 'profession.'" Laurie could have been describing Pender and his young apprentice. What Archie was getting was basic training in acrobatics and, beyond that, something beyond price: how to entertain an audience.

The first thing Pender taught Archie was how to make an entrance. It involved rushing out from the wings and diving through the stage floor, courtesy of a "star-trap"—a trapdoor cut in segments like a pie that is flush with the stage. A star-trap is usually used for magic acts, but it comes in handy for the occasional acrobat. After the acrobat (or magician) passes through, the pieces of the star-trap spring back into place. Since most of the audience was seated beneath the level of the stage, it looked like the acrobat dove right through a solid stage floor. The topper involved four other acrobats huddled below the stage, who hurled Archie up through the star-trap so he could make a startling reentry.

The first few times they tried the second half of the trick, Archie forgot to spread his legs after he rose up through the star-trap, which meant he disappeared back through the floor as quickly as he had risen through it. "I landed on the table [beneath the stage] and up I went again. And I was still too excited to remember to spread out my legs—so down through the trap I went once more."

It was timing, it was physical dexterity, it was remembering to spread your legs. And at the end was the reward: "When the audience roared at me the time I shot up and down through that star-trap, it ruined me forever."

By 1920, Archie was a firmly established member of the troupe. It was in that year that Pender booked his first engagement in America. He could take only eight boys with him, and Archie was one of them. On July 21, 1920, Archie, carrying little more than his talent and a new English passport numbered 5016, left Southampton on board the White Star Line's SS *Olympic*. The passenger manifest correctly asserted he was sixteen years of age, and listed his occupation— somewhat optimistically—as "actor." Destination: the Globe Theater in New York City.

The Pender troupe crossed the Atlantic in second class. Above them, in the deluxe cabin of the *Olympic* were Douglas Fairbanks and Mary Pickford, returning from their six-week honeymoon in Europe.

Shipping manifests are highly democratic; Fairbanks and Pickford were also listed as "actor" and "actress," as if there was no difference between them and Archie Leach.

Archie would remember that he was photographed with Fairbanks while they played a game of shuffleboard. "As I stood beside him, I tried, with shy, inadequate words to tell him of my adulation. He was a splendidly trained acrobat, affable and warmed by success and well-being. A gentleman in the true sense of the word."

The photograph reveals Fairbanks's hair blowing in the ocean breeze, while sixteen-year-old Archie is standing next to him, already extremely handsome and clearly gobsmacked by his proximity to one of his idols.

Fairbanks was a role model for the young acrobat, as he was for half the population of the world. Lithe, with the trim muscularity and skill set of a superb gymnast, Fairbanks was a poor, half-Jewish kid from Denver who recast himself as a show business aristocrat and anglophile, a category that would also describe his son, who would eventually become close friends with Archie. The elder Fairbanks had his suits made on Savile Row by Anderson & Sheppard, his evening clothes by Hawes & Curtis, his shirts by Beale & Inman. He also displayed a perpetual tan in place of conventional movie makeup—traits that Archie would adopt.

But they had more in common than a tan and a taste for English tailoring. Both Archie and Fairbanks had had wretched childhoods, both had alcoholic fathers, both would project professional exuberance with a corresponding private tendency toward depression. And in time, the young man from Bristol would be similarly beloved by the public for the traits that Fairbanks had embodied—athleticism, the projection of optimism, the habit of always turning on his radiant personality whenever a camera was present.

What struck Archie at the time of their first meeting was Fairbanks's entirely sincere noblesse oblige, the way Fairbanks had of enjoying his own celebrity—a trait it would take Archie Leach nearly a lifetime to master. And the clothes. He was entranced by Fairbanks's clothes. A half-century later, he would be talking to Ralph Lauren and describe in photographic detail Fairbanks's appearance and wardrobe. He told Lauren that he really should make a double-breasted tuxedo, "like the one worn by Fairbanks, same lapel and all."

Just before the end of the great swashbuckler's life, Fairbanks would encounter the younger man again and graciously compliment him on a recent performance. Fairbanks didn't remember their first, glancing meeting, but the younger man wasn't offended, nor did he remind him. The fact that he had received a compliment from his idol meant that "my cup overflowed."

The *Olympic* arrived in New York on July 28, and Archie was listed on the manifest as "Archibald Alec Leach." It was attested that he had paid for his own passage, but his occupation had been upgraded to "artist." His marital status was single, his skills were listed as reading and writing, his permanent residence as London, his final destination the Globe Theatre in New York. He asserted that he had £50 in his pocket, and that he was five-nine at the age of sixteen—tall for his age, but four inches and change from his full height.

There was one other thing: the length of his stay was listed as "indefinite." He wasn't kidding; he would not return to England until 1929.

IN 1920, the tallest building in New York was the Woolworth Building, at sixty stories. The scale of the city, its frenetic bustle, made it a different world for a boy from relatively sedate Bristol, where the buildings topped out at five or six stories.

The Pender troupe had been booked to play the Globe Theatre, but after they arrived the venue was changed to the Hippodrome, the world's largest theater, on Sixth Avenue between 43rd and 44th Streets. It was a huge barn, seating 5,300. The size of the theater mitigated against any act depending on intimacy, so the Pender troupe was perfect. When they weren't doing their act at the daily afternoon and evening performances sandwiched between elephant or aquatic acts utilizing the theater's 960,000 gallon tank, the eight boys split domestic duties in their rooms in a theatrical hotel at 46th Street, off Eighth Avenue.

The apartment had a central hallway with rooms on either side. Archie seems to have been the designated dogsbody, delegated to, as he remembered it, "keep accounts for, cater for, and market for, to wash dishes for, to make the beds for, and to cook for every other occupant of that apartment. . . . Thanks to my Boy Scout training, I knew how to cook a stew. . . . It was like a real family. I even learned how to sew and iron." The only day off was Sunday, when Archie would walk to the East Side and gape at the mansions. "I did fantasize about living inside one of those places. I really did. The people inside those places just had to have magical lives. Wasn't I naïve?"

When he wasn't working onstage or slaving at the apartment, Archie took in the city via open-air buses. "The first thing I loved about America was how fast it all seemed," he would say. "The second thing was the ice cream. There were so many flavors, many more than they had in England at the time. Then I made the greatest discovery of all—it was something called a banana split. There was no such thing in England!"

He developed his first serious crush, a twenty-year-old girl named Gladys Kincaid who was on the bill at the Hippodrome. She apparently lied about her age to Archie, who remembered her as being sixteen. (The 1930 U.S. census listed Kincaid as thirty years old, an "Actress, theater" and her mother as "wardrobe mistress.") It didn't go anywhere, he remembered ruefully—he remembered almost everything with a touch of rue—because of his shyness.

After their Hippodrome show closed in 1921, the Pender troupe was booked on the B. F. Keith vaudeville circuit in Cleveland, Chicago, Boston, even playing the acme of vaudeville, the Palace in New York City. A few months after that, Archie began what would become an intensive study of America as the Pender troupe went on the road to smaller cities and towns. During Christmas week of 1921, the troupe was in Syracuse, where they were billed as "Animal impersonators, stilt walkers and eccentric dancers," and where two great comedians had the opportunity to appraise each other in their chrysalis stages.

Variety wrote that, "Apparently figuring that business would be off anyway and that it would therefore be a waste of money to bring in top-notch headliners this week, Keith's offers one of the least attractive bills of the year. The two best acts on the bill are the Bob Pender Troupe and Jack Benny, the latter pulling one line that was so good that it was 'out' after the first show. Benny recalled his last visit here at the Temple—'the place where the strongest man gets the best seat.'"

The *Syracuse Herald* promoted the Pender troupe as "athletes who . . . were hailed at their recent appearance at the New York

Hippodrome with a reception that was astonishing. Perhaps the biggest attraction of the act is the fact that it is not offered in the light of an athletic one, but as an unusual comedy pantomime."

Archie would become friends with many vaudeville veterans, and invariably speak of them with great affection, but he never mentioned Benny. Perhaps it was a case of ships passing in the theatrical night, or perhaps the third act on the bill—Benny—wouldn't deign to speak to the chasers at the end of the bill—the Pender troupe.

ARCHIE LEACH'S VAUDEVILLE CAREER divides neatly into segments:

JULY 1920–SEPTEMBER 1922: Pender's troupe.

SEPTEMBER 1922–APRIL 1923: The Pender troupe minus Archie is back at the Hippodrome in a show called *Better Times*.

JANUARY 1925–JULY 1925: Archie Leach disappears from the trade papers in what seems to have been a lengthy period of unemployment.

AUGUST 1925–FEBRUARY 1926: The act known as Robinson, Janis and Leach tours second- and third-tier vaudeville towns.

These early years were Archie's immersion in the world of American show business, and he seems to have taken full advantage of it. When the Pender troupe played Washington, D.C., on a bill with the Eddie Foy family, they were introduced to ex-President Woodrow Wilson, who was in a wheelchair as a result of his 1919 stroke.

In April 1922, the Pender troupe was in Chicago, playing the Orpheum's State-Lake Theatre, in a mini-vaudeville bill that ran continuously from 11 a.m. to 11 p.m., backing up a movie called *Reckless Youth* starring Elaine Hammerstein. Across town at the Colonial, Will Rogers was headlining the *Ziegfeld Frolic*. Vaudeville was also represented at the Palace, where Eddie Foy Jr. and a couple of his siblings were headlining a bill that included Fink's Mules and Joe Laurie Jr., the monologist who would end his days writing for *Variety* and compiling the first and most valuable book about vaudeville.

The Eddie Foy show was on a much higher level than the show at the State-Lake, because Foy and company only had to do two shows a day compared to the four or so that the Pender troupe did. Archie must have dropped in at the Palace to check out the competition, because that same month he had his picture taken in a companionable group that included Foy, his brother Charlie, and Laurie. The location was Waukesha, Wisconsin, a town the Pender troupe didn't play. Archie remembered that the Foys invited him to join them for breakfast and paid for his meal. (Archie placed the event in Milwaukee, but the fact that they were playing on different bills puts the event in Waukesha.) The boy who had been collecting autographs of music hall artists in Bristol just a few years earlier was probably slightly overwhelmed by his proximity to the vaudeville elite, but he was obviously accepted by the intensely democratic performers, who only cared if you were a pro.

If Elias Leach's occasional letters to his son are any indication, Archie was making an effort to be a good son and was sending money home to his father. In one letter from April 1923, Elias refers to a ten shilling note, "which I thank you very much for it only shows me how much you must think of us at home in sending us the money. I hope my boy that you will never be in want for your generosity towards us." The dutiful support from his teenaged son might also explain why Elias had consented to Archie's apprenticeship in the first place. There is no mention of Elsie Leach in any of Elias's surviving letters to his son.

Archie became fast friends with a man named Don Barclay, whom he had first met when he was just starting out with Pender. The other boys in the troupe had been teaching Archie what they called "the art of makeup," which entailed painting his nose blue, his eye sockets green, and his mouth white. Barclay rescued him, and the two became fast friends. Barclay was older than Archie, so even though Archie was told to call him "Don," his respect for his elders meant that it usually came out "Yes, Don, sir."

Barclay also saved Archie from his own youthful affectations. At one point, Archie went to see the Marx Brothers. Inspired by Zeppo, he began wearing a bow tie that was attached to a rubber band. Barclay thought it was ridiculous and one day pulled the tie out for a good six inches, then let it snap back. That was the last time Archie wore a bow tie attached to a rubber band.

"He was kind to me," Archie would say years later. "He helped me with my makeup. He gave me tips on what to do on the stage and he even helped out with food and lodging. [When] I came to the United States [and was out of work] there was Barclay, lending the helping hand. He put me up in a hotel, bought my food, and gave me money to spend while I was looking for a job. Nobody had ever been so wonderful to me." Long after Archie was no longer Archie but Cary, with a list of friends that included Lady Mendl and Frederick Lonsdale, he would still be happy to work with Don Barclay.

In May 1922, Archie told Bob Pender that he wanted to go home to Bristol. On May 21, Pender wrote Elias Leach:

> I am writing this to inform you that Archie is coming home. He leaves New York by the Cunard Liner *Berengaria* on May 29th and should arrive Southampton June 2 or 3. He has made up his mind to come home. I offered him 35 dollars a week . . . and he will not accept it, as he says he cannot do on it so I offered three pounds ten a week clear & all his expenses paid but he says he wishes to come home. . . . I must tell you he is most extravagant and wants to stay at the best hotels & live altogether beyond his means. . . . He is like all young people of his age, & he thinks he only has to ask and have & I must tell you he has very big ideas for a boy of his age. . . . Mrs. Pender has talked to him but it no use, he will not listen, so I should like to hear if he arrives home safely.

In fact, Archie had no intention of going back to Bristol. The story about going home was a contrivance designed to get him out of his contract. Archie took the passage money Pender advanced him and stayed in New York, beginning one of the most fascinating phases of his life.

CHAPTER THREE

O rry George Kelly was born on December 31, 1897 in Kiama, New South Wales, a small coastal town seventy-three miles from Sydney. Kelly grew to love nightlife, art, and drinking, not necessarily in that order. The drinking was a paternal inheritance. "If you would drink like a Purdue," his mother told his father, referencing her maiden name, "you would drink like a gent, but you drink like a Kelly."

When Kelly was seventeen he moved to Sydney to study, and in 1922 he moved to New York to become an actor. Acting didn't work out, but the man who became known as Orry-Kelly—his friends called him "Jack"—eventually found a viable alternative by becoming one of Hollywood's legendary costume designers.

In New York, he met vaudevillians George Burns, Gracie Allen, and Jack Benny, who all became lifelong friends. Orry-Kelly was living at 10 Commerce Street in Greenwich Village, next to Edna St. Vincent Millay, just around the corner from the Cherry Lane Theatre. As he told the story, "One winter evening, through these same black iron gates walked Archie Leach. . . . He was carrying a little two-foot-square shiny black tin box which held all his worldly possessions, and he was wearing a much shinier black suit. He had been locked out of his hall bedroom.

"I took him in."

Archie Leach's version of this event was slightly different. "I was so poor I couldn't afford a room . . . but luck was with me. Instead of a cold-water dingy room, four of us pooled our resources or lack of them and managed to rent Bert Lytell's charming duplex in Greenwich Village. None of us could afford it alone, but together we managed the rent, though there were times we didn't manage anything else. . . . It was right back of the Cherry Lane Theater, and looked out on a charming little courtyard. Even on the days we didn't know when we'd eat next or which of us would earn something that would supply a meal for all of us we'd look out at the little courtyard and remember how few people had a tree or bush to look at it in New York and it made us feel good."

George Burns was there, knew all the parties concerned, and he didn't feel any need to obfuscate: "I met Cary Grant when he was still calling himself Archie Leach and was sharing an apartment with costume designer Orry-Kelly in New York. We were all starting out together, Archie and Orry-Kelly and Jack [Benny] and me and Gracie. Gracie and Orry-Kelly stayed close friends for their whole lives."

Orry-Kelly dated this event as 1926, but Archie was working for most of 1926, so it's probable that it came two or three years earlier. In any case, Archie and Orry-Kelly were roommates on an off-and-on basis. Every morning, Archie would press his black suit, get on the subway at 14th Street and head uptown to the National Vaudeville Artists clubhouse at 229 West 46th Street. This was the area known to vaudevillians as Panic Beach, where dancers, singers, and actors would wait around for their next audition while cadging a cup of coffee and sorting through the mail that had arrived while they were working out of town. The wisest ones auditioned for everything, even if it wasn't their specialty, in the hope that expanding their skill set would work to their advantage.

If there was nothing on offer for a young acrobat, Archie would listen to all the other unemployed acts tell lies about their glory days on the Pantages circuit, when in reality most of them had been working the Gus Sun circuit—the lowest rung on the vaudeville ladder.

Vaudeville was basically divided between upscale circuits where performers played two shows a day, and downscale circuits where they played three or four shows a day. The former was preferable to the latter in that it paid more because the theaters were in bigger, more cosmopolitan towns; the latter was preferable in spite of the lower pay because there was more work, as much as fifty-two weeks a year, assuming you could put up with the nonstop grind and the smaller audiences.

Everybody who was in vaudeville remembered the hard work, but they also remembered that it was implicitly democratic. "Anybody could be in it," remembered George Burns. "It wasn't restricted to people who could sing or dance or fly through the air—anybody who could do anything that somebody else would pay to see could be in vaudeville." One of Burns's favorite acts was called "The Twelve Speed Maniacs," which consisted of a dozen men who would assemble a Model T in precisely two minutes. The climax of the act came when they drove the car offstage.

The song-and-dance man Donald O'Connor was born into vaudeville at the same time Archie Leach was struggling to create a niche. O'Connor remembered the friendly atmosphere, the way the showgirls hugged and stroked him, the way the great magician Thurston would help him with his correspondence school homework. Between the days spent at the theater, and the long train rides to the next engagement, it was easy to forge friendships that lasted the rest of their lives.

"There were acrobats and magicians," said O'Connor, "but there were also crazy acts, unclassifiable acts that were a series of non-sequiturs. Swayne's Rats and Cats, which was a small arena on the stage where rats would chase cats. That was the entire act! There was an act called Think-A-Drink Hoffman, who would come out in a tux with a portable bar and a cocktail shaker. 'Anyone like a drink?' he'd ask. The audience would request drinks and he would make them Manhattans and Grasshoppers while keeping up a stream of patter. The audience loved him. Of course, by the time he finished his act, they were pretty smashed! A great act in vaudeville was never written down; it was made up over the years."

Around the corner from the National Vaudeville Artists Clubhouse was a lunch counter called Ye Eat Shoppe, which offered meals for 65 cents and 45 cents. After opting for the 45 cent meal, Archie would have coffee with some friends. At dinnertime, Archie would troop back to Commerce Street and tell his roommate about his day. Orry-Kelly was earning a living by making colorful hand-blocked neckties, which Archie took to wearing. His doctor, Berson by name, liked his tie, and bought a range of the neckwear. In turn, Dr. Berson's other patients began buying the ties, and Orry-Kelly cut Archie in for a commission.

It was about this time that Archie met a man named George Tilyou at a party. Tilyou liked the young man and got him a job stilt-walking at Coney Island's Steeplechase Park, which was owned by Tilyou's family. Archie remembered his salary as $40 a week, which sounds high for an out-of-work vaudevillian, but his memory for money was good, so it's certainly possible.

Archie quickly learned that stilt-walking presented certain occupational unpredictabilities that he could have done without. Small children, for instance. Archie on stilts presented what he called "a tempting target for aspiring Jack the Giant-Killers. Saturdays and Sundays were hazardous." He grew used to what he called "the rearguard shove. . . . I dreaded the lone ace who came in zeroing in out of the sun, flying a small bamboo cane with a curved handle. One good yank as he whizzed past and he'd won the encounter hands down (my hands down)." Stilts put you high in the air, so Archie grew used to doing an expert tuck and roll. Mainly, he scuffled.

Just how much he scuffled is proved by the National Variety Artists Yearbook from mid-1924. Over the space of four-hundred-odd pages, several thousand vaudeville artists are advertised, including Jack Benny and Burns & Allen (they had the same agent). The acts on offer ranged from Eddie Cantor and Al Jolson, whose vaudeville days were far behind them, to one Al Lydell, "America's Foremost Portrayer of Senility." But Archie Leach is nowhere to be found. In 1924, four years after his arrival in America, even the basement level of vaudeville was far above Archie's head. He was stuck with stilt-walking, and even that was presenting problems.

George Burns thought that part of the problem was that Archie "was a rotten stilt-walker. I mean, he always looked like he was about to keel over, and there just isn't too much work for a stilt-walker with a bad sense of balance." Burns said that when Archie wasn't stilt-walking he was selling ties out of a suitcase on Broadway with one eye peeled for the cops. It seemed that Archie and Jack Kelly had upped their game. Burns reported that Orry-Kelly would buy a dozen ties for a dollar apiece and paint them, after which Archie sold them for three dollars apiece. Archie did the stencils for the ties, while Orry-Kelly did the detail work. "We did so well," wrote Orry-Kelly, "that I offered him a 50-50 split if he could keep his mind off his blondes and the NVA, and not mess up too many ties. We signed the ties Kelly-Leach. This way Archie could work from dinnertime until the early hours of the morning, and still have his days free for auditions and his blondes."

While Archie was struggling, George Burns and Gracie Allen were doing just fine. Archie had met Burns when he was known as Nat Burns, was courting Gracie Allen, and was already a close friend of Jack Benny's. "He was the best-looking guy I'd ever seen," said Burns. "We used to have dinner together once in a while. At the automat everything was cheap."

Archie admired Burns's impeccable timing as well as his sangfroid. It was Burns who told him of the crucial importance of ingratiating yourself with the audience without making the effort obvious. "If the audience likes you, it makes getting laughs easier," Burns would say.

"George was an absolute genius," Archie remembered, "timing his laughs with that cigar. . . . The straight man says the plant line, and the comic answers it. He doesn't move while that line is said. That's the comedy line. . . . As soon as it's getting a little quiet, the straight man talks into it, and the comic answers it. And up goes the laugh again."

When Burns and Allen played the Palace, the acme of vaudeville, Archie and some friends chipped in and bought a lavish $25 bouquet to be presented to the act as the audience was applauding. When, Archie asked, should the flowers be presented to George and Gracie? "After the third encore," said Burns. "Now, *that's* confidence!" remembered Archie.

At some point, Bob Pender became aware that he had advanced Archie money for a return trip to Bristol that Archie had never made. Pender began to make noises about prosecution. In a commendable display of fatherly loyalty that managed to ignore his son's situational ethics, Elias wrote Archie a typically unpunctuated letter of pointless advice:

> Well if he does try and get you out of your engagement while you are over there it only shows how jealous he must be of your success and being on your own bat. Now Archie directly you get informa tion about what he intends to do to you try and get in touch with the national vaudeville artists institute and ask them if they take up such cases as yours for these kinds of artists clubs generally employ a lawyer if needed to fight a case for a member without the member paying him as they have what is known as a sinking fund

for these things and are only too willing to do their best for their member's welfare.

When they weren't making ties, Jack and Archie painted. At one point, the mob bought the nearby house of composer/conductor Walter Damrosch and converted it into a (highly illegal) casino. Jack and Archie painted green frogs on the walls of the music salon in what Orry-Kelly recalled as "sort of Paul Klee feeling . . . the frogs looked like licentious old men."

Orry-Kelly was gay, allowing for some random collisions with heterosexuality—he would be a customer at Lee Francis's bordello in Hollywood, and drunken party sex with Norma Talmadge resulted in a public engagement. (Since Talmadge was just getting over a marriage to George Jessel, it would have been a definite step up.) Orry-Kelly wrote his memories of Archie in the early 1960s, when relations between the two men had been frigid for years. He goes out of his way to make frequent mention of Archie's girls, but never explains what besides financial desperation impelled Archie to room with a gay man. In later years, Grant would instruct Orry-Kelly to "Tell them nothing," regarding their early days in the Village. "I don't know why," Orry-Kelly wrote. "There was really never anything to hide; he had always lived a perfectly normal life."

For his part, Grant would always shy away from acknowledging his friendship with Jack Kelly. In Grant's version, Kelly lived in the apartment above him, where he was rooming with three other "non-actor types" named Thayer Ridgeway, Eric Erickson, and "Amby" Holland.

What is clear from Orry-Kelly's memoir is that Archie's supreme object of contemplation was neither men nor women, but Archie. His charm was remarkable, but so was his narcissism and, occasionally, his temper. One day Orry-Kelly found him looking in the mirror. After some study, Archie said, "There's no division between my jawbone and my neck." He began exercising by jutting his chin to the left, pulling it back sharply, then to the right and back again. Orry-Kelly believed that this exercise was one of the reasons his friend retained a trim jawline into his sixties.

Whenever Archie had any money he would go to the movies to study technique, because he was coming to the conclusion that his

future lay in comedy, not acrobatics. Although Archie's natural incli-
nation would always be toward the brisk, he liked Stan Laurel and
Harry Langdon, despite the fact that Laurel worked methodically and
Langdon worked paralytically.

Archie and Jack Kelly met Minnie Chaplin, the wife of Charlie's
beloved brother Sydney. Syd and Minnie had an open marriage, and
Minnie made her interest in Archie quite obvious. As far as Archie
was concerned, a possible screen test Minnie offered at Warner Bros.,
where her husband was under contract, was far more interesting than
Minnie.

Orry-Kelly and Archie threw a party they hoped would entice
Minnie to hurry up and arrange that screen test. Jack Benny was
there, and so were Burns and Allen. Burns took over the party with
his singing, which offended the more aristocratic Minnie. She got up
and walked to the window overlooking the courtyard, whereupon
the undiscouraged Burns went outside and sang toward the window
where she was standing. Jack Benny, who was always Burns's best
audience, began pounding the floor in hysterics. Archie ignored the
entertainment and sat by Minnie, excluding the vaudevillians who
were entertaining themselves, if not the guest of honor.

After the party was over, Orry-Kelly upbraided Archie for high-
hatting his friends. Archie responded with a closed fist to his roommate's jaw, knocking out both a tooth and Orry-Kelly. It was not
the first time Archie proved adept with his fists; Orry-Kelly saw him
cold-cock the actor James Hall with one punch. After Kelly woke up,
he looked into Archie's bedroom, where he saw him sound asleep,
with a bottle of gin perched on the night table. Orry-Kelly began
yelling and ordered Archie out of the house, but the bad boy stalled
by bringing his victim some orange juice into which he poured some
gin to kill the pain.

"Then, what was known in those days as the 'Archie Leach charm'
took over," remembered Orry-Kelly.

Drawing back the window curtain, showing the thickly falling snow,
Archie went into a Stan Laurel sad-eyed bit, then a Harry Langdon,
then every comedy routine he could think of. He even did a back flip
and, taking a leap, ran halfway up the wall and, hanging onto the
ledge, looking out the window, likened me to the cruel slave owner

in *Uncle Tom's Cabin:* "You ain't going to throw [me] out into that cold, cold snow, are you, Simon Legree?"

Orry-Kelly relented, and so did Minnie Chaplin. She finally lined up the screen test, but first insisted on Archie taking her to Coney Island for dinner. Archie was mortified when he was recognized by some of his stilt-walking friends. "Why run away?" asked Orry-Kelly, after Archie told him of his embarassment. "It would have been so much simpler to tell the truth. Let people like you for what you are, just be truthful, it's so much easier."

Archie thought that was ridiculous. It would take him nearly forty years before he appreciated Orry-Kelly's wisdom. There appears to be no actual record of a screen test with Warner Bros. Orry-Kelly said that the general reaction was that Archie was too much the matinee idol. So Archie went back to the NVA and to Doreen Glover, the showgirl he kept company with for a few years.

IN AUGUST 1925, Archie latched on with an act that became known as Robinson, Janis & Leach. Constance Robinson was the woman, Jack Janis the other man, and the act had been written by one Jean Dalrymple. The skit involved a girl engaged to a dull but pleasant man, until she meets a staggeringly handsome competitor. "The casting people kept sending me Rudolph Valentino types and I kept saying 'No,'" said Dalrymple. "In came Archibald Leach. He was absolute perfection. He was a little shy, had a peculiar walk, and a strange accent, but he was ideal. . . . Oh, he enchanted me!" She wouldn't be the last woman staggered by the boy from Bristol.

In fact, the "strange" accent was one of the first signs of Archie's capacity for a protean level of self-invention. Bristol is only a few hours from London, but the Bristol accent is nothing like that of the City. Rather, it's a West England accent, a laborer's dialect that places an L on the end of every word ending in a vowel. India is pronounced "Indial." Similarly, "Europe" is "Yerp," and "Bristol" is "Brissle." The Bristol accent is hyper-local—"It doesn't extend 40 miles outside of the town," says the English diplomat Sir Peter Heap, who was raised there.

For an actor, a Bristol accent would be deadly unless he wanted to spend his career playing farm foremen, so Archie had been working to get rid of it. "I was very conscious of my lack of education when I started," he would tell one friend. "I didn't want it to show, so I invented an accent. . . . The rest I stole from Noel Coward." Betsy Drake, who would become his third wife, said that "In Cary's day you got nowhere—*no*where—with a lower class accent."

Actually, Grant only thought he stole a lot from Noel Coward, who never had Archie's energy. But Archie understood that, with any luck, what begins as flagrant imitation can eventually be converted into an authentic projection of an individual personality. "Everything starts with pretense," he would say late in his life. "One *pretends* to do something, or copy someone or some teacher, until it can be done confidently and easily in what becomes one's *own* manner."

The accent he eventually came up with is usually categorized as "mid-Atlantic," a suggestion of an accent more than an actual accent. Sir Peter Heap says that "Most English people wouldn't think Cary Grant's accent was English at all." Along with the mid-Atlantic accent, there was a touch of Cockney, which he picked up from his years with the Pender troupe, where most of the boys were from the East End of London.

Robinson, Janis & Leach seem to have broken in their act in St. Louis, at the Grand Opera House in late August of 1925. After that, they mostly played small cities and tank towns, generally three shows a day—a matinee and two evening shows. Their agent was a Chicagoan named William Jacobs, who had a minor specialty in animal acts—he handled two different mule acts, one called Blake's Mules, the other Fink's Mules ("Something with a kick"), not to mention "The Intellectual Bulldog," who was named Snoozer when he wasn't onstage.

Archie was in the small time, but in America instead of England. With Pender in England he had worked up to six performances a day, while in America it was about half that. But there were still all-night train rides to the next town. "Had to sleep in the coach car," he recollected, and there was no such thing as a private room. "Meals were cans of beans heated on radiators. You'd wash clothes in the bathtub."

Working the road exacerbated Archie's pervasive sense of loneliness, not to mention rootlessness. "On the night trains, I'd look into the windows of the houses along the way and see people living ordinary lives. That was my goal. To live in my own home."

Because he was now acting, not tumbling, he began to have the classic actor's nightmare, where he was onstage and didn't know the lines because he hadn't studied them. The other actors stared at him, but in the dream Archie just stood there, flop sweat pouring down. The dreams were only the tip of what became a free-flowing river of anxiety. "I used to apologize for every little thing I said or did, or hadn't said or hadn't done, or forgotten to say, etc. I used to apologize for living." His mother had projected her anxiety onto a son who had absorbed all of it.

Jean Dalrymple said that Archie had a bad habit of giggling after every funny line, but nobody seemed to mind. *The Billboard*, the vaudeville trade paper, caught Robinson, Janis & Leach at the Majestic Theatre in Chicago and outlined both the act and the audience's response in the issue of September 26, 1925: "Two men and a girl offer a comedy dialog in which the man is short on a dinner check. Fifteen minutes in one and a half [scenes]; two bows."

At the end of September, they played Davenport, where they were billed second of six acts; at the beginning of October, they were in Des Moines, working on a bill that also featured the movie *Parisian Love*, starring Clara Bow. The *Des Moines Register* said that the act involved "a skit combining comedy patter and singing." They played Minneapolis's Seventh Street Theatre with Frank Braidwood, "the cowboy vocalist," and Jerome and Newell in "A Chink Episode." Later that month, they were in Milwaukee.

In November, they played Decatur, Illinois, with the movie accompaniment being *Lorraine of the Lions* with Norman Kerry. After that they were off to Bloomington, where they were billed third out of five acts and the movie was a Mack Sennett short, *Super-Hooper-Dyne Lizzies*.

They laid off for two weeks then went back to work in Detroit, where the *Free Press* barely acknowledged their existence: "Robinson, Janis and Leach add a lot of nonsense in their act, *The Woman Pays*, which is not as romantic as it sounds." From Detroit, they took the train to Huntington, Indiana, where they worked with an act called Kennedy and Peterson, "Hokum Ala Carte" and a movie entitled *The Lady Who Lied* with Lewis Stone and Nita Naldi.

January 1926 brought them to Asheville, North Carolina, where the *Citizen-Times* said that "Their contribution to the stage is of the skit variety, comedy patter and singing . . . a bright little tid-bit with much travesty, brightly told and some good songs." After that it was on to Tampa, billed third out of five acts, among which was "Bee Jung, Flying Venus of the Air." The *Tampa Tribune* was unimpressed: "Robinson, Janis and Leach in 'The Woman Pays,' offer a light comedy skit that pleases, though it lacks distinctive merit in any one particular." Then St. Petersburg and Miami at the beginning of February 1926, followed by West Palm Beach and Pensacola.

They zigzagged to Nashville, where they shared the bill with Lola Arlene, a "water nymph" who worked with four trained seals, not to mention "The Eminent Girl Saxophonist." The *Nashville Tennessean* obliquely referred to Archie as one of two "dapper male comedians." *

What his immersion in American vaudeville taught Archie Leach is not hard to quantify: it taught him everything. Vaudeville spawned acts that privileged vivid personalities above all—the projection of personality was the only way to differentiate between acrobats, between jugglers. James Cagney spoke for his entire profession when he wrote that, "Vaudeville . . . has had the greatest single effect on my life, both as an individual and as a performer. I still think of myself essentially as a vaudevillian, as a song and dance man.

> The vaudevillians I knew by and large were marvelous people. Ninety percent of them had no schooling, but they had a vivid something or other about them that absolutely riveted an audience's attention. First of all, those vaudevillians knew something that ultimately I came to understand and believe—that audiences are the ones who determine material. They buy the tickets."

As far as Archie was concerned, vaudeville's contribution to his skill set was timing. "I learned to time laughs. When to talk into an audience's laughter. When not to wait for a laugh. In all sorts of theaters, of all sizes, playing to all sorts of people, timing laughs that changed at every single performance."

---

* James Cagney would later claim that he replaced Archie in an act known as Parker, Rand & Leach, which then became Parker, Rand & Cagney. The newspapers mention a couple of bookings for Parker, Rand & Cagney, one in May 1925 in Asheville (*Asheville Citizen-Times*, 5-14-25), another in December 1925 in Cincinnati (*Cincinnati Enquirer*, 12-13-25). There is no extant mention of an act called Parker, Rand & Leach. Vaudevillians generally had deadly accurate memories, but Cagney was either mistaken or Parker, Rand & Leach flew far beneath the radar.

It follows that Archie eventually became similar to Cagney and a lot of other fellow vaudevillians in that he was always true but rarely particularly subtle. When he wanted to, he would simply seize a comedy scene, sometimes with mugging that could verge on the outrageous: cocking his head, whinnying and grumbling sotto voce, arching an eyebrow, or drawing his head back like an appalled ostrich. But it was always done stylishly, rhythmically. He would be foolish, but he would never be a fool. He would learn that if he amused himself there was a good chance he would amuse the audience.

This basic attitude was in line with the traditions, not just of American vaudeville, but of America—casual, disrespectful of authority, romantic around the edges but uncomfortable with mooniness and suspicious of the sentimental.

These were years in which Archie grew completely comfortable with America, up to and including its national game. He remembered that he first played baseball in New Orleans. He figured that if he could play cricket he could play baseball. It turned out that he could indeed hit the ball, but it took him a while to grasp the fact that in baseball you have to run after you hit the ball.

When he was becalmed in New York in these years he would take in a game from the third base seats at the Polo Grounds, which is why he became a confirmed fan of the New York Giants. This attachment was eventually transferred to the Brooklyn Dodgers, and after the team moved to the West Coast, to the Los Angeles Dodgers. He was always a knowledgeable fan, attentively reading box scores as well as the daily game stories. Sitting in the seats, talking to the fans around him was also crucial in helping him learn colloquial American English.

His talent was gradually being refined, as were his tastes, but what remained unresolved was Archie's passionate need for show business fame. The realization that just being a working professional was never going to be enough hit him one day when he was passing by the Winter Garden Theatre. He saw a crew erecting Al Jolson's name in lights, and he suddenly started crying. He realized that he wanted, *needed* what Jolson had—an incandescent level of stardom acknowledged by the entire world. "He was a legend. Great singer. There was nobody bigger in the twenties. *Nobody*. . . . And Jolson had gotten there . . . because he was the absolute best."

Archie may have been living a hand-to-mouth existence, as well as working toward a distant goal, but he was concerned with respectability, with doing the right thing. In 1927, he took out a life insurance policy, and made "Elias Leach, my father," the beneficiary.

It was Reggie Hammerstein, the younger brother of Oscar Hammerstein II, who suggested that Archie try his hand at musical comedy. It needn't take the place of vaudeville, he told Archie, but it would give him a fallback when bookings grew scarce. Reggie took him to Arthur Hammerstein, who thought Archie had the makings of a younger—and cheaper—Jack Buchanan. He promptly cast him in a small part in *Golden Dawn*, which premiered at the end of November 1927.

Golden Dawn was the product of gilt-edged creators with a long roster of hits in their immediate past: book and lyrics by Oscar Hammerstein II and Otto Harbach, a score by Herbert Stothart and Emmerich Kalman. But credentials are no guarantee. *Golden Dawn* is the only extant musical about the African slave trade, an embarrassment then, an embarrassment now. The libretto involves a blond girl named Dawn who is captured by an African tribe as a young girl. She is all set to be the tribal princess until an escaped POW shows up. Love walks in, and the natives get restless. The songs included "My Bwana," "Jungle Shadows," and "When I Crack My Whip." Called an "overheated colonialist fever dream" by one theatrical historian, *Golden Dawn* nevertheless ran for a respectable 184 performances. Besides playing his nominal part, Archie also understudied the leading man.

At this point in his career, Archie's primary influence was the aforesaid Jack Buchanan, probably because for young English actors in this period, style was at least as important as talent. Maybe more so. "We all had our blue serge suits and played tennis and backgammon," he said. "I used to emulate actors like Buchanan and A. E. Matthews. I used to keep my hand in my pocket so"—and here he struck an appropriately casual pose—"but only because I was so nervous I couldn't pull it out."

Archie was living in Yorkville, at 325 East 80th Street, when he signed a contract with Hammerstein on January, 12, 1928. He was to be paid $75 a week for the 1927–28 season, with yearly options through 1933 which would bring his salary to $800 by the conclusion of the contract.

Golden Dawn might have been embarrassing, but it got Archie on Broadway, which meant he was definitely on the upswing. In 1928,

Archie bought a Packard Phaeton, a monster with a 143-inch wheel-base that made every turn a near-miss adventure. Archie adored the car. "I washed, polished, scrubbed, waxed, patted, doted upon, and finally even learned to drive, that car."

Hammerstein next cast him in *Polly*, which proved to be a rockier ride than *Golden Dawn* had ever been—Archie was replaced while the show was out of town. It wasn't a disaster, though, because he was soon cast by Marilyn Miller to replace Jack Donahue in the great Ziegfeld hit *Rosalie*.

It was around here that Archie formed a double act with his vaude-ville pal Don Barclay, who had appeared in a couple of Ziegfeld's *Follies*, and made some silent comedies. Both of them were between gigs, so Barclay and Archie were invited by a friend to use a cottage he had on Long Island, where they devised a satirical mind-reading act, with Archie as a fraudulent psychic.

Barclay & Leach got scattered fill-in bookings, but Barclay said that the act broke up in Newark when a theater manager insisted he get a better straight man. The two men would be friendly for the rest of Barclay's life. Barclay worked in small parts in Hollywood—his last movie was *Mary Poppins*—and became a noted caricaturist distin-guished by working in nearly every military theater in World War II, including time spent with a one-man USO show attached to General Claire Chennault's Flying Tigers in Burma, China, and India.

After the Hammersteins sold Archie's contract to the Shubert Brothers, in January 1929, the Shuberts put him in a show called *Boom Boom*, opposite Jeanette MacDonald. Archie played Reggie Phipps, and his occasional girlfriend Doreen Glover was in the show as well.

MacDonald thought the script was atrocious, and she wasn't too sure about Archie either. They had a duet entitled "Nina" in which MacDonald sang, "From toes to her forehead/This bimbo was *torrid*/I mean this tamale was *hot*," to which Archie would respond, "She kissed with such *pash*/that she'd scorch your *moustache*/And that's hot enough, is it *not*?"

MacDonald was an extremely ambitious woman, and she could tell that *Boom Boom* was not going to do anything for anybody con-nected with it. "This," she told J. J. Shubert, "is the rottenest show I've ever been in!" As for Archie, "He was absolutely terrible," said MacDonald, "but everyone liked him. He had charm."

The Shuberts discounted tickets, but *Boom Boom* barely ran for nine weeks on Broadway, closing on March 30, 1929. Nevertheless, the Shuberts sent it out on the road, to Pittsburgh, Cincinnati, Detroit, and Chicago, after which MacDonald bailed. A month later, in mid-1929, Ernst Lubitsch signed her to play opposite Maurice Chevalier in *The Love Parade*, and she was officially in the Big Time.

The Shuberts thought Archie had possibilities; an interoffice memo dated July 29, 1929, says that "Mr. Lee Shubert . . . said it would be okay if Leach was signed with us for next season. He is." The new contract was signed on July 12, 1929, and ran until September 30, 1930. Archie was guaranteed twenty-five weeks of work per year at $300 per week. The contract was exclusive except when it wasn't— if there was no employment from the Shuberts for five consecutive weeks, Archie was allowed to work in vaudeville, film, or concerts, but he had to drop whatever else he was doing and come when the Shuberts called. There was an option for an additional year at $400. The option would be exercised on April 29, 1930.

After the road tour of *Boom Boom*, Archie was seized by homesickness and booked a trip back to Europe. He arrived in Liverpool aboard the White Star's SS *Adriatic* on July 22, 1929. His occupation was listed as "actor," and he stayed at the Regent Palace Hotel in London. After London, he went to Paris, where he took in the Folies Bergère, then it was off to Southampton, where he watched the Cowes Regatta, and finally, back to Bristol for the first time in nine years.

Archie overextended his finances on the trip, and he had to wire E. R. Simmons, the Shuberts' casting and wardrobe director, for an advance to get home. Simmons was a flamboyant man—Agnes de Mille described him as "a homosexual with outrageous proclivities"— and was generally known as "Ma" Simmons by the chorus boys he hired. On August 15, Archie wrote Simmons an extended thank-you note in his graceful handwriting. It's an unusually emotional letter for Archie, and indicates the extent of the rigorous self-education he'd been engaged in since he left Bristol. His spelling and punctuation are impeccable, and the content shows a flair beyond many returning natives.

> It's all so interesting—my hometown after so many years—seemingly different and still, looking back to my childhood, so familiar. I've experienced the greatest thrills exploring boyhood haunts—treading

those same sidewalks, remembering incidents of days gone by. I've walked and walked those memorable districts, far from where Dad lives now, and before turning each corner visualized what lies around it and then hesitated, fearing that it might all be altered—but no, once around the corner and it's all just the same—seemingly a little smaller, but actually the same. . . .

Forgive a rather lengthy letter, Mr. Simmons—you're busy, I know, but the pen's raced on—homecomings don't happen every day and I'm naturally full of it—cue for chorus of questions—"full of *what*?" . . . meantime all the best that I know. Sincerest, Archie Leach

Archie left for New York on August 17, arriving nine days later. His reentry papers listed his address as the National Vaudeville Artists Club, 229 West 46th Street. That fall, the Shuberts tentatively penciled Archie into a revival of their *Greenwich Village Follies*. It was a revue they first produced in 1920, the first few of which had been directed by John Murray Anderson. Archie had already done comedy, gymnastics, and had expanded into singing, so a revue was a logical extension.

As it happened, the *Greenwich Village Follies* was canceled. Instead, Archie was slotted into *A Wonderful Night*, a rewrite of *Die Fleder-maus*. Archie felt out of his depth, until the comedian Fred Allen took him to the Woolworth Building. They went up to the observation tower, and Allen pointed Archie toward Broadway. "You could barely see it, it was so tiny," he remembered. "I suddenly got a very good perspective on how small I was and how small my problems really were."

A Wonderful Night opened in October 1929, and Archie was right to have been worried—his reviews were withering. "Archie Leach . . . feels that acting in something by Johann Strauss calls for distinction [but] is somewhat at a loss as to how to achieve it." Another notice pointed out that "Archie Leach sometimes managed to miss the proper note entirely." The bad reviews did not affect Simmons's attention to detail, for he ran what is generally known as a tight ship; his notes are granular and unyielding: "On the velvet curtains, on the side where Smith is, all the marks of the hands are shown. The curtain should be steamed so that these marks of the hands do not show."

Archie did not escape unscathed. Among Simmons's notes for Scene 3 in *A Wonderful Night*: "Please tell Archie Leach not to handle the maid so much. He does this before his wife and spoils the effect afterward. . . .

Also, when Archie Leach and the Maid dance and slap hands and she strikes the pose (which is a good laugh) they must pick up the scene immediately, because if they wait too long for the dialogue it drops the following scene right into the cellar." The show's timing could not have been worse—it opened a few days after the stock market crash, but it still managed a reasonable 125 performances before closing in February.

SHOWS OPEN, SHOWS CLOSE, the stock market goes up and the stock market goes down, but overall Archie was doing well. He was living at the Belvedere Hotel on West 48th Street, and in May 1930, he bought yet another Packard, a 1927 Sport Phaeton. The total price was $819, and Archie made a $300 down payment, with the balance paid off in monthly installments of $44.

So far, so good, but he was still prey to brooding. He had fallen in with a group that included Moss Hart, Preston Sturges, and the actor Sam Levene. They all met regularly at a restaurant called Rudley's at 41st and Broadway. Moss Hart remembered Archie as "a disconsolate young actor." The playwright Edward Chodorov said that they mistook Archie's accent as Australian, which explained his nickname of Kangaroo, which was sometimes replaced by Boomerang. "He was never a very open fellow," Chodorov said, "but he was earnest and we liked him." Archie listened a lot more than he talked, so of course a tableful of writers found him good company.

Although he was working regularly, it would appear that depression was already a boon companion of Archie's, which could have been exacerbated by the fact that his friends were all verbally brilliant. His magpie personality was already formed, and he began adopting traits of people he admired and making them his own. Mainly, he felt he needed to divert attention from the fact that he had left school at the age of fourteen—more of a sensitive issue in England than America.

Archie was on tour with a Shubert show called *The Street Singer* in Boston when, four days before Christmas in 1930, he gave what seems to have been his first interview, to *The Boston Globe*. "ENGLISH ACTOR PRAISES AMERICANS" was the headline, and Archie took the opportunity to philosophize on the differences between English and American actors:

The United States has the cleverest actors. It seems to me that the Americans are a Nation of actors. In England there are few persons who appreciate the histrionic art.

The Englishman wants to act natural on the stage. He wants a part in which he can be himself. He doesn't want to rant and rave or over-act. He is much happier when he can be a well-bred English gentleman of the sort that can be met anywhere in polite society. That is why there are so many politely sophisticated English comedies.

In the United States the average man with ambitions to become an actor expects to be a quite different person from what he is in real life. He sees nothing wrong in subordinating his well-bred personality into something quite rough and tough and wicked. Indeed, the American actor much prefers to be different on the stage from what he is in real life.

Archie went on to talk of Bristol, at which point he segued into fantasy, claiming that he graduated from Clifton College and served as a cabin boy for three months a year on transport boats between Southampton and Le Havre. He then steered back to truth by mentioning that he came to America with the Pender troupe.

He . . . frankly admits that he would like to be an international star. His heart's desire is to alternate between London and New York in light comedy. . . . He scoffs at the idea that he is cut out for sentimental roles. . . . "I want light comedy, and I am not romantic in any feature."

This mélange was not atypical of young actors nursing strong ambitions in the midst of an infirm apprenticeship. And there was one other sentence that foretold his future: "Mr. Leach is a businessman as well as an actor."

THE RESPONSE TO *The Street Singer* was affected by the spread of the Depression, and when the production moved to Toronto, the Shuberts asked Archie to take a pay cut from $400 a week to $275. After he agreed, they sent him a letter thanking him for his "splendid cooperation . . . and the assistance given us during these trying times."

Archie's next engagement for the Shuberts was in the summer of 1931, when he worked at the St. Louis Municipal Opera. The suggestion seems to have come from Orry-Kelly, who was friends with Milton Shubert and had worked at the St. Louis operation the year before. Archie's singing voice would always be on the warbly side, more the voice of a music hall entertainer than a singer. In spite of that, and the fact that Milton Shubert grumbled that Archie was "such a lousy actor," he got the job.

Shortly before he left for St. Louis, Archie was hired by Paramount to make his motion picture debut in a short called *Singapore Sue*. The contract is dated May 8, 1931, and it's generic, with blank spaces for names and fees. Paramount agreed to pay him $150 for six days of work beginning May 13, 1931, and $25 extra per day for anything over six days. Modest money for a modest beginning.

Singapore Sue was written and directed by Casey Robinson, a young screenwriter who would go on to a notable career with credits on such pictures as *Captain Blood, Dark Victory*, and *Now, Voyager*. *Singapore Sue* captures Archie at the stage of his career when he was not just handsome, but pretty, without the harder masculine edge that he would develop in a few years. Archie isn't billed in the film, but Anna Chang, Joe Wong, and Pickard's Chinese Syncopators are. Because of his inexperience with a camera, Archie comes on too strong, a musical comedy sailor rolling his eyes and flashing his teeth at the title character. It's probably a reasonable replication of one of his stage performances, and it's pretty dire—eagerness verging on shamelessness.

Despite Archie's inexperience, Casey Robinson was impressed and wanted to help. "I wrote a note to important executives at Paramount, none of whom I knew at the time, urging them to screen the short, not for my work but for that of a young actor whom I felt to be a sure-fire future star." It was another nudge for the young actor to think seriously about a movie career.

Archie was a young man on the make, enjoying all the perquisites of a handsome young man in the theater and not averse to violating the social speed limit. Or, for that matter, the actual speed limit. Just after the film finished shooting, on May 21, near Galesburg, Illinois, Archie and "an employee" named William Smith were heading toward the engagement in St. Louis. Smith told Archie he was driving too fast, but Archie ignored him and flipped the car. According to an article in the *St. Louis Post-Dispatch*, Smith "suffered various physical injuries and a severe shock to his nervous system." Smith ended up filing a suit against Archie in the St. Louis Municipal Court asking $15,000 in damages. Although Archie was noted as "one of the Municipal Opera principals," it is doubtful he had $15,000 to his name.

The adjudication of the case is uncertain; what is certain is that Archie spent his summer in St. Louis playing in eleven shows: *Three Little Girls, The Street Singer, Music in May, Nina Rosa, Rose Marie, The Countess Maritza, The Three Musketeers, A Wonderful Night, Irene, The Circus Princess*, and *Rio Rita*. It was a mélange of hits and obscure operettas alike that would provide a steady stream of royalties for the Shuberts until the generation that liked operettas died out. The year before Archie was there, a young ingénue named Irene Dunne had performed in St. Louis in *Nina Rosa* and *The Circus Princess*, as well as *The Desert Song, The New Moon, Blossom Time, Maytime, The Student Prince*, and *Show Boat*.

Archie kept at least one program from that summer in St. Louis. It's for *Nina Rosa*, an operetta with a libretto by the prolific Otto Harbach, music by Sigmund Romberg, and lyrics by Irving Caesar that ran for the week of June 22. Archie was playing a character called Don Fernando, and was billed fourth, beneath Guy Robertson, Leonard Ceeley, and Gladys Baxter. The costumes were by Orry-Kelly, although it's possible he had actually executed them the year before, when *Nina Rosa* had also been done by the Municipal Opera.

That summer Archie wrote an article for the *St. Louis Post-Dispatch* that constituted one of his few pieces of outright make-believe. He asserted that he had gone into show business after a misbegotten career as a boxer, and again claimed a partial higher education. After that, "Father took me back, even if I wasn't a champion, and sent me off to college . . . the principal thing I learned in college was that I wanted to go on the stage."

Clearly, he was nervous about his humble beginnings and lack of education. Archie finally drops the myth-spinning and writes about the Pender troupe. "I have never gotten over the idea that I would like to be a comedian. When the audience roared at me the time I shot up and down through that star-trap, it ruined me forever, I suppose. I am quite sure that if Beel Jackson or Battling McJuggins or Bruiser

O'Lannigan or some other husky aspirants that I fought with years ago had only left me a cauliflower ear I would be a clown today."

And then he came as close as he ever would to a performing manifesto: "You don't do a half-bad day's work when you make an audience forget its troubles in laughter at your humors."

AFTER THE SEASON IN ST. LOUIS, Archie felt it was time to make a move. In August, he asked the Shuberts to release him from his contract, and they obliged him. "I hereby release you so that you can take the engagement you speak of, as I do not wish to stand in your way," wrote J. J. Shubert.

At just about the same time Shubert gave him his release, Archie was hired for another Broadway show. *Nikki*, Archie's farewell to Broadway, as well as his farewell to the name Archie Leach, began life as a series of short stories in *Liberty* magazine by John Monk Saunders, the author of *Wings*—the winner of the first Best Picture Oscar in 1927. Saunders followed *Wings* with more aviation movies: *The Legion of the Condemned* and *The Dawn Patrol*. He broke up the monotony by writing a series of short stories about ex-fliers. It could fairly be said that Saunders got a lot of mileage out of his material—he converted the stories into a novel entitled *Single Lady*, which he sold to Warner Bros., who made a good 1931 film adaptation called *The Last Flight* starring Richard Barthelmess.

Saunders wasn't done yet. A few weeks after *The Last Flight* opened, he had rewritten the novel as *Nikki*, a musical starring Fay Wray, who just happened to be Mrs. Saunders. Archie's salary was $375 for the first three weeks, $500 a week thereafter. The play opened at the Longacre Theatre on September 29, 1931, with a score by Philip Charig and lyrics by James Dyrenforth. Besides Fay Wray and Archie, the cast included Douglass Montgomery and Louis Jean Heydt.

In all of its versions, it's the story of a disaffected, damaged group of ex-fliers in the years after World War I, who pursue their postwar occupation of alcoholism while traveling around Europe and mooning about Nikki. Critics of the novel had pointed out that what Saunders had written was a thin gloss on Hemingway's *The Sun Also Rises*, a charge he angrily denied.

Archie was playing Cary Lockwood, whose burned fingers compel him to hold a glass with both hands. It was the same part Richard Barthelmess played in the movie, and Archie appears to have been a late addition to the cast—as of the first week of September, his name didn't appear in the cast list.

The publicity mostly centered on Fay Wray, which was understandable, although Archie did get a photo in the *New York World-Telegram* on opening night. The reviews for the play were, in the main, terrible: "We are moved to express the hope that Mr. Saunders will now wind up Nikki's career in proper fashion by taking the script out and burying it somewhere" (*New York World-Telegram*). "The rest is noise and dullness, suggesting that, if the sun also rises, it also sets, and, in this case, not gently."

Even though Archie ended up with Fay Wray at the curtain, he wasn't singled out, but rather lumped in with the acting also-rans: "The others who play most ably include . . . Archie Leach." "Archie Leach and Louis Jean Heydt do the best they can with the rather sketchy roles allotted to them." Most of the reviews didn't mention him at all.

The program for opening night included a biography of the twenty-seven-year old Archie:

Archie Leach was born in Bristol, England, and has appeared in English musical comedies and vaudeville. He came to this country to appear in *Better Times* at the New York Hippodrome, and toured in vaudeville for several years, returning to England to play in *No, No Nanette* and *The Arcadians* [!]. Then in the USA he appeared in several of Arthur Hammerstein's productions. Later he was signed by the Shuberts for three musical productions, the last of which was *The Street Singer*. During the past summer he was with the St. Louis Municipal Opera Company.

All in all, a reasonable gloss on Archie's professional past, omitting the more humiliating jobs, emphasizing the interest that the more reputable producers had taken in him. A few weeks after opening, the play moved to the Cohan Theatre, accompanied by salary cuts of 25 percent. By that time, a caricature of the principals had appeared in the papers. It was a fair approximation of both Douglass Montgomery and Archie—gleaming black hair, cleft chin, long eyelashes.

There was some heavy flirting going on between the star and her leading man. Wray found Archie a generous actor. "He had an outstanding quality and he made me keen about getting to the theater every night," she said. "It was really very nice and he was very generous. If I had a scene where the focus was to be on me, he made sure that his back was to the audience so that it all went to me, you know. He was a very dear human being."

For the rest of their lives, Archie would call her Nikki. The mutual infatuation might have led to something, except for the fact that Wray was not prone to adultery. "I was married. The timing was not right for romance."

Victoria Riskin, Wray's daughter, says that in her mother's telling it was as if there was a light around Archie. "It was a very strong connection," said Riskin. "She was going through a tough marriage, and the fact that Archie was attracted to her and made her feel good about herself was wonderful at a difficult time. He reminded her that she was attractive, lovely. The other people who were attracted to her around this time were less romantic, but Archie made her feel beautiful. He was obviously a complicated man, but she didn't see the complications. She saw him as a totally positive force, a sparkling, lovely human being."

Nikki closed on October 31, 1931, and Archie was once more at liberty. At the closing night party, Archie was introduced to Irene Mayer Selznick, the daughter of Louis B. Mayer, and wife of David O. Selznick. The conversation centered on two topics: whether Archie should go to Hollywood, and Fay Wray. "He was very stuck on her," Irene said. Wray was at the party as well, and for the rest of her life she remembered Archie, dressed in white tie and tails, gazing at her with an unrelenting focus.

Archie's decision was quick in coming. *Singapore Sue* wouldn't be released until the summer of 1932, by which time his first three feature films were already in release. In early September 1931 Archie began the long drive from New York to California. He was going into the movies.

He was still carrying a blazing torch for Fay Wray, because he called to tell her he was headed for California and hoped to see her there. Archie drove across the country accompanied by Phil Charig, the composer of *Nikki*. The first night in Hollywood he got a room at the Warner Kelton Hotel. The next day he rented an apartment on North Kingsley Drive, between Hollywood Boulevard and Franklin. It was the old part of town, and firmly declassé, but it was what he could afford.

Archie's transition from New York to Hollywood, from vaudeville and the theater to the movies, was heralded by a new name that was noted in the *New York Herald Tribune* on December 18, 1931. "CARY GRANT WITH PARAMOUNT" was the headline. "Cary" came from his character's name in *Nikki*, while "Grant" was evidently picked out of a list of generic surnames. The accompanying story said that the actor formerly known as Archie Leach had left for Hollywood sometime earlier.

As far as the newly christened Cary Grant was concerned, Hollywood felt different than New York, and it felt radically different than Bristol or London. New York was mired in the Depression, with the unemployed lining up for charity at soup kitchens. Hollywood was full of Mediterranean architecture and had a climate to match. While the movie studios were struggling, some were struggling more than others, and there was nothing like the suffering that was going on in New York.

Archie didn't know it at the time, but the movies would not only survive but flourish, while vaudeville had already begun to wither and die. Broadway revues were beginning to siphon off vaudeville stars, and radio would only speed up that process until movies completed the transition. Vaudeville was inexorably slotted into the status of a stepping-stone for more lucrative—and far less stressful—entertainment venues. In May 1932, the Palace, the most prestigious vaudeville house in the world, began showing movies along with vaudeville—the beginning of the end of an entire performing discipline.

Archie Leach had been in the right place at the right time. Cary Grant's instincts would be even better. As the historian Will Coates has noted, Archie could easily have gone back to England, spent a few years in the English music hall, perhaps even made it to the West End, then transitioned to an appropriate English movie studio—Ealing perhaps. He would have become something of a star in largely parochial English films, after which he would probably have been forgotten. Instead, he committed to America and to being part of the huge talent pool in American movies—the making of an acting legend.

On September 19, 1932, E. R. Simmons from the Shubert office wrote to "Mr. Cary Grant" in care of Paramount Pictures.

"I am so glad to hear from everybody that you are making a great success of your new venture," wrote Simmons. "I do hope it will continue and land you just where it was your ambition to go." Simmons asked Grant if he could look up a young Los Angeles singer named Liana Galen, who was supposed to have a beautiful coloratura voice. "Can you find out something about it and let me know? Also try and find out from people who have heard her sing and who are musically inclined, what they think about her possibilities. As to her looks, you are probably a better judge than most of the people I know out in California." If there was a reply, it doesn't survive.

Just short of eight years later, on March 11, 1940, John Monk Saunders, newly divorced from Fay Wray and in helpless thrall to the bottle, would wrap the sash of a robe around his neck and hang himself in a cottage in Fort Myers, Florida. By that time, the man he had known as Archie Leach was one of the biggest movie stars in the world.

CHAPTER FOUR

P. G. Wodehouse put it best: "The talkies had just started, and the slogan was Come one, come all, and the more the merrier. It was an era when only a man of exceptional ability and determination could keep from getting signed up by a studio in some capacity or other."

As far as the general public was concerned, sound landed with *The Jazz Singer* in October 1927, but talkies didn't attain tidal-wave proportions until the summer of 1928. At first the novelty value of sound was enough to propel the films of great silent stars to remarkable heights. The first talking films of stars as various as Mary Pickford, Harold Lloyd, and John Gilbert were among the most financially successful films of their careers.

But the second talkie had a way of earning less than the first, and the third had a way of earning less than the second. It turned out that the audience that was flocking to movies with sound often wanted new stars to go with the new technology. James Cagney, Edward G. Robinson, Bette Davis, and William Powell would have been unthinkable in silent movies. (In fact, Powell did make silent movies, where he usually played skulking heavies.)

The man formerly known as Archie Leach would always have been an attractive bet for movies—looks like his are a qualifier all by themselves. But what would eventually make Cary Grant special was a very unusual bundle of skills: the face of a perfect leading man and the soul of a gradually accreting physical and verbal comedian who would, with time and seasoning, be able to play brooding and cynical. In short, a man for all movie seasons.

Grant found Hollywood awash with his countrymen. Even in the silent days there had been a British group in Hollywood—Ronald Colman, Clive Brook, H. B. Warner, et al. But sound created a seller's market for actors who had an easy way with the King's English. Boris Karloff had been a jobbing actor in silent pictures, but he became a star in *Frankenstein*. Then there was Leslie Howard, Laurence Olivier, Herbert Marshall, and, soon, David Niven and Ray Milland, and an endless stream of character actors: C. Aubrey Smith, Basil Rathbone, Nigel Bruce, George Arliss, etc.

The newly christened Cary Grant should have fit right in, even if nobody could quite figure out his accent. Most of the British actors tended to cluster around the Hollywood Cricket Club, which played every Sunday. If members didn't play, they could discuss cricket scores and the randy doings of the Prince of Wales.

But Grant hung back—an archetypal cat who walked by himself. The crucial barrier between Grant and the rest of the English contingent was that of class. Aubrey Smith had gone to Cambridge, Basil Rathbone to Repton, Boris Karloff to Uppingham, John Loder to Eton, and Clive Brook to Dulwich. Grant would eventually become friends with David Niven, who had gone to Stowe and Sandhurst, but then everyone became close with Niven, who had a genius for friendship. Niven's standard line would be that when he started in Hollywood it consisted of gentlemen trying to be actors. Then it became actors trying to be gentlemen. Eventually, it became neither trying to be both.

Another issue was the fact that Grant had very little stage experience, and what he did have was trivial, whereas most of the Hollywood British had been on the boards for decades. They had done Shakespeare and Shaw, while Grant had done Shubert musicals. As Sheridan Morley would observe, "Grant was actually the founder of a new generation of Hollywood Britons, one which would stretch forward through . . . Ray Milland to Michael Caine; they were to be an oddly stateless lot, owing allegiance to individual directors rather than to any formal dramatic training, and they were survivors because the cameras, recognizing original film artists rather than resting stage players, loved them with an especial devotion."

Grant was obviously studying this strange, exotic kingdom with a very close eye, and with an unusual degree of objectivity. "There's no getting around it," he told one reporter. "Everybody knows that when a leading man is at his peak, he's already slipping." At the same time, being a run-of-the-mill professional profile held little attraction. "I've always wanted to be an actor, a really first rate actor, with a reputation like—like Fredric March."

But he was a stranger in a strange land in need of guidance. He asked for and was given Fay Wray's old dressing room, and went to see Jack Haley, who had landed at Paramount in 1930. Haley gave him good advice: "The first thing you learn is not to use your stage makeup. So find a good makeup person. And don't talk to the leading actress. She'll steer you wrong. She's your competition. Talk to the character people. They'll teach you the ins and outs." So the young man sidled up to Charlie Ruggles and Arthur Treacher and the rest of the skilled character actors floating around Paramount. He listened. And he learned.

Slowly.

His first picture for Paramount was initially called *He Met a French Girl*, which was providentially changed to *This Is the Night*, a charming, slavish imitation of Ernst Lubitsch. Grant's first day of moviemaking in Hollywood was Thursday, January 21, 1932, on stage 5 at Paramount. Grant played Stephen, a young javelin thrower on his way to the 1932 Olympics who gets sidetracked by romance in Paris and Venice. His costars were Charlie Ruggles, Roland Young, and Lily Damita, who would eventually marry Errol Flynn, after which they proceeded to make each other miserable. Grant worked two and a half weeks on the picture, for which he was paid $450 a week—loose change compared to Damita's $2,500 a week, or, for that matter, Roland Young's $2,000 a week.

A few months after Archie arrived in Hollywood, so did Orry-Kelly. Archie had become Cary, but as far as Jack Kelly was concerned he still acted like Archie—Orry-Kelly said that his friend spent most of his first few months at Paramount worrying about whether or not the studio would pick up his option. Decades later, Grant would write that, "From my younger man's viewpoint, [the contract] promised fame and fulfillment, stardom and serenity. I wouldn't know then that, although I would gain the contemporary fame of an actor, and the stardom, such as it is, I would still be seeking fulfillment and serenity 30 years later."

Orry-Kelly was broke, but couldn't summon the courage to tell his friend the true state of his finances. Grant was drawing his $450 a week, but the most he felt he could afford was an 85 cent fish dinner on Vine Street. "Every time I'd start to say something during dinner, [Grant] would be full of his own plans. Other times, taking a drive after dinner, I'd pluck up the courage, but before I'd get started, he would say, 'Kelly, you talk too much—I'm thinking.'"

Finally, Kelly broke down and told Grant the truth about his perilous financial state. Grant said he was sorry, and that Kelly was welcome to his couch. The next day they went apartment hunting and found a larger place for $28 a month, including breakfast. Archie advanced the money, and he and Kelly were once again roommates. After six months, Paramount picked up Grant's option, but without giving him a raise; he was still earning $450 a week.

Kelly noticed incremental changes in his friend. Grant marked the occasion of his option pickup by buying another Packard, trading in his 1927 model on a new 1932 Packard Model 900 Coupe Roadster. He gave the dealer a $250 down payment, with monthly payments of $250. One day while they were out in the car, Grant mused, apropos of nothing, "The woman I marry is going to already own a mink coat, and a diamond bracelet." Did Kelly by any chance think he should marry Doreen Glover, the dancer he had been seeing off and on?

Kelly thought it was a silly question. She was a lovely girl. Why not?

"Well, you know, Doreen is of German extraction. Germans get fat. In ten years I may be a big star and she may be a big, fat blonde."

"Oh, for God's sake, Cary, [then] don't marry her. You can't love her!"

Grant got angry and threw Kelly out of the car, but Kelly was used to that. In any case, his luck was about to change. A few months later, Walter Herzbrun, Grant's agent, took Kelly to Warner Bros., where he was hired to design costumes. He would stay there for eleven years and do yeoman work for Bette Davis, designing her wardrobes for *Dark Victory, The Letter, The Little Foxes, Now, Voyager*, and *Mr. Skeffington* among others, not to mention classics such as *The Sea Hawk, The Maltese Falcon*, and *Casablanca*. He would eventually win three Academy Awards, for *An American in Paris, Les Girls*, and *Some Like It Hot*.

Grant gave some consideration to keeping the loose domestic partnership with Kelly going, but Kelly was no longer sure he wanted to live and eat on Cary's schedule, which was pretty much a prerequisite for the arrangement. "I suggested he take an apartment nearer Paramount and share it with Randy Scott."

That, at least, was Orry-Kelly's version. He would never have much good to say about his off-and-on roommate, the reason for which could well have been his irritation with Grant's single-minded focus on Grant at the expense of everybody and everything else. For instance: Shortly after Orry-Kelly started working at Warner Bros., Grant told Kelly to make his apologies to Bebe Daniels; he wasn't going to be able to get to her party, even though he'd accepted the invitation.

"When the hell are you going to learn manners?" asked Kelly. "At least call Bebe."

"Who the hell do you think you're talking to? You owe me $360.48!"

"For what?"

And then Kelly remembered that all those months when he hadn't been working Grant had always made entries in a little book after they'd had dinner. Then there were the Friday night fights they attended, which cost $3.30 apiece. And the string Grant collected in little balls, and the brown wrapping paper he folded neatly and saved, and the book matches he stockpiled. And then Kelly understood about the $360.48.

Of course, the reason for his disaffection could have been something deeper than bad manners. Jack Kelly hung around his friend for years despite what he retrospectively depicted as a nonstop procession of condescension, self-absorption, and anger, not to mention an occasional punch—slavish masochism worthy of *The Blue Angel*.

Grant later apologized to Kelly about his demand for money. And when Kelly handed him $360.48 wrapped up with a rubber band, Grant seemed embarrassed. "I was tight," he said by way of explanation. "You really don't owe me that." But he took it anyway.

What is clear is that Grant early on had a sense of what it took to get ahead. His starting salary of $450 a week was very respectable for a Hollywood beginner in the pit of the Depression, and was probably attributable to the fact that he had Broadway credits, however minor. But he understood that disposable juvenile parts would only lead to being disposed. He needed decent parts in decent films, which would become a near-impossibility at Paramount, simply because Gary Cooper had dibs on every good script.

When Paramount assigned him to *Devil and the Deep* opposite Tallulah Bankhead, Gary Cooper, and Charles Laughton, Grant knew the set wasn't going to be big enough to accommodate him amidst so many star egos. "He didn't want to play it because he knew it wasn't a very good part," said Bankhead, "but I said I wanted him. Get *me* being so grand." Her instincts proved correct.

In fact, Grant had landed at a studio in deep trouble. Paramount was being inexorably drained by its huge chain of 900 movie theaters, each of which was worth far less than its mortgage in the economic environment of the Depression, which had sliced attendance by about a third. The expansion of the theaters had largely been the doing of Adolph Zukor, who had no intention of taking the fall; he would euchre his founding partner Jesse Lasky out of the company within a year. Lasky would declare bankruptcy, while Paramount went into receivership.

With financial and management chaos hovering, Paramount funneled almost all of their effort and most of their quality material into a few premiere stars such as Gary Cooper and Marlene Dietrich. Everybody else had to more or less fend for themselves, which would become a considerable problem for Grant, who lacked both experience and leverage. That he made it more or less unscathed through five years at Paramount would be a testament to his considerable survival skills and his unforced star quality.

Grant's early years at Paramount consisted mostly of bad parts, bad films or both. And, to be honest, sometimes bad performances. He had obviously looked at his showboating turn in *Singapore Sue* and been appalled—in his early films at Paramount he pulls back, but entirely too much. He seems stiff, inhibited. To work in vaudeville you had to *present*, had to assert a personality. Musical comedy on Broadway demanded at least as much, especially if your singing skills were as limited as Grant's. But in his early years in the movies he's little more than a male ingénue who allows himself to be photographed.

He must have realized that he wasn't bowling anybody over with his talent, so he decided to add ingratiation to the recipe. Budd Schulberg, the son of studio head B. P. Schulberg, remembered Grant personally delivering an Airedale named Gent to the Schulberg household.

Gent would become one of Budd's favorite dogs. As for Grant, it constituted service with a smile.

Past nominal mentions of his spectacular looks, nobody seemed to know what to make of him. The perennially befuddled columnist Louella Parsons had little to say about Grant other than her regret over his name change. Parsons thought it was unfortunate that Archie Leach had been "burdened with the name Cary Grant. When Cary and Gary Cooper are at a party, you get tongue-tied trying to differentiate."

After featured parts in his first two films, he was relegated to what amounted to a small part in another stinker called *Merrily We Go to Hell*, for which he earned $400 for one week, $450 for a second week, and $225 for a third week—Paramount was clearly trying to save money whenever it could.

Grant didn't begin to get onto a fast track until his fifth film: *Blonde Venus,* opposite Marlene Dietrich, directed by Josef von Sternberg. His salary was still only $450 a week—Dietrich was getting precisely ten times as much—but that didn't matter. It was a lead in a Sternberg picture with a great star, although if Grant had been fully aware of the psychodrama he was walking into he might have chosen a different set of coworkers.

The studio executive and biographer Steven Bach knew both Sternberg and Dietrich and his analysis of the relationship between director and star was that they had an affair during *The Blue Angel*. "Marlene admired him, knew what he stood for, felt affectionate respect for him. But my guess is that she said something like, 'You should know that I'm married with a child, and Richard Tauber is around the corner, and there's a girl waiting for me at the bar.' And Jo, the open wound looking for a deeper wound, said, 'I know. It's okay.' When they got to Hollywood, Gary Cooper showed up, and she said, 'But Jo, you knew,' and Jo said, 'I know. It's okay.' And then he went home and bled. He couldn't break away, and he was too proud to beg."

This barely veiled sexual masochism is the reason that the seven Sternberg-Dietrich films demand cryptography as much as criticism. Nearly alone among his generation of directors, Sternberg was completely a creature of the movies; he had never worked in the theater, never learned how to get a laugh or carry a dramatic moment, and had never had to relate to an audience. The result was that his films are closed systems of signs with veiled meanings.

Sternberg was slavishly submissive to Dietrich in private, and overcompensated with aggression and grandiosity in public. "Jo was walking pain, a monster of ego, which was his defense against the pain," said Steven Bach. "You'd sit with him at a screening of one of his pictures and he would say, 'Pay no attention to the credits. I wrote the script. I wrote the music.' Once I asked him, 'But isn't this Rimsky-Korsakov?' 'Well, I conducted the orchestra.' Nothing could ever be enough for this man. He was a wound sealed over by a mask of inscrutability. He was desperately unhappy, and it only got worse because after he was retired the recognition and the glory that he felt he deserved was not forthcoming."

Dietrich was having an affair with Maurice Chevalier during *Blonde Venus*, and Maria Riva, Dietrich's daughter, felt a mingling of love and pity for the director. "When a man is madly in love with a woman, and is doing everything in his power artistically—which was Jo's life—to prove it to her, and walks past a closed dressing room door knowing what's going on behind that door, you have to forgive him if he's a little sadistic on the set. Jo was like Orson Welles—his own best invention. These are talents that are so vulnerable they must invent a persona for the world so that they can't be hurt, or have their fragility damaged. Extremely talented, but they don't have emotional stamina."

Faced with subterranean sexual currents and the tense atmosphere that always existed on a Sternberg set, Grant wisely chose to keep his head down. "I wasn't going to get mixed up in that," he told one friend. The critical event happened on the first day. "Your hair is parted on the wrong side," Sternberg snapped at the young actor. He grabbed a comb and changed the part to the right side. Grant kept it that way for the rest of his life.

"Josef von Sternberg yelled at her all the time," was the gist of Grant's recollections. Actually Sternberg yelled at everyone. "Jo loved to throw you," Grant remembered. "I could never get a scene underway before Jo would bawl out 'Cut'—at me, personally, across the set. This went on and on. I felt like someone doing drill who kept dropping the rifle, but wasn't going to be allowed to drop out of ranks."

Blonde Venus is the one where Dietrich performs on stage in an ape costume, takes off the furry hands and the head, then sings "Hot Voodoo" backed up by jungle drums. Grant plays Dietrich's rich boytoy, whom she keeps around because she's trying to earn enough money to take care of her sick husband (Herbert Marshall) and young son (Dickie Moore.)

The Sternberg-Dietrich films are veiled retellings of their affair. Grant is saddled with the Jannings/Menjou/Atwill/Sternberg doomed-to-be-dumped part, but without the masochism, or, unfortunately, the irony. He's dazzlingly handsome, but he doesn't project anything beyond his looks, which seem oddly indistinct compared to what they would be in a few years. What's missing is attitude. Grant's performance is indistinguishable from what Leslie Howard would have given. He's just there. On the other hand, Dietrich does wear a gorilla costume.

Initially, Dietrich liked Grant, for his looks as well as his industriousness. "There's a young, handsome Cockney Englishman by the name of Cary Grant, that Jo cast as the lover," she wrote her husband, who was conveniently back in Europe. "What do you think he does? To make more money, he sells SHIRTS on the set, and he's so charming that people come from all over the lot to buy them from him!"

The reason Grant suddenly took an interest in wardrobe was an investment—in May 1932 he had become a partner in a men's store on Wilshire Boulevard called Neale Smart Men's Apparel. By July, the store was in arrears and it appeared that some of Grant's investment had been siphoned off. "I hate to be continually writing you about our bills but as you know the light and telephone companies don't fool around," wrote someone named Lester to Grant on July 19.

> The burglar alarm people are ready for trouble they inform me that unless the bill is paid by tomorrow noon they will attack. The premiere [*sic*] carpet co and Western showcase are also of the same mind. . . . The first attachment of the store and your personal assets would throw the store into the board of trade which would make you liable for all bills plus the merchandise returned as returning mdse 90 days prior to liquidation constitutes creditor preference.
>
> In plain words if we are [forced] to liquidate you will be responsible for about $5,700 instead of $2,800. You will not get over $1000.00 in the stock. . . . You rarely have heard me say anything alarming but I can't impress you any too strongly with the danger you are in right now.

It was a harsh lesson, one that he never forgot. For the rest of his life, Grant maintained a horror of debt and kept spotless records of what he owed and was owed.

In later years, Dietrich didn't care for Grant—her private comments about him tended toward the caustic—and it's probable that her general air of artificiality would have turned him off as well. In January 1933, he was asked about the recent trend inaugurated by Dietrich of women wearing men's clothes. He responded with a waspish, "If women want to wear men's clothes, let them do men's work."

Despite their mutual uninterest, Grant and Dietrich would occasionally run into each other around town—they were both guests at Countess Dorothy di Frasso's infamous Tape Recording party in 1935. The Countess—she was born Dorothy Taylor and inherited millions from her father—invited Claudette Colbert, Clifton Webb, Betty Furness, George Cukor, and William Haines, along with Grant and Dietrich to what she promised would be a marvelous party. What the guests didn't know was that di Frasso had microphones hidden all over the garden.

A few weeks later, she once again threw a party for the same roster of guests, except this time there was entertainment—she played the recordings her guests didn't know they'd made. Evidently the guests were not amused; Webb and several others made di Frasso promise never to play the recordings again. It all sounds like the setup for an Agatha Christie murder mystery, but di Frasso lived until 1954. A photograph of the party survives; the group is posed in front of a gigantic larkspur, and Grant is wearing a white suit with a white ascot.

AFTER BACKING UP A MAJOR STAR in a film directed by an A-list director, Grant got another leg-up later the same year when Mae West cast him in *She Done Him Wrong*. West described the casting process during an audience/interview in 1973, in her pearly cocoon of an apartment at the Ravenswood in Hollywood, which featured a nude statue of her on a pedestal by the living room and huge mirror mounted on the bedroom ceiling ("So I can see how I'm doin'").

"We were just about ready to start shooting and we hadn't gotten a leading man yet. I was in the casting office trying to pick somebody out, but every actor was in a picture, working. They just didn't have enough men around. I had just left the casting office and was walking down the studio lot. A guy came around the corner and, Oh Boy! He was the best-looking thing in Hollywood. I took one look at him and said, 'If he can talk, I'll take him.' So he opened his mouth and I said, 'He's it.' 'For what part?' they asked me. 'For the lead, what else?'"

West's story may have been exaggerated—Grant was getting tryouts opposite Paramount's biggest female stars and at least one of their best directors, so the studio was obviously high on him. In any case, the film provides her with some of her best moments. "Why doncha come up sometime, see me?" she asks in her matchless Brooklynese, a line invariably misquoted as "Why don't you come up and see me sometime?" Grant, playing a minister, says he doesn't have time. "Say, what're you tryin' to do, insult me?" she replies. She sings "A Guy What Takes His Time," continues pressing and, minister or no minister, he folds. From this experience, Grant began to formulate a theory that when it came to movies, it was better to be wanted than to want, a profound lesson he would illustrate for the rest of his career.

The picture was shot quickly, in about three weeks, for the modest cost of $275,000. Grant had gotten a raise, because his salary amounted to $3,000, compared to the star's $20,000. *She Done Him Wrong* was released in February 1933 to tumultuous commercial response, so Grant was again paired with West in *I'm No Angel*, released in October 1933. Once again, Grant doesn't get the girl so much as he allows the girl to get him.

West gave Grant his first big break, but he was always uncharacteristically un-gallant about her, possibly because her ego demanded that she get all the good lines, as well as the close-ups, with everybody else in the cast relegated to the status of courtiers. Even *Variety* noticed the imbalance: "Cary Grant does nice work as the sweetheart, but is at all times overshadowed by Miss West."

"When I first met her," he remembered, "I was astonished how tiny she was, barely five feet. And not at all svelte. She had a flabby belly which always wiggled when she walked. She talked badly. Not dirty. I mean when she was called to set, she'd yell, 'I ain't ready!' That kind of bad. She was actually a prude. . . . She dealt in a fantasy world;

the heavy makeup she wore was one sign of her insecurity. We were all very careful with her."

In between the two pictures with West, Grant made *The Eagle and the Hawk*, a World War I aviation picture costarring Fredric March, Jack Oakie, and stock footage from *Wings*. "Cary Grant wasn't like he is today, I'll say that," said Mitchell Leisen, Cecil B. DeMille's art director who was being groomed as a director by Paramount. The special effects department had rigged up a set where the walls and ceiling would collapse while the actors ducked under a table. "Mr. Grant . . . was off tap dancing in a corner and wasn't paying attention. The special effects department touched the wire off accidentally, but everybody dived into their positions except Mr. Grant. He just stood there looking up and got it right in the face so badly they had to send him to the hospital."

March and Oakie were unscathed, but Grant had a gash in his cheek that necessitated plastic surgery. Luckily it healed with no scarring. A couple of days later, on March 10, 1933, Oakie and March were shooting a scene that was interrupted by the Long Beach earthquake. As far as the actors were concerned, *The Eagle and the Hawk* was memorable; as far as the public was concerned, it was a forgettable vehicle for a couple of young leading men.

It's yet another aviation picture by John Monk Saunders, with March as the brave commander gradually destabilized by the fact that all of his pilots get killed. There's a lovely ten-minute sequence with a luminous Carole Lombard, who gazes at March as if he's an ice cream sundae on a hot summer day. March had already won an Oscar for *Dr. Jekyll and Mr. Hyde* and gives an effective, underplayed performance, but Grant, playing a misanthrope with a temper—perilously close to type-casting—tends to declaim his lines rather than speak them. It's a typically bitter picture by Saunders, with an ending that was cut for a 1939 reissue. Originally, after a close-up of a plaque honoring the deceased March for his war efforts, the camera pulled back to reveal Grant passing by, carrying a bottle in a paper bag—he's a derelict, another victim of war. But the reissue version, which is all that's available now, ends with the shot of the plaque, taking the sting out of the ending.

In Grant's first year with Paramount, the studio cast him in ten pictures. Grant didn't impress the critics, the public, or his coworkers. But the studio correctly thought there was something there beyond good looks—a sense of something held in reserve. In a word, possibilities. Paramount decided to keep him around a while longer.

DESPITE THE DISASTER OF NEALE'S, Grant showed no particular hesitance about spending money. In May 1933, he bought yet another Packard, a 1932 Coupe 8 roadster. And he moved into a rented house at 2285 West Live Oak Drive near Griffith Park, with another Paramount actor named Randolph Scott. They had met in 1932, on the set of a movie called *Hot Saturday* in which they costarred with Nancy Carroll. Cary is the rich playboy, Randy the virtuous childhood sweetheart who calls off the marriage because he thinks Nancy has been unfaithful. Complications ensue.

At this point, Grant and Scott were two extremely handsome young actors with indefinite personalities and uncertain futures. Scott was a Virginian who had played football at the University of North Carolina and was already regarded as one of the most sincere gentlemen in show business.

He and Grant hit it off immediately. Their first joint interview had appeared in July 1932: "Over at Paramount they have a little list. There are ten names on the list, some of which are still unknown to the moviegoing public, and Paramount confidently believes that someday each of these ten will be a star in his own right."

Grant and Scott were both on the list. The article went on to give potted bios of both men, which are reasonably accurate, although Grant reduced his age when he ran away from home from fourteen to twelve, amplified his father's occupation from tailor to clothing manufacturer, and made himself a prep school graduate instead of a dropout.

Randy Scott's scrapbooks, filled with newspaper stories gathered by a clipping service, attest to their busy social lives in the latter days of 1932. The boys were everywhere, social butterflys on a mad whirl. When Amelia Earhart visited Paramount in July, Grant and Scott were there to greet her along with Tallulah Bankhead, Marlene Dietrich, Claudette Colbert, Helen Hayes, Gary Cooper, Adolphe Menjou, and Harpo Marx. In September, Grant threw a party at the Cocoanut

Grove for Helen Kane with entertainment by Phil Harris and his band. The guests included Johnny Weissmuller and Randolph Scott.

On the 26th of November, Grant threw another party; the guests included Orry-Kelly, Vivian Gaye, and Randy Scott. On the 30th it was a theater party thrown by the writer Tiffany Thayer where other guests included Richard Boleslavsky and his wife, Lowell Sherman, and Fuzzy Knight.

In November, Scott stopped dating Martha Sleeper and started going out with Vivian Gaye. By 1934, Scott and Gaye were said to be engaged, which coincided with a newly formed relationship Grant was having with Virginia Cherrill. Soon, there was talk of a double wedding: Grant and Cherrill, Scott and Gaye, all of it taking place in England: "Cary will meet Virginia in England, and escort her to Kent to visit his parents before the nuptials." Scott and Gaye never did marry—she would eventually become the second wife of Ernst Lubitsch, and was heartily disliked by all of his friends.

Grant's relationship with Cherrill was his first comprehensively disastrous relationship with a woman who wasn't his mother. Orry-Kelly was a witness to Grant's first glimpse of Cherrill, although he mistakenly dated it as early 1933, when it actually seems to have been a few months earlier. There was also a difference of opinion as to whether the site was Marion Davies's Ocean House or a small party at the house Grant and Scott were sharing. Either way, accompanying Vivien Gaye to the party was a gorgeous blonde with milky skin who looked familiar. It was Cherrill, the leading lady of Chaplin's masterpiece *City Lights*, now far more glamorous than she had been as the blind flower girl.

"The mink coat and the diamonds," mumbled Jack Kelly, recalling Archie Leach's requirements for a wife. "He gave me a hard look and I knew he would have liked to kick me in the shins. Gone was the Archie Leach full of fun. He was adjusting the mask of Cary Grant—a mask that became his career, a career that became Grant." Cherrill was indeed a stunning beauty, although not really an actress—Chaplin had pulled a performance out of her by first miming what he wanted her to do, then demanding she imitate him.

What was certain is that, as Grant remembered, "I fell in love with her the moment I saw her . . . she was the most beautiful woman I'd ever seen." The only problem was that Cherrill was having an affair

with Oscar Levant. (She liked 'em complicated.) Grant was unde-
terred and began a full-court press, with multiple phone calls to the
house that Cherrill shared with her mother. Cherrill had seen Grant
in *Blonde Venus*, and found him attractive, but she held back because
of the relationship with Levant.

One night she and Levant were in bed when they were startled by
the sound of crunching metal. Cherrill looked out the window and
saw Grant in his Packard enthusiastically ramming Levant's old Ford.
Cherrill wisely kept the drapes drawn, and Grant finally drove away.
"The Ford was a wreck," said Cherrill in tapes recorded in 1994, two
years before her death. Cherrill must have been thrilled by the display
of alpha aggression, because she segued from Levant to Grant almost
immediately.

Cherrill was entranced by Grant's humor and charm, but there
were places that were clearly off-limits. His past, for instance. "Cary
never talked about his background more than he could help. . . . He
never mentioned his mother." At this point, he still believed that his
mother had abandoned the family and then died; Cherrill remembered
that "I thought she'd gone off with some other man. It wasn't a topic
that Cary wanted to discuss."

Cherrill's characterization of Grant was nearly identical to
Orry-Kelly's, especially when it came to Grant's fierce ambition. "Cary
was driven," Cherrill said. "Randy Scott always worked hard and took
care to keep himself in good shape, but he wasn't set upon becoming
a star. Cary never lost sight of his goal."

TRACKING GRANT'S AND SCOTT'S personal and professional
advancement in those first few years in Hollywood makes it clear
that they were far down the pecking order in what was basically an
apprentice system. Hollywood in that era was fueled by publicity and
talent, where men and women were noticed as much for their off-
screen life as they were for their on-screen skills. In 1933, photos of
Grant and Scott began appearing in the movie magazines: "Randolph
Scott and Cary Grant, who live together, have a Damon and Pythias
friendship which started when they both signed contracts with the
Paramount studio."

Rumors began floating around Hollywood, but as Cherrill saw it there was nothing to notice, because she and Grant were very happy, in bed and out. "Douglas Fairbanks once told me that Cary said I was the best lover he'd ever had. Well, it was mutual. . . . Cary was crazy about women. He didn't like me to wear makeup and he hated it when other men started eyeing me up . . . but he was great in bed—and so funny. We'd sometimes roll out on to the floor we were laughing so much. And Randy—Randy was a darling. We used to double-date, back in the early days, when he was dating Doris Duke. Randolph Scott was no more gay than Cary was."

The problem was Grant's turbulent personality, which tended to derail the emotional intimacy he claimed to desire. Cherrill signed a photo to her boyfriend, who evidently already had a habit of drifting away: "Cary—Remember me? Virginia—June 1933." There were weekends at San Simeon, where the prudish William Randolph Hearst made sure that unmarried couples had separate rooms. On one of these weekends, Marion Davies told Cherrill that Hearst had thoughtfully paid for Davies's abortions, "so as not to embarrass his wife." Cherrill said that she wasn't absolutely sure if the story was true, because Marion had a tendency to blather when she drank, which was often.

Grant's scapegrace ways got him into trouble when he and William Randolph Hearst Jr. "borrowed" a biplane at the San Simeon airstrip. "Cary was foolish enough to come with me," said Hearst Jr. "We got the kind of paper bags one found at the corner candy store and filled them with flour. We buzzed around and threw the bags on the hangar's asphalt roof. It was great fun because you could see where they hit."

Unfortunately, neither Hearst nor Grant realized that the bags of flour were damaging the hangar's roof, not to mention frightening the guests. When they got back to the house, Grant's bags were packed and on the front porch, which was how Hearst Sr. let a guest know he had worn out his welcome. Someone must have interceded, because the banishment was postponed.

Cherrill was enchanted by Grant's skill set—exuberance mixed with a certain danger. She was fond of recalling a night at either the Ambassador or the Biltmore. Grant was in white tie and tails.

One of the guests tapped Cary on the shoulder, told him that he remembered seeing him as a kid in vaudeville on the East Coast. I'm not sure how pleased Cary was about that; he didn't like talking about those early years.

This man swore that Cary had been one of the best acrobats he'd ever seen outside a circus. The guy asked Cary if he was still up to performing one of his old stunts. "Give me $50 and I'll do any stunt you like," Cary told him.

Cary just walked up to the band leader and asked him for a roll on the drums. He stripped off his jacket and tie and waited for the roll—500 people staring at him—and then he flipped over backward with a twist and run in the middle and he landed back—just like that—perched flat on his feet again. . . . It was wonderful. Everybody in the place started to applaud. And then Cary walked over to the guy's table and simply stretched out his palm for the fifty. He got it.

In her old age, Cherrill preferred to talk about the Cary she loved, not the Cary that occasionally frightened her, but when pressed she'd get specific about his volatility, his jealousy and a temper that could easily ascend to rage. "Randy was good with Cary, when he was around," said Cherrill. "But he wasn't always there. It's not like you read in the books. They lived in the same house and they got on well, but they didn't necessarily lead the same lives. They had different lives."

Grant wanted to get married. Cherrill didn't. "I could never be happy with a man who made me feel so trapped," Cherrill said. "God, how we argued." In the last quarter of 1933, the papers were full of breathless items about the presumed impending nuptials between Grant and Cherrill. Nothing happened, because Cherrill was worried. "Being an obsessive man, he wouldn't let the idea go. But I'd been married and divorced already. I didn't want to get involved in something that was going to be a bust. Besides, I wasn't ready to settle down."

They were driving to Mexico for a vacation when an argument broke out. Grant yelled and threatened Cherrill, or she thought he did. When he pulled into a gas station, she got out and waited for a bus to take her back to Los Angeles. Another time she wanted to go to England, but Grant didn't. He started by telling her she wouldn't like it, and ended by forbidding her to go. She promptly flounced out of the house, out of California, and went all the way to New York, where she bunked with Laurence Olivier and his wife, Jill Esmond, who were doing a play.

There was a knock on the door, "and in fell Cary. He'd had a drink or two by then." Cherrill ended the fight by leaving for England anyway. "I was really crazy with love, and at the same time I was so scared of the way Cary behaved sometimes."

Grant followed her. On November 18, 1933, Cherrill arrived in Plymouth, England, aboard the SS *Champlain*. Grant, Randy, and David Manners were right behind her on the SS *Paris*, traveling first class. On November 22, the three men threw a party billed as "Three Licentious Old Men From Hollywood." The food was delicate and French, the champagne only the finest (Mumm Cordon Rouge 1923, Traminer 1924). Guests included Ruth Draper and Mr. and Mrs. W. L. Mellon. As the party was winding down, all the guests signed a menu. David Manners drew a smiley face with "Hello! Kid" written next to it. Another guest wrote, "A ship which did Carry Grant is a happy ship."

And finally, there was this: "To my spouse, Cary. Randy."

Grant and Randy arrived in London on November 23, 1933, and stayed at the Hotel Savoy. To kill time, he went to Bristol to see his father. According to Cherrill, it was at this point he was told that his mother had not abandoned the family, was not dead, but was institutionalized. Cherrill said that he did not visit her immediately, but tried to digest this stunning news. Grant told several different stories about his discovery that his mother was still alive. In some of them he found out only when his father died in 1935, but he confirmed Cherrill's version to Dyan Cannon, his fourth wife.

In this version, his father first called him in Los Angeles and told him he needed to see him, to tell him something that he couldn't tell him in a phone call. As might be imagined, the reunion was a fiasco. Grant showed up in a fancy car loaded with gifts. Elias was glad to see his son, but he gradually grew resentful about his son's success. Elias was drinking, but he wouldn't drink with his son because he thought the boy was too bloody grand.

"He actually asked me to meet him in a pub at Bristol," Grant said. "I almost didn't recognize him. He'd pretty well ruined himself with drinking. Jowls hanging, bloodshot eyes. He just looked like an old, broken-down alcoholic."

Finally, Elias blurted it out. "It's about your mother. She's not dead."

I wasn't sure I hadn't heard him right. I thought maybe by now he'd gotten wet brain from drinking so much. So I asked him what in the hell that was supposed to mean.

He said it again. "She's not dead." . . . He was acting like this was something he had to get off his chest but resented me bitterly for being the one he had to tell.

Grant said that after he assimilated the news, he drove to Fishponds to see his mother and found an old, white-haired woman who said, "It's been a long time."

"I went crazy," Grant would say about this revelation. He would also say he went on an epic bender that resulted in having to be dried out in a sanitarium.

The problem with this story is that it leads directly to the question of why Elsie stayed in Fishponds for several years after Grant found out the truth. (Elsie's medical records aren't any help; they don't specify whether her release came at the request of a doctor or a relative.)

Grant may have been profoundly ambivalent about his mother, but it's hard to imagine him letting her stay institutionalized for such an extended length of time. There is a teasing reference in a 1933 article in the *Bristol Evening Post* about how one day "the real story" behind Grant's visit might be told, "but not yet, and not by me." The writer went on to say that the "secret" was known "to only a small number of people in the city, and is essentially a personal matter." If, however, it was to become known "it would make Bristolians proud of their splendid son."

What is certain is that the earliest surviving letter from Elsie to Grant dates from 1937.

All this emotional upheaval would account for the lengthy gap between his arrival in England at the end of November and the wedding to Virginia Cherrill in London in February. Randy Scott only stayed in England for two weeks, sailing back to America on December 6. In the interim between arrival and the marriage, Cherrill met Elias, whom she termed "a nice old man, a working type, very friendly."

And then, possibly out of a mingled love and pity for her lover's utterly compromised emotional life, Cherrill finally agreed to marry Grant.

Cherrill said that the day before the wedding Grant once again visited his mother. Grant's memory of the meeting was a preview of coming attractions, a stew of thwarted devotion and damage.

I went to Fishponds where Elsie had a very small and almost completely empty room. I rushed to hold her and she put up an elbow to stop me. She was small, but she was strong. It was like trying to cuddle up to a porcupine.

"Who are you? What do you want?" she asked, pulling away from me.

"Mother," I said, "It's me, your son, Archie."

"You're no son of mine," she screamed. "You don't look like my Archie. You don't even sound like my Archie."

Grant went on to say that it took several visits to Fishponds to even have a civil conversation with her. "She always kept me at arm's length, as if there was a part of her mind that was convinced I was an imposter. And, I suppose, in a way, she was right. The Archie she knew with a working class accent and clothes was now this slick film star. Even the part in my hair had changed."

On February 9, 1934, he and Cherrill married—his first, but by no means his last lunge for the security of home and family.

The wedding day had an air of frantic improvisation about it. "They made their appearances . . . in relays," wrote one clearly unimpressed reporter. "Grant showed up without his fiancé. He telephoned. She arrived. They were wed."

It didn't get any smoother. Rushing from Caxton Hall to catch an ocean liner, Grant and Cherrill jumped into separate cabs, then Grant got out and got into her cab. They traveled back to America on a Cunard ship, and the voyage was smooth in more ways than one. "They gave us the biggest suite on the ship," said Cherrill. "We spent a lot of time in our rooms."

They arrived back in Hollywood on February 26. The newspapers covered the difficult adjustment: "Randolph Scott refusing to move from the Hollywood hillside home where he and Cary Grant 'bached' for several moons—even when Cary returned with Virginia Cherrill for a bride. . . . But Virginia telling Scott he's welcome and she's adding the feminine touch to the menage and everybody's happy."

With his brain roiling with the reality of his mother's existence, Grant had to attend to his career as well as a new marriage. It was not going to be a smooth fit.

CHAPTER FIVE

A Paramount star navigating sound with some difficulty was Harold Lloyd, who had a triumphant run in silent pictures, but whose get-up-and-go personality seemed jarringly out of place in the Depression. Lloyd had been releasing his productions through Paramount since 1926 and had been their premier comedian, but by 1933 that was beginning to change. After Grant completed his second picture with Mae West, he had been slotted into *Alice in Wonderland*, a stiff with a bunch of Paramount stars in disguises—W. C. Fields was Humpty-Dumpty, while Grant drew the Mock Turtle. (In fact, Grant wasn't in the costume at all, and only dubbed the voice.)

As it happened, Harold Lloyd's wife, Mildred, had wanted to play Alice. Lloyd didn't want his wife working, so Mildred didn't get the part, which went to Charlotte Henry. But it was during *Alice in Wonderland* that Grant and Lloyd got to know each other and became friends. They had a lot in common—Lloyd's mother was a battle-axe, his father a drunk, and he had been drawn to the theater at a very young age as a means of escape. In just a few years the relationship would figure in one of Grant's great comic triumphs.

In the spring of 1934, Virginia had a miscarriage, which seemed to have had the unintended effect of provoking Grant's sexual paranoia. "Every man I spoke to instantly became his enemy," remembered Cherrill. "He didn't want me to go to work; he didn't even like to go out in the evenings. And when we went home, he liked to drink.

85

And when he'd had a drink or two and got angry, he used to kick and hit me."

After a few months of her husband's brooding and abuse, Cherrill took a job in Hawaii making a movie for Lois Weber—her last directorial effort. When Virginia returned from location, things were worse. Grant was morose and his jealousy continued, often in absurd directions. "He was so jealous. Even of my *mother*." On September 10, she left him and went to her mother's house, but relented and came back, after which they traveled to Illinois for a visit with her family. Grant was on his best behavior and things seemed fine.

When Cherrill and Grant got back to Hollywood, Archie Leach, their Sealyham terrier, darted out the back door and never came back. A fortnight later, they were at the Cocoanut Grove. Cherrill was talking to Sir Guy Standing, a sixty-one-year-old British character actor. Grant took Standing's attentions amiss. He leaned across the table and told Standing he better think twice about making a pass at Cherrill. That broke things up in a hurry. They went home and went to bed. Cherrill woke up to find Grant standing over her, his hands around her throat. "You hate me enough to want me dead?" she gasped. That broke the spell, but Grant had broken the marriage.

Cherrill got up, got dressed, and went back to her mother's. After a day or two, word reached Louella Parsons, who called. Cherrill told her the marriage was in bad shape. "Was [the trouble] brewing for some time, or was it sudden?" Grant was asked. "Sudden," he replied.

On October 4, Grant called his wife. His speech was slurred, his manner imploring. After they hung up, Cherrill called back. The houseboy answered and she told him to check on her husband. The houseboy came back to the phone to say that Grant had passed out. On the night stand was a bottle marked "Poison." At 3:28 a.m., Grant was dropped off at Hollywood Hospital.

Once his stomach had been pumped out, Grant told the doctors he had only been drunk. "I had been drinking most of the day before, and all that day. . . . You know what whiskey does when you drink it all by yourself. It makes you very sad."

"I'm ashamed of getting drunk," he told a reporter. "In Hollywood, a comedian can get drunk, but a 'straight' man can't. I'm a 'straight' man, and people won't like it." Whether the event was a suicide attempt or simply a binge is unclear, as is the identity of the "people" he referred to—his employers or his audience. To the end of his life, Grant insisted that there was no suicide attempt. "I just got drunk and passed out," he said forty years later. "Dead drunk. That's all there was to it. The papers had a field day with the story. But it didn't hurt me. Not one little bit."

What is certain is that in the first week of December 1934, Cherrill sued her husband of ten months for divorce. She asked for $1,000 a month in alimony and $2,500 for lawyer fees. She said that her soon-to-be-ex "used vile and opprobrious language," and was abusive when he drank. Grant was ordered to pay $167.50 a week in temporary alimony, whereupon Cherrill upped the ante and said Grant had not only been surly when drinking but had threatened to kill her. Privately, Grant would say, "My first wife accused me of being a homosexual." Years later, Cherrill not only denied ever saying any such thing, but to the end of her life insisted that, whatever his issues, Grant was far from homosexual.

Grant's attorneys seem to have counseled him to cut his losses. An out-of-court property settlement was quickly negotiated—Cherrill accepted half of the value of their house, which was valued at $50,000. When the first decree of divorce was issued in March 1935, Cherrill testified that Grant was "sullen, disagreeable and morose." And then she went back to Oscar Levant, although she always insisted that "I missed Cary all the time. You have no idea. . . . I was carrying a torch for Cary for years after we parted."

Cherrill would make only two more movies, both in England opposite the young James Mason. In 1937, she married the ninth Earl of Jersey. Eventually she had a happy union with husband number four, Florian Martini, a Pole who flew for the RAF during World War II. In 1945, she financed the Savile Row operation of Hardy Amies. In return Amies designed her seasonal wardrobe for free.

"We were never one," Grant would say in summation of his first marriage. "We were always competing, as I was with most of my wives. . . . Perhaps she thought being married to me would help her career, but it only increased her resentment. She was a cold woman."

It's possible that Cherrill was simply a convenient substitute for Fay Wray. In September 1934, when Wray went to England to make some films, Grant sent her a corsage for the voyage, leading her to once again consider the possibility of another life, one that didn't involve John Monk Saunders.

When Wray returned to Hollywood, she and Grant had lunch together. She seems to have been prepared for a romantic rush, but all they talked about were their careers. It was the first time there had ever been awkwardness between them. Interestingly, when Wray had a baby in September of 1936, she named the child Susan Cary Saunders. Grant remained on the edge of Wray's life for decades. When Wray finally left Saunders, Grant sent Susan a stuffed Santa Claus at Christmas and took Wray to a New Year's Eve party at Jack Warner's house. The next man in Wray's life would also figure prominently in Grant's: Clifford Odets.

For her part, Virginia Cherrill echoed Orry-Kelly by saying that "I was in love with Cary; Cary was in love with himself. I didn't stand a chance." But then she would relent and say, "Just Cary and Florek [Martini]. Truly, they are the only men I ever was in love with. Just them. Nobody else."

BY 1934, times in Hollywood were changing. In the middle of the year, the Production Code, heavily promoted by the Catholic Church, was installed as the law of the movie land. It banned a long list of on-screen behaviors, including overt sexuality and "sexual deviancy on the screen."

Before then, the Paramount publicity department had set up photos of Grant and Scott around the house, sitting across from each other at the dining room, frolicking by the pool, and generally acting like a congenial couple. In late 1933, Billy Wilkerson, the publisher and editor of *The Hollywood Reporter*, had published a screed inveighing against "long-haired . . . males," around Hollywood, ending with a warning that Grant and Scott "were carrying the buddy business a bit too far." *The Hollywood Reporter* had already established itself as ground zero for homophobic slurs, often inaccurate—also tossed into the presumably boiling pot were James Cagney and Gary Cooper.

Edith Gwynn wrote the paper's gossip column and suggested how some movie titles could be easily cast with current stars: Garbo could be *The Son-Daughter*; Marlene Dietrich could be *Male and Female*, while Grant could be featured in *One-Way Passage*. The *Reporter* kept at it. A few years later, the paper ran a gossip item that "Cary Grant,

Randy Scott, Betty Furness and Cesar Romero and some more took a serious (but not too serious!) pledge not to marry for five years." (Furness had been a date/escort for both Grant and Scott.)

Wilkerson was setting himself up as a corrosive industry alternative to the fan magazines, which were primarily chattels of the studio publicity departments, but occasionally would slip in shards of reality. A *Photoplay* profile of Cesar Romero was titled "Bachelor by Choice." Most of the article consisted of gush about Romero's good looks while taking the time to throw up a yellow caution light: "Still he seems slated for bachelorhood." The implications could hardly have been more blunt.

Even the most vanilla fan magazines were noticing Grant and Scott, as in "We Can't Afford a Hollywood Marriage," in October 1933 *Hollywood* magazine. A few months earlier, in March there had been a story entitled "They Keep Bachelor's Hall" in *Silver Screen*. A few years later, there was a story entitled "Movie Bachelors at Home," in *Screenland*, in which Grant was quoted as saying, "Every morning when we aren't working we jump out of bed into our bathing trunks [and] make a run for the surf." *Photoplay* waited until 1939 to publish "The Gay Romance of Cary Grant."

As the historian Anthony Slide noted, either everybody was incredibly naive, or the transparent bravado of Grant and Scott's life together defused the obvious conclusion. People who refused to acknowledge they had anything to hide could not possibly have anything to hide. And that's the way it stayed until the 1960s, when the publicity stills of the two men's domestic life began to circulate all over again, resulting in an entirely different set of conclusions.

No other trade paper went as far out on a limb as *The Hollywood Reporter*. What made all this interesting was the fact that Wilkerson, although "incredibly homophobic," according to his son, invariably surrounded himself with gay men at his paper. Almost all of his secretaries were gay men, and in later years Mike Connolly, his star columnist, was also gay. "When it came to my father's business, he put his morals in his pocket," says William Wilkerson III.

Wilkerson had run speakeasies in New York during Prohibition and was close with the mobster Johnny Rosselli, who did a lot of Wilkerson's dirty work for him. (In later years, the lawyer Greg Bautzer would be a smoother version of Rosselli in service to Wilkerson.) Wilkerson knew the mob, knew the score. When he arrived in Hollywood he had $250 in his pocket, and immediately began throwing rocks at the town's largest commercial entities—the movie studios.

He became very close to all the publicity heads at all the studio, and it is highly doubtful he would have taken his shots at Grant and Scott without permission from Paramount. It's even possible that the studio nudged him into printing the items.

"That stuff [about Grant and Scott] could easily have come from Paramount," says Wilkerson's son. "One of the jobs of a publicity head is to keep their people in line. Howard Strickling, the head of publicity at MGM, was a very close family friend, for instance. It was a weird but symbiotic relationship. My father was bosom buddies with Strickling and [Fox publicity chief] Harry Brand, and he absolutely hated their bosses, the guys that ran the studios—Mayer, Cohn, and the rest. On the other hand, Joe Schenck was a lifelong friend. A lot of his friendships were based on trading for blind items."

The *Reporter* items resulted in a lot of raised eyebrows around Hollywood, but Grant and Scott carried on as if nothing had happened. They always would. Chris Scott, Randy Scott's son, would assert, "My father had an endless number of humorous stories he used to tell us about the days with Cary when they were new to the movie industry. . . . From the information I gleaned from the stories all those years ago, Cary and my father were quite the rogues with the ladies." Chris Scott went on to address the rumors that had floated around Hollywood until they were disseminated to the public by Charles Higham in the 1980s, shortly after promulgating the novel theory that Errol Flynn was a Nazi spy.

> Most of the photos which appeared . . . were publicity photos which had been taken and posed for by Cary Grant and my father at the request of the studio. . . . These were not the kind of pictures that you or I might have taken as memories of our time together. They were posed and contrived. . . . Someone was directing the poses from behind the lens of the camera. . . . I can tell you honestly, having grown up with [my father] that he was not gay.

Chris Scott was certainly correct that the pictures were commissioned by the Paramount publicity department. He is also correct in that nobody who worked with his father thought he was gay; Budd Boetticher and Burt Kennedy, who directed and wrote a distinguished series of Scott westerns in the 1950s, both thought the story was absurd. "No actor was more of a man than Randolph Scott," asserted Boetticher, who remembered the time Scott started to explain his "true friendship" with Grant. Boetticher began to laugh and said, "Believe me, if ever I had one inkling of gayness in my system, I would beg you to introduce me to your pal."

Yet the *Hollywood Reporter* items about Grant and Scott imply something quite different, as did stories spread by the society photographer Jerome Zerbe, the longtime companion of the journalist Lucius Beebe, who was known around newsrooms in the mid-twentieth century as "Luscious Baby."

Zerbe, categorized as "handsome and flirtatious," by one acquaintance, was born to a well-off family in Euclid, Ohio, and attended Yale, after which he began a lifelong run as a social butterfly. He worked as the staff photographer for both the Rainbow Room and El Morocco in New York, and made occasional trips to Los Angeles. Zerbe would be paid by the venue where he was working, and his photographs of celebrities wining and dining would be shipped to newspapers that could run them for free. Result: free publicity for everybody.

According to Zerbe he moonlighted sexually with both Grant and Scott at a time when the fan magazines were busily reporting that Grant and Betty Furness were a hot item. "Night after night," reported Brendan Gill of *The New Yorker*, "[Grant] took the good-natured Furness out to dinner and returned her to her apartment promptly at ten o'clock, after which Zerbe and he and assorted companions went out on the town."

As it happens, Zerbe was an inveterate diarist, as is attested by his collection at the Beinecke Library at Yale. The diaries are a matchless record of the breathless whirl of the 1930s *beau monde* on both coasts. Zerbe's first visit to Hollywood began in May 1935, when he stayed at the Garden of Allah. His initial mention of the people involved is on Thursday, May 23, when he goes to Paramount—"saw Carole Lombard & Randolph Scott," followed by lunch at RKO and dinner at the Bruce Cabots'. On May 25, he notes "3:30 Randolph Scott's apartment until 6:40." By May 30 he was at "Orrey Kellys [sic]—a madhouse there. Lloyd Pantages drove me back at 9:45 and out on town."

Zerbes's first meeting with Grant occurred on June 3, when he photographed both Irene Dunne (at the Wilshire Golf Club) and Grant (at Paramount). After dinner he went over to William Haines's house. On June 4, 1935, he took some photos at MGM, then went back to Paramount for more shots with Grant. "700 Randy Scott dinner, Vendome & quiet evening with him here in [illegible] flat."

Sunday, June 9, was a big day: "Lunch at the Countess di Frasso's, who left on afternoon plane for New York. Everyone there. Mary Pickford, Cary Grant, (Dolores) del Rio, Clifton Webb, Fay Wray, Tom Tyler, etc." On Sunday, June 16, he attended one of George Cukor's poolside parties along with William Haines and Haines's partner, Jimmy Shields. That night he was at a party thrown by Carole Lombard for two hundred close friends in Venice, among them Grant, Marlene Dietrich, and Richard Arlen. On the 19th he was at Paramount and had lunch with Grant, with "cocktails first in his dressing room."

On June 25, it was "cocktails Cary Grant, with Frank [Horn, Grant's secretary], Marian Marsh, Betty Furness and Fred Brisson.*

"We all had dinner Vine St. Brown Derby & then to 'The Drunkard' which was hilarious. The Trocadero & home quite late." The next day he was "up late with hangover." On June 28, "Day at beach at Swimming Club with Cary Grant, Frank Horn, Betty Furness." On June 30, Frank Horn stopped by Zerbe's place "late evening," and the next evening it was dinner "with Cary Grant, Betty Furness and Frank Horn to [American] Legion wrestling match, which was a riot. All back here for a drink."

On July 4, Zerbe attended Hedda Hopper's party at a beach house in Santa Monica. There were about forty people there, including Grant, Betty Furness, W. S. Van Dyke, Mary Pickford, and Gene Raymond. On July 12, Zerbe had a screen test at Columbia, which he termed an "interesting and exhausting experience." That night he went to boxing matches, then over to Grant's, and got home about 3 a.m. Two days later, he had dinner with Grant and Furness, then went back to Grant's place with him and Frank Horn for a "quiet evening." He got home about 1:45.

The July 4th party with Hedda Hopper began what seems to have been a lifelong friendship. In 1935, she was not yet the public

---

* Horn was a homely, bald gay man who had met Grant in 1931, during his summer at the St. Louis Municipal Opera.

termagant she would become after starting her column in 1938, but a medium-unsuccessful character actress. After Hopper began her column, she differentiated herself from the motherly Louella Parsons by adopting a sharp, finger-wagging style that resolutely played favorites. Unfortunately for him, Cary Grant was never a favorite, and Hopper indulged in the journalistic equivalent of semaphores to tell her readers what she thought: "Noel Coward and Cary Grant took up where they left off about a month ago," she wrote in October 1940. "I mean Noel was Cary's house guest." In years to come, Jerome Zerbe would stay at Hopper's house whenever he was in town.

By November, Zerbe was back in New York, and on the second of the month he had breakfast at the Waldorf with Grant. A day after that, Zerbe went over to the Drake Hotel to meet Grant and Frank Horn, where they went out to breakfast. On the 4th, there was another breakfast with Grant and Horn, with "Frank over in afternoon." A day later, it was El Morocco, with Lucius Beebe. "I'm joined by Cary Grant, Betty Furness & Frank Horn."

In January 1936, Zerbe sees *Sylvia Scarlett*, "in which Cary Grant is swell." In August 1937, he was back in Hollywood, where he was badly beaten by a man he had picked up. "Face a mess. Really a sight. Stay in bed with ice packs all day. Cary Grant, Ruth Pidgeon etc. call. Feel like hell." On September 6, he spent the afternoon with Grant and a girlfriend. On September 11 he left for New York.

Zerbe didn't come back to Hollywood until 1941, when he again stayed at the Garden of Allah. On June 19, he went to Hedda Hopper's new house to take photographs of various stars helping her move in—Grant, Rosalind Russell, Robert Stack. He was back in 1943, this time as Hopper's houseguest. On December 15 he dined alone at Romanoff's, where he saw Randy Scott, also dining. On December 19 he had a quiet day with Hedda. That night he joined Randolph Scott and a friend, "who are on their way overseas for 8 wks to entertain the boys."

And there the diary entries from Hollywood stop. Zerbe occasionally alludes to people spending the night, but they aren't Randy Scott or Cary Grant. He usually sees Grant and Scott separately, mostly the latter. When Zerbe sees Grant he's usually with a girlfriend. As a matter of fact, Zerbe saw Lili Damita and Errol Flynn at least as often as he saw Grant or Scott.

Examining the record compels admiration for the way Grant played his cards. He was extremely smart, almost cunning, or, perhaps, just profoundly indifferent. There is plausible evidence to place him inside any sexual box you want—gay, bi, straight, or any combination that might be expected from a solitary street kid with a street kid's sense of expedience. What you saw in Cary Grant depended on which team you were rooting for.

What all this overlooks is that neither Archie Leach nor Cary Grant ever played on any team but his own.

CHAPTER SIX

In the late summer of 1935, Grant and Randy Scott upgraded to a rented place on the beach at Santa Monica. The address was 1018 Ocean Front, a house built in 1923. Cary and Randy were accepted by everyone, including William Randolph Hearst Jr., who said that "there were girls running in and out of [Grant and Scott's beachhouse] like a subway station."

Betty Furness, his frequent date in this period—later she would become a TV pitchwoman for Westinghouse and still later President Lyndon Johnson's assistant for consumer affairs—would remember Grant as "beyond any question the most attractive, charming, funny, sweet, marvelous man I've ever known," and would take angry exception to Brendan Gill's characterization of her as a beard.

Grant and Randy Scott would spend more than six years together, in between their respective first and second marriages. "Cary is the gay, impetuous one," wrote one reporter who visited the house. "Randy is serious, cautious. Cary is temperamental in the sense of being very intense. Randy is calm and quiet. Need I add that all the eligible (and a number of the ineligible) ladies about-Hollywood are dying to be dated by these handsome lads."

Grant's explanation for continuing to tie up with Scott centered on his already existing reputation for thrift: "Here we are, living as we want to as bachelors with a nice home at a comparatively small cost. If we got married, we would have to put up a front. Women—particularly Hollywood women—expect it."

As Carole Lombard noted, "Cary opened the bills, Randy wrote the checks, and if Cary could talk someone out of a stamp, he mailed them." Moss Hart would note that if he visited Grant for more than a few days he would be presented with a bill for his laundry, phone calls, and incidentals.

The people who came to the Santa Monica house remembered it as a happy place. Among the attendees at the Sunday brunches were Noel Coward, Dorothy Lamour, Douglas Fairbanks Jr., Cesar Romero, and Hal Roach. Errol Flynn and David Niven, who were living down the beach at a house they called Cirrhosis-by-the-Sea, were regular drop-ins. Roach would become a good friend of Grant's; when he and his first wife had marital troubles, Roach crashed with Grant and Scott. At all times, Grant was a smooth host, losing his aplomb only once, when Greta Garbo came for lunch. "Oh, I'm so happy you met me," he told her.

AMIDST THE PREDOMINANTLY LETHAL PROCESSION of pictures Paramount was giving Grant, there are several ludicrous standouts. *Kiss and Make-Up*, released in July 1934, casts Grant as Dr. Lamar, who runs a beauty salon with high-pressure salesmanship. His primary creation is Eve, played by Genevieve Tobin. Eve is the ex-wife of Edward Everett Horton, who adored her before all the surgeries. Eve wields her newfound beauty like a cudgel and betrays Lamar, who ends up with his loving but plain secretary. It's not that Grant is particularly miscast; anyone would have been miscast in an unplayable part in a movie that should never have been made, let alone released.

Then there's *Wings in the Dark* (February 1935), which is truly something special. It's about a blind pilot. Grant loses his sight in a stove explosion, and when Myrna Loy—on loan from MGM—is imperiled during a daredevil flight, the sightless Grant climbs in his plane and guides her back to the airport. As photographers take pictures of the triumphant couple, Grant sees the lights of the flashbulbs—he won't be flying blind for long!

It's one of those movies that steadfastly refuse to acknowledge their own lunatic premise and thereby descend into self-parody. It took six writers to concoct *Wings in the Dark*, including an original story by Nell Shipman, a heroine of silent outdoor dramas, while the screenplay is by Jack Kirkland, whose play *Tobacco Road* ran for years, and whose daughter, Gelsey Kirkland, danced for years. By far the best performance is given by the dog star known as Lightnin', who is typecast as Grant's seeing-eye dog. Loy found Grant extremely attractive, but preoccupied by his failed marriage to Virginia Cherrill.

In 1946, Alfred Hitchcock would cast Cary Grant and Claude Rains in *Notorious*. Rains evinced a coolness toward his costar that confused people, as Grant hadn't done anything to cause it. In fact, Grant had done quite a bit, but the incidents had occurred years earlier during the production of another Paramount turkey called *The Last Outpost*. Grant and Rains were cast as British officers escorting a group of Armenians across Mesopotamia. Grant falls in love with Rains's wife, which leads to Rains's convenient death.

The director was Charles Barton, who had risen through the ranks at Paramount and had recently been promoted from a job as assistant director to William Wellman. Herbert Coleman, the script supervisor on the picture, would later ascend to the rank of associate producer and second unit director for Alfred Hitchcock, but this was his first exposure to Grant, whom he termed "arrogant, egotistical, pompous."

Grant didn't like Barton, didn't like him at all. Part of the problem was that Grant had already come to the realization that the better the director, the better the picture, and the better the picture, the better for Cary Grant. He had asked for an A-list director in pre-production but had been turned down.

Grant bridled at Barton and asked Claude Rains to join him in asking for another director, to which Rains replied, "Don't try using me to solve your problems. I'm very happy with Charlie's direction." Grant continued agitating. After two weeks Barton told the studio he wanted out. The studio assigned Louis Gasnier, who hadn't directed an important picture since *The Perils of Pauline* in 1914. On his last day on the picture, Barton told the crew what had happened. As Herbert Coleman remembered, "Grant must have wondered what had happened overnight. He was ignored by everyone. The wardrobe man was slow to bring his coat and just tossed it on his chair. [The script supervisor] was always preoccupied when [Grant] fumbled his lines and looked to her for help. It was the same with everyone: the propman, makeup man, and hairdresser."

What made it worse was that Gasnier "adored the tall, handsome English actor and fawned over him . . . he staged every scene to feature Grant, even when the scene demanded the focus on Rains, or one of the other actors."

The crew began to openly refer to the picture as *The Last Out-house*. When it was released, the reviews were what might have been expected. *Variety* said that "Out of this mélange of melodrama, travelogue, history, jungle clips and whatnot the mainstreeters can expect nothing but negligible returns." Maybe the picture wouldn't have been much better under Barton, who spent most of his career directing Abbott and Costello, but the crew as well as Claude Rains found Grant's behavior unprofessional.

It might have been the first time that Grant openly agitated for a better director, but it wouldn't be the last. Cary Grant was now in the Cary Grant business full-time. *The Last Outpost* was just another bad movie for Paramount, but Grant was still on the upswing. On May 3, 1935, Paramount picked up his option for another six months beginning June 7 at a salary of $1,500 a week.

ELIAS LEACH DIED ON DECEMBER 1, 1935, at the age of sixty-three. His death certificate lists the cause as "extreme toxicity," a period euphemism that could have referred to anything from chronic alcoholism to septic shock. Grant ascribed his father's death to "liver disease."

Elias was buried at Bristol's Canford Crematorium & Cemetery on December 5. In yet another example of his furious temper, there seems to have been an incident at the funeral involving Grant smashing a photographer's camera. After that, he reached a rapprochement with the Bristol press, an informal agreement whereby he would make himself available for a quick interview and photo op whenever he arrived in town in return for privacy for the rest of his stay.

Grant was in England when his father died, making a film that was released in America as *Riches and Romance* (The English title was *The Amazing Quest of Ernest Bliss*.) According to his costar, Mary Brian, Grant did the film in order to see Elias before he died. Brian had risen to stardom in the 1924 version of *Peter Pan*, in which she played Wendy. She was pretty and had charm, but was an indistinct actress who tended to serve as a foil for stronger, eccentric leading men—Gary Cooper in *The Virginian*, W. C. Fields in *The Man on the Flying Trapeze*, etc. She had left Paramount just as Grant was arriving, and the two began a relationship during the production.

> We had cars that took [us] to the [studio] and we decided we should go in the same car. And we had a lot of time to talk, and we liked each other. And it just evolved. Sunday would be the only time we had off, and we went exploring London. They had asked me to do a pantomime. Well, I couldn't because I was still doing the stage thing, but I had never seen a pantomime. . . . We went to pantomimes, we went to all the kinds of stage things that he had done. He loved to go to those shows. And there were a lot of parties and things in London. And it evolved into quite a romance.

Brian said that Grant's reaction to his father's death was muted: "I don't think it was as traumatic as it might have been because he hadn't seen that much of his father for quite a number of years. I don't mean he wasn't fond of him, but it wasn't as if he'd been with him day after day. He never discussed his mother or his father with me. And it wasn't that he was drawing back. He just wasn't ready."

The death of Elias served as an impetus to get Elsie out of the asylum. She was finally released in July, 1936, after which Grant moved her into a comfortable house at 93 Whiteladies Road, Clifton, and arranged for an allowance for her. On September 30, 1937, Elsie Leach wrote to her son for the first time. The envelope was addressed to "Mr. A.A. Leach, Cary Grant, 'Actor' Paramount Studios." The address is crossed out with a stamp that says NOT AT THIS ADDRESS. "Just a line enclosing a few snaps taken with my own camera," she writes. "Do you think they are anything like me Archie? I am still a young old mother. My dear son, I have not fixed up home waiting to see you. No man shall take the place of your father. You quite understand.

"I am desperately longing waiting anxiously every day to hear from you. Do try and come over soon . . . please do answer." Elsie's fixations would never change; on November 15, 1938, she wrote that "My darling Archie I have always lived for you and your father. I have been over this morning to his grave with some flowers. My darling if anything ever happens to you I have no desire to live."

It's clear that Grant was taking care of the practicalities, but he seemed uncertain about how to proceed psychologically. On a small 4 x 6 card, he wrote out a telegram to an unnamed person, probably one of the lawyers he hired to disburse money for his mother's care: ABLE TO SAIL HOME FOR SHORT VISIT IMMEDIATELY BUT NEED YOUR ADVICE KNOWING SITUATION REGARDING CONDITIONS AFFECTING MOTHER AS WOULD LIKE SEE HER BUT UNABLE DUE IMMIGRATION LAWS TO BRING HER BACK SO CONSIDER CAREFULLY AND ANSWER TODAY REGARDLESS LENGTH OF MESSAGE.

The slightly garbled tone of Elsie's initial letter would be repeated in most of her correspondence over the years, accompanied by a vagrant strain of religiosity. With the exception of the war years, Grant would generally travel to Bristol to see her at least once a year; when he was in America, he would call her every Sunday morning. If he couldn't call, he would send her a telegram in explanation. His letters to her were effusive and reassuring, but on the emotional level he found her intensely stressful. "When I go to see her, the minute I get to Bristol I start clearing my throat," he told one friend.

GRANT'S RELATIONSHIP WITH MARY BRIAN continued after they got back to Hollywood. She noticed his attitude toward money, but she told Anthony Slide, "It wasn't that bad. He was frugal. But I understand that, because I am sort of a child of the Depression. He came from a poor background. He made very smart business moves, which is to his credit. But I never found him stingy."

Brian enjoyed the Sundays at the Santa Monica house. "He'd come in, pick me up at Toluca Lake, take me down there, always on

Sunday—he was working the rest of the time—and there were people at the beach house. And he would take me home that evening."

Brian did not believe that the relationship between Grant and Scott went beyond friendship, and left no doubt that she could vouch for Grant's sexual bona fides. "People misinterpret a lot of things. If I say this, it sounds conniving and I don't mean it that way, but Cary kind of invented himself in a way. He invented the characters he played. I don't think he was [gay]—not in my experience. I know it's been rumored, but I've never believed it."

Brian and Grant were together for about a year and a half, and discussed marriage, but the relationship ended before they got to the altar. Brian indicated the shoals were a result of her own character: "I'm kind of independent. I guess it could have been smoothed over, but I got on a plane and went back to New York and signed up for a show. A straight show for the Shuberts. [Cary] just hit his stride at that time. He couldn't get away. I was tied up and couldn't get away. A lot of time went by, and that is what happened."

Brian never had a bad word to say about Grant. She ended up marrying George Tomasini, Alfred Hitchcock's favorite film editor. As a friend of Brian's would say, "Mary always had the best affairs."

IN 1935, Henry Hathaway was directing *Lives of a Bengal Lancer*, a period action picture with Gary Cooper and Henry Wilcoxon. It was Hathaway's first big picture after years of assisting and directing B westerns. After a week of production, Hathaway went to the front office and demanded that Wilcoxon be replaced—he was trying to dominate every scene and was in any case too rough for the part, which had been written as a gentleman.

Wilcoxon refused to pull back, telling Hathaway, "I can't help it if I'm the stronger of the two men. If Cooper and I and a girl were out on a boat and we got into a storm and the boat sunk, who would she turn to? She'd turn to me." Agnes de Mille was standing nearby and was heard to mutter, "I'd rather drown with Cooper."

The studio suggested replacing Wilcoxon with Cary Grant. "You mean that Cockney guy with the long neck and the big ears?" asked an appalled Hathaway. "He's no gentleman." In telling this story,

Hathaway would explain that Grant had seemed very Cockney when he arrived at Paramount. What was worse was that he was a Cockney fashion plate: "Always used to wear a scarf to hide his neck, and he had big ears and wore a little hat. . . . I would have been worse off than I was before."

Hathaway settled for Franchot Tone. The picture was a great success and Hathaway was off on forty years of high-end directing. And Grant had to wait for *Gunga Din* to prove he could be a convincing action hero.

GRANT MAY HAVE BEEN in the Cary Grant business, but his attitude indicated he was ambivalent about his client. A *Photoplay* magazine profile in August 1935 was written by a former Paramount publicist and constituted a frank admission of failure. "The Cary Grant publicity campaign proved to be the greatest flop of my press agent career. I worked like a fiend for months, I dragged scribes in droves to his dressing room, onto the set, into his home.

"My efforts were rewarded with a mere dribble of stories concerning the facts of his birth, education and stage career and then things came to a complete and dismaying standstill."

The problem was Grant's childhood. After he was told his mother had died, he shut down. "He missed all the elementary lessons in the art of expressing to outsiders his hopes, his dreams, and his despairs. . . . His closest companion was silence." The article went on to note his "hyper-sensitivity," mentioned his rooming with Orry-Kelly during the 1920s, his best friend Randolph Scott, and noted his "soundless writhing" at anything approaching a personal revelation in print. The publicist had come to believe that "Cary Grant will never know peace as long as his name spells news." Allowing for the breathless tone, the piece captured the essential duality of Grant's character—ardently pursuing fame while resisting exposure.

There would be many stories about the beach house. Grant had become friends with Dorothy Lamour, a rising starlet at Paramount, who worked with Randy Scott in *High, Wide and Handsome*. Lamour was temporarily married to bandleader Herbie Kay, and thought Randy Scott was "one of the finest men in Hollywood." She became a regular guest at the Sunday soirees. One Sunday afternoon, Lamour and eight other guests were finishing dinner when she mentioned how tasty the chicken had been. Grant looked at her and said, "Dottie, that wasn't chicken, it was rabbit." Lamour happened to like rabbits and got rather nauseated at what she had just eaten.

Edmund Goulding, a very good writer/director (*Grand Hotel, Dark Victory, The Razor's Edge*), used to tell a story about one of Grant's parties. It was in honor of Gertrude Lawrence, who was in the midst of an affair with Douglas Fairbanks Jr. She was coming to Hollywood for the first time, and Fairbanks suggested that he and Cary throw a party at the beach house and split the costs. Grant agreed, and the party went off without a hitch. When Grant presented Fairbanks with the bill, everything was itemized, down to cigarettes and napkins. Because there were two bathrooms at the beach house, the list concluded with "two rolls of toilet paper—20 cents."

When Fairbanks was asked if the story was true, he shook his head and said with a sheepish grin, "I'm afraid, old boy, it's the truth."

PANDRO BERMAN ALWAYS CLAIMED that *Sylvia Scarlett* was a nasty joke that Katharine Hepburn and George Cukor devised for the sole purpose of humiliating him. "I despised everything about it," Berman said. "It was a private promotional deal of Hepburn and Cukor. They conned me into it and had a script written. I said to them, 'Jesus, this is awful, terrible, I don't understand a thing that's going on.'"

Berman's frustration began in pre-production, when he spotted an actor for the part of a young artist whom he greatly preferred to Brian Aherne, who had been tentatively cast. "I had tested a young fellow that I thought was very attractive and that I wanted to put into the film. And Katharine raised such hell against him and was so anxious to have . . . Brian Aherne . . . that I had to abandon the whole concept of using Errol Flynn long before he became a star."

The story of *Sylvia Scarlett* involves a girl disguised as a boy who attracts both women—her stepmother wants to instruct her in the art of kissing and what comes after—and men: Brian Aherne gets "a queer feeling" whenever he looks at her. The premise is that Sylvia (Hepburn) has to adopt drag in order to help her scapegrace father

(Edmund Gwenn) escape an embezzlement charge. They meet a Cockney sharper named Jimmy Monkley (Grant) on a train and before you can say "Let's put on a show!" they form a traveling act preciously called "The Pink Pierrots." At this point, the movie is charming, but it has lurching tonal shifts that only get worse when the focus shifts from the travails of The Pink Pierrots to Hepburn's romance with the handsome but invariably dull Aherne.

In these days of gender fluidity *Sylvia Scarlett* is an unexpected gift found beneath the Hollywood tree, but in 1936 it must have been what-the-hell-were-they-thinking stupefying. Even John Collier, soon to become an eminent short story writer, was stunned by the offer to work on the picture for eight weeks at $500 a week—far more money than he'd ever earned as a writer. "I'd scarcely seen a motion picture in my life," he remembered. "I didn't know a thing about screenwriting." Typically, it was all a misunderstanding. Hugh Walpole, who had just written *David Copperfield* for Cukor and David Selznick, had recommended Collier, but Cukor was told Evelyn Waugh was going to be hired. When Collier showed up, Cukor was confused, but acquiesced.

"Cukor put up with it as well as he could and he was very pleasant about my working for him . . . and a rather amateurish film emerged. . . . But it did have bits that weren't bad." Collier gave most of the credit—if that's the proper word—for the film's virtues to cowriter Mortimer Offner, who Collier said was a very good writer who helped with structure, which was only one of the things that Collier knew nothing about. "Believe me, there was never anyone in Hollywood at that time who knew less about writing motion pictures."

Everyone agreed that there was one good thing about *Sylvia Scarlett*. "Cary Grant's performance in this picture was magic," Katharine Hepburn would assert. "He was his true self . . . slightly plump and full of beans. His energy was incredible, his laughter full and unguarded. Teddy Gwenn and I were his stooges." More to the point, for the first time *Sylvia Scarlett* unleashes Cary Grant—as a movie star, as a leading man with the skills of a comedian who can also function as a character actor. He combines energy, humor, and charm with more than a touch of class-based anger. "You have the mind of a pig," Sylvia tells him at one point. "It's a pig's world," Jimmy replies.

Jimmy Monkley is more or less Archie Leach as described by Orry-Kelly and Virginia Cherrill—glittering, hard, blatantly out for himself but with irresistibly seductive overtones of fun and danger. Jimmy Monkley also has some of Elias Leach's gift for incremental self-destruction—Jimmy refers to himself as "a little friend of all the world, nobody's enemy but me own." For the first time Grant had a part that enabled him to connect to his inner self. He's not pretending to be Noel Coward or Herbert Marshall; he's achieved transparency, partly as Archie Leach, partly as Cary Grant.

Perhaps it was losing a woman he loved, perhaps it was the psychic dislocation wrought by the death of his father and the rediscovery of his mother, but for the first time Grant digs into his own painful experience, his own past, his mingled confusion, disgust, and bumptious energy to inform a little masterpiece of characterization. Shaped by Cukor, who directs with more drive than was his wont, the contrast between the barely animated profile Grant had been displaying and Jimmy is like the sun emerging on a dim gray day.

The filmmakers knew they had birthed something strange. After a very difficult preview in December 1935, George Cukor wired Hepburn and accentuated the positive:

OUR LITTLE LOVE CHILD LAST NIGHT AUDIENCE GENERALLY INTERESTED THROUGHOUT STOP A BIT CONFUSED ABOUT THE STYLE OF THE PICTURE APPLAUDED FOR FULLY A MINUTE AFTER IT WAS OVER STOP REVIEW IN REPORTER NOT FAVORABLE STOP DAILY VARIETY QUITE FAVORABLE AND EXTREMELY NICE ABOUT YOU STOP LA TIMES RESPECTFUL AND ENTHUSIASTIC SAYING IT IS A MOST EXTRAORDINARY PICTURE STOP WE ALL DID OUR BEST AND I THINK NONE OF US HAVE BEEN DONE IN BY IT ALL STOP I THINK YOU ARE ABSOLUTELY LOVELY IN IT.

Although *Sylvia Scarlett* was a notable box-office bomb—it lost $363,000 on a cost of $641,000—it was Grant's breakthrough within the industry. Cukor could be waspish about Grant as well as appreciative, sometimes in consecutive sentences. He enjoyed telling Grant that if he hadn't been so well directed by, um, George Cukor, he would have spent his career playing blind aviators. "He was extraordinarily good-looking," Cukor remembered. "In fact, too good-looking; a bit too much like a model. . . . In person he seemed like someone with no humor, but he was slick and bright and very agreeable. . . .

Cary Grant wasn't really a trained actor. Cary Grant was in the theater, and then he had a lot of his training here. He was at first a rather wooden man, and then suddenly he discovered, I'm a comedian. And he found good directors helping him a great deal. In fact, if you see him with Mae West he's rather awkward. But in the meanwhile he had been working and had experience . . . and suddenly when he got the right part, in *Sylvia Scarlett*, he flowered; he suddenly felt the ground under his feet. It was a well-written part, well directed, and he knew what this character was, and he gave a marvelous performance.

He felt an audience like him for the first time, he felt he was in command. I've seen that happen. It's a combination of part and experience that makes it happen.

Cukor appreciated what he called Grant's "native intelligence," with one cavil. "Mind you, he's better when he's well directed."

To which the author and historian Gavin Lambert replied, "Who isn't?"

And then Cukor got to the crux of the matter: "You see, he didn't depend on his looks. He wasn't a narcissist; he acted as though he were just an ordinary young man. And that made it all the more appealing, that a handsome young man was funny; that was especially unexpected and good because we think 'Well, if he's a Beau Brummel, he can't be either funny or intelligent,' but he proved otherwise."

The irony is that Grant wasn't any fonder of the picture than Pandro Berman. "The whole joke was far too private," he would grumble. Grant's reviews were, for the first time, excellent. *Variety* said that "Cary Grant doing a petty English crook with a Soho accent, practically steals the picture," while *The New York Times* said, "Cary Grant, whose previous work has too often been that of a charm merchant, turns actor in the role of the unpleasant Cockney and is surprisingly good at it."

In years to come both Cukor and Hepburn tended to go into an Alphonse and Gaston routine whenever the subject of *Sylvia Scarlett* came up—each of them claimed it was the other's idea. Nearly thirty years later, after he had directed *My Fair Lady*, Cukor sent a letter to Leland Hayward, who had been Hepburn's agent when *Sylvia Scarlett* was made. "Do you think, with *My Fair Lady*, I have overcome *Sylvia Scarlett*?" Cukor asked. "Have I, at long last, paid my debt to society and rehabilitated myself?"

Hayward's reply gave no quarter. "George, *Sylvia Scarlett* was a terrible sin. I haven't seen *My Fair Lady* yet, but if it grosses as much as people say it is going to, it is possible that not only GOD, but I will forgive you for *Sylvia Scarlett*. I shall never forget that preview night as long as I live!"

As far as Hepburn was concerned, the only good thing that came out of *Sylvia Scarlett* was a relationship with one of Grant's friends. They were shooting near Trancas Beach when an airplane circled overhead and landed in a field next to the location. "That's my friend Howard Hughes," said Grant. He made the introductions, and it wasn't long before Hepburn and Hughes formed one of the more unlikely couples in Hollywood history.

WITHIN THE INDUSTRY, *Sylvia Scarlett* made Grant something of a hot ticket, and Paramount began making money on him. In February 1936 they loaned him to Walter Wanger for a picture called *Big Brown Eyes*, for which Wanger paid Paramount $17,500 for Grant's services. *Big Brown Eyes* is one of the unheralded gems in Grant's catalogue, a snappy comedy-drama directed by Raoul Walsh about the world's best-dressed police detective (Grant) going up against a gentleman jewel thief and his minions (respectively, Walter Pidgeon, Lloyd Nolan, and Henry Brandon under his real name of Henry Kleinbach). Both of the leads are interested in a manicurist (Joan Bennett channeling Joan Blondell). It's basically a cheerfully disreputable pre-Code film unaccountably made after the Code, with speedy cross-talk that prefigures *His Girl Friday*.

"What would you do if you bought a girl a present and she wouldn't accept it?" asks Walter Pidgeon thoughtfully.

"Give it to my wife," says Lloyd Nolan.

Big Brown Eyes shouldn't be oversold, but it captures Grant solidifying the transition that had begun with *Sylvia Scarlett*. Age was beginning to work in his favor; there was now a hardness in his jawline accompanying the ambition in his eyes.

A few months later, Grant was again loaned out, this time to MGM for a Jean Harlow vehicle called *Suzy*—another drippy World War I romance in which Grant plays a French aviator. (By now, Grant should have reflexively avoided any movie in which he played a pilot.) This time Paramount was getting $12,500 for a few weeks of Grant's time.

Grant hated the script and began his first meeting at MGM by refusing to play the part. This led to a conference with Grant, his agent, MGM general manager Eddie Mannix, producer Harry Rapf, and screenwriter Lenore Coffee.

Grant's agent began by outlining his client's objections, when Grant broke in. "The part is completely wrong for me and I won't play it."

"Even though it were made completely right for you?" asked Coffee.

"That would be impossible," he replied.

"Difficult, yes. Impossible, no," said Coffee. She asked Grant to work with her in an empty office and go through the script one page at a time. Grant stood up. "Where can we go?" he asked.

Once they found an empty office, Coffee arranged two copies of the script, two legal pads, and some pencils. She began by studiously applying some soft soap: "In truth, I am very much on your side for you are at a critical stage in your career, moving into leading man parts, and then on to being a star."

He looked at her. "You think I can be a star?"

"But of course. So, being on your side, I want to make this part a stepping-stone, for it would be a fine thing if your first part of this sort was with Jean Harlow, which guarantees you an audience. That puts me on both sides. Now let's get to work."

Coffee pulled one of the scripts toward her. "Whenever we agree on a rewrite of a scene, or a completely new one, I want you to make very clear notes of it on the blank facing page of your script, and do this throughout the script, and guard it with your life! Sleep with it under your pillow. Never let it out of your hands."

Grant was staring at her with an uncomprehending look. "The reason," she explained, "is if I fail to write or rewrite scenes as we have agreed, you can produce this script as proof."

Grant's body language began to loosen up. This woman seemed to be on his side. They began rewriting from his entrance. "His detachment from himself *as* himself, and as the actor playing a part, was amazing," remembered Coffee. "When he gave a flat 'no' I knew it meant just that. Then we'd improvise variations of the scene, and this he began to enjoy."

By the time they got to page 30, Grant began making suggestions of his own—good ones. Before dinnertime rolled around, he told Coffee, "I think this is going to work."

"It wouldn't have worked without your help," she replied.

The reality was that Grant's initial instincts had been correct—the script was unsalvageable, a typical example of MGM at its patchwork worst, in which a slew of writers (four were credited, including Dorothy Parker) contribute scenes that might be individually good but never coalesce into a coherent whole. For his trouble Grant got third billing, after Harlow and Franchot Tone.

Nobody except Grant seemed to notice that Harlow was in failing health. He remembered her as "a sweet, frail little thing," and she wore a succession of wigs to cover up that fact. She was widely beloved on the MGM lot, but she was drinking too much, complaining about pains in her lower back, and underwent an abortion during shooting—she was madly in love with William Powell, who couldn't bring himself to marry another actress after his disastrous turn with Carole Lombard. Harlow didn't tell Powell of the pregnancy for fear of losing him. By the time they got to retakes, Harlow had to rest between shots with ice packs over her eyes. She would die of renal failure slightly less than a year after *Suzy* was released, at the age of twenty-six.

In spite of all the difficulties, *Suzy* constituted a marginal success for Grant: "Cary Grant . . . is something more than just a leading man," wrote Welford Beaton in the *Hollywood Spectator*. "Since his outstanding performance in *Sylvia Scarlett*, his talents for varied characterizations have been recognized, and in each new venture he makes good."

The key point in all this was Grant's objectivity, his dawning recognition of the divide between the kind of man he was, and the kind of man he wanted—*needed*—to portray. Most movie stars are fine with parts that reflect aspects of their actual personalities, which lessens the gap that acting has to fill. But with occasional exceptions, Grant wanted to put as much space between Archie Leach and the construct known as Cary Grant as possible. This would inevitably create a terrible disconnect and make living with himself, let alone with other people, nearly impossible, but in 1936 establishing a no-man's-land was necessary.

After Suzy's *Sylvia Scarlett* and *Big Brown Eyes*, Grant spent the next year in a holding pattern. *Wedding Present* was a mediocre comedy back at Paramount. Still, he was attracting interest from major Hollywood players. In mid-1936, Charles Feldman, one of the most innovative thinkers among the brigades of agents that patrolled the territory between Hollywood and Culver City, wrote a memo outlining his desire to sign Grant.

"It is too bad we slipped up on the Grant matter, as he had just signed with [rival agent Harry] Edington giving [Edington] four months after the expiration of the Paramount contract which has six months to run to negotiate for him. There is still the faint possibility of getting this man inasmuch as he is not going to sign any long-term contract with any producer and is going to free-lance."

Feldman was a suave charmer widely known as the Jewish Clark Gable, who maintained a strictly prestige clientele: Marlene Dietrich, Claudette Colbert, and, later, John Wayne and William Holden, among others. Feldman was intrigued not just because of Grant's gradual ascending confidence and general aura of glamour, but because of his obvious intelligence.

The years before World War II are generally regarded as the apex of the studio system and of exclusive contracts that tied actors to one studio, but there was an undercurrent of change. Agents like Feldman and Leland Hayward were at least ten years ahead of their time—they understood that premier talents actually had enormous leverage when it came to bargaining with the studios, even though most stars refused to realize it, preferring the sure thing of guaranteed contracts.

Ronald Colman, for instance, had left Goldwyn to freelance and had landed a deal at Fox that gave him story approval, $100,000 per picture, and 10 percent of the gross—a deal MGM matched in order to get him for *A Tale of Two Cities*. Colman told Irene Dunne to replicate his strategy, which she did. So did Claudette Colbert. Dunne's theory was that between overlapping short-term deals with Columbia, Universal, and Paramount, "I'd get at least one good feature a year, and it worked for the next 15 years. And when I turned down roles, as I frequently did, nobody could suspend me for months on end."

As it turned out, Feldman didn't sign Grant, but the two men liked each other and Grant would occasionally use Feldman as a trail guide through the Hollywood thickets, especially after he decided to forgo agents altogether.

Leaving Paramount was a momentous decision. Even though Paramount offered him $3,500 a week to kick off his next contract, Grant decided to freelance. His reasoning was unassailable. If he stayed, he would have continued to take the castoffs from Gary Cooper, William Powell, or Clive Brook.*

On February 4, 1937, Grant signed a four-picture deal with Columbia Pictures. It mandated that the four pictures be completed within two years, and that he be paid $50,000 apiece for the first two films, and $75,000 apiece for the last two. Columbia was buying ten weeks of Grant's time for each picture, "unless any such photoplay shall be directed by Frank Capra, in which event the Producer shall be entitled to 12 weeks of the Artist's services for said compensation." Grant had to furnish all of his own clothes for modern pictures—the studio agreed to compensate him for any clothes that were ruined—while Columbia agreed to furnish period costumes. There was an option for an additional four films over another two-year period, for which he would be paid $100,000 a picture.

At all times, he would have either first or second billing and would always have first billing over any other male actor. Columbia also agreed that all of Grant's pictures would be "Class A" productions with negative costs of at least $400,000, and would be directed by "a director of first-class reputation and standing in the motion picture industry as a director who customarily directs Class A productions."

What is interesting is the shared commitment that both Grant and Columbia had to making sure that he was surrounded by the best the company could offer. Grant was trying to maximize the possibility of the films being good. If the setting had quality, it could only enhance the star.

The contract also allowed him to work elsewhere. Grant's agent Frank Vincent—Harry Edington's partner—promptly lined up a similar deal at RKO, where Grant's stock remained high despite *Sylvia*

---

* Powell had left Paramount in 1932 for Warners, but Grant's basic point was unassailable.

Scarlett. These were propitious deals, and the money was good for someone who could not yet be considered a genuine star, although he was clearly on the verge. But there was still an element of risk; figuring two pictures a year, he would still be grossing less than what had been on offer from Paramount. He was betting that by taking a little less in the immediate future, he could make more in the long term. The most important feature was potential—at Paramount, he would be one star among a dozen; at Columbia and RKO he would be first among equals. All he needed was better pictures, and, courtesy of Columbia and RKO, he was about to get them . . . but not right away.

Grant's first picture for Columbia was *When You're in Love*, a vehicle for the opera singer Grace Moore, while his first picture for RKO was *The Toast of New York*, opposite Frances Farmer and Edward Arnold. Farmer later said that he was "an aloof, remote person, intent on being Cary Grant playing Cary Grant."

Neither picture was an appreciable advance on the movies Grant had been making at Paramount. Nevertheless, as 1936 turned into 1937, Cary Grant was very much a man on the rise. He spent New Year's Eve in Los Angeles with Howard Hughes, Alfred Vanderbilt, and Darryl Zanuck and his wife. He was beginning to sculpt an image off-screen similar to what he was constructing on-screen—as a member in good standing of café society. Only the best need apply.

CHAPTER SEVEN

━━━━━━━━━━

The stardom that Lenore Coffee prophesied for Grant finally began to coalesce in 1937. It seemed sudden, but it wasn't really. After the unprepossessing *When You're in Love*, Grant made *Topper*, released in July, and *The Awful Truth*, released in November.

Most critics rush past *Topper* in a hurry to get to *The Awful Truth*, but there is a connection. *Topper* was produced by Hal Roach, while Leo McCarey, who produced and directed *The Awful Truth*, had learned comedy at the Roach lot, where he wrote, directed, and eventually became head of production. If you wanted situation comedy, you couldn't do better than the Roach lot, where Laurel and Hardy flourished.

Topper is the first film where Cary Grant appears in full. In his first scene, he's sitting on top of the driver's seat of his car, steering with his feet. He's a trust-fund baby, happy and—this is key—playful. Constance Bennett, playing his wife, is equally loose, equally relaxed; it's a pity they never worked together again. If you didn't know better, you'd say Leo McCarey could have directed the entire picture, but it was actually directed by Norman Z. McLeod, a high-end journeyman with W. C. Fields's immortal *It's a Gift* to his credit.

Topper is the one about the Kerbys (Grant and Bennett) who meet their demise in an auto accident, and spend the rest of the movie as ghosts, luring Roland Young's title character out of a life of glum respectability into the pursuit of pleasure. It was precisely that aspect of the story that worried Joseph Breen, head of the Production Code Administration. In a letter dated March 19, 1937, when *Topper* had just started shooting, the Breen office gave the script cautious approval, provided that there would be no offensive material "in connection with the business relative to the embroidered panties and . . . there will be no sexual implication, or suggestive flavor, in Marion Kerby's efforts to rejuvenate Topper."

When it came to panties, Breen maintained an eagle eye. He saw the picture in June and approved it, with the exception of a couple of lines that had to be excised. Among others, there was the question, "Was she a strip-tease girl?" to which Topper replied, "She was a strip-tease *artist*."

The Kerbys might be dead, but that doesn't mean they can't have fun. The film eventually hammers the invisibility gags into the ground, but it's still notable for Grant's birthing of his screen character, for some beautiful art deco sets, and for Roland Young's absolute command of dry wit.*

Blithe and witty even when dead, Grant's George Kerby is a delightful performance in a good movie. It was his first comprehensive portrayal of a man who has it all—a raffish rich guy with an attractive store of bohemian charm. Shot in a snappy six weeks, Grant did the picture for $75,000. Constance Bennett, who only a few years earlier had been the highest-paid female star in the business, was obviously in decline—she got only $40,000. Bennett gives a first-rate comic performance, but her performance off-camera was less attractive. When Roach signed her for the picture, he told her that her traditionally haughty behavior would not be acceptable on the Roach lot, where everybody liked each other. Roach's warning didn't help; she was continuously condescending.

As for Grant, he asked Roach to make sure that he didn't have any love scenes with his leading lady. The producer wasn't sure if Grant simply thought she lacked sex appeal or that the Bel-Air Circuit would hoot at any love scenes because of her well-earned

---

* In the 1930s, the mother of film historian Alan Rode lived in an apartment house in the flats of Beverly Hills. Among the other tenants was a high-end hooker whose regular customers included Roland Young, who would show up for his regular appointment in a chauffeur-driven Cadillac. Topper!

reputation as a manipulative piece of work. The end result was that Grant and Bennett play their roles as rowdy siblings rather than lovers.

Topper cost $720,625, and MGM, the releasing organization for Roach at the time, reported receipts of $840,860, a figure that was undoubtedly revised upward after Roach sued them for underreporting income. There was a lot of that going on in Hollywood. When *Topper* was reissued in the 1940s by an outfit called Film Classics, Roach ended up suing them for underreporting income as well.

The Awful Truth began as a Broadway vehicle for Roland Young that was made into a movie in 1929 with Ina Claire. Leo McCarey convinced Harry Cohn that the play could be redone economically with an up-to-date spin and cast. As Irene Dunne observed, it's still basically a play, with nominal sets and a small cast. But nobody noticed the cramped surroundings, because Grant and Irene Dunne were in the foreground. "We just meshed from the first moment," said Dunne. "He's a generous actor. He can afford to be—any man that gorgeous— who'd be watching little old me?"

The most comprehensive, as well as the funniest recounting of the making of *The Awful Truth* derives from Ralph Bellamy, who gave Leonard Maltin chapter and verse regarding Leo McCarey's singular methods of production.

It seems that Harry Cohn sent Bellamy a script and told him to pay no attention to the part as written. "Well, why are you sending it over," asked Bellamy, "and why am I supposed to read it, if I'm not supposed to pay any attention to it?"

"Just to get your reaction," answered Cohn.

Soon afterward, screenwriter Mary McCall Jr. called and said that she would be rewriting the Roland Young part so that Bellamy could play it. Shortly after that, Dwight Taylor told Bellamy that he was working on *The Awful Truth*. When Bellamy asked if he was collaborating with Mary McCall, Taylor said she had nothing to do with the project. Weeks went by. Bellamy ran into Dorothy Parker and Alan Campbell, who told Bellamy that they didn't know anything about Dwight Taylor, let alone Mary McCall, but they were thrilled with the progress they were making on *The Awful Truth*. Bellamy, they were sure, was going to love his part. (It should be pointed out that neither McCall, Taylor, Parker or Campbell got screen credit.)

More time elapsed until Bellamy got a phone call to report to Columbia to start *The Awful Truth*. Bellamy was alarmed and called Cohn, who told him, "Just leave it to Leo McCarey. Leo McCarey is a great director, and we're going to be all right. I'm not going to tell you anything." Bellamy pleaded for some kind of guidance, and Cohn finally relented, telling him his character would be from Oklahoma. Now in full panic mode, Bellamy went to McCarey's house, where the director told him "Don't worry, don't worry."

"It all seemed so indefinite, and nebulous," remembered Bellamy.

Come the first day of production, Bellamy showed up with a pile of clothes; as with Grant, Bellamy had to supply his own wardrobe, and since he knew nothing about the plot, he didn't know what kind of clothes to wear.

He had Irene sitting at a piano in front of the camera, and she was saying, "Leo, you can't ask me to do this." Irene and I said hello, and Leo said, "Can you sing?" I said, "I can't get from one note to the next." He laughed. "That's exactly what I want." He said, "You're an Oklahoman." I said, "What kind of Oklahoman?" He said, "Just be an Oklahoman for the moment; I'll tell you about the rest of it later. Do you know *Home on the Range*?" I said, "I know the words, but I can't sing it." He said, "It's perfect! Irene, do you think you could do it?" She said, "You know I don't read music very well." And Leo thought this was funny.

The camera was all set up, and Leo said, "Let's try one." The camera's running, she's playing *Home on the Range*, and I'm singing, and it's just awful. We finished, there's no place else to go, and nobody said "Cut." We finally looked up and McCarey was doubled up under the camera. He finally said, "That's it! Cut, Print it."

Irene and I didn't know what the hell we were doing.

According to Bellamy, it was at this point that Cary Grant came in and did a scene, after which he was deeply upset. At the close of the first day of shooting, none of the actors had seen a script. "Irene was in tears. Cary went to Harry Cohn and said, 'I'll make you one of two propositions. Either let me play Bellamy's part as it is written for Roland Young, or let me out of this and I'll do another picture for you for nothing.'"

On the second day, McCarey showed up with a piece of paper on which he had written the shots and the business for that day, which involved Bellamy, Grant, and Dunne, some doors, and a dog. McCarey chuckled gleefully for the entire day. In Bellamy's recollection, within a few days, everybody was in love with everybody else, and the actors were soft putty in Leo McCarey's supple Irish hands.

To a great extent, this account was confirmed by McCarey.

I'd say, "See everybody at nine o' clock tomorrow morning," and I'd go home not knowing where we were going to start. I'd say, "Well, I know that there's a knock at the door, and Irene Dunne opens the door and admits Cary Grant, so let's put the camera here and I'll see what to do in the morning."

So somewhere along the line, I got the idea that Irene opens the door and says, "Well, if it isn't my ex," or something like that. "What brings you here?" And he says, "Have you forgotten the judge? The judge says this is my day to see the dog." And the scene developed from there.

In other words, the actors went home without knowing what scenes they'd be shooting the next day, which is something perfectly calculated to make actors extremely nervous. Since Grant tended to be a nervous actor anyway, his level of anxiety can be guessed, as can the response.

Edward Bernds, the sound man on the picture, said that McCarey's stories might have been slightly exaggerated. "Every evening, he would have a conference with the writer. However, he did improvise in ways." Frank Capra had temporarily left the studio—he would come back one last time for *Mr. Smith Goes to Washington*—and McCarey was now Harry Cohn's prize director. "McCarey had such a reputation that Cohn wasn't going to interfere," said Bernds. "McCarey would be playing piano on the set and pretend to be thinking."

Beneath his catch-as-catch-can ebullience, McCarey was a strange case—profoundly gifted, profoundly Irish. He was simultaneously alcoholic, deeply religious, and sexually promiscuous while married to his wife for forty-nine years. He would eventually become the highest-paid man in Hollywood, and quite possibly, in America, all the while regarding himself as an artist above "pattern pictures." "He was funny, entertaining, cut your balls off if he had to," said Dore Schary. McCarey lived far beyond the speed limit, so it follows that, while he respected his leading man's talent, they were never going to be bosom buddies.

"Cary Grant was impossible," said McCarey, referring to him as nervous, insecure "and uncertain." McCarey confirmed that Grant tried to get out of the picture. "He offered $5,000 to repay Harry Cohn for the expenses that he had incurred. And I heard about it and I said, 'Well, if that isn't enough, I'll put in five and make it ten.' . . . It was strained all the way through."

Grant even called his friend Hal Roach to use whatever leverage he might have with McCarey to get him out of the movie. Roach thought Grant was being silly and dodged the request. McCarey eventually convinced Grant to hang in there, but Roach would spend the rest of his long life amused by Grant's spotty judgment of comic potential. Everybody's memory was in agreement about one thing: by the end of the first week the picture was flowing.

What McCarey gave Grant was the inestimable gift of freedom, letting Grant improvise to his heart's content. An actor who can do that with wit, not to mention in character, is gold. It should be emphatically pointed out that improvisation took place in rehearsal, not during actual takes. As Edward Bernds pointed out, "Improvising in takes is not professional. It wouldn't matter much if they improvised lines, but if they improvised moves, you were dead. The mike man had to know what was happening."

Grant derived his professional personality from bits and pieces of other actors—a bit of Fairbanksian dash here, a pinch of Noel Coward there. And now he began to see that there were things about Leo McCarey that were very attractive, things he could use. McCarey was tall, dark, and handsome, and possessed interesting, tetchy mannerisms. Peter Bogdanovich, who would do an oral history with McCarey in the last few years of his life, would say, "All those little grunts—that's very Leo. McCarey was a lot like what Cary Grant picked up on: very dry, laid-back in humor. . . . Once he digested it, Cary took what he got and ran with it."

Since McCarey obviously had confidence in him, Grant began to feel secure. Pauline Kael brilliantly characterized Grant's transition from stock leading man to something more:

No doubt he felt absurd in his soulful, cow-eyed leading man roles and tried to conceal it; when he had nothing to do in a scene, he stood lunged forward as if hoping to catch a ball. He became Cary Grant when he learned to project his feelings of absurdity through his characters and to make a style out of their feeling silly. Once he realized that each movement could be stylized for humor, the eyepopping, the cocked head, the forward lunge, and the slightly ungainly stride became as certain as the pen strokes of a master cartoonist. . . . He brought elegance to low comedy, and low comedy gave him the corky common-man touch that made him a great star.

Besides his growing trust in his director, Grant found that he also loved working with Irene Dunne—he came to believe she had the best internal clock of anybody he'd ever worked with. "Irene Dune's timing was marvelous," Grant said late in life. "She was so good that she made comedy look easy. If she'd made it look as difficult as it really is, she would have won her Oscar."

Dunne liked to pretend that comedy was comparatively easy for her, hence not as satisfying as drama. She would tell John Kobal that "[Comedy is] is something like having a musical ear." In fact, Dunne worked very hard on comedy; at night and between setups, she would reread her script and try different line readings and timings in order to coax as much humor as possible out of the material. After McCarey said, "Print," she would head for her dressing room to begin the process all over again for the next shot. Comedy was serious business for Dunne, if not McCarey.

Dunne may have been the least neurotic movie star of all time, and somehow she and the nervous Grant developed a magical rapport. They amused each other on-screen and off because Dunne was the female equivalent of Grant. Not in physical dexterity, or in vitality—Dunne worked in real time, while Grant was faster than life—but in the way she could suggest a hidden layer of bemusement that was strictly between her and the audience. As with Grant, she's in the movie, completely fulfilling her duties to her character and the other actors, but she's also slightly outside the movie, observing and keeping score with a subtle air of what-fools-these-mortals-be. Between them, they define irony, not in the postmodern sense, which often leans toward the cruel, but in a shared, gentle complicity.

The difference between them is that Dunne never completely loses her dignity, while the joy of seeing Grant at his comic best involves watching his dignity be stripped away an inch at a time. Grant might have looked like a romantic leading man, but his willingness to play the fool implied an indifference toward his own good looks. As Jeanine Basinger noted, "Grant was smooth, but his pants might fall down." The more mayhem he endures, the more we love him.

Both Grant and Dunne understood movie acting's delicate balance. The camera prefers actors whose emotions can be discovered surreptitiously. Actors used to projecting toward a theater audience can be too big for the camera, but they can also pull back too much, thinking that nothing is required, when in fact nothing is just nothing. Both Dunne and Grant learned the perfect calibration of movie acting by the hard process of doing it. At first Grant had projected little beyond his looks and his way with clothes, and the result was an inert 8 x 10 glossy that moved but wasn't moving. But Grant's intelligence finally began to inform his relentless observation, and working with actor's directors like Cukor and McCarey made him realize that projection was mandatory.

"Cary was quite a mumbler," Dunne told James Harvey. "He'd go mmmm-mmmm-mmmm—he'd throw in little yeses and nos and mumbles all the way through. . . . He was a lot of fun to work with. He was a lot of fun *between* scenes as well—and I was probably his best audience. I used to die laughing at him, and of course the more I laughed the more he went on."

And then there was McCarey: "When anybody asks me my favorite director, I always say Leo McCarey, and then a very close second was George Stevens. But Leo, well, he was another one that when you were doing a scene and if he liked it, he'd just laugh. And he got the crew to laugh. Oh yes, he was a joy." At the end of her life, Dunne's favorite leading men were Grant and Charles Boyer, simply because "Even if I were not in a movie with them, I'd enjoy seeing them."

The Awful Truth was previewed at the Pantages Theatre on October 5, 1937, to a tumultuous response. *The Hollywood Reporter* gave it a rave, and Billy Wilkerson wrote one of his front-page editorials hailing McCarey and the stars, one of whom had been the target of sniggering articles in Wilkerson's paper just a few years before. "This new Columbia smash is, unquestionably, the funniest picture ever made, packing more laughs than any of the Keystone comedies in their greatest day, more humor than you could get in ten big humorous attractions, offering more SOLID ENTERTAINMENT than we have seen or heard in all our years looking at pictures." The review went on to compare *The Awful Truth* to *It Happened One Night* and *Mr. Deeds Goes to Town*.

That's Hollywood.

McCarey was flooded with congratulatory telegrams. Pat O'Brien wrote, PARDON ME WHILE I BURN INCENSE TO AN IRISH GENIUS. THANKS FOR A GREAT PICTURE LEO GRAND PERFORMANCES FROM GRANT TO DUNNE TO BELLAMY TO DOG . . . I WOULD HAVE BEEN SATISFIED TO HAVE PLAYED ONE OF THE FIGURES ON THE CLOCK. GRATEFULLY . . .

Kay Francis wired that she was STILL WEAK FROM LAUGHING. And Gregory La Cava wrote, DON'T YOU REALIZE THAT WHEN BETTER PICTURES ARE MADE COLUMBIA WILL NOT MAKE THEM. HAVING LEARNED THE AWFUL TRUTH AM NOT ONLY LEAVING TOWN BUT WILL NOT RETURN. IMAGINE WHAT YOU COULD HAVE DONE WITH PANDRO BERMAN AT THE HELM.

Grant was also in the preview audience and sent a telegram to McCarey that is the first surviving evidence of his abiding concern for the finer details of movie production: MAKE ME HAPPY BY GOING CLOSER ON GOODBYE NOW AT DOOR AND REPLACING STRINGY HAIR MUSICALE SEQUENCE ALSO LINE IN VANCE HOME I WOULDN'T DO THAT IF I WERE YOU AS PRESENT MOOD RELIANT UPON POSTCARD OH YES AND MAKE A DETOUR AROUND THAT CORNER STEPINFETCHIT ROUTINE STEP. AT LEAST GIVE THESE CONSIDERATION AND I WILL LOVE YOU ALWAYS. AGAIN THANKS LEO ALTHOUGH IT SOUNDS SO INADEQUATE. CARY.

The Awful Truth was a rarity—a comedy nominated for six Academy Awards (Best Picture, Best Actress, Best Supporting Actor, Best Screenplay, Best Director, and Best Editing). The only winner was Leo McCarey.

For the actors, it was a joyous experience, but McCarey was left with a bad taste in his mouth. Harold Lloyd, whom McCarey had directed in *The Milky Way*, stopped by the set for a visit, but Harry

Cohn refused to let Lloyd interrupt the shooting. "When McCarey found that out, he went livid," reported Edward Bernds. "He went up to Harry Cohn's office and nobody knows what happened there. . . . Cohn needed McCarey because he had lost Capra, so he sent [cinematographer] Joe Walker as an emissary to McCarey, who [told Walker] 'I'll never work for that SOB again.'" He never did. McCarey went over to RKO on a two-picture deal, the first of which was *Love Affair*, again with Dunne, this time opposite Charles Boyer.

McCarey would always reflect exasperation about Grant's spikes of anxiety that no amount of praise or success could alleviate. It is a fascinating psychological tic, for nowhere do any of the people who knew Archie Leach when he was working in vaudeville or the theater describe spasms remotely like what became part of Cary Grant's working life in the movies. The difference, of course, is that Cary Grant was an incrementally devised artificial construct, whereas Archie Leach was the authentic man. Archie had no particular problem being Archie, but playing Cary Grant would easily provoke the emotional equivalent of flop sweat at the risk of being exposed as an impostor.

In the part of the soul where it's 3 a.m., almost everyone feels that they're faking it. When Archie Leach had to play Cary Grant, it was always 3 a.m.

GRANT WAS NOW A FULL-FLEDGED MEMBER of the In Crowd, as was shown by his presence at William Randolph Hearst's seventy-fourth birthday party at the end of April 1937. The place was Marion Davies's gigantic Santa Monica beach house, which was modeled after George Washington's Mount Vernon. The guest list included five hundred of Hearst's most intimate friends, including Grant, Leslie Howard, Clark Gable, Carole Lombard, Tyrone Power, Sonja Henie, Dolores del Rio, Maureen O'Sullivan, Hal Wallis, Mervyn LeRoy, and Ernst Lubitsch. The party had a circus theme. Grant and Paulette Goddard came dressed as acrobats—in his case, typecasting—while Hearst was dressed as a clown. Shortly after the birthday party, Davies sold a million dollars' worth of her jewelry to bail Hearst out of a deepening financial crevice that had been slowly widening since the stock market crash, which had failed to stop his manic overspending.

In between parties—Grant and his fellow British expatriate Ida Lupino would occasionally favor gatherings with medleys of bawdy English music hall songs—he returned to polishing his extraordinary performing skills. *Topper* and *The Awful Truth* began an astonishing run of films that included *Bringing Up Baby, Holiday, Gunga Din, Only Angels Have Wings, His Girl Friday, My Favorite Wife, The Philadelphia Story, Penny Serenade,* and *Suspicion.*

With the exception of *Bringing Up Baby,* revered now but a flop at the time, these were all critical and commercial hits, and they were proof positive of Grant's remarkable ability to suss out quality projects, as well as amplify them with his own efforts. The only pictures that might have been considered disappointments in this otherwise triumphant procession were *The Howards of Virginia,* a ghastly stiff about the American Revolution directed by Frank Lloyd, and *In Name Only,* a high-end soap with Carole Lombard and Kay Francis.

Holiday was based on a play by Philip Barry that had already been made into a movie in 1930. Grant plays Johnny Case, engaged to a rich girl played by Doris Nolan. Her brother is Lew Ayres, a psychologically castrated alcoholic, and Katharine Hepburn is her sister. Hepburn seems tinny and unfelt in her climactic speech, but other than that George Cukor brings all the actors safely into port. The material is played more seriously than seems necessary, but Grant's physical equilibrium—at one point he does a cartwheel, at another a fine nip-up—is as impressive as his comic equilibrium.

These comedies emphasized that Grant's burgeoning comic success was built on the control of his body that he had learned in vaudeville. Acrobatics are about coordination, which demands timing—the crucial element of comedy. When Grant played a heavy drama his body perceptibly tightened and stiffened; the loss of buoyancy radiated a seriousness that could easily ascend to threat. Grant's body language would be the core strength of his performing style, the foundation upon which everything else was built. In comedy, his movements would appear supple and uncontained, prone to explosions while always maintaining a beautiful balance. But when he played serious drama, his arms would invariably be tight against his body, his posture rigid and unyielding.

The films of this period that have sustained are undoubtedly the collaborations with Howard Hawks, which began with *Bringing Up Baby.* Hawks had been brought to RKO by Sam Briskin, the studio's production head since 1935, who gave the director a contract for two years at $2,500 a week, plus a profit percentage. Hawks's first project was *Gunga Din*, with a Ben Hecht/Charles MacArthur script, which was ready to go by April 1937. But RKO couldn't find three leading men to front the picture. Ronald Colman turned the project down, and MGM refused to lend out the triumvirate of Clark Gable, Spencer Tracy, and Franchot Tone. The project was put on hold until a cast could be lined up, so Hawks went looking for another project.

At this point, Hawks had been drawing a salary for more than a year without anything to show for it. At the same time, Briskin had a problem, and her name was Katharine Hepburn. *Sylvia Scarlett* had marked the beginning of a succession of flops: *Mary of Scotland*, *A Woman Rebels*, and *Quality Street*. *Stage Door* had done fairly well, but that had also featured Ginger Rogers, Lucille Ball, and Eve Arden, and it was thought that the ensemble was largely responsible for the film's success.

In May 1937, Hawks told Briskin that he wanted to make *Bringing Up Baby*, from a story by Hagar Wilde in *Collier's* magazine. Personally, Hawks was dour and mostly nonverbal, but he had the remarkable gift of making brilliant, high-spirited comedies. Hawks went to work with Dudley Nichols, and the lead female role was assigned to Hepburn. The studio sorted through Fredric March, Ray Milland, Fred MacMurray, and Leslie Howard before settling on Grant for the role of the harassed paleontologist.

As Briskin examined Hepburn's financials, he came to the conclusion that *Bringing Up Baby* had no commercial chance unless it was made for a price, and that price was $600,000. Nevertheless, the final script came in at a whopping 202 pages, and the budget estimate was $767,000—too high.

By now, Briskin needed to get a Hawks picture in production or risk looking very bad to the stockholders. Besides that, Cary Grant had a play-or-pay deal—if Briskin canceled the picture, he had to pay Grant anyway. So Briskin reluctantly okayed the picture, despite his worries about the budget.

Six weeks before the start of production, Briskin's assistant Lou Lusky wrote a memo that should have frightened RKO:

> I know, because the gentleman has said so in so many words, that he's only concerned with making a picture that will be a personal credit

to Mr. Hawks regardless of its cost—and your telling him the other day that it would be suicidal to make a Hepburn picture for seven or eight hundred thousand dollars I know made no impression on him at all. . . . Hawks is determined in his own quiet, reserved, soft-spoken manner to have his way about the making of this picture. . . .

With the salary he's been getting he's almost indifferent to any-thing that might come to him on a percentage deal—that's why he doesn't give a damn about how much the picture will cost to make.

Briskin was hoping Hawks could be transformed into a company man, if for no other reason than gratitude for his generous contract, but that didn't happen, not at RKO, not anywhere. Hawks would always keep his eye resolutely on the prize—making good Howard Hawks movies, irrespective of whatever studio happened to be financ-ing, or how much they had intended to spend.

Hawks came up with the idea of Grant wearing glasses as a prop indicating character. "You're gonna play a Harold Lloyd character," he told Grant, which led to Grant projecting a continual sense of civilized dismay, if only because he's always a beat behind the other charac-ters. "Cary went over to talk to Harold about it," said Sue Lloyd, the comedian's granddaughter. "Then Harold worked with him on being the shy, retiring type with the glasses. Hawks wanted Cary to do his version of Harold's fumbling and nervous gestures."

Shooting began on September 27, 1937. By now, Grant felt the wind at his back. "Cary was so funny on this picture," remembered Hep-burn. "At this point his boiling energy was at its peak. We would laugh from morning to night." Nearly every morning, Hawks and company would rewrite the dialogue, which meant that each day produced less footage than the production department had estimated. Hawks simply ignored pleadings to speed things up. And then Hepburn got sick for seven days, and she also had some trouble finding her comic rhythm.

"The great trouble," explained Hawks, "is people trying to be funny. If they don't try to be funny, then they are funny." Hawks was initially unhappy with Hepburn's performance, so he went over to Walter Catlett, an entertainingly dry comedian who had spent years in the Ziegfeld *Follies* and had a good-sized part in the picture.

"Walter, have you been watching Miss Hepburn?"

"Yeah."

"Do you know what she's doing?"

"Yeah."

"Will you tell her?"

"No."

"Well, supposing she asks you to tell her?"

"Well, then I'll have to tell her."

Hawks asked Hepburn to talk to Catlett, whom she found so illuminating on the subject of playing comedy that she asked Hawks to keep him on the picture as an unofficial comedy coach.

"From that time on," said Hawks, "she knew how to play comedy better, which is just to read lines."

About a month into production, Sam Briskin was forced to resign, at which point Hawks's pace slowed even more. By the time he was finished, a fifty-one-day schedule had ballooned to ninety-three days, and the budget had expanded to more than $1 million. There was also a sizable amount of post-production work, because Grant almost never worked on the same stage as the leopard, which was tied into the scenes with the actors courtesy of prodigious optical effects work by Linwood Dunn. Hepburn was somewhat braver; there's a remarkable scene where the leopard companiably nudges Hepburn's thigh, said thigh anointed with perfume to attract the cat. To torment Grant, Hepburn and Hawks dropped a stuffed leopard through the vent of Grant's dressing room. He wasn't amused.

In the short run, both Lou Lusky and Sam Briskin were proved right—*Bringing Up Baby* lost $365,000, or just about the amount Hawks went over budget. In the long run, it didn't matter, because the picture became a classic screwball comedy, and Hawks and Grant quickly collaborated on two more pictures: *Only Angels Have Wings* and *His Girl Friday*.

Bringing Up Baby concerns itself with David Huxley, a paleontologist whose only goal in life is to assemble a complete brontosaurus skeleton. He's short one part: the intercostal clavicle. His search for funds to get said clavicle puts him in harm's way, that is to say in the sightline of Susan Vance, a daffy heiress who finds meaning in first pursuing, then hobbling David both physically and psychologically. In the process Grant runs the gamut of emotions from dismay to frustration to several varieties of panic, all of it beautifully paced and irresistibly funny.

The moviemakers of the 1930s must have greeted the arrival of Grant like an answered prayer. In *Bringing Up Baby*, he has a habit of distracted mumbling to indicate put-upon frustration at his life being turned upside down by a troublesome woman in pursuit of her missing leopard. Grant's Huxley is not only a great comic performance, it's fully thought out in terms of physical effects. When David runs, he moves in an awkward hobble, as if his knees are tied together.

Hawks and Hepburn spend the entire running time thinking up new ways to humiliate the hapless David. Hawks even gets Grant into drag—a rather fetching negligee with marabou-trimmed sleeves. Confronted by May Robson, David explains, "I've lost my clothes."

"Well, why are you wearing *those* clothes?"

Exasperated, he yells, "Because I just went *gay* all of a sudden!" giving a little hop in the air to accent "gay." It's a prodigiously inventive performance, and Hepburn matches him moment for moment—his perpetual retreat motivated by her perpetual pursuit.

The basic joke, repeated with variations in most of Grant's comedies, was the gradual but increasing discombobulation of his impeccable surface. Complacence would be displaced by unease, which gradually ascended to panic. (You could tell Grant was panicked because a lock of hair might fall over his forehead.) Cary Grant was invariably classy, but rarely dignified, at least not for long.

His secret was an unmatched ability to lend shadings of seriousness to comedy—his performance in *Holiday*, for instance—and vice versa. He never displayed only one color, no longer played a person with only his perfect profile. There was an edginess about him—the fretful tone in his voice, the strange accent, and the abiding sense that beneath his calm surface well-oiled gears were whirling faster and faster. "I know I should run," he mumbles at one point, "but I can't."

This cycle of films made Grant the paragon of romantic comedy for his own generation as well as succeeding ones. In 1935, by which time he had made more than twenty films, Grant had received less than one percent of the votes in the popularity contest held by the trade paper *Motion Picture Herald*. By 1938, he was one of the most popular leading men in the movies.

Romantic comedy is an insufficiently respected genre that didn't really do much for the careers of other frequent practitioners such as Melvyn Douglas, Ray Milland, or in the modern era, Jennifer Aniston or Matthew McConaughey. But Grant was to romantic comedy what Fred Astaire was to dance—he made something that is extremely difficult look easy. Basically, romantic comedy is a battle of the sexes, and since sex was forbidden under the Production Code, the combat had to be expressed verbally or, on occasion, physically, which is where Grant's comprehensive dexterity proved invaluable.

A lot of the romantic comedies of the period involve the problems of rich people, a strategy that seems counterintuitive until you see the movies—*Holiday, Bringing Up Baby*, and *My Man Godfrey* depict a world where the rich are crazed by their privilege, a posture calculated to make all the members of the proletariat who paid to see these movies feel better about their lumpen lives. Nothing dates faster than comedy, but Hawks's best—*Twentieth Century, Bringing Up Baby*, and *His Girl Friday*—stand up to the passing generations as well as any comedies ever made. They're raucous, but the flamboyant nature of their characters and settings means they never seem overplayed.

In all of these pictures, and many others, Grant lets us see a familiar outline, then takes us a shade deeper than we expect, without ever completely sacrificing humor or charm. It was a perilous balancing act, and it left him a nervous wreck for most of his life.

RUDYARD KIPLING WROTE his narrative poem *Gunga Din* in 1892, about a native in India who gives his life in service to the Raj, leading the narrator to cry out, "You're a better man than I am, Gunga Din." MGM thought about making a movie version as early as 1928, but after a couple of scripts nothing moved forward. In 1934, the producer Edward Small optioned the poem from Kipling, and completed the purchase two years later, after Kipling's death, for £5,000. In April 1936, Small hired William Faulkner to write another script. Faulkner's efforts bore no resemblance to the film that emerged except for the curtain line.

That same year, RKO bought the property from Small. Hawks set to work on a new script with his longtime collaborators (*Scarface, Viva Villa, Twentieth Century*, etc.) Ben Hecht and Charles MacArthur. The work went well—on October 27, 1936, Hawks, Hecht, and MacArthur wired the head of RKO:

HAVE FINALLY FIGURED OUT TALE INVOLVING TWO
SACRIFICES, ONE FOR LOVE, THE OTHER FOR ENGLAND,
WHICH NEITHER RESEMBLES BENGAL LANCERS NOR
CHARGE OF THE LIGHT BRIGADE AND CONTAINS
SOMETHING LIKE TWO THOUSAND DEATHS, THIRTY
ELEPHANTS, AND A PECK OF MAHARAJAHS STOP WE
HAVE THIS NOW IN A COCKTAIL SHAKER AND HAVE
POURED OUT SOME THIRTY-FIVE PAGES OF GLITTERING
PROSE WHICH LOOK GOOD. BEST REGARDS.

The script was completed by February 1937. The collaborators
took the basic idea of Kipling's poem, fused it with *Soldiers Three*, and
stole a primary plot point from Hecht and MacArthur's 1928 play *The
Front Page*: Ballantine, one of the three soldiers, is preparing to leave
soldiering to get married, which provokes his friends into spending a
great deal of time and comic effort trying to sabotage his plans—the
same premise accompanying Hildy Johnson's plans to leave journalism
in *The Front Page*. At the end of the Hecht-MacArthur script, Ballantine and his girl get married and leave the fort. Cutter and MacChesney
take a look at Ballantine's enlistment form, then wire ahead to arrange
for his arrest for desertion—*The Front Page* all over again.

After casting problems arose, Hawks elected to make *Bringing Up
Baby* instead, after which RKO paid him $40,000 to cancel his con-
tract. Pandro Berman was named the new production head at RKO,
and handed *Gunga Din* to George Stevens, a younger and, Berman
thought, more malleable director who had done splendid work on
pictures as varied as *Alice Adams* and *Swing Time*. Stevens brought in
Joel Sayre and Fred Guiol to rewrite the last third of the script and cast
Cary Grant for $75,000, initially in the romantic part of Ballantine.
But with his evolving instinct for maximizing his strengths and mini-
mizing his weaknesses, Grant was instead drawn to the part of Cutter,
an insolent Cockney who could be turned into an antic action hero.
Everybody agreed Victor McLaglen would be an ideal MacChesney.

It was Grant who brought Douglas Fairbanks Jr. into *Gunga Din*.
Fairbanks had recently made a considerable hit as Rupert of Hentzau,
the dashing heavy in David Selznick's production of *The Prisoner of
Zenda*. He had been dubious about the part until his father told him
he was being idiotic. Senior explained to Junior that *The Prisoner of*

Zenda had always been a success and that Rupert was "was one of the best villains ever written. He is witty, irresistible and as sly as Iago." Furthermore, the part was actor-proof: "Rin-Tin-Tin could play the part and walk away with it," Fairbanks told his son.

Grant approached the younger Fairbanks, who appraised him as "a remarkable guy with an agile mind (which, *he* said, was replete with complexes) and a treasure of a friend." Fairbanks wondered how he was going to fit in—an American in a sea of Brits. Grant kept after him, sending him the new script. Fairbanks liked the script, but it wasn't clear which of the two remaining sergeants was his. Fairbanks asked Grant who he wanted to play and in spite of his yen for Cutter, he said, "Whichever one you don't want! I want us to be together in this so badly—I think the two of us, plus old McLaglen as our top sergeant . . . will make this picture more than just another big special." The two men still couldn't come to a decision, so they flipped a coin. It's the sort of unlikely story that fills Hollywood biographies, but it was confirmed by both Fairbanks and Grant.

To the end of his life, Fairbanks was moved by Grant's unselfishness, but he made a profound observation about his friend that explains a great deal about Grant's grasp of the essentials of success: "He had always been most concerned with being involved in what he guessed would be a successful picture. If he proved right, he reckoned it could only rebound to his credit." In other words, the movie was the setting for the actor, and if the setting was shoddy, the actor would reap little credit no matter how hard he worked. For the bulk of his starring career, Grant was always careful to work with either good writers or A-list directors, preferably both—it increased the odds of success, and success breeds success.

Fairbanks was earning $117,187—more than Grant—and McLaglen brought up the rear with $62,991. George Stevens was low man on the totem pole with a salary of $58,050. For the title character, Stevens tried to get Sabu, who had become a star with *Elephant Boy* and *The Drum*, but Alexander Korda wouldn't lend him out. Stevens instead cast Sam Jaffe, who had gained notice for his portrayal of the mad Czar in Sternberg's *The Scarlet Empress*, and as the ancient High Lama in Frank Capra's *Lost Horizon*.

The Hecht-MacArthur script mostly took place indoors, but the rewrite by Sayre and Guiol introduced the Thuggee cult as the unifying factor for the heavies and made it an outdoor picture. The Thuggees killed more than a million people in India before they were vanquished by Lord William Bentinck, the governor general of India, between 1827 and 1835. (The period of the film was at least fifty years after the Thuggees were destroyed, but nobody seemed to notice.) Sayre and Guiol also minimized the weak replication of *The Front Page* in the Hecht-MacArthur script.

Stevens's choice for location work was Lone Pine, three hours outside Los Angeles, at the base of the Sierra Nevada mountains, where Stevens had photographed westerns early in his career. He knew that the rock formations in the Alabama Hills could easily stand in for the Khyber Pass if only because other movies about the Raj such as *The Lives of a Bengal Lancer* had been shot there.

Production began in July 1938, with a schedule of sixty-seven days and a budget of $1.49 million. Three hundred and twenty-seven actors and crew lived at the site. "This, of course, was appalling," remembered Grant, "and a little nerve-wracking here and there. But we had a great cavalier with us, a fellow called Doug Fairbanks Jr."

Although Fairbanks was American, he aspired to be English, wanted a happy set, and set about making it so. Fairbanks brought his English butler with him to Lone Pine, which turned out to be a good idea because of a stuntman and sound man who took an instant dislike to each other and kept threatening a brawl. "Doug would put on his best manners," said Grant, "and served Pimm's—we had all sorts of things while we were making the film. And he'd get these fellows together. Well, they couldn't fight, you see, while being entertained by the principal . . . so we had very few fights in the camp. And these were fellows who could knife fight."

Besides volatile stuntmen there were circus people around to handle the elephants, so George Stevens had his hands full. Grant observed people carefully, and he realized that Stevens was someone special. "Nothing was going to stop him from accomplishing his purpose. Nothing. No other producer, no studio heads, nothing. He was going to do it his way. Now, he might . . . permit you to believe that you were doing it your way, but you weren't at all—you were doing it his way. And we all knew that."

Luckily, the actors all liked each other. Fairbanks and Grant were already pals, and Victor McLaglen fit right in. "Vic was lovely," said Grant. "A sweet, good, great man—like a big bear. We all loved him."

Six weeks had been set aside for location work, but that plan soon disappeared into the rearview mirror. Doug Fairbanks said, "We couldn't get much work done in the morning because, although it was a good script . . . we kept thinking of different minor ways of altering it. So George and Cary Grant and myself would sit around most of the morning and try out the scene, rehearsed and made alterations, send them in to be rewritten, revise them again, then sit around some more and have some coffee . . . George would have a beer or two perhaps." *Gunga Din* would be the first film of Stevens's artistic maturity, when, as Marilyn Ann Moss wrote, he would be "chronically late, chronically expensive and chronically big at the box office."

Part of the problem at Lone Pine involved the weather. It was summer, and the temperature could go up to 110, but there was also a snowstorm that put whitecaps on the mountains in the background. (Stevens shot close-ups until the snow melted.) Then there were three days of dust storms that damaged some sets. The cast remembered the experience as glorious, full of comradely fellowship and good times. Stevens allowed his stars to improvise and devise bits of business at will, more or less in the manner of the great Laurel and Hardy comedies he had photographed ten years earlier. All the actors were circumspect around leading lady Joan Fontaine, oblivious to the fact that she was engaged in an intense location affair with her director.

Stevens remembered the shoot as an extended improvisation, and all the better for it, but improv ended where Grant was concerned. "He was a master technician," said Fairbanks, "meticulous and conscious of every move. It might have looked impetuous or impulsive, but it wasn't. It was all carefully planned."

Actually, Grant was becoming extremely adept at working out all sorts of things. Fairbanks remembered that every morning before rewriting and shooting, Grant would hurl himself into currency trading. Fairbanks said that Grant would sell English pounds and buy Italian lira or German marks.

Since learning the value of concentrated relaxation, Grant was in his element, free and easy with his suggestions, many of which Stevens adopted. "All the way through this film we don't know what we're going to do next week," Stevens remembered. "There's a great deal of vitality that comes from this, and we were enormously excited and pleased . . . with what we were doing throughout." But the front office was frantic, and for the first time Stevens perfected his foolproof method of dealing with worried executives: pretend to listen, nod sympathetically, then do what you were intending to do in the first place.

At one point, Pandro Berman announced he was coming to the location for a serious weekend confrontation with his out-of-control director. When Stevens was apprised of Berman's imminent arrival, he took off for the weekend, giving Berman his choice of cooling his heels at Lone Pine or going back to Hollywood. He went back to Hollywood.

Generally, Grant didn't have much feeling for animals, but he bonded with Annie, the elephant. "I was with Annie and I had my lunch sent up, because I got tired of getting up and down off that damn thing. And I had pants that were very difficult to wear, because I had them—they were reinforced because an elephant's hairs are so strong that if you ride it for a while they break through the material.

> I had an umbrella up there; they fixed me up with an umbrella and lunch and I had a book. And Annie got so accustomed to me—and this is absolutely the truth—that the man hadn't arrived that took care of the elephants. And he asked me if I'd go out there and sleep out there with Annie, and I said "Sure." It was hot anyway, and I went out and slept on a cot alongside Annie, so she'd quiet down, because she'd be all over, otherwise. . . . And she did, she calmed down. I patted her a couple of times and kicked her a couple of times. It was all fine with her.

After the film was finished, Annie died in a fire, and Grant was upset—"I had become very fond of Annie."

After eight weeks on location, Pandro Berman ordered the company back to Los Angeles. In September, a rough cut was assembled and the executives were sufficiently impressed to authorize another two weeks at Lone Pine for the climactic battle. The sequence entailed 1,500 extras, several hundred horses, and four elephants. Stevens outlined his shots on paper and rehearsed the action with the cast in slow motion until everyone was sure of the mechanics, rehearsed again at half-speed, then finally shot it.

By the time the movie was finished, Stevens had shot for 104 days instead of the planned sixty-seven. Released in January 1939 as a harbinger of one of the greatest years in the history of Hollywood, *Gunga Din* was loved by the critics but didn't quite recover its high cost. (It went into profit on a 1941 reissue.)

Everybody loved the picture except Rudyard Kipling's widow and Indians. In the case of the former, Stevens and company had cast Reginald Sheffield to play Kipling accompanying the regiment during the final battle—an invention on Stevens's part, as Kipling never saw combat during his years as a journalist in India. In the film, Kipling witnesses Din's sacrifice and is inspired to write his epic poem. Caroline Kipling asserted that the filmmakers had held her husband up to ridicule. They hadn't, but they were disinclined to argue the point in court. RKO matted out Sheffield so the character of Kipling magically disappeared from the film. (The original version has been restored.)

In the latter case, the film critic for *The Bombay Chronicle* called the film "Imperialist propaganda of the crudest, the most vulgar sort and depicts Indians as nothing better than sadistic barbarians. . . . All the British characters are honest, jolly souls while all the 'natives' are scheming, treacherous, unscrupulous devils. All but one!! The solitary exception is Gunga Din, the faithful water carrier—loyal unto death, despite the insults and curses that are invariably showered on him by his White Masters." The film was banned in India, and, in what was billed as an act of sympathy, in Japan.

The Bombay critic's arguments were accurate, assuming you have the strength of character to resist one of the movies' most exhilarating Boys Adventures. As *Variety* noted in their review, the film is "a magnificent narrative poem spun into vigorous, ecstatic action," an opinion echoed by *The New York Times*, whose critic said that "All movies should be like the first 25 minutes of *Gunga Din.*"

Cutter, Ballantine, and MacChesney are carefree, overgrown adolescents, using the Hindu Kush as an extended recess, oblivious to the possibility of death. The film is emotionally anchored by Sam Jaffe's touching performance as Gunga Din, a real man of pride and pain. At the end of his life, Stevens said, "I made the film long ago and I made it just in time. If I'd experienced another year, I'd have been too smart to make it." Certainly, the film is the last completely carefree movie from Stevens, whose films began to gravitate toward the morose.

Despite the travails of production, everyone involved with the movie knew they had accomplished something memorable. Certainly, it cemented the lifelong friendship between Grant and Doug Fairbanks Jr.—the two always addressed each other as Cutter and Ballantine.

*   *   *

IN THE FIRST WEEK OF NOVEMBER 1938, Grant was in Paris, where he accompanied Marlene Dietrich and Jack and Ann Warner to Maxim's for dinner. Dietrich was in the midst of one of her typically tempestuous affairs, this time with Erich Maria Remarque, who referred to her as a "steel orchid." Remarque decided to skip Maxim's and visited an art dealer, where he bought a Cézanne watercolor. A week later, Remarque and Dietrich accompanied the Warners to dinner. "Simple man," wrote Remarque about Warner in his diary, "Somewhat crazy wife. . . . In one room two girls were making love. Ann Warner was very interested in it." Grant returned to America with Dietrich and Remarque on the *Normandie*, where they again socialized with the Warners, as well as Ernest Hemingway. Hemingway was incapable of meeting anybody he regarded as competition without trying to humiliate them, so he spent the crossing telling Dietrich that Remarque was "worthless," certainly as a writer, probably as a man.

Hobnobbing with the elite of café society and world literature must have been a very peculiar experience for Grant, calling upon all his performing skills. Hollywood was full of people who had risen out of flotsam, changed their names, capped their teeth, altered their hairlines—everyone was passing, one way or the other. Dietrich was a true daughter of Berlin—smart, mordant, sexually ambitious not to mention ambiguous, with a withering sense of appraisal armored by her narcissism. Grant's armor was his gleaming surface, his charm, his quick grasp of personalities and situations, and his capacity for sudden withdrawal. That was enough.

RIGHT AFTER *Gunga Din*, Grant was back with Howard Hawks for *Only Angels Have Wings.* Grant plays the same part John Wayne would play in Hawks's *Rio Bravo*—a taciturn, omni-competent leader of men, in this case a group of mail pilots in South America. Despite playing a typical Hawks leading man, Grant is outfitted with a spectacularly flamboyant, unlikely wardrobe that would not have been out of place in a Shubert musical.

Hawks's problem on the picture was Rita Hayworth. Hawks liked his women tart, knowing, and as tough as the men, and Hayworth was basically sweet and feminine. He thought she was irretrievably stupid and let her know it. Hayworth remembered that only Grant's kindness and compassion got her through the picture.

Only Angels Have Wings has garnered its share of adherents over the years in spite of Grant's wardrobe, topped off by a show-stopping white hat wider than anything Gary Cooper ever wore. The hat wasn't the worst of it. That was what Manny Farber called "razor-creased trousers that bulge out with as much yardage as a caliph's bloomers and are belted just slightly under his armpits."

The story takes place on a distant South American escarpment populated by a fraternity of tough fliers who don't seem at all surprised when in wanders the one man in the world who not only betrayed Thomas Mitchell's kid brother but who married the woman Grant loved and lost. The dialogue is terse, the bravery is stupendous, and everybody keeps a stiff upper lip, not to mention a straight face. It does look good—cameraman Joe Walker made his blacks glisten.

AFTER MARY BRIAN, Grant began keeping company with the actress Phyllis Brooks. They went everyplace together, although Grant's official residence remained with Randy Scott at 1018 Ocean Front. The front of the house faced the ocean, the back of the house the highway. There was parking space for two cars—Scott's Cadillac, Grant's Packard. There was a swimming pool, a walled patio for privacy, a small dining room. Over the garage was another bedroom that was mostly used as a den, with a bar, a piano, and some backgammon tables.

Cesar Romero was there, Reginald Gardiner was there, and Gloria Vanderbilt's first husband, an agent named Pat de Cicco, was there. Also in the ménage was Albert Broccoli, a cousin of de Cicco's who would eventually strike platinum by producing the James Bond movies.

Brooks's family objected to what they saw as a clear case of immorality. "My mother was a tight-thinking person, a strict Victorian," Brooks said. "Things were a lot different in those days. There were moral clauses in your contract. Nobody dared live together . . . it would have been utterly scandalous."*

Brooks said that Grant asked her to marry him, then presented her with what amounted to a prenup specifying that Brooks's mother would never be allowed in their house. Brooks wasn't much fonder of her mother than Grant was, but there was a further issue. Grant wanted her to give up her career, which was a problem as she was the main support of both of her parents. Caught between the competing demands of her boyfriend and her parents, Brooks capitulated to her parents. She ended up marrying Torbert Macdonald, the Harvard roommate of John F. Kennedy and a future Massachusetts congressman. She would always call Grant "the love of my life."

Brooks kept her letters and photos from Grant in a trunk at her mother's house so her husband wouldn't find them. Years later, she went to the trunk and found it empty. Her mother had burned everything.

Grant had applied for American citizenship, but pulled it after England declared war against Germany—he didn't want to give the impression he was bailing on his native country when she was in trouble. Before that, on December 12, 1938, Elsie wrote him one of her loving, garbled letters: "I read in newpaper suggestion you thinking of changing your nationality. I hope and trust you will do what's right in the sight of God. I have always trusted in him. My darling I am sending you this Christmas parcel hoping you will be pleased to find it useful. It is very fashionable colours I like. I do so my darling so wish you were nearer. I could see you more often and do for you."

In fact, Grant would not see his mother until after World War II. While it is doubtful that Elsie would have wanted to leave Bristol, it is equally doubtful that Grant wanted her in his immediate proximity. Seeing Elsie always rattled Grant. She perceived him as a carefree young man and seemed not to be completely aware of just how famous and well-off he had become. It was so much easier to send money and expressions of love.

---

* Well, *some* people lived together. Among others, Charlie Chaplin and Paulette Goddard lived together, albeit while pretending to a nonexistent marriage. Laurence Olivier and Vivien Leigh also lived together before they married, as did Clark Gable and Carole Lombard, as well as Barbara Stanwyck and Robert Taylor.

PART TWO

1939–1953

"Some people say a star is better off independent," she said.

"Yeah, that's what they say. You hear that all the time, from actors that it don't look so good for their next option. You hear it from actors that the studio only wants them for one picture. You hear it from agents that can't land a contract for more than one picture. Yeah, a star is better off independent, once he got about two million stashed away and don't care if he never works."

—John O'Hara's "Natica Jackson"

"I have spent the greater part of my life fluctuating between Archie Leach and Cary Grant, unsure of each, suspecting each."

—Cary Grant aka Archie Leach

CHAPTER EIGHT

═══════════════

By August 1939, Grant was a guaranteed hot ticket, as was indicated by a memo from RKO's J. J. Nolan to studio head George Schaefer about the studio's production plans for their major stars. After moving past Ginger Rogers, Nolan turned his attention to Cary Grant:

> We have three more pictures to make with Grant during the two-year period commencing September 23, 1939, and his first picture will be the McCarey picture [*My Favorite Wife*]. It is your plan that we should utilize Grant's services immediately following [*His Girl Friday*] which is being made by Columbia. The only property I know of which has had any preparation that Grant could appear in is the McCarey picture. The other possibility, *Passport to Life*, has had no preparation. . . . Incidentally, [Grant's agent] Harry Edington has phoned me asking what the possibilities will be for him to get a picture in between the finish of the Columbia picture and our next picture. I told him that this was impossible as we were going to use Cary in a picture when he finishes with Columbia.
>
> I think in view of this that it is imperative we have a picture ready for Grant, which we all assume will be the McCarey picture, but in the event anything happens I think we should start preparing *Passport to Life*. If nothing happens to the McCarey picture and we can go ahead, then we can use the property *Passport to Life* for Grant's next picture.

Grant's hot streak came to an abrupt end with *In Name Only*, which is what RKO ended up calling the property that had been *Passport to Life*. Under any title, it's a glam soap opera in which Grant plays a rich boy torn between the avaricious wife (Kay Francis) and the idealistic girlfriend who loves him for himself (Carole Lombard). It might have been more interesting if Francis and Lombard had switched parts, but no such luck.

The plot has Grant trying to get a divorce from Francis's manipulative bitch so he can marry widow Lombard, who comes complete with an adorable five-year-old to clinch the deal. The affair begins because she doesn't know Grant is married—he conveniently forgets to mention it, so her innocence is maintained. As for Francis's character, as Jeanine Basinger noted, "In movie terms, the fact that she doesn't love him means she shouldn't have him. . . . Lombard gets him because she *loves* him, and he's sympathetic for the same reason." To quote Dorothy Parker, if you like this sort of thing, this is the sort of thing you'll like, but there's no getting around the fact that Grant is stuck with the George Brent part—a retreat to the generic leading man parts Paramount had dumped on him for years.

The director was John Cromwell, who remembered that he was "perfectly amazed that [Grant] took the part, and nothing was said about meeting or talking about the script. [I was sure he would see] at one reading what his part amounted to, you know, a guy between two dames fighting over him. Can't do anything but take the worst beating in the world, and I thought surely—was that smart? Nothing happened and I was absolutely amazed."

Finally, two days before the picture was due to start, Grant called Cromwell. "He was quite upset about the script and wanted to talk about it. I thought to myself, 'Oh, here it comes.' I didn't know what we were gonna do because we hadn't been able to get anybody. I had had a couple of other choices before him and they had seen through it right away."

Came the day of the meeting. Cromwell had spent the morning devising clever ripostes to what he was sure would be Grant's absolutely sensible excoriation of his part. "All right," Grant began, "on page 10, it says, 'Now, you surely don't expect me to believe that.' But I think that's a little strong. I think it's, 'Now, you don't expect me to believe that?'"

Cromwell was thunderstruck. "It was just as inane and silly as that. I couldn't believe my ears. I could see he had his script all marked and pages turned down so I knew that all meant something that I was to hear about. Instead of betraying my relief by a quick answer, I acted like a fool. I put on a show and I said, 'Mmmm, well, yes, I think . . .' We went through the whole script and that's all there was. When we got all through, Cary got up and said, 'I feel so much better about the whole thing.'" Except for the fact that there was nothing for Grant to do, he acquitted himself professionally, but he must have known something was awry; he never played another part remotely as passive.

Playing an immobile object of desire was an incomprehensible choice which his entire run of pictures since *Topper* had rendered archaic. *In Name Only* banished the comic dervish, not to mention a reliable agent of narrative change. *In Name Only* does offer one intriguing moment: the film concludes with Grant in an oxygen tent while Francis and Lombard face off in the waiting room. As Lombard walks in triumph into the ward room to be with Grant as he (presumably) recovers, the door closes slowly on Francis's wife, standing alone and impotent—a prefiguring of the last shot of *The Godfather*.

In Name Only was still playing sub-runs in American theaters when *Variety* ran a cursory two-sentence obituary for Bob Pender in November 1939. Grant made no public remarks about his mentor's death.

GRANT HAD BECOME FRIENDLY with Gene Lester, the West Coast photographer for *The Saturday Evening Post*. Lester specialized in candid shots of the stars, and worked out of a combination studio/ home at 8504 Sunset, a couple of doors west of La Cienega. Lester stored 16mm prints of movies at his office—a novelty at the time. Most producers had 35mm projectors at their houses, but few stars bothered with the expense of 35mm. Instead they would get 16mm prints as part of their contractual payments from the studio, and store them at Lester's as part of an informal lending library. Lester would show the films at Sunday night parties for a group of young actors that included Robert Stack, Laraine Day, and Bonita Granville. As word spread, stars such as Rosalind Russell, Deanna Durbin, and Lou Costello would drop by to pick up a movie to watch over the weekend.

Grant began using Lester's film library, and the two men developed a guarded friendship—guarded because that was the way Grant wanted it. Lester liked him, but thought it was curious that Grant didn't have a screen on which to show the movies; he'd just aim the projector at a white wall. Sometimes the two men would go out to dinner together. Grant had developed a yen for kosher food, and he and Lester would dine at a delicatessen at the Hollywood Roosevelt. After the matzo ball soup and kreplach, Grant would drop Lester off at his studio and head for Santa Monica with a movie in tow.

AS OF SEPTEMBER 1939, England was at war with Nazi Germany. In Bristol, Elsie Leach cabled her son: DARLING TELEPHONE . . . HOPE YOU SAFE DON'T WORRY ABOUT MOTHER PULLED THROUGH LAST WAR GOD WATCH OVER YOU LOVE ALWAYS.

The war presented a conundrum for Hollywood's English contingent. David Niven came from a military family with a run of bad luck—his great-grandfather had died in the Crimean War, his grandfather had died in the Boer War, and his father had died in World War I. It seemed logical to Niven that he was destined to die in World War II, but he felt honor-bound to return to England and serve in the war effort. On September 30, 1939, Doug Fairbanks Jr. gave Niven a lavish farewell party that included both Scottish pipers and American strippers. The attendees included Grant, Ronald Colman, Laurence Olivier, and George Sanders.

As it happened, Niven spent most of the war training soldiers or in administrative jobs, which is probably the main reason he violated family tradition and survived. Niven would remember that he had been trending toward insufferable arrogance in Hollywood, and that self-sacrifice turned out to be good for him. "I think I was saved from being a total shit by the war," he said. "Going to war was the only unselfish thing I have ever done for humanity."

For the rest of their lives, Niven and Olivier would be contemptuous of British actors who stayed in Hollywood while having endless conversations about how they could stay in Hollywood without seeming to be either cowards or bastards. On the other hand, there was George Sanders. "I admire your courage and all that," Sanders told Olivier, "but *I'm* not going back because I'm a shit and I don't give a fuck who knows it!"

Niven did not include Grant in his personal roster of shits, because Grant made a good-faith effort to join the Navy but was told again and again by the Admiralty, the Foreign Office, and Lord Lothian—the English ambassador in Washington—that he should stay in Hollywood and promote England on the screen.

None of this carried much weight with the English press, which demanded that British actors return "like David Niven." In 1942, *Picturegoer* magazine said that all the English actors still in Hollywood should be filmed only in black and white, "since Technicolor would undoubtedly show up the yellow of their skin."

Alfred Hitchcock came to America in March 1939 to direct movies for David O. Selznick. He immediately became the target of those in the British film industry who felt he had abandoned his country in its time of need. The spokesman for this group was the producer Michael Balcon, who said, "I am surprised and disgusted by the attitude of British people at present in Hollywood; when things become tough here they desert the country and take cover in America. . . . I maintain that they should return at once to this country instead of cavorting about on the dance floors of Hollywood."

Balcon went so far as to single out "a plump young junior technician" he had once promoted as typical of the people lollygagging in Hollywood "while we who are left behind shorthanded are trying to harness the films to our great national effort."

Grant would do his part, donating both considerable amounts of cash and time—his $140,000 salary from *His Girl Friday*, for instance. He wasn't alone—Charles Laughton raised well over a million dollars by doing a forty-eight-hour radio marathon.

Grant's hometown would have a rough time during the war. Bristol would be the fifth most bombed city in the Battle of Britain, enduring seventy-seven air raids, six of them classified as major. Thirteen hundred citizens of Bristol would be killed during the war, the worst night being November 2, 1940, when the Germans dropped ten thousand tons of high explosives and five thousand incendiary bombs into the heart of the city.

The war quickly became personal: in January 1941, Mr. and Mrs. John Henry Leach, Grant's aunt and uncle, as well as their daughter, son-in-law, and grandson, were all killed by a direct hit from a German air raid. Bristol was a target for reasons that extended past destabilizing the population—there was Bristol's shipping business to be disrupted, but the city was also a major center for the manufacture of airplanes. (After the war, airplanes would become a major local industry, along with cigarettes and printing.) A few months later, in March, another uncle, Frederick William Leach, along with his wife and daughter, were killed. Frederick Leach's house was at 4 Belgrave Road, only a few blocks from Elsie Leach's residence at 93 Whiteladies Road. Elsie's survival was mostly a matter of wind drift, i.e., luck.

GRANT WAS ENTIRELY COMFORTABLE ON RADIO. He even had a show of his own in 1939 entitled *Kellogg's Circle*. The show was on NBC and the premiere on January 15 featured a bizarre group of expensive hosts calculated to appeal to all facets of the potential audience: Besides Grant, there was Ronald Colman, Lawrence Tibbett, Carole Lombard, and Groucho and Chico Marx, not to mention Robert Emmett Dolan and his orchestra. It was a mutually exclusive group that would have needed separate writers for each host. All this combined to produce a sky-high talent budget of $27,500 for the premiere, which didn't take into account the money Kellogg's had to pay NBC for the airtime—a lot of cornflakes for 1939. Grant's publicity for the show referenced him as "[A] first rank star of Hollywood. You've seen him in *The Awful Truth, Topper, The Toast of New York, Gunga Din* and other box office hits. As versatile on the air as on the screen!"

Kellogg's Circle ran only thirty-nine weeks, possibly because of the heavy overhead combined with a bad time slot—Sunday nights at ten. Over the years, Grant would appear three or four times a year on radio in adaptations of his own or other people's movies on prestigious—and lucrative—shows such as Cecil B. DeMille's *Lux Radio Theatre*. DeMille's show paid as much as $5,000 an appearance, entailing little more than a single rehearsal and two performances—one for the East Coast, one for the West Coast.*

---

* Grant would undertake one more radio show, in the dying days of radio drama in the early 1950s, an adaptation of his film *Room for One More*, probably done as a means of promoting his new wife, Betsy Drake.

On June 26, 1942, Archibald Alexander Leach, six feet one and a half inches, 178 pounds, brown eyes, dark complexion, was granted American citizenship. He stated that he "intends to reside permanently in the United States . . . [and] had in all other respects complied with the applicable provisions of such naturalization laws, and was entitled to be admitted to citizenship . . . as a citizen of the United States of America." His witnesses included Randy Scott and Frank Horn. Interestingly, Grant signed the certificate with his real name, in a noticeably tighter hand than his signature as Cary Grant. It might be said that Grant was taking care of all family business—that same day he legally changed his name. Archibald Alexander Leach was no more.

Some of Grant's tax papers give an indication of the financial life of a major movie star of the time. In 1942, Grant grossed about $255,000. (His income for 1943 would be over $300,000.) After federal and state taxes and professional expenses were deducted for 1942, his net was about $50,000, or $773,000 in today's money—a good income, although minor compared to what twenty-first-century stars can make because of media expansion beyond anything dreamt of in 1942. Grant's stockholdings at this time were basic blue chips of the period: Pan American Airways, General Motors, Chrysler, U.S. Steel, Coca-Cola.

Grant was increasingly concerned about his mother's welfare. He frequently sent night letter cables to Elsie along the lines of this one from August 13, 1940: "Darling, do let me know how you are as am always anxious God bless love Archie Leach." He cabled to thank her for the birthday gifts she sent him, and asked to be remembered to the family. In return she would cable as well: FROM MOTHER AM ALRIGHT AT PRESENT GOD KEEP US SAFE FROM ENEMIES YOUR ALWAYS DARLING ARCHIE . . . LIVING FOR YOU WONDERING WHEN WE MEET AGAIN.

Grant had retained an English attorney named Edwin Davis to tend to the needs of Elsie and her little dog. Davis would send Grant occasional updates of his expenditures on Elsie's behalf—£17.5 for a silver tray from Mappin & Webb on Oxford Street as a Christmas gift. In one letter, Davis told Grant that he had decided not to give Elsie any more cash because she just stashed it in the bank in order to pay her fare to America after the war. She had what Davis called a "craze for saving." The lawyer was clearly a fan; he ends one letter by telling Grant, "I recently saw your picture called *Suspicion* and thought your performance was a very good one."

Giving Elsie nice things seems to have been pointless; in one letter she tells her son (she would address her letters and cables to Cary Grant, but she always referred to him as Archie in the text and in turn he always signed off as Archie) that "When you come over I have a silver tray and many other things you could have. If you would like me to send, I will do so with pleasure. . . . Darling if you don't come over as soon as soon as the War ends, I shall come over to you."

He never forgot her birthday or Mother's Day, and she never forgot to worry about him, often telling him not to work so hard. In a long letter she wrote him in December 1944, she told him that it had been five years since she had seen him and "I should like to spend a holiday six months in America. . . . I get to see all your . . . films. But its not like seeing you personally."

CARY GRANT WAS NOW A STAR, which meant he didn't have to appear any more conciliatory than he felt. One interview began with an innocuous question about his plans, and he snapped, "Do you mean on the screen, or off the screen? Because if you mean off the screen, it's none of your business." Settling down, he grew more relaxed. "I supposed the way I pick a picture is a form of egomania. I ask myself, 'Would I be interested in the characters, watching them on the screen? Would they take me out of myself?'"

The asperity was contrasted by the studio biographies that were issued, a compendium of truth—Archie Leach was usually acknowledged—as well as purest fantasy: his father's occupation was upgraded to the status of "clothing manufacturer," and there was the sudden appearance of a mythical grandfather named Percival Leach, "an English actor who spent a lifetime in the theater." The coverage reflected Grant's own confusions—a 1942 news story referred to the death of his mother when Grant was ten, even though Grant had known she was alive since 1935.

A handwriting analyst came closer to Grant's real character than most of the magazine and newspaper stories written about him: "The pressure is very, very heavy and is written rapidly. This combination gives intensity and passionate feeling. . . . It isn't wise to cross Mr. Grant or shove him around. He has a strong dominating will and a terrific determination to carry through."

BEN HECHT CONTINUALLY RETURNED TO ONE STORY: gorgeous egomaniacs who can't live with each other and can't live without each other. That describes *Twentieth Century* as well as *The Front Page*. Howard Hawks got the idea of remaking *The Front Page* with Cary Grant as the self-absorbed editor Walter Burns and a woman as Hildy Johnson. Harry Cohn had bought the remake rights to *The Front Page* in January 1939 and Charles Lederer, the nephew of Marion Davies and a close friend of Hecht's, set to work on the rewrite. Lederer did his work in Palm Springs, where Hecht dropped in to assist. Lederer wrote three drafts, and Morrie Ryskind did the final polish up to the beginning of the shoot in September 1939.

Lederer, Hecht, and Ryskind essentially constructed a new first act that put Burns in the picture almost immediately instead of waiting for him to take control in the third act, as in the original play. As for Hawks's idea of making Hildy Johnson a woman, it was a stroke of genius—it gave the bickering and veiled love the two characters have for each other a wider audience without watering anything down.

The only problem was that no one wanted to play Hildy Johnson. Cohn asked Jean Arthur to play the part, but she and Hawks hadn't cared for each other on *Only Angels Have Wings*. Others were sounded out: Ginger Rogers, Claudette Colbert, Carole Lombard, Irene Dunne. All of them passed. With only two weeks until the beginning of production—a start date that couldn't be pushed back because of Grant's busy schedule—Cohn borrowed Rosalind Russell from MGM, where she had just finished *The Women* for George Cukor.

Russell knew that she wasn't even the fourth choice for the part, which didn't please her, but she was determined to make the best of it. Hawks was not an effusive man, and Russell's first scene with Grant passed without comment. She went to Grant and asked if Hawks liked what she had done. "Oh, sure Roz. If he didn't like it, he'd tell you." That wasn't enough for Russell, so she ventured into Hawks's line of sight and demanded feedback. "You just keep pushin' him around the way you're doing," Hawks told her.

After that, it was a happy shoot; Hawks believed that comedy had to be made with a relaxed grip, and he was always willing to give his actors room. Grant dropped in lots of ad libs, including one about Hildy's fiancé, who looks like "that fellow in the pictures—you know, what's his name—Ralph Bellamy." Since Ralph Bellamy was playing the part, it was meta before meta. Russell paid a writer friend for some one-liners, which led Grant to come up to her every morning and ask, "What have you got today?" With everybody slinging dialogue as fast as possible, Hawks told Ralph Bellamy to talk slowly, as someone who can't quite keep up. "I savored every line while those characters chattered all around me," Bellamy said.

His Girl Friday is live-action Looney Tunes, where verbal abuse is a form of both endearment and seduction. At one point, Grant's Walter Burns dismisses a threat by saying, "The last man to say that to me was Archie Leach, just a week before he cut his throat!" The secret of the movie, and of *Twentieth Century* as well, is Hecht's knowledge that the raging egomaniacs are two of a kind; each of them brings the other fully alive, personally and professionally. They belong together.

Hawks shot his picture quickly and cut it even more quickly; it premiered in December, only three months after it began shooting. Manny Farber said that "Cary Grant uses legs, arms, trick hat and facial muscles to create a pixy-ish ballet that would do credit to a Massine." He loved the "very stylized discourse of short replies based on the idea of topping, outmaneuvering the other person with wit, cynicism, and verbal bravado. A line is never allowed to reverberate but is quickly attached to another, funnier line in a very underrated comedy that champions the sardonic and quick-witted over the plodding, sober citizens." Farber used a lot of words to arrive at the same destination as Martin Scorsese, who succinctly referred to Grant's "command of the frame" with a perceptible touch of awe.

His Girl Friday looks better today than it did in 1939—it tells the truth about the nurturing possibilities of the good divorce that follows a bad marriage. "Grant is interested in the qualities of a particular woman," wrote Pauline Kael. "Her sappy expression, her non sequiturs, the way her voice bobbles. She isn't going to be pushed to the wall as soon as she's alone with him. With Grant, the social, urban man, there are infinite possibilities for mutual entertainment." For instance: the feigned exasperation that conceals need.

Grant has the part John Barrymore played in *Twentieth Century*, the part Hepburn played in *Bringing Up Baby*: the pursuer. It's one of the rare remakes that's better than the original—Hecht and MacArthur's original first act is all exposition, with the last two acts full of fire, but Hawks and his writers slam the gas pedal to the floor in the first scene and keep it there. *His Girl Friday* is screwball squared; it's what comedy is all about.

This run of pictures was what Pauline Kael was referring to when she wrote that Grant was a woman's "dream date—not sexless but sex with civilized grace, sex with mystery." With Clark Gable, for instance, "sex is inevitable," but with Cary Grant "there are infinite possibilities for mutual entertainment. They might dance the night away or stroll or go to a carnival—and nothing sexual would happen unless she wanted it to."

"Cary Grant," she concluded, was "the sky that women aspire to. When he and a woman are together, they can laugh at each other and at themselves."

Aside from its intrinsic quality, *His Girl Friday* also provided Grant with the chance to be a Good Samaritan. His friend Frederick Brisson, the son of the Danish actor-singer Carl Brisson, left England for America in September 1939. The ship crossing took twelve days, and the ship only had two movies to show the passengers. One of them was *The Women*, and Brisson developed a crush on Rosalind Russell. When Brisson got to New York, he wired his old friend Grant, who promptly invited him to Hollywood.

When Brisson arrived, he regaled Grant with stories of watching *The Women* multiple times and being fascinated by Rosalind Russell. Did Grant, by any chance, know her? Since Grant was in the middle of shooting *His Girl Friday*, he knew her very well.

The next day, Grant asked Russell to dinner at Chasen's. She was thrilled, and appeared at Chasen's all dolled up, but a Danish gentleman came over and sat down, spoiling what she thought was her date with Cary Grant. Brisson pestered her throughout dinner and she finally gave him her phone number. He began sending her flowers, but she put him off for weeks before finally agreeing to a date. When they married in October 1941, Grant was the best man. After the wedding Russell wrote Grant her gratitude: "Now look what you've done! You black-eyed cupid! For the remainder of my life, I'll hold *you* responsible and when I go to Reno (and I shall if I can't get the great Dane's haircut properly) I'll scream at the judge, 'Grant did this to me.'"

My Favorite Wife essentially began as a sequel to *The Awful Truth*. As McCarey remembered, both Grant and Irene Dunne had space in their schedules if he could set up a picture quickly, so the director signed Sam and Bella Spewack to write the script. "I blush at the originality of the picture we concocted; Irene Dunne disappeared for seven years; her husband married again; Irene reappeared on his wedding night. This was *Enoch Arden, Rip Van Winkle*, and we had a threatened suit from Somerset Maugham and Columbia Pictures who were making a picture of the same type."

As Irene Dunne said, "We were all attached to RKO by this time so we couldn't use the original names but let's face it, they were basically the same people [as in *The Awful Truth*]. Only this time it was the story of Enoch Arden and I was Enoch."

The story involved a wife presumed dead but who returns from a desert island just as her husband has remarried but before the marriage has been consummated. The complicating fact is a handsome man who was also shipwrecked with whom she has spent seven supposedly sexless years. Leo McCarey's first thought for a director was René Clair, but he was booked, so he handed the director's job to Garson Kanin, a young RKO contractee fresh off the successful Ginger Rogers vehicle *Bachelor Mother*.

The first draft script was finished by the end of August 1939, after which the Spewacks returned to New York. McCarey brought on a young writer named Bert Granet for the second draft and to work on the picture through production. "He [McCarey] was a wonderful dialogue writer," Granet told David Chierichetti. "He could come up with new lines during shooting."

While *The Awful Truth* had flowed, *My Favorite Wife* was a grind. McCarey's own inspiration was a sometime thing, perhaps because of his drinking. McCarey had been an alcoholic since the late 1920s, when he was working with Charley Chase at the Hal Roach studio. Chase was one of the worst drunks in the movie business—he would die of cirrhosis at the age of fifty—and keeping up with him after hours was virtually a prerequisite to employment.

It was fairly obvious that McCarey had a full roster of demons, which he did his best to disguise behind a smiling facade. "I think it was Irish guilt," Bert Granet would say. "I don't know what the guilt was about—maybe his earlier success, maybe his love affairs." It's also possible he was concerned about trying to top himself with Grant and Dunne in another marital comedy.

Then came the problems with the Breen office over the script. Joseph Breen was a fellow Irishman but far more straitlaced than McCarey and he didn't think the script was shootable. He sent the script back with numerous "Too much suggestion of DF" scrawled on the pages.

A puzzled Granet asked McCarey what "DF" meant.

"Delayed fuck," replied McCarey.

Granet thought the problem with the picture was the third act. There wasn't one. Granet pointed out that, "Once the second wife finds out the first wife is still alive, there's no good reason to keep them apart without making the first wife a bitch."

On December 2, 1939, the cast sat around a table doing a table read of the completed script. At 5:30 Dunne excused herself to go pick up her daughter from convent school. As soon as she was out the door, Grant began to complain. "He was basically a charming fellow," said Bert Granet, "but he had learned to fight. He said it would be a great script for Jimmy Stewart, but not for him. Kanin said, 'OK, we'll get Jimmy Stewart.' 'That's not what I meant,' said Grant."

Grant continued to bitch throughout the picture. Dunne didn't seem very happy either, but didn't verbalize it. By now, Grant had taken up backgammon to while away the time between shots. He taught Thelma Orloff, Kanin's secretary, to play the game and when the picture was finished gave her a backgammon set. He played the game intermittently for the rest of his life. He would always be a good but conservative competitor, playing for no more than ten cents a point.

Ultimately, McCarey's drinking nearly submarined the picture. Most of the local police forces would spot his car weaving around Los Angeles and drive him home without a ticket, but there were slipups.

(He would be arrested for drunk driving in 1945 and arrested again, this time for creating a public disturbance, in 1946.) Just as the shoot for *My Favorite Wife* got under way, McCarey was driving drunk at 95 miles an hour with Gene Fowler in the passenger seat when he slammed into a 1924 Packard. McCarey dodged death by a hair; the accident report lists multiple burns, gouge wounds, lacerations and contusions, broken bones and a possible skull fracture. The doctor would not commit to "eventual outcome."

After it was clear he would live, his wife, Stella, brought a priest to the hospital to get McCarey to take the pledge. Leo recited the vow but he later told Bert Granet he had his fingers crossed beneath his blanket. McCarey emerged from the hospital with a badly damaged arm and an addiction to painkillers; Irene Dunne said that he was never the same man after the accident.

Granet picked up on something interesting: sexual tension between McCarey and Dunne. It wouldn't have been unusual for McCarey to sleep with his leading lady—he would boast to publicist David Epstein about his affairs, including one with Ingrid Bergman on *The Bells of St. Mary's*. "[Dunne] was married to a man she loved, she was a devout Catholic and I don't really think she was a very highly sexed person," said Granet. "When she was sexy in a movie it was all good acting. She didn't commit any acts of folly, but she was interested in McCarey." Epstein's son Bob said that McCarey told his father the fact that he had never slept with Irene Dunne was the greatest frustration of his life.

Shooting began on December 5. Grant and Dunne had a very good working relationship based on a mutual respect for each other's impeccable timing. Once McCarey got out of the hospital, he was a constant presence on the set and began clashing with Garson Kanin. Eventually, McCarey and Kanin stopped speaking and used Bert Granet as a go-between. The core problem was that Kanin was not as good a director as McCarey; he never mastered McCarey's sense of flow and counterpoint that approached the musical—the apparently casual rhythmic connections between the actors in a scene as well as between consecutive scenes that add up to a cumulative emotional experience.

And there were always problems with the script. On February 1, production stopped and the actors were sent home while McCarey and

Granet did some rewriting. By February 2, visitors were banned from the set. But there were no serious problems with Grant. "He worked very hard," said Kanin. "Almost more than any other quality was his seriousness about his work. He was always prepared; he always knew his part, his lines, and the scene. And he related very well to the other players. He took not only his own part seriously; he took the whole picture seriously . . . he was . . . an exceptionally concentrated man. And extremely intelligent too."

The film wrapped on February 15, but the Breen office demanded trims that left the film a bit short. "We finished the picture," said McCarey, "and we found that after about five reels the picture took a dip, and for about two reels or more it wasn't funny. . . . It was a lot of unraveling of a tricky plot.

> So anyway, the cast was dismissed, the writers went home, the director went home to New York and I sat there with the cutter trying to figure out what to do to save the picture. . . . Then I got the wildest idea I ever had. There was a judge in the opening who was very funny and he dropped out of the picture—and I decided to bring him back. What we actually did was to tell the judge our story problems in the picture and have him comment on them. And it was truly great. It became the outstanding thing in the picture.

McCarey called Sam Spewack back from New York to write the second courtroom scene and some other bits and pieces that were shot in the second week of March. McCarey estimated that the retakes amounted to about a reel that replaced two reels of dross. The retakes raised Grant's salary from $112,000 to $127,000, while Dunne's went from $100,000 to $112,000. (McCarey's producing/writing salary was $87,000, while Kanin was getting only $25,000.)

There has been leering speculation about the casting of Randolph Scott as the man with whom Dunne is marooned for seven years, but Granet didn't believe Grant suggested it. He remembered accompanying Scott and McCarey to Lucey's bar, across the street from RKO. McCarey said, "Gee it's hot in here. We should take off our coats." It wasn't hot, but McCarey wanted to make sure Scott was in good physical shape for the scenes where he'd be in a bathing suit. It was only after Scott had passed inspection that McCarey hired him.

My Favorite Wife was a successful picture with both critics and audiences, not to mention the studio—the profit was slightly more than $500,000 on a modest cost of $921,000. It's a strange picture, with a strong first act and, thanks to the reshoots with Granville Bates as the bad-tempered judge, a charming finish. But all of McCarey's efforts couldn't prevent a sag in the middle, probably because Kanin paces the picture too methodically—it needed more speed to get past the thin script.

CHAPTER NINE

B y now it was obvious that Grant had evolved into a comedy master. Working in movies had taught him that a performance can't be given *at* an audience, it has to be done *with* the audience, in a spirit of collaboration. Grant learned to project an antic comic spirit that might as well have been an imp sitting on his shoulder.

Comedy is the most difficult of disciplines to discuss, because much of it involves reacting rather than thinking. Grant's most articulate disquisition was given when he was an old man and had had time to intellectualize what he had done in the moment. It is full of appreciation for technique and the instinct that underlies technique and it's mostly in the present tense, as if he was still an aspiring comedian learning his craft in the exhausting world of three-a-day vaudeville.

"Timing," he said. "The secret of comedy is timing."

You come to learn timing over a long period of time. In my case I was in vaudeville. I was a straight man for a comic. The straight man does the timing. The straight man furnishes the lines for the comic, which the comic will answer. Now, when he answers, the laugh goes up; it goes up and cascades over, and the straight man now must talk into that. His first few words may not be too important—"Well, you know what?" "Oh, I'll tell you what . . . " and you add a few words, according to whether the laugh is tapering off, or cut off, or taking a long time to come down.

When you're playing in a different town, maybe for three days, or every week or two weeks, depending upon the length of the run, your timing is often a constant thing. If you play three shows a day, a matinee—the supper show has practically no one in it, but they keep the doors open and they capture whomever they can. But the night show is your big show of the day. So, therefore, your timing is all according to your audiences—the size of your audience, and according to the type of audience they are. You'll find the women don't laugh at what the wise guys laugh at at . . . the night show.

Furthermore, it alters from town to town, because what they laugh at in Wilmington they do not laugh at in Princeton or Wilkes-Barre, or someplace. Because down there, they're all snobs in Wilmington. And then there's the servant class, and the other class don't often go to the theater, but they don't laugh; they only laugh at certain things.

Now, you go to a house like the Chicago . . . and the first show is packed. It is packed with the night workers of Chicago. And you walk out on the stage at noon or 10 in the morning—and . . . it goes through the roof. And you don't expect it, and your timing is off because of it.

The problem with comedy in the movies is, of course, the impossibility of timing for the audience.

Timing on the stage is a simple matter . . . [but in film] it's inflexible. You can't move film. [So] you do the best you can. The mean, or whatever it is, right down the middle. Sometimes you can't find the blessed thing, you know. So you do the best you can according to your instincts over the years. . . . Because there's no use relying upon the crew, because they're too busy to laugh—or they may laugh—but it gets quieter at the last rehearsal. Well, that's the last time they're going to laugh. And you think, "Oh, my God, it's falling on its face." But it's not. You just have to do it the way you hope is for the best.

The core problem was and is that it's easier to make an audience cry than it is to make them laugh, and when you add the difficulty of timing to the equation, the reputed deathbed line of Edmund Gwenn becomes even truer: "Dying is easy; comedy is hard." To which Grant warily added, "That's why so few actors care to become light comedians."

But it was more than that. Whether it was a psychological exit enabling him to escape his childhood for a period of time, or just consummate talent, Grant's sense of fun transcended his good looks and superb timing. It was an infusion of oxygen, not just to the other characters, but to the audience. It carried him through more than thirty years of stardom; it carried him through his professional life.

THE HITS KEPT COMING, interrupted only by *The Howards of Virginia*, or, as it might have been more accurately titled, *Cary Grant— Frontiersman*. Grant plays a Revolutionary War firebrand who can't warm up to his son because the boy has a clubfoot. Grant must have realized how miscast he was, and responds with misplaced main force, giving what can only be called a musical comedy performance, braying his lines as if he's working with Rosalind Russell and Howard Hawks instead of Martha Scott and Frank Lloyd. It's a terrible picture, although Grant does look good in buckskin. Luckily, with great pictures that came both before and after, *The Howards of Virginia* was quickly forgotten.

The Philadelphia Story was a gilt-edged property that MGM didn't screw up. Philip Barry had written the play for Katharine Hepburn, who was on the run from Hollywood and the label of box office disaster. Hepburn had the foresight—courtesy of a loan from Howard Hughes—to tie up the movie rights and personally negotiated her deal with Louis B. Mayer. "He said things that would really charm me," she remembered. " 'You know Mr. Mayer, you are charming me. I know that you are deliberately charming me, and still I am charmed. That's a real artist.' "

What Hepburn wanted was insurance in the form of a cast that would carry the picture across the finish line despite the indifference the movie audience had demonstrated toward her, thereby reestablishing her as a viable star. She asked for Clark Gable and Spencer Tracy, and George Cukor to direct. Mayer said she could have Cukor. He didn't think Gable and Tracy would do it but he would ask. He did and they refused.

He then offered her Jimmy Stewart, who would accept an assignment, and tossed in $150,000 for her to hire another male star. "You
get them," he told her. (In her memoirs, Hepburn would call Mayer
"the most honest person I ever dealt with in my life.")

Hepburn went after her friend Cary Grant and paid him Mayer's
$150,000 for four weeks' work. Aside from the money, Grant's only
other request—it was actually more of a condition—was top billing.
Despite having starred in the play successfully, Hepburn gave Grant
what he wanted. MGM went to the trouble of recording a performance
of the play in order to make sure that the laughs in the movie were
more or less in the correct order and volume.

"*The Philadelphia Story* was the easiest picture I ever did," said
screenwriter Donald Ogden Stewart.

> That is because Philip Barry had written a very good play, and
> Katharine had played it for a year or two in New York. And the
> MGM people had taken tape recordings at the theatre . . . of all the
> laughs. So as a writer I had to hear that goddamned recorder and
> then make sure that those laughs were in the film play too, whether
> or not they belonged there at that particular time.
>
> I got out of the way of Phil Barry's script. . . . As a screenwriter
> you had to learn first of all not to let them break your heart; I mean,
> not to care too damned much because you would start creating and
> the next thing you knew either the producer or the star, Lana Turner
> or somebody like that, wouldn't like a scene, and the writer was
> never right in those days.

Grant and James Stewart had never met until their first scene
together, and Stewart was startled to find that "a more nervous, fidgety
actor I never saw." He initially chalked it up to the way the studios
devised personalities for actors, but eventually realized that Grant,
not a studio, had devised his own screen personality. George Cukor
mostly allowed Stewart to unleash his acting style, which could run
toward the effusive, so Grant dialed back his own performance—he's
watchful, a little wary. When Stewart ad-libbed a burp in his drunk
scene, Grant coolly responded with "Excuse me," which nearly broke
Stewart up—you can see him taking a beat to collect himself before
his next line.

The film's beautiful opening scene—Hepburn breaks Grant's putter as he stalks out of the house, and he responds by grabbing her face and shoving her backwards through the doorway—was written by the producer, Joseph L. Mankiewicz. "Kate Hepburn always plays a strong, rather arrogant woman," said Mankiewicz, "very sure of herself, hell on wheels. What made that picture work was Cary Grant giving Kate a kick in the ass. She got her comeuppance. Otherwise, *female* audiences would not have tolerated it." In later years, Grant would refer to that scene as the perfect setup for the rest of the film, despite the fact that, as Mankiewicz insisted, "Cary didn't want to do it. . . . He said it wasn't manly to push her in the face."

The Philadelphia Story opened in January 1941, and was an immediate smash hit. On the occasion of Grant's thirty-seventh birthday, Mankiewicz wrote him a fan letter: "Whatever success the picture is having—and it is a simply enormous smash—is due, in my opinion, to you in far greater proportions than anyone has seen fit to shout about. . . . Your presence as Dexter and particularly your sensitive and brilliant playing of the role contribute what I consider the backbone and basis of practically every emotional value in the piece. I can think of no one who could have done as well, or have given as much." He went on to say that he felt the profuse coverage of Hepburn's comeback had perhaps caused people to overlook Grant's sterling contribution to the proceedings. "This probably makes suckers out of all the men who have bitten dogs—but Producer thanks Actor. And, brother, that's news. Happy birthday, Cary."

Made for the very reasonable cost of $914,000, *The Philadelphia Story* returned rentals of $3.2 million, for a net profit of $1.2 million. Katharine Hepburn remained a star for the rest of her life.

A LITTLE LESS THAN A YEAR AFTER *My Favorite Wife*, Grant and Irene Dunne would reunite for the last time in George Stevens's *Penny Serenade*, a four-star weepy in which a Japanese earthquake causes Dunne to have a miscarriage. Later, a judge takes away their adopted child, who eventually dies.

"Cary Grant and Irene Dunne had been enormously successful in light, frothy comedy," Stevens remembered. "I had done something like that previously [and] didn't want to get involved again. I guess I was in a mood by this time. And so these poor people became involved in my indulging myself with a story I got from [original author] Martha Cheavens. . . . But they became wholeheartedly engaged in it . . . it was shocking to the audience to see [Grant and Dunne] not having a fine time but relating to two levels of life."

Stevens called on his trusted associate Fred Guiol as well as Morrie Ryskind for the script and made it for $978,606, $140,000 over budget. Grant's salary was $106,250, while Irene Dunne got $85,000. The result was a big commercial success, and an Oscar nomination for Grant because of a tear-'em-up scene in which he begs the judge to relent. It seems slightly overemphatic to some eyes, but Dunne thought the scene was magnificent. It wasn't easily obtained.

"One thing about Cary," she said. "He was afraid of sentiment. He was leery of a scene . . . in which he had to break down and cry. George Stevens had to convince him that he would never regret having exposed his emotions." Dunne thought the scene might earn Grant an Oscar, but it was not to be. "He made everything seem too spontaneous," said Dunne. "[Too] easy. But that is fine acting when people think you're playing yourself."

The film is undeniably effective, and it may have come about simply because of Dunne's preference for drama over comedy. "I love doing comedy and it was always extremely easy for me," she said. "But never satisfying. I always wanted more dramatic things to do." Dunne cherished an incident when she went to a preview of the film. She slipped in after the lights went down and when the credits came on, a woman behind her said, "Oh, another Cary Grant–Irene Dunne comedy." By the halfway point, the woman and her date were both blubbering.

Grant and Dunne wanted to keep working together, but it never happened. "Wish we'd done ten more," said Grant in his old age. "It wasn't for want of trying," said Dunne.

That was the last film in which he ever took second billing. And different ideas were submitted but we'd always be too busy. But it's strange. People thought of us as a team, you know. Around that time I was [at] Bullock's getting a Christmas present for my husband and looking at dressing gowns, and the saleslady said, "Oh, I don't think that would fit Mr. Grant," and I didn't have the heart to correct her. People thought of us as a team, [but] we only made these three movies in four years, and then we unfortunately moved on.

Actually, the problem was not scheduling, it was billing. "Reunions became impossible because we both liked first billing," Grant said. "It's ladies first in [lifeboats,] but not in movies, I'm afraid."

Grant was becoming as intransigent about money as he was about scripts and billing. He had become friendly with David Selznick through his preexisting friendship with his wife, Irene. Selznick had long wanted to get Grant into one of his movies and had set *Claudia*, a movie about a young wife, as a vehicle for Dorothy McGuire. Grant was interested in the part of her husband, but Selznick was flabbergasted after talking to Grant's agent. Nothing would heal Selznick's wounded ego but a letter to Grant in a relentless tone of wounded abandonment.

"I was naïve enough to believe briefly that you might be one of that company of artists . . . to make a contribution . . . by working for somewhat less for me than you are willing to accept from the larger and more exclusively commercially minded producing companies." After getting a load of Grant's salary demands, Selznick was "disabused of this notion."

Selznick thought better of sending the memo, lest he damage his friendship with Grant. Robert Young was borrowed from MGM and played the part.

CHAPTER TEN

Grant and Barbara Hutton first met in June 1939, on board the *Normandie* en route to New York from England. They dined together, but Hutton was married to Count Kurt Haugwitz-Hardenberg-Reventlow, the father of her son, Lance. They made firmer connections some months later when they were reintroduced by Countess Dorothy di Frasso. By that time, Hutton had separated from Reventlow.

The relationship matured quickly; during production on *Penny Serenade*, Irene Dunne remembered that Grant told her his children were going to have blond hair and brown eyes. Grant and Hutton began making the Hollywood social rounds together, even going up to Wyntoon, the Hearst estate in remote northeastern California. "She was very much in love with him," said Marion Davies, "and I'm positive that he was in love with her. He was very sweet with her."

Davies noticed that Grant was always trying to nudge Hutton out of her passivity. He would ask her to go for a walk, but Hutton would say she didn't feel like it. Grant would insist. "They would go off," said Davies, "and the next thing I'd see, he was carrying her in his arms."

Davies believed that the romantic atmosphere of Wyntoon deepened the love affair. "Cary was always gracious and charming to women. He put women on a pedestal, and some women don't belong on pedestals. I never worked with him, though I wish I had. . . . He was a very fine person, with a warmth that was not put on; it came straight from his heart. When he said, 'I'm glad to see you,' you'd know that he meant it."

But Davies couldn't quite penetrate Hutton's bland exterior, and the remark about pedestals indicated she had misgivings, although she tried to put a positive spin on it. "I don't think she was feeling well. She went on a long diet and lost her vitality. I don't think she weighed more than ninety pounds. Very little, she was, and very thin, but very nice. He was crazy about her, and very cute, and they got married right after they left us."

It was the first week of July 1942 when Grant called his photographer friend Gene Lester and invited him and his wife, Gloria, to Lake Arrowhead for the weekend. Lester asked what was going on. "Oh, nothing," Grant said. "I just thought maybe you'd like to come on up and bring your camera up there. It's very picturesque. You'll be able to take some nice pictures. So come on up there and meet with me."

Unfortunately, Lester and his wife had just had a major fight; Gloria Lester didn't want to go anywhere with her husband, and Gene Lester didn't want to drive up by himself. He declined the offer, thereby costing himself thousands of dollars. Cary Grant and Barbara Hutton were married that weekend in Arrowhead on July 8, 1942. Grant had planned on giving Lester an exclusive on the wedding photos. If he'd known what Grant had in mind, Lester would have driven up, furious wife or not, but Grant typically wouldn't inform Lester of his plans. "He was secretive about his private life when we were together," remembered Lester. "I never tried to ferret out what his intentions or what his ideas were."

Lester struggled to come up with an idea for a wedding present. What do you give a major movie star and the richest woman in the world? And then it hit him. Grant was still showing 16mm movies on a white wall, so Lester gave him a movie screen.

Grant's best man was his agent, Frank Vincent, which indicates the store he always put on his business relationships. The wedding was covered by the New York *Daily News*, whose story came with a witty lead: "The richest girl in the world today married a man who used to walk stilts at Coney Island for $5 and five hot dogs a day."

Born in 1912, Barbara Hutton was the granddaughter of F. W. Woolworth, the daughter of Edna Woolworth and the stockbroker Franklyn Hutton. Her father was the brother of E. F. Hutton, who was, among other things, the father of the actress Dina Merrill, who would one day work with Cary Grant. Barbara Hutton inherited $18.4 million when her mother died in 1918; by 1931 the estate had grown to $40.8 million.

Her upbringing was . . . *unusual.* "Grandpa Woolworth used to say, 'Barbara, you're going to be able to buy the whole world,'" she reminisced. "And father always told me if I wanted anything, to buy it and never count the cost. . . . I inherited everything but love. I've always been searching for it because I didn't know what it was."

When Hutton met Grant, she was a veteran of two unsuccessful marriages, the first to the fraudulent Georgian "Prince" Alexis Mdivani, which had lasted only two years, from 1933 to 1935. The Mdivanis were high-end gigolos, marrying rich women whom the Mdivanis reliably made less rich. During the Mdivani/Hutton wedding ceremony the bride did not smile. It would only get worse; a few months later, Mdivani still owed $500 on the wedding. Hutton's second marriage, to Count Reventlow, lasted from 1935 until their divorce in 1941.

Hutton first met Grant in the movies, specifically *Holiday,* which seemed to her to be the story of her life. Lew Ayres, playing Katharine Hepburn's alcoholic younger brother, was Hutton's cousin Jimmy Donahue, Hepburn's father was just like Frank Hutton, and Cary Grant . . . well, he didn't remind her of anybody other than her ideal man. Her infatuation continued when she saw *Bringing Up Baby.*

After the meeting on board the *Normandie,* Hutton went to Palm Beach for Christmas. Between lunch at the Bath and Tennis Club and dinner at the Everglades Club, she wrote Grant regularly and talked to him on the phone. In 1940, Hutton leased Buster Keaton's old Italian Renaissance mansion at 1004 Hartford Way in Hollywood. The couple went to Catalina and danced at the Casino to Tommy Dorsey's Orchestra with Frank Sinatra.

On Grant's birthday they threw a party to introduce Hutton to Hollywood. Everybody was there, even Ronald Colman and his wife, who rarely went to show business parties. Herb Stein, who wrote for *The Hollywood Reporter,* remembered that it was all beautifully done, except for one faux pas. Hoagy Carmichael was quietly playing one of his dreamy songs when Hutton went over to ask for something a little peppier. "You play what you want when you get to it," Carmichael told his host. "I'm a guest here, same as you are, and I'll play what I like while I'm sitting here. You'll get your chance." He was mortified when he found out who the blond lady was.

Sunday night was reserved for parties at Barbara's rented house, where the frequent guests included Jimmy Stewart, David Niven, Marlene Dietrich and Merle Oberon and Alexander Korda. "We chose Sunday evenings because Barbara's household staff had the night off," remembered Grant. "The guests did their own cooking, such as it was, and washed their own dishes. After dinner we gathered in the drawing room and played charades or clustered around the piano and sang." Grant's specialty became a medley of popular songs with improvised, suggestive lyrics.

In 1941, they got closer. Hutton was rapt; even Lance liked him. "He's the nicest friend you've ever had, Mommy," he told her. If she felt comfortable, Hutton would put on some Chinese music and dance. "None of us knew what we were looking at," said Grant, "but she explained the significance of each step and hand movement. . . .

> Years later, after our divorce, I recognized Barbara's interest in dance and poetry as a need for a kind of expression that her life didn't provide. She wasn't your run-of-the-mill society belle, the sort who, as she lolls down the boulevard, peers into every shop window to ascertain whether her reflection is still there. She was intelligent and sensitive but lacked a suitable means of self-expression, a medium of communication that would allow her to vent her frustrations. And I had no understanding of either dance or poetry and I didn't encourage her in that direction, and I think few people did. The lack of encouragement was as much responsible for her unhappiness as anything.

Grant noticed that the Hollywood crowd regarded Hutton the same way the general population regarded the Hollywood crowd—as a rarefied species. He told a story about a party where a director looked at Barbara and blurted out, "Tell me, how does it feel to have so much money?" All eyes turned to Hutton, who lowered her fork, smiled, and said, "It's wonderful." "I wanted to raise her hand and shout, 'the winnah!'" said Grant.

After the Grant-Hutton nuptials, Hutton threw at least two dinner parties each week—Wednesdays, and a black-tie dinner on Saturday. The regulars included Rosalind Russell and Freddy Brisson, Gene Tierney and Oleg Cassini, Alexander Korda and Merle Oberon. It was weighty company for a boy from Bristol, but the marriage seemed well matched at first. Grant was always appreciative of wisdom from any source, and there were times when Hutton could delight him with her insights.

On a trip to Mexico, he and Hutton wandered into a magnificent cathedral and Grant wondered about the poor peons who worshipped in such magnificence. "Each one of these people alone could never afford such splendor," Hutton told him, "but together all of them contribute to make it all possible and they can all walk in it, sit in it, enjoy its beauty and rest. This is their church. It belongs to them."

He hadn't thought of it that way.

CARY GRANT AND ALFRED HITCHCOCK had a lot in common: working-class English upbringing, ambivalence about women, an outwardly cheerful personality concealing a bleakness that could, in Hitchcock's case, ascend toward malice, and in Grant's case, downward to depression. In years to come, when the two men discussed each other, there would be an almost familial intimacy.

Hitchcock's first American film was *Rebecca*, for David Selznick. After that, he never looked back. Hitchcock embodied Flaubert's dictum about living a comfortable bourgeois life in order to be utterly free in his work. He loved good food, good wine, and dogs.

"In England we had an Old English Sheepdog," recalled Patricia Hitchcock O'Connell, his only child, "and my mother bred wire-haired terriers. After she stopped doing that she got a Sealyham and we brought him over with us to America. After that, they had miniature Sealys called Stanley and Geoffrey. In late life they had a West Highland White Terrier called Sara."

On Sundays, Hitchcock would take his daughter to church. Afterward, they'd come back to an English breakfast of kidneys and bacon. "Then, he'd read all afternoon. Not fiction—fiction was when he was looking for a story for a movie. He'd read current events." Hitchcock wouldn't get too high if a film succeeded or too low if a film failed— what gave him satisfaction was the process itself. "He took them pretty much the same. It was a very happy family life. He worked with my mother constantly; she had much more influence on him than people realized. He wouldn't even begin a project if she didn't think it would be a good movie."

Many actors didn't particularly like working for Hitchcock, even as they appreciated his dry humor and calm command of all aspects of filmmaking. The problem was his reliance on storyboards that locked down every moment in every shot. "Your performance was Hitchcock's performance," said Laraine Day, the leading lady of *Foreign Correspondent*. "You read lines the way Hitchcock read the line. You added nothing and you took away nothing. You did exactly as he told you. He had drawn it out on paper. You'd see the scene like a comic strip and that's the way you played it. You'd bring nothing but [your] body to the set."

Grant, in contrast, would find that he loved working for Hitchcock, because the director had already made all the important decisions about the characters, about the script. The weight of choice was lifted off Grant's shoulders and all he had to do was inhabit and enliven those decisions.

Hitchcock had asked Grant to do his only comedy. Carole Lombard had loved working with Grant on *In Name Only*, and had tried to get him to star opposite her in *Mr. and Mrs. Smith*. But by the end of 1940, Grant was booked nearly two years in advance, so she and Hitchcock decided to go with Robert Montgomery. They should have waited.

"Carole Lombard . . . was not really a comedienne," Grant would say with a straight face. "She was no Irene Dunne. Irene Dunne was marvelous. Her timing was impeccable. . . . But Hitchcock called me up to do *Mr. and Mrs. Smith* . . . and I said, 'No, I can't do it, Hitch.' And he said, 'I don't know how to do the damn thing' . . . and it didn't come off; because Hitchcock didn't know about such stuff."

Suspicion, Grant and Hitchcock's first and worst collaboration, was made right after Hitchcock got *Mr. and Mrs. Smith* out of his system. Based on a novel by Frances Iles, it's about a fragile woman married to a quietly murderous man. The novel lets the man escape his crime, but that was an impossibility under the Production Code, which required much finagling with the script and days of retakes after the film was supposedly finished.

Grant was definitely coming up in the world; he was no longer merely a salaried actor, but a participant in the film's financials. For *Suspicion* he received $50,000 plus 2.5 percent of the gross—the same deal he had for *My Favorite Wife*. Grant and Joan Fontaine heartily disliked each other, but that was not an unusual occurrence on Joan Fontaine pictures. On *Rebecca*, Laurence Olivier hadn't liked the picture or his character—"I literally walked through the part—it had nothing to do with the real work of acting," said Olivier. He wasn't crazy about Fontaine either. Olivier told Hitchcock she was no good, and Hitchcock turned around and told her of Olivier's disdain, feeling that that knowledge might stoke Fontaine's insecurities and thereby work to the advantage of her portrayal.

Grant thought Fontaine was manipulative, although he might have justifiably objected to her habit of doing most of her acting by arching her exquisite eyebrows. Grant was usually gallant about his leading ladies, but in private he used the word "bitch" to describe Fontaine. "She was no fun on the set of *Gunga Din* . . . and she was no fun during this. She had one big fat head about herself. It wasn't hard to play someone who looked as if he wanted to kill her." As for Fontaine, she thought Grant was "only interested in himself."

Hitchcock seemed uninterested in giving Fontaine any direction, perhaps because she was basically playing the same tremulous wreck she'd played in *Rebecca*. Fontaine believed that Grant's disinclination to be friendly on the set was because he gradually came to the realization "that it was my picture, that it was a woman's picture. And he is quite a technician, he knows where his lights are. . . . Then one day Cary said, 'You're in my lights.' And I went to the cameraman, I was crying, I'd never been accused of this."

According to Fontaine, the cameraman told her that "You weren't in anybody's lights. He's just uptight because he realizes what is happening to him, which he did not anticipate." Things got worse when the Academy Awards came along. Grant had been nominated for *Penny Serenade*, but lost to Gary Cooper in *Sergeant York*. Fontaine congratulated him on his nomination, but Grant snapped, "'I don't give a damn what you think, and keep it to yourself from now on.' In front of the entire set. And I had nothing to reply. . . . It was very unpleasant; it was a real tantrum, and I was twenty-two at the time." Years later, Fontaine caught up with the film again and her opinion of Grant shifted; she saw how Grant "threw whole scenes to me. He seemed aloof at the time, but he was never the gregarious sort."

Hitchcock thought he had devised a workable ending that could satisfy the Production Code: Grant's Johnny, feeling smug after killing his wife, posts a letter she had asked him to mail, which contains the evidence that will bring him to justice.

It was the sort of ironic snap ending Hitchcock would request from the writers of his TV show, but it was never shot. RKO was in one of its periodic upheavals, and the men who had hired Hitchcock to make the film were fired while the film was in production. In came Joseph Breen, the arch-Catholic architect of the Production Code. Breen ran RKO just long enough to mandate a last-minute sellout of the movie Hitchcock and Grant had spent months making. Johnny was magically changed from a killer to an irresponsible rogue, which made Fontaine's Lina a clinical paranoid.

Until Howard Hawks lost his nerve over the ending of *Red River* and decided he couldn't kill John Wayne, the ending of *Suspicion* is probably the greatest violation of a core narrative by a great director, although Hitchcock had the small consolation of having had it forced on him. Some of the critics objected to the incoherent bowdlerizing—"If this sop of a happy ending was dragged in by the heels . . . it serves only to spoil a great picture," observed *The Hollywood Reporter*—but most didn't: "This is a far finer film than *Rebecca*," said the *New York World-Telegram*. Then there was *The New Yorker*: "Cary Grant finds a new field for himself, the field of crime, the smiling villain, without heart or conscience. Crime lends color to his amiability."

Joan Fontaine got an Oscar for Best Actress, a make-good for being overlooked for *Rebecca*. And the public clearly didn't care about the script; *Suspicion* earned $440,000 in profits—RKO's biggest hit of 1941.

Thanks to Breen, it's a botched picture, most valuable for Hitchcock's sculpting the last piece of Grant's screen personality—a deep reservoir of calculation and bitterness that he would expose only when he felt in absolutely safe hands. Grant would never admit to the emotional synchronicity between him and Hitchcock; he would say that the reason they got along so well was that they both shared a passion for their favorite English sweet: Liquorice Allsorts.

IN THE MIDDLE OF 1941, Frank Capra wanted Grant for the part of Mortimer Brewster in *Arsenic and Old Lace*—the sole sane member of a comically insane family in Joseph Kesselring's farce. With Jack

Warner's help, Capra got his (leading) man. Grant had a commitment at Columbia, but Warners traded Humphrey Bogart to Columbia for *Sahara* in exchange for Grant's services on *Arsenic and Old Lace*.

On September 30, 1941, Grant signed a contract with Warner Bros. to make the film. The bulk of his salary of $150,000 was donated to charities Grant designated: $50,000 went to the Southern California branch of British War Relief, $25,000 for the American Red Cross, $25,000 for the USO in California. Grant also designated that Warners pay his agent his commission directly, rather than have it deducted from Grant's salary. Grant himself took only $50,000 for the film.

In his deeply fanciful autobiography, Capra reported that he shot the movie in four weeks for $400,000. In fact, he shot the picture in eight weeks for $1.1 million. By this time, Grant was one of the few premier stars who was also a freelancer. Outside of a one-picture-a-year commitment at RKO, and a similar agreement at Columbia, he was a free agent. As a result, he was able to leverage his stardom into higher salaries—and, increasingly, profit percentages—than actors under exclusive contract could imagine.

The contract negotiations turned out to be the easy part, because Grant spent most of the shoot fretting that Capra was forcing him into a performance that was too broad: "I tried to explain to Capra that I couldn't do that kind of comedy—all those double takes. I'd have been better as one of the old aunts." Capra's response was that the script was a farce and a farce can't be too broad.

Grant and Jean Adair, playing one of the deranged aunts, had a happy reunion. Twenty years earlier, when he was still Archie Leach, he had contracted a fever on a vaudeville tour, and Adair had nursed him through the illness. Adair had very little movie experience and relied on Grant to properly scale her performance. For his part, Grant gave Capra what the director wanted: uncontained hysteria, a virtuoso display of popping eyes, whinnies and squeals, violent double and triple takes. He was miserable.

Four weeks into the picture, Capra agreed to reshoot some of Grant's close-ups at the end of the shooting schedule. By that time, Philip and Julius Epstein, the screenwriters, had looked at the rushes and were alarmed at Grant's excesses. "We finally got up the courage to say to Capra, 'Frank, don't you think he's a little overboard?'" said

Julius Epstein. "Capra said, 'Oh, a lot overboard, but the next time I'll tone it down.'"

Capra had planned to shoot all of Grant's scenes in six weeks, so the actor could get to Columbia to begin another film on December 1, but Grant told him Columbia's script wouldn't be ready by December 1, and he wouldn't ask for any more money for going past his finishing date. Because of an agreement with the play's producers, the film couldn't be released until the Broadway show had closed, so Warners sat on the film until September 1944, more than two years after it was completed.

The film's production records document Grant's frequent complaints—about the sets, his part, even his wardrobe, complaints that were exacerbated after Pearl Harbor, when Capra, eager to get into the war, decided against retaking Grant's reaction shots. To the end of his life, whenever someone told Grant they loved *Arsenic and Old Lace*, he would stare at them in disbelief, or tell them he thought it was by far his worst performance, or both. "I was embarrassed doing it," he said. "I overplayed the character. Jimmy Stewart would have been much better in the film."

In fact, Capra was probably right. Grant's performance is a whirling dervish of ascending comic panic, inventive and dazzling in technique if not always in effect. The anything-goes nature of the story gave Grant an opportunity for some great ad-libs. As Grant and Peter Lorre are going down a staircase, Lorre tugs on Grant's arm, which leads him to snap, "Don't touch me. What are you doing, doctor? What kind of doctor are you? Stop underplaying, I can't hear you."

GRANT AND GEORGE STEVENS collaborated for the last time on *The Talk of the Town*, which began shooting just six weeks after Pearl Harbor. Ronald Colman and Jean Arthur formed the rest of the starring triumvirate. Interestingly, Grant's salary ($106,250) was larger than Colman's ($100,000), who had been a star for nearly twenty years, and larger by far than Arthur's ($50,000.)

Most of the drama seems to have involved the script, which was a complicated affair between Dale Van Every, Irwin Shaw, Sidney Buchman, and Everett Riskin, the latter of whom had been employed at Columbia and worked on *The Talk of the Town* in a manner that indicates he was functioning as a coproducer. Unfortunately, he left for a job at MGM before the picture began shooting.

This caused much jockeying over the credits, with Riskin sending Columbia's Sam Briskin an impassioned letter outlining his efforts.

Riskin wanted a credit as either producer, associate producer, or coproducer. He was even willing to accept a credit card acknowledging his contribution to the making of the picture. "You can assure Mr. Stevens that I will naturally not even think of making any move to try to force a credit for myself on this picture, but ask him how he would feel if he had completed eighty percent of a job and then, as a result of a set of circumstances, was forced to leave, only to find that six months hard work was taken away without due recognition."

Neither Briskin nor Stevens was willing to give Riskin credit. "Your true contribution to this picture was the taking of a story and developing it through two drafts of the script to the point where Stevens entered the scene, whereupon considerable rewrite was done to the event that Dilg's part was built up to where it would suit Cary Grant, and with that of course came the triangle love story and the complete rearrangement of the scene between Dilg, the girl, and the professor."

With that problem disposed of, the picture moved into production. There was the usual tension with Jean Arthur, who had clashed with Grant on *Only Angels Have Wings* because she thought he was mugging. On *The Talk of the Town*, Grant let her know he thought she was overplaying a scene, and she responded with what he termed "hysterics." Years later, when she was offered a romantic comedy, she said she'd do it "With anybody but Cary."*

With the exception of one other brief dustup late in the shoot, when Grant accused Arthur of upstaging him, it was a smooth shoot, albeit made with Stevens's usual disregard for time allotments; *The Talk of the Town* came in nineteen days over schedule, although only $100,000 over budget.

The Talk of the Town is a morality tale about a young woman (Arthur) who rents her house to a renowned law professor (Colman).

---

* Grant's feelings about Arthur fluctuated. Talking to George Stevens Jr., Grant referred to her as "A very lovely woman. . . . We all adored her and that lovely cracked voice of hers. . . . I always had a vague idea she fell in love with George. She certainly didn't with me; and Ronnie Colman was married, so . . ."

Complications ensue when an accused murderer (Grant) shows up needing a place to hide. The two men meet and become respectful adversaries, in spite of their differing experience of the world. In a world veering toward chaos, *The Talk of the Town* was Stevens's way of asserting an equivalent balance between men of goodwill.

The film begins with a montage of crime and a jailbreak that's shot by Ted Tetzlaff with dazzling virtuosity, but it soon settles into a stagey, claustrophobic groove that's always threatening to become top-heavy. Stevens and his sterling cast manage to keep the pot bubbling, even if you're always aware of the effort being expended.

One day during production, Grant and Stevens were talking about great comic scenes and Stevens mentioned a sequence from Chaplin's *Pay Day.* It involved Chaplin getting on the last streetcar home, with the succeeding rush of humanity gradually pushing him toward the back of the car. He's eventually expelled from the rear of the streetcar.

"My God," Grant said, "that's the story of Hollywood." Grant whipped up a complicated allegory around the theme of the crowded streetcar that attested to the limited duration of stardom's ride:

> Actors and actresses are packed in like sardines. When I arrived in Hollywood, Carole Lombard, Gary Cooper, Marlene Dietrich, Warner Baxter, Greta Garbo, Fred Astaire and others were crammed onto the car. A few stood, holding tightly to leather straps to avoid being pushed aside. Others were firmly seated on the center of the car. They were the big stars. At the front, new actors and actresses pushed and shoved to get aboard. Some made it and slowly moved toward the center. . . .
>
> Adolphe Menjou was constantly being pushed off the rear. He would pick himself up, brush himself off, and run to the front to fight his way aboard again. In a short time he was back in the center only to be pushed off once more. This went on for years. He never did get to sit down.
>
> It took me quite a while to reach the center. When I did make it, I remained standing. I held on to the leather strap for dear life. Then Warner Baxter fell out the back, and I got to sit down. . . . The only man who refused to budge was Cooper. Gary was firmly seated in the center of the car. He just leaned back, stuck those long legs of his out in the aisle, and tripped everyone who came along.

When Joan Fontaine got on, she stood right in front of me and held on to one of those leather straps. I naturally got to my feet, giving her my seat. Joan sat down and got an Academy Award!

As metaphors go, it had a good deal of psychological acuity, mainly because of an unusual degree of objectivity verging on fatalism about stardom, and Grant's overriding awareness that nothing lasts forever—knowledge that had been drummed into him as a child.

It was the beginning of Grant's determination to avoid being pushed off the rear of stardom's car. He understood that it would be so much less stressful if he simply got to his destination, excused himself, and got off before he was forced to leave.

Grant and Colman got along better than Grant and Arthur, but not for long. When the completed film was screened at the studio, Colman and his wife, Benita Hume, were on time, but Grant and Barbara Hutton were running late. After waiting for fifteen minutes, Mrs. Colman asked for the picture to be started. Fifteen minutes into the film, Grant and Hutton arrived, and Barbara asked for the picture to be restarted. Grant and Colman had words, as did their wives. The resulting chill lasted the rest of Colman's life. More than ten years later, Colman was checking into the Plaza Hotel with William Frye, a mutual friend of Colman's and Grant's. Grant was standing in the lobby and asked Frye what he was doing in town. "Ronnie and I are here to catch some shows," Frye said. Grant said, "Well, have a good time," and turned away without speaking to Colman.

HOLLYWOOD HAD TO TAKE WORLD WAR II into account, and did so with varying degrees of emotional honesty. On the high end were movies like John Ford's *They Were Expendable* and William Wellman's *The Story of G.I. Joe*—movies made by men who had an advantage over their fellow filmmakers in that they had been in combat.

Grant wanted to be involved, and seems to have made an honest effort. On June 19, 1942, a telegram addressed to Archibald Alexander Leach was sent to Grant at the Santa Monica house. He was told to report to March Field for a physical as well as to forward his examination papers to be attached to his application to the Army Air Force.

A few days later, a lieutenant colonel in the Air Force sent Jack Warner, Grant's current employer, a letter reporting that "at the present time it is practically impossible to obtain a commission in the Army Air Force due to the temporary 'freezing' order on any new appointment. However, it is felt that Mr. Leach's case is an exceptional one and his services to the Army Air Force will be of inestimable value."

Warner evidently asked for an exemption, and a few days later Grant was deferred until August 15, 1942, to enable him to complete the picture he was currently making. But, the board said, "the board cannot see its way clear to allow the time to make the second picture the RKO Radio Pictures Inc. mentioned in the affidavit submitted."

At this point, Grant's draft status was 2A, and he still seemed determined to get in the Air Force. He got letters of reference from the manager of the Security-First National Bank on Hollywood Boulevard attesting to his generally fine character and the exemplary manner in which he managed his accounts. Grant received another deferment for five weeks on August 12, and at that point it was planned that he would enlist on September 15, after which he would report for duty to the Officer Candidate School in Miami Beach.

On September 8, Grant received a telegram stating that

IN VIEW OF WAR DEPARTMENT INTEREST IN THE PICTURE BUNDLES FOR FREEDOM [later titled *Mr. Lucky*] A DEFERMENT OF YOUR ENLISTMENT FOR COMPLETION OF THIS PICTURE WILL IN NO WISE MITIGATE AGAINST YOUR BEING ENLISTED IN THE AIR FORCES AT THE COMPLETION OF THIS PICTURE STOP PLEASE PRESENT THIS TO YOUR LOCAL DRAFT BOARD AS EVIDENCE OF INTEREST OF THE AIR FORCES IN THE COMPLETION OF THIS WORK.

Shortly thereafter, in an undated letter from RKO vice president Charles Koerner, the studio head quoted from a letter he had just received:

The matter of relieving Cary Grant from the arrangement we were making on his behalf has been satisfactorily cleaned up without any misunderstanding.

Washington suggests that they would like to have Cary Grant's name on their list of people who from time to time might do some temporary service. In each instance, if he is called upon, he will have an opportunity to say "Yes" or "No" to whatever job is proposed and it is not at all certain that they will call upon him in any case.

Koerner went on to ask Grant to "please advise me whether you would care to have yourself lined up with such work."

The sudden short-circuiting of Grant's enlistment, and Koerner's veiled coyness in refusing to specify the source or specific nature of said offer, suggest something more than the typical string of deferments handed out to movie stars who lacked a burning urge to serve. The truth is that Grant's wartime activities almost certainly went far beyond making movies.

Among the most fascinating untold stories of the complicated relationship between the American film industry and World War II is the spy network run by Britain's MI6 out of Alexander Korda's London Films offices. Korda was Hungarian by birth, and, as his company name would indicate, a rapt anglophile by inclination. London Films had offices all over the world, and MI6 installed agents in many, if not all of Korda's offices. In South America the agents reconnoitered for signs of Nazi operations and attempts at influence; ditto in America.

The isolationists in Congress had long been suspicious of Korda's passionately pro-British stance in movies such as *The Four Feathers* and *That Hamilton Woman*. In fact, Korda had been scheduled to testify before the House Committee on Un-American Activities on December 8, 1941, but his testimony was canceled due to larger events in Hawaii the day before.

The FBI was definitely tipped off to Korda's operation in June 1943, probably by a Los Angeles bank employee who noticed that the British consulate in Los Angeles had reimbursed Korda for the salary of an employee in Santiago, Chile. J. Edgar Hoover promptly shipped out a "Personal and Confidential" memo because the man in Chile—Ellerman by name—seemed to be a British agent operating in the Western Hemisphere without having registered with the American government, as required by the Foreign Agents Registration Act, passed in 1938. Hoover was mightily bothered by this, probably because he couldn't control it and anything Hoover couldn't control he viewed as a threat to the Republic, even if it involved an ally.

One of Hoover's subordinates recommended doing nothing about Ellerman, if only because he had not been actively engaged in espionage in the United States. On the other hand, "it is evident that Alexander Korda is being used by the British as an agent to finance British agents in the western hemisphere." It was suggested that Korda be investigated to see if he was doing the same thing within America.

Hoover didn't know the half of it. MI6 had set up an intelligence operation in New York, with Korda's office in Rockefeller Center as the front. The British had shuttered an MI6 operation in New York City in 1938 because of fears that it might lead to a diplomatic incident with an America currently beset by a firmly isolationist Congress. The theory was that closing the MI6 office might lead to a closer relationship with the FBI, but that didn't happen. The result was that the British were completely ignorant of what was going on in America. Which is where Alexander Korda came in.

"There were close to a dozen people involved in the Rockefeller Center office," said Michael Korda, Alex's nephew, the son of his brother Vincent.

It was a much larger office than was necessary to run the London Films operation. Everybody there, even the secretaries, were chosen because they were involved with MI6 at some level.

I strongly suspect that Cary Grant was involved, because that would explain the friendship. Cary would have known what was taking place in the film studios, and the whole purpose of the operation was to have people you could use. Cary knew people all over the world, English and every other nationality. There was always a great degree of affection between Alex and Cary, and some of it must have been based on the war, because a lot of Alex's friendships were based on that.

The purpose of Korda's operation was to funnel independent information about American politics to the English political leadership. This meant that before Pearl Harbor they were essentially engaged in espionage against the United States, whose official stance was one of non-intervention. Korda would tell his nephew Michael that these "were the most difficult years of my life. Only four people [in England] knew what I was doing—Brendan Bracken, Max Beaverbrook, Churchill, and myself."

Korda was not the only filmmaker engaged in spying. Cecil B. DeMille was operating an ad hoc intelligence service for the FBI. Richard Hood, who ran the Los Angeles office of the bureau, would show up in DeMille's office at Paramount and ask him to assign one of his people to check something out. Usually, DeMille gave it to screenwriter Charles Bennett, an Englishman who over time sniffed around events as disparate as an American soldier photographing Fort MacArthur's gun placements, or investigating an English writer named Jeffrey Bernard, who the FBI suspected was a German agent. A lot of what Bennett was asked to do was anti-Soviet in nature, which he found confusing—Russia was America's ally against the Nazis, but the FBI and DeMille were both convinced that the alliance was only temporary.

Similar things were taking place in New York. At the same time Korda opened up his operation, the Canadian-born English intelligence officer William Stephenson opened another Rockefeller Center office that was supposedly concerned with passport and visa control. Stephenson's actual function was planting propaganda with journalists—Walter Winchell was one of Stephenson's favorites—conducting intelligence operations, and avoiding diplomatic incidents at all costs.

The problem for the historian is that none of this was written down, but rather hashed out over brandy and cigars in Westminster or Paramount. Korda and Grant were similar in that they both possessed a considerable supply of guile, habitually played their cards close to the vest, and tended to have good cards. It would have been perfectly natural for Korda to bring in someone with Grant's native intelligence to engage in some light reconnaissance on his own.

Generally speaking, Korda was completely open only with his brothers, Vincent and Zoltan, although Michael Korda doubts that he would have shared the details of his espionage operation with anybody. The danger for Korda was that if he was caught he could be declared an undesirable alien or even prosecuted for espionage, which would have meant the destruction of his film company.

Korda was not invulnerable, but he did have extremely influential friends and supporters within the Franklin Roosevelt administration. There was William "Wild Bill" Donovan, the founder of the OSS and a good friend, as well as Robert Sherwood, who had written scripts for Korda before the war (*The Scarlet Pimpernel, The Ghost Goes West*, uncredited work on *The Divorce of Lady X*). Sherwood spent World War II in Washington writing speeches for FDR and, from 1943 to 1945, serving as director of the Office of War Information.

When Michael Korda was seven years old in 1941, he left England. He and his friend Martin Gilbert had to stall for time in Canada until Robert Sherwood got them into the United States. It's entirely possible that between Sherwood and Donovan, the senior Korda had all the backup he needed, Hoover or no Hoover. Michael Korda says that "I honestly don't think Alex would have worried about J. Edgar Hoover because it's almost certain that Donovan and Sherwood knew about the operation Alex was running out of New York."

The FBI had noticed what was going on only when Korda was reimbursed by the British government, so Korda suggested carrying the operatives on his own payroll—a considerable financial sacrifice. Despite the fact that Hoover was apparently aware of only a few of Korda's operatives, he wouldn't let it go, writing that "Alexander Korda Films Incorporated [has] acted as an intermediary between the British government and persons suspected of acting as agents of the British Government."

Hoover was told to stand down by both Tom Clark, the assistant attorney general, as well as the chief of the Foreign Agents Registration Section. The latter wrote Hoover, "Under the circumstances I do not believe it possible to tell whether . . . Korda . . . acted in violation of the Act, or whether, under the circumstances, either their prosecution or registration would be warranted."

Hoover persisted, ordering a further investigation within fifteen days. The State Department informed Hoover that "no useful purpose would be served by prosecuting Alexander Korda Films and/or Alexander Korda." Nevertheless, Hoover ordered that Korda be interviewed in order to determine the extent of his culpability. As was his wont, Korda was slippery, and the interview wasn't conducted until March 26, 1946—nearly a year after the war had ended.

By 1946, Korda was playing from a position of strength and he didn't bother concealing it. "Mr. Korda was at first rather resentful," noted the agents, as well he might have been. Korda proceeded to spin an ornate series of lies, stating that he had never acted as an agent of the British government or any unit or department of that government, but would have been happy to do so except for the unfortunate fact that he was well known. As he patiently explained to the agents, he was far too conspicuous to do anything as risky, as audacious as what the gentlemen from the FBI were so erroneously suggesting had taken place. Korda left the impression that he admired the FBI's creativity in devising such a thrilling alternate existence for a man who was, after all, only making movies. Korda managed to keep a straight face throughout his bravura display of deceit.

All this goes a long way toward explaining why Korda was knighted while the war was still going on, while Alfred Hitchcock wasn't knighted until more than thirty years later, when he was practically on his deathbed. This also explains the strangely covert nature of Charles Koerner's letter to Grant.

The end result of all this was success. One historian of the period would hail what he called "the President's backdoor cooperation with [operations that caused] disruption of major German intelligence and propaganda efforts. . . . Without British intelligence assistance . . . German success in subverting the United States would have been much more likely."

In the years after the war, Korda and Grant were always trying to find a film to make, but it never happened, although there would be some interesting near-misses. The central irony of the entire episode is that Grant's manifestly antifascist sympathies would be conveniently overlooked in 1944, when the Los Angeles office of the FBI issued a memo entitled "Communist Infiltration of the Motion Picture Industry." The memo named Lucille Ball, Ira Gershwin, John Garfield, Walter Huston, and Grant as among those stars who had "Communist connections." Grant's Communist connections consisted entirely of his friendship with Clifford Odets, who wrote and directed *None But the Lonely Heart*, and was a member of the Communist Party from 1934 to 1935.

Besides his activities for Korda, Grant also did a lot of work for the Hollywood Victory Committee. To take one year—1942—at random, in March he made a personal appearance at the Olympic Auditorium boxing match along with Jack Benny, Joe E. Brown, George Raft, Mickey Rooney, and Lou Costello—the performers were supposed to gin up interest in volunteering for Army Canteen Service.

From April 26 to May 20, Grant was part of the Hollywood Victory Caravan that traveled to thirteen cities. Some actors flew in and out, as their schedules demanded, but Grant was there for the entire run, along with Desi Arnaz, Charles Boyer, Bing Crosby, James Cagney, Bert Lahr, Groucho Marx, Frank McHugh, Ray Middleton, Eleanor Powell, Stan Laurel and Oliver Hardy, Risë Stevens, Merle Oberon, Olivia de Havilland, Joan Bennett, and Pat O'Brien.* There was also a group of va-va-voom starlets including Frances Gifford, Elyse Knox, Marie McDonald, Fay McKenzie, and Arleen Whelan.

A joint function of the Army-Navy Relief Fund and the Hollywood Victory Committee, the Caravan was inspired by an all-star bond show at Madison Square Garden that had been organized by Walter Winchell in March 1942. The purpose of the Caravan was to raise money for families of soldiers killed in combat. No one who was approached turned it down. As Bob Hope said, "Who in Hollywood had the guts to tell the [Committee] he was going to be out of town?"

The Santa Fe railroad donated a special fourteen-car train, with rehearsal space for two portable dance floors, two pianos, and ten musicians. The train set off from Los Angeles on April 26, 1942, and made a cross-country jaunt to Washington, D.C., while the troupe rehearsed. Mark Sandrich headed the production, Melville Shavelson the writing, Alfred Newman was in charge of the music for the ten musicians who traveled with the show, augmented with pickup talent from each city. Special musical material was donated by Jerome Kern, Johnny Mercer, Frank Loesser, and Arthur Schwartz. Alfred Newman's younger brother Dr. Irving Newman went along to handle any medical issues. Bob Hope and Cary Grant split the MC duties. Every performer worked for free.

Each town hosted a parade through the streets. The show usually opened with Risë Stevens singing "The Star-Spangled Banner" and closed with Jimmy Cagney doing a medley from *Yankee Doodle Dandy*. In between, Laurel and Hardy did their Driver's License sketch, Eleanor Powell tap-danced, Frances Langford sang a new Jerome Kern song, and Groucho Marx did his Dr. Hackenbush routine. Besides splitting master of ceremonies duties, Grant did a skit with Joan Bennett.

---

* The Caravan cities were: Washington, Boston, Philadelphia, Cleveland, Detroit, Chicago, St. Louis, Minneapolis, St. Paul, Des Moines, Dallas, Houston, San Francisco.

With such a plethora of talent, audiences were enthralled, which was good because the show usually ran about three and a half hours.

Grant recruited Gene Lester to document the event. "Cary came into [my] studio one day on his way back from RKO and he said, 'We're planning a cross-country trip with about thirty-five to forty stars.' They were talking about taking a photographer along because they did not want any photographers from outside the industry to go on board the train or to go into the shows backstage and so on. They wanted to be able to control this thing. Not to look like it was a blast on the road. They wanted it to look like it was a serious operation."

Grant told Lester it would take about a month of his time. "He said, 'We'll pay for all the materials plus we'll give you some kind of a pittance.' I think for the whole month they gave me $100." That wouldn't have paid for Lester's overhead, let alone his expenses, but Grant got the Victory Committee to give Lester the rights to his photographs, which meant he could sell his shots to any publication that wanted them.

There was a war on, but putting several dozen actors and comedians together on a train is not an environment conducive to sober considerations, or sober anything else. Laurel and Hardy made sure there was a bottle of whiskey in every Green Room; Olivia de Havilland missed a photo on the White House Lawn because she was engaged in more pressing activity with John Huston; Merle Oberon bribed a porter to let her into Jimmy Cagney's room, where she waited for him under the sheets. Cagney told a friend that he was fully prepared to oblige Oberon until he remembered how much he loved his wife and backed off. Claudette Colbert smuggled her husband, a doctor in the Navy, onto the train, which led Groucho Marx to stick a note on her door: "Isn't this carrying naval relief too far?" Bob Hope did what Bob Hope always did and found a couple of obliging girls. Desi Arnaz, having left Lucille Ball back in Los Angeles, attempted to surpass Hope's accomplishments and apparently did, although his relentlessness aroused the irritation of the other stars. As for Grant, he did his job, was friendly but not too friendly, and otherwise kept to himself.

When it was all over and everybody had said goodbye, Joan Blondell and Joan Bennett sent out telegrams to the other participants: ARE YOU GETTING MUCH? When the receipts were totaled, the

Victory Caravan had raised $600,000. Adding in the War Bonds that had been sold as an ancillary benefit, it was estimated the take for the three-week tour was just under $1.1 million.

Grant kept working for the cause. In August, he recorded a radio show for the Victory Committee along with José Iturbi, Bert Lahr, Ethel Waters, and Joan Davis, and there was another radio show in December. In 1943, Grant toured military camps from March 8 to March 30, did one stop in May, and two days at the end of December. Nineteen forty-four brought several camp shows, and in 1945 he went on a tour of military hospitals from February 3 to February 14.

The camp shows must have been fun, because Grant enlisted his old vaudeville friend Don Barclay to encore the mind-reading act they did in the 1920s. Barclay would always insist that his partner was never happier than when performing something absurd or physical that would negate his good looks—anything that would take him back to the catch-as-catch-can days of vaudeville.

"It went something like this," Barclay remembered, using Grant's real name while reminiscing.

"Gentlemen," I would say while Archie clapped his hand to his forehead in deep concentration, "This is a serious test in thought transmission. Professor Knowall Leach will endeavor to call anyone in the audience by name." As I went through the crowd, I'd put my hand on a shoulder, then call to Archie. "This Gentleman is from Buffalo."

"Bill!" Archie would shout back.

"Now here's a stickler, professor. For the love of . . ."

"Pete!"

"No, no, the other kind!"

"Mike!"

And so forth. If Barclay singled out a woman, he would say:

"This girl is an upper and lower, professor!"

"Bertha!"

"And here is one, not deaf, but dumb.'

"Dora!"

"Dumber than that!"

"Belle."

"Right you are professor. Good people, I call your attention to the fact that we use no signals, no code!"

GRANT REUNITED WITH LEO MCCAREY for an RKO comedy-drama entitled *Once Upon a Honeymoon*, a misbegotten attempt to meld the director's genial comedy with the current vicious political and social reality. "I wish I'd never thought of it," grumbled McCarey late in his life, a sentiment shared by audiences as well. "I didn't like it because the public didn't like it. I thought it was very funny. But I knew we weren't on the same wave-length. My public and I were not on the same wave-length."

It was actually a bit more complicated than that. The story and script were by Sheridan Gibney, who told Patrick McGilligan that "Leo was a terrible drunk . . . and I didn't see much of him while I was writing the script. But when we got on the picture, he sobered up—a little. Leo had a genius for casting, and a genius for getting good performances out of actors. . . . His whole idea was to get the most talented, the best possible actors for the parts, and then let them do it. He would never correct the actor . . . but he was very patient and understanding and sympathetic. Always joking, keeping them in good humor."

The problem was that McCarey "would think up little vaudeville routines that he thought were very funny, very often at the expense of important aspects of the story. He thought in terms of gags, like silent comedy people did. Some of the gags I thought cheapened the picture and robbed it of any real comic value."

After a day's work, McCarey would drag Gibney to Lucey's bar and restaurant. "We'd start drinking and be there until two o clock in the morning. I'd get to the studio the next day with a hangover, and some days Leo wouldn't show up—he'd found someone else and gone drinking all night. His wife would call and I'd have to go scouting for him, and I'd usually find him holed up somewhere with a couple of whores. And that day, he couldn't do anything at all. That was Leo."

McCarey seems to have been after something akin to Lubitsch's *To Be or Not to Be*, but he couldn't figure out a throughline connecting the physical comedy (the film's best scenes) and the bleakness of war (the film's worst scenes). Ginger Rogers is at all times impeccably made up with layers of pancake and gleaming lipstick, even when she and Grant are interned in McCarey's idea of a concentration camp, which seems to be a dank basement. The film runs slightly less than two hours and feels like three; it's the sort of ambitious botch that can only be made by talented people, because only talented people would think they could pull it off

The reviews made it clear that it was no *Awful Truth: The New York Times* pointed out the mistake of "trying to mix romantic comedy with tragedy too stark and real." McCarey clearly conflated the film's dicey reputation as compromising its financial success; actually, *Once Upon a Honeymoon* made a profit of nearly $250,000, with Grant earning a base pay of $50,000 for ten weeks of shooting, plus 2.5 percent of the producer's gross with a guarantee of an additional $75,000 in profits within eighteen months.

What came after the movie was more interesting than the movie. Years later, Grant was counseling Peter Bogdanovich about his affair with Cybill Shepherd, the star of several of Bogdanovich's pictures. "Very dangerous," Grant said of set romances. "I always told myself to stay out of affairs with co-stars. And, of course, I didn't. There was Ginger—although that was after the picture."

THE AUTHOR OF *Mr. Lucky* was Milton Holmes, who managed the Beverly Hills Tennis Club and published a short story in *Cosmopolitan* magazine in June 1941 about a draft-dodging gambler who has a change of heart when his brothers are killed in the Nazi invasion of Greece. RKO bought the story for Grant and hired Charles Brackett to work with Holmes on a screen treatment. RKO paid $30,000 to Holmes for his story, plus ten weeks at $500 a week for his work on the script.

Once the story was written, RKO handed script assignments to both Dudley Nichols and Adrian Scott. Neither Scott nor Nichols was aware that the other was working on the same story—an expensive but fairly common method to enable producers to choose the best scenes from two scripts by two highly regarded writers.

Scott's script was used for the picture, although he shared a credit with Holmes. Grant's costar was Laraine Day, who got an interesting view of his bifurcated psyche. On the set, "He knew where the camera was, what he wanted to do, and he worked very hard. He had managed to teach himself a lot of tricks, and he used them and taught them to other people. It was a treat to work with him."

Socially, after the work was done, he was a different creature.

> I have never worked with an actor who wasn't the same off the set . . . with the exception of Cary Grant at the time when he was married to Barbara Hutton. . . . If you went out in the evening with them, or went to a dinner party with them, Cary subsided so as to let Barbara have the spotlight, not to detract from her. It was an effort, I think, to save his marriage, because he was so much in love with her that he was subduing his own wonderful, expressive personality so that she would stand out. After the marriage broke up, I would see him off the set or at the studio in the commissary, and it was back to the Cary Grant that was on the set all the time.

RKO had upped Grant to name-above-the-title status. "The scuttlebutt was that RKO had decided not to have Cary Grant co-star with Irene Dunne and Jean Arthur and people of his own caliber," said Day. "Instead he would be the solo star, above the title and the girls would all be rising actresses coming up, of lesser importance." Laraine Day said that Rita Hayworth was RKO's first choice for the leading lady, but that Grant refused to work with her, believing she might overshadow him.

The director was H. C. Potter, a jazz buff and a good friend of Nat King Cole. Potter threw a couple of parties for the cast, and Cole's trio entertained. Socially, Grant was a different man than he was professionally. "He wasn't *not* friendly [but] he didn't project or capture you like Cary did [on screen], he didn't involve you in anything." Day thought that Barbara Hutton had a sense of humor of sorts, but it's hard to tell if the humor was intentional or not. The story goes that everybody was at a party and Gary Cooper and his wife, Rocky, arrived.

Barbara came up to say hello, looked at a pin Rocky Cooper was wearing, and said, "Oh, Rocky, what a lovely pin."

"Well, thank you," said Rocky, "but it's only costume jewelry."

"Oh, I'm so sorry," said Hutton.

Day said that on the set, Grant turned on his personality, and did all the things he didn't do socially: "being the wonderful Cary Grant, which he *was*. He was so much fun and charming. A little stingy, but fun."

Grant's sense of economy came to the fore during Thanksgiving, when he proclaimed that he and Day would give a turkey to each member of the crew. "I just thought it was funny, because he was the star of the picture, and the turkey should come from him!" Another factor could have been that Grant was making more than $100,000 for the picture, while Laraine Day was making about $750 a week on loan from MGM.

If Grant lacked a certain generosity when it came to money, he didn't lack for generosity on the set. "*Very* generous. If it worked and was good, [if] it worked for him . . . it worked for everyone. And when they were ready to shoot, the first cameraman had a little flute, and he would play some popular little piece of music, and that would let Cary know that they were ready to go and he would come bouncing onto the set. . . . He was fun to work with, and I hadn't had such a good part in so long. And especially in that lighthearted vein, and the clothes and playing a rich girl."

Mr. Lucky is not much more than a star vehicle, but Grant has a scene of scorn and class rage that rings true and looks forward to similar scenes in *None But the Lonely Heart* and *Notorious*. "You think the worst thing that could happen to you is to marry me," he tells his girlfriend. "To people like you, folks like me are animals. We're so *bad*. And you're so very *good*. What do you expect—credit for it? How else did you expect to turn out? You had so much going for you—you ought to be horsewhipped if you didn't turn out right. What are you so high and mighty about? What did you ever *do*?"

After *Mr. Lucky*—RKO's biggest hit of the year, with profits of $1.6 million against a cost of $842,000—Grant knocked off *Destination Tokyo* at Warner Bros., where he encored his steely-leader-of-men persona from *Only Angels Have Wings*. It's a standard-issue World War II submarine movie with what one critic called "an over-diversified cross-section" of humanity, encompassing the expected roster of Irish and Jews and adding Greeks for good measure. It's the first film directed by Delmer Daves—Grant was always willing to take a flier with a first-time director, despite the people around him.

Frank Vincent, Grant's agent, thought his client had lost his mind and swooped in to protect him. An irate Vincent called producer Jerry Wald to complain. "Delmer Daves has never directed a picture in his life! What do you mean he's going to direct Cary Grant! Let him practice on someone else before he deals with my star!"

"Have you talked to Cary?" asked Wald.

"I don't care what Cary says. I'm handling his affairs, and I refuse to let a new man, who's never directed before, direct him."

Wald had no choice but to call Jack Warner and tell him Daves was ruled out as a director. That was followed by another call from Frank Vincent, who told Wald he had talked to Cary and his client had told him that he wouldn't make the picture with anybody but Daves.

Daves asked Grant the reasons for his commitment to the risk of a first-time director. Grant replied that once upon a time Mae West had pointed to him and said, "I approve that young man. I think he'll be my new leading man." He intended to pay it forward whenever possible. He knew Daves, liked him and his writing, and thought it was time for someone to stand up and say, "I have faith in Delmer Daves." Daves was off and running on a considerable career, with a particular gift for strong, pictorially striking westerns: *Broken Arrow, 3:10 to Yuma, The Hanging Tree.* Years later, Grant would watch *Destination Tokyo* on TV and thought it held up well. His comment about Daves was that he was "quite underrated."

Then came *Once Upon a Time*, a flier at whimsy with Grant as a glib theatrical producer who finds a dancing caterpillar named Curly.

Again: a dancing caterpillar named Curly. (Chuck Jones would lift the idea and improve it for his classic cartoon *One Froggy Evening.*)

Once Upon a Time may be the longest eighty-nine-minute movie on record. The only worthwhile thing that came out of it was a friendship with Ted Donaldson, who played the boy who owns Curly.

"This was one of the greatest professional and personal experiences that I have ever had," said Donaldson.

Let me tell you how I met him. He came to the set at Columbia to make a test for Janet Blair, who played my sister. Well, I'm sitting next to my father and I see Grant standing 20 feet away talking with a representative from MCA or the studio. Grant leaves the person he's talking to and comes directly over to me. He extends his hand and says, "How do you do? I'm Cary Grant." Then he turned to my father and said, "You must be Mr. Donaldson. What a great pleasure to meet you." That was my introduction to Cary Grant—Cary Grant introducing himself to me. . . . That's the way it started. And that was characteristic of him.

During the shoot, Grant gave the boy pointillist tips about positioning for the camera. There was a shot of the two of them waiting on some steps, and Grant said very quietly, "Put the one foot above the other on the step. It looks better." Beyond that, he took care to make sure the boy got attention. After the cameraman Franz Planer had taken two hours to light a setup for a two-shot at the end of the picture, director Alexander Hall yelled for the take. But then Grant held up his hand.

"Just a moment now, Al. The set-up is all wrong."

"What do you mean?" asked a nettled Hall.

"It's not a two-shot. It should be a close-up of the kid."

Hall said the two-shot would be fine and tried to coast past Grant's objection, but he wouldn't budge.

"No, no, put my shoulder in to establish that I am there, but it's a close-up of the kid. It's not a two-shot."

"He would not do the scene unless it was a close-up," said Donaldson.

I have told this story many times, and I get a lump in my throat just now as I started telling it. That's where his perfectionism lay. He was concerned with the story and the dramatic effect. He was totally unconcerned with himself and his stardom. . . .

When you take all of that together, the fact that he was funny, taught me games, loved magic and was absolutely charming, well, I came to love the man.

There was only one time that Donaldson saw the sadness. They were waiting for Franz Planer to light another set—Planer was every bit as much of a perfectionist as Grant—when Grant began talking about his stepson Lance Reventlow.

It was the . . . really serious and rather melancholy side of Grant
that I had not ever seen before. He talked about how he just didn't
feel he was able to spend enough time with him. It was very strange
because it was a reversal of roles. I began asking him questions; I felt
that I was trying to almost comfort and help him. It was a strange
thing, but it gave me an insight that made me feel closer to him. . . .
I believe that I came to substitute Grant for my father at that time.
I don't know if he went as far as I did, but I think he came to have
some real fatherly feelings about me. I really believe that.

Donaldson continued as an actor for years, giving a particularly
lovely performance for Elia Kazan in *A Tree Grows in Brooklyn*.
When he graduated from high school in 1949 he wrote Grant and
asked him to come to the ceremony. Grant showed up and sat on
the aisle.

GRANT CONTINUED TO DO HIS BIT for the war effort whenever
he was asked. Sydney Guilaroff, MGM's head hairdresser since 1934,
was working the night shift at the Hollywood Canteen waiting on
tables. The Canteen was a cooperative effort funded by the studios
where food and drink were free for any serviceman who showed up.
Guilaroff asked Grant to come down to the Farmers Market on La
Brea for a fundraiser. He was to sit on a huge pile of potatoes and sell
them for $2.50 apiece, proceeds to go to the Canteen. Grant sat on
the pile until the last potato was sold and raised thousands of dollars.
Another time, Grant was enlisted to sell peanuts alongside Rosalind
Russell, Myrna Loy, and Charles Boyer at a Buy-a-Bomber benefit.

Orry-Kelly was in the Army but on loan to Warners to work on
This Is the Army when he ran into his old roommate. Kelly mentioned
that he had seen their mutual friend Lady Mendl in New York, where
he had been told by a friend of hers that all Englishmen should either
join up or go home and lend their support to their country. Grant
replied by telling Kelly of a conversation he'd had with Lord Lothian,
the recently deceased English ambassador to the United States, wherein
Lothian had told him he should stay in Hollywood and donate his
services and whatever money he could afford to War Relief.

Orry-Kelly was offended by the name-dropping. "I could see now that Grant had gone to the point of no return," wrote Kelly. That evening, Kelly visited Ethel Barrymore, and told her about the encounter. "He Lord Lothian'd me too," she said.

Kelly was beginning a serious battle with alcoholism that centered on bars along Vine Street and drinking companions that included Joe Frisco, Rags Ragland, and the boxer Barney Ross. Drinking made him truculent. One night Kelly was with Norma Talmadge and Constance Collier at Romanoff's. Sitting at the bar were Grant and Sonja Henie. Grant turned around and gave Kelly a halfhearted "Hi." Kelly exploded. His mother, who had helped support them both in their days of starvation in Greenwich Village, and who had always been fond of Archie Leach, had just visited. Her visit had been noted in the trade papers, and Grant hadn't called to say hello.

"Look here, Cary, if and when you are in the mood to say hello, do so. If you are glad to see me, look straight at me—preferably in the eye. But never, never again half-turn and give me that half-English half-Cockney half-arsed 'Hi.' " He then proceeded to remind Grant of his mother's visit. The next day, Grant sent a signed photo to Kelly's mother.

If he was indifferent to Kelly, Grant remained on intimate terms with Alexander Korda. Besides his clandestine activities for MI6, Korda was a patron of the arts and of beautiful women, part-owner of United Artists, a pretty fair director (*The Private Life of Henry VIII*, *Rembrandt*), and a great producer (*To Be or Not to Be*, *The Third Man*). In the early 1930s, Korda had made Merle Oberon his mistress, then made her a star. Still later he made her his wife.

Grant, along with almost every man who met her, was fascinated by Oberon. She was born Estelle Merle O'Brien Thompson in Bombay to a twelve-year-old mother and an unknown father. Oberon concealed her roots by telling people she was born in Tasmania, while her mother spent most of her life concealed as Oberon's maid. After Korda, Oberon would marry Lucien Ballard, a premier Hollywood cameraman, followed by a Mexican industrialist, who was succeeded by the actor Robert Wolders. Each husband checked off a box—Korda was for professional advancement, Ballard was for the maintenance of her screen image, the industrialist was for money, and, finally, Wolders was for love.

In Oberon, Grant got a whiff of a scent he recognized as close to his own—a grim childhood, vaulting ambition fueled by extraordinary looks, and relentless focus.

DOUGLAS FAIRBANKS JR. had gone into the Navy, and rented his house to Grant and Hutton for the duration of the war. Fairbanks was a rigorously correct gentleman and would usually indicate disapproval only in vague generalities, but he remembered that "Barbara had the better of this deal, as Cary was literally the only one of her attachments who neither wanted nor took anything from her. She was such a silly, affected girl—but so sweet in many ways—that I suspected Cary felt sorry for her and thought he could bring her down to earth. He failed, but Barbara was the loser, not Cary."

The house and twelve acres of grounds were at 1515 Amalfi Drive in Pacific Palisades—today it's the home of Steven Spielberg. Grant and Hutton got it for the bargain rate of $600 a month, with Hutton engaging three sets of servants—one group for days, one group for nights, and one group to take care of the other two sets of servants. The house didn't have enough room for the infusion of new employees, so they were parceled out among rented cottages and rooms scattered around the Palisades.

The Hutton-Grant marriage has never seemed to make much sense to posterity, but initially it made a great deal of sense to Hutton, Grant, and their friends. Hutton gave Grant gifts he would not have bought for himself—a Boudin, an Utrillo, some Tiepolo drawings. For a time they were happy.

He was delighted by her sense of humor—her nickname for him was General, after General U.S. Grant. "Barbara had a wonderful word for anything that lacked taste," Grant said.

> "My God, isn't that *ig,*" she'd say. We were once guests in an Italian villa in Hollywood. The house was in good taste except for one thing—there was a huge pink bar that stretched across one whole end of the living room. The owner was exceptionally proud of it, and she finally said, "Don't you just love the bar?" There was a pause, and then I said, "Yes, it's so wonderfully *ig.*" Well, I tell you, Barbara

went ape. She staggered around the room shrieking with delight and she was still doubled up with laughter when we reached the car.

Jill Esmond, Laurence Olivier's first wife, had left England accompanied by her son Tarquin after Olivier abandoned her for Vivien Leigh. They made the crossing to America on a ship called the *Fythia*. The seas were stormy, so the U-boats were in abeyance. Olivier was paying Esmond $800 a month separation and child support, and Esmond was hoping to supplement her alimony with income from acting in the movies. Observing all this was Tarquin: "It was my mother's tragedy that the love of her life was my father. It was my father's tragedy that the love of his life was Vivien."

In New York, Esmond and her son lived for six months with Jessica Tandy, whose first husband, Jack Hawkins, was fighting in Burma. "It was the west side, the wrong side, in a small apartment," remembered Tarquin Olivier. "And after six months my mother had a letter from her dear friend Joan Crawford, who wrote 'Come have a holiday with me.' So we moved to California and lived in the house next to Joan. And then my mother was taken up by Fox and after a year or two I was in movies too, because of my English accent."

Esmond took her son to the Hollywood Bowl, where he fell in love with classical music and began taking piano lessons. "After that, we moved to Pacific Palisades, a nice house at 1535 San Remo Drive. There weren't a lot of houses in the Palisades then; it was mostly lemon groves. We were across the street from Thomas Mann, who would walk over and give me his canceled stamps for my collection. I still have some of them—Hitler stamps and Hindenburg stamps."

Tarquin's hobby involved painting pictures of roses on bottles using a long-handled brush. The only problem was that there weren't that many bottles at his house, so he became proficient at scavenging bottles from the garbage cans of his neighbors. Up the hill from his house he found a can with wonderful bottles in all different shapes and sizes. "I was taking them out of the can and lining them up on the curb when this beautiful lady appeared and asked me, 'What are you doing?'

"I explained that I needed the bottles for my painting, and she said, 'You sound English. What's your name?'

"I told her, and she asked me if I was any relation to Laurence Olivier.

"I told her that I was his son, and she said, 'Well, I adore your parents. Come up to the pool.'"

Tarquin walked with the beautiful woman and found Cary Grant sitting by the pool. The woman explained the situation, and Grant called out to the butler "A bottle of rum for Mr. Olivier!"

The beautiful lady was Barbara Hutton, who had known both of Tarquin's parents in London. With a steady supply of bottles now assured, Tarquin and his mother began spending time at the Hutton-Grant household. Hutton told Esmond that she had fallen in love with Grant without qualifications because he was the only man she had ever known who was indifferent to her money. All he cared about was her.

"She was slim and beautiful," remembered Tarquin. "Cary obviously adored her. She was quite friendly as well. I had these hobby booklets showing what marvelous things you could make with things like matches and corks. I took the booklets to Barbara to show them to her and she was fascinated. We would sit together for hours making animals out of corks and matchsticks. She was very sweet to me."

Tarquin and his mother would often be dinner guests at the Hutton-Grant house. Grant was usually working late at the studio and was around mostly on the weekends. Tarquin and Hutton's son, Lance, used to climb trees together, despite the fact that Tarquin didn't particularly like Lance because he struck Tarquin as "a bit of a thug."

Grant obviously felt protective about his new wife, and tried to limit her access to reporters, on whose attentions she had become oddly dependent. He fired her publicist. "I did the best that could be done," he said. "God knows I've had some idiotic notoriety and I realize that at least she could hide behind that. It took the onus off her and it was helpful. During that time she was moderately happy. She was only recognized when she was out with me."

But over time, the misalliance between them became obvious. Hutton had no discernible purpose beyond a very occasional game of tennis during the day and hosting dinner parties at night. Grant tended toward the industrious, liked order, liked routine, and wasn't particularly social. Hutton gradually realized that Grant was quite different from his screen image—as she put it, he wasn't "fun, laughing, and naughty all the time."

He would come home from the studio after a long day and find a party in progress. After a quick round of hellos, he would ask for a bowl of soup to be sent up and go to bed in time to get up at five the next morning. "If one more phony noble had turned up, I would have suffocated," Grant would say later. Silence began to take precedence over communication. Grant commented that "I was ostracized by all the people I hoped to be ostracized by, and I couldn't have been happier."

On the deeper level, it was a repetition of the pattern he had evinced with Virginia Cherrill, a classic trauma psychology: approach and retreat, exuberance followed by depression and/or rejection, and it would be the norm for Grant's relationships with women for most of his life. Many—most—movie stars focus on projecting variations on some crucial aspect of their authentic personalities: John Wayne's emotional size, Bette Davis's neurotic need to dominate, etc. But Grant was not the smooth operator he tended to play, and this caused a personality that was already divided to become even less coherent.

Tarquin Olivier's story of the final rupture is illustrative. "Cary worked long hours, and didn't get home till seven or eight o'clock. Hutton would often dine alone and got a bit bored. One night he came home and, affecting his Cockney accent, said, 'How's my darling little fat pooch?'"

Grant was referring to her as an adored puppy, but Hutton thought he was referring to her stomach. "The use of that word provoked disaster," said Tarquin Olivier. "She had had a baby, and her waist was not what it was when she was eighteen. With nothing much else to occupy her time, she began obsessing about her weight and the resulting dieting." Grant had plenty of psychological tics of his own, but anorexia was not among them. Hutton became obsessed about her waistline and went on what was referred to as a "coffee diet," which consisted of RyKrisp and caffeine. Grant began pulling away.

Ultimately, the sense is that Grant began to chafe about all the time he had to spend with his wife, despite the fact that one of the reasons he had married her was because he saw her as a reclamation project. "Barbara was more screwed up than I was," Grant would tell a girlfriend decades later. "All she would eat was RyKrisp. She was stick thin. She stayed in bed all day with two female companions holding court beside her. I felt as if I had to ask their permission to talk to my own wife."

Hutton's circle had no more affection for Grant than he did for them. "I don't care how many six-figure donations Grant made to the war effort, he was stingy as hell," said Dudley Walker, his valet in this period.

> Here's somebody who never in his life picked up a tab in a restaurant, if he could help it. And if he did, he'd spend an hour recalculating the waiter's figures. He ran around the house turning off lights to save electricity. . . . He was too cheap to enjoy his own wealth.
>
> He had these four silver-veined crystal liquor bottles, and he used to put little marks on the bottles to see if anyone was knocking it off behind his back. It was all Barbara's liquor anyway. She was paying ten dollars for tea and ten dollars for bacon and ten dollars for chicken from some guy out here on the Strip who was black market. The pantry bill alone, what with help, came to thirty five hundred dollars a month, and all that was being paid by her. But Grant was still worrying about it. He begrudged the help every bottle of Coke they took from the pantry. His rule was no soda between meals, only with your meal. If he caught you drinking a soda, he docked it out of your pay.

According to Walker, the only reason the help stuck around was Hutton, who gave beautiful Christmas gifts and expensive watches at Easter, even gave away her dresses and jewelry after she'd worn them. "You were lucky with Grant if he gave you a five-dollar bottle of men's cologne once a year for Christmas. . . . And he was a bad drinker. He would get real nasty and cold. He would become sadistic. He could be a terrible bastard, that one."

Besides the first sign of what would become Hutton's full-blown anorexia was severe jealousy. Hutton accused her husband of having an affair with Ginger Rogers, which just might have been true although probably not until he and Hutton had separated. Hutton had previously come up with the idea of acting opposite her husband in *Mr. Lucky*, which RKO thought was a dandy idea and Grant thought was "insane." (Grant's careful tending of his career absolutely forbade fliers with amateurs, even if he happened to be married to them.)

Freddy Brisson said that Hutton

> wanted someone to be at home all the time. It was a shame, because Cary loved her. And he was a good influence. Barbara . . . gained

confidence. She no longer felt pangs of guilt because she had money and others didn't. He gave her perhaps the best time she ever had. He was absolutely sweet to her. Until Cary came along, I don't think Barbara was ever exposed to the real world. In the real world, every marriage has its ups and downs. In the real world, people go out and earn a living. But for some reason she rejected the real world. She wanted to inhabit a world of her own creation, a world of unicorns and winged white horses.

What seems to have kept the marriage going as long as it did was Grant's affection for Lance Reventlow, and his desire for another child. According to Hutton, she had three miscarriages in three years. According to Grant, Hutton couldn't get pregnant at all because she had had one ovary removed after Lance was born—part and parcel of her addiction to unnecessary surgery. "Barbara was cut to ribbons long before I knew her," Grant said, asserting she was covered with surgical scars that were generally out of sight. She was, he said, a guinea pig for surgeons.

As for Lance, the boy permanently endeared himself to his stepfather by answering the phone one day and greeting the caller with, "I'm sorry, Mr. Grant can't come to the phone now. He's in confidence." Grant thought it an eminently superior term to "conference," and refused to correct Lance.

"He was a marvelous kid and he helped me realize what I was missing by not having children," he would say years later. "The boy loved me so much he sometimes called himself Lance Grant, which enraged his father, who was always battling with Barbara about the boy."

In mid-1944, Hedda Hopper got Hutton to sit still for an interview. "Oh, if only Cary and I could have a bay some day," she told Hopper. ("Bay" seems to have been Hutton's goo-goo talk for "baby.") "Cary and I both love children. We'd like to have at least three. We're praying, both of us." (Hopper's editor cut Hutton's desire for three children.)

Hutton described her average day, keeping an admirably straight face in the process. In the mornings she played tennis. In the afternoon she would go to the beach to swim or ride with her son, and in the evening she read. When Grant was around they played gin rummy, because Grant didn't like bridge. Grant and Hutton had separate bedrooms, his much larger one reached by going through hers. "This room was built by Doug Fairbanks Jr.," Hutton explained, "and he had lived a long time in England where we all know the man of the house thinks of his own comfort first."

"She so much resembles a delicate Dresden china doll," wrote Hopper in the unedited manuscript.

> A frail shepherdess, I think, comes closer to what I mean. So little, so appealing. . . . Barbara is the shyest, most self-effacing little thing I've ever seen. . . . The love of Barbara and Cary Grant is so deep that I think there's little likelihood of their drifting apart. I'm on a limb saying that, knowing well that nearly every "ideal" Hollywood marriage has hit the rocks sooner or later. But with these two, that ol' devil career is no hazard. Barbara yearns only to be wife, mother and chatelaine.

Grant made sure to be out of the house during Hopper's interview; the stated excuse was a conference with his agent at Lake Arrowhead. Perhaps pique was the reason for Hopper's shot at Grant: "There's a quality of charm of Valentino about Cary, [but] without Rudolph's ingratiating gentleness."

Even though he was only a child, Tarquin Olivier had felt the enveloping chill. "Besides the full-blown anorexia, she started having guests to give her something to fill the time, and Cary got bored with her and left. And that was the end of that."

Grant and Hutton separated in August 1944, with no specific reasons given beyond "Cary isn't happy." They reconciled in October and separated for good in February 1945. In July, Hutton filed for divorce saying Grant caused her "grievous mental distress, suffering and anguish," which seemed to be the result of his disinclination to pretend he was interested in her dinner guests. That same month, he renounced all claim to her money in order to speed up the uncontested divorce, which was granted in August 1945 and became final on September 1, 1946.

Grant and Hutton stayed friendly until her death in 1979. There would be occasional telegrams wishing her a happy birthday or a Merry Christmas, signed by Grant and his wife of the moment, the latter signature presumably to forestall any Hutton fantasies of a reconciliation. "I loved Cary the most," Hutton told one friend. "It didn't work out, but I loved him. . . . I was always my own worst enemy, but my husbands for the most part were pretty rotten, except for Cary Grant. But then he was only a dream."

People noticed that Grant spoke of her with more fondness than he did any of his other wives save Betsy Drake. Grant's final verdict on his second wife was blunt. "I doubt if anyone ever understood Barbara. But then I doubt if Barbara ever understood herself."

Hutton married four more times. After the marriage to Grant was over, she was complaining to her aunt Marjorie Merriweather Post. "Maybe I just haven't met the right man yet," Barbara said.

"Nonsense," replied her aunt. "You've already had too many husbands. You must be doing something wrong."

"Like what?"

Post thought about it for a moment. "Have you tried rotating your hips? I'm told it makes it much better for the man."

WORLD WAR II WAS THE LAST TIME the studio system existed free from crisis; it was hard to make a movie that lost money, and the studios were at full employment. Jill Esmond began getting work at MGM in movies like *Random Harvest* and *The White Cliffs of Dover*, and she and her son observed the casual cruelties of a system where the studio usually had the upper hand.

Tarquin had been madly in love with Judy Garland since he saw *The Wizard of Oz* and when he was working at MGM he sent her a bouquet. This prompted Dame May Whitty and C. Aubrey Smith to give a reception so Tarquin could meet his idol. In a panic attack, he lost his voice, but Garland didn't mind.

> Judy was heavenly. I spent quite a few weekends with her. She was married to David Rose at the time, and she took a liking to me. I think she was scoping out children in preparation to have one of her own. She conceived, but the studio told her that a child wasn't in their plans for her. So she had the child removed, and that's what triggered a lifetime of uppers and downers.

Fay Wray and Robert Riskin, her second husband, moved back to Hollywood in September 1945 after his wartime work for "Wild Bill" Donovan. They hosted a party for their friends Jo and Flo Swerling and invited a group of loyal friends: Grant, Loretta Young, Irene Selznick. During the party, Grant sidled up to Riskin and said, "Be good to her. I was *so* in love with her. But I wouldn't have been a good husband. I pay too much attention to the position of the sofa."

After more than a decade in front of the cameras, Grant was particularly attuned to the nature of celebrity. When he was making a movie, Grant didn't wear much makeup, preferring to define himself by being darker than anybody else on screen—the Fairbanks rule. He correctly sensed that a tan masculinized and amplified his already dark good looks. He preferred a natural tan, but said that he would resort to what was reported as Ben Nye #3, which he would recommend to younger actors if they asked.*

Grant continued with the occasional radio program, especially for William Spier, the husband of Kay Thompson. Spier produced a show called *Suspense*, and his basic gimmick consisted of casting actors against type—Boris Karloff playing a henpecked husband, Jimmy Stewart a murderer, etc.

Grant would do interviews with trusted journalists, and once or twice would even indulge in a guest appearance in a movie, as with a walk-on in Mervyn LeRoy's charming romantic comedy *Without Reservations*, starring Claudette Colbert and John Wayne. That came about only because of his friendship with LeRoy. It was a mark of the respect Grant had for LeRoy, because he tended to be leery about in-jokes unless he was the one making them.

Socially, Hollywood was a hotbed in these years, because most people were in town most of the time. The MGM contingent centered around Gene Kelly's house, where furiously competitive games were the rule, whether volleyball or a version of charades that was known as

---

* Ben Nye, the highly respected head of the 20th Century–Fox makeup department, retired from the studio in 1967, as *Planet of the Apes* was going into production and just about the same time he started marketing his own line of makeup. But Grant was retired by that time, so could never have used Ben Nye #3. The makeup artist and film historian Michael Blake believes it's probable that Nye mixed a base color expressly for Grant's particular needs that might have been similar to Ben Nye #3. It's also possible that he used a Max Factor base that Grant liked.

The Game. If Kelly's side lost, there would be hell to pay. "If it weren't for *you* . . ." he would yell at a $5,000-a-week star. The main event at Kelly's house took place on Saturday night, where you'd find MGM stalwarts such as Judy Garland, Mickey Rooney, Frank Sinatra, Kay Thompson, Lena Horne, Betty Comden, and Adolph Green, as well as outsiders—David Selznick and Tyrone Power.

Then there were the Sunset Strip revels, Ciro's and Mocambo, where the elite went to eat. Grant would occasionally be seen at public events like film openings or luxe private parties, but he was regarded as more or less a loner, one who rarely threw a party of his own.

Grant's address book from this period reveals his friends were mostly professional. There were listings for his broker (Neale Cole), his lawyer (Morton Garbus), his tailor, his bootmaker, his tennis pro. There were also addresses and phone numbers for Fred Astaire, his old vaudeville partner Don Barclay, Rosalind Russell, and Freddie Brisson, James Cagney, Gene Tierney and Oleg Cassini, Ronald Colman, Dorothy di Frasso, Clifford Odets, Cole Porter, Diego Rivera, Jerome Zerbe, and Randolph Scott and his new wife, Pat, who were at 1038 Ocean Front in Santa Monica—down the street from where Scott and Grant had lived on and off for years. There was a list of birthdays for people he was close to: Randy (January 23), Danny Kaye (January 18), William Randolph Hearst (April 29), Frank Vincent (June 17), Howard Hughes (December 24), even Barbara Hutton (November 14).

CHAPTER ELEVEN

=========

None But the Lonely Heart began as a novel by Richard Llewellyn, the author of *How Green Was My Valley*. There is a possibly apocryphal anecdote that RKO paid $60,000 for the property because Charles Koerner, then running the studio, heard that Grant told someone that he liked the book.

With the rights in hand, Koerner called Grant. "Well, Cary," said Koerner over the phone, "we've bought that story for you, but I'm a little vague about the story line, and I want you to give [the producer] Dave [Hempstead] a brief resume of it."

"What story?" asked Grant.

"*None But the Lonely Heart*," said Koerner.

"I haven't read it," said Grant. "A friend of mine told me he thought it was good. That's all I know about it."

It's the sort of story implying a slap-happy groping in the dark that writers of a certain generation liked to tell about Hollywood. In any case, the project went ahead; the script was assigned to Clifford Odets. Grant liked Odets and liked his script, and went to bat to have Odets direct the picture—his first. RKO was not about to refuse Grant anything after his string of hits, so they agreed to Odets and agreed to pay Grant $100,000 plus 10 percent of the producer's gross after $1.5 million.

Perhaps the failure of his second marriage impelled Grant to the most searching work of his life—*None But the Lonely Heart* constitutes his only real examination of his own miserable beginnings and character. "Cary wanted to be a serious actor, and he didn't feel that he was," said Walt Odets, the psychologist son of Clifford Odets. "*None But the Lonely Heart* was an attempt at serious acting, and it's also a story about himself, about Archie Leach."

The script allowed Grant to tap into all his reserves of resentment and anger, as well as touching directly on the pain between a mother and a son, each of whom struggles to express their love for each other, neither of whom can be made whole by that love. Not surprisingly, a lot of people around Grant—his agent Frank Vincent among them— were against the project. Grant had taken twelve years to establish a franchise persona and here he was threatening to blow it up by handing it off to Clifford Odets, of all people.

Since *Waiting for Lefty*, Odets had been the great white hope of the Group Theatre specifically and the American theater generally. After *Waiting for Lefty* he wrote *Awake and Sing!* and *Golden Boy* and appeared on the cover of *Time* magazine. Damaged by the miserable marriage of his parents, Odets vibrated with ideas and emotions, was obsessed with everything he wasn't accomplishing. The writer's intensity could wear out his friends in the Group Theatre. The ones who loved him were led by Harold Clurman, who said, "To be near him was like being near a stove on which a whole range of savory foods was standing ready to be served." Stella Adler wasn't so sure: "Clifford, if you don't turn out to be a genius, no one will ever forgive you."

Elia Kazan was somewhere in the middle: "Everyone wanted to meet him, look him over, ask him questions, listen to what he had to say—and fuck him." Odets was not a handsome man, but he had an electric personality and an insightful intelligence that earned him relationships of varying degrees of seriousness with women as varied as Luise Rainer (his first wife), Frances Farmer (a mistress), Fay Wray (another mistress), and Betty Grayson (his second wife). He and Grant found that they had all sorts of things in common, among them a sneaking feeling that Fay Wray was the one that got away. She would write of Odets, "He was intense—if velvet is intense—so smooth and softly thoughtful was the texture of his comments. His gray eyes widened behind his horn-rimmed glasses when an idea sparked his interest. He walked easily, rhythmically, quietly, like a moccasined Indian."

Kazan knew all about Odets; he had been the angry worker yelling "He's my own lousy brother!" at the end of *Waiting for Lefty*, and had starred in Odets's *Night Music*. They would remain close long after the Group Theatre shattered like a pane of sugarglass. *Night Music* didn't run long, but Walter Bernstein, later to be a noted screenwriter, saw the play and thought Kazan "had no great range, but he was mesmerizing. You did not take your eyes off him. He told me once, long after he had quit acting . . . that he would liked to have played Richard III. He knew what he had."

Kazan knew about compromise, but it could honestly be said that he rarely compromised in his work. The same could not be said of Odets, although in retrospect his reputation for selling out is wildly overstated—if writing *Sweet Smell of Success* is selling out, the line forms on the right.

Odets first came to Hollywood in 1936 to write *The General Died at Dawn* for Lewis Milestone and found the weather, the money, and the women to his liking. Despite that, whenever he was in Los Angeles, his conversation primarily centered on how much he missed New York, and how he couldn't wait to get back. But first there was the matter of making *None But the Lonely Heart*.

"First day of shooting," said leading lady Jane Wyatt, "Cary strolls up to me and says this is the first time on-screen he's ever played himself." Wyatt said that the film's most prominent case of nerves was not Grant, but Ethel Barrymore, who hadn't made a movie in twelve years. "[She] was over the top until Cary worked with her and got her to be minimalist. She got the supporting Oscar because of his generosity in showcasing her."

The other leading lady was June Duprez, best known for the Alexander Korda version of *The Thief of Baghdad*. Duprez found that Odets didn't work on line readings but on mood. "Ohhh, what I learned from Clifford," remembered Duprez.

I learned my craft from him. I mean, I learned how to act. Just by the way he directed. . . . To give you an illustration of what Clifford did as a director [Cary Grant and I] had just come home and we were standing outside the front door, and there was a sort of "good night" scene; and Odets said, "You're there and you're very relaxed. I just want you to feel that you've almost been to bed together, or you're expecting to be." It was all that sort of yawny, very relaxed sort of thing. . . . He just very simply gave you the feeling that he wanted. And you often played right against the actual lines. It was extraordinary, it made it all very real.

Grant was likewise seduced. He was worried about a scene that he thought was overly talky and didn't go anywhere. Odets calmed him by saying, "This man is too insecure to leave a silence." Grant realized that a good writer inserts meaning between the lines as well as within the lines.

June Duprez was no different than any other woman: "I had a terrific sort of crush on him [Odets] while we were making the film." Contrarily, "I never thought anything about Cary Grant at all. Nothing. But there was something about Clifford. He had this extraordinary sort of intensity. It was very flattering to feel that somebody could get so *inside* you and bring that out."

Grant echoed Duprez but from the male point of view: "I enjoyed his stentorian convictions and the courage he has to emphatically proclaim his ever-changing beliefs. A stimulating, generous man."

Grant's tetchy temperament was mostly absent while *None But the Lonely Heart* was made. He loved Odets, he loved the script, and he wanted the picture to be a success. Besides their own growing friendship, there was another thing they had in common—they were both close with Irene Mayer Selznick. Odets found her "an antidote to Hollywood." She would visit Odets at his house in the Hollywood Hills where he was accompanied only by his latest writing project and a standard poodle named Clovis. They would talk and Odets would cook for her, which Irene found enchanting. The relationship sustained because sex never reared its ugly head.

While *None But the Lonely Heart* was shooting, Odets began raving about Grant and his performance to Irene. Irene had known Grant since he had been Archie Leach, and she seems to have always thought of him that way—being Louis B. Mayer's daughter meant she had an innately blasé attitude regarding actors.

Irene thought Grant and Odets were an improbable combination, but Odets insisted that Grant was special. Irene visited the set and found that Odets was right. "Cary's serious side had depth; his charm was just a lovely bonus. I think perhaps Cary was the best present

Clifford gave me." The two formed a bond; after Irene left her husband and Hollywood behind, Grant would invest modest amounts of money in the plays she produced, among them *A Streetcar Named Desire*.

Grant loved the finished picture, but Jane Wyatt had her doubts. "Cary truly burrowed inside Ernie Mott. He should have gotten the Oscar. But his film fans hated him as less than glamorous and he never tried that again. . . . I didn't like Odets' direction. It needed the sure touch of a [John] Ford. Clifford wrote it, but he was trying too hard to direct."

None But the Lonely Heart is a strange, haunting picture without any noticeable forward movement until halfway through, when George Coulouris enters as the Satan character, nicely named Jim Mordinoy, who tempts Ernie Mott to the dark side. Until then, it's a succession of scenes that involve people struggling to connect and failing. "Did you love my old man?" Ernie asks his mother. "Love's not for the poor, son," she replies. "No time for it." All these lost souls wandering in the dark undoubtedly appealed to Grant as a true picture of life as he knew it, but it's dramatically repetitive. That said, the totally committed performances and the mood sustain the picture.

"I'm a lone wolf, barking in the corner," says Ernie Mott to one of the girls he loves, "plain disgusted with a world I never made and don't want none of." Ernie's alternatives are limited to being either a victim or a thug; the problem is, "Suppose you don't want to be neither, like me; not the 'are, and not the 'ound. Then what?"

Grant's performance is less of a revelation to modern viewers—he would play dark and bitter in *Notorious*, among other movies—but in 1944 it had to be startling. Except for the hard fact that embittered men in the slums of London don't look like Cary Grant, he's completely believable as a grudge-holder who can't quite bring himself to be as open as he needs to be if he is to find the love that might save him. Any competent actor can communicate passionate primary emotions like anger, but Grant does something infinitely subtler; he makes Ernie Mott indignant. Ernie has gifts—perfect pitch, for one thing—but refuses to take advantage of them. His only real friend is a bull terrier, and each of them is careful not to ask too much from the other.

Like Archie Leach, Ernie wants out of the life he was born into, and he's willing to do almost anything to get someplace else. Also like

Archie Leach, Ernie desperately wants his mother's love and approval, but she can't give him what he needs, any more than he can give her what she needs. In a devastating farewell scene, as she lies in a prison hospital dying of cancer, they fail each other one last time.

Odets's talent shows in the unforgiving, recriminatory relationships, the unexpectedly touching June Duprez, the sense of ethnic struggle in the pawnbrokers played by Konstantin Shayne and Roman Bohnen as quintessential members of the Jewish underclass.

The film ends more or less where it started, except this time the winds of war are everywhere, and Ernie's survival remains an open question. In a time of prevailing mindless propaganda about the triumph of the human spirit, the unrelieved gloom of *None But the Lonely Heart* must have been a bracing, if unwanted shot to the audience's chops.

Jane Wyatt was right; John Ford would have been the perfect director for the film. He would have cut some of the repetition and given the film more visual power. Part of the problem was that, as James Wong Howe observed, "Clifford Odets had no knowledge of camera. He was a good dramatist, but he didn't understand film technique." (Howe photographed *The Story on Page One*, Odets's second directorial effort, which is less ambitious than *None But the Lonely Heart*.)

Even with Ford's visual mastery, it is doubtful that he would have gotten the rigorous, astringent performances Odets gets from Barry Fitzgerald and Ethel Barrymore—Ford would probably have replaced Barrymore with Jane Darwell. Under Odets's direction, Fitzgerald refuses to twinkle and Barrymore is every bit Grant's equal in the bitterness sweepstakes. *None But the Lonely Heart* is a one-off, and an extraordinary directorial debut that is in some ways every bit as memorable as a masterpiece. As for Grant, he got a nomination for Best Actor for his performance, but it was the year of *Going My Way* and Bing Crosby's smooth, soothing priest.

None But the Lonely Heart was the beginning of one of the deepest friendships of Grant's life. He and Odets shared questing natures, a strong sense of shame about the crevices in their characters, and a deep-seated wariness about Hollywood and themselves—a basic emotional skittishness. Luise Rainer described the morning after she and Odets were married in January 1937. Rainer ran toward him to leap into his arms but Odets drew away, and the moment died.

When Rainer sent Odets a telegram announcing she was pregnant, he replied with another telegram saying, "Dear Luise, Will wire you Monday because now I don't know what to say Love, Clifford." Rainer's immediate response was to get an abortion; her secondary response was to see a lawyer. They were divorced after slightly more than three years of marriage.

JUST BEFORE *None But the Lonely Heart* was released, Grant sent a bound copy of the script to Odets, who responded with a letter:

> Thank you for the very beginning of the film. For the intuition which made you feel the novel as a picture and for what seemed to me the surprising fact that you thought I could direct it as well as write it. . . .
>   You will be proud of your performance. I know that I am! Such reality, constantly moving and warm, I have seldom seen in any film of any nation. It is something new in films, that's all.

This sounds like fervent apple-polishing, but it was sincere. In a letter to the columnist Leonard Lyons, Odets wrote about how much he enjoyed working with his star. "[Grant] . . . is sweet and decent, a good man and, as you will see . . . a surprisingly good actor. What [do] I think of the picture? You will not be ashamed of me."

The film received the sort of respectful, bewildered notices common to dark mood pieces. James Agee thought it was an "almost-good film . . . but I was impressed . . . because Odets was more interested in filling his people with life and grace than in explaining them, arguing over them, or using them as boxing gloves." Manny Farber didn't buy it. "I felt an essential lack of the evil, hardness, hunger, loneliness and frustration that seem to be what the film was interested in. Instead there is a great deal of lush, pretty lighting, settings, view, events, talk and people. The central material is constantly being obliterated." He took particular objection to "Cary Grant's consciousness of his own acting and posing." Other people thought better of it; Jean Renoir thought it was a masterpiece, and it has held up far better than most pictures of its vintage.

As for the audience, people in the big cities tended to like it, while people in small towns recoiled. *Motion Picture Herald* ran a weekly feature called "What the Picture Did for Me," in which small-town exhibitors got a chance to weigh in on the films they ran. An exhibitor in Westby, Wisconsin, let *None But the Lonely Heart* have it with both barrels: "The worst chunk of film I have ever seen. My rather limited number of customers went out of their way to tell me the same thing. Most of them were on their way out after wasting their time through half of it. Even those I counted among the intelligentsia did not like it. I pulled it after one show."

Reviews like that from bread-and-butter venues usually imply a disaster, but *None But the Lonely Heart* did better than a lot of people expected—a brave *flop d'estime*. Made for a reasonable $1.3 million, it lost a modest $72,000. But it was an experiment Grant was careful never to repeat. "The only time I played myself was in *None But the Lonely Heart*, and nobody wanted to see the real me," he said. "So I put Archie Leach away and went back to being Cary Grant."

Clifford Odets remained proud of the picture for the rest of his life. "He valued taking an actor like Cary and being able to give him a different type of opportunity," said Walt Odets. The two men remained close for the rest of Odets's life; Grant helped him out with loans from time to time and regularly let the writer stay at his house in Palm Springs.

In 1947, the movie was singled out by Lela Rogers, Ginger Rogers's blunt object of a mother, as a "perfect example of the propaganda that Communists like to inject." Rogers went on to accuse Odets of being a communist, citing Ernie Mott's line, "You're not going to get me to work here and squeeze pennies out of little people who are poorer than I am."

DOUGLAS FAIRBANKS JR. got out of the Navy at the end of 1945 laden with medals and honors. He arrived back at Westridge to find to his dismay that he needed to spend a great deal of money he didn't have repairing the house and grounds.

Fairbanks noted with approval the large sums of money that Grant had donated each year to British War Relief, but Barbara Hutton had different ways of contributing to the war effort. She had ordered the gardener to dig up grass and shrubs in order to plant potatoes. Rose gardens were infested with weeds, and various fruit, date, and palm trees had been untended.

In addition, Hutton had kept the heat on through both winter and summer, so that some of Fairbanks's prized antique furniture had cracked and buckled. Fairbanks and his wife felt compelled to ask for financial redress, which might have broken the friendship with Grant but didn't. Hutton's lawyers were used to this sort of thing and sent a check with a minimum of fuss. Fairbanks didn't hold a grudge.

"It was nearly impossible to get angry with Barbara for long," Fairbanks wrote near the end of his life. "She had been so spoiled that it was not really her fault that reality was no more believable than an old novel or movie—to take or leave as the mood struck her."

IF ANY MOVIE could have destroyed its star, it would have been *Night and Day*, a shambles of a fantasia on the theme of Cole Porter. The musical numbers aren't bad—Mary Martin sings "My Heart Belongs to Daddy," among others—but the script beggars belief and for once director Michael Curtiz is completely defeated.

Jack Warner had agreed to pay Porter a whopping $300,000 for the rights to his catalogue of songs and his life. The problem was that nothing bad ever happened to Porter until a horse fell on him in 1937. As Orson Welles said, "What will they use for a climax? The only suspense is—will he or won't he accumulate ten million dollars?" Jack Warner opened negotiations with Grant in April 1944. Grant had met Porter years earlier through the Countess Dorothy di Frasso, and the composer thought Grant was ideal casting. Grant's contract wasn't finalized until almost exactly a year later, largely because of what seems to have been anguish over his second failed marriage.

The contract was complicated because Warners was using one of Columbia's commitments with Grant. There was the matter of Grant's contractual expectations at Columbia, which he expected Warners to honor. Billing, for instance. Jack Warner's assistant Steve Trilling noted, "If and when the Cary Grant Columbia assignment is consummated [it is necessary that] we execute a document with Grant assuring him first star billing and no one else co-starred unless they are acknowledged stars, as that has been an understanding with Columbia for the past several years, even though not so stated in the contract."

But even when the deal with Columbia was arranged, Grant refused to sign the contract. "In [Frank] Vincent's opinion, because of Grant's mental condition he possibly would not be ready to make a picture for an indefinite time—certainly not by November 1 or 15," Steve Trilling wrote to Jack Warner on September 26, 1944. "Might be a few months from now, or might be six months from now—and Grant wanted you to thoroughly understand this before giving away one of our big assets to effect the Columbia assignment."

Trilling pointed out that this was no way to run a movie studio, and Vincent agreed, finally saying that perhaps the studio needed to think about alternative casting possibilities. A few days later, Vincent reiterated his client's position. "Grant has too much regard for J.L. [Jack Warner] personally not to be very honest and tell him now, rather than bring it up later, that in his present frame of mind he could not give a good performance—it is something much more important than making a picture with his whole life's happiness at stake." Vincent went on to say that Grant would not be ready to work until December, January, or perhaps as long as six months. Grant's best offer was that he would not make any other movie until he made *Night and Day*, but he could not in good conscience commit to any date at all.

When Grant finally signed his contract, one clause specified that Warners rather than Grant pay Frank Vincent his commission; another was that the studio outfit Grant's home with two premium 16mm projectors, "complete with change-overs, and one (1) screen." With movie projectors, he needed prints, and Warners also agreed to give him 16mm prints of his Warner Bros. pictures.

Between Grant's emotional situation and the difficulties of constructing a script, there was a feeling of unease about the picture from the beginning. Even before they started shooting, assistant director Eric Stacey asked a studio functionary how best to proceed with Grant. Stacey needed Grant at the studio for wardrobe and makeup tests, but according to Grant's contract they had to start paying him when he reported to work for music rehearsals. Stacey was worried that if Grant started on payroll too early, the film would be over budget before it began.

The producer was Arthur Schwartz, a songwriter who had never produced a movie before. Steve Trilling sent a script draft by Stephen Morehouse Avery to Philip Epstein, half of the brilliant twins who wrote *Casablanca* and *Yankee Doodle Dandy*, among others. Trilling wanted Epstein's opinion.

"I read it and I really feel that if it were shot just the way it is now everybody might be pleasantly surprised," Epstein began.

Many individual scenes are not bad at all—they could be improved of course (the Bible was re-written several times and being orthodox I feel the first version was the best) [but] lots of scenes are superior to the average musical picture dreck (*Music for Millions, Thrill of a Romance*, etc.).

The story of course is not good but how many musical pictures have good stories (*Yankee Doodle*'s story stank—I defy you to tell it back to me—my listening salary is the same as my writing salary).

Having buried the lede, Epstein then dropped the bomb:

The point is this: I'm pretty sure that under the pressure of day-to-day on-the-set changes, the results might be pretty tragic—and I say that knowing that Steve Avery is a very good man. Cary Grant just hasn't got a part commensurate with his stature as a star and I doubt if anything at this this late date will change it.

Epstein closed by offering a less than helpful suggestion: "What do you think of the idea of making Cole Porter a producer and having him do the life of Arthur Schwartz? I'm charging you absolutely nothing for this idea."

A production date of April 30, 1945, came and went while new writers struggled. The film finally got under way on May 12, 1945, and immediately devolved into a series of competing tantrums from Grant and Curtiz, accompanied by demands from the Breen office to castrate Porter's suggestive lyrics. Grant's anxiety over another failed marriage was now topped off by the fact that he was utterly miscast. Many days he would halt production with some complaint. Grant insisted that he be allowed to supervise the costuming for both the male and female performers; another time he was upset because a quarter-inch of his cuffs were showing, whereas the proper length was only an eighth of an inch. At one point, Curtiz threatened to quit, and by the time the picture was halfway through production the director and his star were spending most of the day in their respective corners glaring at each other in mutual loathing.

When it came to Grant's complaints about the script, he was on solid ground. The dialogue was bad and there were no characters for the actors to play, other than Monty Woolley, who was playing Monty Woolley—as he always did.

Woolley presented his own set of problems—Eric Stacey sent a memo to Jack Warner informing him that Woolley had been late on several occasions because he was "under the influence of alcohol." Burdened by a miserable star and a drunken costar, the picture ground down. Grant brought on William Bowers to write just ahead of the camera. Bowers had done an uncredited polish for Grant on a recent picture, but he was rendered impotent by the intractable premise, as was everybody else.

Grant's costar Alexis Smith had just gotten married to Craig Stevens, and Grant offered her his gloomy accumulated wisdom on the subject of marriage: "Never get divorced. You may as well stick with this one because you just keep marrying the same person over and over."

Smith studied her leading man and noted "the way he never gave too much to a scene. He was a minimalist. You see, he was making love to the camera. His costars somehow got in the way, but he was only interested in how it all looked up on the screen."

Sixty-nine days into production, the unit manager wrote in a memo that "They do not know how the end of this picture is going to be done. They have been writing this story for two years and still it is not on paper." The ongoing problem for the writers was that Porter's homosexuality and his Boston marriage to his wife, Linda, were obviously off-limits, so the script devolved into lead-ins and lead-outs to the songs, with Porter's accident with a horse and its aftermath being saved for the climax. But the accident also presented a problem, because if the script got into the weeds of Porter's failed rehabilitations the picture would become incredibly grim, which nobody wanted. The best the roster of writers could come up with for Porter's distance in his marriage was a passionate attachment to show business—the same bland narrative Hail Mary that served as the reason for Al Jolson's failed marriages in *The Jolson Story* a few years later.

Grant clearly gave up on the picture; he plods through it with an air of grim determination that never even comes close to passing for engagement. He settles back into the position he had adopted in his earliest years in the movies—being photographed.

On the last day of production, Grant walked up to Michael Curtiz and told him, "If I'm chump enough ever to be caught working for you again, you'll know I'm either broke or I've lost my mind." Grant was not a man to casually burn bridges—he never worked for Curtiz again. Post-production ground along. On the day after Christmas, Grant was called to the studio for some dubbing, but Eric Stacey was sure to clear it with the studio first, just in case Grant charged overtime.

Grant knew he had just made a loudly barking dog. When the film was released in August 1946, *The New Yorker* review was particularly brutal:

> Although [Grant] is getting on in years now, he is compelled by the script to depict the composer . . . as a Yale undergraduate . . . and to indulge in such painful juvenile activities as leading a chorus through that song about Eli Yale and a bulldog. Apart from having to attend college at an age when most Yale men would be working for the Luce publications, Mr. Grant is forced to break into song every now and then, which is rather too bad, since his voice, although resonant, is no more mellifluous than the average subway guard's.

None of this mattered. *Night and Day* was the most expensive picture Warner Bros. made that year, at a staggering cost of $4.4 million—more expensive than *Gone With the Wind*. It earned $7.4 million, more than *Mildred Pierce*, more than *The Big Sleep*. It was Warners' second-highest grosser of the year, behind only *Saratoga Trunk*.

GRANT HAD HIRED A LAWYER named Stanley Fox to handle his divorce from Hutton. The firm of Fox, Goldman & Cagen was in the same building as Frank Vincent, and it's probable that Vincent referred his client to Fox. Vincent died in 1946, after which Grant bought Vincent's house on Beverly Grove Drive in Beverly Hills, where he lived, amidst nearly continual remodeling, for the rest of his life. Grant eventually replaced his late agent with Lew Wasserman, except he never actually signed the MCA agency agreement. When necessary, Wasserman and Stanley Fox would negotiate on Grant's behalf, and split the commission, a concession Wasserman made to nobody else. Fox became Grant's business manager and, eventually, business partner for the rest of the actor's life.

GRANT AND ALFRED HITCHCOCK had stayed in touch. In 1945, they were talking about a modern-dress version of *Hamlet* to be made for a new production company with Hitchcock's friend Sidney Bernstein as the third leg. The group planned to form a corporation to make several pictures, with Grant receiving about half of the stock. There was also the possibility of making the film in England, largely for tax reasons. Perhaps, wrote one of Hitchcock's lawyers, "the picture prior to release can be sold to the California company in consideration of the assumption of the liabilities incurred in the making of the picture. Such a sale would not result in any tax to the English company."

But the plans were stymied when Hitchcock and Grant were sued by one Irving Fiske, a playwright who had already written something called "Hamlet in Modern English." Hitchcock won the case when it finally came to court in 1954, but by that time Grant was too old to play Hamlet. Besides, Laurence Olivier's 1947 version had won the Oscar for Best Picture and there wasn't enough interest in another version to warrant going ahead.

The prospective *Hamlet* is interesting primarily because of Grant's willingness even to contemplate such a project, not to mention the complicated financial schemes underlying the movie in order to maximize profits and minimize taxes—a feature that would become a prominent part of Grant's professional raison d'être.

From one of his worst movies, Grant rebounded with what might have been his very best: *Notorious* got under way on October 22, 1945, with a budget of $1.7 million. Grant was on board for $75,000 as a down payment on 10 percent of the first $3 million in gross receipts. *Notorious* was the high-water mark of the Hitchcock-Grant collaborations; as Peter Bogdanovich nicely observed, "Hitch brought out the bass notes in Grant's persona," never more so than in *Notorious*.

The ostensible inspiration for the picture was a 1921 *Saturday Evening Post* serial by John Taintor Foote, but the actual inspiration was the loose confederation of Brits who did reconnaissance for MI6 during World War II—the Korda connection again. Hitchcock's friend and former screenwriter Charles Bennett and the actor Reginald Gardiner had been encouraged to go to bed with women with untoward fascist leanings—not that they needed much urging. One of Gardiner's affairs with a suspected Nazi became a problem in his marriage.

The idea of sex as just another tool for determining political loyalty interested Hitchcock, and beginning in late 1944, he and Ben Hecht—who was making $5,000 a week—constructed a script about duplicity, colliding motives, and conflicting loyalties. Audaciously, they made the ostensible heavy, eventually played by Claude Rains, more sympathetic than either of the leads. "The script writing moves thru a molasses covered paper," Hecht wrote to his wife, Rose, in early 1945, "but it moves." Indeed it did.

All this was theoretically under the watchful eye of David O. Selznick, but the producer was preoccupied by his careening, budget-busting production of *Duel in the Sun* as well as by generalized emotional chaos. Irene Selznick had left him, demanding he give up gambling and Jennifer Jones. He gave up neither and instead launched into *Duel in the Sun*. Selznick's original plan for *Notorious* was to star Joseph Cotten as Devlin, but Hitchcock wanted Cary Grant. Selznick thought Grant's salary, percentage, and general attitude were more trouble than they were worth. In Selznick's eyes, *Notorious* was one problem picture too many, said problem being that Hitchcock and Selznick basically didn't get along and Selznick didn't like the script outline.

And then Selznick made a crucial mistake, one of many he made in this period: he decided that *Duel in the Sun* would not be released by United Artists, but by the Selznick Releasing Organization—a company he intended to set up from scratch. This meant that he needed money, a lot of it, on top of the millions he was pouring into *Duel in the Sun*. He sold *Notorious* to RKO for $800,000, which included the script, Ingrid Bergman, and Hitchcock. Besides that, Selznick was to get 50 percent of the net profits. It was a steep deal, considering that RKO still had to ante up for Grant and pay for the actual production, but it worked out nicely for all concerned.

The sale was finalized in mid-July 1945, but Grant was tied up with *Night and Day* until October. As far as RKO was concerned, that was fine, because the script needed more work. They hired Clifford Odets. Ben Hecht had left, partially because he had a short attention span at the best of times—he was always juggling several scripts and probably had a more pressing deadline on another project. But Odets was a very strange choice, considering that Hitchcock was nothing if not a director of rapt visuals and story structure, and Odets was about character, not narrative.

Odets might have been hired at Grant's suggestion, but the problem with that possibility is that Hitchcock never included Grant in consultations about a script, or even asked his opinion, as, for instance, he regularly did with James Stewart on *Rear Window, The Man Who Knew Too Much*, and *Vertigo*—pictures on which Stewart was both a financial and creative partner. As Patrick McGilligan, Hitchcock's best biographer, says, "Hitchcock loved Grant, but didn't think of him that way."

Odets finished his 136-page script in late September. He ramps up the atmosphere, broadens the emotions of both Devlin and Alicia (Bergman), as well as the philosophical stasis of Alex Sebastian (Claude Rains). "That ocean doesn't stop," Alicia says to Devlin, before they kiss. "Far off the pounding surf. FADE OUT."

Selznick had no official leverage over the production at this point, but he let Hitchcock know that he hated the Odets script: "The characters have lost dimension," he wrote. Alicia had become "a cross between Bankhead and Bacall," and he asserted that the exposition was "bald" and the characters didn't "talk like real people." RKO thought it was imperative that Odets do a second draft.

"We all of us have to stop sometimes and seriously sum up, asking ourselves who and what we are," Devlin says to Alicia in the rewrite. "I won't stand here in moral judgment. But the past is a heap of dead leaves, and what I'm trying to do now is confirm in you your possibilities."

It sounds like something Odets would say to a girl he was trying to impress, and the overly earnest speech derails Devlin's deviousness and implacability, which in turn derails the suspense of the ending. Selznick was now seriously riled, and urged RKO to open their checkbook and once again pay Ben Hecht $5,000 a week. Hecht read Odets's script and didn't like it any more than Selznick had. In one marginal note next to some of Odets's dialogue, Hecht writes, "This is really loose crap!"

The final film is all Hitchcock and Hecht. The plot they came up with involves the American government pimping a woman to a Nazi sympathizer after she has already developed a well-earned reputation for sleeping around—an intriguing premise that cheerfully violated every component of the Production Code. The Breen office's voluminous file on *Notorious* attests to the difficult dance the filmmakers had to do throughout production and, beyond that, the difficulty of making any kind of story involving sex that the Code couldn't render infantile.

The RKO story editor sent the first-draft script to the Breen office in mid-May 1945, with the unusual request to give the script "your very earliest attention. If you have any queries on anything, will you please put a call through to me." Clearly, they knew they had a problem picture on their hands.

A week later, Breen's response was unyielding: "I regret to be compelled to advise you that the material, in its present form, seems to us to be definitely unacceptable under the provisions of the Production Code." The objections were almost entirely based on the character of Alicia, whom Breen termed "a grossly immoral woman, whose immorality is accepted 'in stride' in the development of the story and, eventually is portrayed as dying a glorious heroine. . . . There is, too, in contrast with her immoral characterization, an almost complete absence of what might be called 'compensating moral values.'"

Breen went on to suggest that the filmmakers consult with the FBI, the Navy, and the government of Brazil. "I think you know that the industry has had a kind of 'gentleman's agreement' with Mr. J. Edgar Hoover, wherein we have practically obligated ourselves to submit to him, for his consideration, and approval, stories which importantly involve the activities of the Federal Bureau of Investigation."

And so the juggling began. Hecht, Hitchcock, the RKO story editor, and Hitchcock's secretary Barbara Keon consulted with Breen's second-in-command, Geoffey Shurlock, and agreed that the character of Alicia "would be changed in such a way as to avoid any direct inference that she is a woman of loose sex morals." Hecht rewrote the ending so that Alicia could survive and go off with the hero.

In early July, a new draft went out to the Breen office and met with an identical response. "The present characterization of the girl as a woman of loose sex morals is unacceptable and could not be approved in a story of this sort." Specific objections were raised to some of Hecht's dialogue: "What this party needs—is a little gland treatment." Also noted was the frequent characterization of Alicia by the word "tramp."

What RKO hoped was the final script went out on September 19, and again Breen objected to the characterization of Alicia: "We suggest rewriting this sequence to get away from the present flavor that these officials know they are hiring a promiscuous woman. It might be possible to rewrite it so as to indicate that they decide to hire her because they know that Sebastian was once very much in love with her, omitting all innuendo as to her immoral character."

Hecht followed Breen's advice in regard to Sebastian and Alicia, and more or less finessed the rest. As they got closer to production, RKO began sending the Breen office pieces of the newly revised script as they emerged from Hecht's typewriter. On October 22, they sent fifty-four pages, then ten to fifteen pages at a time. Nothing was too petty for Breen's objections: "We suggest checking with your Brazilian technical expert as to the advisability of these derogatory references to Brazilian food." Pages were shipped off to Breen even after the picture started shooting. As Hitchcock was finishing the movie in late January, script pages were still being vetted by Breen.

This was a ridiculous way to make a movie, but it was part of the devil's bargain the studios had entered into in order to avoid censorship boards of varying standards in all forty-eight states. In June 1946, the Breen office reviewed the finished picture and didn't say a word about the extended love scene between Grant and Bergman in which they nuzzle and kiss for several minutes. Rather, they asked for the deletion of a scene between Alicia and the elderly yachtsman in the beginning of the picture in order to get away from the clear inference that they were sleeping together. Also, they wanted cuts to reduce the amount of drinking in the party sequence and the removal of a shot of a drunken woman's head in a man's lap. RKO agreed, and the cuts were made. The Breen office finally, grudgingly, issued a seal of approval for the picture.

Other than the internecine warfare with the censors, *Notorious* seems to have been a smooth shoot, allowing for the fact that Hitchcock refused to speed up his pace to hit a theoretical budget. He cared far more about the quality of his movies than he did his good relationship with the studio—or the Breen office—and wouldn't be rushed.

Hitchcock and Claude Rains bonded, and Ingrid Bergman's wounded Nordic sincerity proved a perfect counterpart to Grant's obsidian bleakness. Hitchcock and Ben Hecht had constructed a deep, dark part in Devlin, an FBI agent who's conflicted, manipulative, and angry. As David Thomson noted, "What it amounts to is taking the audience expectations—'Oh, it's Cary Grant again'—and letting us see a degree or two more deeply, without sacrificing fun, romance, adventure, and being at a popular movie." This is the film in which Grant gets to have it both ways—behind the rigorously maintained facade, he communicates the simmering rage that a wounded soul lugs around as a burden.

Grant found that he liked Ingrid Bergman a great deal. She was beautiful, but lots of actresses are beautiful. What made Bergman special was her indifference to her looks, her clothes, to everything except her art.

Bergman and Grant had a volatile screen chemistry—she was one of the few actresses who could rouse him from his tendency toward self-absorption. Like Grant, Bergman had a slow-burn sensuality that made them well matched. But that was as far as it went—he had no sexual interest in her. Even the famous love scene that went on for two and a half minutes failed to arouse the performers. Ben Hecht had scripted the scene with numerous double entendres, but Hitchcock told his actors to try improvising the dialogue between kisses. "Hitchcock said discuss anything you want to discuss," Grant said late in his life. The topic of discussion involved a chicken dinner. "We talked about who was going to wash the dishes. It's a very cuddly-looking scene. Noses are a difficult business in the kissing scenes." Hecht was unimpressed. "I don't get all this talk about a chicken," he said.

Grant usually projected something positive—wit, energy, impudence. But in *Notorious* he radiates only contempt and anger. It's a completely contained performance, and the clear implication is that if Devlin ever cuts loose, objects—or people—will be broken. It's a performance of ominous intent and it gives the film a malevolent energy.

After all the hassles with the Breen office, *Notorious* was finally released in July 1946 and acclaimed by critics and audiences alike. *Notorious* cost $2.7 million and returned $7.1 million in rentals for a clear profit of a million dollars. As for *Duel in the Sun*, it proved a great commercial success, but the profits were eaten up by the huge overhead of the Selznick Releasing Organization.

Bergman went to New York to publicize the movie and spent a lot of time with Grant. One night they walked in the rain down Fifth Avenue. They took their time window-shopping, each of them secure in the knowledge that they could afford anything they saw in the stores. At the hotel, undoubtedly by prearrangement, Grant introduced her to Howard Hughes, who was looking to add another notch to his belt. Irene Selznick joined them and they went dancing at El Morocco, where Hughes upped the ante.

"I'm so lonely, I'm so terribly lonely," Hughes told Bergman. "You know I have no friends."

Bergman wasn't buying it. "Then it must be your own fault, because you don't go out and look for friends. Anyway, I'm having a good time; you're not lonely tonight, are you?" Shallow expressions of muted sympathy were as far as Bergman would go with Hughes, probably because she was enmeshed in a serious affair with Robert Capa.

Grant and Hitchcock again began to discuss a partnership, either officially or unofficially. They began to work on a story called "Weep No More," but Grant was ultimately noncommittal. Besides, he didn't enjoy long lunches as much as Hitchcock. The project finally ran out of gas.

Hitchcock had come to the conclusion that Grant was the perfect leading man, a decision he never doubted, not even when Grant drove him crazy. Grant was almost always his first choice for every film, including *Rope*, the Patrick Hamilton play about homosexual thrill killers. Grant didn't say yes, and he didn't say no. Hitchcock's dream cast was Grant as the professor who introduces the two killers to Nietzsche, with the boys to be played by Montgomery Clift and Farley Granger—Hitchcock's malicious humor was tickled by the prospect of casting gay actors as gay characters.

But, as Arthur Laurents, who was working on the script, said, "Since Cary Grant was at best bisexual and Monty was gay, they were scared to death and they wouldn't do it." Grant and Hitchcock had an argument over the project, which ended with Hitchcock saying he would never work with the actor again—a vow he always found a way to ignore.

Decades later, when a friend told him how much he liked *Notorious*, Grant replied, "Yeah. That's the one Hitch threw to Ingrid." Hitchcock would try to make it up to him in the future; in *To Catch a Thief* and *North by Northwest*, he threw the pictures to Grant.

CHAPTER TWELVE

With ten years of above-the-title stardom behind him, Grant's modus operandi was now obvious. With the exception of *None But the Lonely Heart* or *Notorious*, Grant tended to stick to the sort of thing that had already proved successful for him. "It's his conviction that it's up to him to find out what people like in Grant," wrote Pete Martin, the Hollywood correspondent for *The Saturday Evening Post*.

> [Find out] what they expect of him, then do it. Many Hollywood stars don't see their own pictures. If they do, it's usually in the plush-insulated solitude of a studio projection room. Grant sees each of his films in the regular-run movie houses. He studies the reactions of different audiences. If one of his pieces of stage business or one of his gestures rings the bell, it's apt to be in his next picture two or three times.

Grant wasn't actually that programmed, but he did think along narrow lines. Personally, he went through the days with a touch of asperity that was not far below the surface, and he didn't care who knew it. Autograph seekers were a particular annoyance. He would often call them "morons," and refuse to submit to their requests. "Fifteen kids descend upon you," he complained. "It would be nice if they just said, 'How are you?' or 'It's good to see you,' but they say,

'If you don't sign our books, we won't go to see your lousy pictures.' My reaction is to say, 'Fine. Don't go.'"

Along with his sense of audience expectations, Grant had very finely attuned antennae for the political realities of Hollywood. He understood that a certain amount of clubbing was mandatory. "Grant patronized the Trocadero, my father's nightclub," said William Wilkerson III, the son of Billy Wilkerson, the publisher and editor of *The Hollywood Reporter.* "But my father would always complain that since Cary didn't drink, he couldn't make any money off him. Cary was a huge cheapskate. Not as bad as Myron Selznick, who never threw a party and was a herculean freeloader. Myron always won the door prize for cheap, but Cary was in the running."

Grant obviously didn't hold a grudge over Wilkerson's sneering articles about his relationship with Randolph Scott, or pretended not to.

Cary understood my father's basic vulnerability—that if you charmed and kow-towed to him, he would do anything for you. But if you lied to him or tried to sweep things under the rug, hell would have no fury like his.

Grant's English charm was front and center. Socially, Cary presented himself as the Cary Grant you saw in the movies. If he ever gardened, he probably gardened with a cravat. His charm was like an ectoplasmic shield around him; a lot of people were never aware of how cheap he was. I heard stories about people finding half-eaten sandwiches in his refrigerator because he wouldn't throw anything out.

Women *loved* him. He was quite intelligent and could charm the pants off anybody. He was the sort of man who's an asset in any social circumstance. A very smart cookie in that he seemed conscious of his limitations. He was one of the few English actors who had no real desire to play Shakespeare. All the other English actors had the theater and drama in their DNA. Cary knew he was a great light comedian, and for the most part he lived by that. You have to respect that level of self-awareness.

Grant would occasionally launch halfhearted defenses about the skinflint charge. "I had a valet once," he recalled as an old man. "Said I never picked up a dinner check. Now, how would he know that, since he never dined with us? The fact is, I didn't pick up dinner checks. It was arranged so that they were automatically sent to my house. He also said I was so cheap I cut the buttons off my old shirts before throwing them away. Well, why not? They were very good buttons, and it was nice to have them if I lost ones off my good shirts."

The image of Cary Grant rummaging through his button box looking for a match in order to get another year or two out of a shirt should be cherished—it would have made a great scene in a Cary Grant movie. This level of thrift was not an unknown trait in Hollywood. "My mother had that to some extent," said Victoria Riskin, the daughter of Fay Wray. "When she died, I found a box of buttons she had kept. And a box of safety pins of different sizes. And stamps that hadn't been canceled. That sort of thing is a response to early poverty—a sense that you never know when things are going to go south and what you might need when that happens."

Mostly, Grant was a guest rather than a host, but in March 1946 he made an exception, when he, James Stewart, Eddy Duchin, and screenwriter John McLain threw a party at the Clover Club on Sunset Boulevard. According to Jimmy Stewart it was Grant's idea. Mike Romanoff catered, and more than two hundred people were invited, including the Jack Warners, the Lew Wassermans, the Charlie Chaplins, the Henry Fondas, the Alfred Hitchcocks, L. B. Mayer, the Randolph Scotts, the Fred Astaires—everybody who was anybody.

Stewart's date was Rita Hayworth, newly sprung from her marriage to Orson Welles. "Around two o'clock or so," Stewart remembered, "Rita said, 'We've been working all week, and I'm tired.' So I took her home—and came back alone." When Stewart got back to the Clover Club, Hoagy Carmichael was playing the piano and Bing Crosby was singing.

Just another night in Hollywood.

RKO REMAINED COMMITTED to the Cary Grant business. Dore Schary, who was running production at the studio, cast him in *The Bachelor and the Bobby-Soxer*, alongside Myrna Loy and Shirley Temple. Grant's deal was $50,000 plus 10 percent of the producer's gross in excess of $500,000. The director—and target of Grant's ire—was a young émigré from radio and B movies named Irving Reis.

On the first day of shooting, Reis ordered a print of a Loy take, whereupon she asked for another chance because she thought she could do it better. Reis agreed, and agreed again when she asked for yet another take. Watching on the sidelines, Grant fumed at what he took to be a violation of the director's authority. Had the actress been an imperious diva such as Bette Davis or Joan Crawford, Grant's objections might have been valid, but he would never have put himself in their line of fire.

Grant got on the phone to Dore Schary. "What's going on here?" he demanded. "You've got a director down here who doesn't know what he's doing and Myrna's getting away with murder."

Schary came down to the set to see what was going on, and a furious Reis walked out. When he came back, there was a nervous period during which Reis directed Loy and Shirley Temple while Dore Schary was on call to handle Grant's scenes. After a time, Reis more or less took over again, but he and Grant never got along. Shirley Temple remembered lots of bickering "about details of delivery and stage position." If Reis accepted one of Grant's suggestions, Loy would retire to her dressing room, then eventually return with suggestions that would enhance her part in the scene.

And then Grant caught Temple doing an imitation of him for the crew. Clearly, everybody was against him. He stalked off and complained to David Selznick, who had loaned Temple to RKO. Selznick read Temple the riot act for what he deemed unprofessional behavior and she returned to the set to apologize. Grant accepted the apology, turned to walk away, then stopped. "By the way," he said, cocking his head in an exaggeration of Temple's imitation of him, "it was a pretty good imitation."

The picture emerged as a pleasant, innocuous comedy enlivened by Grant's physical dexterity and Temple's surprisingly lush maturation. It made a clear profit of $700,000 on costs of $1.9 million.

CARY GRANT AND LORETTA YOUNG had begun to believe they shouldn't work together, and with good reason. In 1934 they had starred in a ghastly picture for Darryl Zanuck aptly titled *Born to Be Bad*. It was so terrible that neither Grant nor Young would willingly speak of it, so on the first day of *The Bishop's Wife*, Grant told her, "Loretta, you owe me one good picture." Young heartily agreed.

But after a week of shooting, Sam Goldwyn shut down the picture and fired director William Seiter. He ordered a script rewrite that took six weeks, then hired Henry Koster to take over the direction. Grant cooperated to the extent of taking himself off the payroll for the six weeks it took to retool the script.

Koster was at a delicate crossroads in his career. In 1946, he had finished a terrible picture at MGM called *The Unfinished Dance* and then quit the studio because he didn't think it was a fun place to work and he objected to formula filmmaking. Nearly six months later, he had had no nibbles for work, and had begun to think that L. B. Mayer might have had him blacklisted. Koster was on the verge of returning to Europe to make movies.

It was at that point that Sam Goldwyn looked at Seiter's footage and saw the problem. "The casting was wrong," said Robert Koster, Henry's son.

> Contractually, Cary had to have the title role—not the wife, but the Bishop. Cary's contracts were *tomes*! That was in black-and-white in his deal. But the Bishop was the wrong part for him. So the first thing my father had to do was to talk him into switching to the angel. He told Cary that they had a chance to make a truly memorable movie, and that this picture could be one of the movies he would be proud of. And it worked; he talked him into it.

Goldwyn had admired Koster's work since he left Germany in 1936 as part of the exodus that followed in the wake of Hitler. Koster and his wife were invited to dinner parties at Goldwyn's house. After one party, they were driving home when Koster's wife realized she had forgotten her gloves. Koster turned the car around and walked back into Goldwyn's house to see the producer pouring leftover wine back into bottles. "The end result of the entire experience with Goldwyn," said Bob Koster, "was that my father respected him as a producer, but thought he was a little odd as a person." Henry Koster said that Goldwyn was "absolutely the best producer who was ever in this industry, if only for the simple reason that he always took the best people he could possibly get."

The problems with the picture extended beyond the casting. As with his poetic novel *Portrait of Jennie*, Robert Nathan's source material resisted literal translation. The screenwriters were Robert Sherwood and Leonardo Bercovici—Koster and Sherwood reworked the script after the casting switch—with additional scenes from an uncredited Billy Wilder and Charles Brackett.

None of the actors particularly wanted to be there. Grant was being paid $400,000—his biggest haul up to that time—to make a movie he had little interest in. Grant thought the angel Dudley verged on the smug and was a "rather conceited, impudent, high-handed magician." As far as he was concerned, it was a (big) paycheck, nothing more.

"Mr. Grant is a nervous man," said Henry Koster. "When we discussed a scene, he was never rude or anything. I just saw the perspiration appear on his forehead or his face, and he would start to get very, very tense. When he did a scene, I felt it was against his wish to play it that way or to play the character at all. . . . This is the worst thing that can happen to a director, to work with an actor who doesn't want to play a part and has to do it."

David Niven hadn't wanted to play the rather ill-tempered Bishop, and he was still struggling with the tragic death of his wife, Primmie. In May 1946 she had fallen down the basement steps at Tyrone Power's house while playing a party game called Sardines. She tumbled twenty feet headfirst onto a stone floor, and died several days later of a fractured skull and brain lacerations. She left two small boys and a grief-stricken husband who spent the rest of his life feeling cheated out of the love of his life. Then there was Loretta Young, who was upset by Goldwyn's insistence on a de-glamourized appearance. Even with Henry Koster doing his diplomatic best, Grant's lack of interest showed in a certain detachment and absence of his customary vivacity.

Part of the problem was that Goldwyn ladled a lot of production value over what was actually a simple story. An extraneous ice-skating sequence involved building an ice rink at the studio and importing thousands of pounds of shaved ice to take the place of snow. Although Grant could skate—it gets cold in Bristol—the script called for some pirouettes that were past him, so professional ice skaters wearing masks resembling Grant and Loretta Young were called in, a disguise aided by what seemed to be a sudden solar eclipse whenever the doubles were on-camera.

The film felt top-heavy to Grant, and he was clearly not enjoying himself. Goldwyn came down to the set to talk to the actor. "You want me to be happy, don't you?" asked Grant. "I don't give a *damn* if you're happy," replied Goldwyn. "You're going to be here for only a few weeks, and this picture will be out for a long time. I would rather you should be unhappy here, and then we can all be happy later." As always, Grant worked very hard on the set to make scenes work, although he never got over being rankled about switching parts. It's curious—the Bishop is a terrible part, alternately surly and weak, but Grant seems to have preferred him to the omniscient Dudley.

In short, all the actors were unhappy, and Koster had his hands full. "Miss Young refused to show her right cheek to the camera and Mr. Grant didn't want . . . to . . . either," he said still exasperated nearly a quarter of a century after the events. "Now how do you do a love scene when both people look to the right? So I had to do a love scene and I finally decided to have them both look out the window, he steps up behind her, they both look out the window, he puts his hands on her shoulders and they say their dialogue."

After looking at the rushes, Goldwyn was irate. "What the hell happened to the love scene?" he demanded. Koster explained the situation, whereupon Goldwyn marched down to the set and berated his actors. "Loretta and Cary, from now on you draw only half your salary because you only let me use half of your faces."

The seven-year-old Karolyn Grimes was playing Niven's daughter in the picture (she had just played Zuzu in Frank Capra's *It's a Wonderful Life*), and her memories of the picture revolve around Henry Koster's gentleness, Loretta Young's bad breath, and a sense of fun that Grant shared privately with the little girl. Grant took time between shots to read to Grimes, tell her stories, and more.

> I think he was extremely bright and didn't have to work on his lines that much and he was bored, so he messed around and played. . . . When the star makes noise, so can you. When they had a real skating rink on the set, he took me on a sled every day at lunch—"C'mon Karolyn, let's go!"—and he would pull me around while he was ice-skating. It was so exciting. I loved every minute of it, and I thought he was neatest guy ever.

He just really did like children. I think he loved to be with children, loved to make them happy. He really had a wonderful personality. And I never thought of him as a handsome movie idol, because I was too young to realize that. I saw these people all the time, and I didn't really think too much about it. They were just like everybody else, and he was a friend.

In spite of all the heavy lifting by a slew of talented professionals and beautifully graded photography by Gregg Toland—he would shoot only two more pictures before a heart attack killed him at the age of forty-four—the film seemed slightly underwhelming. (To be fair, *The Bishop's Wife* has become a Christmas perennial on television.)

The odd thing was that nobody seemed to know how to sell the picture. The ads position *The Bishop's Wife* as something close to a screwball comedy, which it definitely was not. "Have You Heard About Cary and the Bishop's Wife?" was one tagline, and underneath a grimacing picture of Grant was "That Bachelor and Bobby Soxer Man CARY GRANT—Women Run to Him—With Their Troubles!" Another ad provided the idiotic tagline: "Want a New Slant? See Cary Grant!" and used a still of Grant taken during a rehearsal of the ice-skating sequence. He's in his shirtsleeves and hanging on to a guardrail as if the movie is a slapstick romp. Still another ad positioned it as a triangle sex comedy: "Cary Grant: 'Just Call me Dudley . . . and call me any time!'" Loretta Young: "Every woman needs a man like Dudley around the house!" David Niven: "All I hear is Dudley this, and Dudley that. What's he got that I haven't got?"

In some markets, Goldwyn found that advertising the film as *Cary and the Bishop's Wife* perked up the box office considerably by implying a romance that the film itself delicately dances around. One way or another, Sam Goldwyn usually got his money's worth; *The Bishop's Wife* returned $3 million in domestic rentals to RKO. Deducting RKO's distribution charge left Goldwyn with just about what the film cost to make, but the shortfall was more than made up by overseas receipts. The total return was $4.6 million.

Henry Koster had gone to Europe on a vacation when his agent Bert Allenberg wired him COME BACK IMMEDIATELY. PICTURE IS A SUCCESS. He was hirable again. Koster would go on to direct many good pictures, including *Harvey* and *My Cousin Rachel*, although his personal favorites of his own work were *A Man Called Peter* and *No Highway in the Sky.*

Grant had been annoyed by Loretta Young's prissy grande dame facade and never really warmed up to her. He told a friend in the 1970s that he thought she was "a hypocrite, going around the set and fining people a quarter or whatever it is for cursing." The hypocrisy derived from the common knowledge that she had had an illegitimate child from an affair with Clark Gable during the shooting of *The Call of the Wild* in 1935. Grant didn't fault her for that. Rather, what tore it for him was the story that came out years later—that Judy, Young and Gable's child, had come home from school and asked her mother if the schoolyard gossip was true—that her father was really Clark Gable. Loretta Young lied to the child, which Grant termed "a cruel thing to do."

The Bishop's Wife was the only time Grant had a chance to work with his friend David Niven, and they got on well. Grant could be opaque about his own motives, but when he wanted to exercise his powers of analysis about other people he was invariably spot on. "He seemed to be terrified of boring or depressing you," he said about Niven.

> [He] felt he always had to be an entertainer. He was more educated, I think more intelligent than I was, but you felt there was always something being held back.
>
> I admired him very much for going back and fighting in the war: that was a wonderful thing to have done. When he came back he seemed in some ways to have changed, but I think that may have been because of that terrible accident to Primmie. He was still distraught about that when we were making *The Bishop's Wife*, and yet there was also still that urge to entertain, to tell stories, not always true stories maybe but marvelous rearrangements of the truth.
>
> He was a funny man and a brave man and a good man, and there were never too many of those around here.

GRANT AND HOWARD HUGHES had been friends since the mid-1930s. Grant was enthralled by Hughes's utter indifference to the world and what it thought, which was more a function of Hughes's tunnel vision than his money. "Most of us are controlled by fear, if only we would admit it," said Grant. "Howard is above considerations of what people may think. He'll start for New York in a shabby old suit with a tooth brush in his pocket. He'll buy a clean shirt when his plane comes down and toss the soiled one into the first wastebasket." Grant may have come for Hughes's money but he stayed for a sense of freedom that he could only dream about.

Hughes's purchase of RKO Radio Pictures in May 1948 would have theoretically been a huge plus for Grant, who still had an agreement for one picture a year for the studio. In fact it turned out to be quite the opposite. Hughes would always view RKO as a convenience—for signing up girls in whom he was interested, for releasing his long-overdue picture *The Outlaw*, for the production of whatever vanity project he decided to make.

Besides that, there was the fact that Grant's and Hughes's ideas about movies were diametrically opposed. During Hughes's congressional testimony in 1947, one of the senators brought up a project that Grant had proposed, with an enthusiasm that Hughes obviously didn't share.

"Mr. Grant, as a matter of fact, told me that he has an idea for a picture which would be made in all different parts of the world," Hughes said. "In other words, one episode would be in London, another in Cairo, and so forth. . . . And he had a thought of doing a movie set of some very supercolossal airplane that would have dance floors and a swimming pool and what have you in it. And this fictitious character was going to travel around the world, and a part of the picture would be made in various parts of the world."

Hughes went on to explain that this was going to be "a Buck Rogers kind of a thing, and the airplane would be one of these rocket ships. It was a kind of zeppelin affair with rockets, as he told me." Grant's idea was to set the movie about ten years in the future, with the hero belonging to a world police force that might be connected to the United Nations. "The plot would concern his adventures as he flies from one country to another battling intrigues against the peace of the world. A different picture would be made about each country." Grant believed that a series of these pictures "would go a long way toward increasing each country's understanding of the other."

The Senate inquiry was mainly focused on the Spruce Goose, Hughes's experimental airplane, and some of the senators thought that the money might have been siphoned off into an impractical scheme for making a movie.

"Did you ever discuss this flying boat with Cary Grant?" asked a senator.

"Oh, well, he may have said, 'I hope you have good luck with it.'" Hughes went on to disabuse the panel of the idea. "I never discussed any thought of making a picture with this airplane."

Clearly, he thought Grant's idea was gimcrack, even though in its vague outline it could have been an outline for *Mission: Impossible*.

In the fall of 1948, Hughes was staying at Grant's house when Dore Schary arrived to tender his resignation as head of production at RKO. (Hughes hadn't owned a house of his own since the early 1930s, preferring to rent friends' houses or stay at the Beverly Hills Hotel.)

Grant's house was one of Hughes's favorites; after he crashed the prototype of his XF-11 reconnaissance aircraft in July 1946, Hughes had recuperated at Beverly Grove. Hughes was still there in mid-1948, when he ordered Dore Schary to fire Barbara Bel Geddes because he didn't think she was sexy. Schary told him he had no intention of being a messenger boy for Hughes or anybody else. When Schary arrived at Beverly Grove, it was obvious that Grant had moved everything of his out, but Hughes hadn't moved anything of his in. "There wasn't a paper, a cigarette, a flower, a match, a picture, a magazine," Schary remembered. "The only sign of life was Hughes, who appeared from a side room in which I caught a glimpse of a woman hooking up her bra before the door closed."

Schary resigned from RKO and became head of production at MGM. Hughes took erratic control of RKO and ran it into the ground in seven years, finally selling it in 1955.

AFTER *The Bishop's Wife* was finished in August 1947, Grant sailed for England on the *Queen Mary*. There were plays to see in London, and his mother to visit in Bristol, the first time he'd seen her since April and May 1946.

He headed back to New York at the end of the month with Frederick Lonsdale and Merle Oberon in tow. Grant was now a close friend of Lonsdale's, the author of *On Approval,* among other plays, which would have provided good parts for Grant had he been a star in 1920. By the postwar era, Lonsdale's importance was fading, but he might have been buoyed by his colorful private life, which would eventually result in a dynasty—his illegitimate daughter Angela became the mother of the actors James and Edward Fox, and producer Robert Fox.

Grant gravitated toward Lonsdale as a real-life equivalent of Grant's on-screen image. Michael Korda knew Lonsdale, and remembered him as a man of "immense charm and wit, at home everywhere." "I get lonesome without Freddie," Grant said, "and it's most inconsiderate of him when he goes east on business and leaves me to my own devices."

While Grant was in London, he saw a play called *Deep Are the Roots,* which starred a young actress named Betsy Drake. He was immediately attracted to her. Oberon was intrigued by Grant's being intrigued and invited Drake to lunch with her and Grant. Grant noted that Lonsdale was every bit as interested in Drake as he was. "Had Freddy been 20 years younger, I would certainly have lost her to him," Grant would remember. Grant and Drake had a good lunch, and he was no longer interested. He was smitten.

Drake was born in Paris in 1923 to Carlos Drake, an American whose father had founded the Drake and Blackstone hotels in Chicago. Her parents divorced, and Betsy had what she retrospectively termed "a difficult childhood—lonely, unhappy. . . . I often wished I was someone else, and liked to pretend I was someone else." She had worked as a model, but the work and the people bored her. Pretending she was someone else seemed a viable alternative. She became an understudy and assistant stage manager, then understudied Eva Le Gallienne in a show called *Therese.*

Drake was not a typical actress, which Grant found attractive. For one thing, acting was far down the roster of things that interested her. Betsy read everything, studied everything, thought about everything, and could talk knowledgeably and wittily about nearly everything. She was interested in metaphysics, ecology, sociology, yoga, and even gourmet cooking. "Most actresses are only interested in one thing—the mirror," Grant said. "But Betsy was interested in the world. She was one of the most determined people I've ever met."

There was undoubtedly a touch of the dilettante in Drake, but she definitely had skills; Grant had been a two-packs-a-day smoker for decades, but after Drake hypnotized him, he quit cold turkey and became a relentless anti-smoking advocate for the rest of his life.

When he set his mind on a woman, Grant was irresistible—Drake was living with him while he was making *Mr. Blandings Builds His Dream House* at RKO—a charmer distinguished by an unusually modern supply of dry, sarcastic wit. It's the one about a middle-class man who is nearly bankrupted by his naïveté in building a home in the country—an evergreen premise imitated a dozen times by inferior movies. Grant was once again paired with Myrna Loy, but by this time he'd learned he could trust her, and they were backed up by a delectable turn from Melvyn Douglas as their lawyer and best friend, who sees disaster inexorably advancing but can't summon the energy to prevent it.

H. C. Potter was essentially a director for hire, and hadn't seemed to have much of a clue about what to do with Mr. Lucky just a few years earlier, but this time he matches a knack for comic understatement with lovely cinematography by James Wong Howe, who gives Potter more precisely framed images than he had had before or after. At one point, Howe tosses off a 360-degree panning shot, just because he can. All this bolsters a funny script by Norman Panama and Melvin Frank. Grant was on board for $100,000 as a down payment on his 10 percent of the gross. Strangely, the picture underperformed, and lost $225,000.

"Cary was terribly funny when he was frustrated, when he was upset," remembered Myrna Loy. "That's one of the things that made his comedy so hilarious, so I immediately decided to play the 'little woman' who leans on him and drives him crazy."

"If you haven't [been married], then you can't understand what it meant to have Myrna play your wife," said Grant. "Even when she fed me lines off camera, I'd look over and she'd be pulling down her hem or straightening a stocking in a subconscious wifely gesture, instinctively doing the things that married women do."

He then went on to analyze the craft of acting as succinctly as anyone ever has: "Acting is like playing ball. You toss the ball, and some people don't toss it back; some people don't even catch it. When you get somebody who catches it *and* tosses it back, that's really what acting is all about. Myrna kept that spontaneity in her acting, a supreme naturalness that had the effect of distilled dynamite" (italics added).

It was a happy shoot; Grant regaled his costars with stories of his early days as a stilt-walker, and anecdotes from vaudeville. "He was very sweet to me, a charming companion full of information and humor and hilarious stories," recalled Loy. "Cary's impeccable timing and delivery, his seemingly effortless performances resulted from hard work, concentration, and a driving demand for perfection."

There was only one small cloud on the blissful horizon. The House Un-American Activities Committee was gearing up for its inquisition in Hollywood. John Huston and William Wyler came on the set one day to ask Loy to join with them in establishing the Committee for the First Amendment. Loy anted up $1,000, as did Melvyn Douglas. Grant didn't want to get involved. When Douglas or Loy would begin to discuss politics or raising money, Grant would remember something that needed his immediate attention and sidle away.

To promote the picture, Paul Macnamara, the publicity man on the picture, came up with a scheme involving the construction of a duplicate of Mr. Blandings's dream house in a hundred cities across the country. Each house would be raffled off on the night the movie premiered in that town. Besides all this, General Electric agreed to supply an all-electric kitchen for the film. Knowing his leading man, Macnamara told Grant he could have his pick of the kitchen appliances when the film was finished. The promotion gradually became the tail that wagged the dog—the house in the movie had no closets or stairs because the script didn't call for them, so frantic adjustments had to be made in the actual houses being built across the country.

When the picture was finished, there was another problem. General Electric's luxurious electric kitchen was nowhere to be seen in the preview version of the picture, and GE was mightily upset. Threats were issued involving lawsuits—*expensive* lawsuits. It turned out that Dore Schary and Hank Potter had cut the kitchen scenes because they slowed the picture down. The scenes were promptly restored in time for the release, pacing be damned.

Decades later, Paul Macnamara was on a plane when a man with thick white hair and horn-rimmed glasses popped up from the seat in front of him. "What about my toaster?" asked Cary Grant. "I never got the toaster you promised me."

SINCE BETSY WAS AN ACTRESS, nothing would do but that she become a star on an equivalent level as her lover, so she worked alongside Grant in a trifle entitled *Every Girl Should Be Married*. Grant also agreed to star in a film for Fox if they would feature Betsy in a romantic comedy called *Dancing in the Dark*, in which her leading man was the eternally witty William Powell. Not bad for a twenty-five-year-old actress with no particular claim to this level of stardom.

Her first pictures proved that Drake was classy, obviously intelligent, with a crisp, sensible, slightly English manner—attractive but not a knockout. She also had a beautiful speaking voice. Irene Mayer Selznick, who had a knack for accurate character appraisal, liked her, said she had talent, dignity, and studiousness.

But.

She lacked that indefinable combination of temperament and sensuality that makes movie stars. "She had no comedic talent," said Irene Selznick. "She was a dramatic actress. My impression is she really wanted to be in the theater and only went to Hollywood because of Cary." Betsy's problem was simple: if she was going to work with Grant, she was going to have to develop a facility for comedy.

Taking a young actress of small training and credentials and costarring her as an act of *lèse-majesté* was a huge step. *Every Girl Should Be Married* was a success, but it could hardly fail to be with Grant taking only $50,000 in salary against 10 percent of the producer's gross in excess of $500,000. The film is mild at best, but it ended up with a profit of $775,000 because of its modest cost of $1.2 million. Grant intentionally reduced his income from the movie in order to make hiring Betsy a more desirable prospect—a true act of love. In his mind, it was a fair exchange.

"I gave her Hollywood on a platter," he would say, "but she gave me something much more valuable—my peace of mind."

CHAPTER THIRTEEN

B etsy accompanied Grant when they left for Europe on the *Queen Mary* on September 1, 1948, to shoot Howard Hawks's *I Was a Male War Bride*. They were planning to stay four months.

The delicious title and the reunion with Hawks promise more than the film actually delivers, although Grant's display of dyspepsia is always entertaining. The film is fitfully amusing but it never quite achieves flight because it's essentially a comedy procedural—the plot mechanics of getting Grant into drag are both endless and pointless, because we don't care about the how or why anywhere near as much as we care about seeing Cary Grant fuming and humiliated.

What makes it memorable is Grant's refusal to camp it up à la Tony Curtis and Jack Lemmon in *Some Like It Hot*. Grant in drag isn't trying to pass as a woman; he's seething, and he has to seethe while displaying skinny legs and an unbecoming Louise Brooks wig. He's very funny, and, as David Thomson noted, the film once again attests to Grant's personal security and intelligence. Even so, the movie feels like a long journey for a small amount of comic delight.

Some of the joy of the film was leached out by the circumstances of its production. Ann Sheridan had recently paid $35,000 to be let out of the final six months of her contract with Warner Bros. When she found out that Barbara Stanwyck had been let out of her contract without paying a cent, Sheridan hit the roof and stayed there; she was still talking about the injustice nearly twenty years later.

On location in England, Sheridan got pneumonia and after she got back to work Grant came down with something worse. As Sheridan remembered it, they were doing the love scene inside a haystack when Grant suddenly announced he hated the scene. Sheridan was surprised because Grant and Hawks had just rewritten the scene themselves. Hawks pointed this out, and Grant replied, "I don't care, it's bloody awful. I don't like it."

This wasn't like Grant, at least not when he was working with Hawks, and Sheridan noticed he didn't look right. She felt his forehead—he was burning up with some sort of dry heat. Hawks called off shooting for the day and that night Grant was diagnosed with hepatitis and a touch of jaundice. Before the illness was turned around, he lost close to forty pounds. "Everyone thought I was going to die," remembered Grant, "but I didn't. I knew I had too much to live for. I loved [Betsy] too much to just go off and leave her alone." It was months before he could go back to work. It must have been a nightmare for Hawks, not to mention the insurance company, because Sheridan and Grant were both paid during the long layoff. The planned European stay of four months turned into something like six.

Because of the illnesses, the picture went far over budget but it was still quite successful, amassing domestic rentals of $4.1 million—Fox's second highest grossing picture of the year behind *Pinky*.

By now, Grant had attained a status accorded to few stars—even other movie stars were struck dumb by his appearance. After Grant saw a preview of the brutal boxing picture *The Set-Up*, he searched out Robert Ryan, the picture's star. "You're Robert Ryan," he said as he stuck out his hand. "My name's Cary Grant. I want you to know that I just saw *The Set-Up*, and I thought your performance was one of the best I've ever seen." Ryan never forgot the moment and talked about Grant's generosity for the rest of his life.

On Christmas Day 1949, Grant and Betsy flew to Phoenix and got married. Howard Hughes was the pilot as well as best man. They honeymooned on Hughes's yacht, which Grant had positioned so that the moon shone through their stateroom porthole every night. Kate Hepburn was delighted and sent a letter: "I don't quite know why the hell I should be so thrilled at the idea of you two being married but I am . . . with all my heart—I wish for the greatest happiness." Clifford Odets sent his greetings from New York: "Let me use one of your favorite phrases & say, 'Bless, you, bless you, bless you!!!' How much happiness & human love I wish you both."

Grant would continue to promote his new wife's uncertain comic abilities. In January 1951, they began a radio series for NBC called *Mr. and Mrs. Blandings*, a spin-off of *Mr. Blandings Builds His Dream House*, but it lasted for only one season. The premise was strong, and the writers were Jerome Lawrence and Robert E. Lee, who would later write *Auntie Mame* and *Inherit the Wind*, among other plays. But Grant took a dislike to one of them and gave him the silent treatment, while Betsy's slight stammer complicated post-production of the shows because her hesitations had to be edited out. William Frye, who was producing the show, remembered that "Cary Grant gave me my first ulcer."

Nevertheless, Grant and Frye became friends. Frye found Grant pretty much the same as everyone else did—a mingling of generosity, intelligence, and snappishness, without much warning as to which would take precedence. If someone asked for an autograph, Grant would ask, "Do you have a dollar?" which generally ended the conversation.

Grant and Betsy had two decoupage lamps that sat on the floor in the living room because Grant didn't care for them. Frye liked the lamps and told Grant they were crazy not to place them on tables or pedestals. One Christmas, the lamps were delivered to Frye's house with a note that said, "U won! And no amount of wrapping can disguise them. Still, merry, merry Xmas Bill. Affectionately, Betsy and Cary."

Similarly, Frye once accompanied Grant to Lyons Moving and Storage on Santa Monica Boulevard, where he wanted to get some things out of storage. The vault was full of Grant's old clothes—Frye estimated there must have been at least 250 suits and fifty to seventy-five overcoats. "Do you see anything you want?" he asked Frye. "Just take it." Unfortunately, Frye wasn't Grant's size, or his wardrobe would have undergone a rapid upgrade.

When Frye arrived at Beverly Grove to pick Grant up for a black-tie premiere, Grant pointed to Frye's studs and said, "What are those?"

"They're Swank. I call them raisins. They cost me $12.50."

"Bill, I think we can do better than that."

Grant walked over to a bookcase and from behind a shelf of books he pulled out a drawer filled with miscellaneous jewelry—watches, studs, cuff links, all with rubies, sapphires, diamonds, and pearls. It was an impressive display—Frye assumed they had all been gifts from Barbara Hutton. "Pick out something," Grant said. Frye chose diamonds and sapphires. After the premiere, as Frye was dropping off Grant, he said, "Oh, wait. You better come in and take off the studs and cuff links."

Grant didn't think much of Frye's wardrobe, but he admired the socks that Frye wore. It turned out that they were custom-made argyles, knitted by a friend. Frye commissioned a pair for Grant, which occasioned a gracious thank-you note: "They fit me perfectly. The large size. I have large feet, ideas, mouth and tax-bills. But you, dear Bill, have largesse. I am deeply obliged to you and properly glad for being so properly clad."

Frye, like most of Grant's friends, liked Betsy and thought they seemed quite happy, although David Niven seems to have had his doubts about Grant's inconsistent taste in women. "Virginia was a frothy extrovert," Niven said, in a rundown on Grant's wives. "Barbara was tucked away behind those battlements, and Betsy is one of the fey people, like [Cary]."

Perhaps fey would be the answer.

THERE HAD BEEN A P.S. on the marriage congratulation from Odets, a thank-you for a loan that Grant had made to him. Lee and Paula Strasberg would always be Clifford Odets's best friends, but his best Los Angeles friends were Grant and Danny Kaye. Supporting those pillars were the remnants of the Hollywood outpost of the Group Theatre—John Garfield, Luther Adler—and then Charlie Chaplin, Hanns Eisler, and Jascha Heifetz.

Odets was relentless in searching out those for whom he felt an affinity. Jean Renoir had opened his front door to find Odets standing there, wearing a raincoat, even though it wasn't raining. "I've got you at last," he said. "I swore that I'd not only see you but that we'd become friends." Renoir was brooding over his career troubles in Hollywood when Odets invited him to a party so he could meet Chaplin. "It was like inviting a devout Christian to meet God in person," Renoir remembered, but he had a commitment he couldn't get out of and didn't attend. But Odets kept up the matchmaking, and Renoir and his wife, Dido, came to know and adore Chaplin.

By the time Grant and Betsy married, Odets had moved back to New York, and they were communicating via letters and phone calls. The relationship had subtly altered from one of coworkers and equals to one where Odets was frequently thanking Grant for his generosity, apologizing for his general depression, and for Grant's patience in listening to Odets's complaints. "There is so little kindness in the world that I can not thank you too much for yours," Odets wrote. "It warms & cheers me & makes you increasingly precious to me."

A few months after Grant's wedding, Odets wired him that Kenneth McKenna, the story editor for MGM, had a copy of Odets's new play, *The Country Girl*. He asked Grant to read it with an eye to a movie production. Grant must have expressed some polite interest, because Odets wrote in May 1950 with the news that Sid Rogell at RKO had decided against it as a property for Grant after a conference with Howard Hughes and Grant.

A month later Odets had to ask for another loan. As always, Grant sent a check. Odets wrote to thank him, mentioning that he had cast Paul Kelly and Uta Hagen in the Broadway production of *The Country Girl*. The play opened in November 1950 and ran for seven months—the last commercial hit Odets would have. The movie version of 1954 starred Bing Crosby, William Holden, and an utterly miscast Grace Kelly, who nevertheless won the Oscar as Best Actress because she was Grace Kelly. The success of the play and resulting movie sale meant that Odets was again able to start repaying Grant's generosity.

In 1952, Odets testified as a friendly witness before the House Un-American Activities Committee. He named names—he and Elia Kazan agreed to name each other, and Odets also offered up J. Edward Bromberg—dead for some months—and a few others, all of whom had been named by others.

"What he needed from me was what I needed from him," Kazan would write in his memoirs. "Permission to name the other." When Kazan got back to his house after meeting with Odets about their testimony, he asked his wife, Molly, what she thought. "I don't worry about you; you'll survive anything. But I do worry about Clifford."

Odets's testimony was oddly bifurcated; after disposing of the unpleasant business of selling out his friends, Odets refused to grovel any further and stoutly defended his liberal political outlook. His testimony was a compressed version of his entire life—he wanted to have it both ways: write great plays in New York and make lots of money in Hollywood; pollinate beautiful actresses while proclaiming the higher morality of the artist; name names and be a good liberal.

Kazan went on to make some of his best films after he testified, but, as he would write,

> What was possible for me hurt Clifford mortally. He was never the same after he testified. He gave away his identity when he did that; he was no longer the hero-rebel, the fearless prophet of a new world. It choked off the voice he'd had. The ringing tone, the burst of passion, were no longer there. What in the end gave me strength drained him of his. I realize now that my action in the matter had influenced him strongly. I wish it had not. I believe he should have remained defiant, maintained his treasured identity, and survived as his best self. He was to die before he died.

This sounds like eloquent overstatement, until you remember that even in *Sweet Smell of Success*, Odets's best late work, the dialogue is almost entirely keyed to contempt (J.J. Hunsecker) and self-loathing (Sidney Falco). Walt Odets says his father never spoke of his testimony in later years. Odets and Kazan remained close for the rest of Odets's life. In January 1955, Odets returned to Hollywood, and he and Grant resumed seeing each other on a regular basis.

GRANT AND KATE HEPBURN maintained a loose, jocular friendship, although more letters passed between Hepburn and Betsy Drake than between Hepburn and Grant. In 1950, Hepburn had been properly nauseated by an atrocious picture Dore Schary wrote and produced at MGM called The Next Voice You Hear, about God broadcasting to the world over the radio. Grant and Drake rubbed salt in the wound by sending Hepburn a copy of a book the oblivious Schary wrote about the film's production. "We feel that the reading of this little book will enable you to relive, and help perpetuate, a memory close to your heart," they wrote her. Grant wrote in a PS, "What ABOUT this book, eh? And there are some PRETTY pictures in it too!"

Grant regularly offered Hepburn the use of his house whenever she needed a place to stay in California. In one letter to Grant she had fun with her well-deserved reputation for bossiness: "It will be fun to see you . . . as naturally you expect me to stay with you. I have a secretary—chauffeur—maid and two automobiles—and I really think it would be simpler for all of us if you moved out and let me take the house."

Some years later, after another visit, she sent him a check for $1.81 to pay for the phone calls for which Grant obviously expected to be reimbursed. Another time she wrote and told him that she had left her bath towel in Betsy's bathroom. It seems that she had forgotten it because she had spent so much time basking in the tub reading Sophocles. "What a lovely house," she complimented him.

Grant and Drake were now regulars at the Selznick house. Daniel Selznick, Irene and David's second son, remembered that "Every Sunday night at Summit Drive we showed movies to the same four people: Cary and Betsy, and Kate and [Spencer Tracy]. We started at 5 o'clock, we broke for dinner, and there was a second picture and sometimes a third." Some of the movies starred Cary Grant, which proved to be a problem. "Cary would threaten to walk out of the room, but then he would stay and watch himself, yelling back to the screen: 'Oh, how could you do such a terrible job in that scene.'"

Grant managed to negotiate the divide between Selznick's first and second wives gracefully. Irene Selznick never remarried, and remained "endlessly fascinating and dangerous," according to her friend Steven Bach. Irene's best friend for years was Katharine Hepburn, perhaps because they shared a curious sense of their own divinity. "Irene thought of David as a problem child she had weaned out of her life," said Bach.

Irene and Grant remained close after her divorce. In fact, their friendship was never affected by anything. In Irene's lovely phrase, "Cary Grant and I took in each other's washing." They wound in and out of each other's lives as long as they lived, as did the people important to each of them. Grant had Howard Hughes—Grant's nickname for him was "Loving Sam," after Hughes's unseemly ways with women—personally fly all of them around New England so Irene could inspect boarding schools for her son Jeffrey.

When Irene was setting up her production of *A Streetcar Named Desire* in New York, she wanted to get back to Los Angeles for Christmas. Unfortunately, every train berth was booked. Cary said he could take care of the problem. He called on Hughes, who sent Irene and her sons round-trip plane tickets. When she got to Los Angeles, Irene sent Hughes a check, which he returned. She wrote him another check, which he also returned. She asked Grant what she should do. He told her to let it go because, he said, "You'll only offend Howard." Irene selected several dozen fine bottles of wine and a four-foot planter decorated with a tiny plane with red and green velvet ribbons and had it all sent to Hughes for delivery on Christmas.

Hughes responded with a phone call on Christmas morning. "Irene, this is Howard."

"Who?"

"Howard. Howard Hughes. The tree is the most beautiful thing I've ever seen. I'm overwhelmed." He went on to tell her that the gift had brought him to tears because it was the first time that anyone had ever done anything so special for him on Christmas. For the next ten years, every Christmas night Irene would receive four dozen red roses; the card was always written by Hughes himself.

A year after the wine arrived at Hughes's house, Grant called Irene and told her that Hughes would like to have dinner with her. She wanted to know why. It seemed that Hughes would like Irene as a woman friend. Irene thought that was ridiculous and said so. Grant said she'd have to tell Hughes herself. Rather than put herself in such an awkward position, she agreed to see Hughes, but for lunch rather than dinner.

They met at 21, which Hughes liked because the wooden walls and ceiling enabled him to hear slightly better than was normal at busy restaurants. He needed her, he explained. "Why should Cary have a woman friend and not I?" Irene pointed out that he had a lot of woman friends, but they both knew that Hughes was not talking about that kind of friend. He went on to say he was lonely, and that the great mistake of his life had been failing to persuade Kate Hepburn to marry him. As it happened, Irene liked to make up her own mind about who her friends were going to be, and she and Hughes remained merely friendly, not exactly friends.

Grant bought a $5,000 share in *A Streetcar Named Desire,* which must have been difficult for him given the ridiculously speculative nature of the theater. It turned out to be a superb investment—just like the friendship.

GRANT HAD STAYED IN LOOSE TOUCH with Barbara Hutton, probably in order to stay close to her son, Lance, possibly because he was carrying a ration of guilt over his inability to help her. In September 1952, Irene was in New York working for Adlai Stevenson's presidential campaign. Barbara Hutton asked Grant to find her a house to rent in Los Angeles for two weeks. He asked Irene to rent her place to Hutton, but Irene said Barbara could simply have it.

Three months later, Barbara was still living in Irene's house, and Irene was in a bind—she had promised the house to Kate Hepburn for January 12. Hutton replied on January 13 to Irene's carefully worded request to vacate the property. She was "more than grateful . . . so kindly allowed Lance and me to stay in your beautiful home for so long a time. . . . If agreeable to you I will move out in a month. If this does not meet with your approval, please do not hesitate to let me know and I will endeavor to make other plans."

She went on to say that "There's been a number of fairly costly repairs in the vicinity of $3,000. Naturally I've been very happy to pay this, and will be grateful if you will be kind enough to let me know the balance which is owing, which would cover rental charges."

Irené was upset. I HAVE NO CHOICE BUT TO ASK YOU TO LEAVE, she wired. THERE WAS NEVER A QUESTION OF RENT . . . YOU OWE ME NO MONEY, ON THE CONTRARY.

Hutton replied via a phone call that made it clear she didn't want to leave, at which point Irene told her she was Hutton's hostess, not her landlady.

"Where shall I go?" Barbara asked.

"People usually go to a hotel," Irene replied. Which is what Hutton finally did, after leaving a number of trunks and crates behind, not to mention a bedroom carpet destroyed by her dogs, which was followed by Hutton's request for a quit-claim. It was all a replay of what had happened when Hutton and Grant had taken Doug Fairbanks Jr.'s house during World War II. Oblivious entitlement has seldom been so stunningly demonstrated; the fact that Irene and Cary remained friends was a testament to the strength of the bond.

In Irene's apartment at the Pierre in New York, one of the features was a model streetcar named "Desire." She would serve particularly valued friends aquavit from a case that Cary Grant had given her. "But she'd only give it to you if she really liked you," remembered Steven Bach. "The supply was running low."

BY NOW, GRANT HAD FIRST CRACK at nearly every script that didn't involve a cattle drive or space aliens. A-list domestic dramas, comedies, love stories all passed through his hands. Had he been as comfortable in his own skin as he was in the persona of Cary Grant, he could have had a different career. Ultimately, the roster of films Grant turned down is nearly as impressive as the roster of films he made.

The most enticing was *The Third Man*, which he passed on because of what amounted to terminal uncertainty. Grant had read Graham Greene's original treatment and was quietly interested in either of the major parts: the corrupt charmer Harry Lime or Holly Martins, Lime's naive chum from college days. Early conversations came down to Grant playing Holly, with perhaps Noel Coward as Lime, although David Selznick, who was coproducing with Alexander Korda, suspected that Grant would opt for Harry Lime when he saw the completed script. Other possibilities for the part of Lime included Orson Welles, while the dark horse for Holly was James Stewart. If Coward took the part of Lime, then Grant would have been an obviously better fit.

Orson Welles was always broke or close to it, and could be had for a flat $100,000, while Grant's services were luxe: $200,000 plus half the net from Europe. Nevertheless, Selznick and Korda were willing to pay the freight because Grant brought a box-office cachet that Orson Welles would not be able to match.

Graham Greene's own feelings could be intuited from his description of Lime in his original treatment: "Don't picture Harry Lime as a smooth scoundrel. He wasn't that. The picture I have of him on my files is an excellent one: he is caught by a street photographer with his stocky legs apart, big shoulders a little hunched, a belly that has known too much good food for too long, on his face a look of cheerful rascality, a geniality, a recognition that his happiness will make the world's day."

Put Greene in the Orson Welles camp.

The script was there, a superlative director (Carol Reed) was there, the money was there. But Grant would not commit, partly because of the comprehensive amorality of Lime's character, partly because of Alexander Korda's famously devious definition of net as something that pertained to everyone but him.*

Finally, Selznick gave up. "Grant is out of *The Third Man*," he wrote on June 16, 1948. "I told him of importance of Reed knowing who was going to play role and after discussion and questions he decided he did not like role of (Holly) and had fears about role of Lime, which however he preferred but would not make up his mind as to either role without [the final draft of the] script." *The Third Man* began shooting in October, and handed Orson Welles the best acting part of his career, with Harry Lime providing the perfect vessel for the actor's intrinsic charm and roguishness.

The most famous of Grant's might-have-beens is the 1954 Judy Garland version of *A Star Is Born*. "I asked him to take the part of [Norman Maine]," remembered the director George Cukor.

> But by that time he was very cagey, very clever about the roles he took, up to a certain point. He asked if he could come over and read the part, and Judy Garland came to the house and the two of them read it out in my garden by the pool. He read it in the most inept, bumbling but, nevertheless, the most marvelous way. Although he read it badly, he would occasionally look up with the most furtive look that was absolutely heartrending and eloquent, and you could see in the character a man who might one day commit suicide.
>
> By that time, I couldn't talk to him vis a vis; just [a director] and an actor. He had begun to put himself into these elaborate business deals that would bring him huge sums of money. You couldn't talk to him about the possibilities of the role the way you could to a big actor like John Barrymore or Spencer Tracy.

---

* Dealing with Korda led Louis B. Mayer to devise a recipe for a Hungarian omelet: "First, steal three eggs . . ."

Cukor took Grant aside after the reading and talked to him as directly as he could: "Cary, you have no idea how good you are in this part. You should play this; it will give your career a whole new dimension. You'll be wonderful in it."

Grant asked if he could have a couple of days to think it over, but the days went by and he couldn't make up his mind. Of course, no answer is in fact an answer, as David Selznick and Alexander Korda had found out. Warner Bros. had conceded to all of Grant's financial demands, so that wasn't it. "He was too careful, too fearful to take a chance," Cukor observed. "He might have felt he didn't have the training or something, but whatever it was, this robbed him of the position he really wanted and that I know he was capable of arriving at. Had he played in *A Star Is Born*, he would have had the Academy Award. Years later, they gave him an honorary one, but it wasn't the same thing."

Grant's choices derived from one simple fact: After *None But the Lonely Heart*, he refused to play another man broken by life; the cost had seemed insufficient to the reward, and he would not expose himself to the required extent.

Cukor put it best: "To have been one of the best actors on the screen and end up as a successful perfume salesman is not my idea of a great career. He could have been one of the very great actors, but he wouldn't take the chance."

It would not do to give the impression that Grant spent most of his time blithely walking away from masterpieces. A lot of the time he also walked away from disasters in the making. In 1948, the same year he couldn't commit to *The Third Man*, Warner Bros. was hot on his trail for *June Bride*, a supposed comedy that ended up starring Bette Davis. Grant was first choice for the male lead, ahead of Fred Astaire, Fred MacMurray, and Robert Montgomery. Jack Warner's assistant Steve Trilling sent the script to Grant along with a note: "Dear Cary, Here it is. . . . Carey Jackson is the part, and I think you will share my enthusiasm. Give me a buzz after you have had a chance to read it. Love and kisses."

Grant wrote his reply on the bottom of Trilling's note, instructing his secretary Frank Horn to "Please return this to Steve Trilling. Write a short note to him—saying that Mr. Grant thanks him for the script and returns it together with his very best wishes, etc." He didn't even bother to say no. Robert Montgomery played the part in what turned out to be a mediocre picture—Bette Davis's grasp of comedy was shaky, and the thought of working with such a tempermental diva would have been enough to drive Grant away all by itself.

GRANT WASN'T SCARED OF DIRECTORS who actually directed, as his preferences for McCarey, Hawks, and Stevens proved. The man who had given Clifford Odets and Delmer Daves a shot at directing now landed on another ambitious writer. His name was Richard Brooks, né Reuben Sax, an ex-Marine with a personality to match who had written some successful novels, some bad films (*Cobra Woman*) as well as some good ones (*Brute Force, Key Largo*). Brooks wanted to direct his own scripts, but Louis B. Mayer couldn't see it. "Anyone can be a director," Mayer told him, "but not everyone can write."

Brooks and Grant ran into each other at Santa Anita, where they were introduced by a mutual friend. Grant had read Brooks's new script, entitled *Ferguson*, and complimented him on it. "I wrote it," Brooks replied, "but, Mr. Grant, my problem is I want to direct it too."

Grant asked him how he got along with people. "Okay," said Brooks.

"Well," said Grant, "if you can write it, you can direct it."

Brooks's claim of equanimity was a flat-out evasion—he would always have an extremely short fuse seasoned with a touch of paranoia. MGM had tentatively placed *Ferguson* on Spencer Tracy's docket, but Grant was looking for something different than *Mr. Blandings Builds His Dream House* and *I Was a Male War Bride*. A movie about a middle-aged brain surgeon forced to operate on a South American dictator at gunpoint sounded different. Not only that, but MGM had long wanted to be in the Cary Grant business, and was willing to pay for the privilege. The clincher was undoubtedly the fact that Grant would be the unquestioned alpha on the set of a first-time director, even if said director was an ex-Marine.

As with Odets and Daves, Grant was supportive above and beyond the call of duty. When a camera crane rolled over Brooks's foot and blood began to leak from his shoe, the studio nurse told him to go to the hospital immediately. Brooks refused, because he knew that MGM would immediately assign another director to the picture rather than close down for a few days.

"If they get another director," Grant told him, "they're going to have to get a new actor. You go to the hospital."

Crisis, as the film would be titled, was an unimportant picture but it offers a good example of the sped-up, budget-conscious system imposed by Dore Schary when he replaced Louis B. Mayer as production head at MGM. Budgeted at a modest $1.5 million, $200,000 of which went to Grant, the production started on January 4, 1950, and finished on February 23. The picture was previewed on April 11 and released July 7.

The studio sensed trouble, and a memo instructed the advertising department to try to cut together a trailer featuring "a light touch." It didn't help. The film received good reviews, but lost $600,000. Once again, the public voted with their wallets and declared that they didn't want to see Cary Grant engaged in life-or-death struggles.

Grant's search for something different but not emotionally difficult continued. *People Will Talk* is a quietly bizarre picture written and directed by Joseph L. Mankiewicz that positions Grant as a brilliant gynecologist who first protects, then marries an unwed mother—the lovely, placid Jeanne Crain. Noah Praetorius possesses such vast stores of knowledge, compassion, and understanding as to give the angel Dudley from *The Bishop's Wife* a run for his money. Mankiewicz was coming off the consecutive smashes of *A Letter to Three Wives* and *All About Eve*, and had grown overly solicitous of his dialogue, as well as of his scenes, which seemed to go on forever. The film was being produced by Darryl Zanuck, who usually took his editing responsibilities very seriously, but he decided to let Mankiewicz have his way with the picture.

Mankiewicz demanded that his actors speak the dialogue as written, not customize it to suit their temperament and breath control. The only dispensation he gave was to Grant, who was allowed to make minor changes. Grant was probably attracted to the picture because it gave him a chance to play a character oblivious to fear or anxiety—someone who wasn't like him at all. He gives an expert, entirely convincing performance, as do Walter Slezak and Finlay Currie in charming, eccentric portrayals of charming, eccentric characters.

In fact, part of the picture's problem is that every character is eccentric, which is fine in comedy, but not in supposedly realistic social drama. In retrospect Grant seems to have been quietly appalled by the picture, perhaps because it lost money. Certainly, the subject matter made the film an outlier in terms of the Production Code. Theaters seemed flummoxed about how to sell it; in Chicago, one theater used a still of Grant and Jeanne Crain in their display ad, with dialogue bubbles over their heads. "But, doctor, I'm not married," Crain is saying, to which Grant replies, "Married or not . . . You're pregnant!" There must have been some pushback, because the ad was changed to Grant replying, "Married or not . . . You're going to . . ."

People Will Talk did about half as well as *I Was a Male War Bride*, bringing in only $2.1 million domestically. Darryl Zanuck was convinced that he knew why the picture flopped, and he informed Mankiewicz of his convictions in several confidential memos. "I still believe that if I had done the things I wanted to do instinctively in the editing of *People Will Talk* we would have had a picture that would have been quite an improvement on the version we released," he wrote Mankiewicz in February 1952. A month later, Zanuck was still obsessing over what went wrong. "The picture was a flat disappointment because it was miscast. You know that I did everything I could to keep Cary Grant out of the role after [MGM's] sad experience with *Crisis*. He is a comedian and he will always be a comedian and thus the people who went in to see Cary Grant in *People Will Talk* were disappointed."

Zanuck went on to assert that the movie would have been considerably better had there been 25 percent more action and 25 percent less talk. Since the picture had no action whatever, it was an entirely fair criticism to which Mankiewicz was completely indifferent, as his later pictures would prove.

On a personal list Grant kept of all of his pictures, he omitted only four: three from his early movie career (*Devil and the Deep, Born to Be Bad, When You're in Love*) and *People Will Talk*. In later years, Mankiewicz would say of his film *The Barefoot Contessa* that it was "the best of my bad pictures," but *People Will Talk* gives *The Barefoot Contessa* and *The Quiet American* serious competition despite its strange, compelling conviction about the value of Dr. Noah Praetorius—the singular man at its center with whom the writer-director obviously identifies. Once seen, it's not forgotten.

Which was no consolation to Grant. A few years after *People Will Talk*, Mankiewicz made *The Barefoot Contessa*, for which his first choice for the part of Harry Dawes—eventually played by Humphrey Bogart—was Gary Cooper. While negotiating for Cooper, the agent Bert Allenberg informed Mankiewicz that Grant was so concerned about his recent run of pictures that he had cut his quote to $150,000 "if only [a studio] could come up with a great script."

The best thing that happened in connection with *People Will Talk* came on July 16, 1951, when Grant placed his hand and footprints in the forecourt of Grauman's Chinese Theatre in connection with the movie's release. Grant's square is tinted green and contains the date, his footprints, two handprints, and his signature. A tourist named Georgia Douglas happened to be there during the ceremony and said, "He was most gracious to the public, shaking hands, joking and standing still while we snapped pictures with our tourist-type cameras."

AT THE BEST OF TIMES, Grant was prone to fretting, and, with the exception of *I Was a Male War Bride*, his recent roster of pictures constituted a succession of critical and financial disappointments. Life with Cary Grant at this point can be extrapolated from a letter Betsy Drake wrote to Kate Hepburn in January 1951. "Each time that I have written a note or letter to thank you for your charming candle holder, which we admire and love, I've taken it (the letter or note) to Cary for approval, spelling corrections, etc. Each time he attempted to rephrase my sincerest thoughts, rewrite my jokes, question my punctuation. Each time I've huffed out of the room after saying, 'Write it yourself, then!' Each time I've been called back and told that it was my duty as a wife to attend to thank you notes." Drake's tone is jocular, but it's clear that Drake was a young wife married to a successful middle-aged man with expectations of perfection from those around him.

Whatever Betsy's domestic failings, Grant still wanted the world to share his high estimation of her, so he tried to make her a star one more time. *Room for One More* was an early version of an anodyne Disney movie, the sort that would star Fred MacMurray. It's about a happily married couple who keep taking in strays of both the two-legged and four-legged variety. It was a domestic premise, and Grant worked best when he was snarkily observing domestic difficulties while keeping one foot firmly planted outside the family circle.

Once again, Grant mentored the children in the picture. A young actor named Larry Olsen had been hired to play one of the sons, but he seemed too old to be Betsy Drake's child, so he was switched to the secondary role of a boyfriend of one of the daughters. "Cary Grant was one of the nicest guys," Olsen reminisced, "an extremely nice fellow. . . . Cary gave everybody gifts at the end of the film, and he even apologized to me that I didn't get the role of the son."

Room for One More made money because it didn't cost much, but in order to make the deal attractive to Jack Warner, Grant took a huge salary cut—he got only a flat $100,000 for the picture, while Betsy got $25,000. Warner Bros. got a Cary Grant comedy for a total budget of $1 million.

It was during this run of pictures that Grant began to feel something gaining on him—the beginning of a serious fear of obsolescence, of overstaying his welcome. On the positive side of the ledger, there was his marriage to a woman who was not merely clever but actually intelligent—to use Grant's favorite metaphor, Betsy could catch the ball *and* throw it back, in life if not necessarily on the screen.

Of course, there were people who thought Betsy was a beard, most prominently Hedda Hopper.

It wasn't that Hopper was particularly homophobic—she was close to Cole Porter and George Cukor, among others. But if she smelled hypocrisy, watch out. Unless, of course, it involved Hedda Hopper. When Raymond Burr was threatened with being outed, she wrote him that she would tell any lies necessary in order to maintain his cover. Of course, Burr was employing her son William Hopper to play Paul Drake in the TV series *Perry Mason*, so it was easy for her to convince herself that her hypocrisy was actually maternal loyalty.

"Hedda Hopper was a bitch," Grant would say years later with finality. "I don't mean to speak ill of the dead, but she was. She just liked hurting people."

Monkey Business would be Grant's last picture for Howard Hawks, but the premise was very high concept—a youth serum is accidentally dumped into a water cooler, causing staid middle-aged people to revert to the emotional age of ten. It starts well, but grows slightly tiresome as it proceeds.

On the plus side, the young Marilyn Monroe was a delectable addition to the cast, leading to one of the film's best lines. As Monroe sashays past Charles Coburn and Grant, Grant raises a questioning eyebrow about her status as Coburn's secretary.

"Anyone can type," Coburn says.

Grant always had sensitive antennae for psychological displacement, and he sensed Monroe was troubled. His public comments were predominantly kind, characterizing her as shy and quiet and somehow sad.

Privately, he was more blunt, and seemed to take some offense at the competition Marilyn gave him in the race for the Most Disastrous Childhood.

> Marilyn was a very calculating girl. She was never late on *our* set, I'll tell you that. She was trying to get me to go to bed with her while she was trying to get Howard to do the same thing! We both knew it and—I can speak only for myself—it just turned me off—completely.
>
> Plus, I never believed all those stories she told about her childhood and being a poor orphan and her mother being cuckoo. She'd tell them to *strangers* at the drop of a hat. The girl had no subtlety, no discretion. She was much too blatant for me.

Monkey Business seems to have been a slightly uneasy shoot—Hawks disliked Ginger Rogers, calling her "Virginia" (her real name) throughout the picture, which put the actress on the defensive. Grant had to work with a chimp, which he found less threatening than the leopard in *Bringing Up Baby*. Hawks again made use of Grant's physical dexterity; at one point he does a one-armed cartwheel. "Cary Grant contributed a lot for his part," said the actor Robert Cornthwaite. "He had a remarkable memory of the games he had played as a kid, which he used for his character, and he brought a wonderful childlike quality to it."

Monkey Business was made in a quick eight weeks but proved yet another disappointment at the box office, earning only $2 million for the studio—the forty-seventh top grossing picture of the year. Some later critics found much to be delighted about, but in the twenty-first century it feels like one of Hawks's more laborious films.

And now Grant began to seriously ponder the door marked "Exit." He had made three financial and critical disappointments in a row—*Crisis, People Will Talk*, and *Monkey Business*. Of his recent pictures, only the innocuous *Room for One More* could be considered a (modest) financial success. He was middle-aged and increasingly conscious of it. The fact that Hollywood was changing fast was not to his liking. The studios were retrenching, severely cutting back production and costs in the wake of television, and to top it off, the new breed of actors that had become stars were the antithesis of Cary Grant— Method-oriented seekers of emotional truth such as Marlon Brando and Montgomery Clift. The fact that few Method actors would ever be noted for their light touch, or that Brando had cited Grant as one of the few movie actors "you could learn from" (the others included Paul Muni and Spencer Tracy), didn't seem to help. Grant was beginning to feel like a stranger in his adopted hometown.

In a sense, he always had been. Socially and psychologically, he was the guest, not the host. With *Penny Serenade* and *None But the Lonely Heart* he had made calculated stabs at official recognition, at sincere dramatic acting. But his pursuit of an Academy Award would go unrewarded until an honorary Oscar in 1970. It seems to have been an issue; when Harold Russell, a World War II veteran who had lost his hands in an explosion, got his Academy Award for *The Best Years of Our Lives*, Grant had whispered, "Where can *I* get a stick of dynamite?" It was not the most graceful remark of Grant's life, but a revealing one nonetheless.

It was back to romantic comedy for *Dream Wife*, again at MGM, this time with Deborah Kerr. The director was another first-timer, the screenwriter Sidney Sheldon, who had somehow won an Oscar for the unremarkable screenplay of *The Bachelor and the Bobby-Soxer.*

Dream Wife featured a ridiculous premise about Grant's character marrying a Middle Eastern princess for political reasons. It was one of those pictures that start with everybody rapturously in love, and end in recrimination and embarrassment.

MGM production head Dore Schary personally produced a picture or two a year, and he took on *Dream Wife* as one of his projects. The trouble began before the picture started shooting, when Harry Cohn called Sheldon and told him, "Be careful . . . Cary Grant is a killer. He likes to run things. Why do you think he picked you to direct the movie? . . . He's setting you up. He figures that with an inexperienced director, he can get away with murder."

Cohn was proven right. Inspecting the sets, Grant said, "If I had known it was going to look like this, I never would have agreed to do the picture." When Sheldon cut some lines from the script, he said, "If I had known you were going to cut those lines, I would never have agreed to do this picture." When he saw his wardrobe, he said, "If I had known they expected me to wear this, I never would have agreed to do this picture."

All this was part of Grant's process. But Sheldon was nervous, and it got worse when they actually started shooting. On the first day of production, Grant flubbed a line and Sheldon called "Cut." Grant turned to him and said, "Don't ever say 'Cut' when I'm in the middle of a scene," completely undercutting the first-time director in front of the crew. Sheldon wanted to quit the picture, but the assistant director said to hang on, Grant would calm down. He did, but he continued to test Sheldon's authority despite the fact that the two men were social friends.

When *Dream Wife* was screened for the MGM executives, they were pleased; when the picture was previewed for the paying public, they began to get worried; when it was released, they were suicidal. *Variety* called it a "highly contrived piece of screen nonsense . . . the loose handling reflects occasionally in the performances, notably Grant's."

Howard Strickling told Sidney Sheldon that Dore Schary ordered the picture thrown away—no booking at the Radio City Music Hall, minimal advertising—because "[Schary] can't afford to have his name on a flop." *Dream Wife* lost nearly $500,000 and deserved to. It's dismal, the worst picture Grant made as a name-above-the-title star. What's truly distressing about the picture is how cheap it looks—by 1953, $1.5 million didn't buy much at Metro.

Dream Wife set Grant's internal warning siren to High. There could be no doubt about it; he was now a falling star.

The photographer Murray Garrett told a story that indicated just how rapidly times were changing. Garrett had gone to a party at the Beverly Hills Hotel where he went down on one knee to take a picture of Van Johnson dancing with one of MGM's top female stars. They were twirling around, doing the Lindy.

The next day Garrett looked at the negative and saw that the woman in question hadn't been wearing underpants. "It wasn't as bad as the famous Carmen Miranda shot," Garrett remembered, "but it was still very obvious."

A panicked Garrett called Howard Strickling, who was obviously irritated at a photographer having the temerity to call him directly. "At MGM, you could call almost anybody by their first names," said Garrett, "but not Louis B. Mayer or Howard Strickling.

> I told him what I had. I told him I was not going to put it in the mail. I told him I was going to drive to Culver City and put it in his hand. I told him that if it got out, it would be on his end, not mine. I wanted it out of my office.
>
> I was thinking long-range. *Confidential* magazine had just started publishing. I had been offered $30,000 for shots from Lew Wasserman's birthday party, and after I turned it down the offer went up to $50,000.

After Garrett gave Strickling the film, the temperature suddenly shifted. "Nothing was ever said to me directly. I was simply treated differently after that. Gable suddenly became available for a layout, and he never had been before. Not to me. You had access to anybody if you were working for *Time* or *Life*, but lower-echelon publications or photographers didn't have it so easy. But after that, I never had to ask for anybody; they asked for me."

In the Hollywood of 1943, letting those pictures out would have been career suicide for a photographer. First, nobody would have printed them. Second, Louis B. Mayer would have instituted and enforced an industry-wide blackball of anybody who even suggested bartering for them. But in 1953 somebody would have printed them, or portions of them, Louis B. Mayer was no longer running MGM, and nobody had the power to institute an industry-wide blackball anymore. Power and control were shifting, and not in a way that worked to the advantage of the studios.

In many respects, Grant's creative conservatism was working against him, but the interesting thing is that his conservatism was in direct opposition to his willingness to swim against the political and social tides. In other words, he was a Republican, but a highly independent one. His defense of Ingrid Bergman was repeated when Charlie Chaplin's reentry permit was rescinded by the attorney general after he was safely out of the country, effectively exiling him to Europe after his back was turned. Most Republicans were lining up behind Joe McCarthy and his subordinate witch-hunters, but Grant stood up for Chaplin, telling anybody who would listen that not only was Chaplin a great artist, he was not a communist.

He respected outliers with integrity, people who went ahead and did as they pleased, whether anybody else liked it or not. In the early 1950s, Mae West made one of her many comebacks in a revival of her play *Diamond Lil*. It was more or less the mixture as before, but it was Mae West in the flesh, and theaters were packed. Despite Grant's oft-stated doubts about West, when her show played Hollywood Grant took Betsy Drake, Leslie Caron, and Arthur Loew. The play was full of double entendres of various degrees of outrageousness, but it was a great deal of fun.

After the show, Grant knew that his attendance was required back-stage. He knocked on the door and West's maid asked the group to wait while she got herself prepared to meet her admirers. Ten minutes passed, after which the door opened.

West was a tiny woman, about five feet tall, which meant that she always wore platform shoes in public. When Grant and his party walked into her dressing room, she was standing on a miniature stage about a foot high, with two pink spotlights directed at her, which took years off her age. She opened her arms and exclaimed, "Cary!" He walked toward her and they hugged. They chatted for a bit, and then the audience was over.

Neither Caron nor Arthur Loew knew quite what to make of this bizarre apparition, but Grant told everybody to go see her whether they thought she was funny or not. She was *sui generis*, one of a kind. He explained that West was the only woman who had ever done what she had done, and that nobody would ever do it again.

WITH THE FLOPS ADDING UP, Grant decided to take some time off, maybe even retire. Try to enjoy the comfortable life his labor had earned him. For a period of about a year, Grant turned down every film offer. He had been interested in making *Dial M for Murder* for Hitchcock, thereby scratching the murderous itch left over from the abortive *Suspicion*. But Jack Warner told Hitchcock he didn't think the audience would accept Grant as a murderer. Hitchcock correctly thought Warner's real objection was to Grant's salary demands—Warner believed Grant was unnecessary for a presold property like *Dial M for Murder*, which had been a successful play in both New York and London. Hitchcock hired the much cheaper Ray Milland.

One afternoon in 1954, Grant went over to Humphrey Bogart's house. That year Bogart had *Beat the Devil, The Caine Mutiny, The Barefoot Contessa*, and *Sabrina* in release. Billy Wilder had offered *Sabrina* to Grant, but he had turned it down. Wilder then made a mistake and hired the saturnine Bogart, who was immune to the charms of both Wilder and the script and looked old enough to be Audrey Hepburn's weathered father. "He was a shit," said Wilder, "because he knew that I wanted to have Cary Grant." The casting also made Sabrina's decision to run away with Bogart at the end of the picture perverse; it would have made sense only if Sabrina was a nurse.

Grant didn't regret turning down *Sabrina*, let alone *A Star Is Born*, but he was still fretting, wondering about what to do next, if anything. "You get all the good parts now, Bogie," he said. "How do you get so many of them?" Bogart's answer was simple: "Because I keep working." He explained that work begets work—if you keep the cards moving around the table, sooner or later you'll get a good hand. Grant took this under advisement, but still seemed doubtful. And so he sat and stewed.

And then, just like that, everything changed. Alfred Hitchcock had a script and nobody but Cary Grant could play it. It was called *To Catch a Thief*.

PART THREE

1954-1986

"I think I became what I portrayed."

—Cary Grant

"There's a lot to be said for making people laugh. Did you know that's all some people have? It isn't much, but it's better than nothing in this cockeyed caravan."

—From Preston Sturges's *Sullivan's Travels*

CHAPTER FOURTEEN

===========

Grant was brooding in the Far East when he got the telegram. It was from Alfred Hitchcock saying, more or less, come back, I've found a wonderful new actress.

Her name was Grace Kelly, and of course Grant had seen her in *Dial M for Murder* and *Rear Window* as well as a small role in *High Noon*. "We made *To Catch a Thief*, and she was the best actress I ever worked with, with all due respect to Ingrid. But Grace, she was really there in a scene. She really listened. Unlike most actresses, she wasn't worried how she looked or what angle the camera was shooting her from."

Grant sounds like he was a bit in love, a typical response that led many to overrate Kelly as an actress—any equivalent comparison of her and Bergman's skills is moony hyperbole, as Kelly would probably have been the first to admit. Grant gave every indication of wanting to work with Kelly many more times, but, as he put it, "She had the indecency to marry [Prince] Rainier. And that was the end of that."

What is certain is that Grant met his equal in polish and elegance. *To Catch a Thief* is a great picture only if you think impeccably executed entertainment ascends to art, and it probably does. Certainly, it's far more pleasurable than most clinically judged aesthetic masterpieces. Oddly, the reviews weren't great. *Variety* said, "Billed as a comedy-mystery, it stacks up as a drawn-out pretentious piece that seldom hits comedy level. As a mystery it fails to mystify, although it does confuse. . . . This film won't enhance the prestige of either the stars or the producer-director."

Nevertheless, the film has worn beautifully, perhaps because its virtues are extinct. It offers Grant and Kelly, a genuinely witty script by John Michael Hayes that drapes Grant in the dramatic equivalent of one of his custom-tailored suits, the Riviera captured in glowing Technicolor, all mixed with absolute confidence by a master confectioner of movie moments. Grant embodies the motto that guided Hitchcock in the making of his Paramount films: "Beautiful people, beautiful scenery, a love story and suspense."

Grant's two favorite directors would always be Hawks and Hitchcock—the former because of his loose grip and willingness to rewrite and improvise, the latter because of his calm control, imperturbability, and a passion for order that made improvisation irrelevant. "Oh, Hitch is *great*," Grant said. "You walk on his set for a scene and the set is *everything* you thought it would be, just as you envisioned it—never *anything* out of place or wrong. And he's so *patient*." Shortly before he died, Grant said, "If Hitch said I'm going to make a movie of the telephone book, I'd be there." It was an exaggeration—Grant would turn down several Hitchcock pictures—but a pardonable one.

> Each of those directors permitted me the release of improvisation during the rehearsing of each scene—rather in the manner that Dave Brubeck's musical group improvises on the central theme, never losing sight of the original mood, key or rhythm, no matter how far out they go. [These directors] permitted me to discover how far out *I* could go with confidence, while guided by their quiet, sensitive directorial approval.

The admiration went both ways. "One doesn't direct Cary Grant," Hitchcock told Peter Bogdanovich. "One just puts him in front of a movie camera."

Grant had been doing nothing since *Dream Wife*, even going so far as to tell reporters he was retired. "It was the period of the blue jeans, the dope addicts, the Method, and nobody cared about elegance or comedy at all," he would complain in his best reactionary mode.

But Grant liked the script of *To Catch a Thief*, and he liked it even more when Hitchcock agreed to take a salary cut in order to be able to afford Grant. Grant negotiated the best deal he would ever have as a working actor without any production responsibilities: a straight 10 percent of the gross. Hitchcock's deal was $150,000 plus 10 percent of the profits after the film earned twice its production cost, but Hitchcock's percentage only kicked in after Grant's percentage was deducted from the total. By comparison, Grace Kelly was practically a day player, costing the picture a flat $80,000.

The part of John Robie, reformed cat burglar, fit in with the psychological pattern that Hitchcock saw as a component of his favorite actor: a man with an ambivalence toward women. As Patrick McGilligan points out, "In *Suspicion*, Grant plays an apparent cad who wants to kill his wife; in *Notorious*, he can't bring himself to believe in love. Now Grant was cast as a lone wolf, a man every bit as tense, self-absorbed and narcissistic as the actor himself."

Hitchcock's associate producer was Herbert Coleman, the same Herbert Coleman who had developed a dislike of Grant twenty years earlier on *The Last Outpost*. Coleman found that Grant still exhibited a nearly bipolar swinging between professional extremes. On one hand, he wanted to be "matey," be accepted as a good coworker; on the other, he insisted on the lofty perquisites of an upper-echelon star. C.O. "Doc" Erickson, the production manager, had his hands full for matters on- as well as off-screen. "We have not been able to locate a satisfactory car for Francie's convertible, even though Hitch has agreed to accept almost anything we can produce," wrote Erickson. "Speaking of cars, we were unable to obtain a [Cadillac] convertible for Grant, either, so he may turn right around and go home. But, then, he may call the president of General Motors and get one flown over."

Grant's contract called for an air-conditioned limousine, either a Lincoln or a Cadillac, complete with liveried chauffeur. Erickson spent a lot of time wrestling with Grant over the car:

> I wasn't able to locate a Cadillac, and told him that, as he came down the gangplank. In his usual charming manner, he replied that he didn't want a Cadillac in the first place. He wanted a Ford or some small inconspicuous car. He didn't see why he needed a chauffeur since he enjoys driving himself. I told him we had two possible choices for a valet and/or secretary and he thought this was

completely ridiculous. However, I am not so naive as to believe that the wind may not blow in another direction next week. The ironic part of the story is I'm having just as much damned trouble finding a Ford or Chevy.

The right car was finally ordered from England and delivered to the location in France. After several weeks of the limousine, Grant came to the realization that the limo might make him seem ostentatious, if not pretentious. The limousine was returned and he contented himself with a roadster with a chauffeur in street clothing. But it didn't last; after a week of being one of the boys, he went back to Erickson and asked "Where's my limousine?" which meant that it had to be flown back to France.

Hitchcock would not have accepted such expensively capricious behavior from any other leading man, but for Grant he swallowed, smiled, and nodded. For Hitchcock, Grant was a smoother approximation of what John Wayne was for John Ford—an idealized projection of what the director would like to have been. Grant was his favorite actor—not a category with a lot of competition.

"Hitchcock likes me a lot," Grant confided to one actress, "but at the same time he detests me. He would like to be in my place. He'd very much like to be in my place, because he *imagines* himself in my place."

The production was headquartered at the Carlton Hotel in Monte Carlo, where Grace Kelly was domiciled with Oleg Cassini, and Grant with Betsy. Kelly had sent Cassini a postcard as she left for the location that contained the imperious sentence: "Those who love me shall follow me." Like a good subject, Cassini had followed, only to find that Kelly had changed her mind; she told him that she had to focus on the film and wouldn't have any time for him. "I cannot have my work disturbed. Even the man I marry will have to realize that," she said. Cassini must have been completely besotted—he stayed in France for the two months of location work and Kelly managed to fit him in, here and there. Toward the end of the shoot, she agreed to marry him, an agreement that would be submarined by Kelly's parents, who refused to allow her to marry a twice-divorced man.

On Sundays, Kelly and Cassini socialized with the Grants and the Hitchcocks. One Sunday they went on a sightseeing tour of Monaco. They peered through the gates trying to get a glimpse of the gardens.

John Michael Hayes thought they should have the production office call the palace and arrange a tour, but the location work wrapped before Grace could inspect the gardens of which she would soon be part-owner. She and Prince Rainier wouldn't meet until mid-1955, on a visit to France after she won her Oscar for *The Country Girl*.

Aside from the satisfaction of making a beloved movie, Grant's enduring friendship with Grace Kelly was another bonus of the production. When she married Rainier in 1956, Grant, Frank Sinatra, and Rita Gam were the only Hollywood people invited. (Sydney Guilaroff was also there, but he was working—he designed Kelly's hairstyle and also made a toque hat for her.)

During the location work, Grant insisted on quitting at 6 p.m., so he could have dinner at a civilized time. Hitchcock was displeased; quitting at six was fine at the studio in Hollywood, but location filming was expensive and required the cast and crew alike to pull together and work hard to minimize expense. Grant didn't care; he left the set at 6 p.m. whether Hitchcock liked it or not. The only other major star who behaved in this manner that combined fuss-budgetry with imperiousness was Spencer Tracy. The reasons were similar—Tracy was a nervous alcoholic, nothing like the solid, phlegmatic man of the people he played. For fretful personalities such as Grant and Tracy, acting was far riskier than it was for performers with more of a synchronicity between themselves and what they played.

Eventually, *To Catch a Thief* fell more than a month behind schedule. The final cost was nearly $3 million, an overrun that was quickly forgiven when the film opened in August 1955 and earned four times its cost, helped along by an advertising campaign that featured the tagline "It's Hitchcock . . . It's Monte Carlo . . . It's Cary Grant and Grace Kelly!" Below that were huge head shots of the two stars, bracketing "Alfred Hitchcock's *To Catch a Thief*." What else needed to be said?

Cary Grant was back.

GRANT HAD LONG BEEN THE MASTER of the no-information interview (the modern master of the form is Tom Cruise), so it stands to reason that the conversation in which he revealed his true feelings about the movie business was not about him.

The subject was Barbara Hutton and the journalist was Dean Jennings, who was writing a book about Grant's former wife. The interview took place a few weeks before Grant left for the Riviera to shoot *To Catch a Thief*. When Grant stuck to the subject he did little but talk about how generous Barbara was, and how fond he was of her, which naturally raised the question of why the marriage failed. But in the course of a three-hour interview, Grant freely vented about his ambivalent (at best) or resentful (at worst) feelings about Hollywood, journalism, stardom, and the public that professed to love Cary Grant. It's a zero-sum soliloquy that sounds like something Elias Leach might have uttered if he'd ever had any success in life.

"Anyone who has two dollars creates envy in the world," Grant announced.

> You know it and I know it. Look at Lindbergh. He was a hero, then he was a bum. So was Jack Dempsey. So were many other highly publicized fellows. The less publicity . . . the better off they would have been. As soon as Barbara arrives at that status, the better off she will be. . . .
>
> I need the good will of the press. I need the good will of the people that sell the pictures. I don't give a damn, really, and I don't think it matters. It only matters if you're in a good picture. It doesn't mean a damn thing what people write in our business. . . . I know what it is to be out on the street with everybody gawking, poking each other in the elevator the moment you get outside your room. Or walking down a theater aisle. I don't give a damn. I look right back. . . .
>
> I can't go into any shop but that the girl doesn't say "Just a minute" and she goes into the back room and calls her friend Minnie who works down in a beauty parlor and who comes running. And Minnie in the meantime has called someone else and told them, "Quick, call so and so . . ." Even at my great age. You don't know what it's like, our business. . . . They turn on you and rip you limb from limb. Any second. Out of envy. . . .
>
> Anyone who doesn't get it always says, "Oh, my God, it must be wonderful." But when you get it from morning to night, it is no longer wonderful. We're absolutely stupid to be embarked in this business where our face is connected with our accomplishments.

Such as they are. . . . Two writers said to me the other day, "We've just done the work of our lives." And I said, "How?" And they said, "We went out into the park with the children and played football. We couldn't have had a more wonderful time." I damn near cried. I can't go out in the park and neither can anyone else in our industry. . . .

No dear public ever did anything for me. They only go to see the picture when it's good. None of them are philanthropists, I can tell you that. . . . We just satiate the morbid curiosity of people . . . but alas, I must take it because that is my business. I'm connected with it and my bank account thrives on it. . . . Because if we have money, they say, we must necessarily be happy. That ought to be true. But money is no cure. . . .

Demand is created. It's a circle. Nobody's waiting eagerly, with their little two dollars in their hand for a book to come out. It's foisted upon them. They're advertised into it. But you can't undo it any more than you can undo television now. You throw millions of people out of work. If a man lived in the middle of the desert he wouldn't give a damn about it because he couldn't get it. And he wouldn't be saying, "My God, I wonder what happened to Barbara Hutton?" Or Cary Grant. He wouldn't give a good goddamn. . . .

I've always felt like this. Everybody knows it. This is nothing new. Any columnist in town would tell you this. Hedda Hopper calls me and asks me a personal question. I say, "None of your goddamn business." We're enemies for all of three days. Then she gets it somewhere else and misquotes it and gets it all balled up and that's her fault. It doesn't affect my character or myself one bit. I only have to live with me, not with people's impressions of me. Public relations hasn't a damn thing to do with my career. My God, there are people who have murdered their grandmothers, but if they give a great performance in a great picture, their careers will zoom.

I'm a hard customer. I've developed it. I've had to fight, scratch, kick in this world. [Barbara] hasn't. She will never be that way. She's too tender and sweet to have been born in this materialistic generation.

When Jennings suggested that Hutton's interest in poetry might be satisfied by setting up some sort of foundation, Grant snorted.

The people who are poor—they would ask "What the hell is poetry? Where's a good steak?" These are the people who make themselves heard aggressively, and there you are . . . they're the people who write letters to the editor. They're the little reporters who are having a tough time making ends meet. The world is filled with them. I wouldn't advise her to do such a thing . . . much as I'd like to help the starving young poets, the starving or struggling young anyone.

This self-pitying procession of grievances characterizing Grant as a helpless victim of the movie-industrial complex would be mirrored in Clifford Odets's play *The Big Knife* and its main character, the movie star Charlie Castle, who loathes both himself and his business— high ideals and hopes traded for fame and fortune. The public said they loved him, but Grant saw that public as a gigantic Janus-faced beast who could turn on the object of their supposed affection in a heartbeat. At one point in the interview, Grant mockingly slips into the eager tone of the movie star doing press: "Would you care to hear about my new picture? I'm very eager to talk about it. I get 10 percent of the gross."

GRANT HAD GIVEN UP GOLF, abandoned tennis, and now contented himself with travel with Betsy. Their preferred method of travel involved cargo ships with cabins to rent out. They would board at the harbor in San Pedro and settle in. In Grant's mind, it had all "the luxury of owning a yacht without having to keep it up. Travelling via cargo-carrying boats is the world's greatest treat. There is no such silliness on them as Captain's dinners. There is no 'organized recreation' by Pursers who are about to plan your day with such idiotic games as shuffleboard, badminton or deck tennis.

No one bothers you. No one even looks at you. The crew of a cargo ship doesn't know or care who you are. Usually there's only a handful of passengers; 10 or 12, and none of them are interested in anyone's autographs. They leave you alone and will usually thank you to leave them alone. The meals are plain but wonderful. The grog is strong, if you happen to want grog. The ships are spotless, and the quarters are wonderful. And you get all this for a fraction of a so-called luxury liner, with its hundreds of crew, hundreds of passengers, not to mention paper hats and confetti.

When they wanted a simpler getaway, they would get in the station wagon and head for Palm Springs, Santa Barbara, San Francisco, or Las Vegas, despite the fact that neither Grant nor his wife were gamblers. When not traveling they stayed home and enjoyed Betsy's cooking. "Sometimes [she] has a dozen or so pots simmering at the same time," asserted Grant.

In fact, Betsy's cooking was the source of much discussion around Hollywood, and there was always a persistent rumor that Alfred Hitchcock, who took food seriously, was unimpressed by her efforts. It is said that his portrayal of the well-meaning but incompetent wife-chef in *Frenzy* was based on Betsy Drake's gift for devising what Hitchcock considered inedible meals.

In DECEMBER 1955, Universal Pictures compiled a comprehensive list of the financial requirements of every leading man in the movie business. Humphrey Bogart, Gary Cooper, and Spencer Tracy were clearly out of Universal's reach—they all got $250,000 against 10 percent of the gross. Kirk Douglas ($200,000 up-front, with 50 percent of the profits after the studio broke even) was a maybe, as was Robert Mitchum, who was getting $150,000 plus 25 percent of the net profits. Alan Ladd was getting $150,000 against 10 percent of the gross, but he was tied up with Warner Bros. Errol Flynn was more or less broke and could be had for a flat $150,000.

On the way down but still valuable was Joel McCrea, who got either $75,000 flat or $50,000 plus 17.5 percent of the profits. Randolph Scott got $150,000 plus a percentage and an ownership position. Less valuable was George Raft, who got $30,000, while David Niven was in a temporary trough, getting only $50,000–$60,000 at a time when Jack Palance was getting $92,500 per picture.

William Holden was far ahead of the pack; he was listed as requiring "Ownership. Own company. Booked far in advance." And James Stewart was in a league of his own: "Availability problem. Ownership complications. Recent deals far beyond anything we have been prepared to offer, including ownership."

All this is a window into a time that drove the founding generation of moguls crazy. Attendance had declined by 50 percent since 1947, and here were actors getting percentages of the gross, not to mention ownership of negatives. The drumbeat of stars as well as directors demanding larger and larger pieces of the action would drive Darryl Zanuck to quit running 20th Century–Fox and force Jack Warner, among others, to severely cut back on production and slash budgets in order to maintain some level of financial viability.

In a declining market, stars who could guarantee a decent gross such as John Wayne ("Unavailable" according to the Universal document) could demand and get those terms. And then there was Cary Grant. He was listed as "Might get for 50 percent if he were anxious to do property."

Grant had been one of the first freelance actors to get a percentage years before, but as of 1955 he had been lapped by several actors. That was about to change. Soon, Grant would set up his own production company in order to attain the coveted status of "Ownership" referred to in the Universal document. His production activity wouldn't add to his portfolio of signature pictures, but it would make him extremely wealthy.

GRANT KNEW THAT HE COULD NOT RELY on Hitchcock to come to him with custom-made properties on a regular basis; he had to come up with material on his own, which is what led him to the idea of remaking *Mandy* (also known as *Crash of Silence*), a touching film Alexander Mackendrick made about a deaf girl who is sent to a special school where she is brought out of her shell. "She'll find a home in every heart!" brayed the advertising. "She'll reach into the heart of every home!"

After *To Catch a Thief*, Paramount was anxious to stay in business with Grant, and when he suggested an American remake of a British movie, they tugged their corporate forelocks and said, "Brilliant!" Mackendrick was summoned from London and arrived in Hollywood, where he was met by Alan Pakula, then a young assistant to studio head Don Hartman. "Don received me with open arms and said 'What do you think of the project?'" remembered Mackendrick.

"I said, 'What project?'

"'Oh, God, didn't [Mackendrick's agent] tell you? OK—we've got a contract with Cary Grant and what he wants to do is remake *Mandy*, shot for shot, with him playing the Jack Hawkins character.'" Nothing interested Mackendrick less than remaking his own movie, but he was a stranger in a strange land and he couldn't think of a way to gracefully tell Hartman of his overwhelming apathy. The next day, Hartman personally drove Mackendrick to Palm Springs, where he had dinner with Grant and Betsy at their house while they all watched television.

"A butler with white gloves brought in trays with little legs underneath, and put down very good steaks in front of us, and we all watched television together. It was Noel Coward's *Blithe Spirit*. I ate this steak, looking from the butler to Cary Grant to Betsy Drake, to the television set, thinking, 'What am I doing here?'" Mackendrick told Grant he'd like to think about the project, even though he had no intention of following through. His first American film would not be *Mandy*, but *Sweet Smell of Success*, and Grant's plans for *Mandy* never went beyond his initial enthusiasm.

All this meant that Grant still needed a project, preferably about children. He had liked *Room for One More* because he got to play a father, and had told Melville Shavelson and Jack Rose, that picture's screenwriters, that if they could ever come up with something similar, he wanted to see it. With *Mandy* losing steam, Grant asked them if they had another idea for a domestic comedy.

They had been looking but hadn't found anything.

"Well," Grant said, "I found one, would you like to hear it?"

Grant told them the story—a governess becomes infatuated with both her widowed employer and his children. Marriage follows.

"Who wrote that?" asked Shavelson.

"Betsy," replied Grant.

"Cary, that's a wonderful story," said Shavelson. "How much does she want for it?"

The price was $30,000, not bad for an original story with a huge star attached. The negotiations began. Shavelson told the studio that Grant "will not commit until you buy it because he doesn't want

[Drake] to think that you bought it only because he committed. So you've got to put up the money now."

Paramount cut the check and Shavelson and Rose began work on the script. At that point, Grant popped by to tell them he was leaving for Spain to make a picture for Stanley Kramer "with Sinatra and some Italian girl." Shavelson went to the front office and told them they needed to get Grant's signature on the contract because he and Jack Rose were pulling large salaries and the studio had nothing in writing that tied Grant to the project. D. A. Doran, a studio executive, hurried to the airport and told Grant that Shavelson and Rose were making great headway on the script, but Grant needed to sign the contract before he left, otherwise Betsy might find out that the studio only bought it "because you said you were gonna be in it." Grant signed, and the dominoes began to fall on one of the most painful episodes of his professional life.

Grant's contract with Stanley Kramer for the film that became *The Pride and the Passion* consists of sixty-nine pages of agate type that provides an interesting window into the perks of major stardom of the period. His base pay is set at 10 percent of the gross. Past sixteen weeks of shooting, he was entitled to an overage of $18,750 a week. He had veto powers over any costar changes should Sinatra or Sophia Loren drop out; he was guaranteed $300,000 if the picture was canceled or abandoned; he had veto power over the cameraman—had Franz Planer been replaced, Grant's preferred replacements were Robert Burks or Milton Krasner.

Grant even had 10 percent of Kramer's piece of the soundtrack album. George Antheil's score was owned by the Sands Music Corporation, which was affiliated with Sinatra, and was part of his deal. Capitol Records paid 24 cents for each album sold, which was split between Kramer and Sands. In turn, Sands agreed to pay Antheil six cents per album. Grant's overall 10 percent of the soundtrack entitled him to 1.2 cents per album.

The Pride and the Passion was meant to extend Stanley Kramer's directorial franchise beyond the furrowed-brow social problem pictures he had been producing. Grant was impressed by Kramer's command of the difficult location sequences, and was initially enthusiastic about the picture's prospects. But the finished picture revealed that Kramer had little feel for the epic, and in any case the script—about a group of Spanish revolutionaries transporting a giant cannon six hundred miles to fight the French, only to be opposed by the British, who want their cannon back—was overwhelmed by the cast.

Sinatra was on his worst behavior, alternating between indifference and recalcitrance. He refused to stay on location with the rest of the company. Instead, he was at the Hilton in Madrid, three hours from the location. Two weeks before location work was scheduled to end, Sinatra told Kramer he was leaving because . . . he felt like leaving. Grant would later tell a friend that the reason Sinatra stalked off was because Sophia Loren was allowing Grant to monopolize her time and she had stopped speaking to Sinatra.

Kramer had to complete Sinatra's scenes on a Hollywood sound-stage that looked noticeably phony compared to the visual splendor of the locations. Sinatra would pull the same stunt a few years later, leaving the Hawaiian location of *The Devil at Four O' Clock* and forcing Mervyn LeRoy to cobble together a crucial climactic scene between Sinatra and Spencer Tracy with the latter working with a double.

Tracy soured on Sinatra after his unprofessional behavior, but Grant didn't seem to mind—the two remained good friends for the rest of Grant's life, and Grant asked Sinatra to introduce him when he received his honorary Academy Award in 1970.

Grant and Loren were more than friendly. In her memoirs, Loren referred to "a great friendship, a special partnership." It began with Grant introducing himself at a cocktail party by saying, "Miss Lol-loloren, I presume? Or is Miss Lorenigida?" a dig at her rival Gina Lollobrigida. Luckily, Loren laughed, and relaxed.

"I liked looking Cary over, looking at him eye to eye, not missing out on those genteel gestures, the way he bent his head to one side while he eyed you with intelligent attention. I got to know him, to appreciate his sense of humor, I knew how to make him smile."

Grant asked her out to dinner, and she was flustered—Loren had grown up watching Grant, Tyrone Power, and Clark Gable in an Italian movie house that looked like the one in *Cinema Paradiso*. It was hard for her to make the transition to Grant as a human being, let alone as a man. Grant persisted: "Yes, darling, you and me, out for dinner."

They took off in his red MG, for a long drive in the Spanish countryside. "He told me things about himself and about filmmaking, but lightheartedly. 'Hollywood is a simple fairy tale; if you understand that, you'll never get hurt.' "

The relationship deepened. During Loren's scenes, he began to function as a codirector, advising both Stanley Kramer and Loren on her presentation. "He didn't want her to have the image of an Italian sex symbol," remembered Kramer. "He thought she was beyond that. . . . He never hesitated to say, 'Why don't we do another take? I don't think her line was clear there.' Or, 'I think she can do a little bit better, don't you think so Sophia?' He encouraged her and bolstered her. As he did everybody."

Loren was attracted by his maturity, his wisdom, his interest. As for Grant, he was stunned by her sensuality, her Roman warmth. He told her about his childhood, his mother, his days with Bob Pender and the comic highlights that infiltrate the memories of every young performer who has become an older, successful performer. They began to fall in love.

There was only one barrier to their happiness. Well, two.

1. Grant was married to Betsy Drake.

2. Loren was in a relationship with Carlo Ponti, an Italian producer who was also married.

In later years, Loren would imply that her relationship with Grant was emotionally intense but sexually chaste, although the notes Grant wrote her indicate a depth of emotion that would have been impossible to sustain if all they were doing was holding hands.

Grant got on the phone to Hollywood, to Mel Shavelson and Jack Rose, who were industriously working on *Houseboat*, as Betsy's story was now titled.

"How are you boys coming on the screenplay?" Grant asked.

"We're doing very well, Cary."

"Well, I just want you to know, I just met the new Garbo."

"What do you mean?" asked Shavelson.

"There's this Italian girl, this Sophia Loren. Would it make much of a change to change [the female lead] to an Italian girl?"

Since Shavelson and Rose were writing the script for the starring duo of Grant and Betsy Drake, a sudden shift to an earthy Italian girl did indeed present problems. On the other hand, they were Hollywood scriptwriters and Cary Grant was a star.

No problem at all, they replied, after which they hung up the phone and proceeded to a page one rewrite.

On their last night in Spain, Grant proposed marriage to Loren. "I need more time," she said in the time-honored tradition of a woman who's stalling.

"Why don't we get married first, and then think about it?" he replied.

What made all this even more remarkably awkward was the fact that Betsy had arrived on the set of *The Pride and the Passion* and noticed that her husband couldn't take his eyes off his costar. At some point they must have had it out, because Betsy sailed back to the United States while the film was still shooting. The name of the ship was *Andrea Doria*. The ship left Genoa on July 17, moved on to Cannes, Naples, and Gibraltar, where Betsy boarded.

On July 25, 1956, about sixty miles off the coast of Nantucket, the *Andrea Doria* collided with a Swedish liner called the *Stockholm*. The *Stockholm* stayed afloat, but the *Andrea Doria* lurched, tilted, and began to take on water. It didn't sink for some hours, which is why only forty-six people died. Betsy lost a lot of jewelry and the manuscript of a book she had been writing, but she survived. She was a woman with a good sense of humor—"Well, I guess I lost *everything* to the Italians this year!" she told her husband.

Despite the best intentions of all concerned, there was only pain to be derived from *The Pride and the Passion*, and it spread outward from Betsy Drake to Grant to Stanley Kramer to United Artists. Produced for the reasonable cost of $3.7 million, *The Pride and the Passion* returned $6.7 million worldwide, accruing a loss of $2.5 million. The profits from Kramer's previous film, *Not As a Stranger*, had been cross-collateralized against the returns from *The Pride and the Passion*, so Kramer had to sell both movies to United Artists in order to get out from under his losses from the latter picture. Only Grant did well, financially if not creatively. In later years, Grant would ironically refer to the film as *My Pride and My Passion*.

CHAPTER FIFTEEN

In what was probably the early part of 1952, Leo McCarey wrote an undated memo to himself—a sort of spiritual pep talk. "My aim is to reestablish myself as a creative producer—director-writer, and to regain my autonomy . . . so that neither Hollywood nor our country need be ashamed, either at home or with our foreign release."

After 1945's *The Bells of St. Mary's*, a sequel to *Going My Way* that was the most successful film RKO had released up to that time, McCarey had made *Good Sam*, a Gary Cooper vehicle that made a little money but was regarded as a disappointment. And then he sold his Rainbow Productions, which had produced *The Bells of St. Mary's* and *Good Sam*, to Paramount.

There followed three years of planning and political upheaval during which McCarey was a friendly witness during the House Un-American Activities hearings in October 1947. It was a strangely irrelevant testimony; McCarey gave every indication of wishing he was elsewhere. What seems to have happened is that McCarey, like Gary Cooper, did not want to testify, but the committee wanted them for marquee value. Both McCarey and Cooper negotiated what they would and would not say in advance, which resulted in them saying as little as possible.

Robert Stripling, the committee's chief investigator, asked McCarey if *Going My Way* and *The Bells of St. Mary's* had been successful in Russia.

"We haven't received one ruble from Russia on either picture," replied McCarey.

"What is the trouble?"

"Well, I think I have a character in there that they do not like."

"Bing Crosby?"

"No; God."

Stripling went on to ask McCarey if he had noticed communists in any specific group in Hollywood. "Yes, I have, particularly in the writer's group," said McCarey, before specifying the ways in which writers could slant stories: "In the suppression of ideas that are pro-American. Many a script never sees the light of day because it is rejected before we ever get to read it. . . . The dialogue in the script could be ostensibly quite innocuous but they can cast a character so repulsive when you take one look at him you don't like the man who is portrayed as a capitalist, a banker or whatever part he is portraying."

Although McCarey said that he had personal encounters with communist writers who tried to insert propaganda into his pictures, Stripling never asked for any names, nor did McCarey offer any. When Stripling asked him a leading question about producing anticommunist pictures to counter the commie wave, McCarey demurred, saying "Pictures should be entertainment. . . . I believe it only tends toward causing more enmity if we are partisan and take any sides in our pictures."

In his letter to himself, McCarey enumerated his roster of professional errors. He believed that selling Rainbow had been a cataclysmic mistake. "After heading a corporation that acquired assets of over two and a half million dollars, I suddenly found I had not only sold out my assets but I had sold myself out, too." McCarey went on to enumerate his plans for the future. *The Bells of St. Mary's* would soon return to his ownership, after RKO's seven-year lease on the picture expired. McCarey figured that a few years after that, the picture could either be reissued, depending on the status of Ingrid Bergman—persona non grata because of her affair with Roberto Rossellini—or remade.

Then there was the awkward matter of the profits from John Ford's *Fort Apache*. McCarey had loaned Ford $360,000 to help finance the picture in exchange for 7.5 percent of the film's profits. Ford's Argosy Productions had paid off the loan with interest, but McCarey failed to sign a release. Paramount, which had bought Rainbow, offered to sell what was now their 7.5 percent of *Fort Apache* back to Ford for an additional $40,000, but Ford was disinclined to pay twice for one loan. Ford and McCarey were united by many things, but McCarey's fumbling of their financial transaction could have put a serious strain on their friendship.

And beyond those matters was the ownership of the film McCarey had just finished, the film that would be called *My Son John*. It was, he believed, the film that would put him back on top both critically and commercially.

My Son John is one of the legendary disasters of auteurist studies, a film that is every bit as chaotically bad as its dismal reputation would indicate. McCarey targets communism's potential impact on the American family, and he eases the audience into the picture with overplayed domestic comedy that segues into an anticommunist tract. It was, to say the least, a bad-luck movie.

McCarey began production in March 1951, and was obviously writing the script as he went along because he was still shooting when Robert Walker, the star of the film, died on August 28. With Walker or without him, Helen Hayes, who was playing Walker's mother, said that every day was chaos. After Walker's death, McCarey shut down the picture so he could figure out what to do, then went back for another twelve weeks of shooting and post-production.

My Son John is an obvious paraphrase of Hitchcock's *Shadow of a Doubt*. Both pictures involve a beloved relative coming back to small-town America after a long time away, with an intimate family member gradually tumbling to the fact that the intervening years have turned him into a monster—a serial killer in the case of *Shadow of a Doubt*, a sneering, effete communist in the case of *My Son John*. In both films, the FBI is shadowing this aberrant creature.

The director had to patch together an ending from a rehearsal recording Walker had made of his final speech and some close-ups of Walker that Hitchcock had shot for *Strangers on a Train* and gave McCarey out of professional courtesy. One shot mattes Walker's head and shoulders from *Strangers on a Train* into a cab where he meets his death from a commie assassin. McCarey used his own voice to dub a few lines for Walker and it wasn't even a close match.

McCarey was oblivious to the picture's problems. "I have much confidence, as is possible in our unpredictable business, in its grossing over $4 million, and because of its subject matter, there is no ceiling.

Properly handled, it could do comparable business to *Going My Way* or *The Bells of St. Mary's*."

When it was finally released in April 1952, the reviews mimicked the political sympathies of the reviewer. The Hearst papers loved it, as did the American Legion. *The New York Times* and other liberal papers castigated it. Unfortunately, whether on the right or the left, few people went. With all of the overtime and reshooting, *My Son John* had blown far past its announced $1.8 million budget; it returned domestic rentals of less than $900,000 to Paramount—Leo McCarey's own private *Hindenburg*.

McCarey seems to have turned to God for help—much of his correspondence of the period consists of letters to and from Catholic clergy who want to show *The Bells of St. Mary's* or *Going My Way*. For a time he was working with John Wayne on a couple of projects, undoubtedly because John Ford urged Wayne to do what he could for McCarey. In 1953, Wayne set up a McCarey picture called *Hands Across the Sea* at Warners, but McCarey got cold feet. McCarey then developed a project on Marco Polo, and Wayne unsuccessfully tried to sell it to Jack Warner.

In December 1954, McCarey agreed to appear on *This Is Your Life* to honor his old friends Stan Laurel and Oliver Hardy, but he showed up three sheets to the wind for the live broadcast. The show's producers didn't want to put McCarey on-camera, but he pulled himself together and managed to tell an apocryphal anecdote about days gone by at the Hal Roach studio without tipping off his condition.

And then McCarey turned to *Adam and Eve*—not Mark Twain's version, but an adaptation of the Bible story that McCarey cowrote with a nun. It was "a two and a half hour show with three people in it," wrote John Wayne with a perceptible touch of wonder, not to mention concern.

McCarey had been contemplating *Adam and Eve* since 1947, and largely structured the story after Genesis. The story takes place in the Garden of Eden, beginning with Eve waking up and finding Adam next to her, followed by some gassy pontification about the glory of gender differences. The second act involves the exodus from Eden, and the third act is about life outside Eden. There is no serpent.

McCarey had tabled *Adam and Eve* in favor of *Good Sam* and *My Son John*. He had tentatively chosen Ingrid Bergman for the part of

Eve, but her domestic troubles put her temporarily beyond the reach of American movie producers. *Adam and Eve* got far enough along at Warners to make a 1955 trade ad of forthcoming pictures, along with *The Searchers, The Old Man and the Sea,* and another potential gem: *The Ed Sullivan Story,* starring none other than Ed Sullivan.

John Wayne's take on *Adam and Eve* was that it was "A wonderful story but terribly dependent on a big and expensive background." Jack Warner seems to have feigned interest as long as Wayne was in the room, but the temperature lowered whenever Duke wasn't around. After the project died at Warners, Wayne sent a letter to Howard Hughes in the hope that RKO might be interested in picking up the project. Nothing.

At that point, Wayne told Jack Warner that if Warners didn't have a script lined up for him, they could just use that slot for him to appear in a McCarey picture that Warners could release. Wayne was enthusiastic because there was a possibility of Ingrid Bergman making the picture her comeback vehicle. Jack Warner shied away because, "She's not in public favor and we'd get in trouble with the Catholic church." Wayne responded by saying that McCarey had cleared things with the Catholic church and had even supplied Wayne with the proper responses for any public criticism that came his way.

McCarey must have groused around town about the nonresponse he had gotten to his projects for Wayne, because Wayne wrote him a letter just before leaving town to make *The Searchers,* enumerating chapter and verse of all the projects that McCarcy proposed and what Wayne had done to make them happen.

"I don't know what the hell else I can do to be on your side, Leo," wrote Wayne. "I'm sure it is plain to you that I have put in a great deal of honest effort in the past two years trying to consummate a deal that would make it possible for you and me to work together." The truth was that if McCarey couldn't get a John Wayne picture off the ground in the mid-1950s, he was not just dead, he was decomposing.

Cary Grant knew McCarey was in deep trouble—the entire industry knew he was in trouble. In the latter part of 1954, Grant sent him a couple of scripts he thought had possibilities. Signaling that he was still willing to work with a director widely regarded as damaged goods might have been one of the most selfless acts of Grant's professional life—at least as brave as approving Clifford Odets to direct *None But the Lonely Heart.* McCarey replied that he didn't have the time to develop either of the scripts because "I am up to my 'ears' in two other scripts. . . . Here's hoping that in the not too distant future we do an excitingly different picture together."

It was Jerry Wald who finally threw McCarey a lifeline. The idea was to take McCarey's classic *Love Affair*, which had starred Charles Boyer and Irene Dunne in 1939, and do a modern remake in color and CinemaScope. Wald's original idea was to do a remake with music, similar to *High Society*, MGM's successful remake of *The Philadelphia Story*. That premise was under discussion in August 1956, but Wald and Fox production chief Buddy Adler decided on a straight remake without music, which simplified things. The picture came together quite quickly and was shooting within six months.

Love Affair had been written by Delmer Daves, reputedly after an incident wherein Daves had fallen in love with a woman on a transatlantic cruise, even though he was involved with another woman back home. Sometime later, Daves and McCarey had a commitment at RKO but no story, so Daves mentioned his personal history and the two set to work. *Love Affair* had been a hit, and could be again. Having given up the battle for relevance after *My Son John*, McCarey decided to take Wald's offer and retreat to the past.

The script for the remake is nearly identical to the original—the script charges for *An Affair to Remember* would total $3,541.77, while the story rights, i.e., negotiating the deal with RKO, which released the original, and getting clearances from the original writers, totaled $220,000.

Grant was clearly everyone's first choice for the Boyer part, and his already expressed willingness to work once again with McCarey may have been the decisive factor in getting 20th Century–Fox to agree to finance. McCarey's first choice for the Irene Dunne part was Ingrid Bergman, and he went so far as to wire her at the end of 1956 inquiring as to her availability "to do new version of 'Love Affair' with Cary Grant or Yul Brynner, directed by yours truly." Bergman eventually passed, but Grant quickly agreed to make the picture, preferably with Deborah Kerr.

Throughout pre-production, Grant was his reliably touchy self, but he made his complaints through George Chasin of MCA, and through Chasin to Jerry Wald rather than directly to McCarey. The primary focus of Grant's worry was a ridiculous suspicion that McCarey and Wald would turn the film into a B movie. Specifically, he was upset because there would be no location work done in Naples for the sequence where his character visits his grandmother. He felt that Wald and McCarey had promised "that this would be an authentic film and that we would shoot . . . in Naples and New York." (One of the few changes McCarey made in the new script was to move the climax to the Top of the Mark in San Francisco rather than the Empire State Building in New York City, because he and Wald both felt New York was overexposed.)

In a four-page letter to Fox's production head Buddy Adler, Jerry Wald defended his and McCarey's reasoning: "The original film was shot entirely at the RKO Studio. . . . In the original film you never saw Boyer and Dunne leave the boat. All of this was accomplished by a dissolve to a studio set of the Exterior and Interior of the Grand-mother's house. . . . There were never any shots of NAPLES in the original film."

Grant also complained that the route of the ship didn't exist on any known cruise itinerary. "Grant's argument," wrote Wald, "is that everybody will know that this is a fake trip and that it will ruin the authenticity of the picture. McCarey and I have gone over this point many times, and we both finally came to this conclusion: this is a love story."

Up to this point, Wald is maintaining his temper, but his irritation becomes clear as he cuts loose with underlining and caps for emphasis:

> If the audience is going to get out a piece of paper and start retracing the route of our mythical ship, then we have no film at all, because this story DOES NOT DEPEND ON THE REALISM OF WHERE A BOAT LEAVES AND WHERE IT ARRIVES.
>
> Leo's original version was made by brilliant performances by Boyer and Dunne, by the capturing of beauty on the screen—the beauty of the growing love between two people, the beauty found in Boyer's grandmother and her philosophy of life. We feel that with Grant and Kerr we will be able to top the original version.

Wald and McCarey eventually compromised by moving the end-ing back to New York. There was much scurrying around about the casting of the parts of the grandmother and Kerr's fiancé. McCarey and Wald's preferred choice for the latter part was Michael Rennie.

"We're afraid that we're falling into the same trap that happened in the original film with Lee Bowman," wrote Wald. "Bowman had no weight and as a result Leo was forced to chop a good many of the scenes Bowman was in from the picture. . . . Perhaps with Leo's Irish charm and my training with Harry Cohn (God forbid) we might be able to convince [Rennie] to do the part at the right price. If this could be arranged many of our worries would be out the window."

Wald eventually concluded that the part was too small for Rennie and that maybe James Daly would be better. The search went on: Van Heflin was considered, as were Wendell Corey, Leif Erickson, William Lundigan, Tony Randall, and Lloyd Nolan. (Richard Denning got the thankless part, thus repeating the mistake with Lee Bowman.) For the part of the grandmother, Wald thought Eugenie Leontovich was a possibility, as were Ruth St. Denis, Helen Menken, Pola Negri, or Eva Le Gallienne. Wald had seen *Three Coins in the Fountain*, and thought Cathleen Nesbitt "fails to have the frailty and old world charm of [Maria Ouspenskaya] in *Love Affair*." Nevertheless, Nesbitt got the part and played it beautifully.

While all this was going on, there was much intramural discussion about the possibility of a musical number for Grant and Kerr, and the problem of the title—RKO didn't want the film to be called *Love Affair*, so McCarey and Wald needed an alternative. The musical number was eventually passed off to an annoying children's choir in the last fifteen minutes of the picture. Among the suggested titles were *Affair d'Amour, Affair de Coeur, Love Is Not So Simple, Physical Attraction, Nothing in Common but Sex* (Wald was clearly getting punchy), *Private Affair, Something to Remember*, and *You Are My Love*. McCarey's choices for the title had been *From This Day On* and *An International Affair*, but when New York liked the title *An Affair to Remember*, Wald and McCarey acquiesced.

Once he got past his issues about the ship's itinerary, Grant's primary emotion seemed to have been gratitude to be working for McCarey. "Good comedy is based in amusing circumstances, amusing situations," Grant told columnist Sidney Skolsky.

Nowadays, comedy writers seem to deal more in insults—the kind of gag insults prevalent on radio and television. Perhaps it isn't their fault. The crop of young writers we have nowadays were born in

war, hot or cold, have heard nothing but war and violence since they
were born. Light comedy must be an amusing slant on life. Very few
writers these days feel funny about life. Also, I think comedy must
have a certain amount of grace—which very few people, writers or
anyone else, do these days. The old time writers who gave us the
great comedies, did. But most of them are dead. Frederick Lonsdale,
Philip Barry. Of course, there's still Terence Rattigan. . . .

But I'm happy to say this *An Affair to Remember* picture . . .
while it's primarily a wonderful love story, has some delightful light
comedy situations, some very witty dialogue—all written by Leo
McCarey—that should get merry chuckles from audience, not the
vindictive kind of laughter that comes with the insult-type of gags.
This kind of story is hard to find because writers aren't writing
them. When I do find one, as you see, I'm very happily working in it.

Nowhere in this mildly reactionary monologue does Grant mention that the reason *An Affair to Remember* was such a throwback is
that it had been written in 1939, when Frederick Lonsdale and Philip
Barry were still alive and working.

As the film neared production, Buddy Adler pestered the filmmakers
with memos that attest to a nose for irrelevant detail that rivaled
Grant's:

I believe we should change the dialogue in which Cary states that
he "never worked a day in his life." In the original picture, the
part was played by Charles Boyer, and you just naturally accepted
the fact that a Frenchman would, under financial stress, become a
glorified gigolo. It didn't surprise me at all to learn, in that picture,
that Charles Boyer had never worked a day in his life. But when
Cary Grant, says, in this version, that he has never worked a day in
his life, you can't help but ask yourself, "What was this big, strong,
healthy fellow doing during the recent wars? If he wasn't fighting,
wasn't he working either?"

The picture went into production after two full weeks of rehearsal.
Beginning February 12, 1957, McCarey shot the picture in an efficient
forty-seven days at a cost of $2.2 million—$133,000 over budget.
McCarey seems to have been in fine fettle; camera operator Alfred

Lebovitz said that it was the picture he and cinematographer Milton Krasner had the most fun on in their long careers. Krasner would remember that McCarey "was just wonderful, just a pleasure to work with. . . . It was a different way of making pictures. . . . He'd come in in the morning and he didn't have an idea. He and Grant would get into a little talk, and he'd sit down at the piano. . . . He started toying around the piano, then he'd call in the songwriter and say he had an idea for a tune. That's how they got the title song 'An Affair to Remember.'"

McCarey remained relaxed about dialogue. He allowed Grant to say "Happy thoughts"—one of the actor's favorite sayings—when his character bids farewell to his grandmother.

There was one interesting vignette during production. Robert Wagner was on the set watching Grant and Kerr in a scene where they stand by a railing and deliver some dialogue. After McCarey yelled "Cut! Print!" Grant walked over to Wagner. "The most marvelous thing just happened," he said. "I finally figured out how to breathe in a scene!" Cary Grant had been a movie star for twenty-five years, and he was still polishing his technique.

An Affair to Remember was released in August 1957 and . . . did okay. As of the end of 1957 it had earned $3.1 million worldwide, and was still in the red by a million dollars. It would eventually go into profit many times over, but its status as a legendary romance accrued slowly over time, when it began running on television, and was crowned by Nora Ephron's hilarious, heartfelt tribute in *Sleepless in Seattle*. Certainly it did well enough to maintain Grant's status; in 1957, a national poll revealed that America's favorite male movie stars were Rock Hudson, William Holden, Cary Grant, Frank Sinatra, Gary Cooper, Marlon Brando, James Stewart, Burt Lancaster, Glenn Ford, Yul Brynner, Clark Gable, and John Wayne. Grant was still comfortably seated in the streetcar of fame.

The interesting thing about *An Affair to Remember* is how different it is from *Love Affair*, despite the fact they're made by the same director from the same script. The remake offers some of the same erotic discretion—the first kiss takes place on a stairway, with only legs showing—and McCarey keys the first half of the film to a sort of bemused attraction. But McCarey's staging is stiffer, less fluid than in the original, perhaps because he was shooting in CinemaScope for the first time. More importantly, the film congeals toward the end, with not one but two songs, a ballet and relentless plugging of the film's theme song.

But the main difference in tone between the original and the remake derives from the casting. Charles Boyer had an innate quality of gravity combined with passion that Irene Dunne matched with her own skill in light and dark. *An Affair to Remember* feels lighter than *Love Affair* because Grant had irony and buoyancy as well as a sense of duplicity, about himself and everybody else, while Charles Boyer was best at conveying sincerity. Deborah Kerr, a lighter actress than Dunne, met Grant on his own level. All this makes *Love Affair* a more emotionally serious movie than *An Affair to Remember*, even with the duplicated third-act turn toward tragedy.

No one knew all this better than Leo McCarey, who told Peter Bogdanovich that he much preferred *Love Affair* to *An Affair to Remember*.

> The reason I hesitated [to do the remake] was the glaring difference between Boyer as the main attraction and Grant. Boyer gave a much better performance. Much more effective than Grant. If you put the two pictures in a laboratory, Boyer came out much better than Cary. But Cary Grant meant more at the box office.
>
> The difference between *Love Affair* and *An Affair to Remember* is very simply the difference between Charles Boyer and Cary Grant. Grant could never really mask his sense of humor—which is extraordinary—and that's why the second version is funnier. But I still prefer the first.

It is doubtful that anybody but Grant could have pulled off *An Affair to Remember* in 1957—his unaffected sincerity and class combined with Deborah Kerr overwhelm sensible objections to the sugary plot complications.

McCarey made two more pictures at 20th Century–Fox: the middling *Rally Round the Flag, Boys!* with Paul Newman and Joanne Woodward, and a final catastrophe called *Satan Never Sleeps*, with William Holden and Clifton Webb as Catholic priests beset by Chinese communists. McCarey knew the picture was crumbling even as he was making it; he walked off the set three days before shooting was completed. He died seven years later in 1969.

CHAPTER SIXTEEN

s soon as *The Pride and the Passion* was completed, Sophia Loren had left for Greece to begin work on *Boy on a Dolphin* opposite Alan Ladd. When she got to her hotel in Greece, there were flowers and a note from Grant. The envelope read "With only happy thoughts." The note itself read, "Forgive me, dear girl—I press you too much. Pray—and so will I. . . . Goodbye, Sophia. Cary." There were other letters and notes: "If you think and pray with me, for the same things and purpose, all *will* be right and life *will* be good." Years later, she would remember that she "never doubted for a second that Cary loved me as much as I could hope to be loved by a man."

Grant and Loren didn't meet in Greece, but months later in Hollywood, when Grant was shooting *Kiss Them for Me* at Fox. Ray Walston was in the cast, and remembered that during May and June of 1957, Loren was a frequent visitor to the set. Irene Mayer Selznick put it succinctly: "He was desperately in love with Sophia Loren."

Grant was still pursuing marriage, and Loren was still dodging. "She broke my heart," he would say in retrospect. The affair with Loren was aberrant behavior for Grant, who had little history of straying during marriage. He never analyzed his motivations, but did talk about his growing desire for a child. He and Drake had tried for years, to no avail, and in later years he would say, "If only I had started a family with *her*," i.e., Betsy.

Kiss Them for Me was grossly subpar, a naval-officers-on-leave comedy set in 1944, when the background for presumed hilarity was D-Day and the Battle of the Bulge. A few speeches about war's insanity were tossed in to no avail, and Stanley Donen directed with a consummate lack of interest. Jerry Wald had instructed screenwriter Julius Epstein to build up Jayne Mansfield's part as much as possible, because, Wald wrote, "The more we can do to make sure we have Mansfield in the picture, the better it will be for the film."

Casting Mansfield was Grant's idea, and the studio had cheerfully acquiesced; she had made something of a hit in Frank Tashlin's *The Girl Can't Help It*, but didn't want to do *Kiss Them for Me*. As Lew Schreiber, Fox's casting director, noted, "She fought me tooth and nail about the role because she did not like it and I must have had at least a half dozen meetings with her. Her arguments were that it was not an important role and she would be lousy in it, and the end result proved she was right."

Shortly before the picture began shooting, Buddy Adler wrote a memo to Wald and Julius Epstein that indicates he was still obsessed by the question of yet another Grant character's apathy about World War II:

> On page 105, [Grant's character, Crewson] tells Gwynneth that before the war he "assisted his father-in-law" and that his father-in-law did nothing but cut coupons and Crewson handed him the scissors.
>
> No matter how we try we're not going to make Cary Grant look like a kid. Even before the war he wasn't a kid. Therefore, if he never did anything but assist his father-in-law, also doing nothing, this makes Grant seem pretty much of a no-good.

Grant attempts to make up for the script's shortfall by trying hard, and Suzy Parker as Gwinneth is a true stunner, a pre-Raphaelite vision come glowingly alive. Unfortunately, Parker needed silent movies if she was going to act—she couldn't read a line.

Donen's explanation for the picture was that it was a movie he didn't really want to make. He referred to *Kiss Them for Me* as the kind of movie that "makes you want to kill yourself. The problem with making a movie is you can never get a divorce. It's yours forever."

The critics and the public smelled failure, and the film returned only $1.8 million in domestic rentals, not even recovering its negative cost.

A year or two after the film was released, Donen got a call from Spyros Skouras, the president of Fox. Skouras wanted a meeting. "Mr. Donen," Skouras began,

> I've looked over your list of credits. I could be wrong, but I think all the pictures you made were commercially successful, except one. That one was a picture called *Kiss Them for Me*, which you made for 20th Century–Fox. That picture was the biggest embarrassment to me I ever made. It's a story about how the big industrialists of World War II were insensitive to the problems of working men. And you directed that picture. Explain to me how you did this horrible thing to me.

Donen began backtracking.

> You have to understand. I didn't produce that picture. Jerry Wald sent me the script, told me that Cary Grant was going to be in the picture and we want you to direct it. I read the script, and said absolutely not. Then Cary Grant called me and put the pressure on me . . . so I said I'd do it.
>
> Mr. Skouras, I didn't prepare the script, I didn't cast it, I just came over and told the actors where to stand. I was like a traffic cop.

Skouras looked long and hard at Donen.
"Mr. Donen. Are you Jewish?"
"Yes."
"Have you ever heard of a Jewish traffic cop?"
Checkmate.

Donen would say, "I will never again say I'm not responsible. It was fifteen or twenty years too late to do that picture. If you do it, you're responsible."

NOW FIRMLY ENSCONCED IN MIDDLE AGE, when he was in Los Angeles Grant drove a 1957 black-and-silver Rolls-Royce Silver Cloud which he kept for more than a decade. He had bought his Palm

Springs house at 796 Via Miraleste in 1954, 1.5 acres encompassing an Andalusian-style farmhouse and casitas built in 1930 by the architect John Byers. The main house was white stucco with windows that flooded the house with light. The living room had exposed beams and a forty-foot ceiling. There was a pool, a stone terrace, and a variety of trees. Wallace Neff designed some additions in the mid-1950s, including a guest wing that brought the compound up to six bedrooms and six bathrooms spread over three separate living spaces, each with its own kitchen. Via Miraleste was Grant's designated getaway until he sold the place in 1972.

In Palm Springs he drove a 1956 Ford station wagon, white with a red interior, while Betsy drove a pale green 1957 Thunderbird. He and Betsy had gradually come to consider Palm Springs their real home. The house on Beverly Grove felt less than home mostly because it was unfinished. The house in Palm Springs, on the other hand, had thick walls, a pool, lots of vines and bougainvillea, palm trees, a lemon tree. Between pictures, Grant would live in Palm Springs, and when he was working he would slip away to the Springs for the weekend.

In those days, Palm Springs was an extension of Beverly Hills; you saw the same people in both places. Harold Lloyd's granddaughter Sue got to know Randolph Scott in Palm Springs, as well as Cary Grant, because her grandfather's house there was adjacent to Grant's.

If I had a screaming fit, Harold and Mid [Mildred Davis, Lloyd's wife] would tell me Cary didn't want to hear children screaming and would call the police. That always shut me up in a hurry.

Randy was gentle and very sweet. You never thought of him as a movie star. He was perpetually tanned, just like Cary. Lean and tall and soft-spoken. *Never* got angry or even upset. His wife, Pat, would get mad. I think she drank. From a child's point of view, she was far more severe.

Chris and Saundra, Randy's kids, were adopted. The kids had a side wing of the house, and the other wing was for Randy and Pat. He was an older parent. So was Jimmy Stewart, but Jimmy was more involved with his kids than Randy. Randy would take us to ride ponies, or have someone else do it. My mother-in-law, Nancy Gates, made *Comanche Station* with Randy. She loved him, but then everybody loved Randy.

Scott would always bring his personal rocking chair on location, so he could be comfortable while reading *The Wall Street Journal* between setups. One night he called Budd Boetticher and vented about a story that was making the rounds of the studio. The (apparently false) story was that Rock Hudson and Tab Hunter had been having an affair and were seen walking hand in hand around the studio. They would supposedly sit in the screening room watching each other's films, putting up their feet on the seats in front of them to blot out the other actors in the shot.

"Isn't that the most disgusting thing you have ever heard?" Scott asked Boetticher.

"Yes," Boetticher replied. "It is the most disgusting thing since I heard about you and Cary Grant."

Scott burst out laughing and promptly calmed down.

Cary and Betsy would often host other couples at their house, although apparently not Randy and Pat Scott. Deborah Kerr and her husband, Tony Bartley, stayed with the Grants in Palm Springs, as did Judy Balaban and Jay Kanter, Audrey Hepburn and Mel Ferrer, Dina Merrill and Stan Rumbough Jr.

A favorite pair of houseguests were the costume designer Adrian and his wife, Janet Gaynor. "Betsy and I remember every moment spent in their company with fondness and delight," Grant wrote Irene Mayer Selznick. "They are, quite as you once told me, dear intelligent unassuming undemanding and utterly charming people. . . . Of the very few married couples we know, they have become, in the past, and too short months, our closest friends."

Grant told friends that he had lost the gene for reading fiction, although he professed an appreciation for Eudora Welty's short stories: "I admire people who can concentrate on a fish or a leaf and know more about them than most of us can suspect about a human being." When it came to music, he preferred Bach to Beethoven, but he liked almost any kind of music played well except rock 'n' roll, which left him cold and always would. His favorite singers were Frank Sinatra and Ella Fitzgerald. When it came to actors he liked "Both Tracy's, Spencer and Lee." Added to that were both Hepburns (Katharine and Audrey), Ingrid Bergman, Grace Kelly, and Deborah Kerr. For exercise, he was loyal to swimming and horseback riding—he rode whenever he was in Palm Springs.

After reading Winston Churchill's *Painting as a Pastime*, he dabbled for a time in oils. What did he do with his paintings? "I hide them, in storage or somewhere." He sometimes slept nude, sometimes in pajamas, depending on the weather or his inclination. He preferred his bedroom windows to be open so long as the air was warm.

He was amused by his ranking as one of the Ten Best Dressed men in the world, because his only real secret was to buy the best clothes from the best tailors in the best material available. Since men in the studio system had to wear their own suits, Grant bought them by the half-dozen. He warned friends against anything too trendy or extreme and told them to simplify their lives by wearing classic clothes.

He bought clothes from Cifonelli Rome, and from various Hong Kong tailors. In England, he went to Sir Charles Abrahams, where he allowed pictures of him being fitted in return for getting the clothes for free. As his father would have said if he'd thought of it, a fair exchange is no robbery.

He preferred the English cut, where the armholes are slightly higher than in America. Whether the suit was English, Italian, or Hong Kong, it was carefully contrived for the camera. "Once, I had a director who complained my suit didn't fall right across the back. I said, 'But I'm not going to turn my back to the camera.'"

He didn't wear belts, suspenders, or garters; his pants had adjustable waist tabs with buttons, and some of his suits were outfitted with a slide buckle waistband. He was a stickler for putting clothes on hangers and putting shoe trees in his shoes. His ties always had rounded edges, and he liked single-color or dark colors. He never wore bright ties or loud checks, and seldom wore bright colors.

The result of all this was the passionate approval of people who lived and breathed fashion. Edith Head's appraisal: "I consider him not only the most beautiful but the most beautifully dressed man in the world. His is a discerning eye, a meticulous sense of detail. He has the greatest fashion sense of any actor I've ever worked with. He knows as much about women's clothes as he does about men's."

Grant often recalled his father's advice about buying the best clothes you can afford. "The average wage earner . . . would save money in the long run if he could buy only one good suit and pair of shoes. I can't be accused of talking through my hat on this because I was penniless at one time, but when I began to earn my own livelihood,

I'd stick to my father's dictum. If I couldn't afford a good pair of shoes I didn't buy any. That went for everything I owned."

Along the same lines, he believed that Cartier or Tiffany offered better value than any of the competition, let alone a friend who can get it for you wholesale. "The advantage of buying something good is that it outlasts eight others, not only in initial outlay, but in always looking better. You'll save money in the long run . . . and consequently feel more comfortable."

When it came to women, his pet aversions were affectation, baby talk, and heavy makeup. He disliked food that was cooked without imagination, even though he was the first to admit that "I can't cook at all." After the layoff that followed the fiasco of *Dream Wife*, he had come to a born-again appreciation of work. "I'm in the fortunate position of being able to choose. I tried not working. I prefer working. I enjoy working more than not working. I love acting. And now that the motion picture industry has a five-day week, I have enough leisure to enjoy my work doubly because we have the weekend to relax.

He was sure about many things, especially retirement. "Never," he said. "You might as well die."

INGRID BERGMAN HAD BEEN EXILED by Hollywood and castigated on the floor of Congress when she had twins out of wedlock with Roberto Rossellini. She was Ilsa in *Casablanca*, she was Maria in *For Whom the Bell Tolls*, she was Joan of Arc, she was a nun in *The Bells of St. Mary's*, for God's sake—literally.

Despite the stiff wind of public and political disapproval, Grant had sent her letters and cables of support, as had Hemingway, John Steinbeck, and Helen Hayes. More importantly, he spoke out for her in public: "Ingrid Bergman is a fascinating, full-blooded yet temperate woman who has the courage to live in accord with her needs, and strength enough to accept and benefit by the consequences of her beliefs in an inhibited, critical and frightened society." There were not a lot of public pronouncements of equal weight from people as eminent as Grant.

After more than six years in limbo, during which Bergman occupied herself by making a group of often beautiful, resolutely uncommercial movies with Rossellini, she made an American comeback with

Anastasia, a huge critical and commercial hit that brought her an Oscar for Best Actress. It was *the* comeback of the postwar era, and Bergman asked Grant to accept her Oscar if she won. He did so with grace and a sense of the politics of the moment: "So, dear Ingrid, if you can hear me now or will see this television film later, I want you to know that each of the other nominees, and all the people with whom you worked on *Anastasia*, and Hitch, and Leo McCarey, and indeed *everyone* here tonight, send you congratulations and love and admiration and every affectionate thought.

"Come back home, Ingrid," he concluded. "We miss you." And, in a manner of speaking, she did, opposite Grant in a picture called *Indiscreet* directed by Stanley Donen. It began as a 1953 play by Norman Krasna called *Kind Sir*, starring Charles Boyer and Mary Martin, directed by Joshua Logan. Despite the gilded résumés of everyone concerned, the play underperformed, running a modest 166 performances. Every studio passed on making a movie version.

Donen and Krasna were friends, and Donen thought that *Kind Sir* could make a wonderful film, so Krasna gave him a free option to see if he could set up the project. Grant agreed to star, which meant the picture would get made. Grant and Donen both wanted Bergman for the film, so Donen flew to Rome to make his pitch. It was the easiest sale he ever made. "I know you're frightened and nervous," Bergman told him. "I want to put you at your ease. I'm going to do the movie no matter what it is."

Indiscreet was the beginning of Grant's career as a producer, and the legal documents are instructive of both his own desire for control and money, and the way the movie business had altered to accommodate stars. It was a terrible negotiation. "My lawyer would say to me, 'We're never going to get this contract finished,'" said Donen.

> I would go to Cary and say, "Cary, for God's sake, won't you just give this up and settle this? In the end you're not even going to know how much money you have. It's just a number on the page. It doesn't mean anything to you. It's just going to be another digit on your numbers."
>
> He didn't see it that way. And eventually I didn't care. The picture got made because of Cary. We got the backing and other actors because he was in it.

Indiscreet was a coproduction between Grandon (Grant and Stanley Donen), Donen Productions (Norman Krasna was president), Winkle Radio Productions (Winkle was Betsy's favored pseudonym, and Stanley Fox was president), and Warner Bros. The picture was wholly financed by Warners, who agreed to distribute the picture for eight years, after which the picture would revert to Grandon and Donen Productions. The up-front money paid out was $150,000 to Winkle and Donen, $300,000 to Grant, $75,000 plus 10 percent of the profits over a gross of $4 million to Bergman, and $25,000 to Donen. In addition, there was $125,000 to Paulfilm SA, a Panamanian corporation that was paid off for waiving its rights to Bergman's services, and $100,000 to Donen Productions. After the picture paid off its costs, the profits were to be split 25 percent to Warners, 65 percent to Donen and Winkle, and 10 percent to Grandon.

The matrix for ownership deals for actors was complex. Actors had been getting percentages since the 1920s, when Rudolph Valentino got a piece of *The Eagle* and *The Son of the Sheik*. But it was Bing Crosby who moved things to a whole new level in the late 1940s, when he decided against taking a full salary in favor of a piece of the gross—a very large piece of the gross. Crosby and Bob Hope personally cofinanced both *Road to Rio* and *Road to Bali* and co-owned them. (Crosby sold his half to Hope in the 1960s, and Hope turned around and sold the pictures to NBC.)

On both *White Christmas* and *High Society*, Crosby had received 30 percent of the gross after the films earned back their negative and distribution costs. Crosby took only what amounted to scale up front, while his percentage would be paid to one of his companies, thus qualifying as capital gains instead of straight salary—the taxes on the former amounting to about half of the taxes on the latter. (The gold rush for *White Christmas* included Irving Berlin, who also got 30 percent, and Danny Kaye, who got 10 percent.)

Giving away at least 70 percent of the profits of a studio's most commercial movies would seem to be a quick path to bankruptcy. It was obviously untenable for any picture that wasn't a sure thing, and sure things are few and far between in the movie business. The balance of power, which had been firmly grasped by studios for roughly fifty years, had passed to the talent.

The upshot of the new reality was that Warner Bros. was essentially acting as a bank, without any leverage over content. When Jack Warner suggested that *Irresistible* was a better title than *Indiscreet*, Donen coolly informed him that "after discussing it thoroughly with Cary we prefer *Indiscreet*." And so the title remained *Indiscreet*.

Indiscreet is an unusually intense romantic comedy because it's about two middle-aged people, both of whom are aware that this may be their last chance at the brass ring. The plot involves Grant as an unmarried diplomat who tells women he's married because he prefers nonbinding relationships. He meets an actress (Bergman), who is weary of her life and ready for something else. It's well directed by Donen, especially during a scene in an elevator taking them to their adjacent rooms. Grant simply stares at Bergman as she makes up her mind. Will she or won't she? It's one of the most thrilling seduction scenes in movies, and nobody says a word.

Donen believed that it was *Indiscreet* that taught him how to direct actors. He was used to creating emotion through movement, either by the camera or actors or dancers. But there was a scene with Grant and Bergman over a breakfast table, where he tells her he's moving to London to be closer to her. "That's the event in the scene," remembered Donen. "And they don't talk much, and she's fixing him breakfast, and she sits him at a little table in the kitchen and [positions] the plates and the juice and the eggs. It's all about what they're feeling about each other. And I realized I had to get that; I couldn't just stage the physical places. I had to stage it completely differently." Donen shot that scene in 1957. Eight years earlier, when he had codirected *On the Town*, "I thought I knew everything."

As before, Grant and Bergman meshed beautifully, the love story bringing out their shared gravity. Donen believed that Bergman "was so good on camera because she had a completely rooted quality . . . she was completely at ease. She never seized up while acting. Her concentration was complete. She was in her element." Grant's take was similar—Bergman was the ideal screen partner of his later years: mature and good-humored, without temperament, incandescent on-screen. "We had a wonderful time making the film. I found her a joy to be with."

But one day Bergman turned to Grant with an indecent amount of amusement and said, "Do you realize that together you and I are one hundred years old?" She was exaggerating, but not by much; Grant was fifty-three when they shot the film, and Bergman was forty-three. Grant was not delighted by the remark, but she would occasionally repeat it anyway.

At the end of the picture, Grant gave his costar a gift: the key she had held in *Notorious* as Hitchcock's camera plummeted to a close-up of it in her hand. Grant had taken the key after the scene, and kept it for more than ten years. He put it in her hand and said, "I've kept this long enough. Now it's for you. For good luck."

The financials on *Indiscreet* give a glimpse into Grant's acumen as a producer. The film's entire negative cost was a mere $1.5 million, and that was before deducting $220,000 in rebates under the English Eady plan. The cost was about half of what a picture costarring Grant and Bergman might be expected to run in the late 1950s. Worldwide rentals came to $6 million, which meant profits of around $3 million split among Warner Bros., Grant, Donen, and Bergman. And Grant, Stanley Fox, and Donen ultimately owned the picture.

In the new world of the 1950s, giving actors who contributed nothing more than their performances a large piece of the action staggered men who had been in Hollywood for decades, but Jack Warner was willing to go along to get along. When it came to *Indiscreet*, everyone was happy. Just how happy was shown a few years later, when Warners vice president Steve Trilling wrote to Donen. The ostensible reason for the letter was asking Donen where they should send his 16mm print of *Indiscreet*. With that request out of the way, Trilling moved on to a naked plea for another Grant-Donen project: "Apparently the deal you consummated was a very profitable one for yourselves particularly. In any event, we like you . . . we like Cary . . . we like your business . . . and if you would like to achieve as good or, I hope better, results than with *Indiscreet*—why not continue [with] the old established firm?"

AFTER *Indiscreet* was in the can, Grant took a cultural cross-pollination tour to Moscow and Leningrad with Sam Spiegel, Howard Hawks, and Truman Capote. Spiegel showed *On the Waterfront* and *The Bridge on the River Kwai* and in return the Western contingent watched Soviet films. Grant had the odd experience of comparative anonymity. "Nobody knew who I was. It was the first time in twenty-five years I could walk down the street without people pointing at me." After he left Russia, he spent Christmas in Bristol with his mother.

Since he had a large investment in *Indiscreet*, Grant went on the road to promote the film, speaking in theaters in nine cities in the U.K. and Ireland—Kingston, Hammersmith, Glasgow, Edinburgh, Dublin, Birmingham, Liverpool, Leeds, and Belfast. He was petrified the entire time. His ability to quickly get up to performance speed in front of a movie camera vanished when he was out of that milieu.

It took him years to get over his stage fright, and he finally figured it out. "It finally came to me that the audience wasn't making me nervous. I was making myself nervous. Nobody ever buys a ticket hoping to see a lousy show. Or to hear a terrible speech. Or to see any performers fail. They want every actor to be Olivier. They want every ballplayer to hit home runs and make impossible catches. That way they can tell their friends they were in the theater or the ball park when it happened."

AT LONG LAST, Melville Shavelson and Jack Rose finished the script for *Houseboat*. Grant showed up at Paramount and took them to lunch at Lucey's, which meant Shavelson would have to pick up the check.

"Tell me the story of *Houseboat*," asked Grant.

Shavelson began the story and Grant stopped. "Wait a minute. You changed the leading lady to an Italian girl?"

"Well, Cary, you [told us] you had found the new Garbo."

"That bitch. I'll never make a picture with her again as long as I live. If she's in it, I'm out."

Shavelson and Rose were both stunned. As Shavelson expected, Grant stuck them with the check. Shavelson was curious and began making inquiries about just what had gone on in Spain. According to Shavelson's memoir, Grant had indeed been having an affair in Spain. Scuttlebutt had it that Grant had actually had more than one, starting with his chauffeur and flipping the switch when he saw Loren.

According to Shavelson, "They had a brief, passionate romantic episode, and then Sophia had brought Cary down to earth by telling him she was in love with Carlo Ponti, even though he was a married man like Cary. Carlo had made her a star and although he was a dozen years her senior, she preferred him to Cary. Grant went wild. You do not turn Cary Grant down. You may turn him, but you don't turn him down. He had never been rejected before, by either sex."

Grant wanted nothing to do with *Houseboat*, but he had conveniently forgotten the contract he had signed at the airport. *Houseboat* was the first of three pictures he was to make for Paramount over the next ten years. His compensation was fixed at 10 percent of the gross—the same magnificent deal he had gotten on *To Catch a Thief*. According to Shavelson, Grant offered to make two additional pictures for Paramount if they would only let him out of *Houseboat*, but given the fact that there were no other prospective scripts that could work for him, Paramount decided to stick with the original plan. "[Paramount] made him make the film after he had split up with [Loren]," said Shavelson.

For Betsy Drake, the humiliation was complete; not only had her husband been publicly unfaithful, her screenplay had been tossed out. On October 2, 1957, a memo went out at Paramount: "This is to advise that Betsy Drake has requested us not to mention her name or her pseudonym, B. Winkle, in connection with the motion picture *Houseboat* or in respect to any screen credit in connection therewith or in connection with any publicity or advertising thereof, and we have agreed to comply with her request."

As *Houseboat* went into production, things were tense and they stayed that way. "I just didn't want to be around her," Grant would say. "Then we started making the film and I fell in love with her all over again!" One of Hedda Hopper's spies listened in on a phone conversation between Grant and Loren. Grant reiterated that he would be willing to immediately divorce Betsy and get the final decree in Mexico. By his figuring they could be married in three weeks. Loren's response was unyielding: "No . . . No . . . No." "Cary went out of his mind," Hopper reported to a friend.

Hopper's informant was probably Martha Hyer, the second female lead in the picture. Although she was a bland actress, Hyer's career had been infused with a sudden burst of oxygen that coincided with her relationship with Hal Wallis, the most powerful producer at Paramount. (Wallis eventually married Hyer after the death of his first wife.) Hyer remembered that she picked up the phone in her dressing room one day and discovered that she had been patched in to what amounted to a party line. Grant was talking to Loren, saying, "If only you'd marry me . . . we'd take a tramp steamer around the world, and we'd have the child you've always wanted."

Stories like this illuminate Grant's essential misreading of the woman he was infatuated with—Loren was born illegitimate and grew up poor. After she matured into a stunning movie star, she never gave any indication that she wanted to travel via tramp steamer, let alone risk the sure thing of Carlo Ponti. The Hyer story also justifies Grant's suspicion of most of the people around him, and his difficulty in relaxing even in his private life. The reason he often acted as if people were out to get him was that people *were* often out to get him . . . or embarrass him.

Shavelson said that Loren came to him and asked, "Doesn't Cary know I am truly in love with Carlo and isn't Cary a married man, and will you please ask him to stop chasing me? I can't work." Grant finally resorted to begging. "If you can, and care to, have someone leave a note for me at the desk," he wrote her. "A few words—any words. I need something from you today, as all days."

Houseboat must have been a nightmare for Grant, who had grown used to getting the material things he wanted, and who was now living out every man's nightmare—head over heels in love with a woman who won't reciprocate, or, rather, won't reciprocate in the way he wants. Beset by alternating waves of desire and anger, Grant was on his worst behavior. At one point, he became convinced that Loren was sleeping with costar Harry Guardino. It was an understandable error—Guardino was actually sleeping with her maid.

Shavelson, who had only directed two previous pictures, both with Bob Hope (*The Seven Little Foys* and *Beau James*), was completely overmatched. "That was my third ulcer," he remembered. "Cary Grant made life hell for everybody on that picture and everybody on the set during it. . . . *Houseboat* was the most trouble of all the pictures I've made." On top of everything else, Grant was too preoccupied to keep up his tan, so the proper color had to be applied every morning, which Shavelson thought was the height of movie star absurdity.

Shavelson remembered that Grant had become enamored of something called sleep learning—putting a tape recorder under his pillow at night. He told Shavelson that he was learning French in his sleep. Shavelson didn't buy it, especially after the sound man on the picture came to him with a story. Betsy had asked the sound man to fix her tape recorder because it wasn't working correctly. There was a tape in the machine so the sound man listened to it. There were the voices of Cary and Betsy saying over and over again, "Cary Grant you are the greatest actor in the world. Cary Grant, you have nothing to worry about. Cary Grant, stop worrying."

A few days before the shoot concluded, as Grant and Loren were playing the marriage scene that served as the finale of the picture, Loren and Carlo Ponti were married by proxy in Mexico. The marriage was illegal in Italy, and would cause them problems down the road, but it was a clear signal that the possibility Grant represented had been discarded. "All the best, Sophia," he told her on the set. "I hope you'll be happy."

Grant was careful not to ladle his misery over the heads of the children in the picture. Paul Petersen was ten when he worked with Grant in *Houseboat*, and he says that "He was wonderful. He taught me so much. What I loved then and still appreciate was that I never asked a question he didn't have time to answer. I remember him sitting in a chair on the set, wondering out loud if he would use a single take, a double take, or maybe a triple. And he explained them all to us. Oh, the discipline he had, yet he made it look effortless. I chatted his ear off, but he was great with me." Grant even assumed some of the prerogatives of the director, as he carefully explained to Petersen the technique of acting in front of a process screen, and the dramatic or comic purpose behind every scene.

Ultimately, Shavelson said that "There was a tension between [Grant and Loren] all the time . . . but . . . it worked for the picture. That was the important thing." This was Shavelson's retrospective judgment, when the stresses had been largely filed away. But as soon as the picture was finished, he checked himself into the hospital. "Cary was a large part of it," said Shavelson. "He apologized while I was in the hospital." Shavelson never worked with Grant again.

For all of the tension on the set, if the viewer is unaware of the situation there is no trace of dissension or even passive aggression in *Houseboat*. It's choppily directed—Shavelson never quite mastered the art of seamless camera placement—but in all other respects, both

Grant and Loren function as high-end professionals. Grant never made the other two pictures on his Paramount contract, which was canceled in August 1959, probably because he was in the process of firming up a deal at Universal that was even richer. Or maybe he just felt Paramount needed to be punished because they had forced him into making a picture he didn't want to make.

In later years, Grant would talk about Sophia Loren only in generalities, unless the conversation was with someone he regarded as a good friend, in which case he would let the hurt show.

There was only one consolation. "We certainly ripped up a few bull rings in Spain, I can tell you *that*," Grant told Peter Bogdanovich.

ESTRANGED FROM BOTH BETSY AND LOREN, Grant was at loose ends during the shoot of *Houseboat*. Across town in Burbank, Orry-Kelly was working on *Auntie Mame* with Rosalind Russell, when his phone rang.

"Last night I dined with Bill and Edie Goetz and I saw there the most enchanting picture of five little Samoan boys. I would like to buy something similar." There was a pause. "Do you know who this is?"

Orry-Kelly knew very well who it was. He and Grant hadn't had an actual conversation for more than ten years; when they ran into each other at a restaurant or a party, they would just nod. But Grant was shooting *Houseboat* and was getting in touch while simultaneously letting Orry-Kelly know he was still part of the in crowd. The conversation was brisk. When could he see some of Kelly's paintings? Where was his studio? Could he come over right away?

Grant arrived and bought about ten of Kelly's small paintings for gifts. After that he came over several times a week while the picture was shooting. Orry-Kelly intuited that conversation about Sophia Loren was off-limits, and the marriage with Betsy Drake was on life support. If Bill and Edie Goetz, the doyennes of Beverly Hills society, who owned the best art collection in town, weren't throwing a party, Grant seemed to have no place to go.

Grant told Orry-Kelly that Betsy had hypnotized him, with the result being that he wasn't smoking or drinking anymore. Orry-Kelly thought that was odd, because Grant was sipping a glass of wine as he talked about not drinking anymore.

"Your yellows and golds are your best," Grant said, gazing at the paintings. "You should paint in them all the time." He asked Kelly out to lunch, and after that Kelly suggested dropping in on Rosalind Russell on the set of *Auntie Mame*. She was happy to see the man who had introduced her to her husband, and was talking to Grant and Kelly in the mirror while getting ready for an afternoon shoot. Kelly mentioned that they had driven over in Grant's Rolls, and Cary chimed in and said he had another just like it in London.

"I'm going over for ten days," said Russell.

"Why don't you use my Rolls?" said Grant, who then offered her the use of his chauffeur.

Russell was delighted. And then Grant said, "When you arrive in London, call MCA, my agents. They will give you the rental fee and the cost of the chauffeur."

There must have been a slight hitch in Russell's head when her eyes went to Orry-Kelly. "I think, Mame," he said, "they're about ready for you on the set."

After Grant left, Russell told Kelly, "We mustn't talk about this."

Orry-Kelly would return to this story often, and he would compare Grant to another star who began life mired in poverty: Joan Crawford: "I don't know how many changes Crawford had as Lucille LeSueur when she danced in the Shubert Winter Garden. But I do know Cary had just a little tin box and what was on his back. Even then he was never shy or reticent—always alert and aware. He was just as indestructible as Joan. He might have started out as a bad stage actor, but he studied and learned the magic of the magic lantern."

And there the similarities ended. The problem, as Kelly saw it, was one of generosity and its lack and, beyond that, of belief. "While Cary Grant was worth millions and still had his first twopence, the overgenerous and extravagant Crawford had spent more than her last nickel. . . . In Cary's case, his faith ended with himself. When we were both young, our biggest brawls were over his *not believing*. He had no *faith*. I realized his torture. For many years his mother had been mentally ill. When I told him, 'You must have faith of some kind,' the battle would be on. . . . I don't know how he felt about faith, or about the truth."

Kelly pressed Rosalind Russell for her thoughts on her friend. "It strikes me that Cary never has had any social poise," she said. "He dares not be around people more than twelve minutes. He flits around, hiding from his own shadow, hoping nobody will notice, or that his shadow may expose the image he has created for himself. Yet, there's no one really like him—or you, for that matter—and at times I'm glad there aren't."

Grant shadowed Orry-Kelly for much of his life and afterward. Orry-Kelly stopped drinking around 1960, and died in 1964 of liver cancer. He went out on top—his last jobs were designing the costumes for *Gypsy* and *Irma la Douce*. The pallbearers at his funeral included George Cukor, Billy Wilder, Tony Curtis, and Cary Grant.

A MONTH BEFORE *Houseboat* was released in November 1958, Grant and Betsy Drake separated. Grant issued a press release:

> After careful consideration and long discussion, we have decided to live apart. We have had, and shall always have, a deep love and respect for each other, but, alas, our marriage has not brought us the happiness we fully expected and mutually desired. So, since we have no children needful of our affect, it is consequently best that we separate for a while. We have purposefully issued this public statement through the newspaper writers who have been so kind to us in the past, in order to forestall the usual misinformed gossip and conjecture. There are no plans for divorce, and we ask only that the press respect our statement as being complete, and our friends to be patient with, and understanding of, our decision.

The syntax suggests that Grant wrote the statement himself. Grant and Drake would stay in loose touch for the rest of his life. He would occasionally forward some clippings that he thought she would find interesting. "Only yesterday, Ray Stark, yes Ray Stark, asked about you," he wrote her in 1976. "I said I would telephone you and inquire how you are. And I will. I'll telephone soon, hoping to find you very well and happy."

They didn't divorce until July of 1962. Betsy's last film of the nine she made was 1965's *Clarence, the Cross-Eyed Lion*. Richard Brooks, who was generally kind in his remarks about Grant, said that "In the last few years of their marriage, I was with Betsy and Cary any number of times. Betsy had simply stopped functioning either as an actress or in any other field in which she had once been interested. It was pathetic to see her not functioning."

Drake agreed with Brooks. "When I was married, I regressed . . . I became a totally subservient wife. I swallowed all the myths. All the women in my generation were brought up to believe husbands' careers and desires came first in every sense. I drank white wine because Cary liked white wine. And I ate well-done roast beef although I hated well-done meat."

When Hedda Hopper reported that Drake's divorce settlement consisted of some property worth $80,000, Orry-Kelly called Hopper to add another layer of spite. "He's worth eight million," Orry-Kelly told her. "I hope she does better than that. Grant is the original man who came to dinner as far as I'm concerned. He used to make my Greenwich Village apartment his home when he was doing one-line bits in plays. I'm still waiting for him to buy me a cup of coffee." Actually, *Variety* reported that Betsy received more than $1 million in cash in addition to a percentage of Grant's earnings from the thirteen films he made during their marriage.

Betsy told reporters that she was still in love with Grant, but that "he appeared to be bored with me. I became lonely, unhappy, miserable. . . . He showed no interest in any of my friends." In other words, more or less business as usual. And then there was Sophia Loren.

It would become clear that Drake felt badly used, and Grant seems to have agreed with that judgment. Grant's summation of their marriage is notable for its respect, if not its passion: "Betsy was good for me. Without imposition or demand, she patiently led me toward an appreciation for better books, better literature. Her cautious but steadily penetrating seeking in the labrynths of the subconscious gradually provoked my interest."

Betsy's feelings were far more conflicted. As far as she was concerned, Grant was destructive. In later years, after rumors regarding Grant's sexuality became public, she said much the same thing that Virginia Cherrill said, and Dyan Cannon would say, only less circumspectly: "Why would I believe that Cary was homosexual when we were busy fucking?" At the same time, there was doubt. "Maybe he was bisexual. He lived 43 years before he met me. I don't know what he did."

Grant seemed to have a nagging sense that Betsy had given him far more than he had given her, a premise she completely agreed with. "Cary always spoke of you with the greatest admiration," Betsy would write Kate Hepburn in 1967. "He speaks nicelier (nicelier?) of you than of me." In another letter, Betsy made jokes about devising scenarios whereby she could steal her ex's Diego Rivera.

Betsy went on to have a highly productive life that had nothing to do with show business, which had come to seem an awkward script combining the unpleasant combination of humiliation and pain. "I dreamed of being in the theater," she said. "I never dreamed of marrying an actor. I wanted to marry a writer. I thought that was more dignified." She wryly observed that she "divorced the whole town as well as Cary, and they divorced me. Suddenly I was divorced, movie work was uncertain, I was searching for something . . . and I knew a thing or two about trauma."

In 1971, under the name Betsy Drake Grant, she published a novel through Atheneum entitled *Children, You Are Very Little* about an unhappy nine-year-old girl in 1932—the same age Betsy was that year. She enrolled at Harvard, where she got her master's degree in education. She became interested in psychodrama, i.e., role-playing in order to work out trauma. The UCLA Neuropsychiatric Institute was receptive to some of her ideas and she became director of psychodrama at the institute, while spending four years doing therapy at Mount Sinai Hospital. She maintained a private practice while also teaching at UCLA and Pepperdine, and published at least one scholarly article, in the March 1975 issue of the *American Journal of Orthopsychiatry*. She believed that she got such good results with children "because I take the radical position that children are human beings." It was a life far removed from movies, if not from living with Cary Grant.

In time Betsy would move to London, where she became good friends with the silent film star Bessie Love, the actress Faith Brook, and the war correspondent and novelist Martha Gellhorn. Both Betsy and Martha had married petulant, needy men—Gellhorn's first husband was Ernest Hemingway—so they had much in common. "If you ever think you married the world's worst shit," Gellhorn told Betsy, "you're wrong. I did."

Betsy liked men far more than Gellhorn, who seemed to regard them as incomprehensible aborigines from a distant culture. But Betsy was also somehow afraid of men, lonely, and doubted herself. Gellhorn thought loneliness was the baseline human condition and it was absurd to be afraid of anything except a decrepit old age. "A man cannot do anything more than disappoint you," she wrote Drake. "He can't destroy you."

Gellhorn and Betsy traveled together, which ended badly. "You invent complications," Gellhorn informed her. "With all your feelings, you have never stopped to look at yourself: a woman who sulks when events don't work out as desired, who has innumerable absolute needs which are not life and death matters, but your absolutes, who has to be kept happy or else by golly it's miseryville all around. . . . Try growing up."

They patched things up. Eventually, Betsy began a relationship with Jack Rose, Mel Shavelson's writing partner. She was living in London and Rose was in Hollywood, but every so often the planets would align and they would get together. The conversations must have been interesting. Martha Gellhorn's sight failed, as did her overall health, and she committed suicide in 1998. Betsy Drake never remarried. She died in 2015 at the age of ninety-two.

Certainly Drake found a deep solace in her psychotherapy work. And perhaps she loved nature, as did her friend Martha. "Count one's blessings," Gellhorn advised her. "There is the sapphire sea, with white caps beyond the reef because the Northeast monsoon is blowing a treat. There is the moonstone sky by day and the brilliant moon-lit star-lit sky by night. The air is satin and soft and warm. There is no sound except the sea, the rattling of palms in the wind . . ."

CHAPTER SEVENTEEN

Within mid-twentieth-century show business, Grant was the equivalent of the finest dividend-bearing stocks, but his status didn't seem to give him much consolation—he still fretted constantly. In an interview for the *Hollywood Reporter*'s twenty-fifth anniversary, he vented about professional insufficiencies that only he noticed: "When I was just starting out, I knew all the answers. Today, when I have the misfortune to see some of my early pictures, I go into a severe case of the shudders. In my salad days I saw no reason for worrying about the playing of a scene. Today I am, if anything, over-critical, except that I don't think that one can really be over-critical."

He went on to recount asking for extra takes on *To Catch a Thief* after Hitchcock had ordered a scene printed.

> It seemed to me, sitting there in the projection room, that I missed the entire point of what I was trying to put over. Or I'd say, "That can't be me there. What was I thinking of to do this, when I was supposed to do that?" . . . But go to the rushes I must, for if I am not interested in how Cary Grant looks up there on that giant screen—and in Technicolor, yet—who, may I ask, is?
>
> The only way I know of driving home what I'm trying to say is this: if you or your friends have a home movie camera, try this test. Let someone turn the camera on as you do something—walk, pick up a book, turn and greet someone or do anything else that you had

definitely prescribed doing before the camera started turning. . . . Practice it, a couple of times before you do what you're going to do. Then have them shoot you with the camera.

When you see the results you will invariably say, "What on earth was I trying to do with my hands? Why did I fumble that book, instead of just picking it up? Where did I get that conception of how to walk? What happened to my carriage? Why the stooped shoulders?"

Only by such an ordeal can you start to understand what an actor with a conscience goes through when he sees himself on the screen.

These were years in which Grant was turning down scripts right and left: *Around the World in 80 Days, The Bridge on the River Kwai, Lolita.* And once again Grant dodged a job offer from Billy Wilder. The Wilder picture was *Love in the Afternoon,* a lovely bauble from an obscure French novel that had previously been made into a movie starring Elizabeth Bergner and represented Wilder's tribute to his beloved mentor Ernst Lubitsch. "I don't like taking a big hit and making a movie out of it," Wilder said. "It's too easy, too uninteresting. I couldn't fuck it up. I like to work with original stories or perhaps some obscure story that you just use a notion from, nothing very substantial."

Audrey Hepburn was quickly cast, and then Wilder went after Grant . . . again. And he got the same response . . . again. "Cannot do it," Grant told Wilder. "Please don't. Don't persist. Look, I like you, Wilder, but I cannot explain it. I just . . . the wrong signals come up in me."

A few years later, Wilder tried one more time. This time it was for *One, Two, Three,* for which he wanted Grant to reprise the fast-talking ruthlessness of *His Girl Friday.* After Grant passed, the part went to James Cagney, who didn't particularly like working for Wilder. "He felt that Billy was too rigid in following his script and didn't allow Cagney as much leeway as he wanted in developing his role," producer Walter Mirisch recalled.

Wilder always had trouble coming to terms with Grant's rejection of such excellent projects, and, by extension, of him. It didn't seem to be personal—Grant would call to congratulate Wilder on his pictures, even going out of his way to say how much he appreciated Tony Curtis's dead-on imitation of him in *Some Like It Hot.*

Grant's shying away derived from an intense dislike of any personality that might be even potentially abusive. Grant liked charmers—Leo
McCarey—or cool, collected customers like Hawks and Hitchcock—
men who never raised their voices. Wilder wasn't abusive, but he did
have sharp elbows and a mouth to match.

"I'd heard he didn't like actors very much," said Grant, "and I'd
already worked with enough of those kinds of directors to last a
lifetime. Humphrey Bogart did [Sabrina] and he looks very unhappy
all the way through." Grant would invoke Stroheim and Preminger,
Teutonic directors with a reputation for being "impolite and outrageous and insensitive." He would also refer to his disastrous experience
with Michael Curtiz on Night and Day. Curtiz was Hungarian, not
German or Austrian, but as far as Grant was concerned that was close
enough. "I could tell stories about Mike Curtiz blowing his top all
day long," he would grumble. Clearly, one unpleasant dance with an
irascible director with an accent was more than enough.

The other potential problem that scared off Grant was probably
the fact that Wilder wasn't particularly collaborative; he expected the
actors to say the dialogue exactly as written, and he was averse to
improvisation. With the exception of Hitchcock, Grant liked directors
who maintained a loose mood. Beyond that, he simply may have preferred a director whose instincts tended toward acquiescence to their
star, and Billy Wilder never acquiesced to an actor in his life.

After a brief flirtation with Yul Brynner, Wilder went with Gary
Cooper for Love in the Afternoon, and his age and gentleness had
the opposite effect of Bogart's age and bitterness in Sabrina—Cooper
made the dynamic more April-November than April-September, and the
emphasis on time's fleeting nature made the movie even more touching.

GRANT HAD BEEN PAYING 90 percent tax on his income for years,
but his essential conservatism kept him from various tax havens—
Switzerland, etc. Numerous stars had gone to Europe, only to come
back a few years later because of homesickness.

There was still a lot to complain about. "It's a shame that smog
has ruined this city," he grumbled. "I can remember what a wonderful
town it was when I first came here. It's not so wonderful anymore."

The vagrant mood passed; Grant stayed in California for the rest of his life. Balancing the dark moods were some of the cheerful commonplaces that filled his conversation: "Happy Thoughts"; "God Bless"; "You look thoughtitive."

He was making more money than ever. On pictures that he didn't produce, Grant's quote around this time averaged a guarantee of $400,000 against 10 percent of the gross. If the picture did well, he'd easily earn $1 million for his troubles. He would occasionally accept less—he did *An Affair to Remember* for a flat $300,000—a bargain for Fox (Deborah Kerr got $200,000). He got a whopping $450,000 for the dire *Kiss Them for Me*, but no percentage.

Although Grant had been getting a percentage on top of his salary since the early 1940s, in many cases the percentage had a ceiling. On *Notorious* and *Mr. Blandings Builds His Dream House*, Grant's percentage was capped at 10 percent of the first $3 million in gross, meaning his pay topped out at $300,000 per picture. (*I Was a Male War Bride* was capped at 10 percent of $2.5 million, i.e., $250,000.) There were certain pictures on which he had 10 percent in perpetuity, such as *The Bachelor and the Bobby-Soxer*, *Every Girl Should Be Married*, and *To Catch a Thief*, but those were exceptions.

On the pictures he produced with Stanley Fox (*Indiscreet, Operation Petticoat, The Grass Is Greener, That Touch of Mink, Father Goose, Walk Don't Run*) Grant was paid a modest salary by his company, but he and Stanley Fox owned the picture after the initial release period—usually seven years—and got 75 percent of the profits, with the releasing company getting the remaining 25 percent for the privilege of putting up the money. With the exception of *Indiscreet*, these were not distinguished pictures. Rather, they were straight commercial opportunities—not cash-grabs exactly, but calculated choices that would present Grant as the audience wanted to see him and bring in a reliable stream of revenue.

IN 1958, Alfred Hitchcock once again dropped into Grant's life with a script that carried with it the usual bountiful terms. Grant's deal for *North by Northwest* was $300,000 for twelve weeks of work. Beyond twelve weeks, Grant was to get $25,000 a week. In addition, he was to get 10 percent of the gross after the film earned twice its negative cost, "payable in annual installments." Along with Grant's 10 percent of *To Catch a Thief*, it would prove to be the most advantageous deal of his career.

North by Northwest is an exhilarating exercise, but Hitchcock made it hard on himself the whole way. For one thing, he made the decision to jettison James Stewart after the financial failure of *Vertigo*. Stewart was every bit as expensive as Grant, although much easier to work with. But Hitchcock felt that the fact that Stewart looked his age was one of the reasons *Vertigo* underperformed. Rather than acknowledge a diffuse and, at its core, completely unbelievable story, Hitchcock pinned the blame on his star.

North by Northwest was a difficult proposition from the beginning, because Hitchcock was making his movie at MGM, and the corporate culture at MGM was in steadfast opposition to a director such as Hitchcock. Traditionally, MGM was a studio devoted to stars shepherded by powerful producers. Directors were more or less interchangeable. But the old MGM culture was gasping for air in the late 1950s, when in-house producers such as Pandro Berman and Joe Pasternak were increasingly passé. If the stock price was any indication, so was MGM.

Something else seemed to be called for, so the studio signed Hitchcock. They were paying him $250,000 plus a percentage, but it was never going to be an easy fit. MGM's Floyd Hendrickson did some background checking and wrote a memo outlining what it was going to take to make a movie with Hitchcock: "Over the last ten years in making deals . . . Hitchcock has been given increasingly greater control over every facet of the making of his pictures until now Paramount functions practically as a facility setup for him. . . . [MGM] should be prepared to give him everything."

In order to get Hitchcock, MGM had to give him complete artistic control of the picture, and that was not the only reason people in the Thalberg building were sweating. Over in Rome, William Wyler was making *Ben-Hur* without any meaningful studio supervision because producer Sam Zimbalist had dropped dead soon after the start of production. MGM had ceded de facto control of the most expensive picture in its history to a director who was renowned for overshooting, not to mention overspending.

Another issue: MGM had hired Hitchcock to make *The Wreck of the Mary Deare*, a novel for which the studio had paid a great deal of money, but the director hit a creative wall while working on the script with Ernest Lehman. Hitchcock peremptorily made an executive decision and jettisoned *Mary Deare*, after which he and Lehman started writing what amounted to a Hitchcock anthology, the romp that Lehman had always wanted to see Hitchcock direct. If the studio wanted a Hitchcock picture, they had little choice but to capitulate.

The project went through a number of titles—*In a Northwesterly Direction, In a Northwest Direction, The CIA Story, Breathless, The Man in Lincoln's Nose*—before finally settling on *North by Northwest*. MGM's preferred cast was Gregory Peck and Cyd Charisse, the latter because she was under contract and the studio didn't know what to do with her now that musicals were faltering at the box office.

Hitchcock hadn't cared for Gregory Peck in *Spellbound*, let alone *The Paradine Case*—stolid, no humor—and Charisse was an obvious nonstarter. There was only one actor for *North by Northwest*, and MGM had to hire Grant, who was much more expensive than Gregory Peck. Hitchcock then hired Eva Marie Saint for $100,000 and costumed and directed her to incarnate Grace Kelly as much as possible, while James Mason got $75,000 to play the silken heavy.

The studio originally planned to shoot the picture in its widescreen process Camera 65, but that went by the wayside as costs mounted. Originally budgeted at $2.3 million, the picture went more than a million over that, not counting studio overhead. The picture was so expensive that Hitchcock had to jettison his planned credit sequence and have Saul Bass concoct the titles out of stock footage of New York City.

Hitchcock and Ernest Lehman worked smoothly together, allowing for numerous narrative dead ends they had to surmount. As with his hero Roger Thornhill, Lehman wrote the story without any particular idea of where the narrative was going, which turned out to be beneficial. "Since I never knew where I was going," said Lehman,

I was constantly painting myself into corners, and then trying to figure out a way out of them. As a result, the picture has about ten acts instead of three, and if I'd tried to sit down at the beginning and conceive the whole plot, I could have never done it.

Everything was written in increments: moving it a little bit forward, then a little bit more, a page at a time. "Okay, you've got him out of Grand Central Station. Now he's on the train, now what? Well, there's no female character in it yet. I better put Eve on the train. But what should I do with her? . . ." Always asking, "What do I do next?" So, in the end, the audience never knows what's coming next, because I didn't either.

The only time Hitchcock got angry with Lehman was over his habit of inserting camera directions into the script. "Why do you insist on telling me how to direct this picture?" Hitchcock asked him. "Why do you insist on telling me how to write it?" replied Lehman. There was no good response. The two men agreed to disagree, and Hitchcock ignored most of Lehman's camera suggestions.

As soon as his contract was signed, Grant began to bridle. He had confidence in Hitch, but the more he studied the script the more it seemed to vaporize. There was no there there. A contributing factor might have been Grant's realization of just what he had let himself in for; he was scheduled to work on eighty of the eighty-five production days. His complaints would only increase once the picture started shooting.

"Suddenly all Cary could think about and talk about was how desperately he wanted out of the movie," said Ernest Lehman. "The role was all wrong for him. The picture would be a disaster, et cetera, et cetera. Apparently Hitch was accustomed to this sort of thinking from Cary, so he just shrugged his shoulders and held fast." The only time Hitchcock got actively angry at his star was when Grant told Lehman that he didn't think Hitchcock had a touch for light comedy—within earshot of Hitchcock, who was "furiously offended."

The complaints came in waves. Grant would be quiet for a while, then his anxiety would spike. "This isn't a Cary Grant picture, it's a David Niven picture," he told Lehman. Grant evidently considered Niven "more 'road company,'" Lehman said. "Not as suave. On a lower level." He complained about having to do all the exposition—stars didn't do exposition, character actors did. Grant was careful not to do any complaining around his costar. "If Cary had any problems, he never showed it," said Eva Marie Saint.

Contributing to Grant's low-level panic about the script was an unusually laborious shoot that encompassed a lot of locations—New

York City, Long Island, Chicago, Rapid City, Bakersfield, then Hollywood for the interiors. It was during the Chicago locations that Grant asked Saint to attend a Judy Garland concert with him. As they entered the auditorium, heads began to turn and there was an audible rustle of conversation that moved over the crowd, as people told each other that Cary Grant had just walked in.

"I was overwhelmed by the experience," remembered Saint. "I sat there and before the show began, I said, 'I just don't know how you handle this.' . . . And that's when he said, 'Eva Marie, because they saw [us] tonight . . . it enriched their evening because they were excited and they'll tell friends about it. They'll say they saw Cary Grant. And that's a good feeling. I did something and made their lives a little brighter.'" As far as Saint was concerned, Cary Grant was welcome to the experience. "I wasn't ready for it, and I couldn't handle it."

Otherwise, her experience of working with Grant was entirely positive. On the set, Grant invited everyone to help make a scene work, even a rookie like Martin Landau, who was making his first movie but who was treated as a full equal by the star. "You just always felt that he was with you every minute," said Eva Marie Saint. "Not only for *his* close-ups, but for your close-ups too."

Hitchcock wouldn't allow the actors to do any casual paraphrasing of the script—the actors had to speak it as written, just like Billy Wilder. James Mason, doing a gorgeous job as the heavy, liked Hitchcock and he liked Hitchcock's films, but he wasn't particularly stimulated by the experience; he echoed Laraine Day and compared acting for Hitchcock to being "animated props." Mason had never worked with Grant before and found his actual demeanor the polar opposite of his casual screen character. He was, according to Mason, "conscientous, clutching his script until the last moment."

Hitchcock gave Eva Marie Saint only three specific directions and those came before the start of production: Lower your voice; don't use your hands; look into Cary's eyes at all times. "He wasn't being facetious," remembered Saint. "That really worked, certainly on the train . . . well, all the scenes, looking right at him." Once shooting began, Hitchcock didn't give her any direction at all other than blocking. Similarly, there was little rehearsal. "We were both very well prepared and just enjoyed working together."

The dialogue on the train sequence, as Ernest Lehman noted, isn't really dialogue, it's repartee, or, if you prefer, foreplay. As Saint observed, that meant that "You have to be working with the other actor who's in tune with that. Cary Grant was. And I love that it wasn't just straight dialogue. A lot of it came off the looks that we had to give one another."

During one scene, Saint had too much light on her and her eyes were involuntarily squinting. Grant stopped the scene and said, "Excuse me, there's too much light on me. Could you check that?" As the crew was relighting the shot, he told Saint, "I saw you squinting." "You're a prince," she said. "Thank you." Saint also noted that when Grant went over stills, he would cross out shots where Saint wasn't flattered by the photography, even if he looked fine.

Saint began calling Grant Thorneycroft, a play on his character's name of Thornhill, and she and Grant began sending each other gag telegrams on days when one of them wasn't working. At one point, Saint was in her room at the St. Regis when a telegram from Grant arrived. "All right, all right. So now you're in the St. Regis. I'm still in the doldrums and in a tizzy. Thorneycroft."

Hitchcock had little passive-aggressive ways of getting back at Grant for the grief the star gave him. Hitchcock had Martin Landau's suits surreptitiously made by Grant's tailor, who was instructed to cut them in precisely the same way he cut Grant's—a state secret. Landau was working on his first day when Grant sent over a minion to ask where he had gotten the suit.

Hitchcock had instructed Landau in precisely what to say. "I got it in Wardrobe at Universal, a month or so ago."

The minion nodded, walked over to Grant, then came back to Landau. "I'm sorry, Mr. Landau, but Mr. Grant says that's not possible."

The reason it wasn't possible was that Grant's suit had been made by Kilgour, French & Stanbury on Savile Row. The Beverly Hills tailor Quintino made five or six copies for use in the movie. According to the clothing historian Matt Spaiser, the suit was made of light worsted wool in a blue/gray fine glen plaid pattern. There were darts to shape the front, and the shoulders were padded. "The trousers are very similar to what Sean Connery wore in the Bond films," wrote Spaiser, with a long rise, double forward pleats, turn-ups and side adjusters.

Connery's adjusters had buttons, but Grant's were two strips of cloth tightened with a clasp.

One day on the MGM backlot, Grant passed the hairstylist Sydney Guilaroff, who asked how things were going. An obviously gloomy Grant mumbled, "I don't know." Later that day he came over to Guilaroff, who was working on Eva Marie Saint's hair. "I'm just lonesome," he said. "I guess I need a little mothering." Guilaroff believed that Grant suffered from clinical depression.

Some of the discontent was just exhaustion—North by Northwest was always going to be a lengthy shoot, but nobody thought it would last as long as it did. Little things became big things. Grant was eating a lot of salads to maintain his weight, and nobody in Bakersfield had ever heard of a salad, which increased his general disgruntlement.

Mainly, though, Grant focused his ire on money. Finally, he went to Herbert Coleman, Hitchcock's associate producer, and demanded to know when the picture would be finished. Coleman replied that they needed Grant for five more days, and what was the problem?

"Because I'm working for nothing!" Grant said.

"$5,000 a day is nothing?" asked Coleman, referring to Grant's per diem for the overage.

"Every dollar of that $5,000 goes to the Internal Revenue Service."

"You were the one who insisted on going on salary two months before our start date," retorted Coleman. "Your guarantee . . . was all paid to you before we started shooting."

The conversation began to get heated as the aggrieved actor began enumerating chapter and verse of the various ways in which he was being taken advantage of. "When [Grant's agent] told me Hitch wanted me for the picture, I told him I had an offer from Fox and I would take the one that started first. When I told him the start date of the Fox picture, he told me Hitch would start two weeks before Fox."

Grant was fuming and Coleman had to come up with something to placate him. Later that day he went to Grant's dressing room and suggested he work his last five days for nothing.

"That's what I'm doing now," Grant groused.

"Hear the rest of it, Cary. You're taking a vacation in London as soon as we finish. Work for nothing for the next five days, and I'll give you a drawing account for 5,000 English pounds for just one press interview for North by Northwest. Tax free."

That calmed the fractious actor and the picture was completed without further aggravation. Once it was edited, Grant had a private showing and gave editor George Tomasini notes, the primary one being to shorten his scene in the police station. He also noted his dislike of the scene where he's driving drunk. He thought he looked "baggy."

North by Northwest started shooting on August 27, 1958, and didn't finish until a week before Christmas, with the costs adding up to $4.3 million—more than a million over budget. Besides the money, MGM was worried about the running time. The picture was a lengthy 2 hours and 16 minutes, and MGM tried to get Hitchcock to trim it—the scene in the woods between Grant and Saint after she feigns shooting him at Mount Rushmore became the focus of the disagreement. Looking at the scene dispassionately, MGM might have had a point, but Hitchcock had final cut and kept the scene, not to mention the long, cumulatively funny silences in the lead-up to the crop-dusting sequence.

Bernard Herrmann had just finished the score for the pilot episode of *The Twilight Zone* when Hitchcock hired him to compose the music for *North by Northwest*. Herrmann chose to use a driving Spanish dance rhythm known as the fandango for the main title. It didn't seem to make much sense for a movie that takes place entirely in America, but Herrmann had a genius for music embodying a movie's psychological DNA. Herrmann's inspiration became clear when he explained that his use of the fandango was inspired by Grant's "Astaire-like agility," which was never more apparent than in the crop-dusting sequence, where he sprints through the cornfield like an Olympic athlete.

All the stresses and strains were forgotten when *North by Northwest* was released in July 1959—it was a critical and commercial hit immediately upon release and became the sixth top grossing picture of 1959. Grant, Hitchcock, and Mason combine to form the movie equivalent of a perfect dry martini. Everyone liked *North by Northwest* except Manny Farber, whose proletarian instincts made him suspicious of Grant's ever-present polish. He decried "senility catching up with Cary Grant's charm technique."

Ernest Lehman's script initially strips away much of what had been working for Grant for nearly thirty years. In Grant's other pictures for Hitchcock, his character feigns innocence, even as he carries a full ration of moral or practical guilt. Roger Thornhill actually is innocent, but he's also a glorified salaryman in a great suit, worried about inconsequential appointments and responsibilities. His initial befuddlement is sharpened by the desperate, forced improvisation of being pursued across the country because of a case of vastly mistaken identity. It is only then that the traditional Cary Grant character comes into focus, including his contempt for the woman he loves, who happens to be a double agent recruited to sleep with the enemy—a direct lift from *Notorious*.

Shortly after the film opened, Grant was walking through the MGM commissary when he saw Hitchcock eating lunch. The two hadn't really made up their many disagreements on the shoot, but all that was put aside as Grant walked over, knelt down on the floor and ostentatiously salaamed the director. "[Hitchcock] once told me, 'If a director can get eighty five percent of a writer's intentions onto the screen, the writer should consider himself very fortunate,'" said Ernest Lehman. "Well, he got a hundred percent of *North by Northwest* up on the screen!"

North by Northwest would be the last time Grant worked with Hitchcock, and in retrospect he knew how lucky he had been.

> Hitch and I had a rapport and understanding deeper than words . . .
> I always went to work whistling when I worked with him [author
> note: !!!!!] because everything on the set was just as you envisioned
> it would be. . . . He was a tasteful, intelligent, decent and patient
> man who knew the actor's business as well as he knew his own.

The two men stayed socially friendly. In June 1965, Hitchcock wrote Grant enclosing a story that Leo McCarey had given Hitchcock. "The story material contains a proposition that I should play a leading role with you," wrote Hitchcock, who begged off in the next sentence. "In view of the fact that I am preparing a new picture (which you should be in) I don't see how I can give it any consideration at this time."

Grant would write Hitchcock a thank-you letter at Christmas 1967 for "such elegant and interesting books," as well as for the perks of "having been associated with your films [and giving], such dividends of personal publicity." He closed by wishing "dear dear Hitch" (Grant's ultimate expression of affection) a Merry Christmas.

Beneath glad-handing public statements, each of them implicitly understood the other's strong and weak points. They also understood their shared covert natures. In 1966, Hitchcock was speaking to a group of young English writers when he told them that likability was a quality that could not be faked in movies. The public, he said, had adored Grace Kelly because she was indeed likable. And for all of Hitchcock's efforts, they had rejected Tippi Hedren because she was not. There was, he said, only one actor in the world so formidably skilled that he could fake a charm he did not in fact possess. Any guesses?

"Cary Grant?" offered one young man.

"Correct," said Hitchcock.

CHAPTER EIGHTEEN

On August 31, 1959, Hedda Hopper wrote a letter to her friend Gardner Cowles, the editor of *Look* magazine. She began by complimenting him on a recent profile of Shirley MacLaine, and then got down to cases.

> The [story] on Cary Grant was the damndest mishmash I have ever read. Whom does he think he is fooling? This will probably surprise you: he started with the boys and now he has gone back to them. . . . The chauffeur Cary talks about is the one he took over from Betsy who employed him when she was making a picture in London. Then later Cary took him on and it was Grant who brought him to this country. He was chauffeur, valet and pal. You can even go further. Grant introduced him to his social friends and now Cary is using a lot of pretty girls to cover up. I used to like him, but no more.

Cowles replied a few days later, telling Hopper "I have long suspected a few things about Cary Grant. You are probably aware that [Cowles's wife] Fleur has had quite a crush on him in recent years."

Hopper had increasingly positioned herself as a provincial guardian of traditional American values marooned in the cesspool of Hollywood. She was a nativist, an isolationist, and had functioned as the Madame Defarge of the Red Scare, cheering on the House

333

Un-American Activities Committee against suspected communists, former communists, or premature antifascists.

Hopper had manifold prejudices—"If you see a nigger around the house, don't be scared, it's only Jackie Robinson," she had yelled to her maid as the great athlete waited in her foyer. But Hopper was not easily dismissed. She read widely, had astonishing energy. Within the film community her sourcing was generally regarded as accurate. "She had spies *everywhere*," said Robert Wagner.

Hopper had plenty of lesbian and gay friends, as older, divorced women who have left sex behind often do, and she rarely gay-baited in her column. There is, however, plenty of it in her correspondence— she referred to Adlai Stevenson as "Adeline" or "Adelaide," because of rumors about his sexuality.

It was curious. Grant and Hopper had long cooperated with each other, although you can tell from their interview transcripts that there was no warmth between them, and a complete absence of candor on Grant's part. On Hopper's part, she separated his work from his personality—in 1958, she told her editor, "If you haven't seen Grant and Bergman in *Indiscreet*, run don't walk to the theater; you'll have a real treat."

But a month after that, she was fulminating about him:

What a ham he is! He had two articles on the same day and I damn near swooned. He is a fine actor, but an awful ham and I am a little tired of his Yogi exercises and his wife's hypnotism—of her, too. They are greedy for money and they have the first five cents they ever made. Now Betsy is not only writing, but going to do some TV shows, thereby robbing an actress of a job—one who needs the job. Enough of the Grants!

Hopper would die in 1966 at the age of eighty, still in harness, still glorifying in her power, still demanding that stars young and old kiss her ass. Four years before her death, she sent a picture of Grant and Randolph Scott to Ken McCormick, her book editor at Doubleday. "I think the one of Cary Grant and Randy Scott will tickle your funny bone, but not theirs. We don't have to caption this; speaks for itself."

Whatever her general batting average when it came to journalistic accuracy, Hedda Hopper had been wrong about Grant's relationship with his chauffeur. The truth of it would have made a great story, if only Hopper had been able to see past her animus to figure it out.

The chauffeur's name was Ray Austin, a stuntman who had been introduced to Grant in 1955 by Grant's own double, Paul Stader. Austin was a Cockney and Grant "took a shine to me," he remembered. "I was more Cockney then than I am now, and Cary used to love doing Cockney for fun. So we would do Cockney rhyming slang, old music hall stuff.

"One of us would say, 'That's Life,' and the other would reply 'What's that?'

"'A magazine.'

"'How expensive?'

"'Thirty-five cents . . .'

"And on and on it would go.

"The English working-class thing was the tie between us. In those days, I was a good acrobat, good on the parallel and horizontal bars, so we used to play around an awful lot on grass or sand, balancing and things like that. He enjoyed going back and polishing the skills he had developed with Bob Pender."

Grant told Austin that he had to get rid of his accent—"You never get anywhere speaking Cockney," he told him. "No one wants a Cockney in America."

When Grant came to London to make *Indiscreet*, he had Austin pick up his Silver Cloud. The two men would drive the Rolls to places like Bath to eat sausage and mash, fish and chips. Occasionally he would tell Austin, "Let's go up there," meaning to Bristol, to see his mother.

And when we got there, he'd say, "For God's sake, come back in an hour and half or two hours." He couldn't take it for very long.

I was in the house with his mother three times. Most of the time she would just sit there and not say a word. There was no contact whatever. The first time, I had to pick up a large hamper Cary had sent her from Harrod's that she had never opened. The second time I dropped him off shortly after he had a color TV delivered, just when they were really new. He came back out and said, "She hasn't even opened it up." So I went in and we set the TV up, but then she didn't want to turn it on.

He would get in the car after visiting her and slump in the seat. "I give up," he would say. "I don't know what to do. I can't get through."

I would say something on the order of, "Well, she was sick for a long time, it takes time," and so forth. And he would say, "I don't have a lot of time!"

His childhood was like a black cloud hovering over him.

Austin was part of the small Grant circle for several years, and says that he never saw any sign of anything but a functioning heterosexual. "He was a man's man. Never once did I see any intentions of that kind. He never went near my backside, not ever.

"I have to tell you we had some naughty times together. He had a lot of fans. When we did the promotional tour for *Indiscreet* across England, we did a theater thing. I would be in the audience with a microphone and people would ask questions. In one of the cities, two young ladies came up to me after the show and made it known that they wanted to meet Cary. We all met and had a truly wonderful evening at the hotel. Once in Monaco I had to get a young lady out of his room because the press was outside and they suspected there was a girl in there."

Austin came to America and worked on the stunt team for *North by Northwest*. Grant's relationship with Betsy was in breakdown, "because of Sophia. That capped it." Grant asked Austin to keep an eye on Betsy, so he moved to Drake's small house in Mandeville Canyon, to an apartment over the garage. "I'm sure she's seeing someone else," Grant told Austin, although she wasn't. "He had said the same thing in England, when he was doing *Indiscreet*, and I had told him she was never out of line."

But an attractive young man in close proximity to Betsy and her wounded ego was a dangerous combination. Betsy and Austin soon began an affair. "Revenge for Sophia?" asked Austin rhetorically. "Tit for tat? It could have been. Absolutely. And then she said, 'I'm going to tell Cary because I want us to be together.'"

Just about that same time, Grant asked Austin to be part of the stunt team for *Operation Petticoat*, scheduled for location work in Key West. "I was a young man, which is to say a great deal of the time I was an idiot. Betsy didn't want me to go, but I went on the picture. And I met a young lady named Dina Merrill." Merrill was Grant's niece through his marriage to Barbara Hutton so they had a preexisting familial relationship. Austin and Merrill soon embarked on a location affair centered in and around the Blue Dolphin Motel. As with Drake, Merrill made remarks indicating she wanted to divorce her husband, the multimillionaire Stan Rumbough Jr., and marry Austin.

There are few secrets on a film set, so of course Grant heard about Austin's affair with Merrill. He took Austin aside and launched into a Come to Jesus talk: "You're a fool. You're going to get hurt. She's one of the richest women in the world. Do you think she's going to give up everything and marry a stuntman? Do you know who her husband is? A man named Stan Rumbough. He's got more muscle than you've ever seen. He can have you wiped off in a night, disappear you from the face of the earth. Ray, you're going to get hurt."

When the film moved back to Hollywood, Austin was bouncing between Merrill's suite at the Bel-Air Hotel and Betsy's house in Mandeville Canyon. And just when it seemed Austin's life couldn't get any more complicated . . . it got more complicated. During a trip to Palm Springs, Betsy told Austin that she knew about Dina Merrill because Cary had told her, but she was prepared to forgive him. More than that, she was going to tell Cary about their relationship. Whoever told Grant about the affair—Austin thought Louella Parsons got there before Betsy Drake did—the result was banishment.

> The next thing I knew the shit had hit the fan. Cary said to me, "I told you you were going to get hurt. None of this is going to happen. And I am never going to speak to you again." And he never did. I tried to remind him that he wasn't with Betsy anymore, that he was going to divorce her anyway. "But I haven't divorced her yet," he said, "and you were going to look after her for me, and she was having an affair with you."

The hypocrisy was and is breathtaking—Grant was eager to divorce Drake because of his extramarital affair, but went into a towering snit over Drake's affair after they had separated. "He couldn't bear the fact that she might be with someone else," said Austin.

> And from his point of view, I was a Cockney he'd brought to America and I'd run off with his wife. If I'd been Marlon Brando, who he

didn't like, it wouldn't have meant a thing, but a Cockney boy from London? A stuntman? It was unheard of.

Did I feel guilty? God, yes. I knew I was fucking up my relationship with Cary. We had had a lot of fun, a lot of laughs. We had this English working-class thing based on the places we both knew. I really hated myself for messing the whole bloody thing up.

Believe me, when Cary Grant cut you dead, you were *dead*. A couple of years earlier he'd told me how he did it. "If you want to hurt someone, you take them off the planet. They simply don't exist. You focus on something behind them, sweep your eyes across them, do not recognize them anymore." And that's what he did to me.

Austin survived and eventually flourished. He went back to England, where he became a successful second unit director, then came back to America, where he directed over three hundred hours of episodic television.

IN 1959, Chris Scott, Randolph Scott's son, took a girl to dinner at Trader Vic's in Hollywood. On his way to the men's room, Chris ran into Cary Grant and introduced himself. "He looked for a moment and smiled. 'Nice to see you, Chris. How is your father?'

"'He's very well, sir.'" The two men exchanged a few more pleasantries then went on their respective ways.

Back at the dinner table, Chris Scott was exerting the maximum amount of charm on his date and getting nowhere. At that point, Grant walked by and stopped. "Why hello, Chris," he said. "This must be the charming young lady you were telling me about." He turned to her and said, "My name is Cary Grant."

"I thought she would faint right there," Chris Scott remembered. "I can see why women used to swoon over him. I can likewise see why men might feel a little insecure around him. He was everything a man is supposed to be . . . sexy, handsome, and he spoke as smoothly as satin."

Grant's few moments with Scott's date softened her up considerably. Chris Scott remembered that "I will be grateful to Cary Grant for that kindness for the rest of my life."

The house in Bristol where
Archie Leach was born in 1904.

A late-in-life photo of Elias
Leach, whose taste in clothes
was still evident despite his
limited circumstances.

From his mother, Elsie Leach, Archie got his dark complexion and his fretful temperament.

Young Archie Leach.

Downtown Bristol as Archie Leach knew it. The tall building slightly to the right of center is the Hippodrome Theatre.

The beautifully appointed Hippodrome Theatre in Bristol, where Archie Leach fell in love with show business.

A teenaged Archie Leach in the Bob Pender troupe.

October, 1920: Archie Leach (center) has his picture taken with Douglas Fairbanks Sr., who is returning from his European honeymoon with Mary Pickford on the *Olympia*. As with most adolescent boys of the time, Leach worshipped Fairbanks's joie de vivre. Unlike most adolescent boys of the period, Leach would first replicate, then expand upon Fairbanks' exquisite taste in clothing centering on the English cut. The boy on the right is another member of Bob Pender's troupe of acrobats.

Beginnings: Grant, Thelma Todd, Roland Young, and Charlie Ruggles in Grant's first feature, 1932's *This Is the Night*, in which he plays an Olympic javelin thrower. Seriously.

Tennis anyone? In his early days at Paramount, the studio treated the slightly baby-faced young actor to a series of generic glamour portraits that, like Grant at the time, lacked a specific identity.

Grant's career was given a large boost by costarring with Mae West in two pictures. Here he is with her in *She Done Him Wrong*.

Grant and Virginia Cherrill, certainly among the most beautiful of Hollywood couples, shortly before their engagement in 1933.

One of the Paramount publicity photographs of Randolph Scott and Cary Grant at their seaside home circa 1935 that caused much comment at the time . . . and since.

Grant, Alex D'Arcy, and Irene Dunne along with the object of their affections, Skippy—the same dog that played Asta in the Thin Man movies—in Leo McCarey's *The Awful Truth*.

Grant and Irene Dunne engage in an arched-eyebrow contest in *The Awful Truth*.

Momentarily attired in a fetching peignoir, Grant attempts to explain his predicament to the unsympathetic Katharine Hepburn, May Robson, Leona Roberts, and Skippy in *Bringing Up Baby*.

17

Grant rehearsing with Ronald Colman for a radio broadcast in 1939.

18

Grant, Victor McLaglen, and Douglas Fairbanks Jr. in George Stevens's *Gunga Din*, the movies' most enthralling Boys' Adventure. Next to Grant is Sam Jaffe as the title character.

Grant and Sam Jaffe as the loyal Bisti in *Gunga Din*, here luring Annie the elephant across a rope bridge on location at Lone Pine. The iron stakes driven into the rocks to hold the bridge are still visible more than eighty years later.

The temperature in Lone Pine during the production of *Gunga Din* regularly topped 100 degrees. Here, in a candid, the stars try to cool off between shots.

Grant, Thomas Mitchell, and Jean Arthur in Howard Hawks's *Only Angels Have Wings*, which broadened Grant's acting palette by casting him as a resolute, unemotional leader of men.

Cary Grant and Rosalind Russell harass Billy Gilbert and each other in Howard Hawks's *His Girl Friday*, which would have to slow down to go a mile-a-minute.

George Cukor at his most intense directing Grant and Katharine Hepburn in *The Philadelphia Story*.

Grant and Irene Dunne confront multiple tragedies in *Penny Serenade*.

Grant in earnest conversation with Barbara Hutton, his second wife.

Grant with Joan Fontaine in the compromised *Suspicion*, his first picture for Alfred Hitchcock, which endured considerable reshoots because of squabbles with RKO and the Breen office.

Part of the Hollywood Victory Caravan that toured the country during World War II. Grant stands next to the Metropolitan Opera's Rise Stevens. Next to Stevens are Charles Boyer and Desi Arnaz. Kneeling are Joan Blondell, Oliver Hardy, and Stan Laurel.

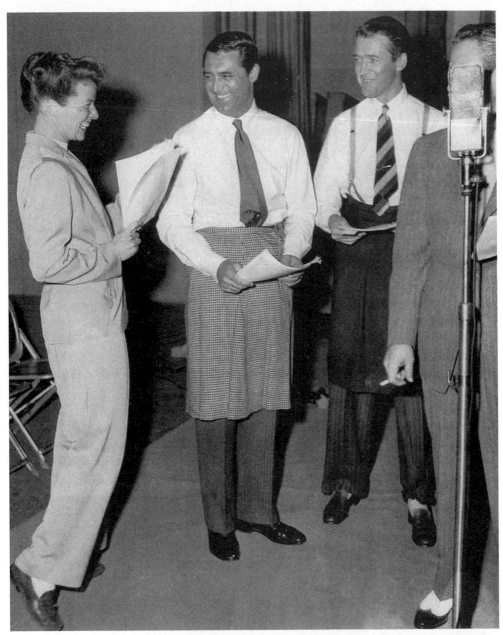

A few years after the movie version of *The Philadelphia Story*, the stars reunite for a radio broadcast. Grant celebrated by wearing an apron—Hepburn's least favorite piece of clothing.

Grant and Ethel Barrymore gave devastating performances as a mother and son unable to find peace with each other in Clifford Odets's *None But the Lonely Heart*.

Grant's most frenzied comic performance is undoubtedly in Frank Capra's *Arsenic and Old Lace*, here with Josephine Hull and Jean Adair.

Grant, Ingrid Bergman, and Claude Rains form an unforgettable triangle alongside the forbidding Madame Konstantin in Alfred Hitchcock's *Notorious*.

Grant as the angel Dudley, with Loretta Young and James Gleason in *The Bishop's Wife*.

Jim Blandings (Grant) faces impending bankruptcy while his wife (Myrna Loy) ups the financial ante in the drily hilarious *Mr. Blandings Builds His Dream House*.

Grant dons an amusingly unlikely Louise Brooks wig for *I Was a Male War Bride* opposite Ann Sheridan.

Grant in a portrait with third wife, Betsy Drake.

With the young starlet Marilyn
Monroe and a spectacular pair
of glasses in Howard Hawks's
Monkey Business.

Grant with his old vaude-
ville pal Don Barclay, who is
presenting him with Barclay's
caricature of Grant.

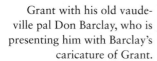

Grant and Grace Kelly on the hills above Monaco in Hitchcock's *To Catch a Thief*.

Grant and Sophia Loren in
The Pride and the Passion.

Grant and Deborah Kerr in the movie that launched a million crying jags: Leo McCarey's *An Affair to Remember*.

Grant and Ingrid Bergman share a scene with Picasso in Stanley Donen's touching late-life love story *Indiscreet*.

Twilight of the Gods: Grant rehearsing for the 1958 Academy Awards with Clark Gable, Bob Hope, and David Niven.

Grant and Sophia Loren reunited for *Houseboat*, the making of which gave the director an ulcer.

Grant's friend, the stuntman Ray Austin (left) joins Grant, Eva Marie Saint, and James Mason on the South Dakota location of *North by Northwest*.

One of the most justifiably famous scenes in movie history: Grant and the plane that's dusting crops where there are no crops in Hitchcock's *North by Northwest*.

Grant on location for *North by Northwest* with the greatest suit in movie history, Alfred Hitchcock, and the VistaVision camera.

The leading men of Universal Studios in 1962: Rock Hudson, Grant, Marlon Brando (in costume for *The Ugly American*), and Gregory Peck.

Grant loved playing the grumpy, perennially put-upon *Father Goose*, if only because he didn't have to obsess about his wardrobe.

49

Hail and farewell: Grant in *Walk, Don't Run.*

50

There are thousands of photographs of Grant with his daughter, Jennifer, and fourth wife, Dyan Cannon, but this one best captures the giddy joy that fatherhood brought him.

A deeply emotional Grant receives his honorary Oscar in 1970 from his friend Frank Sinatra.

52

IN MEMORY OF ELIAS
WHO DIED DECEMBER 1... AGED 6... YEARS
THE HUSBAND OF ELSIE LEACH
REUNITED JANUARY 22ND 1973.

The grave of Elsie and Elias Leach in Bristol's Canfield Cemetery.

53

The happily retired Cary Grant
in Nassau circa 1973.

Grant and an old friend in 1974.

A year or two before his death, Grant was photographed with his teenaged daughter, Jennifer.

Grant and his last wife, Barbara Harris, shortly before his death.

When the divorce from Betsy finally came through in July 1962, Grant wrote his mother: to say that it was inevitable, but they remained friendly.

The tailored nonchalance didn't extend far beneath the surface, and Grant knew it. Grant's affair must have made him even more conscious of his failures. "I am not proud of my marriage career," he would admit. "It was not the fault of Hollywood, but my own inadequacies. Of my own inconstancy. My mistrust of constancy . . . I feel fine. Alone. But fine. . . . My wives have divorced me. I await a woman with the best qualities of each. I will endow her with those qualities because they will be in my own point of view."

As an unwitting admission of social confusion, the idea that women have no intrinsic qualities other than those imposed on them by a man is hard to surpass. Grant's core problem was outlined by Elia Kazan: "Actors get trapped in a personality that's partially their own invention. It made them a commodity, it made them saleable. . . . You've got to find some way to smash the wall that makes you the merchant and . . . the merchandise." It was a problem Grant would not solve until he made the drastic decision to stop selling the merchandise.

Cary Grant embodied perfection, but Archie Leach knew all too well how imperfect he was. Grant had been seeking some way to unify the two disparate halves of his personality for decades, and he would come to believe that what finally enabled him to get beyond his fears was not acting, not fame, not psychotherapy, but LSD.

Betsy had long been interested in psychotherapy and had consulted with Dr. Mortimer A. Hartman, a Los Angeles internist who was experimenting with psychotherapy and had undergone years of classic Freudian analysis. At some point, Hartman got sidetracked into experimenting with LSD—at the time, the drug was legal. After her consultation with Hartman, Betsy had taken the drug.

Betsy told Grant of several doctors she knew who had come to believe in the reparative effects of LSD, among them Hartman. "He's the man who saved my life," Grant said. "I am not exaggerating. I was so confused and lost when I began seeing him."

Distraught over the collapse of his marriage, not to mention his inability to convince Sophia Loren to marry him, in 1958 Grant began LSD treatments with Hartman and, later, with Dr. Oscar Janiger— more than a hundred sessions in all.

"LSD empties the subconscious and intensifies the emotions a hundred times," said Hartman. "It also breaks down memory blocks so that past experiences, even childhood ones, may be vividly relieved. Further, it provides far-reaching insights into one's own self and one's relationships with others. Some who have taken it feel that they have finally gained an insight into the purpose of life." In other words, one-stop shopping for the psychiatrically constipated.

LSD had been around since 1938, when Dr. Albert Hoffmann formulated the first dose in an attempt to develop a circulatory stimulant out of a rye fungus. His twenty-fifth attempt at the stimulant turned out to be LSD, which didn't do a thing for the circulation system but had entirely unexpected properties.

Mortimer Hartman had a small, dark office on Lasky Drive, off Rodeo Drive. There was a back entrance where patients could enter and exit without anybody being the wiser. Grant wasn't the only celebrity LSD patient Hartman and other Los Angeles doctors had. In fact, the town was a nest of psychedelic dilettantes that included English expats and media eminences: Henry Luce, his wife, Clare Boothe Luce, Christopher Isherwood, Gerald Heard, Anaïs Nin, Aldous Huxley, André Previn, Edie Wasserman, Esther Williams, Judy Balaban Kanter, and Jack Nicholson, who took 150 micrograms in Dr. Oscar Janiger's office on May 29, 1962. Nicholson later incorporated his experiences into his script for Roger Corman's *The Trip*, starring Peter Fonda and Dennis Hopper—who was also a patient of Janiger's. Esther Williams called LSD an "instant psychoanalyst."

When Grant wasn't working, he would go to Hartman's office once a week, arriving at nine, leaving at three. He never called Hartman about any distress.

In the beginning, Betsy would accompany Grant to the sessions and wait for him in the outside office in case anything went wrong. "It was monitored," said Grant.

The dosages were small. But unfortunately, LSD was known as a drug, and drugs have a bad connotation. It connotes heroin. When, in fact, to come down, you had to take a drug, you had to take a cigarette. . . .

I laid down on a couch. The doctor read a book over in the corner with a little light. He played music associated with my youth. Like

Rachmaninoff. It would last three or four hours. . . . You would
see nightmares, your fears, the scenes associated with nightmares.
I learned to forgive my parents for what they didn't know. And my
fear of knives. If I see a sharp knife, I cringe.

In some respects, Grant's LSD experiences were typical. "I passed
through changing seas of horrifying and happy sights, through a montage of intense hate and love, a mosaic of past impressions, assembling
and re-assembling; through terrifying depths of dark despair, replaced
by glorious heavenlike religious symbolisms. Session after session.
Week after week."

One time, Ray Austin and Stanley Fox accompanied Grant to
Hartman's office. Fox did not partake and left, but Austin tried it and
found that LSD scared the hell out of him. Grant had told Austin that
LSD would take him back to the womb, but Austin didn't enjoy the
scenery. "The session was four or five hours," remembered Austin.
"You couldn't leave after taking it, because you could crash the car.
You had to stay there and just hang on." After that, Grant carried
on alone.

In years to come, renegade adherents of the drug would disdain a
controlled environment. Hunter Thompson would write that he preferred to just swallow the acid and hang on, "which is probably just
as dangerous as the experts say, but a far, far nuttier trip than sitting
in some sterile chamber with a condescending guide and a handful of
nervous, would-be hipsters."

Grant's estimation of his motivation centered on his overwhelming
dissatisfaction with himself. The first breakthrough came one day
when Grant was writhing on the sofa in Hartman's office. "Why am
I turning around and around this sofa," he asked the doctor. "You
don't know why?" the doctor asked.

"No, but I tell you this: It better stop soon."

And Hartman said, "Cary, it'll stop when you stop it."

Deep inside the LSD, Grant realized that Hartman had spoken
truth. "*I* had to take command. *I* had to take complete responsibility
for my own actions and stop blaming my mother and my father and
everyone else." Put it another way: "I learned that no one else was
keeping me unhappy but me; that I could whip myself better than any
other guy in the joint.

And then I said, "I'm unscrewing myself, aren't I." And that's what happened in more ways than one. . . . When I broke through this way, I lost all the tension that I'd been crippling myself with. I lost all my inhibitions. The day this all became clear to me, I lost it all, but I gained something more. Myself. And on that day I shat all over the rug in the doctor's office, and I shat all over the floor.

Grant was not speaking metaphorically. He would describe the office accident several times—once as defecating in his pants—and he would come to see it as the physical manifestation of a psychic explosion. It wasn't all humblings and humiliations; another time Grant said that "I imagined myself as a giant penis launching off from Earth like a spaceship."

More typically, "I was noting the growing intensity of light in the room . . . and at short intervals as I shut my eyes, visions appeared to me. I seemed to be in a world of healthy, chubby little babies, legs and diapers, and smeared blood, a sort of general menstrual activity taking place. It did not repel me as such thoughts used to."

He began extrapolating other insights, such as the revelation that he was trying to take revenge on his mother by consistently undermining his relationships with wives and lovers. "I was punishing them for what she did to me." In time, Grant began to refer to Hartman as "Mahatma."

"I took LSD with the hope it would make me feel better about myself," he said. "I wanted to work through the events of my childhood, my relationship with my parents and my former wives. I did not want to spend years in analysis. . . . Either something was wrong with me, or obviously, with the whole sociological and moralistic concepts of our civilization."

Ultimately, he concluded that the only person who couldn't relax and accept Cary Grant was Archie Leach—the man inside. "I had lots of problems over the years, but they were Archie Leach's problems, not Cary Grant's."

And at the end of it all was something perilously close to gobble-dygook: "I learned that everything is or becomes its own opposite. A theory I can sometimes apply, but would find difficult to convey.

"It took . . . years, but it was necessary for my evolution."

Soon, Grant was proclaiming to anyone who would listen how LSD had changed his life for the better in the passionate, vague manner of a fifteen-year-old after his first tussle with a hash pipe. He urged Clifford Odets to try the drug, and Odets thought enough about the idea to ask his psychiatrist her opinion. She thought it was a bad idea and Odets never did try LSD. Mae West heard about what her costar was saying around town and responded completely in character: "What is Cary fooling with that stuff for? Why doesn't he come up and see me sometime? I'll straighten him out."

IN 1959, Cary Grant and Stanley Fox set up shop at Universal Studios with a service comedy called *Operation Petticoat*. The director was Blake Edwards, at the beginning of a notable career. Unfortunately, Edwards and Grant butted heads. "I couldn't believe his choices," said Edwards. "He was very lucky throughout his life that he got certain directors who were strong enough to impose their will on him. Left alone, I don't know what would have happened. . . . He would come up with things that were just . . ."

At this, Edwards broke off and told a story about a scene he had begged Grant to play. The script involved Tony Curtis and Gavin MacLeod stealing a huge pig and getting stopped by the Shore Patrol. To get the pig past the cops, they dress it up as a sailor. Edwards realized that the scene would be much funnier if it was played by Grant—his straight-faced dignity and sangfroid refusing to be rattled by a costumed pig.

"I gave him every argument I could come up with," said Edwards. "He said that people would not associate him with a pig. . . . The writers and I got down on our knees and said, 'Look, Cary, do it anyway. You own the film; you can get rid of the scene if you don't think it's any good, but let us show you what we're talking about!'

"No good. Missed one of the great comedy moments. To this day I'm sorry about it. It's one of the few things I regret in my career."

Edwards left no doubt that the experience of directing Grant was simultaneously educational and stressful. "I learned a great deal about personalities and politics. . . . I was there by virtue of the fact that Cary Grant had agreed to give this newcomer a break. I was really in great jeopardy of being off the film before I got started and I had to, at one point, sit down and really examine myself. I learned something about myself—that I didn't have to go quite that hard to prove my point." Head-butting with a recalcitrant Grant undoubtedly prepared Edwards for coping with Peter Sellers on the *Pink Panther* pictures.

Tony Curtis's main memory of working with his acting idol was a piece of advice Grant gave him about wine. "Cary . . . told me the way to judge a fine bottle of white wine was that after chilling, it should taste like a cool glass of water. 'It's so artful that it's artless,' Cary said." Curtis extrapolated that to an overall approach to his craft—simplicity is best, i.e., never let them catch you acting.

Working opposite Grant was Dina Merrill, the daughter of Marjorie Merriweather Post—about whom Merrill was ambivalent—and E. F. Hutton—whom she adored. Merrill had grown up as the cosseted princess of Mar-a-Lago and provoked her mother's dismay when she decided to become an actress.

> I had the most magical bedroom—the door handles were squirrels with long tails. In the bathroom the tiles around the tub had nursery rhymes on them. That's how I learned to read. . . .
>
> Cary was fine. He was relaxed, very much himself. I'd met him when I was seventeen, when he was married to [Merrill's cousin] Barbara. From what I remember of her, she was a nutcase, but he was a thoughtful, kind man. We were doing a scene in the movie and a little extra girl began crying. She thought she was going to be outfitted in a beautiful dress, but the scene called for something torn and bedraggled and she was terribly upset. Cary took an assistant aside and told him to buy the little girl the finest dress he could find and give it to her after the scene.
>
> He told me, "Through LSD, I discovered that I hated my mother. But now I think I could be a good father."

He was less candid with the actress Joan O'Brien. She had been working with Grant for a day or two when costar Madlyn Rhue took her aside and told her Grant was upstaging her—subtly shifting his position during a shot so that only the back of O'Brien's head would be visible to the camera. Normally an actor pulling this stunt is quickly set right by the director, but Blake Edwards probably didn't want to risk irritating his star any more than he already had. O'Brien didn't want to think Grant would do something so petty, but she had to admit that he was an absolute master of screen technique and wouldn't do it accidentally. O'Brien responded by giving him some of his own back. "I'd get in there—and it was kind of fun—forcing him to meet me halfway. I'd then turn sideways so the camera would pick up more of me."

Grant would never have tried such a stunt on Ingrid Bergman, Irene Dunne, or any other experienced actress, but O'Brien was making only her second film. Moreover, she was trained as a singer, not an actress, and had been hired for her bountiful figure, which was the point of a laborious running gag about her causing a backup pile of sailors whenever she tried to navigate the narrow passages of the submarine.

O'Brien found Grant good company when he wasn't trying to edge her out of camera range. "He was a very warm, down-to-earth, straightforward guy. With his legendary screen image, I thought he might be difficult or hard to work with. But he wasn't."

Despite Grant's obstinance and Edwards's disaffection, *Operation Petticoat* was a huge hit—rentals of $10 million against a modest negative cost. *Variety* estimated that Grant's piece of the picture came to about $3 million.

GRANT'S RELATIONSHIP WITH THE PRESS remained generally one-sided. He did hundreds of interviews and rarely said much. When the reporters' notebooks emerged, so did Grant's bland facade. But LSD changed that, as the Hollywood columnist Joe Hyams found out.

In the spring of 1959, Hyams interviewed Grant on the Key West set of *Operation Petticoat*. Grant talked, not about the film, or even psychiatry, but also LSD. "For the first time in my life I was ready to meet people realistically," he told Hyams.

> Every man is conceited but I know now that in my earliest days I really despised myself. It's when you admit this that you're beginning to change. Introspection is the beginning of courage.
>
> I was always professing a knowledge I didn't have. If I didn't know about a subject I would disdain it. I was very aggressive, but without the courage to be physically aggressive. I was a bad-tempered man but I hid it. . . .

Now everything's changed. My attitude toward women is completely different. I don't intend to foul up any more lives. I could be a good husband now. I'm aware of my faults, and I'm ready to accept irresponsibilities and exchange tolerances.

Hyams believed all of this was related to Betsy. At this point Grant was unaware of her affair with Ray Austin, and was desperate to reestablish a harmonious relationship with the woman who had led him to LSD and enlightenment. Hyams was taping the interview and knew he had a reportorial gold mine. He asked Grant if he could publish all this. "Not yet, but the time's coming and I'll let you know when I'm ready."

A few weeks later, Grant showed up at a class Hyams was teaching at UCLA so he could be interviewed by twenty-five journalism students. While Grant answered their questions, he calmly worked his way through a couple of sandwiches, a banana, and a small carton of milk. He reiterated the passionate enlightenment LSD had given him, and allowed that he didn't think he had ever been a good husband.

Hyams's co-instructor was Lionel Crane, who wrote for the London *Daily Mirror* and had also interviewed Grant in Key West. After that class Crane told Hyams that Grant had told him everything he had said was on the record and that the *Daily Mirror* had already published the interview. That night, Hyams went to the theater and saw Grant sitting nearby. He was alone, but a few rows away Betsy Drake was sitting with a man. "That's my wife," Grant told Hyams. "Isn't she beautiful?" He added that he wasn't concerned about the other man because, "She would be incapable of being unfaithful. None of my wives have been unfaithful; neither have I. This has never been the problem." If Hyams's mind flashed to Sophia Loren, he didn't mention it.

Hyams asked permission to publish the interview and this time Grant agreed, specifying that he could only use the quotes that had already appeared in Lionel Crane's article. Hyams wrote his articles, but when the series was announced for publication, Grant called and said he didn't want the stories running in America. Hyams told him that it was too late, that the presses were running, and Grant replied, "You better find a way to stop them or you'll be discredited. I'll tell the press that I haven't seen you at all. . . . It's your word against mine and you know who they'll believe." The phone rang again a few minutes later. It was Stanley Fox, and again Hyams explained that it was too late.

Hyams's story encompassed three installments and ran in both the *Los Angeles Times* and the *New York Herald Tribune*. Things got even dicier when Grant, or Stanley Fox, or both, panicked and denied ever having been under psychiatric care. Then Grant said he had never spoken to Hyams about LSD or anything else. "I've never had an interview with Hyams on any subject," he told the *Los Angeles Times*. He then accused Hyams of lifting quotes from the London *Daily Mirror*.

And just like that Hyams's access to movie studios suddenly dried up. "For the first time I realized the tenuousness of my claims on the world in which I operated, and how quickly the press, my friends included, turned on anyone in trouble." Hyams believed that Grant had reversed his earlier decision because of a planned article in *Look* magazine about his LSD experience. The appearance of Hyams's article had violated his contract with *Look* and killed the deal.

For Hyams, this was all highly dangerous. A columnist depends on press agents and studios for interviews, and Grant's charges were turning off the spigot. Hyams insisted that yes, he had interviewed Grant, and had used some quotes from the English paper, but had only done so on Grant's instructions.

Grant's assertion that he had never done an interview with Hyams was quickly proved false when photographs surfaced of Hyams and Grant talking in Key West. In June Hyams filed a $500,000 slander suit against Grant, possibly the first and only time a journalist has sued an actor. While the lawyers maneuvered, Hyams and Grant retired to their respective corners.

During two 12-hour depositions, Hyams produced the tapes of his interview with Grant and was questioned about a wide variety of things that had nothing to do with Cary Grant. Hyams's lawyer smelled a settlement, simply because he didn't think Grant would show up for an equivalent deposition. "He won't want to go through with it," he told Hyams. "They made it tough on you to discourage you, but now that it's their turn they'll chicken out."

The next day the case was settled. If Hyams dropped his suit, Grant would cooperate with an as-told-to life story and Hyams could keep any monies paid for the stories. Hyams thought that Grant would back out, but he didn't. He greeted Hyams at the first interview as if they were old friends, never mentioning the lawsuit. The interviews were detailed, if not particularly emotional. When Hyams sent Grant the completed manuscript, Grant asked if he could make some changes in the beginning. In fact, he set about rewriting the entire series, but Hyams thought the changes were positive.

For much of the next year, Grant's rewriting went on until Hyams began to believe that Grant was stalling. Finally, Grant said he was satisfied and the manuscript could go to market. Hyams was stunned when the *Ladies' Home Journal* offered $125,000 for the memoir, which would be broken up into three installments.

"There are mis-spellings and some of the grammar is awkward," Grant wrote in a note to the editor. "If a reader notices these things, he'll say 'Cary doesn't know how to spell' and he will be right. . . . Let the readers judge me as I really am and not by an image they may have of me as polished up by someone else."

In May 1962, Hyams had an off-the-record conversation with Hedda Hopper, who wanted to know what was happening. Hyams told her that "Our lawyers got together out of court. . . . Grant is doing his own writing. The *Ladies' Home Journal* is enthusiastic about the material received. I get the money. Grant decided if his life story was going to be done, he was going to write it."

Hyams then asked for a favor, one pro to another. "The announcement is supposed to be a joint announcement. If it comes out that I've made a statement, they can say I violated our contract. And he might be capable of that.

"I got a taste of what he can be like. He's a unique type of fellow. Hedda, my children's education hinges on this money—my possible retirement from the newspaper business hinges on it." Hopper kept her promise to Hyams and didn't print anything.

Published in the early part of 1963 in three successive issues of *Ladies' Home Journal*, the articles may well have provided more emotional honesty than readers were prepared for:

> I have spent the greater part of my life fluctuating between Archie Leach and Cary Grant; unsure of either, suspecting each. Only recently have I begun to unify them into one person: the man and

the boy in me, the mother and the father and all people in me, the
hate and love and all the degrees of each in me, and the power of
God in me.

Grant misspelled his mother's maiden name as "Kingdom," said
that he was separated from his mother when he was nine, and at
another place accurately stated it happened when he was eleven. He
disputed his reputation as a cheapskate and inserted pointless diatribes
about autograph seekers and the absurdity of people who criticize the
movie industry while remaining comfortably outside it.

The editors mostly let Grant have his own way, probably more than
they should have. They silently corrected most misspellings and gram-
matical errors, but otherwise the articles sound like Grant—they're
full of his circuitous phrasing and the vocabulary of an autodidact
who lived with an unabridged dictionary close by.

In today's media environment, the articles would provoke a
firestorm, not to mention a plethora of cable shows on the order of
"Cary Grant: What Went Wrong?" In 1963, people read the articles,
shrugged, and moved on. The public had its own idea of Cary Grant,
separate and distinct from Grant's ideas about Cary Grant.

Hyams's lawyer had wisely told him not to let Grant know how
much money was on offer, but Grant or Stanley Fox learned the
amount from the *Ladies' Home Journal*. Naturally, Fox called Hyams
to complain. "Since you've admitted that Cary did most of the work,
enough for you to remove your own name from the byline, don't you
think he ought to participate to some extent in the money paid for
the article?"

"But, according to our contract, I'm to get all the income from
his life story."

"True. But we're not talking about the contract anymore. That's
over and done with. What I'm talking about is something else, something equitable for Cary, who spent a lot of time working on the
articles. Fair's fair."

How much? Hyams wanted to know.

"Enough, say for a new Rolls-Royce."

At this time, a new Rolls-Royce cost about $22,000. Hyams knew
that because he'd already priced one for himself. Hyams asked for
some time to think the matter over. He called his lawyer, who told him

he was crazy even to consider agreeing to such a thing. Nevertheless, Hyams decided to cut his emotional losses. He called Fox and agreed to give Grant the money for the Rolls.

Hyams didn't know, and Fox didn't tell him, that Grant already had two Rolls-Royces. Which, of course, was completely beside the point.

BY APRIL 1962, Grant had moved his LSD treatments to Dr. Oscar Janiger, a psychiatrist who was a cousin of Allen Ginsberg. Under Janiger he took his seventy-second acid trip. Janiger's sessions took five hours, and he screened his patients for any obvious physical or emotional disturbance. Assuming they were healthy, they were administered LSD in the morning and allowed to do whatever they wished for the rest of the day—take a walk in a garden, draw or paint, listen to music. Everybody was assigned a designated baby-sitter, a hardy veteran who could talk a patient down in case of a bad trip.

Grant's response to LSD varied depending on circumstance—mental state, the setting, the vibe from others in the room. What is clear is that Grant's assertions of a realignment of his ego, and of a radically altered viewpoint, is consonant with the recent research of writers such as Michael Pollan. The primary sensation attested to by patients successfully treated by LSD is a shedding of the old, compromised self, and the formation of a new identity for a new phase of life. For a man who had long struggled to integrate Archie with Cary, along with their respective divided loyalties, it must have been a godsend.

Many people besides Grant ascribed nothing but positive results to the drug, but others had disastrous experiences. Anaïs Nin believed that her access to her inner life, i.e., her fantasies, was greatly increased by LSD. Nin eventually referred the author and screenwriter Gavin Lambert to Janiger, after which she confessed to Lambert that her acid trip was traumatic. "On LSD the world seemed to her terrifying," said Lambert. "This, to me, was extremely interesting, because Anaïs Nin's life was a high-wire act of lies. She had two husbands . . . and neither of them knew about the other. And I think that her whole high-wire act became very naked to her under LSD and she couldn't take it.

She was a creature of such artifice, and then suddenly the artifice was stripped away."

Grant's comments about his experiences with LSD suggest that something similar may have happened to him—that LSD exposed the sham elements of both show business and Grant's ego. The result might have been a gradual impulse to make a gracious exit from the world of movies and public life in general, in favor of a private life where he had always been unable to find satisfaction. It was a risky move, but it was a move he came to believe was imperative.

A reporter once asked Grant if he was at peace after LSD. "You join humanity as best you can," he sighed.

> I like myself as far as I've gone, though I do wish my vocabulary were better. Otherwise, I think I'm a fairly decent fellow. I no longer have hypocrisies. You know, it's interesting. You can tell how secure a woman is by the amount of makeup she wears, did you ever notice? Ingrid would wear no makeup and have a shoelace tied in her hair. She had no knowledge about fashion or such matters. She just showed up and did her work. Women who wear all that makeup, there's some faking going on.

NINETEEN SIXTY-TWO was a busy year for Grant. In the spring Timothy Leary came to his office at Universal for a meeting. It was a by-product of Leary's meeting with Dr. Janiger, who wrote Leary a cautious acknowledgment for a meeting "regarding our common interests" on May 9.

Leary was nervous about meeting Grant because of his obvious contradictions. On the one hand, Grant was America's highest-profile proselytizer for LSD; on the other hand, he was Mr. Old Hollywood. If contradictions make us human, Cary Grant was one of the most human people on the planet.

Leary was ushered into Grant's cottage office surrounded by a lawn and flowers and complimented Grant on his surroundings. Grant's reply indicated he was interested in getting down to cases: "It is comfortable, isn't it? Do you think it would be a good place to take LSD?"

"Really should have a fireplace," Leary said.

"You're absolutely right. We'll have to do something about that." Grant promptly picked up a phone and ordered that a fireplace be installed in his office.

After putting the phone down, Grant asked Leary detailed questions about his work at Harvard and responded with enthusiasm. "What a movie this would make. Professors and prisoners. Sinners and saints. Jails and chapels. It's crying to be filmed." Leary was impressed that Grant had not only done his lab work but had done his homework.

Leary thanked Grant for proselytizing for LSD. "Not at all. I'm eternally grateful for the experience. LSD changed my life. I've lived more, felt more, enjoyed life more in the last few years than I had dreamed possible. My relationship with my mother, my love for my mother, is the greatest gift that LSD gave me. For years I had little contact with her. Didn't talk about her. Didn't like to think about her. . . . Since my LSD revelations, I've been over to see her regularly. She's in her eighties and still a lively, intelligent, wonderful person. LSD gave me that treasure."

Leary asked Grant about making a movie about LSD, and he replied that there was nothing he'd rather do. "He could see himself in the part of a Harvard professor discovering the key to the universe." The problem was getting a good script. "In Hollywood," Grant told Leary, "Shakespeare's advice still holds: 'The play's the thing.' Put on paper the grandeur and the splendor and the romance and the revelation of LSD, and then I'll be begging for a part in the movie."

This conversation led Leary on a decades-long journey to write a movie script about LSD, although Roger Corman beat everybody to the post in 1967 with *The Trip*. If Corman had only known Grant was interested, he could have replaced Bruce Dern as Peter Fonda's guide.

After their meeting, Grant kept some distance between him and Leary, indicating that he had reservations. In April 1963, Frank Ferguson, who was working with Leary on something called IFIF (International Federation for Internal Freedom), wrote Grant a letter asking him to join with Leary, as well as Janiger and such film industry friends as Ivan Tors and Aldous Huxley in their activities. There was no reply.

In January 1964, Leary wrote Grant a rather late thank-you note for their lunch from nearly two years before, bringing him up to date on various documentary and book projects, and appreciation for "the radiance and humor with which you are working your way through the social dance. . . . We feel at times as though our 5 1/2 room house is a space-ship hovering over the planet." He then invited Grant to come for a visit, which never took place.

By the late 1960s, reports of bad trips on LSD were skyrocketing and the drug began to be vilified in the media, criminalized in legislatures, banned globally, and classified by the FDA as a Schedule I drug of no medical value. Until it was outlawed, Oscar Janiger administered LSD to Grant and nine hundred others. Dr. Mortimer Hartman, however, was eventually suspended from his profession by the state of California.

In actual practice, as far as most of his friends and coworkers were concerned, Cary Grant after LSD was not noticeably different from Cary Grant before LSD. Stanley Donen, who directed him before and after the treatments, said, "Did I notice any real changes? Not really. He was still exactly Cary Grant after LSD. He had the same attitudes, except he felt more secure perhaps." The screenwriter Peter Stone disagreed; he thought Grant was entirely too blissed out.

> Everything was uncritical after LSD. It wasn't real. It was beatific. You'd say, "Cary, stop it. You're making me crazy." He'd say, "I'm not making you crazy. *You're* making you crazy. . . ."
>
> It gave him equanimity. It was cosmic in its scope. Up was down. Black was white. In was out. Everything was a cycle . . . He could literally stop any discussion by one of these tautologies.

Grant babbled about his LSD experience to anyone who would listen. Glenn Ford, a neighbor of Grant's, took up Transcendental Meditation because of Grant, as well as ESP and what Ford's son Peter would delicately term "mind-enhancing experimentation."

It all seemed to confirm the opinion of those who observed the gap between who Grant played and who he was. Take, for instance, the devastating thumbnail portrait from George Sanders: "Cary Grant, witty, sophisticated and debonair on screen, in life prey to theosophical charlatans, socially insecure and inclined to isolation."

David Niven had noted the crucial importance of enthusiasm in Grant's personality, said enthusiasm occasionally leading him to faddish extremes. There was what Niven remembered as Grant's "health food period," which led Grant to install a state-of-the-art juicer in his kitchen. "Fearful throbbings and crunchings followed us into the garden where we were given a pre-luncheon cocktail of buttermilk, wheat germ and molasses. When the sinister sounds died down, we re-entered the house to find that the machine had gone berserk and had redecorated the kitchen from top to bottom, covering walls, windows, ceiling and linoleum flooring with fibrous yellow paste."

AFTER HE AND DRAKE SPLIT, Grant occupied himself with other women. There was a dancer named Jackie Park, who had participated in some of the weekend orgies orchestrated by director Edmund Goulding. Park had vague ambitions to be an actress but instead opted for the easier alternative of becoming a mistress to rich and powerful men. Grant insisted she try LSD, which led her to Dr. Hartman, whom she ended up marrying. The marriage didn't last, and she moved on to be the mistress of Jack Warner, who put her on the studio payroll for $350 a week. It couldn't have been anywhere near enough. Park spent four or five years with Warner before he gave her a $5,000 check by way of farewell.

Whatever his psychic state, the consecutive smash hits of *Indiscreet, North by Northwest*, and *Operation Petticoat* meant that all of Hollywood was a buyer's market as long as Cary Grant was the seller. At this stage of Grant's career, it was clear that he wanted to color within already established lines. Certainly, Lew Wasserman and his wife, Edie, had accomplished a major seduction when they lured Grant's company over to Universal to make *Operation Petticoat*, cannily bracketing an older, established star with a younger star, making something that appealed to all components of the audience.

Wasserman and Grant had had an unofficial business arrangement since the 1946 death of Grant's agent Frank Vincent. The truth was that Wasserman might have paid Grant for the privilege of, first, representing him, then distributing his pictures, even if the financials were heavily weighted in Grant's favor. Wasserman and MCA had bought Universal early in 1959 for $11.25 million, and one of the first deals he did after the purchase was to bring Grant and Stanley Fox into the fold. Grant's company was entitled to 75 percent of the profits or 10 percent of the gross, whichever was larger. After seven years in release, the negatives of Grant's films reverted to his company. As Grant would note of a fellow Englishman with an equivalent sense of his worth, "Chaplin always owned his own pictures."

"Grant was a bauble," said Mort Engelberg, a successful producer at Universal. "Universal had been associated with Abbott and Costello and Ma and Pa Kettle before Wasserman took over, and Lew wanted to change the culture, as well as tell the rest of Hollywood that Universal was being reinvented."

Around the studio, Wasserman was respected as well as feared—no one wanted to be the target of one of his Vesuvial eruptions of temper. Socially, Wasserman was totally charming and loved to tell stories. Engelberg enjoyed curling up and basking in the stream of anecdotes about Wasserman's humble beginnings in Cleveland, where he had been an ancillary member of the Mayfield Road Mob that helped found Las Vegas.

One of Wasserman's favorite stories involved Ben Hecht and Sam Goldwyn. In 1950, Goldwyn wanted Hecht to work on a picture called *Edge of Doom*. Hecht turned him down. Goldwyn tried again, and Hecht still wasn't interested. Goldwyn threw more and more money at him and Hecht finally capitulated. The picture was a huge flop—to this day few people have heard of it, let alone seen it.

A few years later, Goldwyn bought the movie rights to Frank Loesser's *Guys and Dolls*. Hecht called his agent and said he'd love to write the screenplay. The agent called Goldwyn, who replied, "Absolutely not! He was associated with one of my biggest flops!"

Along with Alfred Hitchcock, whom Wasserman brought to Universal right after he made *Psycho* at Paramount, Grant became the primary jewel in the Universal crown, a marker laid down by Wasserman that indicated his intent to class up what had been a cheap-jack operation. Soon, Wasserman would give Gregory Peck and Marlon Brando similar production deals at the studio, to go with homegrown talents such as Rock Hudson and Tony Curtis. The bulk of Universal's money would still come from their lucrative but creatively anonymous television operation, but the presence of Grant, Hitchcock, and Brando helped camouflage that fact.

"Lew Wasserman's secret was that he wasn't really in the movie business, or even in the TV business," said Mort Engelberg. "Lew was in the money business."

After Grant set up shop at Universal, Wasserman usually gave him whatever he wanted, and since Grant was not in a particularly ambitious phase of his career, the relationship was quite comfortable. But there were times when even Wasserman came up short. Grant wanted to make *Bell, Book and Candle* opposite Kim Novak for Columbia, but Wasserman had the unpleasant task of telling him that Columbia had promised the part to Jimmy Stewart—one of Wasserman's good friends, and Kim Novak's favorite actor on earth.

Losing the picture with Novak bothered Grant; he would mention her as one of two actresses he would have liked to work with. The other was Natalie Wood—Grant was a particular fan of her performances in *Love with the Proper Stranger* and *Inside Daisy Clover*. He was also friends with her husband, Robert Wagner, who Grant thought did the best imitation of him.* Grant gave some thought to working with Wood in *Gypsy*—he would have played Herbie, the vaudeville partner of Mama June, but was probably scared off by Herbie's third-banana status in the script.

Grant continued to cheerfully resist all entreaties to appear on variety or talk shows, usually by saying, "No, no, no. I can't stand talking about myself." Actually, his reason was simple: "I don't believe you should compete with yourself."† In time he would even turn down the American Film Institute Life Achievement Award, because it mandated an acceptance speech, the idea of which "terrified" him.

Despite Grant's oft-stated aversion to television and the idea of giving himself away for free, Wasserman proposed packaging *The Cary Grant Show* for television.

"Do you really think I should appear on television?" asked Grant.

Absolutely, said Wasserman, who assembled a group of MCA agents to explain their ideas. They thought an anthology format would be best—Grant could introduce each show, perhaps appear in five or

---

* Grant was right; Wagner's imitation is a virtuoso display centering on Grant's character in *Gunga Din*, complete with an accurate facsimile of the trumpeting call of Annie the elephant.

† There is an urban legend to the effect that Grant appeared in 1950 on an early Cliff Arquette show called *Dave and Charley*—Charley being Charley Weaver, Arquette's homespun character. Grant was a fan of the show and supposedly played a hobo with two lines of dialogue. No kinescope of the show was made, so the appearance is impossible to verify.

six episodes per year. They outlined the vast amounts of money stars such as Loretta Young and Dick Powell had made by going into TV. Not only that, it had revitalized David Niven's career and increased his movie salary. This, they figured, was their best shot at getting Grant to agree—his passion for money just might outweigh his contempt for TV.

They proposed what amounted to an MCA production, similar to *Alfred Hitchcock Presents*: MCA writers, MCA directors, MCA actors. Grant realized that the show would be as much about strip-mining cash from the creative team's efforts for the financial glory of the agency as it would be about Cary Grant. He stood up and summarily ended the meeting.

ALL OF UNIVERSAL'S PREMIER TALENTS were gifted with cottages on the lot, private residences that included a kitchen, dining room, office space, and other perks, the costs of which were picked up by Universal. (Hitchcock was first among equals—he had an entire building for his production activities.)

Peter Stone, who would become Grant's favorite writer, said that "We all used to sit on the front porch of our bungalows in the afternoon and chat with everybody." Peggy Lee or Cy Coleman might drop by for an impromptu musicale; Tony Curtis would knock on the window to see if Cary was available. The producer Robert Arthur and writers Maurice Richlin and Stanley Shapiro were in the bungalow next to Grant's and he would regularly walk over, lie down on the couch, and chat.

Grant had a designer work magic in the bungalow with a dispatch that eluded him in his own house. There were chocolate brown leather chairs, a brightly colored Argentinian rug, and trompe-l'oeil paintings on all the flat surfaces—birds, flowers, and clouds. It was personalized with a wedding picture of his parents displayed in a Cartier frame, and a photograph Ingrid Bergman had given him of Grant doing a delightful jig in *Indiscreet*. Off to the side of the building was a walled-off area where Grant could work on his tan.

Shapiro and Richlin noticed that Grant was at pains to educate himself by improving his vocabulary. He kept a notebook full of words he found interesting—"avuncular," "attrition," "exacerbation," "hypertrophies," all the way through the alphabet, all written down in his sweeping hand. He also kept two notebooks of jokes—not terribly good ones, it must be said—and another full of reminders and miscellany—interesting places to travel, medical advances, and so forth.

Universal's corporate culture soon got used to Grant's particular sensibility, his strange mixture of entirely sincere courtesy and oblivious narcissism. Grant took pains to be pleasant and charming to all the Universal employees. Around lunchtime he would sit on the bungalow steps to get some sun. Word got around and secretaries of all ages, sizes, and sexes would be sure to saunter casually past Grant's bungalow around noon. Grant would always respond courteously to every greeting.

Grant's bungalow was close to the office of Bob Rains, a Universal advertising executive. One day he asked Rains for a sketch pad so he could outline a few ideas he had for the promotional campaign for one of his films. By the time he was finished, there were rough sketches for art as well as ad copy. Rains didn't think any of them were very good, but he said the politic thing: "Looks interesting, Cary."

"Now, just because these are my ideas, Bob, please do not feel you have to use them. After all, you are the expert on such matters. I'm not."

About three weeks later, Rains had prepared some ideas for the ad campaign and presented them to Grant. He gave them a great deal of attention, moving them around the bungalow to see what they looked like in different light, on the couch vs. on the floor and so forth. And then he said that he thought they were terrible. "Every one of them. The entire dozen. There is not one I like. Might I suggest you never again use the individual who dreamed up these concepts. He certainly knows nothing about advertising."

Bob Rains was a smart man; he didn't tell Grant that all of the ad concepts had come directly from Grant's rough sketches.

CLIFFORD ODETS HAD BEEN PAYING OFF his indebtedness to Grant as late as *An Affair to Remember*, when a check had arrived accompanied by a case of claret. The two men remained close, despite the writer's privately expressed contempt for *Operation Petticoat*, which struck Odets as unforgivable. "My father admired him as a man and as an actor," said Walt Odets, "and my father was angry about him doing this trivial, trashy stuff. Oh, I heard a lot about *Operation Petticoat*. I thought the criticism was unfair. I thought Cary should have the career that he wanted to have. I understand someone with his background wanting security. Having money was important to him."

Grant and Odets were united by the fact that they were both searchers and both fundamentally dissatisfied with themselves. They also shared a complicated relationship with money and what it represented. "My father was insecure about money," said Walt Odets. "He kept canvas bags of coins in his closet. But at the same time, he had no interest in accumulating money. He used to tell me, 'If you die with money in the bank, you've lived your life badly.'"

Grant spent election night 1960 at Clifford Odets's house. In his thank-you note, he told Odets how pleased he was to be included, and what a delightful group it was, including Odets's children, Walt and Nora. He even seemed to have been pleased by the election of John Kennedy.

Odets loved Grant, both for his personal generosity and for their shared feelings of being thwarted in some primary way. At the same time he seemed to resent Grant's creative compromises, which he expressed in both his play *The Big Knife* and some undated notes Odets made for a play called *The Actor*, involving a famous actor who's opening in a new play in Boston. While rehearsing, he takes his niece shopping. "A thousand things distract him and [he] has no happiness or human connection, no glamour or zest for the theater." The actor attempts to articulate what the theater means to him, but fails. In the end, he dies and leaves his legacy to his niece. At the top of the page, just below the title, Odets wrote "Cary Grant."

Odets had moved back to Los Angeles after the failure of his play *The Flowering Peach*, on which he spent three years and made a grand total of $4,500. Walt Odets observed that his father "only really made money on two plays in New York: *Golden Boy* and *The Country Girl*. In both of them he took the Jews out of the plays. He knew how to write a moneymaking play, he just didn't want to do it."

Odets's creative problems were complicated by the financial drain of his daughter, Nora, who was born brain damaged. Odets was determined to solve her problems. "My father's secretary told me that my sister's medical bills could run in the $2,000 a week range," said

Walt. "My father hired psychologists, endocrinologists, every medical professional you could think of. He was determined to fix her, and it was a mistake, because she couldn't be fixed."

Grant began to act as a sort of surrogate father for Walt in those areas where his father was not interested. Clothes, for instance. Clifford Odets dressed like a *schlub*—khakis and whatever shirt or sweater he could pull over his head. "Cary thought I should have good clothes," remembered Walt. "He would pick me up in his Rolls and we'd go about four blocks to Dick Carroll's, a men's store on Santa Monica. Fake British. Expensive. I don't know if Cary was paying for it or my father was, but Cary would pick out clothes and ties for me and give me advice. He told me when you wear black tie, you shouldn't wear black socks, but rather dark blue, because black socks have more of a sheen and they look lighter than they are. Dark blue looks blacker than black does."*

By now, Grant was a member of Odets's extended family, and vice versa. Both Odets and his son had liked Betsy because she was simultaneously sweet and smart, but now Grant was alone. "We'd go out to dinner and I'd get a Shirley Temple," said Walt Odets.

And then Cary's health food nut would come out. He wouldn't allow me to eat the maraschino cherry because the red dye was carcinogenic. I couldn't use colored toilet paper because the dye would give me cancer.

He would give me gifts that my father made me give back. He gave me a fancy telescope, an astronomer's telescope really, professional grade. I must have said something that made him think I'd like it. And my father said that it was too extravagant, not a gift for child. And he made me give it back. He gave my sister Nora a pearl necklace, of real pearls.

When he would come over to Odets's house, Grant would usually wear tasseled loafers without socks. Walt asked why he didn't wear

---

* Dick Carroll remembered that Grant started buying in his store around 1950 and gravitated toward navy blue suits and dark sharkskins with a very clear finish. "He wore a lot of solid satin ties," Carroll said, "usually a very, very elegant gray. . . . I never saw him wear a flowered tie and I never saw him wear a striped one. He was very pointed in his tastes and he never deviated."

socks and Grant took off one of the loafers and explained that the shoes were custom-made with extra padding and they were more comfortable that way. Walt noticed that unlike the rest of him, his feet were ugly—"peasant's feet."

The crucial thing was the importance that Grant felt about explaining all these details to the boy. Walt Odets would become a psychologist specializing in the gay experience—he knew he was gay by the time he was twelve or thirteen—and he would retroactively contemplate the psyche of his friend.

When Cary was young, he wasn't handsome, he was pretty. That makes a lot of people think you're gay even when it's not true. He seemed more feminine to me than my father did, because Cary dressed the way gay men dress—he paid attention, and straight men usually don't. But he was trying to be Cary Grant. I never had a sense of his sexual identity; it honestly never occurred to me.

Speaking as a psychologist, in retrospect I think Cary was one of those people who felt perpetually unlovable. It came out in his pursuit of other people—the craving he had for my love as a kid. Attachment was *so* important to him. He had a kind of longing about him. Things like explaining about the shoes seemed very important to him, and I think it was because it was a way of making a connection.

When you're famous on that level, when you're Cary Grant or Marilyn Monroe, you can't make connections. People see Cary Grant and Marilyn Monroe, but that's not who you are, not really. Why did he feel unlovable? I think he carried a lot of shame. The way he would dress, and the Rolls-Royce, and being Cary Grant were all a way of addressing the shame he felt. Shame about his background, perhaps shame about things he'd done early in his life.

It always felt to me that he was looking for himself. That's where all the wives came in. It's very difficult for a person to sustain a relationship when they feel unlovable. There's nothing another person can do to make you feel lovable. Cary would be more and more demanding because he was either determined to get love, or, failing that, determined to get confirmation that he was unlovable. And then he would simply withdraw, to hide his unlovability from being seen. I just don't think he ever found himself.

Becoming famous when you're young obstructs self-discovery. The same thing happened to my father. Cary was an actor, not being himself, and then he invented Cary Grant and everything was completely obstructed by that. When we were out together in Beverly Hills, people usually didn't approach him, or interfere. He was an object of awe.

Being famous, visibly famous, is a terrible fate.

CHAPTER NINETEEN

=================

Grant made another one of his typically conservative decisions when he turned down *Tender Is the Night*. David O. Selznick had owned the property for years, and had come after Grant for the part of Dick Diver in 1951 in a package that included George Cukor directing and Jennifer Jones as Nicole. But script is always a problem for people adapting Fitzgerald—plots barely exist, and the beauty is all in his lambent voice and command of emotional twilight.

By 1960, Selznick no longer had either the money or the credibility to get the picture off the ground, but he was working with Jerry Wald to set up the picture at 20th Century–Fox. Wald, supposedly the inspiration for Budd Schulberg's Sammy Glick, had become the studio's most reliable producer, with such recent hits as *Peyton Place*, *The Long, Hot Summer*, and *An Affair to Remember* to his credit.

On January 27, Wald wrote Grant at the Savoy Hotel in London to assess his interest in a proposal Wald had made six days earlier in a cable. "Having heard nothing in reply I am wondering if you received it, hence this note. I know how you like to plan ahead and will be interested to hear whether or not you would consider doing *Tender Is the Night*. I know you've read the property and now that I have become associated with it I will be most anxious to have your reactions to the script. Please advise."

Grant would have been the perfect Dick Diver—layers of unease and emotional ambiguity conflated with authentic concern for a damaged, adored wife who is fundamentally wrong for him. Whether Jennifer Jones remained the problem, or Grant simply didn't want to work in a picture that would inevitably mirror some of his own psychological conflicts, nothing came of the offer. After a serious flirtation with William Holden, Selznick ended up selling the property to Fox, who made it in 1962 with the dour, completely miscast Jason Robards Jr. opposite Jennifer Jones, everyone laboring beneath a script that failed to capture Fitzgerald's elegant mingling of hope and despair.

Grant also dodged *Can-Can*, leaving some bruised feelings behind. Despite his previous unfortunate collision with the work of Cole Porter, Grant approved of the property and had even begun working with Fox's vocal coach Ken Darby. At this point, the picture was to be produced by Nunnally Johnson with the ballets choreographed and danced by Roland Petit and Zizi Jeanmaire. "Eventually, as so often happens," grumbled Nunnally Johnson, "Cary withdrew himself, after giving me every reason to think that he liked the part."

Stanley Donen offered him the part of the Devil in *Damn Yankees*— no dice—and he wisely passed on *Let's Make Love* with Marilyn Monroe. Grant had been tentatively slotted for *Lawrence of Arabia* when the picture was on Alexander Korda's docket in the late 1930s. By 1962, he was too old, but Sam Spiegel wanted him to play Allenby. Spiegel was nervous because Peter O'Toole, the actor chosen for Lawrence, was virtually unknown and the producer was understandably eager for as much commercial insurance as possible.

David Lean thought casting Grant would be a mistake that could unbalance the picture. "Bugger and blast the star system," Lean wrote his producer. "I tell you [Jack] Hawkins would make a mighty good stab at the Allenby part." Lean got his way, but it's doubtful that Grant would have taken a supporting part in any picture, no matter how prestigious—he was a star, with a star's prerogatives. Actors supported Cary Grant, not the other way around. In due time, Jack Warner would offer Grant the part of Professor Harold Hill in *The Music Man*, to no avail, as well as Henry Higgins in *My Fair Lady*, but he famously replied about the latter, "There's only one actor who can play the role, and that's Rex Harrison. Furthermore, if he isn't in it, I won't go to see your picture."

He didn't tell Warner that the role he would actually have liked to play was Eliza Doolittle's scapegrace father, Alfred P. Doolittle, who has one bang-up number, "Get Me to the Church on Time." The reason Grant didn't volunteer for the job was that he had admired Stanley Holloway since his days with Bob Pender, and wasn't about to euchre the old music hall star out of his career part.

Jack Warner couldn't be discouraged. He would also offered Grant his choice of parts in the musical *1776*, but, said Grant, "I was retired by then, and J.L. should have been by then too." When *1776* was reissued for the Bicentennial in 1976, Grant went to see it. "I really dodged a bullet with that one, didn't I?" was his only comment.

Generally speaking, the pictures Grant turned down in the final phase of his career are invariably more interesting than the ones he made. He also rejected Stanley Kubrick's adaptation of *Lolita*, thereby handing James Mason one of his career plums. Grant would have altered the picture's dank chemistry; the picture would have been sexier, and Humbert would have been less pathetic, more dangerous. Of course, the part also constituted a huge risk that might have alienated his loyal fans, and he obviously felt that at this stage of his career risk was something to be avoided.

And there was another teasing possibility. On September 28, 1961, Ray Stark sent Grant a package along with a letter thanking him for a good lunch—he particularly liked Grant's meatloaf and asked about the recipe. Stark enclosed a script of the William Wyler/Bette Davis classic *The Letter*, and wrote that, "We would be very willing to work out a deal with you whereby we would develop a screenplay with (you) having the choice of producing, acting or both."

Whether Grant was interested in the part of the weak husband, or the casually intrigued attorney who breaks down the murderess and forces her to deliver the blood-curdling curtain line, "With all my heart, I still love the man I killed!," is unknown. Stark was legendarily devious, and the flirtation stands as yet another example of the creative impulses Grant often stifled.

A project that was more in his wheelhouse was John Huston's *The Man Who Would Be King*, the screenplay of which was offered to Grant in July 1960. Huston had originally written it for Humphrey Bogart and Clark Gable, but Bogart had died, and Grant would have offered a considerably peppier chemistry with Gable. Grant was interested, if in his own particular way: "I've read it twice and am still uncertain whether it's fair, good, or perhaps, even excellent," he wrote

Paul Kohner, Huston's agent. "I am a man of no decided thought. . . .
Has [Huston] the time to mess around with me?"

The offer from Huston would have returned Grant to the character
he established in *Gunga Din*, but it didn't happen, whether because
of Gable's death in November 1960 or Grant's now normal demand
for ownership of the negative. *The Man Who Would Be King* had to
wait until Sean Connery and Michael Caine enabled Huston to create
one of his greatest pictures.

WITH THE EXCEPTION OF *Indiscreet*, none of the pictures Grant
produced were particularly notable, but they were usually successful.
Grant was at his ease, and why shouldn't he have been? He had chosen
the stories and hired the directors, including the smooth Stanley Donen.

If the best of them was *Indiscreet*, the worst was *The Grass Is
Greener*—civilized adultery amongst the English monied classes,
except nobody actually sleeps with anybody they aren't married to.
And the casting was gravelly: Deborah Kerr, Jean Simmons, and
Robert Mitchum, who replaced Grant's preferred casting of Rex
Harrison. Jean Simmons was coming off the huge hit of *Spartacus*,
but accepted fourth billing because it was the first comedy she'd
been offered in years. "Cary Grant . . . was a fuss-budget," she said.
"Everything must be just so. Then he'd come forth with the most
amusing, polished take, so seemingly effortless." The cameraman
Christopher Challis had to put up with Grant's worrying and it wasn't
easy. He remembered that Grant was "a consummate artist" never
"in any way unpleasant," but was also "the biggest 'old woman' I
have ever worked with."

Robert Mitchum was a philosophical anarchist who could hardly
have been more tempermentally different than his costar, and his
appraisal of Grant was subtly withering. "Very charming. But no
sense of humor. I mean, he's very light and pleasant, but his humor is
sort of old music-hall jokes. 'What's that noise down there? They're
holding an elephant's ball. Well, I wish they'd let go of it, I'm trying
to get some sleep.'"

Mitchum's preferred relaxant was marijuana—he grew his own—so
Grant's taste in drugs struck him as extreme and possibly dangerous.

"I guess that was when he was coming off his LSD treatment. He was a little weird. . . . Whenever the camera turned off me and onto him, I'd go for a drive." Then there was the question of Grant's economizing on the small things, the better to afford the big things. "We had lunch one day," Mitchum said, "and Deborah Kerr leans over to me and whispers, 'Eat all you can.' I said, 'I'm not hungry.' She said, 'I don't care, eat it all.' I said, 'Why?' She says, 'Cary's paying.' . . . But he was a very pleasant fellow."

But not always. John Mitchell, the sound man on the film, recalled that "He was very polite, charming some might say, but he left me with a feeling that I should be on my guard. He was very helpful and even warned me that he was the bane of sound men by using very little voice."

> Moments before the cameras rolled for a scene he was checking that every hair of that immaculate hair style was in place, when through the headphones I heard him muttering, "I like me."
>
> On another occasion, Deborah and Jean Simmons came on set wearing beautiful model gowns complemented by some exquisite jewelry. Again, over the headphone I heard him call Stanley over to say, "Get those jewels off them." In reply to the query, "Why?" Stanley was told that the audience would be looking at the jewels, not at Cary Grant!

If Mitchum wasn't fooled by the experience, neither were the press or public. "A generally tedious exercise," said *Variety*, and *The New York Times* said that Grant looked "mechanical and bored."

For *The Grass Is Greener*, Grant asked if he could limit his publicity efforts in New York to two newspaper interviews and an opening night appearance. Bob Rains agreed, and then Grant asked that the studio pick up the tab for a two-day stop on the way to New York and another on the way back. No problem.

It wasn't until the bills came in that Rains realized where the stopovers had been. Grant had first flown from Los Angeles to Hong Kong for some suit fittings, then to New York for the opening. He then went back to Hong Kong for the final fittings, then flew back to Los Angeles. "Not only did he turn in his hotel bills, and meal receipts for those four extra days, but also the cost of the suits," remembered

Rains with perceptible wonder. Grant noticed the stricken look on Rains's face and said, "You did agree to pay all my expenses for those stopover days, didn't you?"

The odd thing was that costs for publicity and promotion are always added to the cost of the picture in question, so Grant's company was paying its share for the trips to Hong Kong, as well as the suits. Rains came to the conclusion that "Grant knew but really did not care. The money . . . was not coming out of his pocket or checkbook directly, thus he wasn't paying."

The Grass Is Greener earned only about $2 million in domestic rentals and struggled to break even. The problem was that Grant had reached that stage of an acting career where some edge in the writing or direction was necessary if he was to be fully engaged, and *The Grass Is Greener* was simply a boulevard comedy *sans* passion.

If critics occasionally wondered about Grant's steadfast commitment to playing one thing, people within the industry didn't, even people of a different generation who might have been expected to scoff. "When you look at [Sean Connery's] Bond characterization, everybody says, 'Oh, well, he's just charming,'" observed Sidney Lumet. "Well, shit, that's like saying Cary Grant was just charming. There is more acting skill in playing that kind of character. What he's doing stylistically, is playing high comedy. And that is extremely difficult to do, which is why there are so few of those actors, so few Cary Grants and Sean Connerys."

ROBERT MITCHUM'S GRADUAL DISENCHANTMENT with Grant was replicated by another, more casual acquaintance. Mel Brooks was working at Universal with a producer named Marvin Schwartz, who idly informed him that Cary Grant's office was adjacent to his own. Brooks kept watch until he observed Grant pull up in his Rolls, get out of the car, and go into his office. Brooks remembered that Grant was wearing a double-breasted gray suit with chalk stripes.

Brooks never expected to be in such close proximity to one of his idols, so he called his brother Lenny in Brooklyn. "He's in the next bungalow," Brooks told his brother. "I can't ask him for his autograph. It's gauche.

"Lenny said, 'What's gauche?'

"The next day I'm walking down the path to the commissary, and I hear a voice behind me. [Here Brooks slips into a faultless imitation of Grant's voice.] 'Mel Brooks, I can't believe it. It's actually Mel Brooks!'

"I turn around. It's Cary Grant. He has the record Carl Reiner and I had just made, *The 2000 Year Old Man*. And he's heard it already.

"You're a mirage," said Brooks. "You shouldn't talk to me."

"Where are you going?" asked Grant.

"The commissary."

"Can I go with you?"

There's only one answer to that question. In the commissary, Grant had two poached eggs on whole wheat toast with black coffee. Brooks had fruit, cottage cheese, and coffee with milk.

"I paid," Brooks remembered.

They ate together again the next day, and by the third day they were learning all about each other. "What's your favorite color?" asked Grant.

"Blue," replied Brooks. "What's yours?"

"Yellow.

"What do you drive?"

"A Rolls-Royce."

"I like a Buick."

"What's your real name?"

"Kaminsky. What's yours?"

"Archie Leach."

Recounting all this, Brooks paused to wonder at the strangeness of it all. "We're finding out about ourselves, me and Cary Grant. It's kind of wonderful.

"The fourth day, he's still having poached eggs, I've switched over to melted cheese." By Friday, Brooks had had enough, of both the poached eggs and of paying for lunch. "He was such a *schnorrer*," Brooks said. He told Marvin Schwartz that if the phone rang and it was Grant, "I'm not in."

BY NOW, GRANT HAD BECOME a male Marlene Dietrich—reviews would automatically note his undiminished professional skill, then segue to contemplating an agelessness that managed to avoid any of the hardshell signs of plastic surgery. There were frequent rumors that Grant availed himself of the services of Dr. Paul Niehans's Clinique la Prairie in Vevey, Switzerland, which specialized in supposedly rejuvenating live cell therapy injections involving placenta extracted from pregnant sheep. The treatments became popular among elderly members of the jet set—Gloria Swanson, Noel Coward, and Dietrich herself. There is a possibly apocryphal, but nonetheless delicious story of Kay Thompson, Dietrich, and Coward singing a rousing chorus of "I've got EWE Under My Skin."

Alas, the Niehans story turns out to be yet another urban legend; Grant's passports show only one trip to Switzerland, in January of 1963.

Despite—or because of—his state of preservation, the audience had come to love Grant in much the same way that they loved actors of the same generation—Clark Gable, Gary Cooper—but with one difference. Those men had aged, sometimes alarmingly, but Grant managed to look forty-five for fifteen years, after which he managed to look sixty for a decade, and did it with an astonishing lack of apparent effort. He was a Dorian Gray for the Age of Anxiety.

Katharine Hepburn knew him well as both actor and man, and summed him up objectively as "A personality functioning. A delicious personality who has learnt to do certain things marvelously well. He can't play a serious part or, let me say, the public isn't interested in him that way, not interested in him at all, which I'm sure has been a big bugaboo to him. But he has a lovely sense of timing, an amusing face and a lovely voice."

Grant remained quite close to Irene Mayer Selznick. She understood the movie business and the people that populate it in the same way that the Windsors understand royal succession. Because of her lofty viewpoint, Irene found most of the inhabitants of modern Hollywood lacking in the splendor that is a by-product of a century or so of success.

Irene was ferociously intelligent, as well as ferocious. She was, as her son Dan would say, "relentless." When Dan told his mother that his cousin Judy Goetz was marrying the producer Richard Shepherd, Irene replied, "Oh, you mean Richard Silberman?"

Dan was embarrassed and muttered something, and his mother continued, "Well, his father's name is Silberman, doesn't that mean *his* name is Silberman?" Since Grant had always made a humorous fetish out of being born Archie Leach, Irene liked his sense of humor about himself. At least he didn't dissemble about his ignoble beginnings.

"The only actors Irene had good things to say about were Cary Grant, Tyrone Power, Janet Gaynor and Katharine Hepburn," said the renowned editor Robert Gottlieb, Irene's close friend and executor of her estate.

> Gaynor because she was the only actress friend she was allowed to have by her father. L.B. Mayer thought actresses were unsuitable companions for his daughter. "She's a nice girl and a top star," her father told her. "It's all right if she's your friend." Janet was like an older sister—a woman friend Irene listened to and trusted.
>
> She also trusted Grant and Power. She liked Tyrone Power because he was intelligent, sensitive, had a major career and was not particularly happy. She felt the same way about Grant and for the same reasons. People loved Tyrone Power; he was congenial and outgoing and gentle with people, and he would go to bed with them whether they were men or women because it was the kindest thing he could do. Irene was interested in psychology, interested in therapy. As a young girl she wanted to be a doctor, but her father forbade it—that would mean she would go to college and he didn't believe in college for women. She had a lot of therapy herself.
>
> Besides Grant, how many charming and talented British people were there in Hollywood? Ronald Colman's group was far too fusty. Irene liked Grant and she trusted him, and she didn't trust many people.

The critic and author David Thomson got to know Irene well when he wrote the authorized biography of her husband, and he had more ambivalent feelings than Gottlieb. "I would say Irene and Grant were confidantes in quite a deep way. I had the impression she knew about his confused sexual life, but to her dying day she wouldn't speak in specifics. She fancied herself an authority on abnormal psychology; she certainly knew her father and she were both abnormal experiences."

The correspondence between Grant and Irene reflects trust and devotion. Grant told her that he regarded her as his best friend; he would fly to the East Coast to take in her theatrical productions during their out-of-town tryouts and offer advice. In one undated note, he offers up a casting suggestion, probably for her production of *Bell, Book and Candle*. His first choice was Robert Montgomery, but his second was "Joseph Cotten, Joseph Cotten, Joseph Cotten hm, pretty good JOSEPH COTTEN. Yes indeed, Joseph Cotten."

Unfortunately, Grant's years of hobnobbing with Dorothy di Frasso and Frederick Lonsdale had tilted him toward a snobbish perspective. Shortly after his excellent suggestion of Joseph Cotten, Grant gave Irene a different suggestion: "JOHN WAYNE!! If only he could be induced. Most attractive, pleasant, intelligent and SUCH a good actor."

Grant often ruminated about casting, especially if he was an investor. When Irene was planning her production of Enid Bagnold's *The Chalk Garden* in 1955, Grant had reservations about Wendy Hiller for the part of the governess opposite Gladys Cooper's chilly grande dame—a woman who maintains a garden but can't make anything grow. Hiller, Grant wrote, "sometimes uses a strange range of voice, a seeming though only occasional disturbing [affectation] from high soprano to contralto in one sentence," he noted. "Have you seen Peggy Ashcroft recently? Peculiar, but perhaps interesting casting."

Wendy Hiller proved unavailable, and Grant fretted. "Where is an English Uta Hagen? Could your character be American—and BE Uta Hagen?" he asked rhetorically in mid-April. Grant went on to say that he liked the play but had one criticism: "No one character in the play seems to speak in simple words for simple minds. The effect lingers that each character deals only in phrases suggesting complex thought. . . . It all had some abstruse quality which interested me mildly but not quite fully."

A little more than a month later, Grant had a brainstorm and cabled Irene: THINK ME NOT MAD WITHOUT GIVING MY NEXT WORDS FULL CONSIDERATION . . . IF YOU HAVE STILL NOT CAST THE GOVERNESS HOW ABOUT BETSY? He went on to say that Betsy was just about the right age, that she embodied the breeding as well as the vague peculiarity the part called for, and her slight stutter could even be an asset to her characterization. He closed by asking for the courtesy of a reading for Betsy in New York.

There the matter seems to have ended. In the end, Siobhán McKenna played the part on Broadway and Peggy Ashcroft played it in London. But Grant had a point—Betsy probably could have played the governess and brought more star power to the show than Siobhán McKenna. Irene's dodging of Betsy's casting didn't affect their friendship; Grant continued to invest with Irene, including her last show, a Graham Greene comedy entitled *The Complaisant Lover*, that starred Michael Redgrave and ran for 101 performances. If Grant lost money, it wasn't much—he capped his investment at $2,500.

GRANT WAS COMFORTABLE AT UNIVERSAL because it felt like home. He even allowed himself the occasional luxury of dressing down—a story meeting was likely to see Grant unshaven, with his slacks and untucked shirt wrinkled. In public, however, he invariably presented himself as the public wanted to see him.

"He's just like Cary Grant," thought Peter Bogdanovich when they met in 1961. Bogdanovich noted "his extraordinarily dark and deep-flowing eyes [and] his buoyant spirit," both of which were part and parcel of the unique acting ability that made audiences accomplices rather than observers. The primary difference between Grant off-screen and Grant on-screen was his open and infectious laugh. "He was a hell of a laugher," said Bogdanovich. "His eyes would tear—he really laughed. I never saw him do that in pictures. He had a very effervescent, ebullient laugh. Never laughed without his eyes watering excessively. Maybe that's why he didn't do it on the screen."

Of the pictures Grant produced, the only truly embarrassing one is *That Touch of Mink*, with Grant as a millionaire who tries to get Doris Day to go to bed with him. It's useless—she won't put out, and neither will the film. Not only is the premise unworthy of him, so is the execution—hideous Eastmancolor pastels. Nevertheless, a salary of $600,000 plus 10 percent of the gross and ownership of the negative made the picture seem enticing—until it wasn't.

It's one of those films that make you realize the truth of Stanley Kramer's remark about the basic trick of being Cary Grant—the surface diffidence that distracted the audience from what amounted to cold commercial calculation: "When he exhibited himself," said Kramer, "he was 'Cary Grant'—the handsome leading man, star-incarnate. Grant never gave the appearance of being 'commercial,' and he was probably as commercial an actor that ever lived."

Part of the problem with the picture was Grant's antipathy for Martin Melcher, Doris Day's grubby husband, who used his leverage to get undeserved credits as a producer on her films. "He was in on a pass, as they say in society," said Grant. "He meddled in everything. I hate to speak ill of the dead, but the best thing that ever happened to that poor woman was when he died."

The film was typical of the consciously archaic films that Ross Hunter and other producers were making for Universal throughout the 1950s and much of the 1960s—movies for old ladies pining for a comeback from Constance Bennett but who were willing to settle for Lana Turner. Most of Grant's peers from the 1930s were dead and had been struggling to maintain their status before they died. James Harvey pointed out the all too obvious portable shadows that follow Gary Cooper around throughout *Love in the Afternoon* in a vain effort to minimize the huge discrepancy in appearance between him and Audrey Hepburn.

But there were no floating shadows in a Cary Grant movie; indeed, Doris Day required more soft-focus than Grant did. Grant's apparently permanent middle age was coming to seem the only laudable point of what were increasingly mechanical performances. But the trouble went deeper than that. Not only were the performances simulations of other, better times, so were the films. Grant had locked himself into a format that was slowly becoming obsolete and there is every indication that he sensed it.

Throughout the shoot of *That Touch of Mink*, Grant was preoccupied with trivialities—the paintings on the walls of the set representing his character's office, or his costar's wardrobe. "I saw girl after girl wearing clothes that a real girl, in the same circumstances, could never afford," said Grant. "I took [Day] to certain fashion houses that I knew had the type of dress a girl could afford. Remember, she played a secretary. I took her to Anne Klein, who had a range of clothes, very reasonable. But there was a deeper reason. Not only did girls wear clothes beyond their means, they often cost the studio too much."

Hitchcock or McCarey would have ignored him or told him—nicely—to butt out, but Grant was now working for directors who wouldn't confront him because he had hired them. Delbert Mann had made some good movies—*Marty, Middle of the Night*—but he had more of an affinity for drama than comedy, and besides that, he had never run into an actor like Grant before. Mann had directed *Lover Come Back*, Day's previous picture, which went into the Radio City Music Hall and broke all records, so he was recruited to direct *That Touch of Mink*.

The problem was that Mann and Grant couldn't find a meeting place. "Cary and I just didn't get along," said Mann. "I figured finally that he was at the end of his acting career and he was very tired of acting. It no longer excited, no longer interested him. He was making a lot of money on the picture, but he was just disinterested."

Mann was particularly disturbed by the attention Grant paid to Day's wardrobe. "He spent a lot of his time worrying about Doris' . . . shoes. He flew her and himself to New York to get shoes for her to wear in the picture. I said 'Oh, brother.' Cary was always amiable, pleasant as could be, smiling, told stories, usually in a Cockney accent. But I knew somehow that Cary, deep down, knew that he was Archie Leach from [Bristol], and that someday the clock would strike, the [carriage] would disappear and he would turn back into Archie Leach."

On the superficial level, Doris Day found Grant congenial. "I like Cary Grant very much, because he's a perfectionist, which I am. Perfectionists work well together because they think alike. He wants everything to be just so, and so do I. . . . And of course, I think he's maybe the best actor in all of Hollywood. There's no one better. He's never won an Academy Award and I will never understand that. I think he should have about ten on his mantel."

But Day found Grant uninterested in any kind of connection, which bothered her—she was a straight-shooter from Ohio and liked a happy set. It was obvious that Grant and Mann were not communicating, so Day ramped up her efforts to be helpful and cooperative—a nervous daughter trying to keep peace between two father figures who couldn't find any common ground. "She was just totally adorable," said Mann. It didn't help.

"Cary in one scene did not like the huge brass doorknobs on the door to his office," said Mann.

And he stopped production while the art director was brought onto the stage to change the door knobs. People were sent out for them. They had a gold center with an emerald . . . in the middle of them. Cary would not shoot until the doorknobs were changed. So we sat, and we waited and we waited, and finally a painter came on the set and painted them white.

I liked Cary a lot, always amiable and charming and smiling, and I often said to myself, "What is he really thinking? What is he really like underneath all of this phony charm?" And I never found out; I never felt that I reached a quarter inch into his real personality, ever.

Mann sensed that Grant had erected what amounted to an impregnable wall around his professional persona, and you breached that wall at your—and his—peril.

Just to prove William Goldman's dictum that nobody knows anything, *That Touch of Mink* also played Radio City Music Hall, where it broke the box-office records set by *Lover Come Back*. Grant knew precisely what his audience wanted, and he aimed to give it to them. That said, the picture didn't fool the industry. Even *Variety*, which was invariably friendly to Grant, clucked their tongue over *That Touch of Mink*: "The gloss . . . doesn't obscure an essentially threadbare lining."

That Touch of Mink caused a brief rupture in Grant's growing friendship with Peter Bogdanovich, who saw the film in a preview with Grant sitting in front of him. Bogdanovich didn't laugh once, but lied and told Grant he'd liked the movie. He then told Grant that the process of applying for unemployment insurance shown in the film was incorrect. That irritated the perfectionist, who replied, "No, no! We did a lotta research on *that*, and it is *exactly* the way it's *done*." Bogdanovich said that it didn't really matter, and moved on, but Grant followed up with a phone call in which he again asserted that the matter had been thoroughly researched.

A year later, Grant was passing through New York and Bogdanovich called him. "You didn't like my picture!" Grant said. Bogdanovich insisted through gritted teeth that he had liked the picture, but Grant wasn't having any. "No, you didn't like my picture. But that's all right, it's been quite profitable and a lotta people enjoyed it. But I know *you* didn't like it!"

Grant was at the Plaza Hotel planning some appearances for the movie. The phone rang and Grant picked it up.

"May I ask what you wish to speak to Mr. Grant about?" he said. Pause.

"This *is* Cary Grant, my dear lady."

Pause.

"I can't help it, but I am Cary Grant, and it's too late to do anything about it."

Pause.

Grant hung up the phone and turned to the photographer Murray Garrett. The woman had refused to believe that she was speaking to Cary Grant, because, she said, "Everybody knows that Cary Grant wouldn't answer his own phone. And you can tell him for me that I'll never see another one of his films!"

It was the principal conundrum of Grant's public image, which he had carefully constructed so that he was viewed as a rarefied creature exempt from the duties and penalties that afflicted the rest of humanity. People didn't quite believe in him or his problems even when confronted with incontrovertible evidence that he and they did indeed exist.

Grant and Garrett were barely out of the Plaza on the way to their first appointment when they were surrounded by mostly female fans. Grant said, "Remind me not to walk with you . . . again. You attract too many women." He had a phrase for moments like this, brief appearances in public at premieres and such. He called it "just another walk in the park."

HER NAME WAS MILLIE BLACK. She and her twin sister came to Hollywood in the early 1940s after bailing out of the Northwest, which they found damp and uncongenial. Hollywood was warm and friendly, at least if you weren't working at a studio and had an option coming up. Millie was brunette, her twin sister, Marge, was blond, and they were both lookers. They worked as extras in *Since You Went Away* and had their picture taken with Joseph Cotten.

Millie found her métier as a cocktail waitress around town in the string of bars that flourished in the shadow of the various studios. For a time she worked near the Republic lot, but that studio closed in 1958 so she had to move on, which was all right with Millie. She married the guitarist-bandleader Stanley Black, and eventually they divorced, but she kept working because she enjoyed the camaraderie and the laughs. The professional drinkers—Robert Mitchum, Lawrence

Tierney—and their friends who drank as much as they did were all hilarious.

It was about this time that Millie got to know Cary Grant. He would occasionally stop at her bar near Universal and sit quietly in a booth near the back. Since most of the clientele came from Universal, they didn't ogle Grant. Being quietly accepted without any fuss seemed to be what he needed at this stage of his life.

There was something about Millie that was attracted to damage, to strays, and Grant was obviously at loose ends. He told her that he was sick of being stared at, sick of being photographed. She said that the phrase that captured him at this stage of his life was "world-weary."

One night he invited her to come home with him. It was all very spur-of-the-moment, but he didn't have to ask twice. She wouldn't mention that night unless she trusted you completely, and she never went into detail, but she never claimed it was one of the transcendent experiences of her life one way or the other.

It had been a night with a lonely man, that's all.

THE TENTATIVE UNITY WROUGHT BY CHEMICALS was slowly prodding Grant into the realization that he didn't really need movies anymore. Also contributing was the fact that he was now extremely wealthy. Grant's recent run of pictures accomplished something remarkable, memorialized by *Variety* on November 20, 1963, with a banner headline on page one: "RICHEST ACTOR: CARY GRANT." The article went on to analyze his business deals. *Variety* said that Grant's 75 percent of the profits on the bulk of his Universal pictures stood to make him in the vicinity of $12 million by 1966. First, there was the $3 million that *Operation Petticoat* had brought him. *The Grass Is Greener* had underperformed, but *That Touch of Mink* was slated to put another $3 million in his pocket. *Charade* was still in the pipeline, but it would do even better than *That Touch of Mink*.

The article went on to mention other smart shareholder actors. William Holden would make at least $2 million off his percentage of *The Bridge on the River Kwai*, Gregory Peck a bit less from *To Kill a Mockingbird*, and Doris Day about $1 million each from *Pillow Talk* and *That Touch of Mink*. "But none have clicked into the over-$2,000,000 range as often as Grant and none have the potential already either in the can or on the drawing board that he has. It is small wonder that he sticks with Universal where he can make these kinds of deals and presumably satisfy all sides. His *Petticoat* arrangement, though heavily weighted in his favor, still helped bail Universal out when it was in a genuine slump. It has never been in one since, nor has Grant."

In his fourth decade of stardom, Grant stood at the apex of the Hollywood food chain, so ubiquitous that he was even parodied on *The Flintstones*. "Gary Granite" was a matinee idol in Hollyrock who had the same vocal inflections as Grant. In one episode, Fred Flintstone was pressed into action as Granite's stunt double. Disaster ensues. Fame in the early 1960s could not go any further.

Perhaps it was time to relax a bit. There were other things he could do. Enjoy life, for instance. "I was a self-centered bore until the age of forty," he said. "I didn't have time for reading. Now I'm reading, absorbing, listening and learning about the world and myself. Understanding is as important to growth as patience is necessary to understanding. One must have perspective."

And so it was that Cary Grant began an incremental psychological withdrawal from show business.

CHAPTER TWENTY

G rant's daughter, Jennifer, would say that she thought what drew her parents together was her—the possibility of a baby. In this telling, Grant and his fourth wife were different in almost every way, but they both wanted a child, and once that was accomplished they moved apart.

Dyan Cannon listened to her daughter's opinion and promptly dismissed it.

> That's a sweet answer, but I wasn't thinking about babies when I met him. I was thinking career. When I met him I was told by my agent it was about a part in a movie. After a four-hour meeting I came out of the office and said to my agent, "He didn't mention a part in a movie." And my agent said, "He's interested in you." And I said, "You're crazy."
>
> But he was right and I was wrong. Cary called me every day for three months. He was clever and funny and brilliant and lonely and needed someone to trust. He didn't let go until the day he asked me to marry him. And then everything changed. Everything.

It began in the autumn of 1961, when Grant was idly watching television and came across a show called *Malibu Run*. Guest-starring in the episode was Cannon—voluptuous body capped off by tawny blond hair. Grant's taste in women was nothing if not varied—physically,

Cannon was closer to Sophia Loren than she was to the trim and prim Betsy Drake. He immediately began making phone calls. First he found out who represented her, then he got her private number.

She was born Samille Diane Friesen in 1939 in Tacoma, a nice Jewish girl whose father sold insurance. In 1961, Cannon had only made two movies, the biggest of which was *The Rise and Fall of Legs Diamond*, but she was appearing in a number of TV shows: *Have Gun–Will Travel, Wanted: Dead or Alive, Ben Casey, Bat Masterson*.

Grant worked fast. The day after she came to his Universal bungalow for an interview, he called her at 7:45 in the morning and asked her to listen to an inspirational radio program called *The Daily Word* with him. They listened to the five-minute show together, on opposite ends of a phone line. Then he asked her to lunch, but she begged off. For a while, he settled for listening to *The Daily Word* with her on the phone. All this made Cannon slightly flustered. For one thing, he was fifty-seven—older than her father. For another, he was Cary Grant.

He took her to a party at Clifford Odets's house, where she met Frank Sinatra, Danny Kaye, and Howard Hughes. Not surprisingly, Cannon was most impressed by Odets. "His brilliance was electrifying. . . . He was not handsome, but as your eyes warmed to his countenance, he became beautiful." Odets got her number from Grant and called her for a date, but she told him she was seeing someone—the man who had given Odets her number.

That led to a kerfuffle—Grant thought she had led Odets on—but it was soon smoothed over. By the fall of 1962 Cannon was in New York working in a play called *The Fun Couple* and living with Grant at the Plaza.

Having passed all the preliminaries, it was time for the ultimate test: meeting Elsie. Cannon noticed how Grant's mood deflated the closer he got to Bristol. He gripped the steering wheel tightly and drove with a much heavier foot than usual. "Going back to Bristol dredges up a lot of memories," he told Cannon. "You never know what branch she's going to fly off of." In fact, the first time Cannon went to Bristol, she didn't meet Elsie, because Grant's mother was having a bad day.

The second time was the charm, and Cannon found a small woman with gray hair and posture that would have done a West Point cadet proud. Elsie said "Nice to meet you" mechanically, as though she wasn't really interested. She acted the same way to her son. She referred to Dyan as "Betsy," even though both Cannon and Grant corrected her. Cannon had brought a nail kit for Elsie, and gave her a manicure, including red nail polish, which provoked an explosion. "Get it off," Elsie screamed. "I hate it! Get it off!" She threw the bottle of polish across the room against the white wall, where the red lacquer splattered.

"I don't think she likes me," Cannon told Grant later. "Oh, she likes you," he replied. "She has never once asked to spend any time alone with any woman I've ever brought to meet her." The only pure positive about the initial visit to Bristol was the chance it gave Grant to see his cousin Eric Leach and Eric's wife, Maggie. They were short and plump and Grant clearly adored them both.

Grant had been proselytizing about the miracle of LSD, wanting Cannon to join him. She was resisting, so he flew Mortimer Hartman to London, where Grant introduced him to Cannon. "Talk to her, my wise mahatma," he told the doctor. Hartman gave her the soft sell: "The drug has a dismantling effect. It can tear down our inner walls and help us look at the world, and ourselves, through new eyes. And everything you sense and see is a hundred times more vivid than usual."

Cannon was still unsure, so Grant chimed in. "I'm thinking about our future. This is important to me." Cannon gave in and took the blue pill. All in all it wasn't bad. She saw the words Hartman spoke as letters tumbling out of his mouth; when she looked at Grant she was suddenly in the movie *The Time Machine* as she watched him regress to the age of ten or twelve. Then time sped up and he was an old man, wattles hanging off his neck.

At that point, Cannon asked Hartman to make it stop, so he gave her a dose of Seconal that knocked her out for the better part of a day. Cannon was shaken, not stirred. She told Grant that she would never do it again. "For him, it was the gateway to God," she said nearly sixty years later. "It had saved him and he thought it would make our marriage, or save the marriage. But drugs can't do that."

Cannon was young, no pushover, but pliable in some areas. For instance: Grant would have New York stores send him wardrobes for her on approval. His secretary would make a first selection among the dozens of outfits, Grant would make the final choices, and the rest would be sent back. The outfits Grant had chosen would then be presented to Cannon, who had no choice in what she could wear.

GRANT HAD BEEN WAITING for the arrival of a script from Howard Hawks. But when *Man's Favorite Sport?* arrived, Grant saw it for the stiff it was and backed out. He told Hawks that "I'm not going to play against . . . young girls." Hawks regrouped and got Rock Hudson for the lead, but the film had been structured for Grant's gifts, which were not the same as Hudson's. "Rock tried hard, and he worked hard, he did everything he could, but Rock is not a comedian," sighed Hawks. "And when you have visualized one person in it, and you're trying to get that, it's an awful tough job to do it because you just don't come out right."

Grant quickly hooked up with Stanley Donen again, in a Peter Stone script called *Charade*. Stone was the son of John Stone, a scenarist for John Ford in the silent days who went on to produce Charlie Chan pictures in the 1930s. The younger Stone was an aspiring playwright who had just had his first Broadway flop: *Kean*, starring Alfred Drake. Stone and a writer named Marc Behm had originally concocted *Charade* as a movie, but couldn't sell it so Stone rewrote it as what he termed "an absolutely awful novel . . . unreadable, terrible."

The novel was rejected by numerous publishers, and the objection of a Harper's editor seems perfectly legitimate. "There's a lot of imagination in this manuscript, but the plot is rather diffuse and the stamp business struck us as a little too ornate for credulity." Another publisher rejected it for some of the same issues, but did offer a backhanded compliment: "It certainly would make a splendid movie."

Stone's agent eventually placed the novel, as well as selling an abridged version to *Redbook* for $5,000. Suddenly the story Stone hadn't been able to sell as a script became a hot Hollywood property. There was a murmur of interest from the exploitation producer William Castle, but Stone's asking price of $50,000 for the story and a screenplay was too rich for Castle's blood.

And then Peter Stone's life changed. On January 16, 1962, Stanley Donen wrote Stone a letter telling him that his story "might make a very interesting suspense action film, if one was fortunate enough to get an extremely good screenplay, and, of course, a marvelous woman to play the leading part. I have in mind Audrey Hepburn, and I am hopeful that I will be able to interest her in doing it."

It all came together very quickly. Stone sold the book to Donen, mostly because "he was the only person who hadn't seen it [as a screenplay] and I felt silly selling it to the people who'd rejected it." Donen paid Stone the bargain rate of $750 a week plus expenses to write the script with the aim of getting Cary Grant and Audrey Hepburn to star. The script was written in the spring and early summer of 1962, and shooting began in October. The good fortune of the project followed through with the shoot, which promised to be pleasant and was.

Donen hosted a dinner to introduce Grant and Hepburn. The always shy Hepburn told Grant she was extremely nervous about meeting him, and he replied, "Don't be nervous, for goodness sake. I'm thrilled to know you. Here, sit down. Put your hands on the table put your head down and take a few deep breaths."

While she was trying to compose herself, Hepburn knocked a bottle of red wine onto Grant's suit. She was now not merely nervous but embarrassed and appalled. Everybody wondered how this was going to end. "Cary took off his coat and comfortably sat through the whole meal just like that," said Donen. Hepburn apologized throughout dinner, and Grant was gracious; the next day he sent her a box of caviar with a note telling her not to be concerned. Peter Stone wrote a similar scene into the movie, when Hepburn accidentally flings a scoop of ice cream onto Grant's jacket and he reacts with the same aplomb.

After the film got under way Donen noticed a quiet, unspoken competition between his two stars. Grant regularly monitored the Paris papers to make sure that the pictures they were using of the shoot were the ones he had approved; Hepburn did the same thing. Protestations of endless affection and respect were and are de rigueur in the movie business, at least when there are reporters around, but the business of being a star requires heightened attentiveness at all times.

Donen noticed that for the first time in their collaborations Grant had to harbor his energy. The climax of the film involved several shots of Grant running at top speed, and Donen had to ask him for extra takes. Grant said he would do the scene once more.

Where Doris Day had found Grant impenetrable, Hepburn responded favorably to his reserve, to his habit of keeping himself for himself. He was, she said,

> Sensitive, reserved and quiet. Working with him was a joy. He was expressed and yet reserved. He led a very quiet life. I do, too. I think a lot of it has to do with shyness and wanting to be with people you're comfortable with, instead of having to always break new ground. I think because he was a vulnerable man, he recognized my vulnerability. We had that in common. He had more wisdom than I to help me with it. He said something very important to me one day when I was probably twitching and nervous. We were sitting next to each other waiting for the next shot. And he laid his hand on my two hands and said, "You've got to learn to like yourself a little more."

Grant spread his accumulated wisdom to star and supporting players alike. George Kennedy was playing the heavy, a killer with a flamboyantly theatrical steel claw in place of a hand. Kennedy noticed that Grant would refer to himself in the third person with absolute objectivity: "Cary Grant can't be in a picture like that," etc. And he gave Kennedy a signature admonition: "You must always remember that you are a property, and you must treat that property with respect." Kennedy found it to be the single best piece of advice he ever got about show business. "You must sell yourself like somebody would sell real estate or automobiles. If you treat the property with respect, everybody else falls in line."

Charade was the fourth collaboration between Donen and Grant, but the star still had trouble relaxing. At one point Peter Stone went to costar Walter Matthau and complained, "I'm going crazy. I have to get rid of Cary Grant." Stone was exhausted by Grant's incessant hovering about dialogue changes. Finally, Stone made a break for it; he told Grant that he had to leave in order to meet his lawyer for dinner. Shortly afterward, Stone, Matthau, and some others snuck off for a meal and blessed relief.

Unfortunately, Grant showed up at the same restaurant. Stone tried to cover up; he told Grant that his lawyer had canceled at the last minute. Grant laughed and said, "Don't worry. I understand."

Stone had written a recapitulation scene for Grant about two thirds of the way through the fairly convoluted script. The screenwriter called it "a reviewing the bidding scene," to remind the audience of what was going on. Grant refused to shoot it because, he said, stars didn't do exposition. Donen patiently explained that since Grant's character was the only one who understood the entire plot, nobody else could do the exposition. Grant grudgingly admitted this was true. He then said he hadn't bothered to learn the scene. The dialogue was then written on a blackboard so Grant could read it. Being a total pro, he did it without making it look too obvious, although if you watch carefully you can see his eyes scanning the lines. In the rushes the next day, they watched the scene, after which Donen had spliced in a close-up of another actor saying, "You're reading off a blackboard!" in an outraged tone. Grant took it well.

Charade was a huge hit—rentals of $13 million against a cost of $3 million. As with *To Catch a Thief*, it's a smooth mixture of ingredients seldom combined so successfully: suspense thriller, love story, and comedy that verges on slapstick. The plot, as various publishers had recognized, is far-fetched, but Donen and Stone understood that legendary movie stars can beguile an audience even if said audience doesn't believe a word of the story that surrounds them.

Peter Stone became Grant's favorite writer of the moment, signing a five-picture deal with Universal for a lot more than $750 a week. First up on his dance card was *Father Goose*, which was followed by *Arabesque*—another picture for Stanley Donen—and a script called *Mirage* that became an underrated Gregory Peck vehicle. After Donen had his script for *Arabesque* rewritten, Stone took his name off in favor of Pierre Marton, his favorite pseudonym. He would eventually become an extremely successful Broadway librettist, with shows such as *1776*, *My One and Only*, *Woman of the Year*, and *The Will Rogers Follies* to his credit.

With the success of *Charade*, Grant had fooled them again. But he hadn't fooled Ingrid Bergman, who told him she thought Audrey Hepburn was too old to be acting opposite him. Bergman thought the twenty-eight-year-old Jane Fonda would have been more appropriate.

IN THE EARLY SUMMER OF 1963, Walt Odets told his father that he wanted to take a road trip with a friend. Odets said he wanted

Walt to stay home. Walt went anyway, leaving behind a note that said he'd be back in two weeks. On the appointed day, Walt was back in the house, in his room, when he heard his father's car pull in the driveway. Walt thought his father would read him the riot act, but instead Clifford Odets stood in the doorway of his son's room for a moment, then said, "Good for you!" Walt was clearly going to be his own man; Odets must have felt he could stop worrying.

But there was no time to take satisfaction in his accomplishment. "My father wasn't okay, but he was pretending he was okay," remembered Walt. "He became very irritable and difficult to deal with. Once I walked into his bedroom and he was in his boxer shorts. I asked him why his stomach was sticking out, and he said 'None of your business.' I just turned and walked out. I had startled him and he was trying to pretend everything was okay."

Odets had gone to a doctor about three times in his life, but on August 1, 1963, he could put it off no longer. His son came home to find a note on his bed: "Waltie, I'm going to the hospital for a check-up. Nothing to worry about. We'll talk soon. Dad." Underneath the note were ten one-hundred-dollar bills. Walt had never seen a single hundred-dollar bill, let alone ten of them. He knew what it meant, and he began to cry.

After the cancer was diagnosed, people came from all over America to say goodbye to Clifford Odets, so many of them that the hospital had to set aside waiting rooms as holding pens. Cary Grant came regularly. Odets would be informed Grant had arrived and he would bellow, "Send in Mr. Mott!"—the character Grant had played in *None But the Lonely Heart*.

Elia Kazan and Harold Clurman flew in from New York. At one point during their visit, Odets raised his fist and, in his self-dramatizing way, said, "Clifford Odets, you have so much still to do!" And then he looked at Kazan and said, "You know, I may fool you, Gadge. I may not die." A little later, he beckoned Kazan to come closer. "Gadge! Imagine! Clifford Odets dying!"

That event took place on August 14, 1963. Odets was fifty-seven. Jean Renoir and his wife were there shortly before the end. Odets had asked that a bottle of fine wine from his cellar be brought to him. He asked for three glasses to be filled. The tube was removed from his mouth and he touched the rim of his glass with his lips. Renoir and his wife finished the bottle while Odets watched and smiled.

"Cliff spent the last dozen years of his life writing films to pay bills that were too large for a man who hoped to continue working in the theater," wrote Elia Kazan. "He drove a Lincoln Continental, and had what he claimed to be the outstanding collection of Paul Klees in the country. He worked frequently and was well paid by New York theater standards. But he was always broke or near it, and I believe he died broke or near it."

Kazan's instincts were correct. Odets left behind mountains of manuscripts, a first-rate collection of Klee paintings, a collection of American commemorative stamps, and little else. As the executor of the estate was going through everything, he complained to Danny Kaye that the estate was a mess and there was no cash. "That's my boy!" said Kaye.

As far as Kazan was concerned, Odets was more than a man, more than a great playwright. He was a metaphor. "The tragedy of the American theater and of our lives is what could have been," Kazan said to a gathering of actors a few months after Odets died.

> Forces dispersed instead of gathered. Talents unused or used at a fraction of their worth. Potential unrealized. We all know our problems. We are not kids, we are not students. We know we are here on short leases. . . .
>
> The man who could have been the Lear of this generation is playing a sheriff on a TV series. I don't think he plays sheriffs very well. He could have been a great Lear. The man who could have been the greatest actor in the history of American theater is sulking on a grubby hilltop over Beverly Hills or on a beach on the island of Tahiti. What happened to them? They don't know. Don't look down on them. They are not weaklings. They were idealists too. Nor are they corrupt, confused, or sicker than most; they are your brothers.
>
> We don't do what we want to do. We do what we think we have to do. Or what's worse, what other people want us to do. . . . When we go from flop to flop we are terrified. When we find ourselves in a hit, we are bored to death.

Kazan was specifically referring to Lee J. Cobb and Marlon Brando, but he could also have been thinking about actors who didn't live in Tahiti. He was thinking of how dissatisfaction is so often wired into our being; that there is an intrinsically tragic element in creative lives that remain less than they might have been. He was talking of Clifford Odets, but he could have been talking about Cary Grant.

Irene Mayer Selznick wrote to Grant a few days after Odets died:

> You've been particularly in my thoughts this past sad week. Yes, it is to you I write my letter of sorrow about Clifford.
>
> I've long known that it was a momentous afternoon that Clifford brought me to the set of *None But the Lonely Heart*. I am in his debt for that—and many other rewarding currents. That our real friendship began then, makes it sweeter.
>
> That you added greatly to his life, you must know. I hope you know *how* much. That being so, he added to yours, and thus I send you sympathy on your loss.
>
> Cary, my dear friend, you add greatly to the life of any friend of yours. I value you—and love you.
>
> Blessings—as always.
> Irene.

"I understand things about my father now that I couldn't have known when I was a teenager," said Walt Odets. "Specifically, the things he shared with Cary—vulnerability, feelings of not being worthwhile. He was a very lonely person, particularly after my mother died. Every year my father would write in his calendar, 'Betty's birthday. I haven't mentioned it to the kids. It would upset them.' Or 'Anniversary of Betty's death. Haven't said anything to the kids.' It was the best marriage he ever had, and I'm sure he was impossible to get along with."

Odets had an ambivalence about Grant, but then he was ambivalent about nearly everything, especially himself. But Cary Grant had no ambivalence about Clifford Odets. In honoring Odets, in generously helping to keep him afloat financially, and in refusing to judge his friend as Odets surreptitiously judged him, Grant revealed his own latent idealism and deep respect for a man who traveled his own path no matter the cost.

In a letter he wrote when his wife was alive, Odets had said, "Betty values nothing so much as kindness. If I could understand that, I'd be a much better person."

In fact, he had understood it perfectly. He just didn't know that he understood it.

CHAPTER TWENTY-ONE

Grant gave serious consideration to making *The Cincinnati Kid*—the part of the wily old poker player who ultimately takes the Kid to the cleaners. It was a transparent rewrite of *The Hustler*, with poker substituting for pool, but Minnesota Fats had been a great part for Jackie Gleason, and it could have been for Cary Grant as well. Peter Stone did some work on the script, but Grant drifted away from the project, whereupon Edward G. Robinson took the part and nailed it.

Then Grant slowly came around to a script called *Father Goose*, about a misanthropic bum with a taste for whiskey who is afflicted with a prim schoolteacher and a group of small children during World War II. Universal had originally suggested the project, and Grant wasn't impressed. "The story on which the screenplay is based wasn't very satisfactory and I didn't want to struggle with it. I started to look around for something else, but a couple of Universal executives kept maneuvering. When I couldn't find another vehicle I wanted to do, they convinced me this one would be good given the proper treatment."

The more he thought about it, the more he liked it. His character wore jeans, a shirt with the tails out, and a week's worth of beard. The transition was obvious: "After dressing so carefully for my films for so many years, I wanted to do the opposite," Grant said.

Grant seems to have been tentatively considering a third act for himself similar to the one that had worked for Bogart and Spencer

Tracy: don't fight age; rather, embrace it. Play angry, play grizzled, play grumpy, play drunk. It had gotten Bogart an Oscar for *The African Queen*, which *Father Goose* resembled in some respects, albeit with the addition of a herd of small children to take the edge off.

The basic story had been bought by a B movie producer named Hal Chester, who hired Frank Tarloff to write the script for short money—$16,000. Tarloff was writing *The Danny Thomas Show* at the time and initially turned down Chester's project because all he saw was "a poor man's *The African Queen*." He finally agreed to do the script and made the woman a schoolteacher so a group of children could be added to the mix.

Tarloff's script had more potential than a B movie, so Hal Chester took it to Universal, which was always scanning the horizon for a likely project for Grant. Chester sold the project to Universal for 5 percent of the gross up to a million dollars. Universal also paid $175,000 for a picture Chester had made in England, which they never released. Once the deal was negotiated, Peter Stone came on to do the rewrite.

The initial director was David Miller, an old MGM hand who had landed at Universal and made pictures both good and bad: *Midnight Lace, Back Street, Lonely Are the Brave*. Miller did most of the pre-production, from January to March 1964, when he suddenly left the picture only a month before the start of shooting. Miller's weekly salary of $5,500 added up to $46,750, and was charged to the picture's budget.

What seems to have happened is that Miller clashed with Peter Stone and lost the clash—Grant had no patience for contention on a film set unless he was the cause of it. "He and Peter Stone didn't see eye to eye," was the way Grant explained it. As was typical of him, Grant chose to go with the writer.

With the clock ticking, Grant had to find another director quickly. He settled on Ralph Nelson only three weeks before the picture got under way. Nelson was fresh off *Requiem for a Heavyweight, Soldier in the Rain*, and *Lilies of the Field*, the latter a big success that won Sidney Poitier an Oscar. If Nelson had any problems with the script, there wasn't time to address them, so he had to function as a director for hire. His fee was a flat $125,000. Grant had hoped to lure Audrey Hepburn as his costar, but she decided against it, so he hired Leslie Caron on the basis of her performance in *The L-Shaped Room*.

Four weeks of locations took place around a coconut plantation in Ocho Rios, Jamaica, followed by eight weeks back at Universal. Leslie Caron found Grant to be a lot of fun except when he wasn't. There were days when he would be exuberant, singing his music hall songs, telling stories about selling Orry-Kelly's ties out of a suitcase on Times Square while keeping an eye peeled for the cops.

And there were other days when he verged on the surly, grousing to the assistant director about the child actors, or yelling at the prop man for placing a bottle by his right hand instead of his left. (Grant was born left-handed, had trained himself to be more or less ambidextrous, but still favored his left hand.)

And always there was fretting over the budget. "This film is ruining me!" he constantly complained. "He kept us on our toes," Caron remembered. Grant's fears about the film's costs were not entirely groundless; the expense of *Father Goose* would add up to $3.8 million.

Ralph Nelson seems to have had his hands full. On April 19 he wrote a long, placating letter to Grant, who was worried that he was overacting. Nelson began by complimenting him on both his career and his ineffable style, then he got down to the issue:

> When I laugh out loud at something you do spontaneously, like laughing at Catherine falling through the steps, throwing away an empty bottle, or taking off your pants, it is not through sycophancy. It is a laugh of appreciation because it is funny and it is funny because it is in character, and I don't think overdone. . . .
>
> I hope that gradually you will rely not just on your own instincts but on me. . . . You sought me on the basis of LILIES, and in that I think you saw a truth I tried to achieve in performance—not in camera pyrotechnics or techniques to draw attention to the director. . . . I have great admiration for what you did last week, though you don't feel it is your best work. I hope you don't retrench.

Grant's insecurity is touching as well as saddening; at the age of sixty, coming off a string of hits, he was still unsure of himself, reaching out to people with less experience, less success, and, frankly, less talent, for reassurance. An actor's life is emotionally perilous, right to the end.

Father Goose went over schedule and over budget; budgeted for fifty-eight days, it ended up taking seventy-two, mostly due to its

star. Because the script was off Grant's beaten track, there were lots
of delays while Grant fine-tuned every scene. He would gather the
actors and run the scene as written by Peter Stone, then everybody
would wait while he added jokes and business. The new version, which
was invariably less succinct and less funny than the original version,
would be copied and distributed. That version would be rehearsed,
until Grant realized that it was inferior to the original, at which point
Stone's original would be restored.

During rehearsal of the final version he would return to his vaudeville days and work hard for laughs from the crew, which reassured
him that the scene was indeed funny. All this took time, which is why
Grant was particularly nervous about the budget.

For the parts of the seven young girls, neither Grant nor Nelson
was interested in any programmed professional children. Stephanie
Berrington, who played the bespectacled fifteen-year-old, was actually eleven but tall for her age, and had never acted before. The girls
weren't intimidated by Cary Grant because none of them knew who
he was. Their parents were another matter entirely.

"He clearly loved children," remembered Berrington.

At the time, elephant jokes were all the rage and we used to have
informal competitions to see who could tell the funniest elephant
jokes. He was very current on the latest jokes. We used to do this in
between takes. Unless there was a good reason for him to leave the
set, he usually stayed between takes and talked and joked.

Cary did adlib, and sometimes when he forgot a line, he adlibbed
and it was better than the original so it was kept in the script. . . .
He enjoyed being able to relax and really wasn't a stiff person at
all. He was very down to earth and may have felt he could be more
himself with kids as opposed to adults. He laughed easily and was
very sharp and quick witted. A wonderful companion.

The kids got a kick out of going to the Universal commissary,
where they met Al Lewis, who played Grandpa Munster on TV. They
may not have known who Cary Grant was, but they assuredly knew
who the Munsters were. Lewis invited them to the set of the sitcom,
which was a huge thrill.

Probably because he was surrounded by children, Grant would often speak of his desire for a child. At lunchtime, he would sit in the sun balancing a reflector in his lap to maintain his tan. Peter Stone visited the Jamaican location with a friend, and lunched with Grant three times. Stone had to pick up the check each time.

Throughout the long shoot, Caron found him amazingly lithe and compelling, full of what she called "animal strength."

Caron had a lot going on; her friend Jack Larson came to visit for professional reasons—he was writing the libretto for Virgil Thomson's opera *Lord Byron*—while Warren Beatty came to visit Caron for personal reasons. Some reporters came down to Jamaica to investigate the state of the relationship between Beatty and Caron, and Grant gave her succinct advice about dealing with the press: "Don't talk, don't reveal, don't give away anything."

He instructed Caron to freeze on his punch lines—a stage technique indicating stunned surprise. "Don't move during my punch line or after! Give 'em time to laugh." It's something that rarely happens in real life, but it works onstage and it worked in the movies as well.

Where all this left Ralph Nelson is open to question. With Grant in control of the script and the rhythm of the scenes, Nelson was reduced to the level of a camera mechanic. Grant had arrived at the same point as a lot of other stars. There were better directors around for his particular skill set than Delbert Mann and Ralph Nelson, but Grant was a movie star and movie stars are disinclined to hire directors who want their own way, let alone directors who argue with them.

On July 10, as the picture was about to wrap, a letter went out to the cast and crew:

There will be no conventional closing day party. Instead, Granox Company hopes to follow a particular happy procedure that began with "Touch of Mink." Later, when the film is edited and scored, you will receive invitations to a private showing of "Father Goose" so that you may have the pleasure of seeing the result of your hard and appreciated work.

The showing will be followed by a gala supper dance to which your wives and sweethearts are invited, and also your children, who can be taken home by private bus before the festivities begin; and since the party will be held on either a Friday or Saturday evening, it can continue as late as you like.

So we'll all meet again in about three months and enjoy sharing a few drinks and memories together.

Black tie, dark suit, cocktail or long dress, whichever you prefer . . .

Ska, anybody?

Appreciatively and gratefully,
Cary Grant

Father Goose is basically a formula film, but Grant is far more energized than in any of the movies he had made since *North by Northwest*. He clearly loved playing a suspicious grump who bore more than a glancing resemblance to himself.

Ralph Nelson thought Grant was remarkably good in the film and suggested to Universal that they launch an Oscar campaign for their star. Despite her long-standing antipathy to Grant, Hedda Hopper wrote approvingly of the campaign, and Nelson responded with a letter to the columnist: "It's astonishing to me that the industry has never recognized Cary although he does superbly what everyone recognizes as the most difficult acting: high comedy."

But there was no nomination for Grant, let alone an Oscar, and *Father Goose* returned rentals to Universal that were about half those earned by *That Touch of Mink* and *Charade*. It was profitable, but only marginally. Grant didn't seem to mind; he always spoke with affection of the picture, and it found its natural audience on television, where it was more popular than it was in theaters.

Despite the moody explosions and manifold contradictions between his on-screen and off-screen character, Leslie Caron thought the picture was a positive experience, if only for the prolonged glimpses of the antic Archie Leach. "Except for the fact that I used to crack up a lot, I loved to do comedy, and Cary Grant was . . . well simply the grandest partner one could dream of, and very sweet when in a good mood." To the end of his days, Grant always said that Walter Eckland in *Father Goose* was, along with Ernie Mott in *None But the Lonely Heart*, the character closest to who he really was—self-absorbed and indifferent to many of the things society, not to mention movie stars, pretend to value.

Oddly, the only award *Father Goose* did win was an Oscar for best original screenplay for Peter Stone and Frank Tarloff. Accepting his award, Stone said, "I want to thank Cary Grant, who keeps winning these things for other people."

GRANT'S RELATIONSHIP WITH DYAN CANNON was not exclusive, at least not as far as Grant was concerned. During the production of *Father Goose*, Grant was occasionally seeing a young writer at Universal named June Randolph. She had initially been starstruck by his attentions, but gradually grew restive. "The relationship was definitely one-sided and it was beginning to wear on me," she remembered. Grant would invite her to his office at Universal for tea but Randolph got tired of being summoned and asked him to come to her office instead. He had never been to that part of the Universal lot and got lost. When he finally arrived at Randolph's office, he was clearly upset—his hands were shaking. He was "terribly ill at ease . . . there was fear there . . . and other elements I didn't understand.

"His microcosm circulated around Cary Grant, the superstar. He really only felt safe in his bungalow and at home. By inviting him to my bungalow, I had made a demand on him. . . . I believe it [had] to do with control. Cary had lost control of the situation and thus was shaken."

The relationship drifted away, and he went back to Dyan Cannon.

GRANT'S UNDERSTANDING WITH UNIVERSAL was open-ended— the studio felt free to suggest various ideas to him. Lew Wasserman was very high on Claudia Cardinale, and word came down asking if Grant would consider doing a romantic comedy with her. Grant asked Tom Mankiewicz to come up with a story, which began with a meet-cute in an elevator where the power fails. To calm down the frightened woman, Grant kisses her.

"You meant she kisses *me*," said Grant as Mankiewicz was explaining his story.

"Excuse me?"

"The woman always kisses me first. Even when it seems like a mutual idea, she actually kisses me." Mankiewicz realized that Grant had to be the love object, an affectation that would also be present with Robert Redford when Mankiewicz worked with him in the 1980s. The film never happened, probably because of the age difference—Cardinale was thirty-four years younger than Grant, which probably struck him as too extreme.

Mankiewicz was the son of Joseph Mankiewicz, with whom Grant had made *People Will Talk*. The first time they met, Grant was working on a parallel above the ground and Mankiewicz had to climb up a ladder to get there. Grant walked to the edge of the parallel and asked if Tom was Joe Mankiewicz's son.

With the affirmative answer, Grant extended his hand. "Here let me help you up. That must be an enormous burden." Mankiewicz once ran into Grant at Dick Carroll's in Beverly Hills. Grant was buying socks and underwear, and everyone was watching him while pretending not to. "Doesn't this bother you a little, all of these people staring?" asked Mankiewicz

"A little, but if they ever stopped, I'd be absolutely panic-stricken."

But that never happened, and by this time he probably knew it would never happen. Whenever Grant walked into the commissary at Universal on the way to his usual table by the back wall, everybody's head swiveled to follow his progress. And Cary Grant would walk down the aisle, muttering under his breath, "Yes, it's me, it's me, it's me, it's me . . ."

GRANT WOULD PROSYLETIZE FOR LSD to the end of his days, and insist it opened his mind to the path to serenity. But people who spent time around him observed a serenity that was superficial at best. In 1964, a crew from *Gentleman's Quarterly* arrived to do a fashion spread on Grant in Palm Springs, where he spent a month every winter. He rode every morning, loved the feel and smell of the desert early in the morning.

He was cheerful about all the changes of clothes, suggested shots, and fell naturally into the most flattering poses. Most celebrities are bored with being photographed, but Grant enjoyed it. He was wearing

Levi's, had a deep tan, and looked stunning. He was sixty years old and incredibly charming. Everett Mattlin, the editor who was interviewing him, realized that if Grant wasn't being absolutely sincere, he was nevertheless playing a role that had become second nature to him.

He was interested in the lives of other people, and asked a lot of questions of the crew, expounding on his theories of life, a mélange of Buddhism, acid enlightenment, orgone therapy, and Episcopalian self-reliance. He discussed the uselessness of competition compared to cooperation, the virtues of camaraderie and bonding. He asked Mattlin's cousin, who had accompanied him to the shoot, what she did. When she told him she taught design at a college, he was suddenly sharp with her: "Oh, you're one of those people who try to force your tastes on others, eh?" He went on to say that people should develop their own tastes; he didn't think much of college, and would never send a child of his there. The only way to be truly successful was to get out into the world and learn about it. In other words, model your life after Archie Leach.

That opened the floodgates. War was the result of sexual repression—people held back their orgasms until the withholding exploded in armed conflict. If only people would make love continuously there would be universal harmony. Mattlin thought nationalism had at least something to do with war, not to mention economics, but Grant couldn't see it because it didn't fit in with his Freudian theories about the primacy of sex.

He wasn't angry about all this—his good humor never lapsed—just certain. After the photographer was satisfied, they sat around the pool and talked some more. He mentioned how reasonable the Palm Springs stable's charges were, then asked the crew not to over-tip around town lest they spoil it for the residents.

He fetched drinks and food for his guests and kept talking. Quick sex was unhealthy; men should stay as close to the womb for as long as possible. LSD had taught him acceptance. Indeed, "acceptance" was now a primary word in his vocabulary and, he said, the source of his newfound contentment. Mattlin said that he thought there were things that needed to be resisted, but Grant said, "Anti's only build up more anti's." Besides, what is there to resist, since "all opposites are really the same."

He might have been obliquely referring to his preferred use of counterpoint—he was never just one thing. He worked in a cheerful

Scottish jig while playing an urbane diplomat in *Indiscreet*, wore an exquisite double-breasted suit while playing a cold-blooded newspaper editor in *His Girl Friday*.

Or maybe he meant none of those things. Or didn't know what he meant.

He believed in reincarnation, and he believed that some damage was permanent. Somebody mentioned Marilyn Monroe and he shook his head. "Marilyn was abandoned when she was two. Her ego was destroyed. All the psychiatrists in the world can't save the orphan." It was a subject he understood from the inside.

He told them that he'd had an operation for a forehead cyst and had hypnotized himself so that he didn't need an anesthetic, then healed the incision quickly by taking deep breaths and directing the pure oxygen to his forehead. He had learned how to do that, he said, by getting to know some Sufis during his vaudeville days, whose act consisted of driving nails through their palms without pain.

What is so startling about this interaction is that, although Grant was not technically talking for publication—Everett Mattlin wrote about Grant only after his death—he might as well have been. The years after LSD were years in which Grant would tell people exactly what he thought about whatever subject was at hand. If they liked it, fine; if they didn't, fine. He began to treat an interview less as a PR vehicle to be dispensed with as quickly as possible than as an opportunity for communication. Cary Grant was no longer hiding behind the facade of Cary Grant unless there was a movie camera in view.

At the end of the day, he took the crew to dinner at a Mexican restaurant, where he ate a large meal, then went to an ice cream parlor for dessert. The *GQ* crew was too full for dessert, and thanked him for his time and good humor. When they stopped at a gas station to fill up for the drive back to Los Angeles, Grant's car pulled up alongside theirs.

He was worried they might take a wrong turn and get lost.

CHAPTER TWENTY-TWO

Elsie Leach lived partially in the real world, mostly in her own. Her ideas of the value of money were locked in her childhood experience, yet her memory of the past was precise and she could make shrewd judgments about human beings. She liked to roam around the antique shops of Bristol looking for bargains. When shopkeepers saw Elsie come through the door, they would raise their prices, because they all knew her son was rich, but Elsie habitually, mercilessly, bargained them down. "She did her own marketing and shopping until she went into the nursing home," Grant said. "She didn't want to owe a soul."

Elsie's correspondence of the 1960s is similar in content to her correspondence of the 1930s and 1940s. A telegram might wish her son a Happy New Year but conclude DISAPPOINTED NOT SEEING YOU AM BETTER NOW STILL SAME. Her letters are in a shakier handwriting, and the sentences have little connection to each other: "I went and seen The Films of Charlie Chaplin at the Embassy Cinema, wanted a laugh it was one of his silent Films, I laughed until my Tears running down my face. The house was packed. . . . I should be much happier if I had someone like Mr. Thomas at hand, to talk to, I am happier when shopping away from this house."

The week of her wedding anniversary in 1961, she sent her son a telegram: WEDDING DAY 30/5/98 TERRIBLE LIFE THROUGH ONE MAN IN MY LIFE. A later letter continued the theme: "You see Archie darling your Father have been the only one man in my life [either "desired" or "deserved"] me no man have put asunder I can prove it by body, and you have *all*. You have been born from a true mother I ought to have another man in my life."

After Christmas in 1961, Grant wrote his mother a note of thanks, putting into words what he found difficult to express face-to-face: "for bringing me into the world, and for giving me the great gift of life, and for the love you've had for me . . . and which I now offer you in return; because even if sometimes we have been unable to express the extent of our love to each other, we must have realized that it was there, at all times, beneath every other emotion."

Grant enjoyed Elsie as far as he was able; he told a funny story about her asking him why he didn't do something about his hair. What's wrong with it? he wanted to know. She replied that he should dye it, that everyone dyed their hair. When he said he wasn't going to do that, his mother finally confessed that her son's white hair made her feel elderly.

In October 1963, Grant financed a trip to London for Elsie as well as Eric and Maggie Leach. By the following summer, Elsie was eighty-seven years old and it was increasingly obvious that she could no longer live alone. Eric was concerned about her habit of putting an electric heater on the table by her bed, which resulted in dizzy spells. "Her behavior had become unpredictable," Dr. Francis Page remembered, so he convinced her to move into the Chesterfield, an assisted living facility in Bristol.

Elsie remained physically sturdy, actively resisted medical examinations, and a lot of other things besides. "She did not know how to give affection," said her son, "and she did not know how to receive it either. I tried to give her so many things, but her answer was always the same: 'Why would I want that? Don't spend your money on me!'"

Once a year Grant would fly to London and drive the two hours to Bristol, usually staying at the Grand Spa Hotel. He would always bring gifts, and, if his visit was around her birthday, daffodils. When he came back from the visit he would be quiet, with a grim look on his face. Occasionally, he would talk about what had transpired.

"What do you want from me now?" Elsie asked once. Nothing, he explained. "It's because I love you that I come and see you."

"Oh, you . . ." she would reply, as if she saw through what she believed to be his manipulations. Once in a while he would take a sentimental journey around Bristol. He would often stop at the Hippodrome, where he had first felt the siren call of the theater, and that would reliably cheer him up.

Between Grant's visits, Dr. Page would send him letters reporting on his mother. Usually Page accentuated the positive. "I have just come from a delightful tea party with your Mother! It was amusing and entertaining with no references to [persecution,] other men or anything abnormal."

Other visits were a little grimmer, as in a letter datelined Boxing Day 1965, when the doctor told Grant that he found cheering her up very hard work. "She said she wouldn't open the stocking even tho she had managed to undo the Cherry Brandy which was well down." In another letter, Page informed Grant that "She is far less abnormal than many other . . . men and women with whom I have dealings. She has her little moods and occasionally barricades her bedroom door at night, but I virtually never see anything other than the mildest abnormality of memory or understanding which would pass almost unnoticed in others of her age."

Elsie would take a walk every day, and Dr. Page took her for rides in the country, sometimes for two or three hours. Occasionally she would pay Page for his services, and he would accept the money rather than provoke an argument. She failed to realize that Page was her doctor and did not remember him from one visit to another. Elsie always asked his name so she could tell Archie all about him. On balance, Grant found Elsie's obstinance, her utterly unyielding nature, admirable. (Dyan Cannon described Elsie's psyche as having "the strength of a 20-mule team.")

Dr. Page believed that Elsie had been diagnosed as a chronic paranoid schizophrenic decades earlier, and he more or less concurred. Of course, Elsie's life experience had convinced her that paranoia was justified. Generally, she would order the doctors at the assisted living facility to get flowers out of her room. She tended to think her son was whatever he had most recently played in the movies. "He's a much better doctor than any of the doctors here," she would say.

Page noted how critical she was toward her son, treating him like a misbehaving child, which led to him acting like a child.

Grant's relationship with Eric and Maggie Leach was more conventionally familial. He presciently wrote them about how it would take many years for soccer to replace the American enthusiasm for baseball, golf, or basketball, but also said that he would be willing to invest in any American soccer franchise that offered stock. None of which ameliorated his passion for baseball, which he illustrated by enthusiastically describing the wonders of Nolan Ryan's fastball. "Wish you'd come over and see a game or two," Grant wrote Eric. "Marvelous!"

They stayed in touch to the end of Eric's life, with Grant chiding Eric about making a will, telling him that he had made his years ago and except for some minor changes, it remained just about the same. Grant would enclose clippings from the *Los Angeles Times*, such as one that illustrated what he called "the same deficit spending, labor lazy, over-staffed, wasteful, bureaucratic government road." After Eric died, Grant was solicitous of Maggie, who had a full roster of her own health problems. He tried to calm her anxiety by assuring her he had no intention of abandoning her. "Money. You are, understandably, worried about money. Well, stop worrying. *You'll* do the best you can. *I'll* do the best I can."

IN THE SPRING OF 1965, Alfred Hitchcock and Grant went to a Dodgers game. Hitchcock was wondering whether it would be worthwhile to try to lure Grant into *Torn Curtain*. There was the matter of Grant's now expected ownership of the negative, which Hitchcock didn't like, even though Lew Wasserman might have allowed it. But Grant told Hitchcock that he'd committed to a picture at Columbia that was going to shoot in the fall, and he was going to retire after that. Hitchcock hired Paul Newman for *Torn Curtain*, which turned out to be one of his worst pictures; following on the heels of *Marnie*, it provided irrefutable proof that the director was in decline.

The project at Columbia was called *Walk, Don't Run*. It began as a simple updating of *The More the Merrier*, an amusing George Stevens romantic comedy about the housing shortage during World War II that had starred Joel McCrea, Jean Arthur, and Charles Coburn. Looking around for a suitably modern equivalent, the studio landed on the Tokyo Olympics. Initially, Columbia was interested in Fredric March, Fred Astaire, Bing Crosby, or Spencer Tracy for the Coburn part, but then Charles Walters was hired to direct, and he thought Grant would be interesting playing the part of a matchmaker with no romantic interest in the female character.

But there were problems, mainly with the script. "I worked for eight months, with three sets of writer," said Walters, "but the whole thing wouldn't mix." Nevertheless, Columbia committed to a month of location work in Japan. As a means of spiking interest, Grant announced that *Walk, Don't Run* would be his last film, and he chose Samantha Eggar and Jim Hutton to play the young couple.

While plans for the film firmed up, Grant made his decision about Dyan. They married on July 22, 1965. He told her in an offhand manner that the site would be Las Vegas. Their host was Charlie Rich, who ran the Dunes Hotel and had offered to front the wedding as his present to the couple.

They were both nervous. A few minutes before the wedding, Cannon knocked on his door for some consolation. He looked at her, arms at his side, then said, "What the hell did you do to your nails? They're gaudy, Dyan. It's just not flattering."

In so many ways, he was his mother's son.

Grant and Cannon honeymooned at John Huston's castle in Ireland, and after that it was time to visit Elsie again, which brought about the usual deflation on Grant's part. "Cary," his new wife told him, "we're not visiting a grave. We're visiting Elsie. Whatever mood she's in, just be grateful she's *alive.*" When they got there, Grant told his mother that he and Dyan were now married. "Congratulations, Betsy," she said. "It's *Dyan*, Elsie," they replied in tandem.

As they settled into their marriage, Grant's familiar pattern reasserted itself. He lived an isolated life, rarely calling anybody but Stanley Fox. If the phone rang, it was usually for Cannon. When Grant was around the house he would go barefoot and watch TV. Sometimes he was agreeable and sometimes he wasn't.

"Cary's shell opened and closed and opened and closed," was the way Cannon remembered it. "He wasn't so much temperamental as he was withdrawn, but his moods shifted without warning, or apparent cause. It was like watching TV with someone who was always changing the channel; you were never tuned into the same show long enough to get comfortable." Conversely, just when it seemed the wire was shorting out, the light came on full strength again.

Grant returned to the idea of Cannon trying more LSD but she refused. She was pregnant and she didn't want the baby to have two heads. Grant was still seeing Dr. Hartman, and would occasionally drop acid at home, without supervision, but with a Valium nearby in case things took a dark turn.

The *Walk, Don't Run* company arrived in Japan in September 1965. Most of the athletic competition, with Grant competing in a heel to toe walk, was captured with hidden cameras. Samantha Eggar found Grant fascinating. "Cary insisted that I had to change my hair, and he chose my dress just as he bought his own props. He was on top of everything. He really didn't open up personally at all, even though I was a friend of Dyan's."

After the location work, the company returned to Hollywood to shoot the interiors. One of the actors joining the production was George Takei, just before he was cast as Mr. Sulu on *Star Trek*. Takei was working on a dissertation for his master's at UCLA and brought his books to the set. Grant appreciated both Takei and his effort and responded with practiced self-deprecation.

"You're such a studious young man, George," Grant observed. "Study, study, study. Why do you want to be a smart actor when all you need to be is dumb and handsome like me?"

"Well," said Takei, "since I'm not as handsome as you, I thought I'd hedge my bet by trying to be a bit educated."

"Good idea. Get educated. You'll be so smart that you'll become a producer. And if you're a really smart producer, you'll be paying me millions of dollars to act in your movies. Study on, I say."

When *Walk, Don't Run* was released in June of 1966, the response was mild. Not a flop, not a hit, it returned $5.1 million in worldwide rentals to Columbia. Grant considered it a disappointment on all counts; one of his few comments about the picture was "I can take a hint!" It was and is a halfhearted, unworthy farewell for its star, hampered by the fact that there is far more of a sexual charge between Eggar and Grant than between Eggar and Hutton, a fact the narrative studiously ignores. The film offers the weird premise that a man in his sixties is irrelevant in a romantic comedy except as a helpful matchmaker for the young lovers—a premise deriving from its squeamish star.

Even more damaging is the fact that *Walk, Don't Run* drones on for an interminable 114 minutes. While Grant's timing is intact, he's defeated by Charles Walters's nonstop succession of flaccid medium shots. To keep himself amused, Grant resorts to in-jokes—humming the musical themes from other, better Cary Grant movies—*Charade* and *An Affair to Remember*. *Walk, Don't Run* offers only mild smiles amidst a general lack of energy and invention. It is something that can be said of very few Grant movies—it's dull.

The last scene shows Grant, on a soundstage replica of a Tokyo street, standing beside a taxi that will take him to the airport and home. He smiles up at a pair of Japanese children his character has befriended, blows a kiss, then looks around a movie set for the last time and waves farewell.

Some great stars go out with a definitive statement of their value and meaning—Gable in *The Misfits*, Wayne in *The Shootist*, Lancaster in *Field of Dreams*. Others—Gary Cooper, Cary Grant—aren't so fortunate.

ALL SEVEN POUNDS AND NINE OUNCES of Jennifer Grant was born on February 26, 1966, seven months after Grant and Dyan Cannon were married. From the beginning, Grant was a doting, hands-on father. He had waited a lifetime for this experience and he was not about to miss a moment. He diapered Jennifer himself, and he lined his bedroom with pictures of her. Telephone calls to friends about the glory of his child could go on for an hour, and there was always a stack of photos of Jennifer in his pocket.

But beneath the surface exaltation, he was still beset by alternating waves of need and fear. When Cannon went to the hospital to give birth, Grant gave away her dog, a Yorkie named Bangs. Grant didn't tell her until she arrived back home with Jennifer, whereupon she naturally became distraught. "Bangs is part of our family," she yelled at Grant. "How can you give away *family*? And how could you give away something that belonged to me without talking to me about it?"

"Animals can experience extreme jealousy around newborns," Grant told her, in the patient, patronizing tone that eventually became known as mansplaining, which he tended to adopt whenever he wanted to get his way with a woman. "They can undergo profound personality changes."

"You had no right, Cary! No right!"

It was a classic character reveal. Grant would never have played a movie scene where he gave away his wife's dog, because it would alienate the audience. But in life fear nudged him toward behavior he was helpless to resist.

Cannon's mother told her that she had to let it go for the sake of her marriage and her daughter. "That was the beginning of the end," said Cannon retrospectively. "I honestly don't think that he thought about it past Jennifer and her safety. You see, he wasn't attached to animals, so the dog was abandoned just like Cary had been. It was a principle that went across the board. The movies make Gods out of people. Or maybe it's that we make Gods out of people, and what we eventually find out is that we all have stuff to work through. He had stuff to work through, just as I did. I was so young; I wish I could have helped more."

The truth was that Grant and Cannon were hopelessly mismatched. Grant believed fervently in moderation, as long as it was his within his definition of the term, while his young wife, as their daughter would observe, "Was never a moderate gal. Why have a bite of ice cream when we bought a quart?"

And so it began all over again—the nitpicking, the attempt to mold a grown woman into something he wanted and she didn't. Resistance would stimulate obstinance, and a resulting emotional distance. After a while, Cannon began to feel like an automaton. "I surrendered my very mind to Cary and let him do the thinking for me—except he never really let me in on the actual thinking process. I only got the commandments that came from the thinking, and the less they made sense to me, the more I obeyed them without question." Cannon would come to believe that what frightened Grant was emotional intimacy, which he didn't trust because in his experience it was used as leverage for manipulation, then quickly followed by abandonment.

A damaged child is always a damaged child.

"He was abandoned," said Cannon,

and I don't think he ever healed that in his heart. He felt it would happen to him in every relationship, and if it didn't happen on its own he would make it happen. It's an interesting thing. I once heard Princess Diana say that she never felt loved. But when she passed, the entire world mourned. But it doesn't matter how many people profess love for you if you haven't found it at its source.

I've really thought about all this. Look, I was a nice-looking girl, but there were girls in this town who were drop-dead gorgeous. *What was it about me that attracted him?* Because when he got it he tried to change it. He had a horrible, horrific childhood, and I think it was the hunger and need for approval and love that really drove him. So the conclusion I came to is that he wanted someone to trust. Really trust. And he told me more than once that I was the only woman he ever knew who he could trust enough to have a child.

And he was right. He could trust me. And that's why what happened was such a shattering experience.

The first time Grant and his wife brought Jennifer to Bristol, Elsie responded well. She was tender and loving and cuddled the baby, "transforming into 87 pounds of pure grandmotherly affection," her daughter-in-law remembered. As she passed Jennifer back to her mother she said, "Don't bring her around too often. I'm afraid I'll fall in love with her, and it'll make me too sad when you take her away from me." Dyan told her she should come and stay with them in California. Elsie thought that was a very nice offer. "Thank you, Betsy," she said.

Back at the hotel, Grant was upset. "Why couldn't you confer with me before you invited my mother to come and stay with us?" Cannon responded by saying that he did everything possible for his mother, except the most obvious thing—"to bring her into your life—our lives!"

"I don't expect you to understand. I don't think anyone can."

"Do you love your mother, Cary?"

"Of course."

"Do you believe she loves you?"

A long pause.

"I think she loved Archie."

Besides Grant's (understandable) wariness around his mother, the underlying problem was that Elsie's mental state meant she was unable to apprehend her son's reality. Charlie Chaplin had processed a similar situation with his mentally infirm mother by buying her a house in Santa Monica and hiring a married couple to live with her twenty-four hours a day. She was close by, but he seldom visited because Hannah Chaplin thought her son was Jesus Christ. Seeing her upset Chaplin terribly. But Grant felt obligated to try to make up for those lost years when Elsie had been institutionalized and did his level best to be a dutiful, attentive son.

After Grant and Cannon got back to California and attended a party celebrating the wedding anniversary of Rosalind Russell and Frederick Brisson, they went through a particularly arduous patch. One day Grant trailed Dyan around the house pointing out everything that was wrong with the way she ran the house. She turned the doorknobs and handles too hard, or not hard enough. She was ruining the stove by being too rough with the switches. She hadn't learned to treat things with respect, because she had no respect for herself, or for him, or for anybody else.

Once again Cannon capitulated and they began what she remembered as about a dozen LSD trips in the house, without monitoring. They took their trips on Saturdays, and the results were initially not bad, although Cannon told her husband that she still didn't know what she was supposed to be getting out of the experience.

"Dyan, don't try to interpret it. Just *experience* it."

It didn't help. Nothing helped. And one day Stanley Fox came to the house when Grant was at Universal. "He thinks it might be best if you two separated," Fox told the stunned Cannon. "He wants a divorce." After a moment to catch her breath, Cannon asked him, "Stanley, what kind of a man would ask another man to go to his home and tell his wife that he wants a divorce?"

"Cary Grant's Rift Reported," was the headline in the *Los Angeles Herald-Examiner* on January 24, 1967. They tried a reconciliation. That June, Grant recorded a song by Peggy Lee and Cy Coleman called "Christmas Lullaby" to be released at Christmas, with any profits earmarked for the Motion Picture Relief Fund. He Rex Harrisoned his way through the song, about the emotions a devoted father experiences watching his child sleep. Given the very specific emotions of the song, it was obviously written to order. (Coleman had written a song for *Father Goose* and adored Grant and his particular rhythm; as the songwriter put it, "He walks to the tempo of an English Music Hall tune.")

Cannon tried LSD once more. It turned dark and pitted and she told her husband she would never take the drug again. But Grant tried, as he understood trying, even though he didn't really want her working, because that would interfere with her caring for Jennifer. He ran a script based on Elaine Dundy's novel *The Old Man and Me* past her, and offered to make it with her as his costar. She recognized a desperation move when she saw it, and told him she didn't think it was a good idea.

"I don't know if I have another divorce left in me," he told her.

Cannon filed for divorce in August.

The divorce was arduous and ugly and played out in the papers in excruciating detail, largely because of the stakes: custody of Jennifer. Dyan testified about Grant's "outlandish, irrational and hostile" conduct, which she ascribed to LSD. "I couldn't please him no matter what I'd do or say. He criticized everything I did—the way I carried the baby, the way I fed the baby, the way I dressed and the way I dressed the baby. I couldn't do anything right." She also said that he was a domestic tyrant prone to fits of rage, that he spanked her. She testified that he was taking LSD as late as February 1967, when he called her and told her he was on a trip.

Grant agreed to be examined by two psychiatrists. Dr. Judd Marmor, a shrink to the stars, examined Grant and reported that he had acknowledged spanking his wife for what Grant termed "reasonable and adequate causes." Marmor nevertheless concluded that Grant was entirely rational and perfectly capable of being a competent father. Grant did not testify because he was in the hospital with broken ribs from an auto accident.

In the end, Dyan was granted custody of her daughter and $2,500 a month in alimony for six months, $1,750 for the next eighteen months, and $1,000 a month for the year after that. She got an additional $1,500 a month for child support. The alimony was modest, the probable result of Cannon's soon-to-be burgeoning movie career. Grant was entitled to only sixty days of custody per year, and every other holiday and birthday.

"The rhythm to my parents' post-divorce relationship was staccato," observed Jennifer Grant. "They fought. And if they weren't fighting, they were at best curt with each other."

The squabbling went on for years—over the schools Jennifer attended, over vacations, over houses, over the amount of time Grant could spend with his daughter. Grant evidently never entirely gave up hope of gaining custody, even though he never could bring himself to sling mud, which is what would have been necessary. Grant felt that his visitation privileges were skimpy, and he glumly complained to Peter Bogdanovich, "The women always win in the end."

He was concerned about the inevitable grudges between a divorced husband and wife, but the truth was he and Dyan didn't really like each other very much—Grant rarely used her name, generally referring to her as "Jennifer's mother." He was concerned that Jennifer would pick up the signals and turn on them both.

Eventually, things evened out. "We both wanted it to be cordial for Jennifer, and it was," Cannon said. "We spent a couple of holidays together, and that was nice—good for her and for all of us. I told Jennifer that the divorce was not her fault, because so many kids think that. I told her that 'It's good you love your daddy so much, because he loves you so much. Love him as much as you want, the more the better.' And I really felt that way. I gave her permission to love everybody she wanted to love, [and] he was easy to love."

Years later, someone asked Grant why he chose scripts so well and wives so badly. "In a script, I know what I'm looking for," he replied. "In a wife, I guess I don't."

GRANT HAD EARNED $300,000 in salary for *Walk, Don't Run*. Although Grant and Stanley Fox produced the picture, Columbia was either unable or unwilling to agree to a reversion of the negative to them. The reason was probably because *Walk, Don't Run* was a remake of George Stevens's *The More the Merrier*, and Columbia would have had to include the story rights to the original in the deal, which would have tied up showings of the Stevens Picture. Columbia asked if perhaps Grant would be interested in the negative of some other picture in order to settle the deal. Grant chose *Penny Serenade*, but the handoff was complicated by the fact that George Stevens owned 15 percent of that movie. Columbia offered Stevens a lowball $5,000 for his 15 percent and Stevens said no. One way or another, the deal was completed and Grant became the owner of *Penny Serenade*.

Grant was going through one of his periodic spasms of financial paranoia, the trigger being a bill from his mother's doctor for about £500. Grant bridled at the bill, which resulted in his solicitor sending a letter to the doctor. "The only basis for assessing fees I have been able to find is that of time," wrote Dr. Page in explanation. "I see Mrs. Leach about once a week, sometimes more, sometimes less if I am too busy." He went on to say that the normal weekly charge for long-term medical care of a patient such as Mrs. Leach was five guineas, and he had charged Grant somewhat less than that, even though his services extended far beyond conventional house calls. Page was clearly embarrassed by the complaint and finally offered to reduce his bill to half of the original, or nothing at all if Grant so wished.

In a follow-up letter, Page submitted a new, presumably lower bill, then asked Grant's solicitor to send any further correspondence to his office, "as my wife hates even more than I any monetary discussions." After that flare-up, the relationship resumed on Grant's more economical terms, with Grant even offering to host the doctor and his wife at his house in Beverly Hills if they cared to visit.

Another reason for Grant's financial panic was alluded to in a letter to Eric and Maggie Leach. He asked them to "*Eke* a bit, if you can. This year's bills so far (babies are astonishingly expensive; nurse too) are staggering my accountant and me." He enclosed a check reimbursing them for taking his mother to Torquay, then, oblivious to the irony, asked if they had made any progress in selling the Rolls-Royce he kept in London.

Perhaps some of the discontent was caused by *Walk, Don't Run*, which was not going to return much, if anything, in the way of profits. Despite his announced retirement, Grant was still tentatively thinking about projects. He sent *The Old Man and Me* to Elizabeth Taylor in June 1967. Richard Burton thought the script was good, not to mention commercial, especially if Grant costarred, as was being suggested. Grant cabled Burton that he would only do the picture if Burton directed. "He must be frightened of [Taylor] or something," Burton wrote in his diary. "Perhaps he's a little strange in the head."

But there would be no more Cary Grant movies, not then, not ever, although offers arrived with regularity. Right after *Walk, Don't Run*, Walter Mirisch offered him *Fitzwilly*, an archaic story about an impoverished old lady kept afloat by cons perpetrated by her loyal butler. Grant couldn't have been thrilled by the idea of playing a butler, but he took a meeting with Mirisch anyway. "I reminded him that this was a role that didn't compel any kind of specious relationship for him with a young woman," remembered Mirisch, "but he replied that—although the story sounded charming to him and he wished me great luck with the picture—it would have to be done without him." The picture was made with Dick Van Dyke and proved a critical and commercial disappointment.

In one of Grant's notebooks, he wrote, "The worthiest of men retire from the world." It was a quote, but he could never find out who said it. Nevertheless, it summed up his decision to walk away from the movie business at the age of sixty-two. His friends and associates spent years trying to figure out why a supremely talented man would abandon his profession while still in full possession of his looks and talent. He was insistent and unyielding about leaving his old life behind, except when he wasn't. It all depended on his mood.

"I got tired of getting up at six o'clock and tripping over all those cables and drinking coffee out of Styrofoam cups," said Grant. "It's not as glamorous as you might think. You can never go back. It's not possible. I could make another film, but I'd be playing a different man. People are used to me as a certain kind of fellow, and I can't make that kind of film anymore."

As far as making more movies, "Who the deuce would go to see me? I suppose I could play an old banker or a character in a wheelchair or something—one need not be ashamed about being old, and there are great roles for older actors always—but I've just disassociated myself from that world."

Dyan Cannon would say that "He just got tired of it. 'I've been there and I don't want to do it anymore,' he said. It was something I never understood. Acting got him everything he thought he wanted, and he'd done it for many years. It's true that he was greatly concerned about being so much older than his leading ladies. In the end, he didn't want the muss and fuss of it anymore."

Privately, he would allude to the abortive comeback attempts of Mae West and Jean Arthur. West made a heralded return with *Myra Breckinridge* in 1970 and Grant went to see the movie out of curiosity, only to leave after twenty minutes. He termed the film "execrable." As for Jean Arthur, after *Shane* she had quit movies, only to attempt a comeback in 1966 in a CBS sitcom that quickly folded. Grant was also dismayed at the sad state of Bette Davis and Olivia de Havilland in the 1960s. He was particularly appalled by *Lady in a Cage*, an exploitation film in which de Havilland was terrorized by young thugs. Better not to work, he thought, than work in demeaning trash. "No one will say I didn't know when to get off the Hollywood trolley."

". . . The Hollywood trolley . . ." It was Grant's old metaphor about there being only so many seats on the trolley; if someone new was going to get a seat, that meant someone else, someone older, was being squeezed onto the street. Grant preferred to make his own judgment about when to give up his seat. Garbo, he would say, had the right idea. "If she came back now, it just wouldn't be the same. And the public wouldn't like it if she tried, believe me." Besides, the middling commercial responses to both *Father Goose* and *Walk, Don't Run* were not exactly arguments for hanging around.

And yet every once in a while he would make a feint in the direction of work. Talking to one reporter in 1975, he would begin by asserting his permanent retiree status by saying, "I had enjoyed a full career. What's the old cliché? There's a time to start and a time to stop. I figured I'd reached that point." Then a few minutes later he would flatly contradict himself: "If a really good movie came along with the sort of role for a man of my age that I could play, chances are I might very well accept it."

Almost alone among his friends, Harold Lloyd understood his decision. "Harold had a conversation with Cary about why he retired," said Sue Lloyd. " 'Leave it to the younger people,' Cary said. 'I've been there, I've done it. It wasn't fun anymore.' And Harold agreed; he said, 'There are other things to do in life. There are other adventures. You don't have to keep doing just one thing.' "

Peter Bogdanovich concurred. "It had to do with his looks. I said something once about all these years I'd known him and he had never met my daughters. He said, 'Well, you don't want to frighten the poor things, do you? I mean, they expect to see Cary Grant and in comes this old man in a wheelchair.'

"Oh come on, Cary, you look great."

" 'I don't want to frighten them.' "

The agent Irving Lazar was more specific, saying, "I think he was a great professional who felt he had done as much as he could. . . . He wanted to be remembered as a leading man, the best of his kind, and didn't want to get into movies which he felt were inferior to the ones he had made."

This seems close to the truth—as a discerning, not to mention demanding, critic of his own work, Grant must have realized that *The Grass Is Greener, That Touch of Mink, Father Goose*, and *Walk, Don't Run* were never going to be placed on the same shelf as *Bringing Up Baby, His Girl Friday*, or *North by Northwest*.

With the decision to quit came distance, which bred a sourness about the business in which he had spent his creative life—movies don't really add up to much, he would grumble. What this meant was that he had to justify his decision emotionally, which in practice meant that he began to deride his former profession in the hope that the audience would move on just as he had. "I was never interested in acting in films," he told *The New York Times*. "I was interested in the economics of the business."

And there was another issue. Comedy is a dance on a high wire, and skilled practitioners in Grant's preferred mode were getting thin on the ground. Leo McCarey was retired, Hitchcock was in decline, and Hawks was retreating to the sure thing of John Wayne.*

Besides that, comedy in the movies is quite difficult, Grant claimed, "unlike theater. In my opinion there is no valid excuse for an unamusing play. Consider the time there is for rehearsal and tryout. Actors have the opportunity to test their lines before many different audiences. The author can change his whole play if need be. But once we put a comedy on film we've had it."

Finally, there was the matter of a lack of passion projects. Grant had always been able to step back and observe the components of a film and make a clinical judgment as to the odds of its success. He wasn't always right, but his batting average was extremely high. It was true that his leading man days were inexorably drawing to a close, and he didn't want to spend the rest of his life lunging after foxy grandpa parts in films as mediocre as *Walk, Don't Run*.

Most leading men face the same problem; the smart ones downshift into character parts where the point is not getting the girl (Burt Lancaster), or switch to producing and directing (Clint Eastwood). But

---

* In 1965, Hal Roach showed up hale and hearty at Stan Laurel's funeral, charging down the aisle of the church at Forest Lawn as if it was 1930. But Leo McCarey, six years younger than Roach, shuffled into the church like a decrepit old man. Watching the two men, the actress Anita Garvin could only wonder at what alcohol had wrought. McCarey died in 1969 at the age of seventy-one. Hal Roach lived to be one hundred.

producing for Grant had always been more of a means to an end—a way to keep more of the money—than a genuinely creative endeavor.

So it made sense to step back and try to learn to do the one thing that had always hovered just beyond his reach: relax, and focus on his one true passion project, Jennifer, or, as he often referred to her, "my best production." "If I had known then what I know now," he told one reporter, "if I had not been so utterly stupid and selfish—I would have had a hundred children and I would have built a ranch to keep them on."

He began to fill his time with travel. He enjoyed New York, and made it a point to see the current shows. He went to see the Gwen Verdon musical *Sweet Charity*, based on Fellini's *Nights of Cabiria*, and responded to a duality that others often saw in him.

"You are the strangest actor I've ever watched," he told Verdon when he went backstage.

"Why?"

"Because when you play a scene where you're just so happy, I cry. And when you play a scene where it's very sad, I laugh."

Years after the MCA debacle regarding a Grant TV series, Jack Haley Jr. suggested a TV special about Grant's career. He needn't worry about a speech, Haley said; everything would be scripted by high-end professionals. Grant said no, then backtracked and said if he was paid a million dollars, he might think about it. Haley went to work and six weeks later he had an offer from CBS that included a million-dollar fee, but Grant backed off yet again.

Eventually, he would accept the Kennedy Center Honors, probably because it didn't require a speech. Accompanying the event itself was a quiet dinner at the White House, with President and Mrs. Reagan, James and Gloria Stewart, Douglas and Mary Lee Fairbanks, Audrey Hepburn and Rob Wolders, and Reagan's friend Jerry Zipkin. The Kennedy Center appearance shook loose even more interest in him, which resulted in him having to fend off Barbara Walters, who wanted to feature him on one of her celebrity specials. "Yes, she has asked me, and I said no," he said with a touch of asperity. "I'm not selling anything, not running for office. I don't want to expose my own ignorance to all those people that Barbara plays to."

He made occasional appearances at the Academy Awards to present an award to a friend. His fear of an unscripted screwup, of appearing as something less than the Cary Grant of the movies, kept him from being able to relax without the security of a script. But when the Motion Picture Academy voted him an Honorary Oscar in 1970 he sucked it up and accepted the award.

Grant's attitude toward the Oscars favored the way it used to be. "It was a *private* affair, you see—no *tele*vision, of course, no *radio* even—just a group of friends giving each other a party. Because, you know, there *is* something a little embarrassing about all these wealthy people publicly con*grat*ulating each other."

The award ceremony was on April 7, 1970. Frank Sinatra introduced Grant, who was met with a thunderous standing ovation. He thanked the "extraordinary men" who had put up with him: "Howard Hawks, Hitchcock, the late Leo McCarey, George Stevens, George Cukor and Stanley Donen. Oh, and the writers, Philip Barry, Dore Schary, Bob Sherwood, Ben Hecht, dear Clifford Odets, Sidney Sheldon and, more recently, Stanley Shapiro and Peter Stone. . . .

"And now, before I leave, I want to thank all of you very much for signifying your approval of this. I shall cherish it until I die . . . because . . . probably no greater honor can come to any man than the respect of his colleagues."*

A few years after the award he reminisced about the experience.

When everyone stood up I was all at sea. I thought for a moment I was seeing things. I was so taken back, I don't know how I delivered my speech. I almost burst into tears. It was difficult to bear up emotionally. Then I looked at Frank Sinatra who had a mischievous gleam in his eye and it pulled me together. I guess he realized how deeply affected I was. I've made about 65 movies [actually 73], but in none of them witnessed such a spontaneous reaction on the set or otherwise. It is a wonderful thing to know that others respond to you with warmth and affection. I was most honored and touched.

---

* The inscription on the Oscar reads:
TO CARY GRANT
for his unique mastery
of the art of screen acting
with the respect and affection
of his colleagues.

What startled him was how he had blanked out on some of the scenes in the montage that preceded his award. "In some of them I couldn't even remember being on a particular set or making a particular scene. Some I do. There were some that were very pleasant. I may have enjoyed working with a particular leading lady. But often I don't even remember being there."

An honorary award is usually a deathbed affair given to people who have been overlooked or underappreciated. Neither was exactly the case with Grant—he had had the adoration of critics and audiences alike for nearly forty years, and made it look easy in the process, which was the underlying problem that led to his lack of official awards. "The leading men who get awards have to walk with a limp or act retarded," Billy Wilder snorted. "They don't notice the guy who does all the hard work. . . . You can't just open a drawer beautifully and take out a tie and put on a jacket. You have to take out a gun! You have to be afflicted. Then they notice you."

In OCTOBER OF 1969, Grant attended a screening of *Bringing Up Baby* at the Academy Theater at Beverly and Doheny. It was part of a series of screenings with a star, director, or, as a last resort, the writer of a legendary film who would take questions after the film.

Grant walked down from the back of the theater quickly, almost at a run. He had a stool to sit on, and he kept turning it out of nerves. He talked fast, held the mike in both hands as if it was a prayer object, occasionally tugged at his left ear as he answered questions.

His primary response to the film was wonder at Kate Hepburn's willingness to take so many falls. "Kate, she'd fall anywhere, and she'd trust me. Why I don't know. I started as an acrobat, you know. She did it. Trusted me utterly. Incredible girl. And then she told everybody she taught me."

In the audience was a young writer named John Sacret Young, who remembered that Grant was

> definitely not comfortable. He had a nervous energy that may have been a kind of comfortable because it was him performing. He was full-on Cary, not Archie, but Archie was there, however occluded

by his fantastic Cary creation. There was a remarkable discomfort, like an aura, around the man who on film and in performance seemed often the ultimate in grace. He couldn't keep still. The way the microphone was held, the turning of the stool. The burners were lit and firing, an electricity that was captivating, but I wouldn't be surprised if he came down hard in the aftermath.

Grant's relationship with Universal gradually corroded, as it was bound to if he wasn't making any movies. In 1969, Grant and Stanley Donen sued the studio for $8.8 million on the grounds that Universal hadn't exhausted the commercial television potential of the pictures they had made for the studio. Later that year, the studio informed him that they needed his bungalow, and Grant gave up his filmmaking home.

It was typical of the New Hollywood, or, for that matter, the Old Hollywood: they want you desperately until they don't want you at all. When Ross Hunter produced *Airport*, Lew Wasserman had Hunter's house outfitted with a beautiful projection room, and even gave him a Renoir. After Hunter left the studio, Universal sent over a crew to rip out the projection room and repossess the Renoir, which Wasserman had been careful to keep in his name. Wasserman did the same thing when Rock Hudson left Universal.

Hunter decamped to Columbia to produce *40 Carats* with Audrey Hepburn. But Hepburn's husband was playing around on her and she didn't want to leave Europe, while Columbia didn't want to spend the extra money to shoot the film overseas.

And thus begins a gorgeous tale of pure Hollywood lunacy.

With *40 Carats* gone from Hunter's docket—Columbia would eventually make it with Liv Ullmann, who Hunter correctly thought was too young—the producer was looking for a project, something intimate that would appeal to women. Grant suggested a remake of *Penny Serenade*, which now Grant owned but didn't particularly want. A remake would put some money in Grant's pocket and, if he managed the deal right, take the property off his hands completely. He offered to lend Hunter his personal print of the film, so Hunter set up a party at his house to look at the movie.

As it happened, Grant was on an airplane the day of the screening, and when Hunter called for the print, Grant's secretary said he couldn't possibly send the print over without Grant's permission. Hunter tried to find another print of *Penny Serenade*, but it couldn't be done on such short notice. A friend of Hunter's was sent over to Columbia to look at the 16mm rental prints and bring something back. He grabbed a print of Frank Capra's *Lost Horizon*. That's what they showed at the party, which promptly fired up Hunter with the idea of a remake. No, even better—a musical remake, with a score by Burt Bacharach and Hal David!

The result was one of the resounding disasters of the era. At the premiere, after the film ended Merle Oberon was so appalled she asked to be lifted over the seats to avoid having to walk up the aisle and speak to Hunter. At the glum after-party, a desperate Hunter devised a face-saving story: Columbia had attached his name to the project because it needed a commercial push. Ross Hunter never made another theatrical film.

Careers ruined, tens of millions of dollars lost, all because Cary Grant was on an airplane. If Grant had ever given any thought of going back to the movie business, this intricately interlocking catastrophe that could have been devised for a brutalist David Mamet farce would have dissuaded him.

NONE OF THE CHARGES THAT WERE LEVELED against Grant during the divorce from Dyan Cannon affected his popularity with the public in the least. People read the stories, nodded, and went back to gazing at pictures of him and wishing he'd make more movies. He had long resided in that special group of actors who were more than actors; they were members of the audience's extended family. Any evidence to the contrary was irrelevant.

After his fourth divorce, Grant contented himself for a time with short-term affairs of varying degrees of seriousness. Howard Hawks would occasionally check in, asking how he was doing with women. "Better than ever," Grant would say.

For a time Grant was involved with a woman about town named Cynthia Bouron, who gave birth to a baby girl in March 1970 that she claimed was fathered by Grant. She named Grant as the father on the birth certificate and filed a paternity suit, which was dismissed after Bouron refused to allow a blood test. Bouron's life was a train wreck; she was murdered in November 1973.

Another relationship was with the widow of the agent and producer Charles Feldman, who had married her only a few months before his death. Her dependence on Grant gradually increased, which annoyed him, because, as William Weaver, Grant's secretary in this period, would note, "Grant always found dependency difficult." He edged away.

"I never left any of my wives," he would say. "They all left me." Maureen Donaldson, one of his girlfriends from this period, would insist that what really happened was that "he subconsciously pushed them into leaving or 'abandoning' him. Of course, he never admitted that to me—and I sincerely doubt to himself either." Donaldson too eventually had to leave.

With the exception of Dyan Cannon, Grant's wives had always been distinguished by their lack of vocation. And perhaps that lack had been an attraction for Grant, a subliminal part of a character that wished to dominate without somehow fostering dependency.

Virginia Cherrill had driven Charlie Chaplin mad with her night-clubbing and general lack of interest in acting; Barbara Hutton's only occupation had been spending money; Betsy Drake gave up acting, then gave up writing, in order to focus on the life of a therapist. But Cannon had been very interested in her acting career, which undoubtedly became an issue for Grant, if only because he was in the process of divesting himself from the movie business. What made it worse was Cannon's admiration for his professional skill, which interested him less every year. "I observed one of the greats of all time," said his ex-wife, referring to his on-screen work. "He made it seem effortless, clever and smart."

Part of the problem with his post-Cannon affairs was his acknowledged inability to sustain a relationship. He began making remarks to reporters that verged on the cynical. "Most women are instinctively wiser and emotionally more mature than men. They know our insecurities."

Increasingly, he gave every evidence of thoroughly enjoying his retirement, but it was a strange retirement: unlike most elderly actors, he still got offers, and rooms still stirred when he walked in, but he had little interest in talking about remnants of a different life. In some ways, it was the best of both worlds: he remained famous, but on his terms. This was proven one day when he ran into Michael Caine outside the Beverly Hills Hotel. They were chatting when a female tourist came out of the hotel, noticed them and walked over.

"Michael Caine?" she gasped. "Is it really you? I've been in Hollywood two weeks and you're the first movie star I've seen! I'm just leaving for the airport—this is my final day—and at last I see a real movie star." She looked over at the white-haired gentleman standing next to Caine and said, "You just never see stars in Hollywood, do you?"

"No, ma'am, you don't," said Cary Grant.

Grant had stayed close to Lance Reventlow, his stepson from the marriage to Barbara Hutton. Reventlow didn't particularly like his mother, for what seem to have been good and sufficient reasons. When Lance graduated from boarding school, his mother didn't attend the ceremony, but Grant did. "He was a father to Lance," said Jill St. John, Reventlow's first wife. "He made time for Lance. Always."

Lance had grown into a handsome man with a yen for speed. He raced Formula One cars, and had coffee with James Dean just a few hours before Dean's fatal car crash. Reventlow wasn't surprised by Dean's death—he thought the young actor was reckless. Reventlow eventually tired of racing and shut his operation down in 1962.

In July 1972, Reventlow booked a flight on a Cessna in Aspen in order to survey a couple of ranches he was thinking of buying. Reventlow had logged thousands of hours as a pilot, but the man at the helm of the Cessna was twenty-seven years old and inexperienced. He flew into a canyon, and threw the plane into a stall trying to go over a mountain. The plane crashed, killing everyone on board. Lance Reventlow was thirty-six years old.

"When Lance died, Cary took over," St. John remembered. "On the day of the memorial service, he picked me up in his old Rolls without air-conditioning and handed me a large manila envelope. Inside was every letter and every card that Lance had ever written him. I looked at him and he said, 'If people are going to write you, you should save the letters.' He greeted everyone at the service. He acted as Lance's father—the only one Lance had ever known."

To the end of his own life, whenever Grant spoke of Lance his eyes softened and his gaze turned inward.

*   *   *

GRANT'S LIFE IN RETIREMENT remained carefully ordered. He rose at 6 a.m., and ate breakfast in bed, in his pajamas and a silk dressing gown he had custom-made in Tokyo. While he ate he went through the morning papers, marking articles he would later clip and file. He'd get dressed around nine, usually in slacks and a turtleneck sweater, or denim accented by handmade leather loafers from Maxwell's on Dover Street in London. Then he'd call Stanley Fox or the hapless architects and crew who had been engaged in remodeling his house for years.

If he wanted to, he could have spent hours of every day going to lunches or dinner parties or public events to which he was reflexively invited, but he refused 98 percent of the invitations he received. "There's a banquet every night," he complained to one friend. "Every bloody night out here. There's one for Bob Hope, one for Jack Benny, one for every guy in the world. You can't do them all. I'd rather dine quietly down on the beach." Every refusal letter written by his secretary was checked by Grant, who insisted that the names and addresses on the envelopes be typed in caps. A crooked stamp on an envelope provoked vocal dismay.

Then came an hour in the sun, and lunch, usually eaten on the terrace. He liked English muffins with melted cheese accented by Worcestershire sauce, or, alternately, bacon and eggs and toast and tea, drunk straight. (He liked breakfast almost anytime.) In the afternoon, while his secretary was engaged in filing the articles Grant had clipped that morning, he might play the piano, make more phone calls, or spend time by the pool. Other than occasional horseback riding or some laps in the pool, he did little exercise. If his pants started to get snug, he'd simply eat and drink a little less for a few days, and that usually solved the problem. He never drank before 6:30 at night, and then usually contented himself with a vodka and orange juice or Setrakian, a modestly priced California white wine that he bought by the case.

The household budget for food was only about $100 a month, not counting the coupons that he was careful to clip, and he developed a passion for McDonald's hamburgers that accompanied his affection for Dodger Dogs. Dessert was carefully rationed, but when he indulged, it was often chocolate-covered marzipan.

He would often eat dinner in bed, and then restlessly watch television, remote control in hand. If he came across one of his old movies, he'd watch with some enjoyment. His reading was limited to biography and current affairs, and he didn't listen to much music anymore.

He still paid careful attention to his clothes. He would occasionally tell people that he bought clothes off the rack, but that was a reflex left over from his acting days, when he wanted to create an impression of casually achieved perfection. In fact, the jackets came from Aquascutum in London, the sweaters from N. Peal in the Burlington Arcade in London. His shirts were made in Spain or by a man named Tani in Tokyo. When an order of shirts came in, he'd try on every one. If there was a problem, no matter how minute, back it went, even if it was only a matter of an eighth of an inch on the sleeve. His closets were motorized, like a dry-cleaner's inventory, with rows of dark suits, and below them lines of polished custom-made leather shoes.

He would drive himself around town in his Rolls-Royce, usually badly—he tended to slide from lane to lane without warning. His generosity came out at odd times, on his own schedule. He would tip a waiter or a parking valet $50 or $100, and he was quite generous, often anonymously, to old friends who were having financial trouble. But he preferred to spend $6 for a haircut, and he saved the rubber bands that wrapped his morning copy of the *Los Angeles Times*. When checks came in, he would divide $100,000 into ten separate accounts, and parcel the money out to various banks or savings and loans, depending on which was offering the best interest rates.

He liked game shows such as *Hollywood Squares, Concentration*, and *You Bet Your Life*. He also liked the Phil Donahue show, and retained an enthusiasm for the English comedian Tony Hancock, which fit nicely with his enthusiasm for music hall humor that was often both bawdy and ancient. He reused Christmas tinsel for years. He tended to ignore birthdays unless they were Jennifer's, but would give things that occurred to him. He saw a Chinese silver pipe in Hong Kong and bought it for Richard Brooks because Brooks smoked a pipe. Another time he gave Brooks a twenty-dollar gold coin he had converted into a money clip. After admiring a friend's suit, he gave him an expensive tie that fit perfectly with the suit.

He would recoil from some innocent behavior, citing a mélange of superstition, old wives' tales, and prejudices that forcibly reminded friends that on some level he would always be eccentric Uncle Archie from Bristol. It would usually start with something moderately sensible: he would lecture people he saw smoking, or drinking sugared soda, which had a way of segueing to other issues about which he was equally adamant: animals carried viruses; dyeing your hair can damage your brain. (He believed, in direct opposition to all medical evidence, that Jean Harlow's early death was caused by her hair dye.)

The firmly held, irrational beliefs went on and on. Plants take up oxygen, so he wouldn't have them in his house; sperm is limited and every time a man makes love he loses a portion of his strength; foods prepared with charcoal cause cancer. Some days he would insist that his parents were Anglican churchgoers. Other times he would speculate on Jewish blood on his father's side, but then say that nobody in his family went to church, let alone a synagogue. He had come to a vaguely Buddhist belief that all human endeavor was, on some level, pointless; that our fate is laid out in some cosmic account book and nothing can alter predestined fate. "It's all been written," he said. "Everything we've done. Everything we'll do."

When Maureen Donaldson asked him why he hired gay men as his secretaries, he first said that he had had women secretaries but that they always fell in love with him. And then he elaborated: "Homosexuals, in my opinion, work more diligently than heterosexual men. It's like having a woman, but not having a woman, if you know what I mean. You get so much more value. So if somebody's going to fall in love with me and be my secretary, I'd rather it be a man than a woman. Besides, a man can carry suitcases and take care of things like that, which you just can't get a woman to do."

When he was a working actor, he had constructed a protective cocoon around himself, and retirement strengthened that cocoon. It was hard to get him to go out. He instinctively understood that rationing his appearances and name increased his value, although his retirement did nothing to make him more sympathetic to appearing on anything he regarded as cheap or declassé.

He remained innately shy, and would get noticeably nervous if he had to make a speech or indulge in small talk. He much preferred small gatherings with close friends. When he agreed to present an honorary Tony award to Noel Coward, he was worried that he would sweat so much that it would be visible to the audience. Finally he had some pads sewn into his jacket sleeves so sweat wouldn't drip onto his hands.

He was a regular visitor at the Magic Castle on Franklin Avenue in Hollywood, a private club where magicians entertain other magicians. In the 1970s he was on the Castle's board of directors. There was a large part of him—the Archie Leach part—that remained a devoted fan of the vaudeville tradition, in which magic retained pride of place. Magic wasn't about money, but professional skill, passion, and comradeship among a peer group.

During the 1940s he had been a member of a Los Angeles group called Los Magicos that also included Harold Lloyd, Edgar Bergen, and Chester Morris. Milt Larsen, who ran the Magic Castle, first met Grant when he patronized a magic shop where Larsen worked. Grant told Larsen that he had performed the famous patter song "The Lion and Albert" at the Variety Arts Theatre in New York. Grant also told him that he had performed as Carizini while doing the rosebush trick, probably with Los Magicos.

Grant's particular enthusiasm was for close-up magic, sleight of hand, the most demanding form of magic because it doesn't rely on custom-engineered props. Grant spent his professional career first cultivating, then embodying finesse and dexterity, so it's perfectly logical that he would have gravitated toward other artists who had the same skill set.

His favorite magicians included Al Goshen and Dai Vernon. He would tell Milt Larsen about the Great Cardini, a magician who had toured the upper ranges of the Keith-Albee vaudeville circuit when Archie Leach had been working the small time. One night at the Magic Castle he met Patrick Culliton, the nephew of the actor Wallace Ford. That connection sent Grant off on a hilarious anecdote about a time when he was in Chicago with the terrible Shubert musical *Boom-Boom* and Wally Ford was next door in a show called *The Nut Farm*. According to Grant, the actors in both shows had their dressing rooms rifled while they were taking curtain calls. Chicago, he believed, was a tough town.

Grant didn't bring girlfriends to the Magic Castle, and brought Jennifer only a few times. The people who usually accompanied him were Walter O'Malley, the owner of the Los Angeles Dodgers, and his Las Vegas chum Charlie Rich.

He occasionally filled up his days with trips to the racetrack, especially Hollywood Park. The focused bustle of the tracks reminded him of the studios where he'd spent so much of his life. Among the directors of Hollywood Park were Mervyn LeRoy and Walter Matthau, and LeRoy would often accompany Grant if LeRoy's wife decided to stay home. Grant was not, to put it mildly, much of a gambler—$5 or $10 per race. Once, when he was feeling particularly flush, he bet $50. Maybe.

He would occasionally run into Fay Wray at the track. "He called my mother 'Nikki,' after that play they had done forty years before," remembered Victoria Riskin.

"Hello, Nikki, how lovely to see you," he would say. I completely projected onto him all the things I found in him as a movie star. I was starry-eyed, and my mother's heart would palpitate when she saw him. There was always such a sweet connection.

It's strange but I always got the feeling that he had suffered. I think there was a part of him that was unhappy about everything. Searching. When you see him in the movies, his life seems perfect. Charming, handsome, adored. But inside he was a little bit broken and confused—he had a lot of wounds from his early life. The world looks at you in a certain way and if you know you're not really that person. . . .

There's something about being on the big screen that feeds people who have strong narcissistic needs. It's intoxicating and addicting and if you're not a whole person it can warp you. It takes a lot of self-reflection to realize that you're a human being and not the person on the pedestal. I was lucky; my mother had a balanced personality; she made orange juice for me in the morning and sewed the labels on my clothes when I went to summer camp. She was a wonderful actress, but she was also a great mom.

Grant's most prized possession was either his father's pocket watch, or a gold chain that he wore around his neck that held one of Jennifer's baby teeth in Lucite, and three charms that represented the three religions of his four ex-wives: a St. Christopher medal from the Catholic Virginia Cherrill, a small cross representing the Protestant religions of Barbara Hutton and Betsy Drake, and a Star of David for the Jewish Dyan Cannon.

He continued to expound on the benefits of LSD to anyone who would listen, as well as anyone who was disinclined. He became known as the go-to man for people who were thinking of experimenting with the drug. At one point, the screenwriter Ivan Moffat and Caroline Blackwood had lunch with Grant. (Blackwood was married to Lucian Freud but having an affair with Moffat.) Grant strongly recommended that Blackwood try a course of LSD treatment and recommended a doctor. Blackwood undertook twelve sessions, and Moffat believed that "it certainly had a tremendous effect on Caroline. She suddenly became much clearer in thought, clearer of purpose—and she started to write."

The interesting thing about Grant's attitude toward LSD was that he remained resolutely antidrug. When this blaring contradiction would be pointed out, he would explain that it wasn't a contradiction at all: "LSD is a chemical, not a drug. People who take drugs are trying to escape from their lives. LSD is a hallucinogen, and people who take it are trying to look *within* their lives."

When somebody would call him on one of the convenient dispositions that supported his prejudices, he would say, "I'm now 70 years old and I have lived a lot longer than you have." And that would be that. Age and experience, however subjective, trumped logic or facts. In short, he was what he self-diagnosed as a "series of contradictions"—intensely human, often maddeningly so.

He knew the stories that had been floating around Hollywood for forty years, and they bothered him . . . but not too much. "That I'm a homosexual and that I'm a miserable tightwad. And I care because it hurts. . . . You can't just wave away blithely what people say or don't say."

He began going out with Maureen Donaldson in 1973. She was a young English writer who worked for Rona Barrett and was precisely forty-three years younger than Grant. They were together for four years, and it was Grant's urging that converted her into a photographer. Donaldson found him an ardent, tender lover, at first shy about sex with the lights on. He explained that it was his "chicken skin. You don't want to see that while we're making love. But in the dark you can imagine I'm one of those young men your age." He continually returned to the age disparity—insecurity tinged with suspicion. What was she doing with an old man? There *must* be other, younger men in her life. Donaldson worked on opening him up. The lights came on, and they even showered together.

He always had a tripwire where children or intentional cruelty were concerned. Then, he would allow all his prejudices about animals to be quickly filed away. He didn't have any particular interest in animals, but he drew the line at hurting them—the infliction of pain was the red line. One day he was going to a Polynesian restaurant with Donaldson when they saw a drunk abusing a dog. Grant promptly walked up to the man and offered him a hundred dollars for the dog. The drunk upped the price to two hundred dollars, which Grant promptly handed over, grabbing the leash as the money changed hands.

"What are we going to do with this mutt?" he asked Donaldson as they walked away.

"I don't know, but I love you," she said.

"Good. Then you find a home for this animal."

Similarly, a woodpecker took up residence on the roof of his house, and drove everybody mad with the incessant hammering. Grant's secretary offered to get a gun and kill the bird, but Grant wouldn't hear of it. Instead, he ordered the secretary to tap back in the hope that the woodpecker would be startled and leave. There was much back-and-forth tapping, until the bird magically flew away to harass someone else.

One of Donaldson's friends was Bill Royce, who was slowly brought into Grant's circle by house-sitting when Grant and Donaldson were out on the town—Grant was always worried about thieves, but refused to install a security system.

"He was a much more complex man than he seemed on-screen," said Royce.

And much more contradictory. I'm an adult child of alcoholics, and that teaches you to be hyper-vigilant. Most days, he would be super-cheerful, everything positive. If I called him and I'd say do you need anything? or want me to drop by with food? I could tell within three words if he was in another emotional state. Usually he would get severely depressed about his relationship with Dyan or his access to his child. Jennifer was the absolute center, the priority of his life. If that wasn't going well, or if he thought it might not go well, he would be in a blue funk. His mood would be one or the other. I could be with him for hours, but I never saw a good mood turn dark.

I don't think Jennifer ever experienced the darkness with him. He always presented a happy picture with her. He wanted his limited visits with her to be up, up, up, so she would always want to come back. As far as his relationship with his mother, I think he felt abandoned by her till the day he died. He tried desperately to have a good relationship with her and she always resisted his attempts at affection. If he brought her gifts, she would cast them aside.

Donaldson and Royce were given increased access to the house and Grant, and their marching orders came, not from Grant, but from Stanley Fox. Maureen Donaldson had playfully planted marijuana in Grant's garden, and Fox pointed out that besides damaging Grant's reputation, a bust could affect his already limited visitation rights with Jennifer. "He made it clear to Maureen and I that there was to be no funny stuff. No friends, no weed, no drinking unless Cary invited us. He said all this point blank. Fox reminded me of [Elvis Presley's manager] Colonel Tom Parker."

Royce served as a go-between with Grant and Donaldson as well as an emissary to life on the Sunset Strip—Grant developed an understandable fascination with Pam Grier and Royce accompanied him to several of her movies. Royce gradually developed a relationship with Grant that was somewhere between filial and paternal, with a single embarrassing exception. The two men were in the swimming pool, when Grant got out and was toweling himself off. Watching Grant, Royce realized he was having an involuntary pelvic response to Grant's unselfconscious beauty. Grant noticed and said, "Well, you take care of that, and I'm going up to get some wine and you can come up when you're dried off."

"It didn't anger or embarrass him in the slightest," remembered Royce. "His reaction was so elegant."

Grant's cook and housekeeper was an African-American woman named Willie Watson. "He adored Willie," said Royce. "He stole her from Dyan. She was charming and she was smart; there was something mysterious about her—you always felt she had secrets. Cary spoiled her. Not in terms of salary, but in trips he would pay for, or tickets to Dodger games. Willie mastered the turkey sandwiches he loved. He had gotten the recipe from Doris Day, and they became his go-to food. The crust was sliced off, and there was a thin slice of watercress in with the turkey."

Royce shared with Grant a childhood that could be termed unconventional—he had been adopted by a married couple who were both alcoholics, and he had been in relationships with both men and women. "As I peeled off one layer of my onion, he would do the same."

Like most adoptees, Royce was curious about his birth parents. Grant went behind Royce's back, hired a private detective to find Royce's mother, and had her brought to the house on Beverly Grove. The expected mother and child reunion was hampered by Royce's feeling of abandonment and a resulting emotional confusion. "Cary saw my ambivalence and took me aside. He told me she was only going to be around a short time—she had pancreatic cancer. He told me that if I didn't make it right, I would regret it to my dying day. And then he flew her to Johns Hopkins to see if they could do anything for her.

"People always said Cary was cheap. He wasn't cheap, he was frugal. He respected the value of money. Cary was never cheap when it counted."

Royce was working for a Hollywood fan magazine, and Grant urged him to travel, to get out of town. "It's too insular," he said. "Your value system gets skewed." He insisted Royce read Nathanael West's *Day of the Locust*. "I told him I had seen the movie, but he said, 'No, you have to read the book.'" Grant didn't read that much at this point, although he had a hard time with insomnia and occasionally took Seconal to get some sleep. "He still read John O'Hara; one time I saw him rereading *A Rage to Live*, and he said that O'Hara 'had nymphomaniacs on the brain.'"

Grant's playful spirit came out regularly. He and Royce would play the piano together—Grant could play in a bouncy vaudeville style, while Royce was limited to two fingers. When they were finished, they would traipse out to the patio and pretend to take bows in front of a Hollywood Bowl audience. Grant would bow in Royce's direction and say "You first," pointing to the imaginary throng. "Oh, no," Royce would reply. "I insist." And so on, back and forth, until one of them broke out laughing. "It was just as silly as it sounds, but it gave us both great pleasure," said Royce.

The lighthearted fun would always be put aside whenever the subject of fractured family relationships and their victims came up. Royce remembered one time when William Inge came to the house and Grant asked him to leave the room so Grant could talk to Inge privately.

Royce and Grant even had a conversation about sex. After Royce unburdened himself about his affairs with both men and women, Grant responded by implying he had been basically gay as a young man, later bisexual, still later straight. Randy Scott, he said, had seen their relationship as "locker-room playing around." It had nothing to do with how a man should lead his life. Besides that, at one point Darryl Zanuck had taken Randy aside and told him that enough was enough.

Grant explained sexuality in terms of performance, of acting. He told Royce that to not completely explore one's sexuality would be like an actor playing only one character for life. Everybody, he said, had more than one character inside them. He didn't think homosexual acts were anything to be ashamed of, or, for that matter, proud of. They simply were—part of the journey, not necessarily the final destination.

> I think Cary saw the searching I was doing and trusted me. He had been influenced by the Kinsey report and saw sex as a spectrum. Most people think it's either/or. And there are men like that, but there are also men who are occasionally gay and occasionally straight. I remember one thing Cary said: "England is Victorian, but America is more Victorian than England."
>
> My sense of it was that he found homosexual life unrewarding. As he got older, he wanted children, and he didn't think he had any chance at a child as long as he was living that life.

His conversation with Grant made Royce curious about Randy Scott. He was at the Beverly Hills post office one day when Scott came in to pick up some mail. He was dressed in tweeds, an ascot, had steel gray hair and sported a deep tan, just like Grant. Royce walked over and introduced himself. "Mr. Scott, my name is Bill Royce. I help Cary Grant with his place off Benedict and just wanted to thank you for your movies."

Scott smiled and said "Well, I haven't seen him in a while. Tell Cary I said hello." Royce thought Scott was stunning; he went back to the house and told Grant about how Scott had looked. "Yeah, he was really something," Grant said, in a tone that combined esteem, fondness, and sadness.

*   *   *

GRANT'S HOUSE AT 9966 Beverly Grove was beautifully situated, with a view of the entire shining city of Los Angeles. Beyond the front door was the living room. Off to the left was the kitchen, while the bedrooms and bathrooms were off to the right. Grant's own bedroom was modest, although the bed featured monogrammed white sheets beneath an electric blanket. On both sides of the bed were bookshelves, with pictures of Jennifer as well as pictures of young Archie with his mother. There was his Oscar, as well as the di Donatello Award he'd received in Italy.

The bedroom led to his office, and beyond the office was the terrace where he liked to eat. Just inside the front door was a fireproof vault, which was full of memorabilia of his and Jennifer's life. There were his old passports, an old jacket from his grade school days, Elias Leach's monogrammed watch, his movies on 16mm. Transcending all this were the hundreds of tape recordings and thousands of photographs with which he had documented Jennifer's life since her birth. It also contained autographed gifts he had requested from other famous people he met in his travels—a signed baseball from Hank Aaron, a signature from Neil Armstrong, a signed picture from The Beatles. Jennifer had no particular interest in the home movies Grant had taken of her, but he loved to watch them.

The vault was his way of documenting their lives, and in a round-about way he seems to have felt it was proof of his love for her. Bill Royce thought it went deeper than that. "Next to Jennifer, the vault seemed to be the most important thing in Cary's life," said Royce. "He was terrified that he would die and Jennifer would not remember him."

"I'm just an old, old man," he said one day when he was seventy. "My life is really devoted to Jennifer. She is going to have the kind of childhood I never had. She's going to know at all times where her mother and father are, and she will be totally secure in our love for her, even if we are divorced."

Left unanswered were the questions provoked by this obsessive documentation of his daughter's life. Who tapes and preserves the meandering speeches of their small child? How can any child live up to such admiration? All the love and passion that had been stored up for a lifetime, that he had been unable to freely bestow on parents or wives was released in a continuing deluge upon his daughter.

The problem with the Beverly Grove house was that Grant had used it as a rental off and on for years, and it was in sad shape. The roof leaked, the ceiling was full of water stains, and patches of plaster sagged down. The French doors leading onto the terrace had become warped by rain and cracks had opened up large enough to allow streams of water onto the flagstone floor. Grant discovered some cardboard boxes he had long forgotten containing a Boudin painting and two Tiepolo sketches that had been a gift from Barbara Hutton.*

After positioning a number of pots and pans under the leaks, Grant realized he would have to spend some money on the house whether he liked it or not. And so began years of self-parody that made *Mr. Blandings Builds His Dream House* look like a model of construction efficiency. Grant's secretary reported that two electricians, each earning $20 an hour, spent an entire day changing the position of a single light plug while Grant pondered the perfect location. The light plugs weren't the only things that got switched—so did designers and contractors.

It undoubtedly seemed odd to the contractors, but it wasn't really. Grant relentlessly second-guessed most of his creative choices, so dithering endlessly over decorating a house was very much in character. This oversensitivity to options was why the idea of an autobiography was impossible, despite the size of the advances that were offered—he would never have stopped rewriting. And there was another reason—or another fear: He believed that if he carried his story to the day of writing it would mean his own end was near. "The drowning man sees his life go by as he goes down, and so does the man who goes back over his memories to write about them."

As he aged, he naturally thought about death and made preparations. When Lord Mountbatten was murdered by the IRA in August 1979, he was visibly devastated. After the funeral, he called a friend

---

* According to an inventory dating from the mid-1960s, Grant's collection of paintings was minor by Hollywood standards, a time and place where truly impressive displays of Impressionists were common. There were eight Boudins, a Utrillo, a Watteau etching, a Poussin pencil drawing, and a Diego Rivera. (Grant had Rivera's contact information in Mexico City in his address book.) There was also a painting of fruit by one B. Grant, i.e., Betsy Drake Grant.

and announced, "I'm absolutely pooped, and I'm so goddamned old . . . I'm going to lie in bed . . . I shall just close all doors, turn off the telephone and enjoy my life." He made Maureen Donaldson promise that if he should die during the night, she was not to call the police or even an ambulance, but rather Stanley Fox. "I've gone over this with him many times. He knows what to do. I can trust him to follow my instructions to the letter."

Mostly, however, he exhibited a blithe grace that retirement had helped create. Peter Bogdanovich witnessed an amusing scene in 1973, when he and Grant both attended the American Film Institute's Life Achievement Award for John Ford. Grant had forgotten his ticket and asked the lady at the reception for some help. Name? she asked, looking down at her list. "Cary Grant," he said. She looked up and wasn't sure about what she saw. "You don't look like Cary Grant."

"I know," he said with a smile. "Nobody does."

Occasionally there would be a tacit moment of rue. At a party, gazing at the stunning women clustered around Warren Beatty, he nodded and said, "See that guy? That used to be me." Beatty had been observing Grant at close range since visiting Leslie Caron during the shoot of *Father Goose*, and it is probable that Beatty's general aura of a megastar floating above the seedy *mishegoss* of the movie business derived from the older actor's attitude.

Paul Sylbert worked with Beatty and said, "He learned from Grant . . . picking up these do's and don'ts from hanging around these people and seeing how they operate." For a time, Beatty insisted on using mascara to accent his eyes, and he would adopt a trick often used by aging actresses, as well as actors—put the camera fifteen feet away and shoot close-ups with a long lens, which slightly softens the focus without being obvious about it.

In the fall of 1968, Grant wrote an exuberant self-analysis redolent of Scrooge after his enlightenment:

> I am a sixty-five year old professional man, recently divorced for the fourth time, and father of a two-and-a-half year old daughter. I am happier than I have ever been, yet not as happy as I intend to be.
>
> I am often pessimistic, yet mainly optimistic. I no longer resist, or inhibit, the penetration of knowledge which I trust will eventually result in wisdom!

I enjoy the boundless feeling of love and intend to let it grow forever in me. I intend to try to set a good example to, and live with consideration of, others.

Looking back on my life, I occasionally wish I had known enough to choose a profession that could have been more directly beneficial to others. But, since I didn't, I must take that into consideration in all future endeavors. . . .

It's a good day and a good life!

GRANT'S FRIENDSHIP WITH Harold Lloyd remained strong. "Harold had a private den upstairs, with a phone that only rang in that room," remembered Lloyd's granddaughter Sue.

I hung around up there a lot. One day the phone rings, and it was that distinctive voice: "Oh, hel-*lo*. This is Cary *Grant*. Is Harold there?"

And I said, "Oh yeah. Dad's here, but he's on the throne." And then I couldn't talk to him anymore. I'd seen *An Affair to Remember* and was just incoherent about it. I threw the phone down and ran down the hall.

"Dad, it's Cary Grant."

"Okay, calm down. Just tell him I'm on the throne and I'll call him back in a minute."

So after that, I begged him to let me go to lunch with the two of them, and Harold said, "If you can compose yourself, we're going to go to the Polo Lounge." But at that point he didn't think I would be able to pull myself together.

The first time that I really had a conversation with Cary was when we were in London. I was seventeen or eighteen, and we were staying at the Inn at the Park. We went to dinner with Cary at the White Elephant. Harold and Cary were very interesting together. You would never have known they were comedians. Serious. No joking around. They looked like businessmen, and they acted like businessmen. Suits and glasses.

And yes, Cary was charming. He asked about what I did with Dad. I told him about the Shriner hospitals, and that I went to

Westlake, I read Dad's light meter for him when he was taking pictures and so forth. Cary had a kind of a warmth when he talked to you. He really looked at you. He wasn't grand at all. He was comfortable in his skin and interested in you. In thinking about it, he was a lot like Harold.

Sue Lloyd's experiences with Grant were almost entirely with the professional aspect of his personality, but there was one time when she got a glimpse of his more informal side.

The bisexual thing. I've thought about it. I can tell you that people didn't make a big deal about it. I can see it, kind of. My friend Richard Correll and I went to a party once. My uncle was there with his boyfriend, and Cary was there as well, swirling around in a caftan. And I was blown back. Oh, it had an effect on me. He was swishing around the party. I saw that side of him, and I saw the businessman side as well. Let me tell you, there was a real contrast.

CHAPTER TWENTY-THREE

In 1968, Grant joined the board of Fabergé, Inc. The money was negligible—about $15,000 a year to start, although there were stock options—but the job came with access to the corporate airplane and apartments in New York and London, which may have been the main attraction. Grant had grown weary of the continual buzz of amazement and subsequent harassment that came with flying commercial, or, for that matter, getting into an elevator.

Oddly, he initially preferred a venerable DC-3, a prop plane, as opposed to a jet, until George Barrie, the president of Fabergé, convinced him to go with a jet. Until then, Grant decorated the DC-3 with an ash dining table, bright yellow armchairs, and couches in tomato red and green. It also had a bar and, in case he felt like serenading his friends, a piano. The walls were covered with photographs of Jennifer. He would hop on the plane with Jennifer for a trip to Catalina for lunch, or up to San Francisco to eat at a Chinese restaurant he loved.

Dyan Cannon's career had heated up, as she costarred with talents as varied as Peter Sellers, Burt Reynolds, and Warren Beatty, revealing a pleasingly daffy sense of comedy. Fabergé made it easy for Grant to move around and stay close to Jennifer, who often traveled with her mother to locations. Grant had maintained his disapproval of movie careers, and never offered Cannon any congratulations or kind words about her success.

In time he would serve on the boards of Hollywood Park Race-track, the Norton Simon Museum, Metro-Goldwyn-Mayer, and the MGM Grand Hotel. Cumulatively, the stipends probably covered his overhead. He began spending more time in Las Vegas, which he rather enjoyed, and where his friend Charlie Rich introduced him to Kirk Kerkorian—another tycoon that Grant warmed to. Kerkorian liked to give the impression that he was self-made, but his Armenian immigrant father became wealthy buying and developing land in the San Joaquin Valley before his son was born.

Grant and Kerkorian had much in common. They were older fathers with young children, and their daughters enjoyed bringing their fathers together for a foursome of horseback riding. Both Grant and Kerkorian had ambition, an innate sense of privacy, and a fear of public speaking. In time, they would vacation together, and Grant would serve on the board of Kerkorian's Western Air Lines.

Grant regarded Kerkorian as "a brilliant man" who carefully studied all aspects of an issue before making up his mind, not to mention someone who retained the common touch. In other words, a man much like Grant. For his part, Kerkorian thought Grant was "a true friend. . . . Such a humble, nice man" and a "supersmart" businessman who made important contributions to the boards on which he served.

Fabergé maintained space for Grant at their New York office, and he used the Warwick Hotel for his New York headquarters. He had been there off and on since the early 1950s, in the penthouse—Suite 2704—that had been allocated to Marion Davies when William Randolph Hearst built the place in 1926. After Davies, it had been Franchot Tone's residence. Many of the original furnishings were still in the penthouse, under the wooden beamed ceiling. It had two bedrooms, with two entrances, a kitchen, and a terrace where Grant enjoyed his daily ration of sun.

The job description of "businessman" pleased him; he felt it gave him a relevance that "retired movie star" didn't. He grew to actively dislike talking about the movies, mostly because he had come to the belief that acting wasn't an appropriate job for an adult. "It's all a put-on, isn't it?" he asked Gregory Peck.

The job with Fabergé entailed public appearances, but he didn't seem to mind, because an interview was an interview; he had done a thousand of them without giving up a thing. He explained that selling cosmetics was just like selling movies. "If you sell to the large department stores—as I sold my films to Radio City Music Hall—then the smaller ones fall in. . . . We researched Fabergé's Brut just as you would research a screenplay. Then we ask ourselves where the raw essence can be found (which would be like finding a location for a movie) and how to get the quantities (the prints) in case we've got a hit."

Fabergé's subsidiary Brut eventually went into the movie business and had an initial hit with a romantic comedy with George Segal and Glenda Jackson called *A Touch of Class*. Grant saw it and liked it, telling director Melvin Frank that it was the only picture he'd seen since he retired that he wished he'd made. Maybe, maybe not. Brut promptly ramped up production and made eight consecutive stiffs (*Night Watch*, *The Divine Sarah*, *Whiffs*, etc.) before they got out of the movie business.

Grant's Fabergé salary was soon up to $25,000 a year, and the company also began paying his secretary's salary. There were other perks—an expense account for one thing. He handled company money with the same care with which he handled his own; his friends laughed about his painstaking attitude. "He threw dollars around like manhole covers," said Quincy Jones.

Grant would regularly donate to charities, especially those headed up by friends. Katharine Hepburn—Grant's nickname for her was "Kate the Great"—would call and ask for donations to Planned Parenthood, and he would usually send a check. At least once when Grant was in New York for business, he stopped at her house in Turtle Bay for lunch, and was mightily amused when she served him an ordinary sandwich rather than go out or have something specially prepared. "Now, *that's* cheap!" he complained.

He relaxed to the extent of occasionally playing the piano, jazz mostly, with George Barrie, who played the saxophone. He liked Oscar Peterson, Bill Evans, and Count Basie—pointillists of the piano, where every note counted.

It was in these years that he began to settle into the man he had always wanted to be, in which he would demonstrate an empathetic depth that surprised people who didn't know him, if only because most movie stars are primarily interested in themselves, and Grant had not been an exception to the rule.

"Everyone always talks about Cary Grant's elegance and style as an actor," said Robert Wolders. "But what about his elegance and style as a man?" Wolders was a courtly, astonishingly handsome Dutch native who was studying child psychology when he was shanghaied into acting and a contract at Universal. He met Merle Oberon, who divorced her industrialist husband and married Wolders. They were living in Malibu when Wolders came home one day to find Cary Grant, Laurence Olivier, and William Wyler sitting in the living room with his wife—an impromptu *Wuthering Heights* reunion.

"I was completely overwhelmed by the presence of Olivier, and then Cary did the most remarkable thing. He saw how intimidated I was and he began concentrating on me, on bringing me into the conversation, so that I wouldn't just be sitting there feeling unworthy. Cary made it possible for me to feel at home in my own home. That was just one example of his remarkable sensitivity to other people."

Grant would repeat his kindness when Oberon died in 1979. During the funeral at Forest Lawn, Wolders was overcome and was sitting in one of the limousines trying to pull himself together when he realized that Grant was sitting next to him. "I realize that this is the worst day of your life," he told Wolders. "I just hope that you never again have to experience another day like this." Wolders always considered Grant the epitome of a gentleman.

This growing attentiveness to other people marked the final stage of a life that had long been defined by self-absorption. Friends grew used to Grant adopting the role of comforter-in-chief, a function he performed expertly. When Bill Royce's fiancée died suddenly of an aneurysm, Grant showed up before the ambulance, closed her eyes, and kissed her cheek. The next day he began making all the funeral arrangements. He gave the bereaved survivor a book called *The Thunder of Silence*, the main point of which was that instead of praying, it was best to sit still, stay silent, and listen for God within.

He felt that he had accumulated a store of wisdom through agonizing trial and error and sought to advise people so they wouldn't have to spend years running in circles. Mainly, he told people to forgive their parents as he had forgiven his, and then make the more difficult leap to forgive themselves. "When you forgive someone," he said, "that means you're taking control. You are making the decision to forgive and then you're taking the action of forgiving. That means you have the resolve and the strength to do so. People sometimes think forgiving is an act of weakness. But it's the exact opposite. It's about realizing your own power and your own strength."

The crucial realization was his ability to accept Cary Grant. "I just had the sense, up to that point, of living someone else's life. A borrowed life, as it were. I helped create this guy, but I didn't believe him for one second—even if everybody else did. That's why I pushed all my loved ones away from me. I was afraid they would try to hold me and discover that I was hollow, just a hollow man."

IN MAY 1972, Grant sold the batch of films he had produced through his and Stanley Fox's companies to National Telefilm Associates for what *Variety* reported as "in excess of $2 million." There were five films—*Indiscreet, Operation Petticoat, The Grass Is Greener, That Touch of Mink*, and *Father Goose*. Included in the purchase was *Penny Serenade* and Grant's percentage of *Walk, Don't Run*, although ownership of the film itself was retained by Columbia.*

It was one of the few bad business deals Grant ever made. His and Stanley Fox's thinking undoubtedly ran like this: They looked at the last five or so years of revenue from each film and projected forward in order to approximate net value. In 1972, movies were more or less lumped together with oil wells as a depleting resource. As Grant explained some years later, sounding suspiciously like an MBA, "Most of the revenue was exhausted by that time. In those days the tax on earned income was up to 94 percent, so we tried to spread the income out."

The idea of films being enduring assets that can be smoothly moved to platforms as yet uninvented and continually monetized was too distant to worry about—or so Grant thought. It would be less than ten years until videocassettes arrived and began to completely rewrite the math of movie libraries.

The same year that Grant sold his movies outright, Charlie Chaplin, Grant's role model when it came to film ownership, netted $6 million

---

* The NTA library passed through several hands and ended up as the property of Paramount, which handles the pictures today.

against 50 percent of the profits for *leasing* eleven features for fifteen years, after which the films reverted to his estate. Chaplin's films had never been on television, which accounted for some of the price differential, but Grant and his heirs could have made multiples of $2 million had they simply held on to the pictures and licensed them for home video and what came after. It's highly probable that the outright sale was part and parcel of Grant's psychological divorce from the movie business.

These were years when he proudly showed Jennifer off to anybody whose opinion he valued. In December 1971, he took his daughter to Betsy Drake's house because, he told his ex-wife, "I miss all the old furniture." Drake was uncharmed. "If he'd come with a moving van instead of a child he'd have emptied the house," she wrote Kate Hepburn. "I decided that he was an ass as well as a viper, which he later confirmed by speaking of his admiration for Lawrence Welk."

Although Grant didn't particularly like to talk about the movie business anymore, he still thought about it. He told one friend that he had decided that almost everyone who went into the movie business was a psychological orphan in search of a surrogate family. As for himself, Grant was still searching for the perfect woman. He began going out with Fiona Lewis, a pneumatic brunette from England who had made a small splash in Roman Polanski's *Fearless Vampire Killers*. In 1971, Lewis moved to Los Angeles and had a few dates with Grant, accompanied by Jennifer.

Grant was attracted, but he was put off by Lewis's career choice. "He was plagued by regrets," said Lewis. "He told me he regretted his own career in films and that he'd have been better off raising children. He hated movies and said Hollywood was a sham."

On the first date, Grant was circumspect about his contempt for his former and Lewis's current profession. On their second date they went to Catalina, and he didn't bother being polite. He bore down on the uselessness of a show business life, neglecting to mention that the show business life had paid for his luxe lifestyle in Catalina and elsewhere. Lewis saw that Grant was devolving into browbeating. "I stopped returning his calls," she said.

There were great similarities to the women he was involved with after his marriage to Dyan Cannon, as well as similarities in the way that Grant treated them. They were all young, sensual, and without a great deal of professional success, hence impressionable. Grant made sure to have Jennifer spend time with them—nothing would happen without her approval. In essence, he was casting the role of Jennifer's stepmother the same way he had cast Dyan Cannon as his wife. He wanted someone young, probably because he wanted more children, but he also wanted someone who would, with any luck at all, be more malleable than Dyan.

In line with that, he worked on Maureen Donaldson's appearance, took her to fashion shows, upgraded her taste in clothes, and had a dentist fix a crooked tooth. When some gray hairs showed up prematurely, he wouldn't let her dye her hair.

Finally, a friend of Donaldson's blurted out what had long been obvious: "This man is grooming you to be the fifth Mrs. Cary Grant. He's changing everything about you. . . . I'm not saying there's anything wrong with it, just that you should be aware of it because that's what *you're* doing, and that's what *he's* doing."

ELSIE LEACH DIED ON JANUARY 22, 1973, a few days short of her ninety-sixth birthday. She had been brought a cup of tea, and when the attendant come back to collect the cup, she was gone.

Grant was on his way to a board meeting for Western Air Lines when he got the news and immediately left for Bristol. He wanted no announcement of her death so that he could slip in and out of town without crowds. "No hearse," he ordered. "Above all, no flowers and no ceremony." He went to Bristol to say goodbye to the woman who had given him life, then shadowed that life with the dubious gifts of anxiety and insecurity.

Elsie was buried at Canford Cemetery in the same grave as the husband who had committed her to a mental institution. Canford derives from the Edwardian era, with much of it gradually returning to nature—grass six feet high, monuments tumbling every which way. Elias's and Elsie's resting place is still tended, but hard to find—it's down an unpaved path, on the perimeter of the cemetery. Grant had a new stone placed above their final resting place. The inscription on the stone reads, "In memory of Elias/Who died December 1st, 1935 aged 63 years/The husband of Elsie Leach/Reunited January 22nd, 1973."

Few tombstones contain more inferences and ambiguities. There is no reflexive sentiment, no "beloved parents of Archie/Cary . . ." It is best read as Grant's final attempt to please his mother, who probably yearned to be joined again with the man who tried to obliterate an inconvenient woman from his and his son's life.

It was cold and rainy the day Elsie was buried, and there were only four mourners. After Elsie was buried, Grant realized that he would never again have to return to Bristol out of duty. "With the past now gone, I have the future ahead—with my daughter Jennifer."

"I HAVE NEVER BEEN MORE MYSELF THAN I AM TODAY," he said around this time. "I pretended to be a certain kind of man on the screen, to be Cary Grant, and I more or less became that man in life. Now I can be Archie Leach again." This equanimity didn't stop him from suing 20th Century–Fox for $1 million for using clips from *Monkey Business* in a documentary about Marilyn Monroe. The judge found in his favor but awarded him only $10.

All of this can be understood as part and parcel of a reflexive tending of the Cary Grant franchise. He may have been retired, but he was not averse to talking to reporters, generally in line with the promotion of Fabergé. The interviews ranged widely over his own life to his general philosophy. A question about his marriages would bring forth withering honesty: "In each instance, the woman deserved my love, but honestly, I had none to give. . . . I was wracked with doubts, fears and skepticism. I was unhappy with my past, dissatisfied with the present and fearful of the future."

Other times he would indicate why he had never needed a publicist, riding herd as he did on his own image and its impeccably smooth presentation: "I turned down an interview with *The New Yorker* because the circulation is too limited," he told one writer. "There's a whole country out there that's never heard of *The New Yorker*."

The philosophizing continued: "I've never met a happy actress. Happy actors, yes, but not happy actresses." Occasionally he would express a counterfactual grudge about his mother, implying that Elsie's mental health issues had somehow been voluntary. "It was her way of rejecting society. And rejecting my father."

He was comfortable with his hometown, and in 1975 he went so far as to attend the unveiling of a plaque at the United Nations building regarding the Bristol Basin, a new landscaped area on the east side of New York. The name referred to the fact that the land was constructed on tons of World War II rubble from the Luftwaffe blitz of Bristol that had been brought over to America as ship's ballast.

Grant cut the ribbon, said a few words. After the ceremony, Peter Heap, the deputy head of British Information Services in New York, noticed Grant standing by himself. People were awed by his presence and nobody seemed to know what to say to him. Heap had also grown up in Bristol, and went over for a talk.

Grant had flown in that morning and would fly out again that night. "He seemed a bit shy," said Heap. "He was well-spoken, intelligent and quite self-contained. He wasn't interested in approaching other people at all. The most interesting thing was how sentimental he was about Bristol. He talked a bit about his relatives who died in the war, and we talked about our hometown. It was clear that his feelings about Bristol far exceeded his feelings about England."

That year, David Niven published his enormously successful memoir *Bring on the Empty Horses*. Despite Grant's private grousing that Niven had appropriated events that had actually happened to Grant, he congratulated his old friend. He sent him four copies of the book, asking for inscriptions for himself, a commissioner of New York City who "consoles harassed Mayor Abe Beame," for Maureen Donaldson, "a delightful young (it's no longer possible to find one older than myself) girlfriend," and his secretary. "I must see you soon," he wrote in closing. "You must see me soon, too."

When Jack Haley Jr. produced *That's Entertainment!*, a sparkling compilation of scenes from MGM's heyday that kept the increasingly moribund company alive for a few more years, he asked Grant to narrate a segment. When a scene featuring Jean Harlow came on, Grant began to cry. After the screening, the two men took a walk. Grant told him that he couldn't appear on camera, but could narrate a segment. Haley said that wouldn't work. Grant had to agree, but there was one favor he asked for: could Haley find out who made Fred Astaire's tux for his "Begin the Beguine" number in *Broadway Melody of 1940*?

In 1977, Warren Beatty was determined to lure Grant out of retirement for *Heaven Can Wait*, a remake of the Robert Montgomery vehicle *Here Comes Mr. Jordan*. Beatty wanted Grant to play the angel that Claude Rains had played in the original. Grant was on the receiving end of Beatty's rush, which was among Hollywood's most persuasive. Grant was polite, and even had Beatty over to the house for breakfast. Ultimately, he didn't budge. The fact that one of the film's costars was Dyan Cannon might have been a problem, although she had no scenes with the angel, and much of the bitterness had been papered over by that time.

"Warren reminds me a bit of myself when I was his age," Grant said afterward, with considerable insight. "I think he's afraid of commitment. He should have a child as I did. And he will, late in his life just as I did. And it'll change his life. He will find more happiness that way than he could with any woman."

"I don't need to act," he said, closing off that possibility for good. "Can't you see I'm acting every time I let Jennifer go back to her mother, knowing it'll be days and sometimes weeks before I see her? That's the best performance I've ever given!"

He continued to give the credit for the serenity he was now exuding to LSD, but the suspicion persists that it might just have been the result of abandoning his dance on the high wire of show business. He could finally relax and be who he had been all the time, without having to don the unnerving facade of Cary Grant.

IN MARCH 1979, Grant took part in the American Film Institute's Life Achievement Award for Alfred Hitchcock. The great director was crippled by arthritis and a drinking problem that had crept up because alcohol stifled the pain. Grant sat at Hitchcock's table, along with Hitch's wife, Alma, Ingrid Bergman, James Stewart, and Lew Wasserman. Hitchcock was in bad shape—he seemed not to recognize several people with whom he had worked. Post-career honors for geriatric geniuses can vacillate between the thrilling and the unnerving, and the Hitchcock evening was an example of the latter—a vivid display of old age at its brutal worst. Next to him sat Cary Grant—old age at its best.

Afterward, Hitchcock wrote Grant a thank-you note:

I can hardly write this without a tear in my eye, because of our fondness for each other. How wonderful for you to be present.

May I have the privilege of photographing you again one day, because you can be, you know.

> Affectionately,
> Hitch.

Alfred Hitchcock died just over a year later.

Not all communication with old coworkers was grim. One day Ted Donaldson remembered that it had been precisely thirty years since the high school graduation that Grant had attended, years after they had worked together in *Once Upon a Time*. Donaldson sat down and wrote Grant a letter he had been meaning to write for years, expressing his gratitude for Grant's savvy about screen acting, and the time he had taken to be kind and supportive to a child.

A few weeks later, Donaldson's phone rang and there was that familiar voice on the other end. "May I speak with Teddy Donaldson? This is Cary *Grant*." He had returned from a trip with Jennifer and had just opened Donaldson's letter. They talked about *Once Upon a Time* and how much Grant had enjoyed acting with Donaldson. He closed by telling Donaldson that he had been terribly flattered and moved by the letter, and that he would cherish it always.

THE GENERAL IMPRESSION within show business was that Grant was—or had been—something other than what he had portrayed in the movies. But in November 1980, Chevy Chase brought the backdoor gossip into the hearing range of the public with some remarkably crass remarks on Tom Snyder's *Tomorrow* show. Chase referenced Grant, saying "He really was a great physical comic, and I understand he was a homo . . . what a gal!" Grant generally laughed off this kind of thing—Jennifer Grant remembered that her father's attitude toward the gay rumors was, more often than not, amusement. But the fact that the rumor was repeated on television, and in such a snickering way, enraged him. Jennifer remembered Grant raising his voice, a rare occasion around the house.

Grant sued, and the case was eventually settled out of court. Grant told friends that Chase had apologized. "Actually, of course, he did me a *favor*. I've had it all my life. Guy takes his girl to a picture and there I am, and the girl says she likes me, so the fellow says, 'I hear he's a *fag*!' Now he's just done me a favor, hasn't he? Because if I ever come to that town, who do you think will be the first one around my hotel to see if it's true. His girl! He's done me a *favor*, you see."

Peter Bogdanovich once asked Howard Hawks about all this. Hawks wrinkled his face and snorted. "Every time I see him, he's got a younger girl on his arm. No, that's just ridiculous."

CHAPTER TWENTY-FOUR

As Grant began going around the country doing "A Conversation with Cary Grant," it occasioned a renewed realization of just how remarkable an actor he had been. A spate of articles appeared paying tribute to his accomplishments. One particularly laudatory one was by David Thomson, who sent his piece to Grant in the hopes of luring him into appearing at the Telluride Film Festival.

That was never going to happen, but it did provoke a phone call. On the other end of the line was a sputtering Cary Grant, who proceeded to tell Thomson off for taking unspecified liberties in his article. Twenty minutes after the call ended, Grant called back to announce that "I read it again, and I see what you're doing and I *like* it!"

Grant was thinking of filming his show and during several phone calls asked Thomson what he thought would be the best way to capture the event. "He had a very good-natured side, but he was *so* insecure," said Thomson. "He had no confidence in his own opinion. He was one of those men who go around asking people what they should do, but won't pay attention to any of them. I got the feeling he was still looking for a doctor figure who could peel him. Clifford Odets and Betsy Drake had filled that role, and then [Dr. Mortimer Hartman], and he was looking for someone else who could."

Spasms of insecurity aside, he usually seemed a gracious elder states-man who made a point of taking time with people. When Ryan O'Neal had been preparing to play a variation of Grant in Peter Bogdanovich's

What's Up, Doc?, he asked Grant for some pointers. Grant's response: "Wear silk underwear. Say, 'Where's my drink?' Be comfortable."

Bogdanovich's film opened at the Radio City Music Hall, and Grant proudly told him that twenty-eight of his movies had played America's showcase theater. He then suggested that Bogdanovich stand in the back of the theater and listen to 6,500 people laughing at something he had created. "It will do your heart good!" Bogdanovich took the suggestion and was indeed thrilled and gratified. Grant's only comment about the film came when he congratulated Bogdanovich on its success and said nice things to O'Neal about his performance. He never said he thought the movie was good, perhaps because Grant recognized that Bogdanovich had grafted the comic mainspring of *Bringing Up Baby* into a different time and setting. His lack of enthusiasm could have been subtle payback for Bogdanovich's lack of enthusiasm for *That Touch of Mink*.

Just as Grant had been a token of corporate accomplishment for Lew Wasserman, so now he became a bauble to a new circle of rich friends. Charlie Rich kept a suite at the Dunes for Grant's exclusive use. The MGM Grand would do the same thing after he joined the board of MGM. Just the possibility of his presence added a patina of class.

When MGM split into MGM Grand Hotels and MGM Films, Grant sat on both boards until his death. Bob Koster, the son of the director Henry Koster, had gone into the movie business despite his father's warnings. "It's the worst business in the world," Koster told his son. "For eight or ten weeks, you're all best friends; it's a family. And then after the film you can't get anybody on the phone because they've gone to another film and they're in a different family." After Henry Koster retired, he maintained few friendships in the movie business.

Bob Koster was working at MGM when Grant showed up to attend a board meeting. The meeting was in the executive dining room; to get there you had to walk past the proles in the commissary. Grant walked through the doors and "the entire room went silent," said Koster. "He was older, of course, but still a marvelous-looking white-haired giant. Most movie stars are smaller than you think they are, but Cary was actually bigger than you thought he was. Everybody stopped, all conversation ceased. No other star I ever saw had the same effect he had."

Grant's musical tastes remained attuned to songs with meaning and style. He greeted his daughter's taste in music with contempt.

"Any moron could write that. Baby, baby, love ya love ya, need ya need ya. Hogwash." He still had his sweet tooth, and had a candy drawer with chocolates, marzipan, lemon drops, and assorted hard candies. Whenever he went to England he'd come back with a supply of Cadbury Flake bars. And there was an enduring enthusiasm for fish-and-chips, and bangers at Christmas.

He had always been orderly in his habits, and that hadn't changed. Besides his shared devotion to the *Los Angeles Times* and *The Wall Street Journal*, he would go to about fifteen Dodgers games a year, as well as the playoffs and World Series, sitting in the third-base box of Peter O'Malley, the son of Dodgers owner Walter O'Malley. These were the years of Steve Garvey and Davey Lopes, and Grant eventually bought loge seats of his own. Grant subscribed to *The Sporting News* and kept *The Baseball Encyclopedia* nearby to check statistics.

"He was a baseball fan before I arrived," said Jennifer. "He even played a bit. I think he liked it because it's a family sport. And he didn't play golf."

He grew to believe—or to hope—that he would live to a very old age, maybe even one hundred. His mother had been active until the end, which he thought promised an equivalent life span. He wanted to try a Russian concoction of honey and fresh walnuts that supposedly contributed to the long life span of Caucasus natives.

His favorite restaurants were La Scala at Rodeo and Santa Monica, and at Madame Wu's Garden. When he ate at home, dinner was still usually served on trays in front of the TV. He liked Carol Burnett, *All in the Family*, and *60 Minutes*, especially Andy Rooney. On Carol Burnett, he adored Tim Conway's old man, shuffling along a few inches at a time. It follows that he also liked Benny Hill, who must have yanked him back seventy years to the naughtier performers of the English Music Hall.

After TV, it was time for bed, but he was a bad sleeper in his old age, usually waking up at two or three in the morning, often to worry about something, a habit he never got over. If he couldn't get back to sleep, he'd read. On the weekends, he liked to play backgammon, puzzles, and cards (Spite and Malice was a favorite, a complicated game that requires two decks of cards and many hours).

Depression was rarely present, but occasionally alluded to. At Christmas, he would occasionally say, "You know, when I was a boy, in wartime England, we were lucky if we got an orange in our stocking. . . . That was it. An orange was a true delight." Charlie Chaplin would say the exact same thing as an old man at Christmas, about the days when he was an indigent child in the workhouse.

You can spend a lifetime trying to outrun childhood deprivation, and you will always fail.

He was friendly with almost everybody he met, but his intimates were few: Stanley Fox of course, who agreed with Cary about both money and politics. Frank and Barbara Sinatra, and Quincy Jones were nearly on the same level. Slightly below them were Kirk Kerkorian, Merv Griffin and Eva Gabor, Gregory Peck and his wife, Johnny Carson and his wife of the moment. David Hockney came to the house several times, as did Sidney and Joanna Poitier.

His blessing as well as his curse was his personality, a presentation he had composed in the same studious way a musician writes a song. Most people met Cary Grant and saw only Cary Grant. Ralph Lauren had idolized Grant and his sense of style for years. As Grant's career was winding down in the 1960s, Lauren had committed to memory how Grant's shirts fit, how many buttons there were on his jackets, whether they had single vents or riding flaps. He would shop at the same stores where Grant shopped. It was not enough to admire Grant; Lauren's ambition was to make other men dress like Cary Grant. When Lauren finally met Grant, it was a special experience. "Cary Grant picks me up, takes me down to the track out in California, isn't that unbelievable? What you think he should be like is exactly what he is like."

But Lauren knew about the desperation and high cost of prodigious self-invention, which turned Jimmy Gatz into Jay Gatsby, Ralph Lifshitz into Ralph Lauren, Archie Leach into Cary Grant. After a while, Lauren realized that his idol "looked like he was playing himself, [but] he really wasn't the guy in the movies. You [only] thought he was. And he became it."

It was a brilliant disguise; he could present himself as Cary Grant at will, and because his audience found him to be more or less like his screen self they relaxed and took him at face value, without bothering to wonder about his affinity for and sympathy with other people's emotional distress.

Grant remained a tough critic of his own work. Generally speaking, he avoided it. "If you're watching my movies, you're up too late at night," he told his daughter. "You could be doing something useful with your time, like sleeping." He was indifferent to almost all old movies. No chatter about the old days, no gossip. His daughter couldn't remember a single conversation about his life as an actor.

Some of his films—*Arsenic and Old Lace*—brought him to the edge of nausea: "I'm *way* over the top," he would grumble. Like most actors of his generation, he didn't understand the younger generation's need for acting classes. "If you want to act, get out there and do it. You'll never learn what it's like to be on a set when you're stuck in a classroom. . . . On a set there are lights and sound and marks and all sorts of things to deal with. It's not all about 'acting.' "

He had moved on.

Similarly, now he rarely spoke about his parents, and never about his previous marriages. The pattern was clear and consistent—the past had haunted him for most of his life, and the more it receded, the freer he felt. He lived as much as possible in the present and in his hopes for the future—where Jennifer was. Since the future was promised to no one, only the present had possibilities. He appreciated an ordered life and, by God, he would have an ordered life.

Vacations could be surprisingly domesticated—he still liked going on cruises. "Terrific concept. You unpack once, visit several places and always maintain your traveling home." There were several visits to Monaco, where he and Jennifer would stay at the palace with Grace and Rainier and their children. Grant would help judge the annual circus festival and sit enraptured at the virtuoso trapeze acts. His own acrobatic background came to the fore when he explained to Jennifer that aerialists grasped each other's wrists, because "hands can slip."

The acrobats would jog his memories and he'd talk about his time with the Pender troupe. "The floor was all wood, and to open the show I would run out. . . . I had to practice this many times when the stage was fully lit, because come performance time the lights were out and I had to find a specific point in the floor to dive in. . . . You see there was an invisible trapdoor in the floorboards, so out I run with 'Let the show begin,' and *boom!* I dive straight through the wooden floor! I gave the audience quite a gasp."

His relationship with Jennifer never altered much: mutual adoration. He carefully preserved the first flower she ever gave him, a pansy picked off his front lawn, presented to him on March 4, 1969.

Similarly, he put a candle from her fifth birthday party in an envelope and dated it. Because Jennifer was the hub of his life, as she grew up he gradually expanded his expectations of her, but tried to avoid using his adoration as a bargaining chip.

On her third birthday he wrote her that the IRS rules specified that annual gifts to any one person should not exceed $3,000, and that he planned to make yearly arrangements for that sum to be added to her already existing list of shares and securities. The three-year-old's financial analyst presumably took note.

On the day Neil Armstrong walked on the moon, he wrote Jennifer from Miami, outlining the momentous events that had just taken place. "You are always in my thoughts, Jennifer, and my dearest wish to live long enough to read and study the enclosed brochures with you . . . perhaps on our way to Mars."

On her eleventh birthday, he wrote,

Ten years have passed by since I first saw your dear face. Ten years of loving you. Ten years of regarding you, of thinking of you, and of being with you at every opportunity possible to me. . . .

I am proud to know you. Proud to be seen with you. Proud and happy while watching you swim, ride and play tennis; and in each of our activities together: the Baseball games, the Races, every day at Greenhorn Ranch, the Malls; Everything; Everywhere. . . .

You are the dearest daughter a man could have. You have never caused me a moment's anguish or disappointment. Your qualities are of the best, and if you persist in those qualities throughout life, you will enjoy ever-growing happiness and, by so doing, understand the happiness you bring to others who know you. Especially to me.

Sometimes they would do the routine from *The Bachelor and the Bobby-Soxer:*

"You remind me of a man?"

"What man?"

"The man with the power."

"What power?"

"The power of voodoo."

"Voodoo?"

"You do."

"Do what?"

"Remind me of a man . . ." And so forth.

Underneath the high spirits were high expectations. He cut out hundreds of newspaper articles for her edification. Jennifer's allowance only went so far, so she needed part-time jobs—baby-sitting, clerking. He enjoyed taking her shopping at the Gap, where the clothes struck him as sensible and reasonably priced. He had an affection for Levi's 501 jeans, which he wore until holes appeared.

By the time she was twelve, Jennifer had a checking account and was expected to handle her own accounts, up to and including her quarterly income tax payments. Grant's joy in his child was interrupted only by occasional moments of rue. When Jennifer turned fifteen Grant complained that "I can't remember my own child. I can remember my own child, but I can't somehow capture her in each year of her growth. . . . You can't really capture her clearly."

There it was. The tape recording, the home movies, the obsessive collecting of relics of Jennifer's infancy and childhood were Grant's attempts to stop time—to fix each stage of the person he loved the most in his mind, moment by moment. It was hopeless, if only because the human brain retains flashes rather than a continuum. He thought that perhaps the problem was that he was "quite elderly by the time I had my first child, my only child. . . . It was life, life itself. To watch her, as she breathes and talks and walks; it's marvelous to be part of that event. . . . You can't explain it to anyone else, except to someone who has done it. You never know how much you love them until you have a child of your own."

His fatherly advice was usually by example, but occasionally he would venture into outright admonitions: "You may have a lot more money and a great deal more advantages than the man you fall in love with. That's all right. If you believe in the man, stand by him. It's tough to make a living." A pithier piece of advice was particularly wise: "Don't marry the guy you break the bed with." If he had learned anything, it was that sex was important, but not all-important.

And he asked Jennifer for one other thing: remember him the way she knew him. Books would be written, things would be said, and some of it—most of it?—wouldn't be correct, or it would be accurate but not true, not really. He understood that life is complicated and he was extremely complicated. In any case, he wouldn't be able to defend himself. Jennifer promised. "To me, he was like a marvelous painting," she would remember. "All the art historians wish to break down the motives, and the color scheme, and so on. I would rather know, as I do, his essence."

He did his best to be attentive to friends both young and old. When Cybill Shepherd starred in Peter Bogdanovich's *At Long Last Love*, the first in a regrettable mini-genre of musicals featuring performers who can't sing or dance (*Everyone Says I Love You, La La Land*), the film was greeted with scathing contempt. Grant called her. "If I was still acting, you're the kind of actress I'd like to work with," he told her. Praise from the greatest high comedian of the century sustained her through a deep depression. "I'll always love him for that," she would say.

Hal Roach, his old friend from the Santa Monica period, invited Grant to dinner at his house. The film historian Richard Bann was shadowing Roach for a prospective biography, and Roach told him he could come for dinner too, as long as Bann promised not to talk about movies. Bann discovered that he and Grant had a mutual interest: the Los Angeles Dodgers. They settled in for a good conversation about baseball.

Grant had long believed that the game had a lot of similarities to show business. Both involved finesse, grace, and control, and both placed a premium on making it look easy. Take Jim Eisenreich for instance, a player for the Minnesota Twins who tended to freeze in front of large crowds. Grant saw it as a simple case of stage fright.

Bann remembered Grant as "The man you saw in *Houseboat* and *To Catch a Thief*. He was as charming as you'd hope. As a film fan, the conversation was uneventful, and focused on things happening in their lives." Grant and Roach talked about the Santa Anita racetrack, which Roach had founded and where he would frequently host Grant. The movie business came up only once, when they agreed about the sad state the industry had fallen into since their heyday.

Roach did not mention a recent incident that had taken place over lunch with two editors from Scribner's. Roach was being pursued for a memoir, which he told Bann would be his responsibility—Roach reminisced only under duress. The editors knew about Roach's friendship with Grant and eagerly went over the things they hoped to see in the book, including the (hopefully) scandalous truth about the Cary

Grant/Randy Scott household. Roach promptly pushed away from the table and walked out without a word. Following in Roach's wake, Bann turned and said to the editors, "I guess lunch is over."

GRANT HAD BECOME FRIENDLY with the *Los Angeles Times* columnist Roderick Mann, who regarded him as an older brother. He gave Mann a lot of column material, almost none of it about movies because, said Mann, movies bored him.

Mann turned to Grant whenever he needed a column, and in turn Grant turned to Mann when he wanted to proselytize for one form of enlightenment or another. Mann functioned as Grant's megaphone for extolling LSD and the changes it wrought:

> Each of us is dying for affection but we don't know how to go about getting it. Everything we do is affected by this longing. Quite obviously, that's why I became an actor—I wanted people to like me.
>
> Now everything is changed. My attitude toward women is completely different. I do not intend to mess up any more lives, especially my own. I could be a good husband now. I am no longer unaware of my faults, and I am ready to accept responsibilities and exchange tolerance.
>
> I used to love a woman with great passion, and we destroyed each other. Now I'm ready to love on an equal level. . . . I asked myself a long time ago, what I wanted out of life. Beautiful women? Luxurious houses? And I decided that what I wanted was contentment and peace. And that cannot be bought with money; only with personal endeavor.

In May of 1976, Grant and Mann went to London for a Fabergé trade show. They were staying at the Lancaster Hotel, where they met Barbara Harris, the public relations director. Grant immediately quickened to her—"I'll tell you what I thought of you," he told her a few years later. "I thought you were quite a dish."

Harris was too busy to pay much notice. Grant invited her to lunch, then to the Fabergé event that evening. Grant was waiting for Mann at the wrong place and got to the bar late, where he saw Mann and

Harris talking. He immediately thought Mann was beating his time and got angry, refusing to speak to Mann for several days. Clearly, the girl had captured him.

Barbara Harris was born in what was then Tanganyika in 1950, the daughter of a Royal Army major who had served in World War II and worked as a provincial commissioner in East Africa. She was calm, unflappable, beautiful, with a posh accent to boot—class personified. Grant would pursue her for the next two years. The problem was, of course, their respective ages—Grant was forty-six years her senior.

His approaches were simultaneously circumspect and, yes, charming. In March 1977, he wrote, thanking her for sending flowers to his cousins Maggie and Eric Leach. Later that year, things had obviously moved beyond platitudes: "May not entertain you at all; but it entertained me. Moderately. But then, it takes so little to entertain me." A considerable amount of white space, followed by a single sentence: "Want to try?"

Things moved in a domestic direction. In April 1978, he sent her a picture of some tables and chairs he thought would be appropriate for her new apartment. On reflection, though, he thought the table was too large for the available space. He referred to yet another dinner ensemble he had clipped at some point in the past and would begin searching for. "Meanwhile, unless a permanent pull to Spain proves irresistible to you, I look forward to seeing you in June."

They finally sealed the deal in July 1978, when Grant and Frank and Barbara Sinatra were staying with the Gregory Pecks at their villa in Saint-Jean-Cap Ferrat. They had gathered just before attending the wedding of Princess Caroline of Monaco. Peck noticed that Grant had arrived by himself and asked if there wasn't anybody in his life. "There is a wonderful girl I've known for quite some time in London," Grant replied.

They all suggested he fly her over, Peck pushing particularly hard. Grant relented and got on the phone. To his surprise, Barbara agreed to come. They spent the next two days in Cap Ferrat before heading to Monaco for the wedding.

In August, he wrote Barbara to thank her for the red rose she had sent after her visit. He had placed it in a round Lucite vase in his bedroom, on a white tabletop at the end of the book-shelved sofa, "where it will stay in my happy-sad vision." Later that day he wrote her again, telling her that he and Jennifer were going to a baseball game, which he expected to be perfect because of the balmy weather, marred only by Barbara's absence.

His letters are by turns yearning, gracious, occasionally music hall racy ("Did you hear about the athlete who suggested the lady should get on top because he had a tennis elbow?"). Another rose from Barbara brought the note in reply, "It represents you without thorns . . . and from where I regarded it, eased my lonely hours in bed. Well, it didn't really, of course . . . the rose I mean . . . but you will, won't you?"

Barbara moved in with him. She and Jennifer got along, and Grant's friends appreciated her as well. The relationship seems to have been deepened by its April-October nature; their time together was limited; they knew it and they wanted to make the best of every moment. Grant blossomed, touched her constantly.

He had been wrestling with the remodeling job on his house for years, and the place was still beset with sawhorses and dust. Grant lived mostly in the master bedroom and the library, because they were the only livable rooms in the house. Barbara took charge and quickly ramrodded the remodel to completion. Grant pronounced himself pleased, if only because it was finished.

"Cary was the same man with Barbara that he had been with Betsy and Dyan and Maureen," said Bill Royce. "He was not going to change. What was different was the woman. Barbara was a peacekeeper. She went totally with his agenda. She wanted him to be happy, and she wanted him to be calm. She effected a truce with Dyan so that Cary could be a happier person and make his relationship with Jennifer even stronger. She did anything and everything to please him. And he appreciated her beyond words. When I visited him with Kathy, my wife-to-be, he couldn't extol Barbara enough. He was entranced, and he was the happiest I had seen him in a long time. What he had been looking for was serenity, and he finally found it."

"He so valued Barbara's competence," said Walt Odets. "She had decisiveness and clarity and she was intelligent. She was not someone he had to take care of. Betsy was probably more passive and dependent, and I think Cary had a problem with dependence."

Around the house, Grant remained studiously casual—cotton slacks, shirts with the tails out, socks but often no shoes. As Sue Lloyd noticed with horror, he had also developed a taste for caftans—in his old age, unfettered comfort was of paramount importance—and Barbara sewed him a closetful of them.

Barbara's skill set made her perfectly suited for living with a man his daughter characterized as "sometimes quite difficult." She was a manager, and more than that she was a diplomat, which enabled her to handle him with dexterity. She loved their nest, and shared his reliance on precise detail.

"Barbara has given me a new life," he told Bill Royce. "I lived what to anyone would have looked like a complete life, but something was always missing. And God knows I made my share of mistakes. I treated all my ex-wives like foster mothers. I was suspicious and fearful no matter how hard they tried.

"Barbara gave me a real Act Three. We both know I don't have many more innings left, but I can't get over this feeling my life has just begun."

On those rare occasions when either Barbara or his daughter displeased him, Grant would slide into the silent treatment. If he absolutely had to talk, it would be in a low monotone from which all joy had been surgically removed. Conversely, whichever one of them was still in his good graces would receive special enthusiasm. This withdrawal of the usually sunny Grant was perfectly calculated to drive the offender batty, so the silence rarely had to last longer than a few days.

Barbara's skills even extended to animals. Grant's indifference to four-legged creatures had been long established, but Barbara loved cats, so cats began appearing around the house. A cat named Sausage was actually allowed inside the house, and Grant was magically converted to the feline gospel. It turned out that Sausage belonged to a neighbor, which entailed much negotiation until shared custody was agreed upon. Sausage was eventually killed by a coyote, but after that there was no question that there would be more cats.

He remained extremely attentive to the people in his life, writing thank-you letters and notes and sending gifts. To a friend who was dealing with the impending death of a friend, he wrote advice that ascended to the level of a humane manifesto:

The most difficult thing a man has to do is die. And no one should do it alone.

Sit with him. Comfort him; not with tiring small talk, but with your quiet presence when he opens his eyes and sees you sitting there between his periods of rest.

It is too late for vanity; he won't mind how he looks if you don't mind. Your very presence will help him face the unknown and assure him that he did not live unloved or without being understood; and therefore, life was not without purpose.

GRANT AND BARBARA MARRIED IN APRIL 1981 and spent their wedding night at a Dodgers game. Grant felt his life had been justified by the birth of his daughter, so of course another child was an enticing possibility. Beginning at the age of eighty, he and Barbara tried to conceive a child. When it didn't happen, they were considering artificial insemination with a sperm donor, a plan that was interrupted by his death.

Friends noticed how pleased and content Grant and Barbara were in each other's company. He would tell everyone how lucky he was to have found her. She brought order to his life, and, as with the late-life, much younger wives of moody, hard-to-please men such as Charlie Chaplin and Henry Fonda, devotion to his happiness was probably all he ever wanted from any of his wives.

These were years of relaxation—parties to attend, friends to see. Billy Wilder invited Grant and Barbara to a dinner party at his apartment and after dinner he and Grant went to his den, where he played Carl Orff's *Carmina Burana* on his new stereo. The music was loud and impressively detailed.

"How much is your loudspeaker? How much is your phonograph?" asked Grant.

Wilder decided to have some fun. "Knowing how stingy he is, I say, 'A hundred and eleven dollars.' So he calls his wife, 'Barbara! This machine here. We are crazy, we are crazy. We paid two hundred and fifteen!'

"He says, 'Now, tell me, those two loudspeakers. Tell me, are they included in the hundred and eleven dollars?' And I say, 'No, they were extra.'

"How much?"

"Six fifty apiece."

"Barbara! Barbara!!"

Wilder shook his head. "He was a very, very peculiar man, and he was very stingy. Stingy, Mr. Cary Grant."

Grant and Wilder both served on the board of directors of the Norton Simon Museum in Pasadena, where they would get together once or twice a year, agree to everything Simon wanted to do, then have a superb catered lunch. "[Grant] only came there for the lunch," said Wilder. "He didn't have to pay for it. It's all right. On him it was becoming, it went with his character. If he had also been very generous, then that would [have] disturbed me. Too perfect."

Grant ignored most of what was written about him, although he would occasionally correct the record. He wrote Garson Kanin about a passage in a book Kanin was preparing. He began by taking issue with Kanin's reference to Archie Leach as a chorus boy. "The first small part I played, in a Hammerstein operetta, was hardly more elevated, 'tis true, but I was never in the chorus. I, sir, was a principal!!!" He went on to deny that he had ever "moved in" with "our friend Orry-Kelly." He had, he said, shared a duplex apartment in Greenwich Village with three other aspiring "non-actor types." Orry-Kelly, he said, lived in the apartment above them. As for the hand-painted neckties, he said that Orry-Kelly and a man named Bill Smith had painted them, but that he had indeed been engaged in the retail end of the business.

If Grant and Barbara weren't at a Dodgers game, they would go to Hollywood Park, where he would explain his betting system and continuing interest in making money to anyone who would listen. "I had an opportunity to invest in Santa Anita," he would say, about the first Southern California racetrack, which opened in December 1934.

They were selling shares for $5,000. I, of course, had no belief at all that such an investment could ever pay off. Hal Roach had one block left over in the end but I refused to buy it. Well, of course, Santa Anita was a tremendous success. . . .

So now Hollywood Park is set to open, and again I'm asked to invest. What do I do? Why, I say, "Such an investment could never pay off. Southern California could never support two tracks." And, of course, Hollywood Park is a great success.

Now I am desperate to invest in a racetrack. So they opened one in Las Vegas near where the convention center is today. I begged the fellows who were raising the money to let me put $10,000 into the track, since racetracks were making all the money.

Then one day I was in Las Vegas. A man called Charlie Rich had taken over the Dunes, and he said to me that this racetrack being in Las Vegas, wouldn't make any money.

I said, "Charlie, how can I lose?"

He said, "Look, the people in Vegas, they want action right away. They don't want to wait thirty minutes between races. Besides, in California there is no other gambling."

Well, I go to opening day rather proud of myself for finally getting in on the big score. They are using the Australian tote system, which threw sand on the whole thing. I think it took all day to sort out the bets.

Pause.

I think the track closed down after about three days.

Somewhere around here he would reach into his pocket, peel off two twenties and ten singles and hand the stash to Barbara. "I make $2 bets, you see, because they won't take a dollar-fifty. I've tried." People would take the $50 limit as confirmation of Grant's reputation. "When I was insecure, I used to throw money around to impress people," he would explain. "But then I learned you don't impress people like that. So I became a tightwad, or so people said. When you're a star, you're either a tightwad or a homosexual. I've been accused of both."

He would study the racing form and make his decisions based, not on the horse, but the jockey. "First I bet on McCarron, then on Pincay. And then I alternate. Now, this fellow Stevens is also good, so sometimes I bet on him. Does it work? Of course it doesn't work."

People walked past and noticed that Cary Grant was betting at Hollywood Park and looking fabulous. "Whatever you're doing, it agrees with you," one person told him.

"Losing," Grant would reply.

*   *   *

IN 1981, Grant was at MGM attending the board of directors meeting at which MGM bought United Artists, which had collapsed in the wake of *Heaven's Gate*. George Cukor and the former MGM story editor Sam Marx were hosting a lunch for Myrna Loy in the executive alcove of the commissary. It was the first time she had been back on the lot since 1947. Loy had been dreading it, but brightened when Grant came over to say hello. Loy hadn't seen him since his marriage to Barbara. "Congratulations, you old fool," she said, grabbing his arm. "Solid as a rock," she observed.

That same year, David Niven was diagnosed with amytrophic lateral sclerosis—Lou Gehrig's disease. After the disease had him in its grip, he wrote Grant, addressing the letter to "Dearest Cary-Chum" and expressing sympathy for the loss of Grace Kelly, who had just died in an auto accident. Niven was in receipt of a letter from a prospective biographer of Grant's, and told his friend that all he had to do was send Niven a postcard with "Yes" or "No" written on it, and Niven would know whether to talk to him or not. "Come over again soon for a happy reason and don't fail to let us know. A big kiss to Barbara and blessings to you." Niven never mentioned his illness. He died in 1983, gallant to the end.

Grant continued to turn most of his attention toward his daughter, as he exercised his passion for fatherhood in molecular detail. The actor Rob Lowe tells a story about his inability to get a date in high school until he got a job on an ABC After-School Special. Figuring that gave him some currency, Lowe decided to ask out "the most popular girl in school," i.e., Jennifer Grant. She gave him the address of the house on Beverly Grove. Lowe was stunned when Cary Grant, attired in a white robe, opened the door. Grant graciously ushered Lowe into Jennifer's room, where the two sat on the bed watching Lowe's TV show, while Grant sat nearby making sure nothing untoward happened—a mid-Atlantic version of a duenna. When the show was over Grant complimented him, saying Lowe reminded him of a young Warren Beatty. Rob left, only to see Grant trotting after him in the rearview mirror. Lowe stopped his car and Grant handed over some parting gifts: a selection of products from Fabergé/Brut, including soap on a rope.

When Jennifer graduated from the Santa Catalina School in 1983, her father sent her jewelry that had belonged to her grandmother.

Elsie "seldom wore such things but . . . would have adored to see you today, just as I do today and all days, dearest Jennifer."

He told Gregory Peck, "I just want to see Jennifer have a child. I want to see my grandchild. Then I'll be ready to shuffle off."

His letters to her usually centered on expressions of appreciation that also contained lengthy admonitions about the proper approach to life, but his expectations were not just theoretical. He adored her, but there was a line that could not be crossed and that line was show business. Between Jennifer's sophomore and junior years at Stanford, she told her father that she had applied for a scholarship at the Manhattan Playhouse.

One of his deepest fears had suddenly set up shop on his doorstep. Grant promptly told his daughter that if she accepted the scholarship, he wouldn't pay for her next year at Stanford. Acting was out of the question as a career choice for his daughter. The craft he had elevated to an art was off-limits. If he had turned away from show business, others had to as well. Disobedience had to be sternly confronted until it became obedience.

"He would have been thrilled if she had been a lawyer, a doctor or a businesswoman," said Bill Royce. "He wanted her to be something substantial; he didn't want her to be like her mother."

"He thought acting was a tough life," said Jennifer, "and he wanted me to enjoy the rich life he had made for himself." Jennifer backed down and returned to Stanford, graduating with honors in 1987. It was only after her father died that she became an actress. Although quite beautiful—she looks like a feminine version of her father—she didn't have much success. As with so many children of privilege, she lacked the drive instilled by early deprivation. "I've never had to work for money," she said. "If things weren't appealing to me, I didn't go after them. Did that harm me? I don't know. I can tell you that I don't feel I hit the mark I set for myself."

Jennifer managed to forgive her father; when she gave birth to a son, she named him Cary.

GRANT REMAINED A REPUBLICAN, mostly for economic reasons. His daughter says that "today he'd be a libertarian—his attitude was basically live and let live." With Jennifer, Grant always accentuated the positive, whatever the topic. For instance, he minimized his separation from his mother and their difficult post-reunion relationship. Rather, he would tell his daughter stories that emphasized their closeness—"They were pals," Jennifer says, contradicting her own mother's portrait of a deeply conflicted relationship defined by Grant's inability to accept his mother's eccentricities. As for movies, that had been another life, so long ago, and it had been a struggle. He was so much happier now—why talk about times when he wasn't happy?

"The precision he brought to fathering was the same precision he brought to his craft," said Jennifer. "The character, that gorgeous quality—the determination to make choices. The self-confidence. Needless to say, he didn't believe in acting classes. He was who he was. He wasn't acting in a scene, he was *being* in a scene. He's effortless, he has a lightness to his person. He's a joy to watch—the economy of motion, the grace with which he moved. Miraculous. Even now, I watch him and I smile."

Between Grant's delight in Barbara and Jennifer's blossoming, he seemed to emotionally enlarge, become more buoyant. He ascribed the difference to the years of LSD treatments and to his domestic happiness, but it's just as possible that the feeling of release derived from the fact that he wasn't acting anymore, which in turn meant that he could complete the integration of Cary with Archie. For the first time in his adult life, he was free from the burden of performance; he no longer had to worry about being revealed as an impostor.

IN 1982, Grant was named Man of the Year by the Friars Club. George Burns, Grant's friend from the 1920s, was there and told the audience that he and Grant had been introduced by Abraham Lincoln. It was the beginning of a looping, hilariously digressive speech in which Burns admitted that they had met through

Minta Arbuckle, who was married to Fatty Arbuckle. Now, Fatty Arbuckle was one of the great comedians in silent pictures. His first name was Roscoe, and they called him Fatty because he weighed about three hundred pounds. He came to Hollywood as a stagehand and was discovered by Mack Sennett, who only weighed 145 pounds. . . .

Now, Fatty was a good friend of Buster Keaton, who was also one of the greats. Keaton originally started in vaudeville with an act called The Three Keatons; he worked with his mother and father. . . . Now Keaton was a very good friend of Charlie Chaplin, who was the king of silent pictures. Charlie Chaplin, at that time, was married to Lita Grey. This was before Paulette Goddard. And Lita Grey had her dresses made in a little shop on 45th Street, right next door to Wiennig's restaurant. And Al Jolson used to eat at Wiennig's. And right above Wiennig's was the Jack Mills Publishing Company. Gee, I could stand here and talk about Cary Grant all night . . .

When Burns was finally finished, Peggy Lee sang "Mr. Wonderful," while Tony Bennett, Cy Coleman, and Frank Sinatra all sang as well. Grant's speech was openly emotional: "I find myself tearful with happiness quite often these days. I cry at great talent. I'm deeply affected by the works of certain writers, by certain singers, phrases of music, the perfection of Fred Astaire. . . . Such things can trigger off a complexity of emotions, but you see, to indulge in one's emotions, publicly and unashamedly, is a privilege permitted the elderly."

Myrna Loy was in the audience and wrote Grant a wifely letter after the event: "Dear, dear Cary, I enjoyed every accolade for you and didn't blame you for weeping a bit. I was trying to get a word to you to say blow your nose, and your voice will clear a bit. Of course you would have been *horrified* at the idea. I was proudest of all. Thank you dear—you look divine and I wish your mother could have been there."

That same year, Grant and Barbara attended the premiere of Blake Edwards's *Victor/Victoria* in Century City. The after-party was a mob scene, and when the photographers saw Grant they went into a frenzy. The flashbulbs wouldn't stop exploding—eating a meal was impossible. Finally Grant announced to the other people at his table, "Ladies and gentlemen, I wish to apologize. There is only one remedy, so I will take my leave." After he and Barbara excused themselves, the photographers went away, and the meal went on. With the exception of Garbo, no other star of the Golden Age of movies could have provoked such a rabid response.

For the first months of 1983, Grant and Barbara took a trip around the world on the cruise ship *Royal Viking*. Grant loved the calm rhythm of life at sea, but Barbara was seasick until they got to Hong

Kong. On one or two occasions, he held court in the ship's pub and answered questions about his career. It was not at all painful, as he had expected; rather, it was pleasurable, and it resulted in "A Conversation with Cary Grant."

PETER BOGDANOVICH TURNED TO GRANT frequently over the years for life advice, which was generally offered with a deep sense of the intrinsic deficiencies of human nature. When the director and Cybill Shepherd were the target of bad press, Grant succinctly told Peter, "Will you *stop* telling people you're in *love*!? And *stop* telling them you're *happy. They're* not in love and *they're* not happy. . . . Just remember, Peter, people *do not like* beautiful people."

In 1984, Bogdanovich thanked Grant for his friendship by sending him one of his father's paintings. Grant gratefully accepted with a kind letter of acknowledgment—he never sent personal letters unless it was important.

At their last meeting, Bogdanovich noticed that Grant was walking more carefully than he had been even a year or two before, but was otherwise undiminished. He was "still boyish, enthusiastic, high-spirited, fun-loving, empathetic, funny, full and delightedly aware of who he was and where he had been and what he had done, though he never took himself too seriously."

In May 1984, Grant wrote Kate Hepburn for what seems to have been the last time, sending along a clipping about Spencer Tracy he thought she might enjoy, then thanked her for her contribution to a video that Barbara made for his eightieth birthday. He closed with, "Often, when speaking with our dear friend Irene [Mayer Selznick], I hear of you and think of you with joy and love."

For a man in his eighties, he seemed to be in excellent shape. Of course, if he did sense anything creeping up on him he undoubtedly intended to keep it to himself. Things stayed that way until October of 1984, when he didn't feel well. After several days he went to Cedars-Sinai, where he was told he'd had a small stroke. He canceled a few "Conversations" until he felt up to it. It might have been about this time that he had a ramp installed next to the front stairs at the Beverly Grove house. "That's for when I'm in my wheelchair," he would tell people who looked at him questioningly. In March 1985 he told an audience in La Mirada about the stroke. The man who had spent a lifetime adamantly refusing to let people breach his emotional wall was now talking to strangers about the perils of old age.

Inevitably, he thought about death. "I don't want to dwell on it," he said. "I don't want to attract it too soon. You know, when I was young, I thought they'd have the thing licked by the time I got to this age. I think the thing you think about when you're my age is how you're going to do it, and whether you'll behave well." His mother had simply stopped breathing. "That's a nice way to die," he mused. "You don't want to embarrass your friends."

As he toured around the country he found he had grown comfortable with the audience and enjoyed the repartee.

When he was asked about Barbara, he said, "I'm very pleased with her," then, realizing how odd that sounded, laughed. In Baltimore, a woman called out, "They don't make them like you anymore." He was clearly embarrassed by the remark, and said, "Well, that's a lovely thing for you to say, but as far as you know, I might be a total hypocrite."

He would occasionally grow wistful for the roar of unified public response. "I used to go to the [Radio City] Music Hall a lot . . . and it delighted me. All the audience was in harmony. Through some lift of my eyebrow, they'd forgotten their troubles and problems and laughed at the man on the screen. That was the best reward. Of course, I was also well-paid for my work, perhaps too well-paid. But it was the hearing of their laughter that was truly the reward."

Doing the live shows seemed out of character for a man who had walked away from the movie business. It seemed a bit strange to Grant too, but he gradually developed a theory, which indicates that he didn't miss the industrial process of movie-making, but did miss the positive reinforcement of the final result. "I need confidence. And somehow this helps me. It's an ego trip, there's no question about it. I don't know why I do this. I guess . . . why, because I like it."

Peter Bogdanovich always thought it odd that Grant never invited him to attend one of his shows, until Grant, weary of dodging, finally came clean: "Well, the thing is, I don't really want you *there*. Because I would be telling some story about making a picture and it would be *difficult* for me with you sitting there knowing the *truth* of what really happened. I just don't want you *there*."

The shows weren't about the money—most of the receipts went to charity. They were about proving that he was remembered, that he was loved. He might not have needed the movie business anymore, but he had been performing since he was fourteen and had grown used to applause and appreciation.

A friend believed that what tipped the scales was his need to show Barbara and Jennifer that he still mattered. "He enjoyed interacting with people. He was truly interested in them. But if he hadn't had these two wonderful women in his life, I don't think he would have ventured out on that stage."

Grant had honed his stage presentation until it was smooth. He had a few prepared bits, among them a monologue about the level of technical skill necessary to pull off even a simple scene:

I'm alone in front of the camera. There is no one else in the shot. Now let's suppose I'm doing the simplest thing—speaking a line to someone off-camera. Perhaps I'm supposed to be speaking to Grace Kelly. But Grace is actually upstairs trying on a gown. I'm playing the scene only for the director, let's say it's Hitchcock, who is watching me carefully, and for the sound man, who is listening just as carefully.

I have one line to do. I say to her, "What time can I see you tomorrow?" Hitchcock wants me to take a drink when I say the line. So I raise my glass of iced tea at the same time, which presents several problems. If I bring the glass up too soon, I sound like a man hollering into a barrel. If I put it in front of my mouth, I spoil my expression. If I put it down hard, I kill a word on the sound track. If I don't it seems unreal. I have to hold the glass at a slight angle to keep reflections out of the lens. Then I must hold it a certain way so that the ice in the glass does not interfere with the sound. It has to be absolutely still to keep the ice from tinkling, since cellophane substitutes are not used in a close-up. And finally, I have to remember to keep my head up because I have a double chin. Now we've got the whole thing worked out. But no, there's one more problem. My elbow has to be bent and turned toward my body so as not to obstruct the view of the camera.

And then he would pick up the glass, tilt it, take a sip of water and say, "What time can I see you tomorrow?" after which he gently placed the glass on the table next to him.

Thunderous applause.

For the end of the show, he would bring out a prayer he kept in his wallet and recite it by way of farewell, a summing up of the man he had wanted to be and, at long last, was:

Now Lord, you've known me a long time. You know me better than I know myself. You know that each day I am growing old and some day may even be very old. So meanwhile please keep me from the habit of thinking I must say something on every subject and on every occasion. Release me from trying to straighten out everyone's affairs. Make me thoughtful, but not moody, helpful but not overbearing.

I've a certain amount of knowledge to share, still it would be very nice to have a few friends, who, at the end, recognized and forgave the knowledge I lacked. Keep my tongue free from the recital of endless details. Seal my lips on the aches and pains; they increase daily and the need to speak of them becomes almost a compulsion. I ask for grace enough to listen to the retelling of others' afflictions, and to be helped to endure them with patience.

I would like to have improved memory, but I'll settle for growing humility and an ability to capitulate when my memory clashes with the memory of others. Teach me the glorious lesson that on some occasions I may be mistaken. Keep me reasonably kind; I've never aspired to be a Saint—Saints must be rather difficult to live with—yet on the other hand, an embittered old person is a constant burden.

Please give me the ability to see good in unlikely places and talents in unexpected people. And give me the grace to tell them so, dear Lord.

EVERY SO OFTEN Grant would check in with Walt Odets. He would begin the conversation by saying, "Hel-*lo*, Walt!" sounding just like Cary Grant. The last time he called, Walt could tell he was getting older. "He told me about the show he was doing, and the towns where he'd been. Every time he called, at some point in the conversation he would always say, 'You know, I adored your father.' It was as if he was trying to communicate with my father through me. He was so respectful, so sweet."

He went out of his way to be considerate, whether to strangers or old friends. When a TV documentary about Kate Hepburn needed his permission for the use of clips in which they both appeared, Grant told the filmmakers to "Please use excerpts that make Kate look good. It's her show. So it's important that *she's* the one that looks good."

Sue Lloyd would see Grant occasionally around town, often at the racetrack. He would sit her down, fix her with a penetrating look, and ask her questions: How are you? Are you happy? The last time she saw him was at a ship christening at San Pedro. The cast of *The Love Boat* was there, not to mention the cast of *Dynasty*, and Grant was there with Barbara. Sue told Grant that she was pregnant and hoped it was a boy. "Oh, your grandfather would be so happy," Grant told her. "I hope it's a boy. Harold always wanted another son."

Shortly before his trip to Davenport, Grant was in Dallas at a benefit for the Princess Grace Foundation. Jill St. John was also among the attending celebrities, and she and Grant sat together. The conversation inevitably turned to Lance Reventlow. The wife of the governor of Texas was sitting next to Grant, and she didn't know who Lance was. She leaned over and asked, "Excuse me, who is this wonderful gentleman you're talking about?"

Grant turned to her and quietly said, "We're talking about my son."

In one of his last interviews, Grant was asked how he thought his life might have gone had his youthful desires not boiled down to a few overriding ambitions: Get out of Bristol. Travel. Earn applause. *Live.*

"I think we all find ourselves where we put ourselves," he replied in one of his gnomish stabs at wisdom. "We choose our places. I don't believe in fate. I don't believe in good luck, only good luck in the point of birth. I think of life as a series of plateaus. And since I hope to be on a better plateau, I can't say I'm completely satisfied. . . . The trick in life is not to feel inferior and not to feel superior. There is always another guy who knows more than you, and you must recognize that."

And has there been anything in your life that made you feel inferior?

"I never learned to play the cello."

EPILOGUE

On November 27, 1986, Grant, Barbara, Jennifer, and her boyfriend were all at Beverly Grove. After dinner, they played Trivial Pursuit. Grant liked to insist that his memory had grown feeble, but it was almost impossible to beat him at Trivial Pursuit. That night, Jennifer had a dream. She and Barbara and Grant were on a cruise and she and her father were in a painting class. A young, lean man with a beard came to Jennifer and asked her to bring her father to his cabin. When she got to the cabin, her father was already there. He was kneeling in front of the man, whose hands were on her father's shoulders. Jennifer was afraid, but her father told her to come in, that everything was fine.

With the man's hands still on her father's shoulders, Grant arched his head and began to vomit blood. He was clearly dying. Jennifer woke up crying and ran down the hall to her boyfriend and told him about the dream. She believed that the young man in the dream was Jesus, because there was a resemblance and he exuded kindness.

Two days later, Cary Grant died in Davenport, Iowa. Vincent Canby's obituary in *The New York Times* had no time for conventional wisdom— that Grant was a supremely gifted comedian who perhaps stuck too slavishly to his niche. "To ask Mr. Grant to do a mood piece like *None But the Lonely Heart* or a solemn-faced period spectacle like *The Pride and the Passion* was to anesthetize a large part of the actor's personality. . . . It was like asking Cole Porter to write a hymn."

Grant had typed out his wishes for his funeral in capital letters on lined notebook paper. Among his requests was this: "LIKE GROUCHO MARX I AM ADAMANT ABOUT NOT WANTING EITHER FLOWERS OR EULOGIES WHEN I'M GONE, UNLESS THE EULOGY WOULD IMPRESS MY DAUGHTER AND MY DEAR WIFE THAT I DID THE BEST I KNEW HOW IN EVERY PHASE OF LIFE. FOR MYSELF AND OTHERS AROUND ME. WHEN I DIE, I JUST WANT TO DIE. AND BE REMEMBERED MOSTLY AS A GOOD SON TO MY MOTHER AND FATHER, AND A GOOD FATHER TO MY DAUGHTER AND A GOOD HUSBAND TO MY WIFE."

Grant's will had been signed on November 26, 1984. It is a carefully designed document with all of his flair for the nineteenth-century phrase, as in the authorization of his executors, "to invest and reinvest any surplus money in their hands in every kind of property, real, personal or mixed, and every kind of investment, that men of prudence, discretion and intelligence acquire for their own account."

He bequeathed the house and its furnishings, his art and his cars to Barbara. Everything else was divided equally between her and Jennifer, with Jennifer's money doled out through a trust fund until she was thirty-five. Specific bequests included $100,000 to his bookkeeper, $50,000 to the Motion Picture Relief Fund, $25,000 to Variety Clubs International, $25,000 to the John Tracy Clinic for the Hearing Impaired, and $10,000 to Dr. Mortimer Hartman. His clothes and jewelry were left to Stanley Fox, with the understanding that Fox would distribute them to Grant's friends, including Frank Sinatra, Stanley Donen, Kirk Kerkorian, and Roderick Mann. Jennifer took the remainder of his wardrobe and doled it out to inconspicuous places around town—the shop at the Motion Picture Home was the recipient of Grant's neckties.

After Grant died, Kate Hepburn telephoned her condolences to Betsy Drake. Betsy waited a few months, then wrote to bring Kate up to date. Her initial feelings echoed those of the moviegoing public: "I guess I assumed that Cary would outlive everybody in the world." And then she got personal: "For some strange reason, despite all that happened, despite that I think Cary was, in some respects, perfectly terrible, I loved him and haven't been as involved with anyone else since."

A few weeks later, Betsy wrote Hepburn again. Besides the bequests to what Betsy referred to as "his Mafia friends, [Kerkorian] and Sinatra, etc." he had also left his favorite ex-wife something in his will. Barbara had sent Betsy a crystal and silver decanter, a painting of Drake's, and a money clip Drake had given Grant during their marriage. Accompanying the objects was a note from Barbara. Cary, she wrote, hoped Betsy had forgiven him.

Drake wrote Barbara back, refusing the money clip, the painting, and the decanter. All she wanted, she said, was a paper knife Grant had once brought her from Mexico that she had given back to him for a birthday present. When he had given her the knife, made out of tortoise shell and silver, she had forgotten to give him a penny, which you are supposed to do in reciprocity for the gift. "Thus," she wrote, "began the beginning of the end." In closing, Drake told Barbara Grant that she had indeed forgiven the man she had loved for so many years.

The feeling of loss, of a comforting presence irreplaceably gone, was replicated throughout the world, by audiences as well as family, friends, and filmmakers. Peter Bogdanovich was once asked to name the one actor he would have liked to have worked with. He responded without hesitation: "Cary. He could do anything. Oh, God, he was my favorite. I still *kvell* over the things he did."

Pauline Kael wrote, "We didn't expect emotional revelations from Cary Grant. We were used to his keeping his distance—which, if we cared to, we could close in idle fantasy. He appeared before us in his radiantly shallow perfection, and that was all we wanted of him. He was the Dufy of acting—shallow, but in a good way, shallow without trying to be deep. We didn't want depth from him; we asked only that he be handsome and silky and make us laugh."

In one of his last interviews, Grant had theorized that "the reason we're put on this earth is to procreate. To leave something behind. Not films, because you know that I don't think my films will last very long once I'm gone."

He was wrong, profoundly so. More than a generation after his death Grant's best films still flourish as prime examples of popular art, and audiences still cling to him as an embodiment of gentler times, with the actor's multiple ambiguities lending a sense of psychological depth absent from most stars of the period.

Cary Grant exemplified the truth that Dickens voiced in *Hard Times*, when he has a circus master named Sleary utter what might have been Archie Leach's motto. Sleary tells Gradgrind that it isn't enough always to be working or even learning. Something else is needed to sustain life emotionally. "People must be amused," he says.

Grant's genius was to be simultaneously amused and amusing. The world, he implied, is hopelessly variegated, not to mention bizarre, and imagination is every bit as vital as a flush bank account. In his life, he tended to emphasize the bank account, but in his work he projected a profound appreciation of play.

In so many ways, Cary Grant *was* the movies, a great star who embodied the physical experience of watching movies—a brilliant, centered light made all the brighter by a surrounding darkness— Grant's wariness about the world and most of the people in it. The darkness worked for him as an actor, got in his way as a man. But, as Bill Royce noted, "If great anguish was one product of his childhood, so were great strength and independence."

Cary Grant was not born with style, but he caught it, the way other people catch measles or religion, then developed it and exemplified it. Elegance combined with irony, masculine beauty amplified by a consistent willingness to look ridiculous—an actor with an allergy to the banal, a man who developed a gift for the gentle.

"When I think of him now," says Bill Royce,

> I think of how kind he was. He was one of the kindest people I've ever met. I was a troubled young man—successful professionally, but personally it was another matter entirely. Cary's priorities were Jennifer and his business, but he was willing to take time with me near the end of his life, when time was the most precious commodity he had. It was the time, and the lessons. And the way he refused to judge people. "Don't bemoan your fate," he told me once. "Concentrate on the positive as much as possible."
>
> You don't see much of that warmth in the world today.

Years after he died, Jennifer played a tape recording her father had made one Christmas when she was a small child. On the tape, Grant verbally documents the opening of all of the gifts, and oohs and ahs over a magic trick Jennifer had learned. A friend of Jennifer's listened to the tape, smiled, and said, "That's your problem! That's why you haven't found a man. . . . How could anyone live up to that?"

For his daughter, as well as his audience, nobody else could.

"People keep telling me I've had such an interesting time of it,' Grant said near the end of his life. "But I remember all those stomach disturbances that afflicted me every time I started a new picture. I was an idiot until I was forty, all wrapped up in my own ego. . . . Speaking as Archie Leach, I'm not ungrateful for all that being Cary Grant has done for me."

In the end, he managed to assimilate Archie with Cary, although he seems to have thought of Archie as someone he used to know. "He was very immature compared with me," he once said of his youthful self, "but I quite liked him."

He assiduously maintained Archie's history in his archives—he always kept the autograph of the great music hall star Vesta Tilley he got in March of 1918. It's nothing more than a postcard with Tilley's signature, but it obviously meant a lot to Archie—it's creased and worn, bearing the evidence of being pulled out of his kit dozens of times to show it off. Perhaps he kept the picture because Tilley was a magical performer; perhaps he kept it for other reasons. Tilley quit performing after World War I when she was only in her fifties. She retired to Monte Carlo with her husband; she left the audience wanting more.

Grant could have worked more outside of his comfort zone, tested his limits, but he had to deal with Archie's voice in his head, telling him to be careful. If he wasn't careful, he might lose everything that Cary had brought him. "With all his success, I think he missed out on something that he really wanted and that was within his reach," George Cukor asserted.

> He never had the prestige of a serious actor that he might have had because of his reluctance to take any risk.
>
> Underneath the charm, the great looks, the sophistication, I think he was always unhappy, with great misgivings about himself; but unexpectedly human; unexpectedly there's a warmth and humanity that takes you unawares. He had this wonderful grace, this wonderful gaiety. He was a serious man, something he would cover up; a very private man with a strong streak of melancholia.

Despite a roster of neuroses that would have brought an ox to its knees, Archie Leach recast himself as Cary Grant and forged on, spending more than thirty years of his life in the creation of a triumphant body of work unparalleled in the movies—an unmannered, humorous masculinity embodied in relentlessly nimble and creative performances. His performances don't date.

The world, as is its wont, has moved on in many ways, most of them regrettable. "I can't write about a character that Cary Grant would play," said the writer-producer Judd Apatow. "I don't know how that person talks. I do know that there are people who smoke pot with fishbowls over their heads. That I understand."

Apatow's point is that Cary Grant was an aspirational figure reality could not approach. But Cary Grant was also an aspirational figure for the man who created him—an achievement of genius.

In Bristol, much remains unchanged. The Bishop Road elementary school has a plaque marking Grant's attendance, while an equivalent plaque at Fairfield—now called Fairlawn—was stolen some years ago and never replaced. In 2018, a great-great-grandniece of Grant's was attending Fairlawn.

The Hippodrome, the Bristol theater where he fell in love with show business, still pulls large audiences for touring West End musicals. The Empire, Grant's other favorite theater, closed in 1954. One of its last headliners was "Peaches Page, the Star Without a Bra."

His birthplace at 15 Hughenden Road is marked by a blue plaque, but it's a private residence. Tourists come by regularly, to such an extent that neighbors avoid sitting in their bay windows lest their leisure be disturbed.

In many respects, Cary Grant would recognize Bristol in the twenty-first century, but he would be surprised by its population—Bristol is now multicultural, with ninety-one languages spoken, a town that has successfully made the transition from industrial town to business town. His hometown has honored Grant by erecting a life-sized statue of him on a central plaza. The sculpture by Graham Ibbeson depicts Grant dressed in a tux, carrying a script for *To Catch a Thief*, in jaunty mid-stride on his way to make a wonderful movie.

As the sculpture indicates, Cary Grant attained every artist's desire: He's remembered. More than that, he's loved. With every artist, there is the grim business of separating the imagination that breeds the art from the pain that forms the personality. Luckily for us, Grant's imagination was larger than his fear.

And when it came his time to die, it was a matter of only a few hours. "All death is," he explained to Bill Royce, "is moving from one room to another. Another room where all your family and old friends you've missed and haven't seen in a while are waiting to have you join them." By the end of his life, he had come to believe that what lives once, lives forever. He was right about that, even if the only thoroughly verifiable vehicle for eternal life is art, a discipline he came to distrust and even blame.

As Grant had hoped, he died well. He was holding his wife's hand, telling her he loved her and apologizing for the inconvenience. He was on the road, just like the vaudevillian he had been—a traveling player in demand.

He was always lucky that way.

ACKNOWLEDGMENTS

In his autobiographical articles for the *Ladies' Home Journal*, Cary Grant wrote that, "Often, when I read about myself, it is so *not* about me that I'm inclined to believe it's really about the writer."

I hope that he would—grudgingly?—see this book as an exception to that rule.

In terms of the gratitude sweepstakes, first among equals are Robert Wagner and Jill St. John. Jill knew Cary Grant through her marriage to his stepson, Lance Reventlow, while RJ's friendship with Grant began in the 1950s. Both of them shared their affectionate reminiscences freely.

My friends Sir Peter and Ann Heap of London and Palm Beach offered my wife and me a spectacular guided tour of Archie Leach's hometown of Bristol, which is Peter's hometown as well. They also put us up in London while I continued my research. Peter has never wavered in his passion for Bristol or its soccer team, and to be guided by a member of Her Majesty's diplomatic corps was a rare privilege. To find that Cary Grant's parents were buried in the same cemetery as Peter's parents was a potent reminder of how strangely intimate the world can be.

Carole Phillips hosted a dinner party for my wife and me in London during which she introduced me to Tarquin Olivier, whose memories of Barbara Hutton and Hollywood during World War II provided illumination for a heretofore dim phase of Grant's life.

Ned Comstock worked at the USC Libraries for decades. Every writer of film history is in his debt, and Ned's recent retirement doesn't change that equation. Ned was not only there whenever I needed him, he was there when I didn't know I needed him, in the form of unbidden CARE packages of clips and documents that would arrive on an irregular but welcome schedule. Ned has always been a true friend, and I hope that this book is worthy of him.

With the generosity that has always marked his own marvelous film histories, Anthony Slide shared his interviews with Budd Boetticher and Mary Brian.

Alan Rode gave me support both practical (Alexander Korda's FBI file!) and moral—meals and phone calls whose predominant mode was laughter. Alan's skills as a film historian with a specialty in noir are exceeded only by his gift for friendship.

Finally, Will Coates came on board as my researcher through the good offices of my friends Tracey Goessel and Robert Bader. Not only is Will extraordinarily creative in solving biographical details, my problems became his problems and he proved to have an amazing gift for solutions. Will became more than my legman, he became a good friend. Let me echo Bogart: Will, I think this is the beginning of a beautiful friendship.

Interviews: Ray Austin, Steven Bach, Robert Bader, Richard Bann, Michael Blake, Peter Bogdanovich, George Burns, Dyan Cannon, Leslie Caron, Sydney Chaplin, James Curtis, Mort Engelberg, Douglas Fairbanks Jr., Murray Garrett, Robert Gottlieb, Jennifer Grant, Lisa Stein Haven, Sir Peter Heap, James Wong Howe, George Kennedy, Michael Korda, Robert Koster, Sue Lloyd, Jim Mahoney, Gregory William Mank, Dina Merrill, Patricia Hitchcock O'Connell, Donald O'Connor, Walt Odets, Tarquin Olivier, Robert Osborne, Warren Phillips, Victoria Riskin, Maria Riva, Bill Royce, Daniel Selznick, Jill St. John, David Thomson, Michael Uslan, Robert Wagner, Mae West, Billy Wilder, William Wilkerson III, Rob Wolders, John Sacret Young.

Bill Hooper made it possible for me to examine the voluminous Cary Grant file at the Time Inc. *Time* Research Center Files, MS 3009-RG 13, at the New-York Historical Society.

John Brady offered much moral support and not a little practical support as well. Strength to your pen, John.

I would also like to single out John Sacret Young for his memories and notes regarding Cary Grant's night at the Motion Picture Academy in 1970, and for his friendship and unyielding belief in this book and its author.

Libraries and the men and women who make their materials available are every historian's best friend. To wit:

The Margaret Herrick Library at the Academy of Motion Picture Arts and Sciences: Louise Hilton.

The Shubert Archive: Mark Swartz.

UCLA Library: Simon Elliott and his outstanding associates.

USC Cinematic Arts Library: Ned Comstock.

USC Warner Bros. Archives: Brett Service.

The Louis B. Mayer Library at the American Film Institute: Emily Wittenberg.

The staffs of the New York Public Library's Billy Rose Theatre Collection, the Lilly Library at the University of Indiana, the Beinecke Library at Yale University, and the Columbia University Library.

Backing me up for more than thirty years and all of my books is my wife, Lynn Kalber, without whom I would have written nothing at all. Professionally, I rely on the extraordinary Mort Janklow of Janklow & Nesbit, and his—and my—trusted associates Judythe Cohen and Michael Steger.

None of this would be possible without Bob Bender at Simon & Schuster, who has published me for nearly twenty years. While Bob might regard that span as cruel and unusual editorial punishment, for me it has been the most gratifying of relationships. Every writer should have Bob for their editor. Fred Chase is the copy editor of my dreams: comprehensive, relentless, and funny. In short, the best. Jonathan Karp, the publisher at S&S, and Johanna Li are part of this extremely lucky writer's extended publishing family.

My gratitude and indebtedness to you all.

—Scott Eyman
Los Angeles, New York, Bristol,
London, Lone Pine, Asheville,
Barcelona, Seville, Majorca, Aspen
December 2016–May 2020

NOTES

AFI: The Louis B. Mayer Library at the American Film Institute.
AMPAS: Academy of Motion Picture Arts and Sciences, Margaret Herrick Library.
BOSTON: Boston University, Gotlieb Center.
COLUMBIA: Columbia University Library.
DGA: Directors Guild of America.
LILLY: Lilly Library at the University of Indiana.
NYPL: Billy Rose Theatre Collection.
SHUBERT: Shubert Archive, New York City.
UCLA: UCLA Library.
USC: University of Southern California Cinematic Arts Library.
USC Warners: Warner Bros. Archives.
YALE: Beinecke Library at Yale University.

PROLOGUE

1 *"Cary's still got"*: Douglas Fairbanks Jr. to SE.
1 *Grant told Doug Fairbanks*: Douglas Fairbanks Jr. to SE.
2 *"I don't give autographs"*: Gregory Mank to SE.
3 *Grant was a marvelously skilled ringmaster*: I witnessed his level of skill when I attended his show in Fort Lauderdale.
3 *It was the crowning event*: Quad City Times, 11-29-86, p. 3.
3 *More than sixty years before*: Davenport Daily Times, 9-26-25, p. 7.
3 *At 2 p.m. Grant and his wife*: Nelson, p. 372.
4 *Something was clearly wrong*: Quad City Times, 12-1-86, p. 11.
5 *As the blood slowly leaked into his skull*: I am indebted to Dr. Tracey Goessel for her detailed explanation of Grant's catastrophic stroke.
5 *"By about 8:15"*: McCann, p. 230.

6 *Finally, a Learjet:* Nelson, p. 375.

6 *"It's a hell of a note":* Quad City Times, 12-1-86.

6 *"It was a relatively quick":* Tracey Goessel to SE.

6 *A few days later:* Rempel, p. 256.

7 *"He's a completely made up character":* Bawden and Miller, *Conversations,* p. 116.

7 *"became synonomous with":* Bogdanovich, p. 107.

8 *"He is always fretting":* David Thomson, "Charms and the Man," *Film Comment,* 2–84.

PART ONE

CHAPTER ONE

11 *"It's important":* Feeney, p. 57.

13 *"My family name is Leach":* "Archie Leach," by Cary Grant, *Ladies' Home Journal,* Jan-Feb. 1963.

14 *Archie was baptized:* AMPAS, Cary Grant papers, box 44, f. 614.

14 *Elias Leach pressed men's suits:* McIntosh and Weaver, p. 21.

14 *"My father was a . . . tallish man":* Nelson, p. 29.

14 *"a suburban stone house":* "Archie Leach," by Cary Grant, *Ladies' Home Journal,* Jan-Feb., 1963.

15 *There was an apple tree:* McIntosh and Weaver, p. 21.

15 *head to the pub:* Nelson, p. 33.

15 *That year the census:* Census of England and Wales, 1911, Ancestry.com.

15 *The family legend:* McCann, p. 272.

16 *"I know a thing or two":* Donaldson, p. 57.

17 *"To commemorate King George's Coronation":* "Celebrating 100 Years of Bishop Road School, 1896–1996," p. 11.

17 *"If the ball slammed past me":* Wansell, p. 15.

18 *"I doubt if I was a happy child":* "Archie Leach," by Cary Grant, *Ladies' Home Journal,* Jan-Feb. 1963.

18 *"I am very pleased with this report":* AMPAS, Cary Grant papers, box 44, f. 614.

18 *"Where are my dancing shoes?":* Wansell, p. 15.

19 *"You see, Archie, nobody wants you":* Donaldson, p. 153.

19 *"I think she thought of me as her doll":* Royce, p. 49.

19 *"his only escape":* Donaldson, p. 158.

20 *On February 3, 1915, Elsie Maria Leach:* I am indebted to my friend James Harrison, of the BBC in Bristol, for documentation of Elsie Leach's internment and much else besides.

21 *With his wife out of the way:* Nelson, p. 47.

21 *"I accepted it":* "Archie Leach," by Cary Grant, *Ladies' Home Journal,* Jan-Feb., 1963.

21 *"a cold, cold woman":* Donaldson, p. 39.

22 *"At most I was a steady annoyance":* Royce, p. 97.

22 *The school was coeducational*: Sir Peter Heap to SE.

22 *"I always fancied shoes"*: Diane K. Shah, "Hul-lo, This Is Cary Grant," GQ, 1–86.

23 *he had his slingshot commandeered*: Donaldson, p. 148.

23 *"I washed myself constantly"*: "Archie Leach," by Cary Grant, *Ladies' Home Journal*, Jan-Feb. 1963.

23 *"I hung around the wharves"*: Diane K. Shah, "Hul-lo, This Is Cary Grant," GQ, 1–86.

24 *"the notorious Hanover Street"*: Parker and Hudson, *Stage Door: The Bristol Hippodrome 100 Years*.

24 *The Hippodrome had opened in 1912*: Parker and Hudson, *Stage Door: The Bristol Hippodrome 100 Years*.

24 *"The Saturday matinee"*: "Archie Leach," by Cary Grant, *Ladies' Home Journal*, Jan-Feb. 1963.

25 *On the first page*: AMPAS, Cary Grant papers, Diary 1918, box 37, f. 528.

27 *"I am very sort"*: Nelson, p. 40.

28 *"The said Robert Pender"*: AMPAS, Cary Grant Papers, Box 46, Folder 661.

CHAPTER TWO

30 *"adapted from the old Italian Comedia del'Arte"*: Archie Leach, "From the Ring to the Muny Opera," *St. Louis Post-Dispatch*, 6-7-31, p. 17.

30 *"Most of the great dumb acts"*: Laurie Jr., pp. 20–21.

31 *"I landed on the table"*: Archie Leach, "From the Ring to the Muny Opera," *St. Louis Post-Dispatch*, 6-7-31, p. 17.

31 *The passenger manifest*: Manifest of SS *Olympic*, Ancestry.com.

32 *"As I stood beside him"*: Sragow, p. 43.

32 *He told Lauren*: McCann, p. 58.

33 *"my cup overflowed"*: "Archie Leach," by Cary Grant, *Ladies' Home Journal*, Jan-Feb. 1963.

33 *The Olympic arrived*: Manifest of alien passengers for SS *Olympic*, arrival in New York, 7-28-20, Ancestry.com.

33 *"keep accounts for"*: Donaldson, p. 136.

34 *"Animal impersonators, stilt walkers"*: Syracuse Herald, 12-18-21, p. 12.

34 *"Apparently figuring that business"*: Variety, 12-23-21, p. 26.

35 *In April 1922, the Pender troupe*: Chicago Tribune, 4-17-22, p. 23.

36 *"which I thank you very much"*: AMPAS, Cary Grant papers, box 17, f. 252.

36 *Archie became fast friends*: Pete Martin, "How Grant Took Hollywood," *Saturday Evening Post*, 2-19-49.

36 *At one point, Archie went to see the Marx Brothers*: "Archie Leach," by Cary Grant, *Ladies' Home Journal*, March 1963.

36 *"He was kind to me"*: Frederick C. Othman, "Original Barclay for Your Favorite Bar—Cartoonist Turns 'Em Out in Lots; Overseas to Draw Pin-Ups for Boys," *New York Morning Telegraph*, 3-21-44.

37 *"I am writing this to inform you"*: AMPAS, Cary Grant papers, Pender to Leach, 5-21-22, box 46, f. 661.

CHAPTER THREE

39 *"If you would drink like a Purdue"*: Orry-Kelly, p. 9.

39 *"One winter evening"*: Orry-Kelly, p. 88.

39 *"I was so poor"*: AMPAS, Sidney Skolsky papers, Cary Grant tintype, box 9, f. 108.

40 *"I met Cary Grant"*: Burns, p. 29.

40 *The wisest ones auditioned*: Cagney, p. 29.

41 *"Anybody could be in it"*: Burns, p. 57.

41 *"There were acrobats and magicians"*: Donald O'Connor to SE.

42 *Archie remembered his salary*: "Archie Leach," by Cary Grant, *Ladies' Home Journal*, March 1963.

42 *"a tempting target"*: "Archie Leach," by Cary Grant, *Ladies' Home Journal*, Part three, April 1963.

42 *Burns reported that*: Nelson, p. 50.

42 *"We did so well"*: Orry-Kelly, p. 90.

43 *"If the audience likes you"*: George Burns to SE.

43 *"After the third encore"*: Nelson, p. 52.

43 *"Well if he does try"*: AMPAS, Cary Grant Papers, Box 17, f. 252.

44 *Jack and Archie painted green frogs*: Orry-Kelly, p. 141.

44 *"I don't know why"*: Orry-Kelly, p. 396.

44 *In Grant's version*: Succinctly made in a letter to Garson Kanin, AMPAS, Cary Grant papers, Grant to Kanin, 7-16-81, box 17, f. 237.

45 *Syd and Minnie had an open marriage*: Lisa Stein Haven, Syd Chaplin's biographer, to SE.

45 *Burns took over the party*: Orry-Kelly, p. 99.

46 *"Why run away?"*: Orry-Kelly, p. 102.

46 *The skit involved*: Nelson, p. 55.

47 *"In Cary's day"*: Nelson, p. 29.

47 *"Everything starts with pretense"*: "Archie Leach," by Cary Grant, *Ladies' Home Journal*, March 1963.

47 *Their agent was a Chicagoan*: Display ad in *Variety*, 10-28-25.

47 *"On the night trains"*: Bawden and Miller, *Conversations*, p. 118.

48 *The other actors stared*: "Archie Leach," by Cary Grant, *Ladies' Home Journal*, March 1963.

48 *"a skit combining comedy"*: Des Moines Register, 10-3-25.

48 *"Their contribution to the stage"*: Asheville Citizen-Times, 1-10-26.

49 *"dapper male comedians"*: Nashville Tennessean, 2-16-26.

49 *"Vaudeville . . . has had"*: Cagney, p. 29–31.

49 *"I learned to time laughs"* Wansell, p. 19.

50 *He saw a crew erecting Al Jolson's name*: Donaldson, p. 137.

51 *In 1927, he took out a life insurance policy*: AMPAS, Cary Grant papers, Amendment for the New York Life Insurance Company, 1-20-27, box 24, f. 398.

51 *"overheated colonialist fever dream"*: Hammerstein, p. 111.

51 *"We all had our blue serge suits"*: AMPAS, Jane Ardmore papers, box 12, f. 25.

52 *"I washed, polished, scrubbed"*: "Archie Leach," by Cary Grant, *Ladies' Home Journal*, April 1963.

52 *"She kissed with such* pash*"*: Turk, p. 63.

53 *"Mr. Lee Shubert"*: SHUBERT, E. R. Simmons correspondence, 1928–29, Archie Leach.

53 *The new contract was signed on July 12, 1929*: AMPAS, Cary Grant papers, Shubert/Leach contract, box 31, f. 521.

53 *He arrived in Liverpool*: Passenger manifest for *Adriatic*, July 22, 1929, Ancestry.com.

53 *"It's all so interesting"*: SHUBERT, E. R. Simmons Correspondence, 1928–29, Leach to Simmons, 8-15-29, excerpted in Helice Koffler, "More About the E. R. Simmons Papers," *The Passing Show*, newsletter of the Shubert Archive, volume 32, 2015/2016.

54 *"You could barely see it"* Donaldson, p. 137.

54 *"Archie Leach . . . feels that acting"*: AMPAS, Cary Grant clipping file, "Stage," 4-13-39, Katherine Best, "Up from Tumbling."

54 *"Please tell Archie Leach"* SHUBERT, E. R. Simmons Correspondence, 1928–1929, Tentative Cast Lists and Layouts, 1929–30.

55 *He was living at the Belvedere Hotel*: SHUBERT, E. R. Simmons Production Files, *A Wonderful Night*.

55 *"ENGLISH ACTOR PRAISES AMERICANS"*: *Boston Globe*, 12-21-30, p. 56.

57 *The contract is dated May 8, 1931*: AMPAS, Cary Grant papers, box 6, f. 76.

57 *"I wrote a note"*: Deschner, p. 9.

58 *According to an article*: "Suit Against Archie Leach," *St. Louis Post-Dispatch*, 8-18-31, p. 19.

58 *Archie kept at least one program*: AMPAS, Cary Grant papers, box 51, f. 740.

58 *"Father took me back"*: Archie Leach, "From the Ring to Muny Opera," *St. Louis Post-Dispatch*, 6-7-31, p. 17.

59 *"I hereby release you"*: AMPAS, Cary Grant papers, Shubert to Leach, 8-28-31, box 31, f. 521.

60 *as of the first week of September*: USC, Fay Wray collection, John Monk Saunders scrapbook, *New York, Evening Post*, 9-29-30, *New York Evening Post*, 9-30-31.

60 *"Archie Leach was born in Bristol, England"*: USC, Fay Wray collection, John Monk Saunders scrapbook.

61 *"He had an outstanding quality"*: Drew, p. 84.

61 *For the rest of their lives*: Nelson, p. 62.

61 *"It was a very strong connection"*: Victoria Riskin to SE.

63 *"I am so glad to hear from everybody"*: SHUBERT, E. R. Simmons Correspondence, 1930–33, Archie Leach.

CHAPTER FOUR

65 *"The talkies had just started"*: Wodehouse, p. 9.

66 *"Grant was actually the founder"*: Morley, p. 121.

67 *"There's no getting around it,"*: AMPAS, Cary Grant clipping file, Robin Coons, "Zeal for Work Marks Career of Cary Grant," 3-30-33.

67 *"The first thing you learn"*: McCann, p. 68.

67 *Grant's first day of moviemaking*: AMPAS, Paramount Pictures production records, *This Is the Night* schedule, box 211, f. 2.

67 *Grant worked two and a half weeks*: AMPAS, Paramount Pictures production records, *This Is the Night*, "Cast," box 211, f. 1.

67 *"From my younger man's viewpoint"*: "Archie Leach," by Cary Grant, *Ladies' Home Journal*, April 1963.

68 *"Every time I'd start to say something"*: Orry-Kelly, p. 173.

68 *Grant marked the occasion*: AMPAS, Cary Grant papers, sales agreement, 5-6-32, box 23, f. 398.

69 *"I suggested he take"*: Orry-Kelly, p. 178.

70 *"He didn't want to play it"*: Kobal, p. 669.

71 *Parsons thought it was unfortunate*: Eells, p. 142.

71 *His salary was still only $450*: AMPAS, Paramount Pictures production records, *Blonde Venus*, costs, 1932, box 34, f. 402.

71 *"Marlene admired him"*: Bach to SE.

72 *"Jo was walking pain"*: Bach to SE

72 *"When a man is madly in love"*: Maria Riva to SE.

72 *"Your hair is parted"*: Bogdanovich, p. 101.

72 *"Josef von Sternberg yelled at her"*: Bawden and Miller, *Conversations*, p. 120.

73 *"There's a young, handsome Cockney"*: Riva, p. 151.

73 *"I hate to be continually writing you"*: AMPAS, Cary Grant papers, "Lester" to Grant, 7-19-32, box 41, f. 588.

74 *"If women want to wear men's clothes"*: AMPAS, Cary Grant clipping file, unsourced clipping, 1-25-33.

74 *"We were just about ready to start shooting"*: Mae West to SE.

75 *Grant had gotten a raise*: AMPAS, Paramount Pictures production records, *She Done Him Wrong*, general, 1932, box 187, f. 1.

75 *"When I first met her"*: I have combined two interviews with Grant: Bawden and Miller, *Conversations*, p. 119; Leider, p. 280.

76 *"Cary Grant wasn't like he is today"*: Chierichetti, p. 54.

77 *"Over at Paramount they have a little list"*: UCLA, Randolph Scott scrapbooks, Eileen Creelman, "Talks with Two of Paramount's Newcomers Randolph Scott and Cary Grant," 7-19-32.

77 *When Amelia Earhart visited*: All of these events are documented at UCLA, Randolph Scott scrapbooks, "Greet Amelia," *Hollywood Herald*, 7-16-32; "Cary Grant Party," 11-26-32; *Hollywood Citizen News*, 11-30-32.

78 *"The mink coat and the diamonds"*: Orry-Kelly, p. 180.

78 *"I fell in love with her the moment I saw her"*: Seymour, 113.

79 *Cherrill looked out the window*: Seymour, p. 117.

79 *"Cary never talked about his background"*: Seymour, p. 118.

79 *"Cary was driven"*: Seymour, p. 118.

79 *"Randolph Scott and Cary Grant, who live together"*: UCLA, Randolph Scott scrapbooks, February 1933 photo, unsourced.

80 *"Douglas Fairbanks once told me"*: Seymour, p. 123.

80 *"One of the guests tapped Cary"*: Seymour, p. 130.

81 *"Randy was good with Cary"*: Seymour, p. 131–32.

81 *She promptly flounced out of the house*: Seymour, p. 135.

82 *As the party was winding down*: AMPAS, Cary Grant papers, Transatlantic Crossings and Cruises, menu for November 22, 1933, party, box 50, f. 733.

82 *According to Cherrill*: Seymour, p. 138.

82 *"He actually asked me to meet him"*: Cannon, p. 113.

83 *"I went crazy"*: Donaldson, p. 159.

83 *Elsie's medical records aren't any help*: James Harrison of BBC Bristol.

83 *There is a teasing reference*: McCann, p. 276.

83 *Randy Scott only stayed in England for two weeks*: List of United States citizens sailing from Havre, December 6, 1933.

84 *"I went to Fishponds"*: Royce, p. 68.

84 *"They made their appearances . . . in relays"*: AMPAS, Cary Grant clipping file, "Confusion Marks Nuptials of Virginia Cherrill and Cary Grant," *Hollywood Citizen News*, 2-9-34.

84 *"Randolph Scott refusing to move"*: UCLA, Randolph Scott scrapbooks, "Hot-Cha Stuff," *Los Angeles Herald-Express*, 3-17-34.

CHAPTER FIVE

85 *In fact, Grant wasn't in the costume*: Gregory Mank to SE.

85 *In the spring of 1934*: Seymour, p. 146.

86 *Cherrill was talking to Sir Guy Standing*: Seymour, p. 151.

86 *"Was [the trouble] brewing for some time"*: AMPAS, Cary Grant clipping file, 10-2-34, "Cary, Virginia Quarrel? Oh No! They're in Love."

86 *His speech was slurred*: Seymour, p. 152.

86 *"I'm ashamed of getting drunk"*: AMPAS, Cary Grant clipping file, "Grant Just Drunk, His Shamed Plea in Poison Scare," *New York Daily News*, 10-6-34.

87 *"I just got drunk and passed out"*: Donaldson, p. 203.

87 *She asked for $1,000 a month*: AMPAS, Cary Grant clipping file, "Mate Cruel, Says Actress," *Los Angeles Examiner*, 12-4-34.

87 *"My first wife"*: Donaldson, p. 203.

87 *"sullen, disagreeable and morose"*: AMPAS, Cary Grant clipping file, "Miss Cherrill Divorces Cary Grant," unsourced, 3-26-35.

87 *"I missed Cary"*: Seymour, p. 158.

87 *In 1945, she financed*: Mutti-Mewse and Mutti-Mewse, p. 267.

87 *"We were never one"*: Donaldson, p. 203.

87 *In September 1934*: Riskin, p. 174.

88 The Hollywood Reporter *had already established itself as ground zero*: McCann, p. 128.

89 *"Cary Grant, Randy Scott, Betty Furness"*: *Hollywood Reporter*, March 1936.

89 Photoplay *waited until 1939*: Slide, *Inside the Hollywood Fan Magazines*, pp. 163–64.

89 *"When it came to my father's business"*: William Wilkerson III to SE, as are all the quotes in this section.

90 *"My father had an endless number"*: Scott, p. 171.

90 *"I can tell you honestly"*: Scott, p. 174.

91 *"No actor was more of a man"*: Nott, pp. 2–3.

91 *"Luscious Baby"*: Warren Phillips, former publisher of *The Wall Street Journal*, to SE.

91 *"Night after night,"*: Brendan Gill, "Pursuer and Pursued,": *The New Yorker*, 6-2-97.

93 *"Noel Coward and Cary Grant"*: Hedda Hopper column, *St. Louis Post-Dis-patch*, 10-27-40.

CHAPTER SIX

95 *"there were girls running in and out"*: Nelson, p. 79.

95 *"beyond any question the most attractive"*: Nelson, p. 75.

95 *"Cary is the gay, impetuous one,"*: Architectural Digest, April 1996, p. 282.

95 *"Here we are"*: AMPAS, Cary Grant clipping file, *Modern Screen*, no month, 1939.

96 *"Cary opened the bills"*: Architectural Digest, April 1996, p. 282.

96 *when he and his first wife*: Richard Bann to SE.

97 *"arrogant, egotistical, pompous"*: Coleman, p. 42.

98 *On May 3, 1935*: AMPAS, Cary Grant papers, Herzbrun to Grant, 5-3-35, box 31, f. 521.

98 *Elias was buried*: AMPAS, Cary Grant papers, Greenslade to Grant's solicitors Kerly, Sons & Karuth, 6-27-63, box 44, f. 614.

98 *In yet another example*: McCann, p. 123.

99 *"We had cars"*: Mary Brian to Anthony Slide. I am indebted to him for sharing the transcript of his interviews with Mary Brian.

99 *"Just a line enclosing"*: AMPAS, Cary Grant papers, Elsie Leach to Grant, 9-30-37, box 17, f. 253.

100 *"My darling Archie"*: AMPAS, Cary Grant papers, Elsie Leach to Grant, 11-15-38, box 17, f. 253.

100 *"When I go to see her"*: Nelson, p. 88.

101 *"People misinterpret a lot of things"*: Mary Brian to Anthony Slide.

101 *"Mary always had the best affairs"*: The remark was made by Peggy Lloyd, wife of Norman Lloyd.

101 *"I can't help it"*: Behlmer, *Hathaway*, p. 94.

102 *"Always used to wear a scarf"*: Behlmer, *Hathaway*, p. 95.

102 *"The Cary Grant publicity campaign"*: Julie Lang Hunt, "We Will Never Understand Cary Grant," *Photoplay*, 9–35, excerpted in Gelman, *Photoplay Treasury*.

103 *It was in honor of Gertrude Lawrence*: Orry-Kelly, p. 350.

103 *"I despised everything about it."*: Mann, *Kate*, p. 235.

103 *"I had tested a young fellow"*: AFI, Pandro Berman oral history, August 1972.

104 *"I'd scarcely seen a motion picture"*: Wilk, p. 129.

104 *"Cary Grant's performance"*: Hepburn, p. 232.

105 *"OUR LITTLE LOVE CHILD"*: AMPAS, George Cukor collection, Cukor to Hepburn, 12-9-35, box 59, f. 780.

105 *"He was extraordinarily good-looking"*: I have combined two separate interviews with Cukor, the first is from AMPAS, George Cukor collection, box 65., f. 964, the second AFI, George Cukor seminar, 5-24-79.

106 *"Mind you, he's better"*: AFI oral history, Lambert-Cukor, August 1970 to April 1971.

106 *"You see, he didn't depend on his looks"*: Schickel, *The Men Who Made the Movies*, p. 182–183.

106 *"The whole joke"*: Mann, *Kate*, p. 237.

107 *"Do you think, with* My Fair Lady*"*: AMPAS, George Cukor collection, Cukor to Hayward, 11-17-64; Hayward's reply to Cukor, 11-24-64, box 19, f. 200.

108 *This time Paramount was getting*: AMPAS, Paramount Pictures contract summaries, Wanger contract dated 2-17-36, MGM contract dated 4-2-36, box 11, f. 976.

108 *"The part is completely wrong"*: Coffee, pp. 116–17.

110 *"It is too bad we slipped up"*: AFI, Charles Feldman papers, 7-13-36.

110 *Ronald Colman, for instance*: Kemper, p. 125.

110 *"I'd get at least one good feature a year"*: James Bawden, "Irene Dunne: Legendary Cool," *Films of the Golden Age*, Fall 2012.

110 *On February 4, 1937, Grant signed a four-picture deal*: USC Warners, Cary Grant legal file, Columbia Contract, 2-4-37, f. 2830A.

CHAPTER SEVEN

114 *In a letter dated March 19, 1937*: USC, Hollywood Museum Collection, Hal Roach material, Breen to Roach, 3-19-37, box 1:88.

114 *He saw the picture in June*: USC, Hollywood Museum Collection, Hal Roach material, *Topper*, Breen to Roach, 6-24-37, box 1, f. 88.

114 *Shot in a snappy six weeks*: USC, Hollywood Museum Collection, Hal Roach material, box 1, f. 103.

115 *"We just meshed"*: James Bawden, "Irene Dunne: Legendary Cool," *Films of the Golden Age*, Fall 2012.

115 *"Well, why are you sending it over"*: Maltin, pp. 178–81.

117 *"I'd say, 'See everybody at nine o clock'"*: AFI, Bogdanovich-McCarey oral history, 11-25-68.

117 *"Every evening, he would have a conference"*: Bernds, p. 290

117 *Grant even called his friend Hal Roach*: Richard Bann to SE.

119 *"No doubt he felt absurd"*: Kael, pp. 469, 471.

119 *"Irene Dunne's timing"*: Feeney, p. 68.

119 *"[Comedy is] is something like"*: Kobal, 322.

119 *In fact, Dunne worked very hard*: David Chierichetti, "The Making of My Favorite Wife," *Films of the Golden Age*, Fall 2012.

120 *"Grant was smooth"*: Basinger, *The Star Machine*, pp. 88, 113.

120 *"When anybody asks me my favorite director"*: AMPAS, SMU collection of Ronald Davis, Irene Dunne interview with Ronald Davis, 7-23-82.

120 *"Even if I were not in a movie"*: Harvey, *Romantic Comedy in Hollywood*, pp. 687, 690.

121 *PARDON ME WHILE I BURN INCENSE*: USC, Leo McCarey collection, correspondence, post–*Awful Truth* preview, October 6–7, 1937.

121 *MAKE ME HAPPY BY GOING CLOSER*: USC, Leo McCarey collection, Grant to McCarey, 10-7-37.

122 *"When McCarey found that out"*: Bernds, p. 290.

122 *The guest list included five hundred*: Finch and Rosenkrantz, p. 234.

124 *"I know, because the gentleman has said so"*: Lusky to Briskin, 8-19-37, Howard Hawks file, RKO West Coast archives, quoted in Richard Jewell, "How Howard Hawks Brought Baby Up: An Apologia for the Studio System," *Journal of Popular Film and Television*, Winter 1984.

125 *"Cary went over to talk to Harold"*: Sue Lloyd to SE.

125 *"Cary was so funny"*: Hepburn, p. 238.

125 *"The great trouble"*: McBride, p. 72.

126 *To torment Grant*: Hepburn, p. 240.

127 *Cary Grant was invariably classy*: This section owes much to Jeanine Basinger's *The Star Machine*, p. 373.

130 *"was one of the best villains ever written"*: Fairbanks Jr., *The Salad Days*, p. 272.

130 *"He had always been most concerned"*: Fairbanks Jr., *The Salad Days*, p. 285.

130 *Fairbanks was earning $117,187*: AMPAS, George Stevens collection, *Gunga Din* costs, box 223, f. 2613.

131 *"Doug would put on his best manners"*: AMPAS, George Stevens collection, *George Stevens—A Filmmaker's Journey* interviews, Cary Grant, box 2, f. 25.

131 *"Nothing was going to stop him"*: AMPAS, George Stevens collection, *George Stevens—A Filmmaker's Journey* interviews, Cary Grant, box 2, f. 25.

131 *"Vic was lovely"*: AMPAS, George Stevens collection, *George Stevens—A Filmmaker's Journey* interviews, Cary Grant, box 2, f. 25.

132 *"chronically late, chronically expensive"*: Moss, p. 56.

132 *"He was a master technician"*: Nelson, p. 104.

132 *Fairbanks remembered*: Nelson, p. 92.

133 *When Stevens was apprised*: Moss, p. 59.

133 *"I was with Annie"*: AMPAS, George Stevens collection, George Stevens— A Filmmaker's Journey interviews, Cary Grant, box 2, f. 25.

133 *Caroline Kipling asserted that the filmmakers*: Most of this is from Behlmer, *America's Favorite* "The Rover Boys in India: *Gunga Din*," pp. 87–103.

134 *"Imperialist propaganda of the crudest"*: Behlmer, *America's Favorite* "The Rover Boys in India: *Gunga Din*," p. 100.

134 *"I made the film long ago"*: Moss, p. 62.

135 *"Simple man"*: Gilbert, 216.

136 *"razor-creased trousers"*: Polito, ed., p. 653.

136 *"My mother was a tight-thinking person"*: Nelson, p. 110.

137 *"I read in newpaper suggestion"*: AMPAS, Cary Grant papers, Box 17, f. 253.

PART TWO

CHAPTER EIGHT

141 *"We have three more pictures to make with Grant"*: AMPAS, Paul Becker collection of Ginger Rogers RKO files, Nolan to Schaefer, 8-31-39, box 4, f. 36.

142 *"perfectly amazed that [Grant] took the part"*: Maltin, p. 221.

143 *Lester stored 16mm prints of movies*: Lester, 132.

144 *DARLING TELEPHONE*: AMPAS, Cary Grant papers, Elsie Leach to Cary Grant, 9-2-39, box 17, f. 253.

144 *David Niven came from a military family*: Lord, p. 100.

144 *"I think I was saved"*: Lord, p. 100.

144 *"I admire your courage and all that"*: Ziegler, p. 87.

145 *Niven did not include Grant*: Lord, p. 105.

145 *Balcon went so far as to single out*: Billheimer, p. 76; Morley, p. 176.

145 *Bristol would be the fifth most bombed city*: Parker and Hudson, *Stage Door: The Bristol Hippodrome, 100 Years*.

145 *in January 1941, Mr. and Mrs. John Henry Leach*: AMPAS, Cary Grant clippings, *Los Angeles Examiner*, 1-26-41.

146 *The show was on NBC*: *Variety*, 1-16-39, p. 1.

147 *"intends to reside permanently in the United States"*: AMPAS, Cary Grant Papers, Certificate of Naturalization No. 5502057, box 46, f. 647; also: National Archives at Riverside, California, NAI number 594890; record group title 21, records of district courts of the United States, 1685–2009.

147 *In 1942, Grant grossed*: AMPAS, Cary Grant Papers, Pike to Grant, 8-21-43, box 41, f. 582.

147 *Grant's stockholdings*: AMPAS, Cary Grant papers, "List of Earnings from 1-1-43 to 6-15-43," box 41, f. 582.

147 *"Darling, do let me know"*: AMPAS, Cary Grant papers, Leach to Grant, box 17, f. 254.

147 *FROM MOTHER AM ALRIGHT AT PRESENT*: AMPAS, Cary Grant papers, Leach to Grant, 10-15-40, box 17, f. 254.

147 *"craze for saving"*: AMPAS, Cary Grant papers, Davis to Grant, 1-2-42, box 17, f. 254.

148 *"When you come over"*: AMPAS, Cary Grant papers, Leach to Grant, 11-21-42, box 17, f. 254.

148 *"I should like to spend a holiday"*: AMPAS, Cary Grant papers, Leach to Grant, cable, 7-25-44, box 17, f. 254; letter, 12-4-44, box 17, f. 254.

148 *"Do you mean on the screen"*: AMPAS, Cary Grant clippings, *Motion Picture*, 2-41.

148 *"an English actor"*: AMPAS, Cary Grant clipping file, 1940 studio bio issued by Columbia Pictures.

148 *a 1942 news story*: AMPAS, Cary Grant clipping file, New York *Daily News*, 7-08-42.

148 *"The pressure is very, very heavy"*: AMPAS, Cary Grant clippings file, Shirley Spencer, handwriting analysis, 8-31-42.

149 *Cohn asked Jean Arthur*: McCarthy, p. 283.

149 *"Oh, sure Roz. If he didn't like it, he'd tell you"*: McCarthy, p. 283.

150 *"I savored every line"*: Bawden and Miller, *Conversations*, p. 35.

150 *"Cary Grant uses legs, arms"*: Polito, ed., p. 470.

150 *"Grant is interested"*: Kael, p. 466.

151 *Brisson pestered her*: Nick Thomas, p. 26.

152 *"Now look what you've done!"*: Nelson, p. 113.

152 *"I blush at the originality"*: AFI, Leo McCarey papers, box 20, f. 120.

152 *"We were all attached"*: James Bawden, "Irene Dunne: Legendary Cool," *Films of the Golden Age*, Fall 2012.

153 *"I think it was Irish guilt"*: The section on *My Favorite Wife* derives from David Chierichetti's "The Making of *My Favorite Wife*," *Films of the Golden Age*, Fall 2012. Chierichetti examined the RKO production files, and was friends with Irene Dunne.

153 *He would always be*: Nelson, p. 116

154 *the accident report*: Giddins, p. 319.

155 *"He worked very hard"*: Nelson, p. 115.

CHAPTER NINE

157 *"Timing. The secret of comedy is timing"*: AMPAS, George Stevens collection, *George Stevens—A Filmmaker's Journey* interviews, Cary Grant, box 2, f. 25.

159 *"That's why so few actors"*: AMPAS, George Stevens collection, *George Stevens—A Filmmaker's Journey* interviews, Cary Grant, box 2, f. 25.

160 *"You get them," he told her*: Hepburn, pp. 216–7.

160 *"The Philadelphia Story was the easiest picture I ever did"*: AFI, Donald Ogden Stewart oral history with Max Wilk, 12-8, 13, 20, 1971.

160 *"a more nervous, fidgety actor"*: Bawden and Miller, *You Ain't Heard*, p. 67.

161 *"Kate Hepburn always plays a strong"*: Dauth, ed., p. 177.

161 *"Whatever success the picture is having:"* AMPAS, Cary Grant papers, Mankiewicz to Grant, 1-16-41, box 18, f. 272.

161 *"Cary Grant and Irene Dunne"*: Moss, p. 71.

162 *Grant's salary*: AMPAS, George Stevens collection, "Budget Penny Serenade," box 239, f. 2821.

162 *"One thing about Cary"*: AMPAS, Cary Grant clipping file, Bob Thomas, "Cary Grant Turns 80 with Style," no date.

162 *"I love doing comedy"*: AMPAS, SMU collection of Ronald Davis, Irene Dunne interview with Ronald Davis, 7-23-82.

162 *"It wasn't for want of trying"*: James Bawden, "Irene Dunne: Legendary Cool," *Films of the Golden Age*, Fall 2012.

163 *"Reunions became impossible"*: Bawden and Miller, *Conversations*, p. 123.

163 *"I was naïve enough"*: Behlmer, *America's Favorite*, p. 318.

CHAPTER TEN

165 *Irene Dunne remembered:* Nelson, p. 121.

166 *"I don't think she was feeling well":* Davies, p. 222.

166 *It was the first week of July 1942:* Lester, p. 128.

166 *"The richest girl in the world":* AMPAS, Cary Grant clipping file, New York *Daily News,* 7-8-42.

167 *Barbara Hutton inherited:* AMPAS, Cary Grant clipping file, unidentified clipping dated 1-4-34.

167 *"Grandpa Woolworth used to say":* Van Rensselaer, pp. 9–10.

167 *Between lunch at the Bath and Tennis Club:* Heymann, p. 168.

167 *"You play what you want":* University of Oregon, Dean Jennings collection, Herb Stein interview, box 2.

168 *"We chose Sunday evenings":* Heymann, p. 181.

168 *"None of us knew what we were looking at":* Heymann, p. 181.

169 *"Each one of these people alone":* AMPAS, Cary Grant clipping file, Roberta Ostroff, "How Do You Like Being Cary Grant? I Like It Fine," *West,* 1-9-72.

169 *"In England we had an old English":* Patricia Hitchcock O'Connell to SE.

170 *"Your performance was Hitchcock's performance":* Davis, p. 74.

170 *"Carole Lombard . . . was not really a comedienne":* AMPAS, George Stevens collection, *George Stevens—A Filmmaker's Journey* interviews, Cary Grant, box 2, f. 25.

170 *For* Suspicion *he received $50,000:* UCLA, RKO payroll records, 2-3-41.

171 *Grant was usually gallant:* Donaldson, p. 229.

171 *"only interested in himself":* Bawden and Miller, *Conversations,* p. 181.

171 *"that it was my picture":* AMPAS, SMU collection of Ronald L. Davis's oral histories on the performing arts, f. 139.

171 *"I don't give a damn what you think":* AMPAS, SMU collection of Ronald L. Davis's oral histories on the performing arts, f. 139.

172 *he would say that the reason they got along so well:* McIntosh and Weaver, p. 40.

173 *$50,000 went to the Southern California:* USC Warners, Obringer memo, 10-20-41, *Arsenic and Old Lace* file, 2 of 3, f. 2798.

173 *"We finally got up the courage":* Davis, p. 126.

174 *"I was embarrassed doing it":* Wansell, p. 79.

175 *"With anybody but Cary":* Bawden and Miller, *Conversations,* p. 122.

175 The Talk of the Town *came in nineteen days over schedule:* AMPAS, George Stevens collection, *Talk of the Town* costs, box 267, f. 3115.

177 *After waiting for fifteen minutes:* William Frye, "Gentleman's Agreement," *Vanity Fair,* April 2003.

177 *On June 19, 1942:* AMPAS, Cary Grant papers, Milton Kaye to Grant, 6-19-42, box 51, f. 758.

178 *"at the present time it is practically impossible":* AMPAS, Cary Grant papers, Danvers to Warner, 6-24-42, box 51, f. 758.

178   *He got letters of reference*: AMPAS, Cary Grant papers, Galloway to Adjutant General, 6-29-42, box 51, f. 758.

178   *IN VIEW OF WAR DEPARTMENT INTEREST*: AMPAS, Cary Grant papers, Stratemyer to Grant, 9-23-42, box 51, f. 758.

178   *"The matter of relieving Cary Grant"*: AMPAS, Cary Grant papers, Koerner to Grant, undated, box 51, f. 758.

179   *In fact, Korda had been scheduled*: Michael Korda to SE.

179   *The FBI was definitely tipped off*: Alexander Korda FBI file, Hoover to Conroy, 6-22-43.

180   *"It is evident that Alexander Korda"*: Alexander Korda FBI file, Ladd to Hoover, 11-4-4.

180   *"There were close to a dozen people"*: Michael Korda to SE.

181   *Usually, DeMille gave it to screenwriter Charles Bennett*: Bennett, pp. 141–42.

182   *"Alexander Korda Films Incorporated"*: Alexander Korda FBI File, Hoover to Clark, 1-31-44.

182   *"Under the circumstances"*: Alexander Korda FBI file, Sharp to Hoover, 3-27-44.

182   *"no useful purpose"*: Alexander Korda FBI file, Neal to Hoover, 2-12-45.

182   *"Mr. Korda was at first rather resentful"*: Alexander Korda FBI file, Hood to Hoover, 3-26-46.

183   *"the President's backdoor cooperation"*: Hart, p. 235.

183   *"Communist Infiltration of the Motion Picture Industry"*: McCann, p. 135.

184   *"Who in Hollywood"*: Giddins, p. 193. Giddins's second volume on Bing Crosby also provides the background for this section.

186   *Grant kept working for the cause*: USC, "Reporting Activities of Hollywood Victory Committee Incorporated to End of June 1942, Month of August 1942, and month of December 1942."

186   *In 1943, Grant toured*: AMPAS, Motion Picture Association of America Hollywood office files, volunteers, Geovanetti through Haron, box 33, f. 353.

186   *"It went something like this"*: Pete Martin, "Grant Takes Hollywood," *Saturday Evening Post*, 2-19-49.

188   Once Upon a Honeymoon *made a profit*: AFI, Leo McCarey collection, box 24, f. 165.

188   *"Very dangerous"*: Bogdanovich, " 'You Don't Look Like Cary Grant,' the Lady Said. 'I Know, Nobody Does,' Said Cary Grant." *New York Observer*, 12-1-08.

188   *RKO handed script assignments*: Langdon, p. 56.

189   *"I have never worked with an actor"*: AMPAS, SMU collection of Ronald Davis oral histories, Laraine Day, f. 100, 1979.

190   *"Very generous"*: AMPAS, oral history with Laraine Day, interview by Barbara Hall, 1998.

191   *"Delmer Daves has never directed"*: Deschner, p. 14.

191   *"This was one of the greatest"*: Goldrup and Goldrup, pp. 58–60.

193   *Guilaroff asked Grant*: Guilaroff, p. 244.

194   *"I could see now"*: Orry-Kelly, p. 262.

194   *"Look here, Cary"*: Orry-Kelly, p. 265.

195 *"Barbara had a wonderful word"*: Heymann, p. 193.

196 *"It was my mother's tragedy"*: Tarquin Olivier to SE. All quotes from Tarquin Olivier are from this interview.

197 *"I did the best that could be done"*: Jennings, p. 163.

197 *"fun, laughing, and naughty"*: Van Rennsalaer, p. 255.

198 *"If one more phony noble"*: McCann, p. 132.

198 *"Barbara was more screwed up than I was"*: Donaldson, p. 204.

198 *"I don't care how many six figure donations"*: Heymann, pp. 198–99.

199 *"You were lucky"*: Heymann, p. 200.

199 *"wanted someone to be at home"*: Heymann, p. 201.

200 *According to Hutton*: Van Rennsaeler, p. 258.

200 *"Barbara was cut to ribbons"*: Jennings, p. 167.

200 *"He was a marvelous kid"*: Donaldson, p. 204.

201 *"She so much resembles"*: AMPAS, Hedda Hopper collection, "Barbara and Cary Grant Fight for Happiness," *Modern Screen*, 6-15-44, box 55, f. 1492.

201 *Grant and Hutton separated*: AMPAS, Cary Grant clippings file, New York *Daily News*, 8-16-44.

201 *There would be occasional telegrams*: AMPAS, Cary Grant papers, box 16, folder 229.

202 *"I doubt if anyone ever understood"*: Archie Leach by Cary Grant, *Ladies' Home Journal*, part three, April 1963.

202 *"Maybe I just haven't met"*: Heymann, p. 206.

203 *"Be good to her"*: Riskin, p. 291.

204 *Grant's address book*: AMPAS, Cary Grant papers, address book circa 1942–45, box 24, f. 390.

CHAPTER ELEVEN

205 *There is a possibly apocryphal story*: Pete Martin, "Cary Grant," *Saturday Evening Post*, 2-19-49.

205 *agreed to pay Grant $100,000*: UCLA, RKO payroll records, 3-6-44.

206 *"Cary wanted to be a serious actor"*: Walt Odets to SE. All quotes from Walt Odets derive from my interviews with him.

206 *"To be near him"*: Smith, p. 129.

206 *"Clifford, if you don't turn out"*: Smith, p. 130.

206 *"He was intense"*: Riskin, p. 224.

207 *"had no great range"*: Walter Bernstein, "Loving Tribute to Kazan Nearly Derailed by Politics," *New York Observer*, 12-26-05.

207 *"First day of shooting"*: Bawden and Miller, *You Ain't Heard*, p. 228.

207 *"Ohhh what I learned from Clifford"*: Kobal, p. 589.

208 *"I enjoyed his stentorian convictions"*: "Archie Leach," by Cary Grant, *Ladies' Home Journal*, March, 1963.

208 *"Cary's serious side had depth"*: Selznick, p. 244.

209 *"Cary truly burrowed"*: Bawden and Miller, *Conversations*, p. 229.

210 *"Clifford Odets had no knowledge of camera"*: James Wong Howe to SE.

211 *When Rainer sent Odets*: Smith, p. 336.

211 *"Thank you for the very beginning"*: Nelson, p. 143.

211 *"[Grant] . . . is sweet and decent"*: Lilly Library, Lyons Collection, Odets to Lyons, 7-11-44, folder 1937–1950.

211 *Jean Renoir thought it was a masterpiece*: Renoir, p. 261.

213 *"It was nearly impossible"*: Fairbanks Jr., *A Hell of a War*, p. 264.

213 *"What will they use for a climax?"*: McBrien, p. 290.

213 *"If and when the Cary Grant Columbia assignment"*: USC Warners, Cary Grant legal file, Trilling to Obringer, 8-8-44, f. 2830A.

214 *"In [Frank] Vincent's opinion"*: USC, Warners, Cary Grant legal file, Trilling to Warner, 9-26-44, F. 2830A.

214 *When Grant finally signed his contract*: USC Warners, Cary Grant legal file, f. 2830A.

214 *Stacey needed Grant*: USC, Jack Warner collection, Stacey to Phil Friedman, 4-19-45, folder S (1945).

215 *"I read it and I really feel"*: USC, Jack Warner collection, "Epstein's," Epstein to Trilling, undated, box 6, f. 4.

216 *Woolley presented his own set of problems*: USC, Jack Warner collection, Stacey to Warner, 6-8-45, folder S (1945).

216 *"Never get divorced"*: Nelson, p. 147.

216 *"the way he never gave too much"*: Bawden and Miller, *You Ain't Heard*, p. 205.

217 *"If I'm chump enough"*: Wansell, p. 94.

218 *Wasserman and Stanley Fox*: Nelson, p. 157.

218 *"the picture prior to release"*: AMPAS, Alfred Hitchcock collection, "Preliminary Memorandum on Hamlet Alfred Hitchcock—Cary Grant—Sidney Bernstein," 11-2-45, box 94, f. 1124.

218 *Grant was on board for $75,000*: UCLA, RKO payroll records, 10-19-45.

219 *"Hitch brought out the bass notes"*: Peter Bogdanovich, " 'You don't Look Like Cary Grant,' the Lady Said. 'I Know, Nobody Does,' said Cary Grant," *New York Observer*, 12-1-08.

219 *One of Gardiner's affairs*: McGilligan, *Alfred Hitchcock*, p. 367.

219 *"The script writing moves"*: McGilligan, *Alfred Hitchcock*, p. 369.

220 *"Hitchcock loved Grant"*: Patrick McGilligan to SE.

221 *"This is really loose crap!"*: Leff, p. 208.

221 *"your very earliest attention"*: AMPAS, Production Code files, *Notorious*, McDonell to Breen, 5-18-45. All of the material relating to the script of *Notorious* derives from this file.

221 *"I think you know that the industry"*: Breen to Selznick, 5-25-45.

222 *Hecht rewrote the ending*: Shurlock memo, 6-15-45.

222 *"What this party needs"*: Breen to Gordon, 7-25-45.

222 *"We suggest checking with your Brazilian technical expert"*: Breen to Gordon, 11-1-45.

223 *Hitchcock refused to speed up*: AMPAS, Alfred Hitchcock collection, *Notorious* miscellaneous, box 47, f. 552.

223 *"What it amounts to"*: David Thomson, "Bringing Up Cary, *New York Review of Books*, 8-18-2011.

223 *"Hitchcock said discuss anything"*: Leamer, p. 125.

223 *"I don't get all this talk"*: Billheimer, p. 126.

224 *"I'm so lonely, I'm so terribly lonely,"* Leamer, p. 131.

224 *"Since Cary Grant was at best"*: McGilligan, p. 406.

225 *"Yeah. That's the one Hitch"*: Peter Bogdanovich, " 'You Don't Look Like Cary Grant,' the Lady Said. 'I Know, Nobody Does,' said Cary Grant," *New York Observer*, 12-1-08.

CHAPTER TWELVE

227 *"It's his conviction"*: Pete Martin, "Cary Grant," *Saturday Evening Post*, 2-19-49.

227 *"Fifteen kids descend upon you"*: Pete Martin, "Cary Grant," *Saturday Evening Post*, 2-19-49.

228 *"Grant patronized"*: William Wilkerson III to SE.

228 *"I had a valet once"*: Diane K. Shah, "Hul-lo, This Is Cary Grant," *GQ*, 1-86.

229 *"My mother had that to some extent"*: Victoria Riskin to SE.

229 *Grant's deal was $50,000*: UCLA, RKO payroll records, 6-10-46.

230 *Grant got on the phone to Dore Schary*: Kotsilibas-Davis and Loy, p. 204.

230 *"about details of delivery"*: Black, p. 400.

230 *Selznick read Temple the riot act*: Black, p. 402.

231 *"Loretta, you owe me"*: Bawden and Miller, *Conversations*, pp. 295–6.

231 *"The casting was wrong"*: Robert Koster to SE.

231 *"absolutely the best producer"*: AMPAS, SMU collection of Ronald L. Davis oral histories, Henry Koster, 1980, f. 200.

232 *She tumbled twenty feet headfirst*: Lord, p. 138.

233 *"You want me to be happy"*: Berg, p. 425.

233 *"Miss Young refused to show her right cheek"*: AMPAS, SMU collection of Ronald L. Davis oral histories, Henry Koster, 1980, f. 200.

233 *"I think he was extremely bright"*: Eals, p. 87.

235 *"He seemed to be terrified"*: Lord, p. 144.

236 *"Mr. Grant, as a matter of fact"*: 80th Congress, "Investigation of the National Defense Program." The original AP story was by Ralph Dighton, "Bachelor's Dreams. Grant, Hughes, Have Bigger Things Cookin," and appeared in The *Washington Post* on 8-3-47. Hughes's testimony is contained in "Hearings Before a Special Committee Investigating the National Defense Program United States Senate Eightieth Congress . . . Part 40 Aircraft Contracts (Hughes Air-craft Co. and Kaiser-Hughes Corp.), July 28–31, August 1,2,4,5,6,7,8,9, and 11, 1947."

237 *"There wasn't a paper"*: Longworth, p. 287.

238 *"immense charm and wit"*: Michael Korda to SE.

238 *"I get lonesome without Freddie"*: AMPAS, Cary Grant clipping file, Hedda Hopper, "Cary's Simply Grant," *Chicago Tribune*, 6-29-47.

238 *Oberon was intrigued*: Nelson, p. 165.

238 *"a difficult childhood"*: Larry Swindell, "We Solve Problems by Pretending," *Philadelphia Inquirer*, 10-27-71.

238 *Most actresses are only interested"*: Donaldson, p. 206.

239 *Grant was on board for $100,000*: UCLA, RKO payroll records, 1-13-48.

239 *"Cary was terribly funny"*: Kotsilibas-Davis and Loy, p. 214.

239 *"Acting is like playing ball"*: Kotsilibas-Davis and Loy, p. 215.

241 *"What about my toaster?"*: Macnamara, p. 91.

241 *"She had no comedic talent"*: Nelson, p. 167.

241 *Grant taking only $50,000*: UCLA, RKO payroll records, 5-24-48.

241 *"I gave her Hollywood"*: Donaldson, p. 205.

CHAPTER THIRTEEN

243 *They were planning to stay*: List of outward-bound passengers for *Queen Mary*, 9-1-48, Ancestry.com.

243 *she was still talking about the injustice*: Among others, there is Hal Humphrey, "Horseless Series for Ann Sheridan," *Los Angeles Times*, 8-2-66.

244 *"I don't care, it's bloody awful"*: Kobal, p. 424.

244 *"Everyone thought I was going to die"*: Donaldson, p. 172.

244 *amassing domestic rentals*: Solomon, p. 222.

244 *"You're Robert Ryan"*: Jones, p. 94.

244 *"I don't quite know"*: AMPAS, Cary Grant papers, Hepburn to Grant, undated, box 16, f. 224.

245 *"Let me use one of your favorite phrases"*: AMPAS, Cary Grant papers, Odets to Grant, 12-26-49, box 20, f. 298.

245 *But Grant took a dislike*: William Frye, "Gentleman's Agreement," *Vanity Fair*, April 2003.

245 *One Christmas, the lamps were delivered*: William Frye, "Gentleman's Agreement," *Vanity Fair*, April 2003.

246 *"They fit me perfectly"*: William Frye, Gentleman's Agreement, *Vanity Fair*, April, 2003.

246 *"I've got you at last"*: Renoir, p. 261.

247 *"There is so little kindness"*: AMPAS, Cary Grant papers, Odets to Grant, 12-23-49, box 20, f. 298.

247 *Odets wrote to thank him*: AMPAS, Cary Grant papers, Odets to Grant, 7-12-50, box 20, f. 298.

248 *"What he needed from me"*: Kazan, p. 463.

248 *"What was possible for me"*: Kazan, p. 463.

249 *"We feel that the reading"*: AMPAS, Katharine Hepburn papers, Grant and Drake to Hepburn, 10-27-50, box 66, f. 907.

249 *"It will be fun to see you"*: AMPAS, Cary Grant papers, Hepburn to Grant, 11-7-50, box 16, f. 224.

249 *"What a lovely house"*: AMPAS, Cary Grant papers, Hepburn to Grant, undated, box 16, f. 224.

249 *"Irene thought of David"*: Steven Bach to SE.

249 *"Cary Grant and I"*: Selznick, p. 371.

250 *Grant had Howard Hughes*: Selznick, p. 287.

250 *"Irene, this is Howard"*: Selznick, p. 289.

251 *I HAVE NO CHOICE*: Selznick, p. 372.

252 *"But she'd only give it to you"*: Steven Bach to SE.

252 *Grant's services were luxe*: Thomson, p. 535.

252 *"Don't picture Harry Lime"*: Wapshott, p. 202.

252 *"Grant is out of* The Third Man*"*: Drazin, p. 30.

253 *"I asked him to take the part"*: AMPAS, George Cukor collection, box 65, f. 964.

254 *"To have been one of the best"*: AMPAS, George Cukor collection, box 65, f. 964.

254 *"Dear Cary, Here it is"*: USC, Jack Warner collection, *June Bride*, Trilling to Grant, 3-2-48, box 24.

256 *"If they get another director"*: Daniel, pp. 10–11.

256 *Budgeted at a modest $1.5 million*: USC, Arthur Freed collection, *Crisis* picture estimate, box 9, f. 2.

256 *"a light touch"*: USC, Arthur Freed collection, memo from Frank Whitbeck, 6-8-50, box 9, f. 1.

256 *The only dispensation*: Geist, p. 272.

257 *in Chicago, one theater*: McElwee, *The Art of Selling Movies*, pp. 242–43.

257 *"I still believe that if I had done the things"*: AMPAS, Joseph Mankiewicz papers, Zanuck to Mankiewicz, 2-26-52, box 15, f. 165.

257 *"The picture was a flat disappointment"*: AMPAS, Joseph Mankiewicz papers, Zanuck to Mankiewicz, 3-18-52, box 15, f. 165.

257 *three from his early movie career*: Nelson, p. 77.

258 *While negotiating for Cooper*: AMPAS, Joseph Mankiewicz papers, Allenberg to Mankiewicz, 6-23-53, box 4, f. 45.

258 *"He was most gracious"*: Endres and Cushman, p. 226.

258 *"Each time that I have written"*: AMPAS, Katharine Hepburn papers, Drake to Hepburn 1-30-51, box 63, f. 814.

259 *"Cary Grant was one of the nicest guys"*: Goldrup and Goldrup, p. 224.

259 *Warner Bros. got a Cary Grant*: USC Warners, *Room for One More*, Budgets 8 of 11, f. 1457B.

259 *When Raymond Burr was threatened*: AMPAS, Hedda Hopper collection, Hopper to Burr, 9-16-63.

259 *"Hedda Hopper was a bitch"*: Donaldson, p. 45.

260 *"Marilyn was a very calculating girl"*: Donaldson, p. 232.

260 *"Cary Grant contributed a lot"*: McCarthy, p. 498.

261 *Brando had cited Grant*: Manso, p. 184.

261 *"Where can I get a stick of dynamite?"*: Berg, p. 428.

262 *"Don't ever say 'Cut'"*: Sheldon, p. 237.

263 *"It wasn't as bad as the famous Carmen Miranda shot"*: Murray Garrett to SE.

264 *Grant stood up for Chaplin*: AMPAS, Cary Grant clipping file, "Chaplin No Communist Says Grant," *Los Angeles Daily News*, 2-16-53.

265 *"You get all the good parts now, Bogie"*: Bacall, p. 219.

PART THREE

267 *"I think I became"*: AMPAS, Cary Grant clipping file, Curtiss Anderson, "Cary Grant Keeps Growing," *McCall's*, 10-75.

CHAPTER FOURTEEN

269 *"We made* To Catch a Thief*"*: Diane K. Shah, "Hu-llu, This Is Cary Grant," *GQ*, 1-86.

269 *"She had the indecency to marry Rainier"*: Diane K. Shah, "Hu-llo, This Is Cary Grant," *GQ*, 1-86.

270 *"Beautiful people, beautiful scenery"*: McGilligan, *Alfred Hitchcock*, p. 496.

270 *"Oh, Hitch is* great*"*: Diane K. Shah, "Hu-llo, This Is Cary Grant," *GQ*, 1-86.

270 *"Each of those directors"*: McCann, p. 150.

270 *"It was the period of the blue jeans"*: McGilligan, *Alfred Hitchcock*, p. 493.

271 *Grant negotiated the best deal*: AMPAS, Paramount Pictures production records, "Notes Pertaining to the Hitchcock Contract," 3-30-54, box 215, f. 15.

271 *"In* Suspicion, *Grant plays"*: McGilligan, *Alfred Hitchcock*, p. 498.

271 *"We have not been able to locate"*: AMPAS, Paramount Pictures production records, *To Catch a Thief* pre-production, 1953–54, Erickson to Frank Caffey, 5-23-54, box 215, f. 19.

271 *"I wasn't able to locate a Cadillac"*: AMPAS, Paramount Pictures production records, *To Catch a Thief* pre-production (location), 1953–54, Erickson to Hugh Brown, 5-25-54, box 215, f. 19.

272 *"Hitchcock likes me a lot"*: McGilligan, *Alfred Hitchcock*, p. 498.

272 *They peered through the gates*: Jorgensen and Bowman, p. 176.

273 *During the location work*: McGilligan, *Alfred Hitchcock*, p. 499.

274 *"Anyone who has two dollars"*: The interview is at the University of Oregon, Dean Jennings papers, Cary Grant interview, 4-1-54, box 2. I have slightly reordered Grant's comments to improve the flow.

276 *"the luxury of owning a yacht"*: AMPAS, Jack Hirshberg papers, Cary Grant.

277 *In December 1955, Universal Pictures compiled a comprehensive list*: USC, Universal Collection, "Casting Survey as of Dec. 5, 1955," box 749, f. 26605.

278 *Mackendrick was summoned*: Kemp, p. 138.

280 *Grant's contract with Stanley Kramer*: USC, Stanley Kramer papers, boxes 13 and 14. The details of the Antheil score are from box 14, Zagon to Kramer, 11-7-57.

281 *"I liked looking Cary over"*: Loren, p. 109.

282 *"He didn't want her to have the image"*: McCann, p. 153.

282 *"How are you boys coming on the screenplay?"*: DGA oral history, Melville, Shavelson, chapter 2.

283 *"Well, I guess I lost everything"*: Donaldson, p. 206.

283 *Produced for the reasonable cost*: Balio, p. 101.

CHAPTER FIFTEEN

286 *"We haven't received one ruble"*: Hearings Before the Committee on Un-American Activities House of Representatives, 80th Congress, 1st Session, Leo McCarey testimony, 10-23-47.

286 *McCarey had loaned Ford $360,000:* Eyman, p. 372.

287 *"I have much confidence"*: AFI, Leo McCarey papers, box 18, f. 106.

288 *It returned domestic rentals:* McElwee, *Showmen*, p. 169.

288 *three sheets to the wind:* Richard Bann to SE.

288 *"a two and a half hour show"*: Sheilah Graham, "McCarey Picks Bergman for Eve but Doesn't Know Who Will Help Raise Cain," *Indianapolis Star*, 2-9-47.

289 *"I don't know what the hell else"*: AFI, Leo McCarey papers, Wayne to McCarey, 6-14-55, box 22, f. 145.

290 *"I am up to my 'ears' "*: AFI, Leo McCarey papers, McCarey to Grant, 10-28-54, box 20, f. 124.

290 *Wald's original idea:* USC, Jerry Wald papers, Adler to Wald, 8-17-56.

290 *"to do new version of 'Love Affair' "*: AFI, Leo McCarey papers, McCarey to Bergman, 11-15-56, box 4, f. 17.

291 *"The original film was shot entirely"*: AFI, Leo McCarey papers, box 4, f. 12.

292 *"We're afraid that we're falling"*: AFI, Leo McCarey papers, box 4, f. 12.

292 *"Good comedy is based"*: AMPAS, Sidney Skolsky papers, Cary Grant tintype interview, box 9, f. 108.

293 *"I believe we should change the dialogue"*: USC, Jerry Wald collection, Adler to Wald and McCarey, 1-4-57, box 33.

294 *"was just wonderful, just a pleasure"*: AFI and American Society of Cinematographers seminar with Milton Krasner and Alfred Lebovitz. 1-10-76.

294 *"The most marvelous thing"*: Wagner to SE.

295 *"The reason I hesitated"*: AFI, Peter Bogdanovich interview with Leo McCarey, 11-25-68.

CHAPTER SIXTEEN

297 *"With only happy thoughts"*: Loren, p. 114.

297 *Ray Walston was in the cast:* Nelson, p. 205.

297 *"She broke my heart"*: Donaldson, p. 234.

297 *"If only I had started a family"*: Donaldson, p. 206.

298 *"The more we can do"*: USC, Jerry Wald collection, Wald to Epstein, box 35, f. 2.

298 *"She fought me tooth and nail"*: USC, Jerry Wald collection, Buddy Adler correspondence, Adler to Wald, 1-25-60, box 85.

298 *"On page 105"*: USC, Jerry Wald collection, Adler to Wald, Epstein, 1-15-57, box 35, f. 1.

299 *"I've looked over your list of credits"*: DGA oral history, Stanley Donen, chapter 2.

300 *"if I had a screaming fit"*: Sue Lloyd to SE.

301 *"Isn't that the most disgusting"*: Budd Boetticher to Anthony Slide, Slide diary, 12-23-2000.

302 *"Once, I had a director"*: Diane K. Shah, "Hu-llo, This Is Cary Grant," *GQ*, 1-86.

302 *"I consider him not only"*: McCann, p. 151.

303 *"I'm in the fortunate position"*: AMPAS, Sidney Skolsky papers, Cary Grant tintype, box 9, f. 108.

303 *Grant had sent her letters*: Leamer, p. 208.

303 *"Ingrid Bergman is a fascinating"*: McCann, p. 139.

304 *Krasna gave him a free option*: DGA oral history, Stanley Donen, chapter 2, clip 16.

304 *"My lawyer would say to me"*: Nelson, p. 207.

305 *The up-front money paid out*: USC Warners, *Indiscreet* legal, f. 12751A.

305 *On both* White Christmas *and* High Society: I am indebted to Robert Bader for information on *White Christmas*.

306 *"after discussing it thoroughly"*: USC Warners, J. L. Warner files, Donen to Warner, 11-14-57, *Indiscreet*, f. 2954A.

306 *"That's the event in the scene"*: DGA oral history, Stanley Donen, chapter 1, clip 14.

306 *"was so good on camera"*: Leamer, p. 259.

306 *"Do you realize that together"*: Grant, p. 113.

307 *"I've kept this long enough"*: Leamer, p. 328.

307 *"Apparently the deal you consummated"*: USC Warners, Steve Trilling files, *Indiscreet*, f. 2752A.

308 *"It finally came to me"*: Nelson, p. 213.

308 *"Tell me the story of* Houseboat*"*: Shavelson, p. 70.

308 *"They had a brief, passionate"*: Shavelson, p. 71.

309 *His compensation was fixed*: AMPAS, Paramount Pictures contract summaries, contract with Cary Grant dated 3-23-56, box 11, f. 976.

309 *"This is to advise that Betsy Drake"*: AMPAS, Paramount Pictures production records, Franklin to Carle, 10-2-57, box 106, f. 1.

309 *One of Hedda Hopper's spies*: AMPAS, Hedda Hopper papers, Hopper to Cowles, 8-31-59, box 42, f. 994.

310 *"If only you'd marry me"*: AMPAS, SMU oral histories 269, Martha Hyer, p. 19.

310 *"If you can, and care to"*: Loren, p. 125.

310 *"That was my third ulcer"*: Davis, p. 32.

311 *"Cary Grant you are the greatest"*: Shavelson, p. 72.

312 *"We certainly ripped up a few bull rings"*: Bogdanovich, p. 117.

312 *"Last night I dined"*: Orry-Kelly, pp. 396–97.

314 *"Only yesterday, Ray Stark"*: AMPAS, Cary Grant papers, Grant to Drake, 3-18-76, box 15, f. 189.

315 *"In the last few years of their marriage"*: AMPAS Cary Grant clipping file, Muriel Davidson, "Cary Grant: As His Best Friends (and Ex-Friends) Know Him," *Good Housekeeping*, 11-62.

315 *"When I was married"*: Susan Smith, "Betsy Drake Returns to Movies," *Los Angeles Times*, 10-16-76.

315 *"He's worth eight million"*: Hedda Hopper, "Dewey Martin Set for Disney Film," *Los Angeles Times*, 7-21-62.

315 Actually, Variety *reported*: Carmel Dagan, "Betsy Drake, Actress and Former Wife of Cary Grant, Dies at 92," *Variety*, 11-11-15.

315 *"Betsy was good for me."* "Archie Leach," by Cary Grant, *Ladies Home Journal*, April 1963.

315 *"Why would I believe"*: Robert Trachtenberg documentary.

316 *"Cary always spoke of you"*: AMPAS, Katharine Hepburn papers, Drake to Hepburn, 6-15-67, box 63, f. 814.

316 *In another letter*: AMPAS, Katharine Hepburn papers, Grant to Hepburn, 12-29 67, box 63, f. 814.

316 *"I dreamed of being in the theater"*: Susan Smith, "Betsy Drake Returns to Movies," *Los Angeles Times*, 10-16-78.

316 *"because I take the radical position"*: Larry Swindell, "We Solve Problems by Pretending," *Philadelphia Inquirer*, 10-27-71.

316 *"If you ever think"*: Moorehead, p. 456.

317 *"A man cannot do anything more"*: Moorehead, p. 390.

317 *"You invent complications"*: Moorehead, pp. 452–53.

CHAPTER SEVENTEEN

319 *"When I was just starting out"*: *Hollywood Reporter*, 25th anniversary issue, 11-14-55.

320 *"I don't like taking a big hit"*: Billy Wilder to SE.

320 *"Cannot do it"*: Crowe, p. 12.

321 *"I'd heard he didn't like actors"*: Bawden and Miller, *Conversations*, p. 117.

321 *"I could tell stories about Mike Curtiz:"* AMPAS, *George Stevens—A Film-maker's Journey*, Cary Grant interview, box 2, f. 25.

321 *"It's a shame that smog"*: AMPAS, Cary Grant clipping file, Bob Thomas, "Cary Grant Will Move to Europe, *Hollywood Citizen News*, 3-13-59.

322 *he did* An Affair to Remember *for a flat $300,000*: AMPAS, William "Billy" Gordon papers, *An Affair to Remember*, casting, box 1, f. 1.

322 *He got a whopping $450,000*: AMPAS, William "Billy" Gordon papers, *Kiss Them for Me*, casting, box 4, f. 159.

322 *There were certain pictures*: AMPAS, Cary Grant papers, Garbus to Grant, 10-5-49, box 31, f. 521.

322 *Grant's deal for* North by Northwest: AMPAS, Alfred Hitchcock papers, *North By Northwest*, cast, box 45, f. 526.

323 *"Over the last ten years in making deals"*: Leonard J. Leff, "Hitchcock at Metro," *Western Humanities Review*, Summer 1983.

324 *"Since I never knew where I was going"*: Baer, p. 65.

325 *he was scheduled to work*: AMPAS, Alfred Hitchcock papers, *North by Northwest*, budgets, box 45, f. 525.

325 *"Suddenly all Cary could think about"*: McGilligan, *Alfred Hitchcock*, p. 566.

325 *"Grant evidently considered"*: Baer, p. 69.

326 *"I was overwhelmed by the experience"*: AMPAS, Eva Marie Saint oral history, 2013.

326 *"You just always felt"*: McCann, p. 184.

326 *"conscientous, clutching his script"*: McGilligan, *Alfred Hitchcock* p. 570.

326 *"He wasn't being facetious"*: AMPAS, Eva Marie Saint oral history, 2013.

327 *Saint began calling Grant Thorneycroft*: AMPAS, Eva Marie Saint oral history, 2013.

327 *"I got it in Wardrobe at Universal"*: Mankiewicz, p. 109.

327 *"The trousers are very similar"*: Spaiser, *The Suits of James Bond* website.

328 *"I'm just lonesome"*: Guilaroff, pp. 246–47.

328 *"Because I'm working for nothing!"*: Coleman, p. 285.

329 *"Astaire-like agility"*: Christopher Husted's liner notes for the *North by Northwest* soundtrack.

330 *"[Hitchcock] once told me"*: Baer, p. 75.

330 *"Hitch and I had a rapport"*: Nelson, p. 217.

330 *"The story material contains"*: AMPAS, Cary Grant papers, box 16, f. 225.

331 *In 1966, Hitchcock was speaking*: Hare, p. 105.

CHAPTER EIGHTEEN

333 *"The [story] on Cary Grant"*: AMPAS, Hedda Hopper papers, Hopper to Cowles, 8-31-59, box 42, f. 994.

333 *"I have long suspected"*: AMPAS, Hedda Hopper papers, Cowles to Hopper, 9-3-59, box 42, f. 994.

334 *"If you see a nigger around the house"*: Frost, p. 39.

334 *"If you haven't seen Grant and Bergman"*: AMPAS, Hedda Hopper papers, Hopper to Wendt, 7-24-58, box 7, f. 148.

334 *"What a ham he is!"*: AMPAS, Hedda Hopper papers, Grant to Wendt, 8-25-58, box 7, f. 148.

334 *"I think the one of Cary Grant"*: AMPAS, Hedda Hopper papers, Hopper to McCormick, 6-7-62, box 9, f. 170.

335 *"I was more Cockney"*: Ray Austin to SE.

338 *"He looked for a moment"*: Scott, p. 175.

339 *When the divorce*: Nelson, p. 243.

339 *"I am not proud of my marriage career,"*: McIntosh and Weaver, p. 49.

339 *After her consultation with Hartman*: Roderick Mann, "Cary Grant: The Four Hours That Changed His Life, *San Francisco Examiner*, 12-27-64.

339 *"He's the man who saved my life"*: Donaldson, p. 127.

340 *"LSD empties the subconscious and intensifies the emotions"*: Roderick Mann, "Cary Grant: The Four Hours That Changed His Life," *San Francisco Examiner*, 12-27-77.

340 *Nicholson later incorporated his experiences*: Richard Whalen, "The Trip," *LA Weekly*, 7-3-9-98.

341 *"I passed through changing seas"*: "Archie Leach," by Cary Grant, *Ladies' Home Journal*, April, 1963.

341 *"The session was four or five hours"*: Ray Austin to SE.

341 *"which is probably just as dangerous"*: McDonell, p. 231.

341 *"I had to take command"*: "Archie Leach," by Cary Grant, *Ladies' Home Journal*, April, 1963.

342 *"And on that day I shat all over the rug"*: Donaldson, pp. 127–28.

342 *"I imagined myself as a giant penis"*: AMPAS, Cary Grant clipping file, Gene Siskel, "The Real Cary Grant," *Chicago Tribune*, 12-7-86.

342 *"I was punishing them"*: Donaldson, p. 129.

342 *"I learned that everything is or becomes its own opposite"*: "Archie Leach," by Cary Grant, *Ladies' Home Journal*, April, 1963.

343 *He urged Clifford Odets to try the drug*: Walt Odets to SE.

343 *"What is Cary fooling with that stuff for?"*: McIntosh and Weaver, p. 45.

343 *"I couldn't believe his choices"*: McGilligan, *Backstory* 4, pp. 96–97. Sequence slightly reedited for emphasis.

343 *"I learned a great deal about personalities and politics"*: Deschner, p. 23.

344 *"Cary was fine"*: Dina Merrill to SE.

345 *"I'd get in there—and it was kind of fun"*: Lisanti, p. 30.

345 *"He was a very warm"*: Lisanti, p. 30.

345 *"For the first time in my life"*: Hyams, p. 92.

346 *Hyams believed all of this was related to Betsy*: Hyams, p. 88.

346 *He reiterated the passionate enlightenment*: Hyams, p. 89.

346 *"That's my wife"*: Hyams, p. 89.

347 *Grant's assertion that he had never done an interview*: AMPAS, Cary Grant clipping file, "Cary Grant Denies Being Treated by Psychiatrist," *Los Angeles Times*, 4-20-59.

348 *"Our lawyers got together out of court"*: AMPAS, Hedda Hopper papers, Hyams transcript, 5-10-62, box 62, f. 1777.

349 *Grant misspelled his mother's maiden name*: "Archie Leach," by Cary Grant, *Ladies' Home Journal* March 1963.

349 *"Enough, say for a new Rolls-Royce"*: Hyams, p. 98.

351 *"regarding our common interests"*: NYPL, Timothy Leary papers, Janiger to Leary, 4-27-62.

352 *"the radiance and humor"*: NYPL, Timothy Leary papers, Leary to Grant, 1-11-64.

353 *"Everything was uncritical"*: Nelson, pp. 237–38.

353 *"mind-enhancing experimentation"*: Nick Thomas, p. 55.

353 *"Cary Grant, witty, sophisticated"*: Morley, p. 131.

354 *"Fearful throbbings and crunchings"*: McCann, p. 169.

354 *Grant insisted she try LSD*: Nick Thomas, p. 246.

354 *Wasserman and his men had to split*: Sharp, p. 72.

355 *Grant's company was entitled to 75 percent*: AMPAS, Cary Grant clipping file, Al Cohn, "The Santa Claus of Radio City," *Newsday*, 12-19-64.

355 *"Grant was a bauble"*: Mort Engelberg to SE.

355 *"Absolutely not!"*: Mort Engelberg to SE.

356 *Grant continued to cheerfully resist*: AMPAS, Cary Grant clipping file, "Cary Grant's Vidodge and Why," *Variety*, 2-6-62.

356 *"Do you really think I should appear"*: Sharp, p. 72.

358 *"Now, just because these are my ideas"*: Rains, pp. 111–12.

359 *"My father admired him as a man"*: Walt Odets to SE. All quotes from Walt Odets derive from our interview.

360 *"He wore a lot of solid satin"*: AMPAS, Cary Grant clipping file, Thomas Vinciguerra, "Behind the Seam's," GQ, 9-2000.

CHAPTER NINETEEN

363 *"Having heard nothing in reply"*: USC, Jerry Wald collection, G folder.

364 *"Eventually, as so often happens"*: Johnson and Leventhal, eds., p. 168.

364 *"Bugger and blast"*: Brownlow, p. 425.

364 *"There's only one actor who can play"*: Nick Thomas, p. 259.

365 *"We would be very willing"*: AMPAS, Cary Grant papers, Stark to Grant, 9-21-61, box 5, f. 48.

365 *"I've read it twice and am still uncertain"*: AMPAS, John Huston papers, *The Man Who Would Be King*, correspondence, Grant to Kohner, 7-26-60, box 31, f. 298.

366 *"Cary Grant . . . was a fuss-budget"*: Bawden and Miller, *You Ain't Heard*, p. 197.

366 *"a consummate artist"*: McCann, p. 151.

367 *"We had lunch one day"*: Time Out #724, interviewed by Chris Peachment and Geoff Andrew.

367 *"Not only did he turn in his hotel bills"*: Rains, pp. 113–114.

368 *"When you look at [Sean Connery's] Bond"*: Glenn Kenny, "Prince of the City" DGA Quarterly, Fall 2007.

368 *"He's in the next bungalow"*: Brooks told the story several times over the years, but the best version is with TCM's Robert Osborne, available on YouTube. The remark about Grant being a *schnorrer* is in Pat McGilligan's biography of Brooks.

370 *Grant's passports show only one trip*: AMPAS, Grant papers, passport, issued July 18, 1960, box 46, f. 658.

370 *"A personality functioning"*: Shipman, p. 254.

370 *"Well, his father's name is Silberman"*: Dan Selznick to SE.

371 *"The only actors Irene had good things"*: Robert Gottlieb to SE.

372 *"Joseph Cotten, Joseph Cotten"*: Boston University, Gotlieb Center, Irene Mayer Selznick collection, Grant to Selznick, undated, box 47, f. 6.

372 *"sometimes uses a strange range"*: Boston University, Gotlieb Center, Irene Mayer Selznick collection, undated, Grant to Selznick, box 52, f. 23.

372 *"Where is an English Uta Hagen?"*: Boston University, Gotlieb Center, Irene Mayer Selznick collection, Grant to Selznick, 4-19-55, box 52, f. 23.

372 *"No one character"*: Boston University, Gotlieb Center, Irene Mayer Selznick collection, Grant to Selznick, 4-19-55.

372 *THINK ME NOT MAD*: Boston University, Gotlieb Center, Irene Mayer Selznick collection, Grant to Selznick, 5-29-55, Box 52, f. 19.

373 *"He's just like Cary Grant"*: Peter Bogdanovich, " 'You Don't Look Like Cary Grant,' the Lady Said. 'I Know, Nobody Does,' said Cary Grant," *New York Observer*, 12-1-08.

373 *"When he exhibited himself"*: McCann, p. 143.

374 *"He was in on a pass"*: Donaldson, p. 237.

374 *"I saw girl after girl wearing clothes"*: Diane K. Shah, "Hu-llo, This Is Cary Grant," *GQ*, 1-86.

375 *"Cary and I just didn't get along,"*: DGA oral history, Delbert Mann, chapter 5.

375 *"I like Cary Grant very much"*: AMPAS, SMU collection of Ronald L. Davis oral histories, Doris Day, 1983, f. 99.

376 *"May I ask what you wish to speak to Mr. Grant about?"*: Murray Garrett to SE.

377 *Her name was Millie Black*: I am indebted to Alan Rode for this anecdote about his friend Millie Black.

378 *"But none have clicked into"*: *Variety*, 11-20-63, p. 1.

CHAPTER TWENTY

381 *"That's a sweet answer"*: Dyan Cannon to SE

382 *"His brilliance was electrifying"*: Cannon, p. 61.

382 *"Going back to Bristol"*: Cannon, p. 103.

383 *She threw the bottle of polish*: Cannon, pp. 160–61.

383 *"I'm thinking about our future"*: Cannon, p. 163.

383 *Grant would have New York stores*: McIntosh and Weaver, p. 59.

384 *"Rock tried hard"*: McBride, p. 73.

384 *"an absolutely awful novel"*: William Wiener Oral History Library of the American Jewish Committee at New York Public Library, Peter Stone oral history, p. 32.

384 *"There's a lot of imagination"*: NYPL, Peter Stone papers, Lantz to Stone, 10-14-60, box 18, f. 4.

385 *"might make a very interesting suspense action film"*: NYPL, Peter Stone papers, Donen to Stone, 1-16-62, box 18, f. 4.

385 *"Cary took off his coat"*: Spoto, p. 226.

385 *Grant said he*: Nelson, p. 245.

386 *"sensitive, reserved and quiet"*: Spoto, pp. 227–28.

386 *"You must always remember that you"*: George Kennedy to SE.

386 *"I'm going crazy"*: AMPAS, Cary Grant clipping file, Diane K. Shah, "Grant's Gone, but Not Forgotten," *Los Angeles Herald-Examiner*, 5-3-87.

387 *Grant refused to shoot*: Nelson, p. 246.

387 *But he hadn't fooled Ingrid Bergman*: Bawden and Miller, *Conversations*, p. 125.

388 *"My father wasn't okay"*: Walt Odets to SE.

388 *"You know, I may fool you"*: Kazan, p. 665.

388 *Jean Renoir and his wife*: Renoir, p. 263.

389 *"Cliff spent the last dozen"*: Kazan, p. 663.

389 *"That's my boy!"*: Walt Odets to SE.

390 *"You've been particularly in my thoughts"*: AMPAS, Cary Grant papers, Selznick to Grant, 8-22-63, box 21, f. 340.

CHAPTER TWENTY-ONE

391 *"The story on which the screenplay is based"*: Barbara L. Wilson, "Grant Skips Query on Perfect Actress; Salutes Our Grace," *Philadelphia Inquirer*, 12-6-64.

392 *Tarloff was writing* The Danny Thomas Show: McGilligan and Buhle, *Tender Comrades*, p. 652.

392 *"He and Peter Stone"*: Barbara L. Wilson, "Grant Skips Query on Perfect Actress; Salutes Our Grace," *Philadelphia Inquirer*, 12-6-64.

392 *His fee was a flat $125,000*: AMPAS, Cary Grant papers, *Father Goose*, box 3, f. 24.

393 *"This film is ruining me!"*: Leslie Caron to SE.

393 *the expense of* Father Goose: AMPAS, Cary Grant papers, *Father Goose*, box 3, f. 24.

393 *"When I laugh out loud"*: UCLA, Ralph Nelson papers, Nelson to Grant, 4-19-64, box 9.

394 *"He clearly loved children"*: 2005 Interview with Stephanie Berrington McNutt, CaryGrant.net.

395 *"animal strength"*: Nelson, p. 255.

395 *"There will be no conventional closing day party"*: AMPAS, Cary Grant papers, *Father Goose*, box 4, f. 28.

396 *"It's astonishing to me"*: AMPAS, Hedda Hopper papers, Nelson to Hopper, 11-17-64, box 76, f. 2495.

396 *"Except for the fact"*: Caron, p. 168.

397 *"The relationship was definitely one-sided"*: AMPAS, June Randolph, "Cary Grant and Me," *Cosmopolitan*, 9–69.

397 *"You meant she kisses me"*: Mankiewicz, p. 109.

398 *"Yes, it's me"*: Mankiewicz, p. 110.

399 *"Oh, you're one of those people"*: Everett Mattlin, "And Cary," *Film Comment*, 11-12–89.

CHAPTER TWENTY-TWO

401 *"She did her own marketing and shopping"*: Donaldson, p. 160.

401 *A telegram might wish her son*: AMPAS, Cary Grant papers, Leach to Grant, 1-2-60, box 18, f. 256.

401 *"I went and seen"*: AMPAS, Cary Grant papers, Leach to Grant, 11-2-60, box 18, f. 256.

401 *WEDDING DAY 30/5/98*: AMPAS, Cary Grant papers, Leach to Grant, 5-23-61, box 18, f. 256.

401 *"You see Archie darling"*: AMPAS, Cary Grant papers, Leach to Grant, 6-25-61, box 18, f. 256.

402 *"for bringing me into the world"*: AMPAS, Cary Grant papers, Grant to Leach, 12-29-61, box 18, f. 256.

402 *he told a funny story*: McCann, p. 211.

402 *"She did not know how to give affection"*: Donaldson, p. 160.

402 *"What do you want from me now?"*: McIntosh and Weaver, p. 122.

403 *"I have just come from a delightful tea party"*: AMPAS, Cary Grant papers, Page to Grant, 11-14-64, box 0, f. 302.

403 *"She said she wouldn't open the stocking"*: AMPAS, Cary Grant papers, Page to Grant, 12-26-65, box 20, f. 302.

403 *"She is far less abnormal than many other"*: AMPAS, Cary Grant papers, Page to Grant, 7-7-65, box 20, f. 302.

403 *"the strength of a 20-mule team"*: AMPAS, Cary Grant clipping file, Henry Gris, "A Different Kind of Love," *Coronet*, March 1971.

403 *Page noted how critical*: Nelson, p. 253.

404 *"Wish you'd come over"*: AMPAS, Cary Grant papers, Grant to Leach, 6-9-75, box 18, f. 257.

404 *Grant chiding Eric about making a will*: AMPAS, Cary Grant papers, Grant to Leach, 10-11-77, box 18, f. 257.

404 *"Money. You are, understandably, worried about money"*: AMPAS, Cary Grant papers, Grant to Leach, 8-8-83, Box 18, f. 257.

405 *He told her in an offhand manner*: Cannon, p. 200.

405 *"What the hell did you do to your nails?"*: Cannon, p. 204.

405 *"We're not visiting a grave"*: Cannon, p. 212.

405 *"Cary's shell opened and closed"*: Cannon, pp. 216, 230.

406 *Grant was still seeing Dr. Hartman*: Cannon, p. 221.

406 *"Cary insisted that I had to change my hair"*: Wansell, p. 164.

406 *"You're such a studious young man"*: Takei, p. 205.

407 *"Bangs is part of our family"*: Cannon, p. 239

408 *"That was the beginning of the end"*: Dyan Cannon to SE.

408 *"Was never a moderate gal"*: Grant, p. 98.

408 *"I surrendered my very mind"*: Cannon, p. 242.

408 *"He was abandoned"*: Dyan Cannon to SE.

409 *"Thank you, Betsy"*: Cannon, p. 248.

409 *"Do you love your mother, Cary?"*: Cannon, p. 249.

410 *One day Grant trailed Dyan around the house*: Cannon, p. 254.

410 *"He thinks it might be best"*: Cannon, p. 277.

411 *Dyan testified about Grant's "outlandish, irrational and hostile"*: conduct: AMPAS, Cary Grant clipping file, "LSD Long Used by Cary Grant, Wife Asserts," *Los Angeles Times*, 3-21-68; *New York Daily News*, "Says Dreamboat Cary Took Nightmare Trips," 3-21-68.

411 *"The rhythm to my parents' post-divorce relationship"*: Grant, p. 98.

412 *"The women always win in the end"*: Bogdanovich to SE.

412 *"We both wanted it to be cordial for Jennifer"*: AMPAS, Jane Ardmore papers, box 12, f. 25.

412 *"In a script"*: AMPAS, "Cary Grant clipping file," Lloyd Shearer, *Parade*, 1-18-87.

412 *Grant chose* Penny Serenade: AMPAS, George Stevens papers, Frank Davis to Stevens, 10-12-65, box 240, f. 2826.

413 *"The only basis for assessing fees"*: AMPAS, Cary Grant, papers, Page to Grimes, 7-4-66, 7-9-66, box 20, f. 302.

413 *"Eke a bit, if you can"*: AMPAS, Cary Grant papers, Grant to Leach, 4-26-66, box 18, f. 257.

413 *"He must be frightened"*: Williams, ed., p. 159.

413 *"I reminded him that this was a role"*: Mirisch, p. 261.

414 *"I got tired of getting up"*: Nelson, p. 270.

414 *"Who the deuce would go to see me?"*: AMPAS, Cary Grant clipping file, "Grant Loves Being Himself," *Albuquerque Journal*, 12-26-81.

414 *"He just got tired of it"*: Dyan Cannon to SE.

415 *"I had enjoyed a full career"*: AMPAS, Jane Ardmore papers, box 12, f. 25.

415 *"Harold had a conversation"*: Sue Lloyd to SE.

415 *"It had to do with his looks"*: Peter Bogdanovich to SE.

416 *"I was never interesting in acting in films"*: AMPAS, Cary Grant clipping file, Warren Hoge, "The Other Cary Grant," *New York Times Magazine*, 7-3-77.

416 *Watching the two men*: Richard Bann to SE.

416 *"In my opinion there is no valid excuse"*: Barbara L. Wilson, "Grant Skips Query on Perfect Actress; Salutes Our Grace," *Philadelphia Inquirer*, 12-6-64.

417 *"If I had known then what I know now"*: AMPAS, Cary Grant papers, Guy Flatley, "Cary—From Mae to September," *New York Times*, 7-22-73.

417 *"You are the strangest actor"*: Wasson, p. 220.

417 *Jack Haley Jr. suggested*: Nelson, pp. 201–2.

417 *"Yes, she has asked me"*: AMPAS, Grant clipping file, *Albuquerque Journal* "Grant Loves Being Himself," 12-26-81.

418 *"It was a private affair"*: Bogdanovich, p. 21.

418 *"Howard Hawks, Hitchcock"*: Grant's acceptance speech is on YouTube.

418 *"When everyone stood up"*: AMPAS, Jane Ardmore papers, Cary Grant interview, 4-18-75, box 12, f. 25.

419 *"The leading men who get awards"*: Crowe, p. 14.

419 *"definitely not comfortable"*: John Sacret Young to SE.

420 *In 1969, Grant and Stanley Donen sued*: AMPAS, Cary Grant clipping file, *Variety*, "Cary Grant, Donen Sue MCA-Universal," 8-11-69.

420 *After Hunter left the studio*: Robert Osborne to SE.

420 *Grant was on an airplane the day of the screening*: Robert Osborne to SE.

422 *"Grant always found dependency"*: McIntosh and Weaver, pp. 130–32.

422 *"he subconsciously pushed them into leaving"*: Donaldson, p. 202.

422 *"I observed one of the greats of all time"*: Dyan Cannon to SE.

422 *"Most women are instinctively wiser"*: Feeney, p. 80.

423 *"Michael Caine?"*: Caine, p. 142.

423 *"He was a father"*: Jill St. John to SE.

423 *"When Lance died"*: Jill St. John to SE.

424 *He'd get dressed around nine*: McIntosh and Weaver, p. 86.

424 *"There's a banquet every night"*: McIntosh and Weaver, p. 87.

424 *He never drank before 6:30 at night*: Donaldson, p. 98.

424 *Dessert was carefully rationed*: Donaldson, p. 97.

425 *When an order of shirts came in*: McIntosh and Weaver, p. 89.

425 *But he preferred to spend $6*: Donaldson, p. 100.

425 *He saw a Chinese silver pipe*: Nelson, p. 266.

426 *Plants take up oxygen:* Donaldson, p. 96.

426 *Some days he would insist:* Donaldson, p. 155.

426 *"Homosexuals, in my opinion":* Donaldson, p. 192.

426 *Finally he had some pads:* McIntosh and Weaver, p. 94.

427 *His favorite magicians:* Milt Larson to Will Coates.

428 *$5 or $10 per race:* Grant, p. 60.

428 *"He called my mother 'Nikki,' ":* Victoria Riskin to SE.

429 *Blackwood undertook twelve sessions:* Lambert, p. 250.

429 *"LSD is a chemical":* Donaldson, p. 126.

429 *"I'm now 70 years old":* Donaldson, p. 126.

429 *"That I'm a homosexual":* Donaldson, p. 40.

430 *Grant promptly walked up to the man:* Donaldson, p. 102.

430 *Grant's secretary offered to get a gun:* McIntosh and Weaver, p. 56.

430 *"He was a much more complex":* Bill Royce to SE.

434 *Off to the left was the kitchen:* Donaldson, p. 92.

434 *a signed baseball from Hank Aaron:* Donaldson, p. 93.

434 *"Next to Jennifer":* Bill Royce to SE.

434 *"I'm just an old, old man":* Donaldson, p. 39.

435 *According to an inventory:* AMPAS, Cary Grant papers, box 24, f. 397.

435 *two electricians, each earning $20 an hour:* McIntosh and Weaver, p. 83.

435 *"The drowning man":* Nelson, p. 312.

435 *"I'm absolutely pooped":* McIntosh and Weaver, p. 151.

436 *"I've gone over this with him":* Donaldson, p. 49.

436 *"You don't look like Cary Grant":* Bogdanovich, p. 99.

436 *"See that guy?":* Biskind, p. 465.

436 *"He learned from Grant":* Biskind, p. 248.

436 *"I am a sixty-five year old professional man":* Nelson, p. 284.

437 *"Harold had a private den upstairs":* Sue Lloyd to SE.

CHAPTER TWENTY-THREE

439 *The money was negligible:* McCann, p. 204.

439 *Grant maintained his disapproval of movie careers:* Dyan Cannon to SE.

440 *Grant and Kerkorian had much in common:* Rempel, p. 148.

440 *"It's all a put-on":* Nelson, p. 290.

441 *"If you sell to the large department stores":* McIntosh and Weaver, p. 102.

441 *Grant saw it and liked it: Film Comment,* April 1987, p. 61.

441 *"He threw dollars around":* Nelson, p. 295.

442 *"Everyone always talks about Cary Grant's elegance":* Rob Wolders to SE.

442 *"When you forgive someone":* Royce, p. 122.

443 *"I just had the sense":* Royce, p. 136.

443 *"in excess of $2 million": Variety,* 5-10-72, p. 2.

443 *"Most of the revenue was exhausted":* AMPAS, Cary Grant clipping file, Aljean Harmetz, "Hitchcock's Death May Revive 5 Films," *New York Times,* 7-9-80. I am indebted to David Pierce for explaining a different generation's concept of the value of movies.

444 *"If he'd come with a moving van"*: AMPAS, Katharine Hepburn papers, box 63, f. 814.

444 *"He was plagued by regrets"*: Caroline Graham, "The A-List Confessions of a B-Movie Starlet," *Daily Mail*, 5-20-17

445 *"This man is grooming you"*: Donaldson, p. 177.

445 *She had been brought*: Nelson, p. 309.

446 *"I have never been more myself"*: McIntosh and Weaver, p. 148.

446 *The judge found in his favor*: AMPAS, Cary Grant clipping file, *Variety*, 9-4-74.

446 *"In each instance, the woman deserved my love"*: AMPAS, Cary Grant clipping file, Curtis Anderson, "Cary Grant Keeps Growing," *McCall's*, 10-75.

446 *"I turned down an interview with The New Yorker"*: AMPAS, Cary Grant clipping file, Al Cohn, "Cary Grant: I Became What I Portrayed," *Newsday, Long Island Magazine*, 9-14-75.

446 *"It was her way of rejecting society"*: AMPAS, Cary Grant clipping file, Warren Hoge, "The Other Cary Grant," *New York Times Magazine*, 7-3-77.

447 *"He seemed a bit shy"*: Sir Peter Heap to SE.

447 *"a delightful young"*: AMPAS, Cary Grant papers, Grant to Niven, undated, box 19, f. 291.

448 *"Warren reminds me a bit of myself"*: Donaldson, p. 226.

449 *"I can hardly write this"*: AMPAS, Cary Grant papers, Hitchcock to Grant, 3-13-79, box 16, f. 225.

449 *Jennifer Grant remembered*: Grant, p. 87.

450 *"Actually, of course, he did me a favor"*: Bogdanovich, pp. 117–18.

450 *"Every time I see him"*: Bogdanovich, p. 117.

CHAPTER TWENTY-FOUR

451 *"He had a very good-natured side"*: David Thomson to SE.

452 *"Wear silk underwear"*: Yule, p. 56.

452 *"It's the worst business in the world"*: Bob Koster to SE.

453 *"Any moron could write that"*: Grant, p. 33.

453 *"He was a baseball fan"*: Jennifer Grant to SE.

453 *"You know, when I was a boy"*: Grant, p. 156.

454 *Charlie Chaplin would say the exact same thing*: Sydney Chaplin to SE.

454 *He would shop at the same stores*: Gross, p. 95.

454 *"Cary Grant picks me up"*: Gross, p. 177.

454 *"If you're watching my movies"*: Grant, p. 69.

455 *"If you want to act"*: Grant, p. 67.

455 *"Terrific concept"*: Grant, p. 46.

455 *"The floor was all wood"*: Grant, p. 53.

456 *On her third birthday he wrote her*: AMPAS, Cary Grant papers, Grant to Jennifer Grant, 2-26-69, box 16, f. 214.

456 *"You are always in my thoughts"*: AMPAS, Cary Grant papers, Grant to Jennifer Grant, 7-20-69, box 16, f. 214.

456 *"Ten years have passed"*: AMPAS, Cary Grant papers, Grant to Jennifer Grant, 2-26-77, box 16, f. 214.

457 *He had an affection*: Grant, p. 160.

457 *"quite elderly by the time I had my first child"*: AMPAS, *George Stevens—A Filmmaker's Journey* interviews, Cary Grant, box 2, f. 25.

457 *"Don't marry the guy"*: Grant, p. 150.

458 *"If I was still acting"*: Yule, p. 93.

458 *"The man you saw in* Houseboat": Richard Bann to SE.

459 *movies bored him*: Nelson, p. 262.

459 *"Each of us is dying for affection"*: Roderick Mann, "Cary Grant: The Four Hours That Changed His Life," *San Francisco Examiner*, 12-27-64.

459 *"I'll tell you what I thought"*: Diane K. Shah, "Hu-llo, This Is Cary Grant," *GQ*, 1–86.

460 *"May not entertain you at all"*: AMPAS, Cary Grant papers, Grant to Harris, 6-8-77, box 16, f. 212.

460 *"Meanwhile, unless a permanent pull to Spain"*: AMPAS, Cary Grant papers, Grant to Harris, 4-25-78, box 16, f. 212.

461 *"Did you hear about the athlete"*: AMPAS, Cary Grant papers, Grant to Harris, 9-5-78, box 16, f. 212.

461 *"It represents you without thorns"*: AMPAS, Cary Grant papers, Grant to Harris, 9-5-78, box 16, f. 212.

461 *developed a taste for caftans*: Diane K. Shah, "Hu-llo, This Is Cary Grant," *GQ*, 1–86.

462 *"sometimes quite difficult"*: Grant, p. 109.

462 *If he absolutely had to talk*: Grant, p. 142.

462 *A cat named Sausage*: Grant, p. 125.

462 *"The most difficult"*: Nelson, pp. 264–5.

463 *Beginning at the age of eighty*: Grant, 117.

463 *"How much is your loudspeaker?"*: Crowe, pp. 12–13. I have slightly reordered some of the sentences.

464 *"[Grant] only came there for the lunch"*: Crowe, p. 13.

464 *"The first small part I played"*: AMPAS, Cary Grant papers, Grant to Kanin, 7-16-81, box 17, f. 237.

464 *"I had an opportunity to invest in Santa Anita"*: Diane K. Shah, "Hu-llo, This Is Cary Grant," *GQ*, January 1986.

466 *"Congratulations, you old fool"*: Kotsilibas-Davis and Loy, p. 352.

466 *"Come over again soon"*: AMPAS, Cary Grant papers, Niven to Grant, 11-29-82, box 19, f. 291.

467 *"seldom wore such things"*: AMPAS, Cary Grant papers, Grant to Jennifer Grant, 6-2-83, box 16, f. 214)

467 *"I just want to see Jennifer have a child"*: Nelson, p. 343.

467 *"I've never had to work for money"*: Jennifer Grant to SE.

467 *"today he'd be a libertarian"*: Jennifer Grant to SE.

468 *"They were pals"*: Jennifer Grant to SE.

468 *"The precision he brought"*: Jennifer Grant to SE.

468   *"introduced . . . by Minta Arbuckle"*: Burns, p. 160.

469   *"I find myself tearful"*: McCann, p. 222.

469   *"Dear, dear Cary"*: Leider, *Myrna Loy*, p. 307.

469   *"Ladies and Gentlemen"*: Michael Uslan to SE.

470   *"Will you stop telling people"*: Bogdanovich, p. 113.

470   *"still boyish, enthusiastic"*: Peter Bogdanovich, " 'You Don't Look Like Cary Grant,' the Lady Said. 'I Know, Nobody Does,' said Cary Grant," *New York Observer*, 12-1-08.

470   *"Often, when speaking"*: AMPAS, Katharine Hepburn papers, Grant to Hepburn, 5-29-84, box 66, f. 907.

471   *"I don't want to dwell on it"*: McCann, p. 229.

471   *"That's a nice way to die"*: AMPAS, Cary Grant clipping file, *Variety*, 12-7-83.

471   *"They don't make them like you anymore"*: Greg Mank to SE.

471   *"I used to go to the [Radio City] Music Hall"*: AMPAS, Cary Grant clipping file, Jeff Silverman, "Cary Grant Breaks His Long Silence," *Los Angeles Herald-Examiner*, 5-20-82.

471   *"I need confidence"*: Diane K. Shah, "Hu-llo, This Is Cary Grant," *GQ*, 1-86.

471   *"Well, the thing is"*: Bogdanovich, p. 100.

472   *"He enjoyed interacting with people"*: McCann, p. 225.

472   *"I'm alone in front of the camera"*: Nelson, p. 369.

473   *"Now Lord, you've known me a long time"*: Cary Grant papers, box 46, f. 658.

474   *"Excuse me, who is this wonderful gentleman"*: Jill St. John to SE.

474   *"I think we all find ourselves"*: Diane K. Shah, "Hu-llo, This Is Cary Grant," *GQ*, 1–86.

EPILOGUE

475   *On November 27, 1986*: Grant, p. 167.

475   *"To ask Mr. Grant to do a mood piece"*: AMPAS, Vincent Canby, Cary Grant obituary, *New York Times*, 12-1-86.

476   *"LIKE GROUCHO MARX"*: Grant, p. 157.

476   *His clothes and jewelry were left to Stanley Fox*: McCann, p. 231; *Los Angeles Herald Examiner*, 12-4-86.

476   *the shop at the Motion Picture Home*: James Curtis to SE.

476   *"I guess I assumed that Cary would outlive everybody"*: AMPAS, Katharine Hepburn papers, Drake to Hepburn, 12-1-86, box 63, f. 814.

477   *"his Mafia friends"*: AMPAS, Katharine Hepburn papers, Drake to Hepburn, 1-6-87, box 63, f. 814.

477   *Drake wrote Barbara back*: AMPAS, Katharine Hepburn papers, Drake to Hepburn, 1-6-87, box 63, f. 814.

477   *"Cary. He could do anything"*: Peter Bogdanovich to SE.

477   *"the reason we're put on this earth"*: AMPAS, Cary Grant clipping file, Jeffrey Robinson, "Cary Grant: I've Lived My Life," *Redbook*, 3–87.

478   *"When I think of him now"*: Bill Royce to SE.

479   *"That's your problem!"*: Grant, p. 18.

479   *"People keep telling me"*: Bawden and Miller, *Conversations*, p. 126.

479   *"With all his success"*: AMPAS, George Cukor papers, box 65, f. 964.

480   *"I can't write about a character that Cary Grant would play"*: Maslon and
        Kantor, p. 197.

480   *One of its last headliners*: Parker and Hudson, *Stage Door: The Bristol Hip-
        podrome 100 Years*.

BIBLIOGRAPHY

Atkins, Irene Kahn. *Henry Koster: A Director's Guild of America Oral History.* Metuchen, NJ: Scarecrow Press, 1987.

Bacall, Lauren. *By Myself.* New York: Alfred A. Knopf, 1979.

Bach, Steven. *Marlene Dietrich: Life and Legend.* New York: William Morrow, 1992.

Baer, William. *Classic American Films: Conversations with the Screenwriters.* Westport, CT: Praeger, 2007.

Balio, Tino. *United Artists: Volume 2, 1955–1978.* Madison: University of Wisconsin Press, 2009.

Basinger, Jeanine. *I Do and I Don't: A History of Marriage in the Movies.* New York: Alfred A. Knopf, 2012.

———. *The Star Machine.* New York: Alfred A. Knopf, 2007.

Bawden, James, and Ron Miller. *Conversations with Classic Film Stars.* Lexington: University Press of Kentucky, 2016.

———. *You Ain't Heard Nothin' Yet.* Lexington: University Press of Kentucky, 2017.

Behlmer, Rudy. *America's Favorite Movies: Behind the Scenes.* New York: Ungar, 1982.

Behlmer, Rudy, ed. *Memo from David O. Selznick.* New York: Viking, 1972.

———, ed. *Henry Hathaway: A Director's Guild of America Oral History.* Lanham, MD: Scarecrow Press, 2001.

Bennett, Charles. *Hitchcock's Partner in Suspense.* Lexington: University Press of Kentucky, 2014.

Berg, A. Scott. *Goldwyn.* New York: Alfred A. Knopf, 1989.

Bernds, Edward. *Mr. Bernds Goes to Hollywood.* Lanham, MD: Scarecrow Press, 1999.

Billheimer, John. *Hitchcock and the Censors.* Lexington: University Press of Kentucky, 2019.

Biskind, Peter. *Star: How Warren Beatty Seduced America*. New York: Simon & Schuster, 2010.

Black, Shirley Temple. *Child Star*. New York: McGraw-Hill, 1988.

Bogdanovich, Peter. *Who the Hell's in It*. New York: Alfred A. Knopf, 2004.

Brown, David. *Let Me Entertain You*. New York: William Morrow, 1990.

Brownlow, Kevin. *David Lean*. New York: St. Martin's, 1996.

Bruck, Connie. *When Hollywood Had a King*. New York: Random House, 2003.

Burns, George, with David Fisher. *All My Best Friends*. New York: Putnam's, 1989.

Cagney, James. *Cagney by Cagney*. Garden City, NY: Doubleday, 1976.

Caine, Michael. *The Elephant to Hollywood*. New York: Henry Holt, 2010.

Cannon, Dyan. *Dear Cary: My Life with Cary Grant*. New York: Itbooks, 2011.

Caron, Leslie. *Thank Heaven*. New York: Viking, 2009.

Castner, Victoria. *Hearst Castle*. New York: Abrams, 2000.

Chierichetti, David. *Mitchell Leisen: Hollywood Director*. Los Angeles: PhotoVentures Press, 1995.

Coffee, Lenore. *Storyline: Recollections of a Hollywood Screenwriter*. London: Cassell, 1973.

Coleman, Herbert. *The Hollywood I Knew*. Lanham, MD: Scarecrow Press, 2003.

Crowe, Cameron. *Conversations with Wilder*. New York: Alfred A. Knopf, 1999.

Daniel, Douglass K. *Tough As Nails: The Life and Films of Richard Brooks*. Madison: University of Wisconsin Press, 2011.

Dauth, Brian, ed. *Joseph L. Mankiewicz: Interviews*. Jackson: University Press of Mississippi, 2008.

Davies, Marion. Pamela Pfau and Kenneth Marx, eds. *The Times We Had*. Indianapolis: Bobbs-Merrill, 1975.

Davis, Ronald. *The Glamour Factory*. Dallas: SMU Press, 1993.

Deschner, Donald. *The Films of Cary Grant*. Secaucus, NJ: Citadel Press, 1973.

Donaldson, Maureen, and William Royce. *An Affair to Remember*. New York: Putnam, 1989.

Dotti, Luca, with Luigi Spinola. *Audrey at Home*. New York: Harper Design, 2015.

Drazin, Charles. *In Search of The Third Man*. New York: Limelight, 2000.

Drew, William M. *At the Center of the Frame*. Lanham, MD: Vestal Press, 1999.

Eals, Clay. *Every Time a Bell Rings*. Pastime Press, 1996.

Eells, George. *Hedda and Louella*. New York: Putnam, 1972.

Endres, Stacy, and Robert Cushman. *Hollywood at Your Feet*. Los Angeles: Pomegranate Press, 1992.

Eyman, Scott. *Print the Legend*. New York: Simon & Schuster, 1999.

Fairbanks, Douglas Jr. *A Hell of a War*. New York: St. Martin's, 1993.

———. *The Salad Days*. Garden City, NY: Doubleday, 1988.

Feeney, F. X. *Grant*. Hong Kong: Taschen, 2007.

Finch, Christopher, and Linda Rosenkrantz. *Gone Hollywood*. Garden City, NY: Doubleday, 1979.

Frost, Jennifer. *Hedda Hopper's Hollywood*. New York: NYU Press, 2011.

Geist, Kenneth. *Pictures Will Talk*. New York: Scribner's, 1978.

Gelman, Barbara, ed. *Photoplay Treasury*. New York: Crown, 1972.

Giddins, Gary. *Bing Crosby: Swinging on a Star*. New York: Little, Brown, 2018.

Gilbert, Julie. *Opposite Attraction: The Lives of Erich Maria Remarque and Paulette Goddard*. New York: Pantheon, 1995.

Goldrup, Tom, and Jim Goldrup. *Growing Up on the Set*. Jefferson, NC: McFarland, 2002.

Grant, Jennifer. *Good Stuff: A Reminiscence of My Father, Cary Grant*. New York: Alfred A. Knopf, 2011.

Gross, Michael. *Genuine Authentic: The Real Life of Ralph Lauren*. New York: HarperCollins, 2003.

Guilaroff, Sydney, with Cathy Griffin. *Crowning Glory*. New York: General Publishing Group, 1993.

Hammerstein, Oscar Andrew. *The Hammersteins: A Musical Theater Family*. New York: Black Dog & Leventhal, 2010.

Hare, David. *The Blue Touch Paper*. New York: W. W. Norton, 2015.

Hart, Bradley W. *Hitler's American Friends: The Third Reich's Supporters in the United States*. New York: St. Martin's, 2018.

Harvey, James. *Movie Love in the Fifties*. New York: Alfred A. Knopf, 2001.

———. *Romantic Comedy in Hollywood*. New York: Alfred A. Knopf, 1987.

Hepburn, Katharine. *Me*. New York: Alfred A. Knopf, 1991.

Heymann, C. David. *Poor Little Rich Girl*. New York: Lyle Stuart, 1984.

Hofler, Robert. *The Man Who Invented Rock Hudson*. New York: Carroll & Graf, 2005.

Hyams, Joe. *Mislaid in Hollywood*. London: Pitt-Wyden, 1973.

Irvin, Sam. *Kay Thompson*. New York: Simon & Schuster, 2010.

Jennings, Dean. *Barbara Hutton: A Candid Biography*. London: W. H. Allen, 1968.

Johnson, Dorris, and Ellen Leventhal, eds. *The Letters of Nunnally Johnson*. New York: Alfred A. Knopf, 1981.

Jones, J. R. *The Lives of Robert Ryan*. Middletown, CT: Wesleyan University Press, 2015.

Jorgensen, Jay, and Manoah Bowman. *Grace Kelly: Hollywood Dream Girl*. New York: Dey Street, 2017.

Kael, Pauline. Sanford Schwartz, ed. *The Age of Movies: Selected Writings of Pauline Kael*. New York: Library of America, 2011.

Kazan, Elia. *A Life*. New York: Alfred A. Knopf, 1988.

Kemp, Philip. *Lethal Innocence: The Cinema of Alexander Mackendrick*. London: Methuen, 1991.

Kemper, Tom. *Hidden Talent*. Berkeley: University of California Press, 2010.

Kobal, John. *People Will Talk*. New York, Alfred A. Knopf, 1985.

Korda, Michael. *Charmed Lives*. New York: Random House, 1979.

Kotsilibas-Davis, James, and Myrna Loy. *Myrna Loy: Being and Becoming*. New York: Alfred A. Knopf, 1987.

Kulik, Karol. *Alexander Korda*. New Rochelle, NY: Arlington House, 1975.

Lambert, Gavin. *The Ivan Moffat File*. New York: Pantheon, 2004.

Lamour, Dorothy, with Dick McInnes. *My Side of the Road*. Englewood Cliffs, NJ: Prentice-Hall, 1980.

Langdon, Jennifer E. *Caught in the Crossfire: Adrian Scott and the Politics of Americanism in 1940s Hollywood*. New York: Columbia University Press, 2008.

Laurie, Joe Jr. *Vaudeville: From the Honky-Tonks to the Palace*. New York: Henry Holt, 1953.

Leamer, Laurence. *As Time Goes By: The Life of Ingrid Bergman*. New York: Harper & Row, 1986.

Leff, Leonard J. *Hitchcock and Selznick*. New York: Weidenfeld & Nicolson, 1987.

Leider, Emily Wortis. *Becoming Mae West*. New York: Farrar, Straus & Giroux, 1997.

———. *Myrna Loy: The Only Good Girl in Hollywood*. Berkeley: University of California Press, 2011.

Lester, Gene, with Peter Laufer. *When Hollywood Was Fun: Snapshots of an Era*. New York: Carol Publishing, 1993.

Lisanti, Tom. *Fantasy Femmes of Sixties Cinema*. Jefferson, NC: McFarland, 2015.

Longworth, Karina. *Seduction: Sex, Lies and Stardom in Howard Hughes's Hollywood*. New York: Custom House, 2018.

Lord, Graham. *Niv*. New York: St. Martin's, 2003.

Loren, Sophia. *Yesterday, Today, Tomorrow*. New York: Atria, 2014.

Macnamara, Paul. *Those Were the Days, My Friend*. Metuchen, NJ: Scarecrow Press, 1993.

Maltin, Leonard. *Hooked on Hollywood*. Pittsburgh: GoodKnight Books, 2018.

Mankiewicz, Tom, with Robert Crane. *My Life as a Mankiewicz*. Lexington: University Press of Kentucky, 2012.

Mann, William J. *How to Be a Movie Star: Elizabeth Taylor in Hollywood*. Boston: Houghton Mifflin, 2009.

———. *Kate*. New York: Henry Holt, 2006.

Manso, Peter. *Brando*. New York: Hyperion, 1994.

Maslon, Laurence, and Michael Kantor. *Make 'Em Laugh*. New York: Twelve, 2008.

McBride, Joseph. *Hawks on Hawks*. Berkeley: University of California Press, 1982.

McBrien, William. *Cole Porter*. New York: Alfred A. Knopf, 1998.

McCann, Graham. *Cary Grant: A Class Apart*. New York: Columbia University Press, 1996.

McCarthy, Todd. *Howard Hawks: The Grey Fox of Hollywood*. New York: Grove Press, 1997.

McDonell, Terry. *The Accidental Life*. New York: Alfred A. Knopf, 2016.

McElwee, John. *The Art of Selling Movies*. Pittsburgh: GoodKnight Books, 2017.

———. *Showmen, Sell It Hot!* Pittsburgh: GoodKnight Books, 2013.

McGilligan, Patrick. *Alfred Hitchcock: A Life in Darkness and Light*. New York: ReganBooks, 2003.

———. *Backstory 4*. Berkeley: University of California Press, 2006.

McGilligan, Patrick, ed. *Backstory*. Berkeley: University of California Press, 1986.

———, ed. *Backstory 2: Interviews with Screenwriters of the 1940s and 1950s*. Berkeley: University of California Press, 1991.

McGilligan, Patrick, and Paul Buhle. *Tender Comrades*. New York: St. Martin's, 1997.

McIntosh, William Currie, and William Weaver. *The Private Cary Grant*. London: Sidgwick & Jackson, 1983.

Mirisch, Walter. *I Thought We Were Making Movies, Not History*. Madison: University of Wisconsin Press, 2008.

Mitchell, John. *Flickering Shadows: A Lifetime in Film*. London: Harold Martin and Redman, 1997.

Moorehead, Caroline. *Selected Letters of Martha Gellhorn*. New York: Henry Holt, 2006.

Morley, Sheridan. *Tales from the Hollywood Raj*. New York: Viking, 1984.

Moss, Marilyn Ann. *Giant: George Stevens, A Life on Film*. Madison: University of Wisconsin Press, 2004.

Mutti-Mewse, Austin, and Howard Mutti-Mewse. *I Used to Be in Pictures*. London: ACC Editions, 2014.

Nasaw, David. *The Chief: The Life of William Randolph Hearst*. Boston: Houghton Mifflin, 2000.

Nelson, Nancy. *Evenings with Cary Grant*. New York: William Morrow, 1991.

Nott, Robert. *Last of the Cowboy Heroes*. Jefferson, NC: McFarland, 2000.

Oakie, Jack. *Jack Oakie's Double Takes*. San Francisco: Strawberry Hill Press, 1980.

Orry-Kelly. *Women I've Undressed*. London: Allen & Unwin, 2016.

Parker, Gerry, and John Hudson. *Stage Door: The Bristol Hippodrome 100 Years*. Bristol: Reddcliffe Press, 2014.

Phillips, Brent. *Charles Walters*. Lexington: University Press of Kentucky, 2014.

Polito, Robert, ed. *Farber on Film*. New York: Library of America, 2009.

Rempel, William C. *The Gambler: Kirk Kerkorian*. New York: Dey Street, 2018.

Renoir, Jean. *My Life and My Films*. New York: Atheneum, 1974.

Riskin, Victoria. *Fay Wray and Robert Riskin: A Hollywood Memoir*. New York: Pantheon, 2019.

Riva, Maria. *Marlene Dietrich*. New York: Alfred A. Knopf, 1993.

Robertson, Robbie. *Testimony*. New York: Crown Archetype, 2016.

Rooney, Darrell, and Mark Vieira. *Harlow in Hollywood*. Los Angeles: Angel City Press, 2011.

Royce, Bill. *Cary Grant: The Wizard of Beverly Grove*. Beverly Hills: Cool Titles, 2001.

Schickel, Richard. *Elia Kazan: A Biography*. New York: HarperCollins, 2005.

———. *The Men Who Made the Movies*. New York: Atheneum, 1975.

Schulberg, Budd. *Moving Pictures*. New York: Stein & Day, 1981.

Scott, C. H. *Whatever Happened to Randolph Scott*. Madison, NC: Empire, 1994.

Selznick, Irene Mayer. *A Private View*. New York: Alfred A. Knopf, 1983.

Server, Lee. *Robert Mitchum: Baby, I Don't Care*. New York: St. Martin's, 2001.

Seymour, Miranda. *Chaplin's Girl: The Life and Loves of Virginia Cherrill*. London: Simon & Schuster, 2010.

Sharp, Kathleen. *Mr. and Mrs. Hollywood: Edie and Lew Wasserman and Their Entertainment Empire*. New York: Carroll & Graf, 2003.

Shavelson, Melville. *How to Succeed in Hollywood Without Really Trying*. Bear Manor, 2014.

Sheldon, Sidney. *The Other Side of Me*. New York: Warner, 2005.

Sherman, Vincent. *Studio Affairs: My Life as a Film Director*. Lexington: University Press of Kentucky, 1996.

Shipman, David. *The Great Movie Stars: The Golden Years*. New York: Bonanza Books, 1970.

Slide, Anthony. *Inside the Hollywood Fan Magazines*. Jackson: University Press of Mississippi, 2010.

———. *A Special Relationship*. Jackson: University Press of Mississippi, 2015.

Smith, Wendy. *Real Life Drama*. New York: Alfred A. Knopf, 1990.

Solomon, Aubrey. *Twentieth Century-Fox: A Corporate and Financial History*. Metuchen, NJ: Scarecrow Press, 1988.

Spoto, Donald. *Enchantment: The Life of Audrey Hepburn*. New York: Harmony, 2006.

Sragow, Michael. *Victor Fleming: An American Movie Master*. New York: Pantheon, 2008.

Stadiem, William. *Madame Claude*. New York: St. Martin's, 2018.

Stevens, George Jr. *Conversations at the American Film Institute with the Great Moviemakers: The Next Generation*. New York: Alfred A. Knopf, 2012.

Swindell, Larry. *Charles Boyer: The Reluctant Lover*. Garden City, NY: Doubleday, 1983.

———. *Screwball: The Life of Carole Lombard*. New York: William Morrow, 1975.

Takei, George. *To the Stars*. New York: Pocket Books, 2007.

Thomas, Bob. *Clown Prince of Hollywood: The Antic Life and Times of Jack L. Warner*. New York: McGraw-Hill, 1990.

Thomas, Nick. *Raised by the Stars*. Jefferson, NC: McFarland, 2011.

Thomson, David. *Showman: The Life of David O. Selznick*. New York: Alfred A. Knopf, 1992.

———. *Sleeping with Strangers*. New York: Alfred A. Knopf, 2019.

Turk, Edward Baron. *Hollywood Diva*. Berkeley: University of California Press, 1998.

Turner, George, ed. *The Cinema of Adventure, Romance and Terror*. Hollywood: ASC Press, 1989.

Van Rensselaer, Philip. *Million Dollar Baby*. New York: Putnam, 1979.

Vaughan, Robert. *A Fortunate Life*. New York: St. Martin's, 2008.

Wansell, Geoffrey. *Cary Grant: Dark Angel*. New York: Arcade, 2011.

Wapshott, Nicholas. *Carol Reed: A Biography*. New York: Alfred A. Knopf, 1994.

Wasson, Sam. *Fosse*. Boston: Houghton Mifflin, 2013.

Webb, Clifton, with David L. Smith. *Sitting Pretty: The Life and Times of Clifton Webb*. Jackson: University Press of Mississippi, 2011.

Wilk, Max. *Schmucks with Underwoods: Conversations with Hollywood's Classic Screenwriters*. New York: Applause Books, 2004.

Williams, Chris, ed. *The Richard Burton Diaries*. New Haven: Yale University Press, 2012.

Wilson, Victoria. *A Life of Barbara Stanwyck: Steel-True, 1907–1940*. New York: Simon & Schuster, 2013.

Wodehouse, P. G. *The Hollywood Omnibus*. London: Hutchinson, 1985.

Youngkin, Stephen D. *The Lost One: A Life of Peter Lorre*. Lexington: University Press of Kentucky, 2005.

Yule, Andrew. *Picture Shows: The Life and Films of Peter Bogdanovich*. New York: Limelight, 1992.

Ziegler, Philip. *Olivier*. London: MacLehose Press, 2013.

PHOTO CREDITS

All photographs are from the author's collection unless otherwise indicated.

INDEX

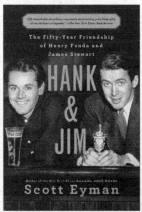

72725